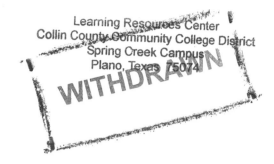

W9-BLM-534

Guide to
Political Campaigns
in America

Guide to
Political Campaigns
in America

Paul S. Herrnson
Editor in Chief

Colton Campbell
Marni Ezra
Stephen K. Medvic
Associate Editors

CQ PRESS

A Division of Congressional Quarterly Inc.
Washington, D.C.

CQ Press
1255 22nd Street, NW, Suite 400
Washington, DC 20037

Phone, 202-729-1900; toll-free, 1-866-427-7737 (1-866-4CQ-PRESS)

Web: www.cqpress.com

CQ Press gratefully acknowledges the permission to reprint the editorial
cartoon on page 3 by Rube Goldberg, the ® and © of Rube Goldberg Inc.
We also wish to thank the National Association for the Advancement of
Colored People for authorizing the use of the poster on page 129 titled
"Protect Her Future: Register and Vote."

Cover design: Rich Pottern Designs

Cover photo: AP Wide World Photos/Robert F. Bukaty

∞ The paper used in this publication exceeds the requirements of the
American National Standard for Information Sciences—Permanence of
Paper for Printed Library Materials, ANSI Z39.48-1992.

Printed and bound in the United States of America

09 08 07 06 05   1 2 3 4 5

Library of Congress Cataloging-in-Publication Data

Guide to political campaigns in America / edited by Paul S. Herrnson.
   p. cm.
  Includes bibliographical references and index.
  ISBN 1-56802-876-8 (alk. paper)
  1. Political campaigns—United States. 2. Political campaigns—
Law and legislation—United States. 3. Elections—United States.
4. Voting—United States. I. Herrnson, Paul S. II. Title.

  JK2265.G84 2005
  324.7′0973—dc22

                        2005018123

Summary Contents

Contents

Tables, Figures, and Boxes

Figures

Boxes

About the Editors

Paul S. Herrnson, editor in chief, is director of the Center for American Politics and Citizenship and professor of government and politics at the University of Maryland. He is the author and editor of dozens of works, including *Congressional Elections: Campaigning at Home and in Washington,* 4th ed. (CQ Press, 2004), and has participated in many aspects of active campaigns for office. He has served as an American Political Science Association congressional fellow and has received several teaching honors, including an Excellence in Teaching Award and a Distinguished Scholar-Teacher Award. He has advised the U.S. Congress, the Maryland General Assembly, the Federal Election Commission, and other government agencies and groups on matters pertaining to campaign finance, political parties, and voting systems.

Colton Campbell, associate editor, works for Rep. Michael Thompson, D-Calif. He has also served as an American Political Science Association congressional fellow for former U.S. senator Bob Graham, as associate professor of political science at Florida International University, and as an analyst in American government at the Congressional Research Service. He is the author, coauthor, or coeditor of several books on Congress and the legislative process, including *Impeaching Clinton: Partisan Strife on Capitol Hill* with Nicol C. Rae.

Marni Ezra, associate editor, is associate professor of political science at Hood College. She has published numerous books, book chapters, and journal articles, many of which focus on congressional primary elections and voter turnout. In addition, she is interested in the use of simulations in political science classes and is the coauthor of the Government in Action series with Julie Dolan (CQ Press, 2002).

Stephen K. Medvic, associate editor, is assistant professor of government at Franklin & Marshall College. In addition to writing several academic articles and book chapters, he is the author of *Political Consultants in U.S. Congressional Elections* and coeditor of *Shades of Gray: Perspectives on Campaign Ethics.* His research and teaching interests include campaigns and elections, political parties, the media and politics, and public opinion.

About the Contributors

Nathan S. Bigelow is a doctoral student at the University of Maryland, where he works as a graduate research assistant with the Center for American Politics and Citizenship. His research interests include political parties, interest group politics, political campaigning, and campaign finance at both the state and national levels. His dissertation will address political representation in the state legislatures.

Barry C. Burden is associate professor of government at Harvard University. He is the coauthor of *Why Americans Split Their Tickets,* coeditor of *Uncertainty in American Politics* with David C. Kimball, and author of numerous journal articles. His research interests focus on electoral politics and representation.

David E. Campbell is assistant professor of political science at the University of Notre Dame. He is the author of the forthcoming book *Why We Vote: How Schools and Communities Shape Our Civic Life.* His research interests include political participation, social capital, and civic education.

Richard S. Conley is associate professor of political science at the University of Florida. He is the author of *The Presidency, Congress, and Divided Government: A Postwar Assessment* and editor of *Reassessing the Reagan Presidency* and *Transforming the American Polity: The Presidency of George W. Bush and the War on Terrorism.* His research interests include the presidency, executive-legislative relations, and comparative executive politics.

Anthony Corrado is the Charles A. Dana Professor of Government at Colby College and a nonresident senior fellow of the Brookings Institution. His publications include *The New Campaign Finance Sourcebook; Inside the Campaign Finance Battle;* and *Campaign Finance Reform.* His research interests include campaign finance regulation, election law, and political reform.

David A. Dulio is assistant professor of political science at Oakland University. He is the author of *For Better or Worse: How Political Consultants Are Changing Elections in the United States* and coauthor of *Vital Signs: Perspectives on the Health of American Campaigning* with Candice J. Nelson. His research generally focuses on the professionalization of political campaigns.

Robert M. Eisinger is associate professor and chair of the political science department at Lewis & Clark College. He is the author of *The Evolution of Presidential Polling.* His research interests include public opinion and the media.

Marni Ezra is associate professor of political science at Hood College. She has published numerous books, book chapters, and journal articles, many of which focus on congressional primary elections and voter turnout. In addition, she is interested in the use of simulations in political science classes and is the coauthor of the Government in Action series with Julie Dolan (CQ Press, 2002).

Peter L. Francia is assistant professor of political science at East Carolina University. He is the coauthor of *The Financiers of Congressional Elections: Investors, Ideologues, and Intimates.* His research interests include interest groups, political parties, campaign finance, and elections.

Peter F. Galderisi is associate professor of political science at Utah State University. He is the editor of *Redistricting in the New Millennium* and coeditor of *Congressional Primaries and the Politics of Representation,* and he has written about realignment in the Rocky Mountain West. His current interests include research on comparative electoral systems and teaching statistical methodology.

Paul S. Herrnson is director of the Center for American Politics and Citizenship and professor of government and politics at the University of Maryland. He is the author and editor of dozens of works, including *Congressional Elections: Campaigning at Home and in Washington,* 4th ed. (CQ Press, 2004), and has participated in many aspects of active campaigns for office. He has served as an American Political Science Association congressional fellow and has received several teaching honors, including an Excellence in Teaching Award and a Distinguished Scholar-Teacher Award. He has advised the U.S. Congress, the Maryland General Assembly, the Federal Election Commission, and other government agencies and groups on matters pertaining to campaign finance, political parties, and voting systems.

Amy E. Jasperson is associate professor of political science at the University of Texas at San Antonio. She is also director of the Media and Elections Studio, which she helped establish in 2002 as a center for political communication research. She has published research in a variety of edited books and journals, including *Political Communication, Polity,* the *Journal of Advertising,* the *International Journal of Public Opinion Research,* and the *American University Journal of Gender, Social Policy and the Law.* Her research interests include the influence of media on public opinion, the impact of political advertising on voters, the relationship between media coverage and advertising, and women in politics.

David A. Jones is associate professor of political science at James Madison University. His articles on media and politics have been published in *Political Communication,* the *Harvard International Journal of Press/Politics,* and *Politics and Policy.*

David C. Kimball is associate professor of political science at the University of Missouri–St. Louis. He is the coauthor of *Why Americans Split Their Tickets* with Barry C. Burden. His research interests include voting behavior, voting equipment, ballot design, and interest group lobbying.

Raymond J. La Raja is assistant professor of political science at the University of Massachusetts, Amherst, as well as an editor of *The Forum,* an electronic journal of applied research in contemporary politics. His research on American political parties, interest groups, and consequences of electoral reforms has appeared in numerous journals and edited volumes. He serves on the Academic Advisory Board of the Campaign Finance Institute in Washington, D.C.

Jan E. Leighley is professor of political science at the University of Arizona. She is the author of *Strength in Numbers,* which examines mobilization and turnout differences across racial and ethnic groups. Her research and publications focus on the contextual determinants of voter turnout and include papers on voter mobilization in the states, early voting, and unions.

Cherie D. Maestas is assistant professor of political science at Florida State University. She has published articles on the role of legislative institutions in shaping political ambitions and the effects of ambitions on legislative behavior. She is co-principal investigator of the Candidate Emergence Study, a multiple-election study of how potential candidates make decisions about running for office in the U.S. House of Representatives.

Tetsuya Matsubayashi is a doctoral student in political science at Texas A&M University. His work has been published in the *American Political Science Review.* His primary areas of research include contextual studies of political participation and public opinion in the United States and in advanced industrial societies.

Stephen K. Medvic is assistant professor of government at Franklin & Marshall College. In addition to writing several academic articles and book chapters, he is the author of *Political Consultants in U.S. Congressional Elections* and coeditor of *Shades of Gray: Perspectives on Campaign Ethics.* His research and teaching interests include cam-

paigns and elections, political parties, the media and politics, and public opinion.

Gary F. Moncrief is professor of political science at Boise State University. His publications include more than fifty book chapters and research articles, and his latest book is *Who Runs for the Legislature?* with Peverill Squire and Malcolm Jewell. His current research interests include the role of states in a federal system, legislative careers, and candidate recruitment.

Nicol C. Rae is professor of political science at Florida International University. His books include *Impeaching Clinton: Partisan Strife on Capitol Hill,* with Colton Campbell, and *Conservative Reformers: The Republican Freshmen and the Lessons of the 104th Congress.* Rae is also a coeditor of *New Majority or Old Minority? The Impact of Republicans on Congress; The Contentious Senate: Partisanship, Ideology, and the Myth of Cool Judgment;* and *Congress and the Politics of Foreign Policy.*

Cynthia R. Rugeley is a doctoral student in political science at Florida State University. Her research interests include voting behavior, elections, and American political institutions.

Roy A. Schotland is professor of law at Georgetown University. He teaches, writes, and speaks on election law and has been particularly active in judicial elections, including writing *amicus curiae* briefs for the Conference of Chief Justices.

Eric R. A. N. Smith is professor of political science and environmental studies at the University of California, Santa Barbara. He is the author of *The Unchanging American Voter* and *Energy, the Environment, and Public Opinion* and the coauthor of *Dynamics of Democracy.* His research interests include public opinion, elections, and environmental politics.

Peverill Squire is professor of political science and a collegiate fellow at the University of Iowa. He is the coauthor of *101 Chambers: Congress, State Legislatures, and the Future of Legislative Studies* and *Who Runs for the Legislature?* with Gary F. Moncrief and Malcolm Jewell.

Clyde Wilcox is professor of government at Georgetown University. His books on campaign finance include *The Financiers of Congressional Elections: Investors, Ideologues, and Intimates,* with Peter L. Francia, Paul S. Herrnson, John C. Green, and Lynda W. Powell; *Serious Money: Fundraising and Contributing in Presidential Nomination Campaigns,* with Clifford W. Brown Jr. and Lynda W. Powell; and *Interest Groups in American Campaigns: The New Face of Electioneering,* 2nd ed., with Mark J. Rozell (CQ Press, 2005). His research interests include campaign finance, religion and politics, gender politics, and the politics of social issues.

Preface

Back in 1816, when John Quincy Adams first used the term *campaign* to describe one of his political efforts, it was considered unseemly for potential officeholders to solicit votes directly from the people. Although political campaigns, by their simplest definition, remain endeavors to collect enough votes to win an election, their shape and conduct have changed significantly over the political life of the nation.

The candidates and others who participate in modern-day campaigning must accomplish a wide variety of tasks to attract voter support. The products of some of these tasks, such as the television ads that saturate the airwaves during presidential elections, are readily visible even to the most apolitical and disinterested individuals, whereas other tasks, including events to raise large financial contributions, often take place in private and among the few political elites who have the funds to host or attend them. Other activities, such as the design of a particular ballot, may be visible and yet unnoticed by voters—until the ballot ends up scrutinized by election officials, as was the so-called butterfly ballot used in Palm Beach County, Florida, in the 2000 presidential election. And still other activities may take place quietly within a campaign organization, such as crafting a theme or conducting opposition research.

Working on this project led me to reflect on the nature of political campaigns and on my own fascination and experiences with them. My curiosity about campaigns first emerged when I cast my earliest votes—in a mock presidential election held in elementary school and in the 1976 presidential election. The campaigns in the latter contest, featuring incumbent president Gerald R. Ford and his successful challenger, Jimmy Carter, were certainly more edifying, but I can still remember the excitement with which I cast my "first vote for president" in Mrs. Kelly's kindergarten class at Oaks School #3 in Oceanside, New York. During and after my college years, I was active in campaign politics, helping to conduct a telephone poll for a House incumbent, going door-to-door to turn out voters for a political party, assisting a successful state legislative challenger to devise a strategy and distill a message, performing the same tasks for a not-so-successful congressional challenger, and or-

ganizing a Capitol Hill fund-raising event to help a member of Congress who had been defeated in 1994 reclaim his House seat two years later. Today, the role of money in politics, campaign ethics, and the impacts of campaign spending, strategy, and national tides on congressional elections are prominent parts of my scholarly research agenda. As director of the Center for American Politics and Citizenship at the University of Maryland, I have had opportunities to advise members of Congress, state legislators, and election officials on these topics and on how to improve voting systems and ballots.

Political campaigns have evolved since my elementary school years, since 1976, and even since 1996 to become more complex endeavors. For people like me who were bitten by the politics bug at an early age, studying campaigns seems an intrinsically worthy and interesting pursuit. But there are perhaps even more compelling reasons to learn about campaigns. From the perspectives of voters, campaigns give substance and meaning to elections. They provide the information voters can use to choose among different candidates, political parties, and issue platforms. They also can supply citizens who are generally uninterested in politics with the motivation to show up to vote. From the perspectives of candidates, campaigns are necessary to unify individual voters into the coalitions of supporters needed to get elected. Campaigns also provide elected officials with justifications for their decision making in office—that is, officeholders routinely link their policy initiatives to their political campaigns, pointing to the substance of their campaign promises and the size of their electoral majorities when claiming a mandate to introduce, expand, cut, or eliminate specific government programs or regulations. Similarly, political parties and interest groups often use their successful campaign efforts to justify pressuring government officials to advance specific policies. On the other side, the candidates, parties, and advocacy groups shut out of power routinely use campaigns to encourage voters to hold those in power accountable for their performance in office. Functioning somewhat outside the normal channels of representative government, initiatives, referenda, and recall campaigns have been used with increasing frequency to challenge the direction of public policy or replace elected officials before their terms in office are completed. And then for the thousands who work or volunteer in elections, campaigns can provide a means of earning a livelihood, increasing political influence or contacts, or having fun while working with like-minded people toward a common goal.

Plan of the Book

Whereas most reference works about campaigns cover small slices of the topic, are written by and for political insiders, or focus on election outcomes, the goal in the *Guide to Political Campaigns in America* is to provide a single source of scholarly and practical insight into a variety of political campaigns and campaign activities. In developing this work, the associate editors, chapter authors, CQ Press, and I aimed to provide a wide audience of students, researchers, scholars, and those interested in election campaigns and politics more generally with a broad foundation of information about all aspects of political campaigns. Among the major subjects covered in the *Guide* are the evolution of campaigns; the strategic context, comprising the institutional, legal, and political arrangements in which campaigns take place; and the voters and financial contributors campaigns are designed to influence. The key participants in political campaigns are examined as well. These include the candidates, the campaign organizations they assemble, political parties, interest groups, and the mass media. In addition, the *Guide* informs readers about the major tasks associated with waging a political campaign: strategic planning, polling and other research, communications, debates, voter mobilization, and fund-raising. Detailed analyses are also undertaken of a variety of bids for specific offices, including the presidential nomination and general election campaigns and campaigns for Congress, governorships, state legislatures, and local offices. Initiative and referenda campaigns, although not campaigns for an office, are described as well. The book concludes with a review of the often hotly debated subject of campaign reform.

Each of the twenty-seven chapters in the *Guide* includes a discussion of one aspect of the campaign process with relevant facts and figures and historic and contemporary examples. The authors, all recognized specialists in their field, have drawn from both the classics and the most recent scholarly literature as well as from hands-on experience. Tables, figures, case studies, boxed features, photographs, and cartoons enrich the chapters and enliven the coverage. The result is an authoritative work that presents the major subjects and themes emerging from the rich literature on political campaigns.

Acknowledgments

In addition to my own background in political campaigns, I also was able to draw on the experiences and knowledge of others when working on this project, including many talented scholars, students, and editors. First, I must thank my associate editors, Colton Campbell, legislative assistant to Rep. Michael Thompson of California's First Congressional District, Marni Ezra of Hood College, and Stephen K. Medvic of Franklin & Marshall College, each of whom assisted in the selection of authors and took major responsibility for editing one section of the *Guide*. Thanks also are due to the individual chapter authors; without their outstanding scholarly contributions the *Guide* would not have been possible. Several top-notch undergraduate students also must be acknowledged for their efforts. Jeffrey Davis, Lisa Epstein, and Jennifer Katkin of the University of Maryland and Jennifer Conklin, Megan Feehan, Amy Miller, Kristyn Miller, Daniel Oakes, and Sarah Steward of Franklin & Marshall College wrote some of the boxes in the chapters, checked facts, and helped to ensure that the prose in the *Guide* was properly pitched to the target audience. Dillard University student Kaletta Moody proofread the manuscript while enrolled in the Summer Research Initiative Program at the University of Maryland. Randy Roberson, manager of the Center for American Politics and Citizenship at the University of Maryland, helped to coordinate the project. Shana Wagger and January Layman-Wood of CQ Press approached me with the concept for this volume and provided valuable feedback and encouragement along each step of the process. Joan Gossett, also of CQ Press, oversaw the *Guide*'s production. Finally, Sabra Bissette Ledent did an outstanding job copyediting the text, helping to join chapters written by a large group of specialists into a publication accessible to a diverse group of readers. To all who participated in the writing and production of the *Guide*, I owe my deepest thanks. To the reader, I promise an interesting and informative experience.

Paul S. Herrnson

PART I

Overview of Political Campaigns

CHAPTER 1

Election Campaigns in the United States

Paul S. Herrnson

Elections are intended to provide citizens and those who are chosen to hold public office with a peaceful and orderly confirmation of power.[1] Elections give voters an opportunity to voice their opinions about the performance of government, various policy issues, and the state of affairs in the nation, their state, or other political jurisdictions. They are the hallmark of representative democracies. In short, without elections there is no democracy.

Campaigns are intended to build the coalitions of voters needed to win elections. They seek to educate voters about the candidates, important public policy issues, and the performance of the government. By attracting voter interest, they help to combat voter apathy and encourage citizens to go to the polls. Regardless of whether they are fought over candidates, parties, or issues, fair and free elections must be accompanied by political campaigns. Just as elections are essential to democracy, political campaigns are essential to elections.

Simply put, a political campaign is an endeavor to collect enough votes to win an election. Contemporary campaigns are much more complicated than they used to be. The candidates and others who participate in elections must adapt to the complex sets of regulations and norms that govern these contests. Among those regulations are the basic rules that determine the requirements for getting on the ballot and for winning a nomination or a general election contest, as well as the statutes that govern campaign finance. The norms associated with campaigning include the expectations of voters, political consultants, party officials, interest group leaders, journalists, and political activists about other factors, including candidates' participation in debates, the volume and tone of campaign communications, and how campaigns raise money and where they spend it. Candidates and others involved in waging election campaigns need to first master these rules of the game. Then they need to survey the landscape of voters who reside in their election districts and make smart strategic and tactical decisions. Waging a well-run campaign does not guarantee victory, but it helps.

This guide to political campaigns is organized as follows. In Part I, this chapter provides an overview of political campaigns in the United States. It is followed by a description of the historical evolution of political campaigns. Part II covers the strategic context, including the laws governing suffrage, procedures for voting, methods of nominating candidates, and issues related to the financing of campaigns. Part III consists of an overview of the electorate and the factors that influence voter choice, including voters' decisions about whether to turn up at the polls on election day and which candidates will receive their vote. Part IV describes the major players in campaign politics—the candidates, campaign organizations, political consultants, political parties, interest groups, and the media. Part V is devoted to an analysis of the campaign process: strategies and tactics, campaign

The "invention" Vote-Getting Machine, by cartoonist and sculptor Reuben Lucius "Rube" Goldberg, satirizes the complexity of the political campaign process. Source: Rube Goldberg Inc.

finance, polling and research, campaign communications, candidate debates, and voter mobilization. And because not all campaigns are alike, Part VI contrasts campaigns waged by candidates for different offices and reveals how they differ from "candidateless" campaigns, such as initiatives, referenda, and recall elections. Part VII concludes the volume by grappling with the subject of campaign reform.

The Strategic Context

Campaigns are waged in a strategic context made up of the nation's political institutions and the broad context in which they work, electoral constituencies, nomination rules, and the specific laws governing elections, including those that determine who can vote and how campaigns will be financed.

The Institutional Context

The setting in which election campaigns, including voting, are conducted is very important. It informs voters, candidates, party officials, interest group leaders, and others who participate in or observe elections about what constitutes legitimate campaign activity, and it structures their election efforts. In the United States, as in most other representative democracies, those who participate in elections are free to communicate their political beliefs, issue positions, and virtually any other information to voters. Voters in turn are free to cast their ballots in secrecy without fear of retribution. Purchasing votes, casting more than one ballot, and intimidating voters are illegal acts. The same is true of tampering with ballots once they are cast. Such abuses of the voting process rarely happen in the contemporary United States or in other mature democracies, including Britain, France, and Japan. These nations' constitutions, election laws, and the traditions embedded in their political cultures minimize the possibilities of fraud and abuse. Such protections should not be taken for granted.

At one time, U.S. elections were rampant with corruption (see Box 1-1). Political parties in some areas, sometimes called "political machines," were notorious for buying votes with cash, jobs, or other favors, and encouraging their supporters to "vote early and vote often." Some political machines were apparently able to perform the supernatural feat of getting dead people to show up at the polls. Elections in some developing democracies also often fall short of contemporary standards of integrity. Organized violence and theft may be incorporated into the campaign tactics used by some candidates and political parties.

The specific institutional arrangements that define various government systems also influence political campaigns. Election laws have a similar effect. Democracies in which power is centralized in a national parliament tend to have party-run campaigns that focus on the parties' performance and platforms, because the ability of party members to get elected and win control of the government are tied to one another (see Chapter 2). Within the U.S. political system, which is characterized by federalism, separation of powers, bicameralism (a legislature divided into two houses), and other decentralizing features, most campaigns are waged by individual candidates, who are responsible for their own tenure. These candidates highlight their own experience, personality, and issue positions, as well as those of their opponent (but in a different light, of course).

Single-member, simple-plurality (SMSP) elections, also known as winner-take-all elections, are used widely in the United States. They encourage political campaigns that are centered around the candidates, not the party. Because this type of election awards an office only to the person who wins the most votes, candidates have little incentive to work as a team when running for office. SMSP elections are conducive to campaigns dominated by candidates representing only two parties. Parties that come in third place or lower usually have little chance of electing anyone, and so they tend to have few followers, wage unimpressive campaigns, and attract minimal media coverage.

Ballot access laws in many states require minor parties to collect a large number of signatures before their candidates can be placed on the general election ballot (Chapters 3 and 4). In this way, many states try to keep some parties from participating in elections. Minor parties therefore play only a small role in elections, except when their candidates attract enough votes to deprive a major-party candidate of victory. This situation arose in the 2000 presidential elections, when Green Party candidate Ralph Nader received over 97,000 votes in Florida, the state that ultimately decided the election outcome. Most of these votes probably would have gone to the Democratic candidate, Al Gore, who lost the state to the Republican George W. Bush by 537 votes.

Electoral Constituencies

Laws governing who can vote and where they can vote also influence the nature of political campaigns. Elections in which large numbers of people are eligible to vote are much different from those that have small constituencies such as the local race for sheriff. To be competitive in elections involving many voters, including presidential and statewide contests, candidates must raise substantial sums of money, hire teams of professional political consultants, and use television and other forms of mass media to reach out to voters. Candidates in local elections, which involve relatively few voters, frequently run inexpensive campaigns that are staffed by amateurs and rely on distributing leaflets, posting yard signs, and knocking on doors.

The nature of elections also changes when specific population groups are included or excluded from the electorate. Only white, male property owners were allowed to vote at the dawn of the nineteenth century. But over the years the Constitution was amended to extend suffrage to African Americans, women, and youths eighteen years

---

BOX 1-1

CORRUPTION IN U.S. ELECTIONS

Jennifer Katkin

In U.S. elections at all levels of government, illegitimate and non-existent voters, including criminals, dead people, fictional characters, and even cats and dogs, have been known to cast ballots. In the 1948 Democratic U.S. Senate primary in Texas, Rep. Lyndon B. Johnson ran against former governor Coke Stevenson. Although immediately after the election Stevenson appeared to be the winner, a recount of the Alice precinct, ballot box 13, in Duval County revealed an additional 203 votes. All but one turned out to be in favor of Johnson, giving him the victory by a margin of eighty-seven votes. It was alleged that George Parr, Johnson's friend and powerful political boss, had stuffed the ballot box—a charge only strengthened when it was discovered that all 203 votes had been cast in alphabetical order. The scandal earned Johnson the nickname of "Landslide Lyndon" for the rest of his political career.

During the 1960 presidential election, complaints were heard about significant voting irregularities, particularly in Illinois. Republicans accused the Cook County political machine, and specifically Chicago mayor Richard Daley, of engaging in a variety of illegal election practices, including miscounting votes, buying votes, and recording votes cast by dead people. The Democratic candidate, John F. Kennedy, carried the state by fewer than nine thousand votes, a victory that resulted from a plurality in the Chicago precincts that just barely outbalanced the rest of the state, which favored the Republican candidate, Richard Nixon. Against the advice of his campaign advisers, Nixon chose not to ask for a recount, reasoning that he did not want to infringe on Kennedy's legitimacy or be labeled a sore loser.

Claims about voter disenfranchisement in Florida and elsewhere during the 2000 presidential campaign are the most recent example of corruption in U.S. elections. In 1998 Florida became the first state to hire a private company to review rolls of registered voters. Using an 1868 law that banned voting by ex-felons (the law was originally designed to limit African American votes), the company purged the rolls of 82,389 Floridians. After the election, 108 eligible citizens who had been denied their right to vote because they were incorrectly labeled ex-felons were informed of the mistake. In addition, 996 ex-felons who had served their time and had their rights restored in other states were prevented from voting on election day, despite a 1998 Florida court of appeal ruling that declared such a denial to be unconstitutional.

Florida was not the only state to come under fire for foul play in 2000. In Wisconsin, a state Democratic candidate Al Gore carried by just 6,099 votes, Republicans claimed that a Democratic activist had offered cigarettes to homeless people in exchange for their votes and that a group of students from Marquette University had voted twice.

---

and older. Other legal reforms made it easier for people to register to vote, enabling a larger portion of the citizenry to exercise the franchise. Rulings by the courts, primarily in the 1960s, further lowered barriers by eliminating literacy requirements, poll taxes, and other measures designed to keep minorities from voting. The National Voter Registration Act of 1993 also facilitated voting by requiring states to allow their citizens to register to vote at motor vehicle bureaus, welfare offices, and some other state agencies. Once new groups of citizens were given the right to vote, candidates, political parties, and the interest groups that participate in campaigns were forced to modify their strategies and tactics, which affected the issues discussed, the groups targeted for campaign communications, and the methods used to reach out to these groups.

Redistricting, the process by which the electoral boundaries for the U.S. House of Representatives, state legislatures, and local governments are redrawn has a similar effect (see Chapter 3). Redistricting normally takes place every ten years, after the decennial census. The information gathered by the census is used to redraw legislative districts so that each is roughly equal in population. The movement of district lines to include new territories and new voting blocs can compel candidates to change issue positions, adjust campaign appeals, and rely on different techniques to reach out to the groups added to their constituencies. In some recent cases, members of the U.S. House of Representatives who had represented districts made up entirely of urban voters had to adjust their campaigns to consider the views of the suburbanites and rural voters who had been added to their districts. Redistricting has been used historically mostly to advantage candidates from one political party over another or to make it easier for incumbents to get reelected. On occasion, however, legislative seats have been redrawn with the specific intent of making it more difficult for incumbents to win.

Nomination Procedures and Ballot Access

The methods candidates use to get their names on the general election ballot have a tremendous impact on the nature of political campaigns (see Chapter 5). In the United States, most candidates are the nominees of a major party. They are placed on the general election ballot through one of three methods or some combination thereof: winning a primary contest, winning a participatory caucus, or emerging victorious at a nominating convention. Still others are declared victors by default because they face no primary opposition. Minor-party and independent candidates may get on the ballot in other ways. In some states, nominees of minor parties that have received significant support in a previous general election are treated like major-party nominees when it comes to being listed on the general election ballot. However, most minor-party and independent candidates must collect a substantial number of signatures to make it onto the ballot. In nonpartisan elections, such as some races for judgeships and municipal offices, candidates appear on the ballot without being associated with a political party. In these contests, candidates usually claim a spot on the general election ballot by collecting signatures, paying a fee, or filing a statement of candidacy.

Candidates who must win a primary, caucus, or some other nomination contest to obtain a place on the general election ballot often assemble a campaign organization independent of their party to raise the funds and develop and implement a strategy to win the nomination (see Chapter 10). That same organization typically forms the core of the campaign team the candidate then uses to contest the general election. As a result, and because many party organizations are relatively weak, these candidates' general election campaigns are conducted relatively independent of party committees. However, as noted earlier, party organizations play an important supplemental role in some candidates' campaigns.

Campaign Finance

Raising and spending money are an important part of almost all campaigns, with the exception of those few that rely on public funding or on unpaid volunteers. As indicated in Chapter 6, the private financing of political campaigns raises some serious issues for the democratic process. These issues include how the candidates, political parties, and interest groups raise the funds needed to participate meaningfully in the electoral process; the impact of public funding on political competition or representation in government; and whether campaign funds are raised in ways that lead to political corruption or the appearance of corruption. Issues of equality and free speech are at the root of many debates over campaign finance. Those who favor regulation of the flow of money in politics emphasize equality, whereas those who consider campaign contributions and spending an extension of personal communication stress free speech.

The federal government and many state and local governments have grappled with campaign finance since the early 1800s, resulting in the enactment of an array of statutes and regulations. Most of the recently enacted statutes limit the sources and amounts of campaign contributions and require public disclosure of all contributions and expenditures. A few states and localities offer public funding to candidates or parties in return for the acceptance of spending caps. The federal government offers this option to presidential candidates.

One of the most provocative issues in campaign finance is the distribution of campaign dollars among candidates. Few scholars argue that too much money is spent in elections, especially when those funds are compared with the billions of dollars spent by fast-food restaurants, soft drink companies, and other well-known advertisers that dominate the airwaves. However, many note that inequalities in campaign spending greatly hamper the efforts of challengers, who are typically outspent by their incumbent opponents. For example, incumbents in the 2002 U.S. House races outspent challengers by an average of 3.75 to 1. Similar spending inequities existed in earlier election years and in 2004, and so they are likely to appear in the future. The typical challengers' inability to raise enough money to mount a viable campaign, critics argue, combines with incumbents' spending advantages, superior levels of name recognition, popularity, media coverage, and campaign experience to produce reelection rates that routinely exceed 95 percent. Uncompetitive elections do little to enhance political accountability.

Another campaign finance issue heatedly debated in recent years is the spending by political parties and interest groups. Some critics argue that the unregulated expenditures by these organizations, which sometimes have amounted to hundreds of millions of dollars in a given election cycle, give them excessive influence over election outcomes and government policy making. They further contend that because the funds used for these expenditures come in amounts and from sources prohibited by campaign finance laws, are not always undisclosed, and are virtually unregulated, the expenditures have the potential to corrupt the political process or give the appearance of corruption. Others argue that because this spending links candidates to issues and does not expressly call for a candidate's election or defeat, it should not be considered "campaign speech" and is protected under the First Amendment.

Despite disagreements over some aspects of campaign financing, critics and advocates of the contemporary campaign finance system agree that it has contributed to the candidate-centered nature of U.S. political campaigns. Under the current system, candidates—not political parties or interest groups—are responsible for raising and spending their own funds. Parties and groups may contribute directly to candidates, help them raise money, and spend money in their behalf, but candidates still bear the major burden of fund-raising and most other aspects of campaigning.

Voters and Voting Behavior

When President Abraham Lincoln intimated in his 1863 Gettysburg Address that the political system was founded to ensure a "government of the people, by the people, for the people," he may have unwittingly directed the gaze of most scholars who study U.S. politics toward the voters. Voters and voting behavior are frequently viewed from two perspectives. The macro-level perspective addresses subjects such as which people are eligible to vote, the impact of voter registration laws on voter turnout, the partisan loyalties of different groups of voters, what determines which voters actually show up at the polls on election day, and the broad impact of elections on policy making. Scholars who study these subjects note that election laws have been reformed over the course of the nation's history to enfranchise more people, but such reforms have not resulted in high levels of voter turnout. Indeed, turnout varies tremendously among different segments of the population. Most of the people who choose to cast a ballot (as opposed to those who choose not to vote) are wealthy, well-educated, middle-aged, married, non-Hispanic whites (see Chapter 7). Voters pay substantially more attention to and know more about politics and participate in campaigns and other activities at higher rates than do nonvoters. And they provide more favorable assessments of politics than do nonvoters. Voters and nonvoters also hold different views of many important public policies.

Partisanship is another important cleavage among members of the electorate. Roughly 80 percent of the contemporary electorate identifies with either the Democratic or the Republican Party. Democratic voters (and politicians) are typically more liberal than are their Republican counterparts. The Democratic Party draws more heavily from the ranks of those less well-off, blue-collar workers, women, youthful voters, ethnic minorities, and racial and religious minorities. The Republican Party counts more men and "upper crust," white Anglo-Saxon Protestants among its staunchest supporters. Nevertheless, as history demonstrates, elections and other historic events can lead to dramatic shifts in the constituent groups that form the political bases of the two parties. These shifts can lead to the emergence of a new dominant party or the replacement of one major party by a new major party. Most major shifts in the partisan alignment of the electorate have occurred after political crises, such as the secession of the southern states from the Union and the Great Depression. Pre–Civil War tensions gave rise to the modern Republican Party and the depression saw the rise of the modern Democratic Party. Partisan alignments are associated as well with major changes in public policy: the Civil War realignment led to the end of slavery and the depression provided the Democrats with an opportunity to introduce Social Security and other programs that gave the federal government a larger role in the nation's economic and social life.

Micro-level perspectives shift attention from structural factors toward the individual and transient political forces that influence voting behavior. As explained in Chapter 8, psychological and short-term political factors are important. People who are more efficacious (that is, have more confidence in their ability to influence the political system) and have stronger feelings of civic obligation are more likely to vote than others, especially when the electoral competition is high and when the political campaigns and the media create an environment rich with information about the election.

Micro-level perspectives also bring to light the effects of individual-level factors and transient political forces on vote choices. Party identification is a major factor in whether a voter chooses to vote for a Democratic or Republican candidate. Other forces that influence an individual's voting decision are national conditions, such as war and peace or the state of the economy, and more proximate considerations such as whether the race pits an incumbent against a challenger or is between two nonincumbents. And the campaigns themselves can be very important (see Chapters 14–26). They can have a major influence on voters' perceptions of a candidate, which, in turn, can influence who votes and how they cast their ballots. Indeed, the lackluster campaign waged by Vice President Al Gore is largely blamed for his failure to perform better in the 2000 presidential election. According to some political observers, Gore's decision to separate himself from President Bill Clinton and the economic prosperity enjoyed under the Clinton administration may have been a major strategic blunder—one that contributed to an election outcome that was so close that the Supreme Court intervened to bring the recounting process to an end.

Political Campaigners

Candidates and their campaign organizations are the dominant actors in most election campaigns. Political parties and interest groups play important supplemental roles, together with the mass media, which, for the most part, consider themselves neutral presenters and interpreters of politics and other public events. All these people and organizations engage in the most visible activities in most election campaigns. However, some elections have no candidates whatsoever: initiatives and referenda are issue-based campaigns that enable voters to enact or repeal specific public policies.

The Candidates

Age, citizenship, and residency are the only requirements people must meet to run for public office—unless they are running for a judgeship, which often requires a law degree. Getting on a primary ballot is usually an easy task that requires collecting signatures or paying a modest filing fee. It is widely believed that most elections are contested by at least two candidates. This is generally true for elections for the presidency, Congress, and statewide offices, but elections for many lower-level offices, including contests for state legislative seats and municipal and local offices often go uncontested.

Why do people run for office? One answer is that running for office may satisfy a set of psychological needs, including an attraction to public life and a strong sense of civic obligation. A second answer, which builds on the first, is that families and mentors play an important role in fostering in some citizens an interest in politics that eventually leads to a political candidacy or some other form of political activism. A desire to achieve a highly valued set of policy goals is yet another answer. Other answers are that people enjoy the social aspects of politics or believe they can help their businesses or advance other economic interests by running for or holding elective office.

Centrally related to the question of who runs for office is the notion of strategic ambition. As described in Chapter 9, strategic ambition is a combination of the desire to get elected, a realistic understanding of what it takes to accomplish that goal, and an ability to assess the opportunities presented by a given political context. Strategic candidates weigh the costs and benefits of running before deciding to enter the political arena. The costs include the financial losses incurred from investing time and money in a campaign, potential career setbacks, and the personal toll running for office can have on both the candidate and the candidate's family. Even when a potential candidate is confident of victory, these costs may outweigh the benefits associated with holding office.

Most politicians who already have held or run for an elective office, worked as a political aide or political appointee, held the post of state or local party official, or worked as political consultants make candidacy decisions that suggest a sense of strategic ambition. They run when their odds of winning are relatively strong—that is, when the current officeholder chooses not to run for reelection, is the subject of a major scandal, is in poor health, or has lost touch with constituents. A favorable redrawing of legislative boundaries, national or local political conditions unfavorable to the incumbent, and other systematic or idiosyncratic factors also can influence their candidacy decisions. By contrast, candidates who have not had significant political experience may not realistically assess their odds of success and run when conditions are less than optimal. Most of these candidates are defeated handily in either a primary or a general election.

Campaign Organizations

Campaign organizations play a major role in some campaigns and are nonexistent in others. The size and professionalism of the team a candidate assembles to wage a political campaign depend on the nature of the office, the size of the constituency, the amount of money the candidate has on hand or might be able to raise, and the anticipated competitiveness of the race. More than half of all major-party candidates running for contested U.S. House seats in 2002 assembled teams of paid staff or consult-

ants to carry out the following activities: management, press relations, issue or opposition research, polling, fund raising, mass media advertising, direct mail, and maintenance of a Web site. More than one-third of these candidates hired professionals to assist with mass telephone calls and provide legal advice. Overall, these candidates typically hired between six and seven professionals to participate in their campaigns.[2] House campaigns in 2004 were reportedly just as professional, if not more. By contrast, less than 30 percent of all major-party candidates who ran in contested races for a state legislative seat between 1996 and 1998 hired a political professional to conduct any one of the campaign activities just listed, and, of these, the typical state legislature campaign employed only one or two political professionals.[3]

Campaign professionals can have a significant impact on elections. Few people would argue that hiring a skilled campaign team and the services of some top-of-the-line consultants is sufficient to ensure victory, in part because incumbents enjoy tremendous advantages over challengers and many legislative districts are drawn to favor one party or the other. However, the experience and expertise political professionals bring with them are widely believed to help campaigns develop better strategies and tactics and implement them more successfully. The effects are especially strong for nonincumbents: those who wage professional campaigns raise more money and win a larger share of the vote than those who rely on amateurs.[4]

Political Parties

Political party labels act as informational shortcuts for voters (see Chapter 8). Voters who have little information about candidates beyond their party labels are able to make some well-founded inferences about the candidates' ideologies and issue positions. By means of such labels, voters also can give credit or cast blame for the state of the economy or some other important issue. In this way, party labels make it easier for voters to hold policy makers accountable.

In addition to helping voters interpret politics and providing them with voting cues, parties historically have played a part in socializing citizens to the political system, drafting candidates to run for public office, helping to structure politicians' careers, conducting election campaigns, organizing the government, and influencing the public policies that emerge from the political process. The broader political environment has a substantial impact on how parties carry out these activities (see Chapter 2). Having once dominated election campaigns, political parties have adapted to the contemporary candidate-centered, cash-driven, highly specialized era of campaign politics. They continue to remain important sources of contributions and expenditures, political expertise, and election volunteers.

Party organizations in the United States have a highly decentralized structure. This structure has been influenced heavily by federalism, the separation of powers, bicameralism, the dispersion of power across the different bodies making up state and local governments, and the political system's heavy reliance on elections as a means of staffing government offices. Chapter 11 describes how autonomous party committees spring up to help elect candidates to individual offices. Each of these organizations seeks to advance the prospects of one or more candidates, and when these organizations join forces, they are better able to advance their individual goals.

The national convention, the party's ultimate decision-making body, is at the top of the party's organizational chart. It convenes once every four years to ratify the selection of the party's presidential candidate, formally kicking off the general election campaign, and to conduct other business. The parties' national committees were originally created to organize the national convention and mount the presidential campaign, but they also have assumed major roles in devising the rules that govern state and local parties. The congressional and senatorial campaign committees assist members of Congress who need it with their reelection campaigns, and they recruit House and Senate candidates and help them to win election. Other party committees at the national, state, and local levels help candidates to campaign for governorships, state legislative seats, and other offices.

Toward the close of the twentieth century, the parties' national, congressional, and senatorial campaign committees, and the committees in some states devoted to electing governors and legislators, became major sources of campaign contributions and campaign assistance. They helped with campaign management, polling, mass media advertising, and other aspects of campaigning requiring in-depth research, technical specialization, or connections with the donors, political consultants, volunteers, or others who possess the resources needed to wage a viable campaign. That said, political parties do not support all candidates equally. Because their goal is to maximize the number of offices their candidates control, they strategically direct most of their campaign assistance to candidates in hotly contested races. By investing in these contests, they are able to reap the biggest rewards for their investments. Party organizations probably will continue to play an important role in campaigns and elections, but the ways in which they perform their functions will evolve in response to political reforms and other changes in the political environment.

Interest Groups

Interest groups, like parties, play an important role in election campaigns. However, interest groups do not have as much influence on elections, or governance more gen-

Presidential and vice-presidential candidates use nominating conventions to kick off their general election campaigns. Texas delegates to the 2004 Republican National Convention in New York City wore cowboy hats and Lone Star shirts to represent their state and to cheer on the reelection bid of fellow Texan George W. Bush.
Source: Scott Ferrell/Congressional Quarterly

erally, as the parties for several reasons. First, interest groups, unlike parties, do not nominate candidates to run under their label on the general election ballot. Thus on a ballot no candidate's name is associated with, for example, General Motors or the American Federation of Teachers. Rather, a candidate is associated with the Democratic or Republican parties, some minor party, or runs as an independent. Second, parties, not interest groups, organize the government. In this way, voters are able to use party labels to hold candidates accountable for the state of the nation or of their state or locality. Third, interest groups do not enjoy the widespread voter loyalty or voter recognition bestowed on parties. Voters have emotional ties to and recognize the centrality of the parties to the political system; they do not have these same emotional feelings or cognitive familiarity with interest groups. This is not to say that interest groups do not play important roles in elections. Indeed, many do.

Cash donations are probably the most recognized, and the most frequently criticized, contribution of interest groups to political campaigns. Some states and localities allow corporations, trade associations, unions, and other organized groups to contribute money directly from their treasuries or operating funds to political candidates. As described in Chapter 12, such organizations must form a separate fund, often called a political action committee (PAC), to contribute to federal candidates and candidates for office in some states and localities. For federal candidates, a PAC can contribute up to $5,000 per candidate for each phase of an election, including the nomination contest, general election, and runoff election (in the unusual circumstance that one is actually held). Only a small number of PACs make the maximum contributions to the federal candidates they support. Most do not possess the resources to give many contributions or large ones. In the 2002 congressional elections, 14 percent of all PACs accounted for 84 percent of all contributions.[5] This concentration of PAC contributions is typical of elections held in the late twentieth century, and it was repeated in 2004.

PACs and other groups that make campaign contributions are generally divided into three groups based on their contribution strategies. Most business-oriented groups, including PACs sponsored by corporations or trade associations, direct the vast majority of their contributions toward incumbents, particularly those in positions to influence policies that are important to their organizations' financial well-being. These groups consider a contribution to be part of a larger lobbying effort designed to increase access to key political decision makers. They are generally not concerned about issues such as a challenger's electability or the closeness of a race.

A second set of interest groups is more concerned with influencing who holds office than with seeking or maintaining access to the legislature's current membership. These groups, which include EMILY's List (a supporter of pro-life Democratic women candidates) and the Republican National Coalition for Life (a supporter of pro-choice Republicans), make contributions to candidates who share their views on ideologically charged issues. The beneficiaries of this largesse include incumbents and their challengers, as well as candidates for open seats. Most "ideological" interest groups seek to back candidates in competitive contests—regardless of whether they are incumbents, challengers, or candidates for open seats—because these races give them with the best opportunity to influence election outcomes.

The third set of interest groups consciously pursues both goals. Most labor union PACs, for example, give the vast majority of their contributions to Democrats, because the Democratic Party is more supportive of legislation that helps workers. However, they contribute a substantial portion of those contributions to incumbents, including those who are a shoo-in for reelection.

Some interest groups, like parties, also provide candidates with specialized campaign assistance, including help with fund-raising, communications, and grass-roots organizing. Other groups may carry out independent campaigns designed to influence the votes of their members and the public. Labor unions, environmental groups, gun owner rights organizations, and groups on both sides of the abortion rights issue may make candidate endorsements and use direct mail, mass telephone calls, and television and radio ads to help their preferred candidates attract voter support.

One of the major differences in the campaign roles assumed by interest groups and parties is that interest groups are willing to become deeply involved in nomination battles, whereas parties usually remain on the sidelines until a candidate has been nominated. Interest groups that participate in elections to gain access to lawmakers are often willing to contribute to incumbents whenever they ask for funds, including during or before the primary season. Interest groups that view elections as a principal means of advancing their policy goals contribute to candidates, including challengers and open-seat contestants and during some primary and general election contests, with the hope of nominating and then electing the candidate who will best represent the groups' issue positions. Another important difference is that interest groups sometimes organize and finance initiative campaigns on specific issues. Parties concentrate their efforts on electing candidates.

Mass Media

News coverage of elections by the contemporary mass media—newspapers and magazines; broadcast, cable, and satellite television and radio; and Web-based outlets—differs markedly from the communications issued by candidates, campaign organizations, political parties, and interest groups. Most journalists strive to be objective collectors and disseminators of information about politics, whereas candidates, parties, and interest groups color the information they distribute to advance their causes. In other words, the mass media by and large report and interpret political news; candidates, parties, and groups try to influence the stories the media report and put a partisan interpretation or "spin" on news coverage. Editorial pages, talk radio programs, and other non-news media also often assume a less neutral role, providing more partisan than nonpartisan coverage.

Most media outlets in the United States are owned by large corporations beholden principally to their profit motives. The drive to maximize profits through advertising revenues influences how elections are covered in the news (see Chapter 13). When the goals pursued by news correspondents and those sought by the corporations that own most media outlets are combined, the result is a set of journalistic norms.

The first norm is that the media rely heavily on politicians for most election-related stories. Campaign media advisories, events, advertisements, and the time that candidates spend with journalists provide the grist for much of the coverage presented to the public. In addition, most media analysis focuses on the "horse race" aspects of the campaign. Journalists turn to polls, campaign finance reports, or delegate counts for nomination races when trying to determine which candidate is in the lead. The candidates' qualifications, personalities, and the campaign teams they assemble provide additional grist for media coverage. Scandals and misstatements, when they are discovered, also attract a great deal of media exposure. Unfortunately for those journalists and readers who would like to see the electorate receive detailed reports on the issues, few election stories focus on public policy matters.

A second norm is that opposing candidates are not treated the same, despite the media's stated goal of covering the campaigns objectively and equitably. Incumbents generally benefit from more favorable coverage, because they are still controlling the levers of power and are very likely to win. This situation applies especially to campaigns for the U.S. House and state legislatures, where free media coverage is particularly important to introducing the candidates to voters.

A third norm is that media coverage tends to gravitate toward competitive elections. Candidates in races with unpredictable outcomes attract more coverage than those in lopsided contests. Challengers who possess more political experience, more money, and a more professional campaign organization often attract more journalistic attention than others, because their races appear to be competitive.

A fourth norm—but one that has not yet received much objective support—is that journalists cover Democratic candidates more favorably than Republican candidates. The evidence for this argument is that more journalists embrace liberal values than conservative ones. What has not been conclusively demonstrated is that those values result in partisan reporting. Indeed, it may be that the conservative views of the owners and editors of most newsrooms may offset those of the correspondents who work for them. It also is possible that for most of the twentieth century the media's tendency to cover politicians in positions of power combined with the Democrats' control of Congress and most state legislatures resulted in less news coverage for Republican politicians. Most of these politicians thus perceived a partisan media bias when a pro-incumbent bias was actually at work.

Regardless of one's opinion of media bias in news coverage, it is important to recognize that op-ed pages and talk news shows are not expected to abide by the standards of objectivity that guide news correspondents. Indeed, these spaces are reserved specifically for the expression of personal opinion—including the candidate endorsements that fill many op-ed pages at the close of the election season.

One thing most researchers agree on is that the mass media have an important influence on elections. The media help set the political agenda, thereby influencing which issues concern voters the most and which candidates are introduced to the public. This may mean that some candidates and issues never show up on the public's radar screen. And they help to frame how news consumers view campaigns, including whether the contests are between a front-runner and a pack of lesser candidates or a political insider and an outsider. Such designations can help a candidate to attract support, gain momentum, and pick up the support of undecided voters.

Campaign Activities

Candidates for most significant offices wage two campaigns: a campaign for votes and a campaign for resources. The campaign for votes is the one most familiar to voters. Its most basic elements are a campaign strategy, research, communications, and voter mobilization. The campaign for resources takes place largely behind the scenes and is invisible to most voters. It involves raising the money needed to mount a campaign for votes and attracting campaign services, endorsements, advertisements, and other forms of assistance from political parties and interest groups.

Campaign Strategy

How many votes does the candidate need to win? Which groups of voters are supporting the candidate? Which groups are backing the opponent? Which groups have yet to make up their minds? Once these questions are answered, a campaign must formulate and execute a campaign strategy to put together a winning coalition. As noted in Chapter 14, formulating a campaign strategy requires research. Demographic research is used to determine the defining characteristics of voters and to divide them into groups that have shared concerns. Research on groups' voting histories will reveal each group's level of voter turnout, its partisan inclinations, and the consistency of its voting behavior. Such research may uncover, for example, that African Americans make up one-third of a district's population, that they are overwhelmingly Democratic in their partisanship, and that they have very low turnout for elections. The finding of low turnout may convince campaign strategists to consider them a less important part of the winning coalition than a smaller voting bloc in the district that is equally loyal and historically has had a very high turnout, such as Jewish voters. Alternatively, the campaign may devote more time and resources to getting out the vote among African Americans.

Polling and Research

Polling is used to learn what voters think about the candidate, the opponent, and the issues that dominate voters' concerns. A well-known candidate who has a reputation for taking strong positions on issues that are at the forefront of voters' consciousness begins the election with a major advantage over a candidate who is not recognized by most voters. Polls and focus groups also are used to test and refine campaign messages. Together, polling and demographic research have a major impact on how and where campaigns spend their money and what they communicate to voters.

Issue and opposition research also influences the substance and tone of the campaign dialogue. Issue research helps candidates to fill out the details of their advertisements and develop a positive message. A pro-environment candidate might use research to pinpoint locations that need protection from corporate polluters. A family values candidate might use research to craft a message that will mobilize conservative supporters without alienating moderate voters. Opposition research, which candidates routinely conduct on the competition and themselves, exposes areas for defense and attack. For example, a candidate whose opponent owns a chemical company that has a history of polluting groundwater will probably discuss environmental issues, unless the candidate has an equally poor environmental record.

A good campaign will use demographic, polling, issue, and opposition research to develop a theme or message to win votes. That message will form the foundation for virtually all campaign communications and will be repeated over the course of the campaign to attract undecided voters and to mobilize the candidate's base. Incumbents often emphasize their experience and appeal to voters to stay the course. Challengers usually recount the benefits of change.

Campaign Communications

Campaign communications can include broadcast and cable TV advertising, radio ads, direct mail, literature drops, newspaper ads, e-mail, mass telephone calls, Web sites, and more (see Chapter 17). One of the ways in which campaigners distinguish among different communications techniques is by whether the techniques are under the campaign's control. The techniques just listed are under the control of the campaign, as contrasted with debates and "free" media (also called "earned" media), which are reported by journalists, and therefore are not under a campaign's control. Candidates, opponents, and news correspondents often seek to put their own spin on free media, which makes those media somewhat riskier than the media a campaign purchases.

Campaigns also routinely distinguish among different communications techniques based on their potential for targeting messages. Some techniques, such as e-mail, direct mail, mass telephone calls, and literature drops, can be targeted very narrowly because they are used to directly contact individual voters or their households. Campaigns can craft a very specific message designed to appeal to a certain group and use one of these communication techniques to deliver that message. Some messages are intended to win the support of the members of an undecided group of voters. Others are intended to shore up or mobilize a candidate's base. The content of these messages is often quite different: those intended to win over undecided voters tend to be more moderate and those targeting a candidate's base more ideologically charged.

Speeches, radio, specialized newspapers and magazines, and cable and satellite TV, although not directly delivered to individuals or households, also can be targeted to groups of people who are known to consume special-

Radio played a major role in Republican Calvin Coolidge's victory in the 1924 presidential race. The night before the election, Coolidge made history when his final campaign speech drew the largest radio audience of the time. Source: Library of Congress

ized programs and channels. For example, a Republican candidate can place an advertisement on a conservative talk show during rush hour and reach huge numbers of conservative voters battling their way home through traffic. Similarly, a candidate of either party who wishes to reach young voters can do so by appearing on MTV.

Campaigns have less control over who comes into contact with broadcast television advertisements and Web site postings. These media are used to disseminate broad messages designed to appeal to more general audiences. Messages aired during network television shows, for example, tend to be more moderate than those included in direct mail or specialized radio shows. For that reason and because of the type of audiences they reach, ads aired over network television can have a bigger effect on the overall political agenda.

Another distinction campaigns make when choosing the techniques to deliver their messages is cost. Broadcast television is by far the most expensive communications medium. The candidates, parties, and the interest groups that weighed in on the 2000 presidential election spent in excess of $255 million between June and November alone. Speeches, grass-roots activities, and Web sites are the least expensive communication techniques, relying

During his 1992 presidential campaign, Democratic governor Bill Clinton of Arkansas appeared on an MTV town hall–style special, during which he played his saxophone and answered questions about his underwear. He later credited the appearance with energizing young people to vote and helping him beat incumbent Republican George H. W. Bush. Source: MTV

mostly on the good will of individuals to listen to, hunt for, or help deliver a candidate's message.

Other distinctions involve the substance of the message. Is it is positive, negative, or comparative in tone? What is the purpose of the communication? Ads circulated early in the campaign season are designed to introduce a candidate to voters. The next set of ads often highlights the candidate's policy positions and reasons for running. They are usually followed by negative or contrast ads that provide unfavorable information about an opponent. Attack ads disseminated by candidates, political parties, and interest groups have become increasingly common in recent years. The final set of communications, often called summation ads, attempt to tie the entire campaign together by reminding voters who the candidate is, why the candidate is running, and why the candidate is better than the opponent.

Debates

Debates are important and unique enough to make up their own category of campaign communications. As noted in Chapter 18, the public expects aspirants for highly visible offices to debate, and many politicians have responded favorably. Every presidential candidate since 1960 and many contenders for Congress and governorships have participated in debates. Presidential candidates can count on audiences of some sixty million voters for their debate performances.

The decision to debate is a strategic one. Because debates are often covered by the mass media, they offer can-

didates an opportunity to be viewed side by side in a neutral setting by a large number of voters. There are, however, pluses and minuses to participating. Candidates who have large leads in the polls have the least to win and the most to lose from debating. Without a debate, they probably could coast easily to victory. But by participating in a debate, they are giving the opponent (or opponents) an opportunity to close the gap. The front-runner might make a factual error or some other gaffe or fail to meet journalistic or public expectations; a candidate far off the lead might give a strong performance; or journalists or others who spin political events might decide that a candidate not in the lead outperformed the front-runner. Conversely, candidates who are not front-runners have the most to gain from debates. In situations in which a candidate is barely behind the front-runner in the polls, a favorable debate showing could help pave the road to victory. Of course, the candidates' (and their advisers') perceptions of their debating skills also influence who chooses to debate.

Debates can assume any one of many formats. A single moderator may ask all the questions, or a team of journalists or other local elites may grill the candidates. In debates that employ a town hall format, the candidates take questions from members of the audience. Debates that allow candidates to question each other and then ask follow-up questions tend to be the most spirited.

Debates have many different effects on the public. They draw the public's attention to the candidates, parties, issues, and elections in general. Debates also can influence how voters cast their ballots. They generally activate or reinforce the partisan predispositions of voters who identify with a party, and they can help to determine how independents or others who are not committed to a particular candidate cast their votes. Meanwhile, debates can encourage both sets of voters to show up at the polls on election day. Debates held in connection with nomination contests have a greater impact on individual voting decisions than debates held during the general election campaign, presumably because in the first contest voters know less about the candidates. Regardless of when they are held and who participates in them or watches them, debates contribute to the campaign process by clarifying the choices available to the voters.

Voter Mobilization

Voter mobilization differs from other forms of campaign communication in that it is concerned less with persuasion and more with urging voters to go to the polls. Carried out by candidates, political parties, and various interest groups, voter mobilization activities target specific individuals. Chapter 19 describes how party registration, race, ethnicity, education, income, age, and group membership are used to target blocs of voters to receive individualized campaign contacts. Once these voters are identified as targets, they are persuaded to go to the polls by means of face-to-face contacts, telephone calls, direct mail, leafleting, and e-mail. Of all of these techniques, face-to-face contacts are the most effective.

Campaign Fund-Raising

All of the activities just described are part of the campaign for votes. With the exception of a relatively few volunteer-staffed, grass-roots–oriented campaigns that take place in small election districts, virtually every campaign involves a substantial campaign for resources. Jesse M. Unruh, the oft-quoted speaker of the California state Assembly during the 1960s, once said that "money is the mother's milk of politics." Given the amount of time and effort contemporary politicians spend on fund-raising, it would not stretch the analogy too far from the truth to add "and most candidates for president, Congress, governor, big-city mayor, and other prominent offices devote a substantial portion of their campaign schedule to time in the 'milking parlor.' " Indeed, one study showed that 55 percent of statewide candidates, 43 percent of U.S. House candidates, and one-third of all state legislative candidates devote at least one-quarter of their personal campaign schedules to fund-raising. The same study showed that 53 percent of all statewide candidates, one-third of congressional candidates, and 9 percent of all state legislative candidates hire campaign aides or political consultants to help them raise funds.[6]

Yet not all elections require the same amount of money or fund-raising effort. The cost of elections depends on the size of the constituency; the costs of advertising in local television and radio markets; the competitiveness of the election; the sums opponents, political parties, and interest groups are willing to spend; and whether voters expect to see their candidates on television. During the 2004 presidential nomination season, President George W. Bush spent more than $219 million by August 31, despite having no primary opponents. Sen. John Kerry of Massachusetts, the Democratic nominee, spent more than $174 million during the same period. Both candidates used substantial portions of these funds to engage in general election–style campaigning before their party's national conventions, after which they each were entitled to receive approximately $75 million from the federal government. In the 2002 midterm election, the typical major-party incumbent House candidate amassed funds of almost $1 million. In 2004 the typical House incumbent broke the $1 million mark, raising more than $1.1 million. Most recent candidates for state legislatures raised

less than $100,000 in pursuit of those offices. With the exception of big-city mayoral candidates, most candidates for local office collected considerably less. But none of these figures include spending by political parties and interest groups, which, in the presidential election and some competitive congressional and state legislative contests, amounted to considerable sums.

Given the costs of elections, it seems reasonable to ask: where does the money come from? Chapter 15 points out that it depends on the candidate. Many challengers and candidates for open seats rely on their own bank accounts for substantial portions of their campaign funds. Incumbents, by contrast, are able to turn to others when financing their reelections.

Beyond the candidates themselves, a small group of individual donors account for a major portion of all campaign funds. Interest groups, including PACs, also are a major source of campaign money, and a relatively small number of organizations provide much of it. Party committees account for substantially fewer campaign contributions. As discussed earlier, donors contribute for a variety of reasons. Many associated with the business world, such as businesses and trade associations, make most of their contributions to gain access to elected officials. Those such as political parties and ideological organizations that care about some salient policy or broad-based ideology are less interested in gaining access than in helping to elect candidates who share their views. Some people also make contributions because their friends ask them to and because they enjoy socializing with other elites. Others contribute for all of these reasons, as well as some idiosyncratic ones.

Politicians ask for money in a variety of ways, including in person, on the telephone, through the mail, via e-mail, and through well-connected third parties. Web sites also have been used successfully by candidates who are visible enough for potential donors to search for the candidates' Web sites. To succeed at fund-raising, those requesting contributions must use solicitations that appeal to the motives of specific donors. Those who contribute for social reasons respond well to requests that are coupled with invitations to fund-raising dinners and other events that provide them with opportunities to rub shoulders with politicians, celebrities, and other big donors. Those who contribute for business reasons respond well to solicitations that give donors opportunities to discuss public policies with incumbents. Those who contribute for ideological reasons react positively to inflammatory direct-mail letters.

Diversity in Campaigns

How campaigns are run depends on the type of office at stake, the strategic context, whether incumbency is a factor, and partisanship. A campaign waged by an incumbent U.S. senator in California will be quite different from a state legislative campaign featuring a challenger in New Hampshire or an open-seat candidate for sheriff in Arizona. Successful campaigns take into consideration the candidate's position in the contest and local conditions and expectations.

Presidential Campaigns

There is no other campaign in the world like that for the U.S. presidency (see Chapter 20). Such campaigns, which are very long and which dominate the news, are waged primarily by candidates rather than by party organizations. They are usually preceded by a highly expensive, participatory, and often publicly contentious nomination process.

Most candidates for a presidential nomination, and for the presidency itself, are experienced politicians with substantial national visibility. They are often drawn from the ranks of senators, governors, and vice presidents. Such candidates are among the few in a position to raise the money and create the organization needed to build a broad-based national coalition of supporters. Candidates begin laying the groundwork for their bids for a presidential nomination years, and perhaps decades, before they actually run. However, the election process actually begins about a year before election day when candidates must begin filing declarations of candidacy to appear on state primary ballots. The process involves competing in a complex system of participatory primaries and caucuses in order to win delegates to the national convention. The candidate who wins a majority of delegates becomes the party's designated nominee.

The presidential general election is every bit as complicated as the presidential nomination contests. As in the primaries and caucuses, voters do not directly cast their ballots for presidential candidates. Instead, the voters, often unbeknownst to them, are actually voting for electors, who, in turn, are entrusted to cast a ballot for president. In all but two states, electors cast their ballots en bloc for the presidential and vice-presidential candidates who won a plurality of the state's popular vote. Thus even if a presidential ticket bests its opponents by only a few votes in a state, it wins all of that state's electoral college votes. To win the election, a presidential ticket must win 270 (a majority) of the 538 electoral college votes.[7]

The presidential election system forces victorious candidates to piece together vote pluralities in numerous states. Although the system places a premium on the large states that possess the most electoral votes, it also encourages candidates to focus on competitive states. During the 2004 elections, both parties' candidates spent a disproportionate amount of time and money in the twenty or so swing states that were up for grabs. Because they were both competitive and large, Florida, Michigan, and Pennsylvania, among other states, were inundated with communications from the candidates. Political parties and interest groups joined the candidates in saturating these states with television, radio, direct mail, and other advertisements. Although sitting presidents typically have substantial advantages in raising money and attracting free media over their challengers, they do not automatically win another term. Since 1956, incumbents have lost two of the seven elections in which they sought reelection.

Campaigns for the U.S. House of Representatives

House campaigns are much less visible than presidential contests. They also are much less competitive—House incumbents typically have a 95 percent-plus reelection rate. Among the factors contributing to this rate are that most House members represent small, homogeneous districts, and they use the resources that come with their offices to improve their name recognition and support among constituents. Most House districts also are specifically drawn with an eye toward improving incumbents' reelection prospects. Finally, incumbents have tremendous advantages over challengers in fund-raising and attracting media coverage. One would be hard-pressed to find an incumbent who was recently defeated because of a lack of funding.

The weakness of the opposition and the campaigns they typically mount also contribute to incumbents' overwhelming reelection rates. As noted in Chapter 21, highly qualified people often choose not to take on a sitting House incumbent, preferring instead to seek another office or wait for the incumbent to retire. As a result, many House seats go uncontested, and those House challengers who do run often have limited political experience and begin the election season virtually invisible to voters, journalists, and potential campaign contributors. The conundrum faced by most challengers is that they begin the election season without the name recognition needed to convince potential individual donors, party leaders, and PACs that their campaigns will be viable. Without substantial campaign funds, they cannot build enough name recognition to attract the support needed to run a competitive race. As a result, most House challengers lose by substantial vote margins. Only once in a few decades do substantial numbers of House incumbents lose. Turnover in the House is more a product of representatives' retirements than of electoral forces.

Campaigns for the U.S. Senate

U.S. senators were originally selected by state legislators, but that changed in 1913 with passage of the Seventeenth Amendment, which called for the direct election of senators by the voters. Six-year terms insulate senators from the constant electoral pressures faced by House members. Because a senator's district is an entire state, senators are less likely than House members to have personal ties to their constituents. This factor contributes to the greater competitiveness of Senate elections, especially in large states where it is difficult to satisfy the needs and aspirations of voters who are racially, ethnically, and culturally diverse. Campaigns and elections play a greater role in fostering turnover in the Senate than in the House.

Another reason for the greater competition in Senate elections is that candidates for the upper chamber typically have more political experience than candidates for the lower chamber. They usually begin their campaigns with greater name recognition, a larger base of constituent support, a larger pool of previous donors, and more political skill. As noted in Chapter 22, because individual senators often maintain a high profile and state borders usually coincide those of television media markets, Senate campaigns spend large sums on TV advertising and receive substantial news coverage. Senate challengers therefore have plenty of opportunities to tell voters how they differ from their opponents, which is important in what are essentially media-driven campaigns. Media coverage, the quality of Senate candidates and the organizations they use to run their campaigns, and the setting in which those campaigns are waged contribute to the competitiveness of Senate contests.

Gubernatorial Campaigns

Gubernatorial elections bear many similarities to elections for the U.S. Senate. Both are high-visibility, statewide contests requiring substantial sums of money. Both also attract extremely highly qualified candidates. As noted in Chapter 23, about one-fourth of all governors have served in another statewide office, such as lieutenant governor or attorney general, or in Congress immediately before election to office. Roughly half have worked in their state legislature at some time before moving into the governor's mansion. Both sets of candidates also assemble very professional organizations and rely heavily on television to reach voters.

As for the differences between gubernatorial and Senate campaigns, some of the most important ones have to do with the institutional environment. First, gubernatorial terms are shorter than Senate terms, lasting four years in forty-eight states and two years in New Hampshire and Vermont. Thus governors spend more time focusing on reelection than senators. Second, three-fourths of the states limit governors to serving no more than two consecutive terms, and governors in one state—Virginia—can only serve one term. The result is more open-seat races for governor. Third, because they are chief executives, governors are held accountable for the state of their states. Therefore, gubernatorial campaigns tend to focus more on a state's employment levels and other economic conditions than do Senate campaigns, which are more concerned about national issues. Fourth, about 80 percent of all states hold their gubernatorial elections in nonpresidential election years, thereby "decoupling" them from the strong national tides that accompany some presidential elections. Some states, including New Jersey and Virginia, encourage an even greater separation of state and national politics by holding their elections in odd years. Fifth, and to a large degree because of these factors, gubernatorial campaigns tend to be somewhat more competitive, expensive, and dependent on state politics than Senate campaigns.

State House and Local Campaigns

Campaigns for state legislatures and most local offices bear little resemblance to presidential, statewide, or even U.S. House campaigns (see Chapter 24). With some important exceptions, particularly in California, state legislative and local candidates run in significantly smaller districts, have significantly less political experience, spend less money, assemble less professional organizations, and rely on fewer specialized campaign techniques. Because of the diversity in term lengths, term limits, the timing of elections, the laws governing campaign financing, and the requirements for candidacy, it is challenging to generalize about these contests. To further complicate matters, some state and local elections are officially nonpartisan; some state legislators, city officials, and others are elected from districts that elect more than one person to office; and some election rules require officials to win a plurality of the vote, while others require a majority and subject the top two finishers to a runoff election in the event that neither obtains a majority. A few places use an instant runoff voting system that allows voters to rank-order candidates by preference or a cumulative voting system designed to facilitate minority representation in at-large electoral systems.

Chapter 23, which describes in detail all these factors and their effects on state legislative and local elections, reveals that many campaigns for these offices are uncontested, and that those in which competition exists are relatively inexpensive because they eschew television advertising in favor of direct mail, literature drops, and other grass-roots activities. One of the major factors that influences whether a race is competitive, or even contested, is the professionalism of the institution in which a candidate hopes to serve. Professionalized state legislatures provide representatives with higher salaries, office space, staff, and additional perks that make serving in them more attractive. These amenities are often exploited by incumbents to improve their name recognition and support among voters. Incumbents in professionalized legislatures devote more time to pursuing reelection than those in less professionalized bodies, and they enjoy somewhat higher reelection rates.

But not all state legislative and local elections are lopsided, grass-roots affairs. In some state Senate elections in California, spending has exceeded $1 million, and the spending in some mayoral contests has been in the millions of dollars. Most noteworthy is the $70 million that Michael Bloomberg spent to become mayor of New York City in 2001. Campaigns for these contests were just as professionally run and media-driven as those for most U.S. Senate races.

Judicial Campaigns

Judicial elections differ from elections for other offices in several ways. Many of these differences can be attributed to the unique role that judges play in the political system (see Chapter 25). First, unlike other elected officials judges cannot meet with constituents to discuss imminent or future decisions. Second, judges cannot make campaign promises to reward their supporters, advance particular causes, or change the law. Third, judges cannot build constituent support through casework, distributing patronage, or using newsletters, franked mail, or press releases to advertise their activities or claim credit for government actions—all of which are routinely done by other elected officials. Fourth, judges' terms in office are longer than those of most other elected officials. Fifth, many judges are appointed for a first term and face no competition in the ensuing retention elections. These factors combine to make the electoral connection weaker for judges than for other elected officials.

Despite these differences, recent trends suggest that judicial elections are changing in ways that portend future elections that more closely resemble those for other offices. The amount of money judicial candidates spend and the time they spend raising it have increased since the late 1970s.[8] Independent campaign spending by political parties and interest groups in judicial elections also has grown significantly. Intensified electoral competition is largely responsible for these other changes. Because judges are expected to administer the law impartially, the growing role of money in judicial elections is a concern.

Initiatives, Referenda, and Recall Campaigns

Despite the centrality of candidates to most elections, some election campaigns are not waged by candidates and do not involve voting for candidates. Initiative, referenda, and recall elections are candidate-less contests associated with direct democracy. These elections are classified as direct democracy, because rather than voting for public officials to represent them in government, voters bypass normal political processes to address a specific issue or problem. These elections stand in sharp contrast to most other aspects of American government, which are based on the republican principle that voters elect public officials who are entrusted to make public policy decisions for them.

As described in Chapter 26, initiatives, referenda, and recall elections take a variety of forms, which are promulgated in state constitutions and statutes. Most initiative processes enable citizens who collect the required number of signatures to place laws and constitutional amendments on the ballot for the voters' approval. Some processes allow the state legislature to address the issue first. Referenda are ballot measures that a legislature submits to voters for their approval. Recall elections enable citizens who are dissatisfied with a public official's performance to force that official to face an election before his or her term of office has expired. Every state but Alabama has provisions for at least one of these vehicles of direct democracy. The federal government does not.

Initiatives and referenda have covered topics ranging from abortion rights to affirmative action to insurance reform to the use of pesticides. For all intents and purposes, getting a measure on the ballot is the first step in an initiative, referenda, or recall campaign. Referenda require the approval of the state legislature. The initiative process is more complicated. Language for measures must be written by state officials, who also draft the title and short description that will appear on the ballot. The drafting process can be contentious because few voters learn the details of an initiative, and so they vote for or against it based on the title or description. Once the ballot language has been approved, sponsors of the initiative must collect a predetermined number of signatures for it to appear on the ballot. This often expensive process may be conducted by a professional signature-gathering service.

The second part of the campaign consists of winning the votes need to approve the measure. The campaign strategy for ballot measures differs sharply from that for candidates, because persona, experience, and imagery are not relevant concerns. The same is true of party identification. Instead, campaigners focus only on the issue. They publicize the ballot title and description, strive to obtain free media coverage, and enlist endorsements and the help of prominent politicians and celebrities. Occasionally, candidates can be found to endorse or even run their campaigns around a specific initiative. At times, an opposing interest will sponsor a counterinitiative to provide an alternative that might divide support for the initiative or confuse voters so much that they do not vote for either one.

Sometimes, an initiative campaign has a third part. Once an initiative has passed, a state legislature may change, block, or decide not to fully fund it. An initiative also may be challenged in the courts. Because they are decided by majority rule and do not benefit from the normal give-and-take of the legislative process, some initiatives violate the individual rights of members of minority groups.

Recall elections are held so rarely that generalizations cannot be made easily. The only successful one held in recent history, in California in 2003, was similar to an initiative campaigns in many ways. In recall elections, the ballot measure calls for removal of an elected official. The required signatures must then be gathered to place the measure on the ballot. In the California recall of Gov. Gray Davis, part of the recall ballot included the name of Arnold Schwarzenegger, Davis's eventual successor, and another 134 "replacement" candidates, each of whom had collected signatures or paid a fee to appear on the ballot. An important way in which recall elections differ from initiatives is that recall elections take place before a normally scheduled election. In California, a special recall election must be held within sixty to eighty days after the secretary of state has certified that proponents of the recall have collected the required signatures.

Although it has been argued that referenda, initiatives, and recall elections are intended to empower ordinary people to change policies or public officials who favor wealthy, well-organized special interests over the general public, critics point out that most contemporary efforts at direct democracy are dominated by wealthy, well-organized special interests, not the general public. Of the many reasons for this, perhaps the most important is that these campaigns tend to be expensive. In this way, they bear similarities to other statewide campaigns.

Conclusion

Clearly, election campaigns in the United States fall short of a standard in which voters educate themselves about the candidates and their stances on the issues, candidates debate one another on the issues and have sufficient resources to communicate their messages, political parties and interest groups provide positive, supplemental information to help frame the major issues of the day, and the mass media devote enough coverage to election campaigns to make it possible for those who tune into the news to cast an informed vote. Reacting to this state of affairs, reformers have put forth a number of proposals to change election campaigns. Reform proposals range from abolishing the electoral college, to altering the way legislative districts are drawn, to changing the way votes are counted. Despite the fact that the Bipartisan Campaign Reform Act and the Help America Vote Act both became law in 2002, the debate over campaign finance reform has been heated and ongoing. Chapter 27 describes several contemporary reforms and the major obstacles that must be surmounted for them to become law.

Notes

1. The obvious exceptions to this generalization are initiatives and referenda.

2. Paul S. Herrnson, *Congressional Elections: Campaigning at Home and in Washington* (Washington, D.C.: CQ Press, 2004), 72–75.

3. Paul S. Herrnson, "The Campaign Assessment and Candidate Outreach Project," Center for American Politics and Citizenship, University of Maryland, College Park, 1998.

4. Herrnson, *Congressional Elections,* 176–177, 190–193; Stephen K. Medvic, *Political Consultants in U.S. Congressional Elections* (Columbus: Ohio State University Press, 2001), 98, 115, 129, 144–145.

5. Herrnson, *Congressional Elections,* 1333–1335.

6. Peter L. Francia and Paul S. Herrnson, "Begging for Bucks," *Campaigns and Elections,* April 1, 2001.

7. The number of electors assigned to each state matches that state's representation in the U.S. House of Representatives and Senate. In addition, the District of Columbia has three electors.

8. But twenty-seven states prohibit candidates from personally soliciting campaign contributions.

Suggested Readings

Berry, Jeffrey M. *The Interest Group Society.* New York: Longman, 1997.

Bowler, Shaun, Todd Donovan, and Caroline J. Tolbert, eds. *Citizens as Legislators: Direct Democracy in the United States.* Columbus: Ohio State University Press, 1998.

Campbell, Angus, Philip E. Converse, Warren E. Miller, and Donald E. Stokes. *The American Voter.* New York: Wiley, 1960.

Fiorina, Morris P. *Retrospective Voting in American National Elections.* New Haven, Conn.: Yale University Press, 1981.

Herrnson, Paul S. *Congressional Elections: Campaigning at Home and in Washington.* 4th ed. Washington, D.C.: CQ Press, 2004.

Maisel, L. Sandy, ed. *The Parties Respond: Changes in American Parties and Campaigns.* Boulder, Colo.: Westview Press, 2002.

Polsby, Nelson W., and Aaron Wildavsky. *Presidential Elections: Strategies and Structures of American Politics.* 10th ed. New York: Chatham House, 2000.

CHAPTER 2

The Evolution of Political Campaigns

Paul S. Herrnson

Elections are, first and foremost, struggles over political power. Political campaigns are the battles that make up those struggles. Although the participants in political campaigns and the strategies and tactics they use have evolved over the nation's history, one principle has remained fairly consistent: the candidates who collect the most votes win. This principle applied to the campaigns held for seats in colonial legislatures before the founding of the United States, and it applies to most modern elections. With some exceptions, most notably the require ment that presidential candidates win a majority of electoral college votes, it applies to nomination contests, general elections, and runoff elections. But the similarity ends there. The earliest campaigns were inexpensive, nonpartisan, and highly personalized, reaching out to only a tiny portion of the population. Contemporary presidential campaigns and some statewide and a few other contests feature huge sums of money, professional campaign organizations, political parties, interest groups, and complicated targeting and marketing strategies—all intended to influence millions of voters.

This chapter traces the development of political campaigns from the colonial period through the early twenty-first century. In doing so, it covers four periods of U.S. history: the colonial and post–colonial era (from the days of the first elective colonial legislatures through the mid-1820s), the party-centered era (from the early 1820s through the early to mid-1900s), the candidate-centered era (from the mid-1900s through the 1970s), and the contemporary era (from the 1970s to the current period). Within those periods, the chapter describes the political institutions, laws, resources, and voters that define the strategic context for campaigns; the candidates, parties, and interest groups that are the major actors in campaigns; and the roles these actors play in candidate recruitment and selection, campaign management, fund raising, public opinion polling, campaign communications, and voter mobilization.

The Impact of the Strategic Context on Election Campaigns

The types of campaigns that characterize a democracy are strongly influenced by the strategic context in which those campaigns take place. The strategic context includes institutional factors such as the constitutional design of the political system, the nature of the offices candidates seek, the laws and party rules governing party nominations or general elections, and some relatively enduring aspects of American political culture such as citizens' traditional ambivalence toward politics, politicians, political parties, and interest groups. The strategic context also includes the methods that candidates, parties, advocacy groups, and others that participate in elections use to communicate with voters. These methods have evolved over time from word of mouth and pamphlets to television advertising, Web sites, and other modern communication techniques. Other elements of the strategic context are extremely transient. They are national factors, such as the state of the economy, presidential popularity, and the mood of the public, and local factors such as the partisanship and competitiveness of the district in which an election is being held, whether an incumbent is seeking reelection, and local conditions and events.

The institutional design of the American political system—including the separation of powers, federalism, bicameral legislatures, and the further decentralization of state and local offices, which formally separates elections for political offices from one another—tends to grant those who hold these offices independent claims to exercise political power. These institutional features also enable voters to hold individual officeholders accountable for their performance in office. In addition, the single-member, simple-plurality (winner-take-all) elections, in which the voters in a given district cast one vote and the candidate receiving the most votes wins, encourage independence among candidates and officeholders and give voters the motivation to make discrete assessments of individual candidates for office. This system contrasts sharply with the party-focused campaigns prevalent in parliamentary democracies, such as Britain, which do not disperse power among different political institutions and do encourage voters to hold individual candidates responsible for their entire party's performance in office.

The widespread use in the United States of single-member, simple-plurality elections also discourages the formation of third parties and minimizes their prospects for success, helping to reinforce the U.S. two-party system. This system differs substantially from those of democracies such as Italy and Germany that use proportional representation—a method in which parties and political groups are allocated seats in legislative bodies in proportion to their share of the vote. Proportional representation lends itself to the formation of many political parties. By tying the electoral fortunes of candidates of the same party together, it encourages those candidates to undertake teamwork in elections.

Campaigns are shaped as well by the nature of election constituencies. Candidates running for offices that have small districts, such as city council, usually confine themselves to grass-roots campaigns. Volunteers canvass door-to-door, distribute leaflets, organize house parties (also called meet and greets), and erect yard signs. The candidate also may meet with local newspaper editorial boards. Candidates for offices that have huge districts, such as the entire nation (the presidency) or a large state (governor or senator), must run much more sophisticated campaigns. The same is true of House members and candidates from large cities. These campaigns require considerably more planning, money, and professional expertise. Many rely on television, radio, direct mail, and mass telephone calls for communication. Even their grass-roots efforts are influenced by sophisticated analyses aimed at targeting voters.

The rules governing the nomination process also influence the types of campaigns that candidates wage. Candidates who must win a party nomination through a primary election—the method used to select general election candidates in most states—or a caucus—the method used in Iowa—create campaign organizations to wage their nomination campaigns. Candidates who are selected in private meetings where dues-paying party members decide among themselves who should win the party nomination do not need to assemble an organization to mount a nomination campaign. Successful candidates who use the first approach, popular today, of creating a campaign organization find themselves entering the general election with a campaign organization that is more or less independent of party committees. The second approach—the private party meetings, which were used in the party-centered era in the United States and continue to be used in most modern industrialized democracies—produces general election campaigns that are primarily conducted by party committees rather than candidates.

Campaign finance is yet another factor in election campaigns. Whether campaigns rely on public funds furnished by the government, funds raised by political parties (or perhaps given to the parties by the government), or funds raised by the candidates from individuals, interest groups, party committees, or their own resources, has a tremendous impact on a campaign's independence from other organizations and how the campaign is conducted. Not surprisingly, candidates who rely on public funds invest little time in thinking about raising money. Those who must build up their own war chests devote substantial time, effort, and expense to fund-raising. Indeed, the money chase in most U.S. elections has evolved into a campaign in and of itself. Elections in which parties raise most of the campaign money or receive the lion's share of all campaign subsidies provided by the government, such as those in most Western democracies, are generally dominated by party committees; candidates are much less in the front and center in these party-centered campaigns.

Broader societal conditions also affect the nature of political campaigns. Public attitudes toward parties, candidates, and politics more generally influence the style and tenor of campaigns. Candidate-centered campaigns typically occur when and where the citizenry is ambivalent about parties and politics. Such campaigns are often characterized by populist themes or antigovernment or antipolitician rhetoric. Party-centered elections are more prevalent where and when voters consider political parties part of the natural order of government and society, such as in the eighteenth-century United States and contemporary Europe.

Finally, technology has a very important effect on how campaigns are conducted. Because campaigns are, first and foremost, about communicating to and mobilizing voters to show up at the polls, candidates able to harness technology to help them reach out to voters are among the most influential in elections. The television age, with its potential for unmediated candidate-to-voter contact, has increased the degree to which campaigns focus on candidates as opposed to political parties. Similarly, the advent of direct mail, e-mail, and computerized databases has given candidates, parties, and interest groups opportunities to tailor their appeals to specific voting blocs.

Campaigns in the Colonial and Post–Colonial Era

Elections in colonial America were quite unlike those of modern times. The electorate consisted of roughly 5 percent of the entire population, because voting was limited mainly to white, male, Anglo-Saxon, Protestant landowners. Politics itself was a part-time enterprise; colonial, and later state, legislatures met for sessions that lasted a few months at the most, and most elected officials received little or no compensation for the time lost from their actual professions.

Because of the tiny electorate and the limited direct financial payoffs for those who were elected, political campaigns were highly elitist, personal, and fairly inexpensive. They resembled extended, semiprivate conversations among the upper crust of society rather than the very public communications of contemporary campaigns that intrude in the lives of virtually everyone who owns a television set. George Washington's election to the Virginia House of Burgesses in 1757 was probably typical. The future first president of the United States let it be known to those eligible to vote for him that he was available to serve in public office. He did this by meeting or corresponding with his neighbors. Political discussions took place without the benefit of political parties, campaign commercials, rallies, or large fund-raising events. Indeed, Washington's total campaign expenses were miniscule when compared with those of a modern campaign. Most of what he did spend was for the refreshments—28 gallons of rum, 50 gallons of spiked punch, 46 gallons of beer, 34 gallons of wine, and a couple of gallons of cider royal—his surrogates passed out to potential supporters at election time (Washington was away at his frontier post). There is no doubt but that the spirits Washington's supporters imbibed helped them to comprehend the richness of his political vision.

The political campaigns held in the new American states did not differ markedly from those held earlier in the thirteen colonies. Much of the campaign conversation, in the form of quiet meetings and correspondence with the few citizens eligible to cast votes, was calm, well reasoned, and centered on the great issues of the day. These issues were the power and scope of local, state, and national governments; economic matters, including the role of those governments in the economy; and other fundamental principles of governance. Candidates did not take to the stump, and there were no boisterous rallies. Nor did the candidates or parties launch public relations campaigns. Electioneering could be more accurately depicted as a small number of gentleman candidates requesting the votes and political support of other gentlemen.

The Party-Centered Era

The transition from the colonial style of campaigning to the party-centered era (a period that extended from the early 1820s to the early to mid-1900s) was brought about by several factors, most notably the massive increase in the number of citizens who could vote in elections.[1] Westward expansion, substantial waves of immigration, and the modification of election laws to allow a larger portion of the population to vote supported a shift toward campaigns that reached out to a wider audience. In response

to the rise in competition among factions in Congress and state legislatures, the members of these bodies began to create party organizations. They realized that public campaigning could be the key to electoral success.

The catalyst for the formation of the old-fashioned political machines that dominated the party-centered era (also known as the golden age of political parties) was the outcome of the presidential election of 1824. In the four-way contest among Andrew Jackson, John Quincy Adams, Henry Clay, and John C. Calhoun, Jackson won a plurality of the popular vote, but he was unable to win a majority of the electoral college vote. As required by the U.S. Constitution, the outcome of the election was then placed in the hands of the U.S. House of Representatives. Rather than vote for Jackson, who had won 41 percent of the popular vote, the House selected Adams, after he received Clay's support. Once sworn in as president, Adams repaid the favor by selecting Clay to be secretary of state, which at the time was a springboard to the presidency. The Jackson forces then charged that this corrupt bargain robbed their candidate of the presidency. Under the leadership of Martin Van Buren, they prepared for the 1828 election by creating a new mass-based party organization to mobilize voters.

Unlike previous political organizations that were largely designed to employ appeals to principle in order to win support from elites (property owners and others eligible to vote), the new, nationally based Democratic Party created by Van Buren and Jackson was founded on the idea of winning elections, controlling government, and using that control to reward supporters with "patronage"—government jobs and contracts. Candidates for Congress and state and local government offices, as well as existing political organizations, agreed to join the new party, because they recognized that they could benefit in both votes and patronage by aligning themselves with the highly popular Jackson. They also understood that, in agreeing to be part of Jackson's election ticket, they did not pledge themselves to support a party platform or campaign on any specific issue stances. Bankers and other wealthy people, unfettered by the lax campaign finance laws of the day, contributed large sums of money to the Democratic Party because they understood that its victories would bring them government contracts, favorable legislation, and other economic benefits. As for the party itself, it relied on a new form of political association currently called the "political machine" or "old-fashioned party organization." This form of political organization was soon adopted by the Whigs, Republicans, and other political parties (see Box 2-1).

The rise of the political machine drastically altered the nature of political campaigns. The principled discussions of the early days among elites were replaced by rallies, speeches, torchlight parades, and other popular events designed to convey a message and mobilize the masses. The machines, led by astute students of human nature,

---

BOX 2-1
ABRAHAM LINCOLN WITH AN INSIDER'S VIEW OF A PARTY-CENTERED CAMPAIGN

In January 1840, Abraham Lincoln, then a member of the Illinois House of Representatives and his party's Whig Committee, wrote the following campaign circular, intended to rally Whigs throughout the state for presidential candidate William Henry Harrison in his (successful) bid to unseat incumbent Democrat Martin Van Buren. Although Harrison was a popular war hero who did campaign in his own behalf, Lincoln's letter illustrates how for most of the nineteenth century election communications and voter contacts were made by party organizations.

CONFIDENTIAL

. . . Our intention is to organize the whole state, so that every Whig can be brought to the polls in the coming presidential contest. We cannot do this, however, without your co-operation; and as we do our duty, so we shall expect you to do yours. . . .

1st. To divide [the] county into small districts, and to appoint in each a sub-committee, whose duty it shall be to make a perfect list of all voters in their respective districts, and to ascertain with certainty for whom they will vote. . . .

2nd. It will be the duty of said sub-committee to keep a constant watch on the doubtful voters, and have them talked to by those in whom they have the most confidence, and also to place in their hands such documents as will enlighten and influence them.

3rd. It will also be their duty . . . on election days [to] see that every Whig is brought to the polls. . . .

Source: A. Lincoln, *Collected Works of Abraham Lincoln,* Vol. 1, University of Michigan, Humanities Text Initiative, www.hti.umich.edu/lincoln (accessed April 18, 2005).

It was not long after their formation that the political machines began to dominate election campaigns. Their control over the nomination process, the resources needed to communicate with the electorate, and the party symbols and labels that gave meaning to voters and helped them to choose candidates turned the parties into the major vehicles for virtually every aspect of the campaign process, from candidate recruitment through voter mobilization.

Candidate Recruitment

The decision to run for public office has always been a very personal one (see Chapter 9). During the era of the political machine, local party organizations played a major role in recruiting candidates for public office. Potential candidates tended to stand out from other party supporters in their popularity, campaign activism, and loyalty to the party organization. They also tended to gradually move up the organization's hierarchy and expand their bases of support until the bosses who ran the machine recognized them as viable candidates and asked them to run for local office. In a less frequently used recruitment technique, the machine bosses would ask prominent community leaders who were not party members to run, ostensibly to give the party ticket more respectability and vote-getting power among more well-established members of the community. Candidate recruitment for higher level offices, such as governor or a seat in Congress, required negotiations among a much larger number of party elites, as local party leaders worked with and sometimes against one another to recruit the candidate who would best represent their organization's interests.

For most of the party-centered era, recruitment for a local office and some higher offices led automatically to the nomination. Where a party organization was dominant, gaining the nomination was tantamount to winning the election. During the golden age of political parties, two general forms of candidate selection appear to have been the most prevalent. The first was a private caucus in which a political boss or a committee of local party leaders chose whomever they wanted to run for each local office and then designated those persons as the party's nominees. Statewide and national candidates were generally selected at conventions at which local party leaders negotiated to determine who would receive the nomination. Candidate selection at all levels was therefore a completely closed-door, partisan affair, involving only a small cadre of party leaders.

The second form of candidate selection, the direct primary, became fairly common during the early 1900s. The shift to the direct primary followed the enactment by many state legislatures of the "good government" reforms advocated by the Progressive movement. These reforms sought to reduce the corrupting influence that political parties and special interests had on government.

---

such as George Washington Plunkett of New York's Tammany Hall, forged and nurtured bonds between themselves and the largely uneducated immigrant masses both during and between campaign seasons by providing these potential voters with food, employment, social opportunities, and other forms of assistance to help them settle into their new homeland. The goal of most of this activity was to build a loyal voter base. The result was the emergence of party identification and strong partisan loyalties among most voters.

The direct primary, based on the participation of voters in the nominating election, thus replaced deal making among party leaders as the means of choosing candidates. Although the goal of such a shift was to wrest away power from party bosses, some local party leaders were able to maintain their control over the candidate selection process by specifying a ticket of party-endorsed nomination candidates and using the machine's political apparatus to campaign for that ticket in both the primary and the general election. Eventually, the direct primary opened the candidate selection process to the involvement of a fairly large electorate, contributing to the end of the golden age of political parties.

Campaign Management

Campaign management encompasses mapping out a strategy, overseeing the day-to-day administration of the campaign, and conducting all the tasks aimed at collecting enough votes to win an election (see Chapter 14). During the party-centered era, party organizations, not candidates, bore the primary responsibility for these activities. Local party committees were mainly concerned with the contests within their immediate jurisdictions. State party committees concentrated on gubernatorial and state legislative elections. The national party, congressional, and senatorial campaign committees in Washington, D.C., directed most of their resources and efforts toward electing candidates to the presidency, the House, and the Senate. Nevertheless, because all of a party's candidates appeared on the same ticket on election day, they were associated with one another in the minds of voters and their destinies at the polls were to some degree tied together. This basic linkage, combined with party leaders' desire to win the spoils that come with holding office, motivated those leaders to cooperate with one another.

The practicality of combining the resources and capabilities of different party organizations also led parties to cooperate in campaigning. During presidential election years, the national committees, and to a lesser extent the congressional and senatorial campaign committees, used their financial, research, communications, and administrative resources to unify their party and organize national campaigns. They raised large campaign contributions, set an issue agenda that favored their party, and arranged for nationally renowned politicians to go on speaking tours. Local party committees capitalized on their proximity to the electorate by gathering detailed information about voters, recruiting volunteer workers, encouraging party supporters to register to vote, and getting those supporters to the polls on election day. State party committees lacked the national committees' financial resources and administrative capacities, and they also were incapable of developing the strong grass-roots ties that characterized local party organizations. Nevertheless, their position within the party hierarchy made them important intermediaries between the other levels of the

Mark Hanna (standing at far right between President and Mrs. McKinley) raised millions of dollars for Republican William McKinley's 1896 and 1900 presidential campaigns. He is considered the country's first national political campaign manager, and his fund-raising practices sparked the first major effort toward campaign finance reform. Source: Library of Congress

party organization. In summary, party committees were responsible for campaign management during the party-centered era.

Fund-Raising

With the emergence of mass democracy, campaigners had to increase the effort and funding they devoted to electioneering. Nevertheless, campaigning remained more labor-intensive than cash-driven during the party-centered era. Most campaign activities consisted of grass-roots efforts carried out by unskilled campaign workers rather than technical services conducted by skilled political consultants and campaign aides. An estimated $10 million was spent on campaigning by both parties in the 1920 general elections in contrast to the several billion dollars spent in 2004. Nevertheless, money was still important in elections. Because campaign finance was not effectively regulated, most funds were raised through activities currently considered illegal in most local, state, and federal elections. Some monies were raised by soliciting large contributions from a small number of organizations and wealthy donors, including business, union, and other interest group leaders who benefited from government contracts. Additional sums were collected by pestering patronage workers for kickbacks from their government salaries. Fund-raising, which did not consume nearly as much time then as it does now, was carried out primarily by party leaders instead of candidates. Economic motives provided the foundation for most campaign contributions. Campaign fund-raisers and donors often viewed a contribution as the price to be paid for the enactment or continuation of favorable public policies, the creation or renewal of government contracts, or sustained government employment.

Assessing Public Opinion

Like fund-raising, assessing public opinion in the party-centered era depended on ongoing personal relationships rather than the technical proficiencies of skilled political consultants. Between elections, party activists developed a rapport with their neighbors and continually monitored their needs, opinions, and political preferences. During the election season, these activists more systematically canvassed election precincts by going door-to-door. In doing so, they learned, among other things, which candidates their neighbors' intended to vote for and what if anything needed to be done to reinforce or change those neighbors' voting intentions. Party canvassers also sought to learn whether those eligible to vote were registered or required transportation to the polls. This information was funneled up the local party hierarchy to the county party leader, who used it to assess the opinions of local voters and to prepare the poll book that would guide the door knocking and other voter mobilization efforts on election day.

The county boss also gave the state party chair a condensed version of this information to assist with planning the state party committee's campaign efforts. The state chair, in turn, passed along the information furnished by county party leaders to the party's national party committee, so that it served as a report on the political mood of voters in the state. Finally, the national party chair used the information provided by the state party chairs to help formulate a national strategy, including the allocation of the national committee's campaign resources.

Communications

Campaign communications, including mass advertising and personalized direct voter contacts, were and continue to be the most visible and most important aspects of political campaigns (see Chapter 17). Campaign advertisements convey the themes, images, issues, and symbols that divide political opponents and give meaning to an election for voters. Campaign communications and direct voter contacts can activate, reinforce, and even change some individuals' voting intentions. During the party-centered era, most election communications and voter contacts were made by party organizations. Indeed, for most of the nineteenth century party organizations, not candidates, bore primary responsibility for communicating with voters. Few candidates actually campaigned in public for themselves, largely because it was considered undignified. Rather, they stayed at home and made speeches from their front porches to voters who traveled from near and far to listen to them. In 1840 William Henry Harrison, a popular war hero, became the first presidential candidate to take to the campaign trail in his own behalf when he traveled across the country to speak at train stations, town squares, and campaign rallies. Despite Harrison's success at capitalizing on his popularity, decades passed before another presidential contender stepped forward to champion his own cause.

Rallies, parades, speeches, and other political demonstrations were among the most popular forms of campaigning during the golden age of parties. Such events not only entertained the voters and presented them with an occasion for socializing, but also served as a relatively effortless way to learn about candidates and issues. Moreover, they were inexpensive and helped party committees at all levels to build electoral support for their candidates. They had the added value of boosting party workers' morale and attracting free media coverage.

Much of a party's written campaign communications were based on the "campaign textbook," a document of several hundred pages written by the party's national committee and distributed to its candidates, party workers, and journalists. This document provided the rationale for a party's campaign. It included statistical tables, candidate biographies, acceptance speeches, and a lengthy, and somewhat biased, comparison of the general election platforms of the two major parties. While lavishing praise on its own party's standard-bearers, the "campaign textbook" colorfully described the opposition party's scandals, mishaps, and missed opportunities.

The campaigns also issued press releases and pamphlets that were intended to provide fodder for newspaper articles and to capture the imagination of voters. Some newspapers were so closely aligned with a specific party that their publishers gave as much priority to improving the party's election efforts as to reporting the news. For example, the editor of Washington's *Globe*, which supported Andrew Jackson's Democratic Party, was so closely tied to the Jackson administration that he became a member of the president's kitchen cabinet (a group of advisers, mostly newspaper editors, who met unofficially and informally with Jackson in the kitchen of the White House). Most of the materials distributed by the national campaigns were written by the parties' national committees. State and local party organizations often printed their own campaign literature, but much of

Painter-politician George Caleb Bingham's County Election (1852) *depicts Missourians lining up to cast their votes publicly as alcohol flows freely. Only white male property owners could vote, and candidates and their representatives could solicit votes immediately before voting. Source: Courtesy of the Saint Louis Art Museum*

and in other ways facilitating voter turnout among their supporters.

Summary

Political campaigns were conducted almost entirely by party organizations during the party-centered era. Party organizations were responsible for recruiting and selecting candidates, managing campaigns, raising funds, assessing public opinion, drafting and distributing campaign communications, and mobilizing voters. The party organization enjoyed tremendous political power during this period, because it was the major link among candidates, voters, and government.

The Candidate-Centered Era

The candidate-centered era emerged during the middle of the twentieth century and continued into the 1970s (see Box 2-2).[2]

it drew factual information and rhetorical flourishes from national party publications to meet local needs. Election paraphernalia, including campaign buttons, billboards, and pennants, also were used to communicate with voters. These were very popular among party workers and loyalists, because they made plain their owners' political loyalties for all to see.

Radio advertisements came onto the political scene at the end of the golden age of political parties. At first, these advertisements were largely financed and controlled by party organizations. Later, during the candidate-centered era of campaign politics, they were financed largely by the candidates.

Voter Mobilization

Voter mobilization, which includes registering voters and ensuring they actually show up at the polling place, was and continues to be a largely grass-roots activity (see Chapter 19). During the party-centered era, precinct captains and other party activists used information collected from voters to target their election day voter mobilization efforts. They sponsored public events to remind voters of the upcoming election and kept careful records of which supporters usually turned up to the polls on election day. Using these records, party workers mobilized local voters by knocking on their doors, arranging for transportation to the local polling place, providing baby-sitting services,

During this period, political campaigns were dominated by candidates, not party organizations. The candidates, who were largely self-selected rather than recruited by parties, assembled their own campaign organizations and bore full responsibility for the conduct of their campaigns. Party activity in most campaigns was minimal. Indeed, in contrast to the parties' golden age, most party organizations during this period were feeble and had little impact on elections.

Changes in the strategic context were largely responsible for the transformation of campaign politics from a party-centered system to a candidate-centered one. The first set of changes consisted of reforms enacted during the Populist and Progressive eras of the late 1800s and early 1900s. The major goal of the reforms was to wrest power from the bosses who controlled the political machines. As noted earlier, the direct primary attempted to achieve this goal by depriving party bosses of the ability to dominate the candidate selection process. One effect of the reform was that candidates began to develop their own campaign organizations to contest primary elections. Successful primary candidates then emerged from the nomination contest with more than their party's nomination; each also possessed a campaign organization with a demonstrated capacity for winning. These candidate-centered organizations existed independently of the party's campaign machinery, and, although they often were augmented to

BOX 2-2

JIMMY CARTER'S CANDIDATE-CENTERED CAMPAIGN

Lisa Epstein

In the 1976 primary season, former peanut farmer and Georgia governor Jimmy Carter was virtually unknown. Carter ran a classic candidate-centered campaign, stressing populist and antigovernment themes. He decided to run for the presidency on his own, without being recruited by party leaders, and he relied on a small group of personal advisers to manage his bid for the presidency. Friends and volunteers from Georgia (called the "Peanut Brigade") descended upon primary states to campaign for him. Lacking the financial backing of party committees or interest groups, he built momentum for his campaign by going out to the people— he would actually stay at the homes of Americans— hoping to build personal relationships. He began his campaign in 1974 and had traveled thousands of miles and visited most of the states before his better-known rivals had even announced their candidacies for the Democratic nomination.

Although Carter did not receive a majority of the support in the Iowa Democratic caucuses, his 27.7 percent showing (the highest among five Democratic candidates) was considered a victory. Carter came in first place in the New Hampshire primary. These victories gave his previously little known candidacy even more momentum. Carter quickly gained more popularity by offering himself as a political outsider who would change the government at a time when the Watergate scandal was still

Source: Burton Berinsky/Landov

a recent memory. Carter's popularity continued to skyrocket, eventually leading him to a victory over incumbent Republican Gerald Ford.

Carter's candidate-centered presidential bid differed from modern campaigns in several ways. He didn't pay for negative advertisements, and there was no money spent by outside groups for this type of publicity. Carter, Ford, and most of the other candidates running for president in 1976 were the first to be governed by new campaign finance reform legislation. They relied on a combination of individual contributions and federal

matching funds for the nomination contest and full federal funding for the general election campaign. The new limits encouraged individuals to contribute directly to candidates rather than to parties in the nomination contest. Because the nominees accepted federal funds they were prohibited from accepting contributions from any sources, including parties, during the general election. The reforms also strictly limited how much parties could spend in federal elections, placing them largely on the sidelines during the contest and further reinforcing the candidate-centered nature of Carter's campaign.

Since the end of his presidency in 1981, Carter has frequently remarked on the damaging impact of money on politics and has said that he could not have run the kind of campaign he did nor won the presidency if he had been forced to meet contemporary fund-raising demands. He has spoken out against interest groups that broadcast television advertisements independently from a candidate, pointing out that while they may not violate federal campaign finance law, they contribute to the growth in campaign costs and can affect an election outcome.

Sources: Laurence McQuillan, "Money Mars Politics, Carter Says," *USA Today Online*, October 1999, www.usatoday.com/news/opinion/e508.htm (accessed August 4, 2004); *Congressional Quarterly's Guide to U.S. Elections,* 4th ed. (Washington, D.C.: CQ Press, 2001).

perform the task, they formed the core of the organization the candidate used to contest the general election.

The Civil Service Reform Act of 1883 and similar reforms enacted in many states established a merit system of civil service, intended to weaken the power of party bosses and their organizations. It thus contributed to the rise of candidate-centered elections. By prohibiting party leaders from soliciting campaign contributions from public employees and preventing them from rewarding party activists with government jobs and contracts, these reforms deprived the parties of much of the money and manpower they had traditionally used to wage election campaigns. This reform and the direct primary combined to make it difficult, if not impossible, for many party leaders to control which candidates received the nomination and to play a central role in nominees' general election campaigns. No longer able to reward party activists with jobs and other government perks or even control who would be the eventual party nominee, party organizations lost much of their clout in government in general and in elections in particular. As a result, candidates became the central actors in election campaigns.

Broader systemic changes in society also encouraged the decline of political parties and the emergence of candidate-centered campaigning. Declining immigration, suburbanization, greater geographic mobility, and expanding education led to the decline of the tightly knit ethnic neighborhoods that were the main constituencies of most political machines. Without the volunteers, contributions, and votes those neighborhoods provided, machines could no longer dominate elections and candidates were increasingly left up to their own devices when mounting their campaigns. Many of the trends associated with the decline of the political machine also were associated with a decline in the influence of party identification on voting decisions and an increase in the number of independent voters, who, lacking partisan loyalty, were and continue to be more receptive to candidate-focused and issue-based appeals.

Technological innovations enabled candidates to rely on nonparty alternatives for campaigning and, indeed, to wage campaigns independent of and sometimes against party organizations. Public opinion polls, television, radio, direct mail (which is printed and addressed using computerized mail-merge technology), and computers provided political candidates with new tools for learning about and communicating with voters. Available at first only from marketing experts, these tools and strategic political advice later became available from professional political consultants, who earned their living by working in politics. Radio, television, and direct mail were particularly influential in bringing about a greater emphasis on the candidates. Increasingly popular with voters, these media were and are extremely well suited to conveying information about tangible phenomena, such as candidate images, but less useful in providing information about more abstract electoral actors, such as political parties. Direct mail also became a fund-raising tool.

Political reforms introduced during the 1970s helped to consolidate the rise of candidate-centered politics. Party reforms drafted by the Democratic Party's McGovern-Fraser Commission and intended to make the presidential nominating process more open and more representative greatly reduced the influence of party bosses in the selection of candidates. And when registered party voters (and independents in some states) were allowed to choose party nominees by voting in primaries and caucuses, the bosses were left largely on the sidelines of a process they had previously dominated (see Chapter 5). This situation was especially true of the Democrats' nomination process, but it also influenced Republican nominations. In some states, Republicans voluntarily emulated the Democrats' reforms, and in others they were forced to adopt them when Democratic-controlled state legislatures wrote the reforms into law. The nomination reforms laid the foundation for candidates instead of party leaders to appeal directly to their party's registered voters (and in some states, voters who did not register with a party) for support that would be crucial to winning the nomination. The primary and general election campaigns then began to focus more on issues that excited political activists than those that appealed to rank-and-file voters.[3]

The Federal Election Campaign Act (FECA) of 1971 and its subsequent amendments further reinforced the candidate-centered election system. As noted in Chapter 6, the FECA placed specific limits on the contributions that individuals could make to candidates, parties, and interest groups. In response to the law, interest groups formed political action committees (PACs) to collect money from group members and contribute it to candidates and parties (see Chapters 6 and 12). The act also placed an aggregate annual limit on the contributions individuals could make during a federal election. This aggregate limit encouraged individuals to direct most of their contributions to candidates rather than to political parties or other intermediary organizations. The provisions for financing the presidential election, which call for matching funds for nomination candidates and an unmatched grant for general election candidates, almost took parties out of the financing of presidential elections altogether.

Candidate Recruitment and Selection

The decision to run for elective office continued to be rooted in the local political context during the candidate-centered era, and it continued to involve personal considerations. However, the transition to that era led to some important changes in the decision process. First, local party organizations became less involved in socializing prospective candidates and encouraging them to run for office. Second, labor unions and other organized interest groups began to play a more active role in candidate recruitment. Third, prospective candidates began to listen not only to party leaders but also to a broader base of political associates when deciding whether to run for office, including issue-oriented political activists, political consultants, and those people who were concerned with more than securing some form of government largess.

These changes, together with the new, more participatory nomination processes, enabled candidates to pursue their party's nomination on their own, without first having to secure the endorsements of members of the local party organization. Although some candidates sought and benefited from such endorsements, others ran without them, casting themselves as outsiders who were running against the political machine. For some candidates, securing a party endorsement became impossible, because party organizations refused to make pre-primary endorsements as a matter of general policy.

The combined result of these changes was that the process of candidate recruitment, which had been dominated largely by political parties, was replaced by one in which candidates emerged—that is, individual candidates and their personal supporters had a greater hand than party bosses and their organizations in deciding who would run for office and win the nomination in most localities (see Chapter 5). To compete in these more open competitions for a party nomination, candidates had to build personalized campaign organizations and draw on nonparty support. This transformation had a tremendous impact on virtually every aspect of election campaigning and is a distinguishing feature of the candidate-centered system.

Campaign Management

In an era of candidate-centered primaries and weak party organizations, candidates began to rely on their own campaign organizations, rather than party committees, to conduct the vast majority of their primary and general election efforts. Campaign management was one area of campaigning that was firmly in the hands of candidates and those they selected to carry out this activity. Candidates and their managers hired staff and political consultants to carry out fund-raising, research, communications, and most other campaign activities; made strategic and tactical decisions; and supervised the day-to-day activities of the campaign. Voter mobilization was one area of campaigning that groups of candidates and party committees conducted cooperatively.

Fund-Raising

The emergence of contested participatory primaries, the rise of candidate-centered campaign organizations, and the greater reliance on modern campaign techniques and the paid campaign professionals that had mastered them forced candidates to raise more money to finance their elections. In 1972 spending in presidential elections reached almost $138 million, including the some $62 million spent by Republican Richard Nixon's Committee

to Re-elect the President, the $30 million spent by Democrat George McGovern's campaign organization, and the sums spent by various party committees and interest groups.[4] During the candidate-centered era, fund-raising became a campaign in and of itself, complete with its own strategies, tactics, and techniques. Even presidential candidates who accepted partial public funding for the nomination contest and full public funding in the general election devoted substantial amounts of time to raising money for their own campaigns, other candidates' election efforts, and their party's war chest.

Different types of appeals were used to attract resources from different donors. Although political parties were not a major source of funds for most campaigns, there was a logic to party contributions. Most party committees committed substantial resources to the reelection of incumbents, including those who had a hand in helping the committees raise money. Because the parties were interested in increasing the number of public offices occupied by their politicians, challengers and open-seat candidates who wished to receive party contributions had to demonstrate to party leaders that their races were competitive enough that party money could make the difference between winning and losing. Similarly, individuals and interest groups that made contributions to advance specific issues or a broad ideology were responsive to appeals based on the notion that a group could make a difference in a campaign.

Those individuals and interest groups that considered campaign contributions to be part of a larger public relations strategy to gain their lobbyists access to the political process contributed most of their funds to powerful incumbents, including congressional and state legislative party leaders and committee chairs whose political views did not coincide with their own. Solicitations designed to remind donors of an incumbent's influence were usually very successful. A combination of appeals generally was used to attract support from donors who had ideological concerns and wanted to gain political access. For example, Democratic candidates in close races emphasized the unpredictability of the outcomes of their contests when soliciting contributions from labor unions, while Democratic leaders emphasized the ability of those candidates to influence the policy process. Most Republicans made no fund-raising appeals to labor unions out of recognition that policy differences gave labor little incentive to support GOP candidates. Finally, some people contributed simply because they enjoyed the social side of giving. Candidates appealed to these donors by dangling before them invitations to rub shoulders with powerful politicians, celebrities, and other elites at gala events and in more intimate settings.

With the decline of political parties and the rise of candidate-centered elections, the responsibility for fund raising largely shifted from the party organizations to candidate campaign committees. In most candidate organizations, one or more persons were responsible for fund-raising. These campaign aides might include a treasurer, an accountant, organizers of traditional fund-raising activities such as cocktail parties, raffles, and dinners, and those with expertise in more modern techniques, such as direct-mail solicitations. Fund-raising appeals centered around the candidate, not the political party. Many candidates raised their funds using appeals based on their backgrounds, experience, and issue stances. But then as candidates learned the fund-raising power of extremist and even inflammatory appeals, they began to rely heavily on distortions of their opponents' records when raising money.

The FECA and similar campaign finance reforms instituted in some states solidified the candidate-centered nature of campaign fund-raising by limiting the contributions that candidates could receive from individuals, political parties, and interest groups. The reforms also required campaigns to fully disclose their financial transactions. The major goal of these reforms was to reduce corruption in federal elections; however, they also had several other effects. First, the strict disclosure requirements of the reforms led to campaign financing that was even more highly centralized and tightly controlled by candidate organizations, further reducing the involvement of party organizations. Second, the reforms prompted some interest groups to form PACs through which they could collect money from individual donors and redistribute those funds to candidates. In the late 1970s and 1980s, the number of PACs skyrocketed, and PACs soon surpassed party organizations in the total amounts of money contributed to federal candidates. As a result, PAC solicitations became a central part of the fund-raising strategies of many congressional candidates. Some House incumbents even raised more in PAC money than in individual contributions.

Assessing Public Opinion

The introduction of survey research techniques and high-speed computers into the electoral arena partially transformed the task of gauging public opinion from a labor-intensive activity that relied on campaign volunteers into a technical operation that required the expertise of professional pollsters (see Chapter 16). Candidates hired political consultants to collect and analyze voter information using statistical techniques. Most of the information collected was used to learn voters' underlying political preferences, positions on salient issues, assessments of the candidates, and reactions to the themes and messages the campaign was considering communicating. Baseline polls became popular for gaining an overview of the electorate, trend polls for learning about basic changes in public opinion, and tracking polls for making short-term assessments of the impact of various campaign activities and events on voters' opinions of the candidates. The use of focus groups—small, carefully selected groups of vot-

ers—enabled candidates to explore voter responses to their campaign messages and advertisements.

Communications

Not surprisingly, during this era most campaign communications were disseminated by candidate-centered organizations and featured the candidates. Candidates developed their own public images, selected the issues and themes that formed their message, and chose the specific forms of media to convey that message. Unlike in the previous era, parties were relatively uninvolved in this process. Party platforms, campaign books, and other types of party-centered communications declined in importance, especially in elections for Congress.

During this period, newsletters, campaign fliers, pins, and bumper stickers remained popular, but they were designed by candidate organizations to promote an individual candidate rather than an entire party ticket. Radio and television, coupled with the adaptation of public relations techniques used by business marketing, proved to be more effective means for delivering candidates' images directly into voters' living rooms. The rise of the candidate-centered system broke the near monopoly that political parties had over campaign communications, substituting candidate control over this process in most campaigns.

Voter Mobilization

Voter mobilization, consisting of voter registration and get-out-the-vote drives, also was affected by the emergence of a more candidate-centered system of election campaigns. Many candidates and their campaign managers developed their own targeting strategies and frequently relied on their own volunteers to contact and mobilize the electorate. However, a significant group continued to rely, at least in part, on local party organizations for assistance with this aspect of campaigning. Local party committees, unlike most candidate organizations, had an ongoing intimate knowledge of and sense of identity with the neighborhoods that composed each candidate's election district. They also possessed the organizational resources to coordinate the voter mobilization efforts of several candidate committees who were seeking the support of the same voters. The same was true of labor unions, groups representing Christian conservatives, and a small number of other organizations. Because many voter mobilization drives had, and continue to have, a multicandidate or party focus, party organizations and interest groups that could harness the needed human resources were in a position to play a significant role in those drives.

Summary

The FECA and the reforms of the presidential nomination process continued a trend toward candidate-centered politics that began with the introduction of the direct primary and was reinforced by the civil service reforms adopted at the turn to the twentieth century. The effects of these reformist impulses were solidified by larger systemic transformations in society, including demographic changes and the introduction of new technologies. Collectively, these developments led to the decline of political parties and the disappearance of party-centered campaigns from many parts of the country. The reforms also provided a legal environment that helped the candidate-centered era to take hold. This system was dominated by self-recruited candidates who assembled their own campaign organizations for the purpose of winning a party nomination and contesting the general election. Candidate-centered organizations became the major locus for the planning and implementation of most campaign activities, and parties moved to the periphery of many campaigns. One side effect of the rise of the candidate-centered system was that fewer challengers possessed the means for mounting vigorous campaigns and incumbent reelection rates began to soar.

The Contemporary Era

The contemporary era of campaign politics and the one that preceded it have many similarities and some differences.[5] Contemporary campaign politics is in some ways a natural outgrowth of the earlier candidate-centered period. As candidates, political parties, and interest groups learned how to navigate around the laws governing campaign finance, and as the Federal Election Commission (FEC), state regulatory agencies, and the courts weakened various provisions of the laws, the strategic context in which politicians and politically active groups operated changed considerably.[6] The passage of the Bipartisan Campaign Reform Act (BCRA) in 2002 led to even more change. Nevertheless, most campaigns remain focused on specific candidates. What has changed is that some outside groups have become very involved in closely contested elections. These organizations conduct independent, parallel, and coordinated campaigns (sometimes called outside campaigns) designed to influence both the political agenda and the votes individuals cast on election day. This independent campaigning has driven up the costs of elections considerably. Candidates, parties, and interest groups spent well in excess of $600 million on the 2000 presidential election, for example.

The weakening and eventual demise of the FECA followed the usual cycle of regulatory politics. Candidates, party officials, interest group leaders, political consultants, and campaign contributors challenged the law in a variety of ways. Some chose to directly challenge its constitutionality. In *Buckley v. Valeo* (1976), the Supreme Court overturned some of the FECA's major provisions, including those that sought to limit the amounts that individuals and PACs spent independently of candidates to influence elections. The overall limits on candidates' campaign expenditures also were overturned, with the exception of expenditures by presidential candidates who accepted public funding. The structure of the Federal Election Commission, which originally had two voting members appointed by the president and four appointed by congressional leaders, was declared unconstitutional and changed to six presidential appointees who required Senate approval.

Other people and groups challenged the law, or even flouted it. Some toed up to the FECA and tested its boundaries to learn what was and what was not permissible. Still others consciously violated provisions of the law to learn whether punishment would be forthcoming and, if it was, the degree of its severity. And then there were those who, given the choice between winning an election and obeying the law, chose to break the law in order to win. Indeed, President Richard Nixon's campaign staff, and perhaps even the president himself, was so worried about Nixon's 1972 reelection that they collected illegal campaign contributions and used them to finance the break-in at the headquarters of the Democratic National Committee in Washington in June 1972. Known as the Watergate scandal, these activities eventually landed several powerful Republican Party political operatives in prison and drove Nixon to resign from the presidency in 1974. Ironically, Nixon had won the 1972 election by a landslide, and his behavior led Congress to enact extremely strict amendments to the original FECA.

Perhaps the most significant challenge to the FECA involved the expenditure of "nonfederal," "soft," or "outside" money (as opposed to the "federal" or "hard" money spent inside the system) to influence federal elections (see Chapter 6). Until enactment of the BCRA in 2002, soft money included contributions made to the parties' national, state, and local organizations from sources and in amounts banned under the federal system. It also encompassed interest group contributions and expenditures made outside the federal system, some of which are still allowed under the BCRA and are made by so-called 527 committees (which take their name from the provision of the Internal Revenue Code that defines them).

Prior to enactment of the BCRA, party soft money contributions to political parties were collected from corporations, unions, and wealthy individuals in amounts that sometimes exceeded $1 million, well in excess of the then $25,000 per year aggregate total for individual hard money contributions.[7] Most soft money was raised and spent by political parties, but other groups, some of which are closely affiliated with party committees, also collected and distributed money outside the federal system in order to influence federal elections. Related to the rise of soft money was the advent of issue advocacy ads. These ads, which are financed primarily with soft money, are nearly identical to hard money ads in that they praise or criticize federal candidates by name or feature their likenesses. The major differences between the two types of ads are that issue advocacy ads *cannot expressly* call for a candidate's election or defeat, and they tend to be more negative.

Soft money and issue advocacy ads offered parties, and continue to offer some interest groups and state and local party committees, advantages. Soft money can be raised in huge chunks from a small number of deep-pocketed sources, and it can be spent in competitive elections where it can presumably have a substantial impact on election outcomes. As pointed out in Chapters 6 and 12, soft money gives those who contribute it political access and presumably influence, and it enables political organizations to spend extra—and once banned—resources to influence campaigns and ultimately the composition of Congress. Soft money and issue advocacy ads substantially increased the influence of political parties and interest groups prior to enactment of the BCRA, and they continue to enhance the influence of organized interests in the post–BCRA period. These forms of participation did not do away with candidate-centered elections, but they did significantly influence many competitive elections.

Candidate Recruitment and Selection

Candidate recruitment and selection in the contemporary era are similar to that during the candidate-centered system, but with a few important differences. First, party organizations have assumed a more important role in candidate recruitment. National party organizations located in Washington, D.C., particularly the Democratic and Republican congressional and senatorial campaign committees, now play significant roles in encouraging some candidates to run for Congress and discouraging others. The same is true of legislative campaign committees in many states. These party committees give only modest encouragement and advice to the many politicians who wish to run for the U.S. Senate, U.S. House of Representatives, or a state legislature, and they expend considerable effort to recruit candidates to run for the few seats they anticipate will be competitive. The committees use various methods to encourage prospective candidates to run, including demonstrating through poll results the candidate's popularity with voters or potential for winning and promising to provide campaign contributions and assistance with fund-raising, communications, and other campaign activities should the candidate win the nomination. In primary contests in which the party leaders who direct these committees believe that one candidate would be more viable in the general election than the others, these leaders and committee staff may actively discourage the others from running. Sometimes, politicians who are ideological extremists are discouraged from running in favor of moderates. Such de-recruitment strategies can be very effective at winnowing the field of potential candidates. However, in the few instances in which they fail and in which party leaders believe one contender would be much stronger in the general election than another, the congressional campaign committees actively back one primary candidate.

A second difference between candidate recruitment in the contemporary era and the candidate-centered era is the role of interest groups. Like political parties, many interest groups are now recruiting candidates for public office. These groups include various labor unions; the Club for Growth, an anti-tax group that supports Republican candidates who favor free-market economics; the League of Conservation Voters, an environmental group that supports mainly Democrats; and EMILY'S List ("Early Money Is Like Yeast [it helps the dough rise]"), which seeks to elect pro-choice Democratic women. Unlike political parties, these organizations are now routinely extremely involved in contested nomination contests. Some provide candidates with endorsements, monetary contributions, and campaign assistance such as volunteers during the primary season. They also may air campaign advertisements on radio and television supporting one candidate (or opposing others); make similar appeals via mail, e-mail, or telephone; and mobilize their members on primary day.

A third difference between candidate recruitment in the contemporary era and the candidate-centered era is that political parties, interest groups, and even some candidates have become much bolder about participating in the opposing party's nomination contests. The 2002 California gubernatorial contest was a particularly noteworthy example. Incumbent governor Gray Davis, who faced only token opposition in his race for the Democratic nomination, spent an estimated $10 million attacking former Los Angeles mayor and moderate Richard Riordan in the Republican primary. His goal was to boost the prospects of conservative businessman Bill Simon, whom Davis and most Democrats considered the less viable of the two opponents. The plan ultimately succeeded, because Simon defeated Riordan by roughly 49 percent to 31 percent in the Republican primary, and Davis went on to defeat Simon by 47 percent to 42 percent in the general election. Ironically, Davis was subjected to a successful recall vote in late 2003, less than a year after his reelection.

Campaign Management

Campaign management in the contemporary era continues to revolve primarily around candidates and the staff hired to mount their campaigns. Candidates are responsible for assembling their own campaign staffs, consultants, and volunteers and for conducting their own election campaigns (see Chapter 10). The influence of political parties and interest groups depends primarily on the resources those organizations can bring to bear on the campaign. In presidential elections, the two major-party candidates, and some minor-party contestants, possess enough financial and personnel resources to wage substantial campaigns. Party committees and allied interest groups typically help presidential campaigns by providing financial and organizational support, communications, and voter mobilization assistance. In return, they may ask a candidate to visit a particular locality, make an effort to boost the prospects of a candidate for lower office, or draw attention to one or more issues when making a speech. The same type of cooperation exists in most gubernatorial campaigns.

Campaign management in most elections for Congress, state legislatures, local and municipal offices—so-called down-ballot races—is dominated by candidate campaign organizations as well. Political parties, particularly congressional, senatorial, and state legislative campaign committees in many states, assist candidates with hiring campaign aides and political consultants and with management, fund-raising, communications, and other aspects of campaigning requiring specialized expertise. These party committees maintain lists of qualified consultants, facilitate matchmaking between consultants and candidates, and provide some campaigns with general strategic and organizational advice. They also hold training seminars for candidates, campaign aides, and political activists.

In a small number of campaigns, however, particularly those featuring a nonincumbent congressional candidate in a very close race, political parties and other groups often play a larger role. Party operatives take a vigorous interest in ensuring that these campaigns hire staff and consultants that have the ability to wage a strong campaign. They help the campaign write a sound campaign plan, and party field staff visit campaign headquarters routinely to provide strategic advice and to report to their party committees about the campaign's progress. Party committees, and some interest groups, may even dispatch some of their personnel to work full time on a few campaigns. Most candidates appreciate the support they receive from these organizations, but that support also can cause tension. The candidate's campaign aides consider themselves experts on the candidate or the local strategic context, and the party and interest group aides consider themselves experts on campaign politics. Some candidates and campaign aides view party and interest group personnel as outsiders and are resentful of the roles they seek to assume in the campaign. Nevertheless, even these candidates and their aides usually accept advice from these "outsiders" because to do otherwise could result in their campaigns being cut off from large contributions and other forms of campaign assistance.

Fund-Raising

Candidates use the same techniques and turn to the same financial sources in the contemporary era as they did in the candidate-centered era. Campaign fund-raising continues to be carried out primarily by the candidates' own campaign organizations (see Chapter 15). Nevertheless, the role of party committees and interest groups in fund raising has increased considerably. The parties' congressional, senatorial, and state legislative campaign committees have become much more influential in directing the flow of campaign money to candidates in competitive elections. The same is true of a relatively small number of interest groups. These party committees and groups influence the fund-raising process in several ways. First, they provide candidates with both lists of potential donors and advice on how to solicit contributions from them. Second, these organizations use letters, newsletters, e-mail, briefings, and other methods to circulate favorable information about the candidates they support to other donors that fall within their sphere of influence. Third, some organizations, mainly party committees, ask powerful officeholders to use their political muscle to encourage donors to contribute to other candidates who are in need of funds. This "buddy system" works particularly well when legislative incumbents are paired with nonincumbents who share their political views. Fourth, interest groups and some party committees actually collect, bundle into one package, and deliver large checks from their members to candidates.

The new role of party committees and interest groups in fund-raising has had important consequences. For one thing, it has contributed to the development of a more nationalized system of campaign finance and has enhanced the parties' and interest groups' abilities to influence the flow of money in that system. Party committees and some interest groups that participate in the financing of congressional and some state legislative elections are now able to start and stem the flow of contributions to individual campaigns. Indeed, a direct effect of these organizations' efforts to channel the flow of money to some campaigns is that others are starved for cash and left unable to compete for votes. One of the side effects of the contemporary system of campaign finance is a concentration of competition in a limited number of elections.

Assessing Public Opinion

Although politicians and political consultants continually refine the techniques they use to gauge public opinion, those used in the contemporary era are, for the most part, the same as those used in the era that preceded it. The major difference between the two eras is that political parties and, to a lesser degree, interest groups have assumed larger roles in taking the electorate's political pulse. As noted earlier and discussed in Chapter 16, some of these organizations take polls to encourage prospective candidates to run for office. These same organizations also use polling data when formulating their own campaign strategies and deciding how to distribute their campaign resources. In addition, party committees and interest groups routinely disseminate the results of national surveys and other research through the newsletters they send to candidates, the media, and political activists. These organizations also conduct polls in a limited number of competitive elections and share the results with the candidates in those contests to improve the campaigns' decision making. Party and interest group polling has increased the influence of these organizations in today's elections.

Communications

With the exception of the introduction of the Internet and satellite television uplinks, only incremental changes have taken place in the techniques campaigns use to communicate with voters (see Chapter 17). What have changed are the roles of political parties and outside groups in helping candidates to gain access to and, in some cases, utilize these techniques. During the 1980s, the parties' congressional and senatorial campaign committees helped candidates to communicate with voters in several ways. Some candidates received basic party issue packages that also were sent to political activists or were given the use of generic TV ads and assistance in customizing them with voiceovers and text. Others benefited from more individualized assistance, including extensive issue and opposition research, help with message development, and the use of party facilities and media experts in writing, recording, editing, and disseminating TV, radio, and direct-mail advertisements.

These organizations continue to provide generic communications assistance to many candidates, but changes in technology have made it more cost-effective for candidates and consultants to tape and edit their own campaign ads. Parties continue to provide candidates with access to generic TV ads, and they furnish candidates, mostly incumbents, with access to satellite technology in Washington, D.C., that enables candidates to interact in real time with their constituents. Most of the communications assistance that parties provide directly to contemporary campaigns is timely feedback on campaign ads. Using streaming video on the Internet, party communications staff typically give candidates commentaries on their ads in a matter of hours, and sometimes even minutes. In addition to the assistance given to campaign organizations, party committees (and some interest groups) also directly communicate with voters to influence the outcome of some elections.

Voter Mobilization

Voter mobilization activities during the contemporary era closely resemble those of the candidate-centered era except for the now higher levels of party and interest group involvement (see Chapter 19). Because state and local party committees benefit from money transferred to them by national party organizations, local party organizations are able to play a greater role in voter mobilization. Similarly, a variety of interest groups, including labor unions, religious-affiliated groups, and 527 committees, are benefiting from financial and organizational improvements that have enabled them to play a larger role in mobilizing voters. By the 1990s, the Democratic Party and labor unions had established an effective voter mobilization program that enabled Democratic candidates to compete with Republicans, even when the former were outspent. The Republicans responded in 2002 by organizing their own nationally directed voter mobilization program called the "72 Hour Task Force," because it was used to mobilize voters during the last seventy-two hours of the campaign. The GOP expanded and refined this program in 2004, making special efforts to register and turnout evangelical voters.

Independent, Parallel, and Coordinated Campaigns

The most distinguishing feature of the contemporary campaign era is the direct voter communications being undertaken by the political parties and interest groups. In what began as soft money–funded, grass-roots campaign activities and generic advertisements designed to claim credit or place blame on a party for the state of the nation, party and interest group efforts have evolved into sophisticated independent, parallel, and coordinated campaigns. These campaigns largely owe their existence to the weakening of the FECA and the continued evolution of the candidate-centered system. In the campaigns, teams of pollsters and other researchers, media consultants, direct-mail and mass telephone experts, and other political strategists plan campaign communications and voter mobilization drives that appeal directly to the voters. Some of these communications are designed to influence the national political agenda or to set the campaign agenda in a specific state or congressional district. Most are used to disseminate a positive message on behalf of one candidate, to communicate a negative message about a candidate's opponents, or to do both. Additional communications are intended to encourage voters to show up at the polls on election day.

Independent campaigns are supported primarily by what federal law classifies as independent expenditures for advertisements or other communications that *expressly* call for the election or defeat of a candidate. Such communications are undertaken almost exclusively in competitive races, and they are generally more aggressive than those issued by the candidate. Independent expenditures must be made with hard money and without the candidate's knowledge or consent. They usually take the form of television or radio ads, direct mail, or mass telephone calls. Parties try to maximize the effectiveness of these expenditures by conducting preliminary polls and other research. Although the FECA allowed PACs to make independent expenditures as of 1974, political parties were not allowed to engage in such expenditures until 1996 when the Supreme Court ruled them permissible in *Colorado Republican Federal Campaign Committee v. Federal Election Commission*. Because they must be made with hard money, independent expenditures were not as attractive an alternative for party or interest group spending as issue advocacy advertising prior to the passage of BCRA. In the 2002 congressional elections, the parties spent just over $3 million and interest groups a bit less than $14 million on independent expenditures. In 2004 parties spent more on independent expenditures.

Parallel campaigns incorporate many of the organizational features used by candidate campaigns and independent campaigns, including polling, issue research, and campaign communications. Some of these communications, however, are coordinated to some degree with the campaigns of specific candidates. The earliest efforts at parallel campaigning were generic party messages, such as the Republican National Committee's televised ad "Vote Republican, for a Change" aired in 1980, and the Democrats' "It Isn't Fair, It's Republican" aired in 1982.

With the loosening of the FECA's prohibitions against using soft money for candidate-focused electioneering during the 1996 elections, the two major parties and some wealthy interest groups began to air issue advocacy advertisements on television and radio, through the mail, and over the telephone. Most of these communications resembled candidate-sponsored communications, and it was often difficult to distinguish between them. The major difference is that the communications issued by the parallel campaigns were more negative or contrast-oriented, and they were more likely to skewer the opposing candidate. By means of issue advocacy, parties and interest groups were able to force candidates to discuss issues they might otherwise wish to avoid. Some candidates thus found themselves campaigning on a political agenda set by an outside organization rather than their own or one set by their opponents. Overall, parties and interest groups were able to use issue advocacy ads to concentrate huge sums of money collected from a tiny sector of society in a small number of hotly contested races. In the 2002 congressional elections, the Democratic and Republican Party organizations in Washington, D.C., spent in excess of $360 million on parallel campaigns. Interest groups spent more than $20 million on television alone as part of their parallel campaigns and at least $100 million more on other campaign activities.

Because of the BCRA's ban on national party soft money and party-sponsored issue advocacy ads, only interest groups (including some with strong partisan ties) were free to engage in issue advocacy during the 2004 election season. Democratic-leaning 527 committees, such as America Coming Together and the Media Fund, and Republican-leaning groups, such as Progress for America, Swift Boat Veterans for the Truth, poured hundreds of millions of dollars into issue advocacy advertising during the campaigns to sponsor television, radio, and direct-mail advertising and voter registration and mobilization activities. These groups' efforts, like those of the presidential candidates and political parties, were concentrated primarily in the most competitive states.

The coordinated campaign takes the form of the traditional grass-roots party campaigning, enhanced by innovations in communications, database management, and voter mobilization. Important elements of the coordinated campaign are voter identification, absentee ballot programs, and other voter mobilization efforts. Contemporary party-coordinated campaigns often involve the parties' national, congressional, and senatorial campaign committees; state and local party organizations; allied interest groups; and federal, state, and local candidates. It is impossible to calculate the exact amount spent on coordinated campaign activities, but the totals were well in excess of $100 million for the 2002 congressional elections and in the hundreds of millions of dollars during the 2004 elections.

The Impact of Campaigning by Political Parties and Interest Groups

The major difference between the contemporary era of campaign politics and the candidate-centered era that preceded it is the bigger role being played now by political parties and interest groups in election campaigns. This begs the question: what effects are party and interest group efforts having on the outcomes of contemporary elections? This is not an easy question to answer because many factors—including the state of the nation, the mood of the electorate, local conditions, the political agenda on which a specific election is fought, and the efforts of individual candidates and their organizations—have an impact on election outcomes. Nevertheless, the effects of party and interest group activities can be measured in a variety of ways.

One way is to ascertain whether parties and interest groups are having an impact on the issues that voters are considering when casting their ballots. It is clear that, although neither major party is able to consistently dominate the national political agenda, both have succeeded in influencing it. During the 1994 midterm elections, for example, the Republicans railed against a Democratic president and a Democratic-controlled Congress that they called corrupt and out of step with voters. They offered as an alternative a national platform called the Contract with America and succeeded in winning control of both houses of Congress for the first time in forty years. Two years later, the Democratic Party spent millions of dollars on issue advocacy advertisements blasting the Republicans for their ideological extremism and for making tactical decisions to twice shut down the federal government in their budget battles with the Clinton White House. This advertising drive helped the Democrats to maintain occupancy of the White House and pick up seats in both the House and the Senate.

A second way to measure the impact of political party and interest group efforts on elections is to ask candidates and those who help them run for office how valuable they find the campaign services they receive from these organizations. Candidates and campaign aides who participated in the 2002 House elections were asked to rate the importance of campaign assistance from local, state, and national party organizations and union, business, and advocacy groups and PACs in aspects of campaigning requiring professional expertise or in-depth research. The candidates and their aides ranked their party's congressional campaign committee highly. Indeed, they gave top evaluations to the assistance they received with campaign management, information about voters, issue and opposition research, mass media advertising, and development of the candidate's public image. Local party committees received the strongest evaluations for assistance with registering voters, launching GOTV (Get out the vote) drives, and signing up campaign volunteers. State party committees were rated next highest for voter mobilization activities. The parties received their highest ratings from candidates in close races, reflecting the parties' strategy of targeting their resources to a small number of close contests in order to win as many seats as possible. Candidates for open seats, which are usually the most competitive and unpredictable House contests, gave the parties substantially more favorable evaluations than did the other candidates. Republican candidates in competitive races gave more favorable evaluations of the assistance they received than did their Democratic counterparts, suggesting that the GOP extended more help to its candidates and did a better job targeting that assistance than did the Democrats.[8]

In virtually every aspect of campaigning, interest groups received somewhat lower evaluations than did the parties for the assistance given in 2002. The exception was fund raising, reflecting the fact that the typical House candidate raises considerably more money from interest group PACs than from party committees. The assessments of House campaigners further indicate that interest groups, especially labor unions and labor PACs, play larger roles in the campaigns of Democrats than in those of Republicans. Interest groups, like parties, target selected races. The information provided by both House and Senate campaigners indicates that interest group campaign assistance tends to be directed more toward competitive contests and to be more important to challengers and open-seat candidates than to incumbents.

A third way to measure the impact of party and interest group campaigning is to evaluate the effect of these organizations' communications efforts on the candidates' abilities to reach out to voters. Gauging the impact of party and group independent, parallel, and coordinated campaigns is much more complicated than assessing these organizations' influence on campaign agendas or candidates' campaign efforts. It requires an analysis of massive amounts of data on the composition of election districts, candidate strategy and spending, media coverage and endorsements, party and interest group efforts, and other factors that can influence election outcomes. The results of such an analysis reveal that party and interest group independent, parallel, and coordinated campaign efforts have a positive impact on the portion of votes House challengers and open-seat candidates collect. These efforts also have a reinforcing effect on the votes garnered by House incumbents, who, as noted in Chapter 21, begin their elections with leads so large that there is little these candidates or other organizations can do to expand them. However, in those House races in which parties and interest groups concentrate their efforts they diminish and sometimes overshadow the efforts of the candidates themselves, thus to some degree neutralizing the impact of candidate strategizing and spending. In summary, all three ways of measuring the impact of party committee and interest group efforts demonstrate that these organizations play an important role in contemporary campaign politics.

Conclusion

Political campaigns in the United States have progressed through many stages, often in response to changes in the larger strategic context in which elections are conducted. Early in U.S. history, before the days of mass suffrage, campaigns consisted primarily of informal caucusing among those few political elites who enjoyed the right to vote. With the rise of mass suffrage and strong party organizations, the party-centered era emerged. During this period, local party machines dominated most aspects of political campaigning, including candidate recruitment, selection, campaign strategy, and implementation of the campaign itself. With the onset of regulatory reform and broader systemic change in society, candidates became more self-selected and campaigns became more candidate-centered. Political parties and interest groups responded to the candidate-centered system by providing campaign assistance to candidates. Then, as the regulatory framework governing elections began to weaken, these organizations also began to increase their roles in elections by conducting independent, parallel, and coordinated campaigns. In response to these election activities, and more general concerns about the role of money in politics, Congress passed the Bipartisan Campaign Reform Act of 2002 (see Chapter 6). This law, other political reforms, and additional changes in the context in which elections are conducted will lead to further developments in the campaign process.

Notes

1. Much of the information in this section is drawn from Paul S. Herrnson, *Party Campaigning in the 1980s* (Cambridge, Mass.: Harvard University Press, 1986), 9–18.

2. Much of the information in this section is drawn from ibid., 19–29.

3. See, for example, Nelson W. Polsby, *The Consequences of Party Reform* (Oxford: Oxford University Press, 1983), 62, 72–81.

4. Herbert E. Alexander, *Financing Politics* (Washington, D.C.: Congressional Quarterly, 1976), 20.

5. Much of the information from this section is drawn from Paul S. Herrnson, *Congressional Elections: Campaigning at Home and in Washington*, 4th ed. (Washington, D.C.: CQ Press, 2004), 12–17, 115–128, 152–158, and from Paul S. Herrnson, "The Bipartisan Campaign Reform Act and Congressional Elections," in *Congress Reconsidered*, ed. Larry Dodd and Bruce Oppenheimer (Washington, D.C.: CQ Press, 2005).

6. On the decline of the FECA, see Anthony Corrado, Thomas Mann, Daniel Ortiz, and Trevor Potter, *The New Campaign Finance Sourcebook* (Washington, D.C.: Brookings, 2004).

7. The aggregate individual contribution limit was increased from $50,000 per two-year election cycle to $95,000 under the BCRA.

8. Herrnson, *Congressional Elections*, 121–123.

Suggested Readings

Green, John C., and Rick Farmer, eds. *The State of the Parties.* Lanham, Md.: Rowman and Littlefield, 2003.

Herrnson, Paul S. *Congressional Elections: Campaigning at Home and in Washington.* 4th ed. Washington, D.C.: CQ Press, 2004.

———. *Party Campaigning in the 1980s.* Cambridge, Mass.: Harvard University Press, 1988.

Johnson, Dennis W. *No Place for Amateurs: How Political Consultants Are Reshaping American Democracy.* New York: Routledge, 2001.

Maisel, L. Sandy, ed. *The Parties Respond: Changes in American Parties and Campaigns.* Boulder, Colo.: Westview Press, 2002.

Medvic, Stephen K. *Political Consultants in U.S. Congressional Elections.* Columbus: Ohio State University Press, 2001.

Sabato, Larry J. *The Rise of the Political Consultants: New Ways of Winning Elections.* New York: Basic Books, 1981.

Sorauf, Frank J. *Inside Campaign Finance: Myths and Realities.* New Haven, Conn.: Yale University Press, 1992.

Wayne, Stephen J. *The Road to the White House 2004: The Politics of Presidential Elections.* Belmont, Calif.: Thomson/Wadsworth, 2003.

PART II
Laws and Regulations Governing Campaigns

CHAPTER 3

Laws Governing Suffrage

Barry C. Burden

In the United States, electoral participation is widely viewed as both a right and a duty.[1] Citizens are expected and encouraged to vote in federal, state, and local elections and to pay attention to public affairs. It is ironic, then, that the Constitution, universally revered as it is, contains no fundamental right to vote. Not only does it defer to Congress and the states to establish electoral procedures, but it also makes no explicit suggestion that the votes cast should even count equally.

Although the trend has been toward making more Americans eligible to vote, during some periods in U.S. history suffrage has been restricted. *Direct* restrictions on suffrage were slowly removed over the last two hundred years, but it has only been since the 1960s that *indirect* limitations on voting rights have been pushed aside. These lurches toward a universal franchise and an equal weighting of votes are the product of changes in American society, an injection of the judiciary into the process, and other factors. The purpose of this chapter is to describe these changes.

Who Can Vote?

The portion of the adult population eligible to vote has grown considerably since the nation's earliest days from a cadre of white, male property owners at the turn of the nineteenth century to all but noncitizens and felons at the turn of the twenty-first century. This section describes changes in voting rights in three domains. *Constitutional* changes include three key amendments giving blacks, women, and young people the vote. Two of these amendments had immediate effects, but one, the Fifteenth Amendment dealing with race, was entirely ineffectual for a full century. *Legislative* changes are more often directed at voter registration, a procedure that presents hurdles unique to the United States. Registration laws are complex and often serve conflicting purposes—they are devised to eliminate voter corruption but can be manipulated to exclude voters. The laws are administered on a local rather than national level, so they vary from one jurisdiction to the next. *Judicial* changes, primarily in the

1960s, affected registration practices, providing some uniformity across the states and eliminating poll taxes and other efforts to disenfranchise minority groups.

Constitutional Changes

It is striking that most constitutional changes take place on the heels of periods of military conflict. Otherwise, voting rights tend to go unchanged. The Fifteenth Amendment, which on paper gave the vote to black men, was added in the immediate wake of the Civil War. Women gained the right to vote in the Nineteenth Amendment, just two years after World War I ended. And the voting age was lowered by the Twenty-sixth Amendment to eighteen years near the end of the conflict in Vietnam. Although the circumstances surrounding each of these constitutional adjustments are unique, it is nevertheless apparent that war and voting are linked.

Revolutionary War to Civil War

Disputes over voting rights began well before the federal constitution was ratified in 1787. Although the Declaration of Independence in 1776 established some "unalienable Rights" and that "all men are created equal," early American law was not heavily based on rights. America's first constitution, the Articles of Confederation, paid little attention to individual rights. The Constitution went a step further in referring to "We the People," but the individual's right to vote is nowhere to be found. Indeed, Article I delegates to the states "the Times, Places and Manner of holding Elections." As a result, suffrage laws in the early republic were determined locally and tended to be strict. Women, blacks, and other minorities were regularly kept away from the ballot box. It would take federal initiative and more than a century of change to bring these groups into the electoral process.

Most states also had property and residency requirements. These were often in place to prevent poor people and immigrants from participating in elections. In the years immediately after the Revolutionary War, all thirteen states had in place some kind of property qualification that was merely a continuation of requirements under colonial rule. For example, in the colonial era New

VOL. XI—No. 568.]   NEW YORK, SATURDAY, NOVEMBER 16, 1867.   [SINGLE COPIES TEN CENTS.
[$4.00 PER YEAR IN ADVANCE.
Entered according to Act of Congress, in the Year 1867, by Harper & Brothers, in the Clerk's Office of the District Court for the Southern District of New York.

In this image published on November 16, 1867, a Union soldier is among those casting their ballots in the nation he had fought to defend but which had denied him the right to vote. Although the Fifteenth Amendment supposedly removed racial barriers to voting, African Americans did not secure full voting rights until the passage of the Voting Rights Act in 1965. Source: Library of Congress

Hampshire steadily increased its property requirements from £20 in 1680 to £50 in 1709, a standard that remained in place through 1776. Some of the property requirements were abandoned soon after the Revolutionary War, but many remained in place until the Civil War.[2]

Residency often had to be established a year or two before a citizen could actually cast a ballot, an extreme requirement by today's standards. In the early 1800s, elites often imposed such requirements based on principle.[3] Many believed that people without local knowledge and a clear stake in the community should not make collective decisions for long-term residents. But residency requirements also were used for less principled purposes: to discourage transient populations from unsettling the electoral status quo in an area.[4]

Debates about property requirements were intense and multifaceted. Supporters of a property requirement argued that a person should be financially independent

to vote; only then could a clear-eyed decision be made. A person on "relief," who depended on charity or government to survive, could not make principled voting decisions; he was too lazy or incompetent to be given the vote. Regardless of the rationale, both groups believed that a minimum standard for "freeholding" (the free and clear ownership of property) should be required. Yet Benjamin Franklin's statement in Box 3-1 points to the foolishness of this point of view. In his persuasive example, he illustrates that property itself does not lead to a reasoned voting choice. Although it would take several decades for this view to become law in most locales, it did indeed slowly take hold.

Reconstruction Amendments

Before the Civil War, elections were white-only affairs in all but a few states. It was not until after the war over slavery that the Constitution was amended to include voting rights for blacks. The Fifteenth Amendment, ratified in 1870, states simply that the right to vote cannot be "denied or abridged . . . on account of race, color, or previous condition of servitude." Although this statement is negative rather than positive, it clearly prohibits the discriminatory voting habits that were so common before the war.

Unfortunately, the Fifteenth Amendment was hardly enforced. It struck down the de jure (legislated) barriers to black participation, but not the de facto (actual) ones. In theory, then, most black men could now vote, but in practice few could. It would take more than a constitutional amendment to eliminate discrimination at the ballot box and ban devices such as poll taxes, which were used to scare off black voters until the 1960s.

In retrospect, the Fourteenth Amendment, ratified in 1868, was more momentous than the Fifteenth. Most important was the statement that no person shall be deprived of "life, liberty, or property, without due process of law" nor shall anyone be denied "equal protection of the laws." This new legal focus on "due process" and "equal protection" would only grow over time as challenges to suffrage laws, ballot designs, and districting practices were raised. It would be almost a century until the courts fully embraced this approach, but the groundwork was laid in the 1860s.

Women's Suffrage

The milestone for women's suffrage came later than it did for black men, but the change was more immediate. The Nineteenth Amendment to the Constitution, ratified in 1920, declared that the right to vote cannot be limited "on account of sex." These words marked the end of both the Progressive era in U.S. politics and a lengthy

BOX 3-1

BENJAMIN FRANKLIN'S VIEW OF PROPERTY REQUIREMENTS

Today a man owns a jackass worth fifty dollars and he is entitled to vote; but before the next election the jackass dies. The man in the mean time has become more experienced, his knowledge of the principles of government, and his acquaintance with mankind, are more extensive, and he is therefore better qualified to make a proper selection of rulers— but the jackass is dead and the man cannot vote. Now gentlemen, pray inform me, in whom is the right of suffrage? In the man or in the jackass?

Source: Franklin quoted in Alexander Keyssar, *The Right to Vote: The Contested History of Democracy in the United States* (New York: Basic Books, 2000), 3.

struggle over women's suffrage that had begun at least seventy years earlier.[5] The women's suffrage movement began with meetings of activists in the mid-1800s, and after a temporary derailment around the Civil War, it developed into a mass movement. Elizabeth Cady Stanton and Lucretia Mott organized the first prominent women's convention in Seneca Falls, New York, in 1848. Women such as Susan B. Anthony began working through state constitutional conventions, political party meetings, and other venues to push their cause.

Until the Constitution was amended, women were granted suffrage in a patchwork fashion. Some women had full voting rights; others had none. For example, widows were usually permitted to vote if their husbands left them with sizable estates, but as property requirements came under greater scrutiny, many observers wondered why a small number of women deserved the vote, while most others did not.

Some partial gains over time, such as the right to vote in school and other local elections, might have contributed as much to stalling the cause as to promoting it. Yet because of these delays activists were able to take advantage of referenda and initiatives—new tools made available in the Progressive era—to put women's suffrage on the public agenda and enlist support. Picketing, marching through the streets, and contributing to the American effort in

World War I were all critical parts of the path to women's suffrage. Indeed, President Woodrow Wilson began supporting the amendment as a "war measure."

The adoption of new social views were helped by western expansion. By 1900, eight western states and territories had fully enfranchised women. Five others permitted women to vote in local elections, and twenty-eight allowed them to vote in school elections.[6] Another dozen states provided for full women's suffrage before ratification of the Nineteenth Amendment in 1920 nationalized the trend. Overall, twenty-seven states passed women's suffrage acts of one kind or another before passage of the Nineteenth Amendment.[7] In fact, women were elected to public office in several western states before ratification.

Lowering the Voting Age

In the late 1960s, some men being drafted to serve in the increasingly bloody and unpopular Vietnam conflict were too young to vote. The time seemed ripe, then, to remedy this perceived unfairness with a constitutional amendment. In 1971 the newly adopted Twenty-sixth Amendment asserted that citizens eighteen years or older could not be barred from voting based on age.

But using the Constitution to lower the voting age is more of a technical solution than a grand philosophical statement. The 1970 amendments to the Voting Rights Act (VRA) had already lowered the voting age in all elections to a possible eighteen, but the Supreme Court ruled that the president and Congress had the power to enact such a change only in federal, not state, elections. The

Parades, petitions, and picketing by the women's suffrage movement helped gain President Woodrow Wilson's eventual support of the Nineteenth Amendment, which was used to build momentum for its ratification in 1920. Source: Library of Congress

quick movement to ratify the Twenty-sixth Amendment the next year was intended to remedy the confusion of having two age standards, one for national elections and another in each state and its localities. The states ratified the amendment in only ninety-nine days—more quickly than any amendment in U.S. history.

Legislative Changes

In some ways, the discussion thus far has missed the forest for the trees. Aside from a small number of landmark constitutional changes, suffrage laws have always had a decidedly local orientation in the United States. Most adjustments to the law have been made by state legislators or municipal politicians—a strong strain of federalism has encouraged a great deal of variety across the states. As Chapter 4 on voting and ballots reveals, the design of ballots and the methods for counting votes are some of the most notorious differences. These variations continued in quite dramatic form even with the Fourteenth Amendment's guarantee of equal protection.

Figure 3-1 Presidential Election Turnout in Alabama and Minnesota, 1872–2000 (percent)

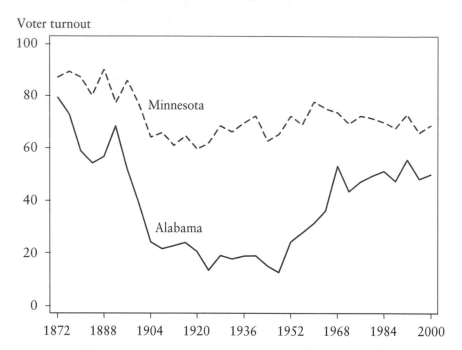

Note: Figure shows the percentage of eligible voters who cast ballots for president.

Sources: Federal Election Commission and Jerrold G. Rusk, *A Statistical History of the American Electorate* (Washington, D.C.: CQ Press, 2001).

Emergence of Voter Registration

Voter registration was one of many reforms tied to the Progressive era. These reforms—mostly enacted between 1890 and 1920—included various measures aimed at opening up government to more citizen participation and making political parties, staffing of the bureaucracy, and elections more democratic. The measures dealt with, among other things, the direct election of senators (they were elected by state legislatures), adoption of the primary election rather than use of party caucuses to choose candidates, the secret ballot, women's suffrage, and voter registration. Stories about people being paid to vote multiple times helped the progressives to convince state governments to create a process for registering voters (and therefore determining their eligibility) before election day. Prior to registration, qualifications were determined at the polling place by election "judges." When, as it often happened, a person's eligibility could not be clearly established, these judges tended to be lenient when deciding which white men could vote.[8]

America's history with registration diverges sharply from that of other industrial democracies. In most other nations, registration is automatic; in the United States the burden of registering falls on the voter. It thus adds an administrative hurdle to the voting process, requiring people to take action before the campaign is in full swing. Some studies have suggested that registration is the main reason why turnout is lower in the United States.[9] Yet other re-

search finds that steps to liberalize registration laws such as extending the "closing date" by which a person must register would have only modest effects on turnout.[10]

Whatever its effects today, voter registration channeled participation and almost certainly depressed turnout when it was enacted.[11] Although progressive advocates were interested mainly in reducing corruption, others used registration to discourage some groups from voting. In the South, with its large black population and strong history of racial hostility, voter registration effectively demobilized black voters. Turnout fell everywhere in the late 1800s, but its decline was sharper in the South. A comparison of turnout in Minnesota, a progressive and mostly white state, with that in Alabama, a southern state with a larger black population, over the years 1872–2000 reveals that registration lowered voting rates in Alabama more than in Minnesota (Figure 3-1). Blacks in Alabama were surely less educated and thus were more negatively affected by registration, but white majorities also purposely targeted blacks—mostly white registrars were able to invoke requirements selectively.[12] It would not be until the 1960s that federal legislation would rectify the situation in Alabama and the rest of the South.

The National Voter Registration Act of 1993 attempted to lower the barriers caused by registration. Known as the "Motor Voter Act," it aimed to increase the participation rates of minorities who were thought to have been disproportionately harmed by restrictive registration procedures.

Registering to vote became easier after President Bill Clinton signed the National Voter Registration Act into law on May 20, 1993. Known as the "Motor Voter Act" it required most states to provide eligible citizens the opportunity to register when they applied for or renewed a driver's license. Source: Clinton Presidential Library

The law required states to tie voter registration to driver's license renewals, provide opportunities for registration in offices that administer public assistance in the form of welfare or other state benefits, and accept mail-in registration forms. Because the increase in registration (and eventually turnout) was expected to benefit the Democrats, they favored the law and Republicans opposed it. In the end, the Motor Voter law clearly increased registration, but voter turnout was hardly affected.[13]

Voting Rights Act

The Voting Rights Act (VRA) of 1965 stands as the most important effort to expand suffrage in the United States. As part of the "Second Reconstruction," the VRA struck down racially restrictive voting practices in the South and elsewhere and brought African Americans (and later other minorities) into the mainstream of American electoral politics. Amendments in 1970 expanded its authority further. Unlike constitutional changes, the VRA immediately squashed racial discrimination at the polling place.

The VRA did three things. First, it affirmed that "the right of citizens of the United States to vote is not denied or abridged on account of race or color." Gimmicks used to disenfranchise blacks would no longer be tolerated. Second, it explicitly did away with literacy tests. Although there were variations, most literacy tests included some combination of a reading test and writing test. Literacy tests had been used to discriminate against blacks, the poor, and other voters in the South and elsewhere for years. Box 3-2 reproduces some of the questions used until 1965 in the notorious Alabama test. On the face of

it, it seems obvious that these difficult questions were not intended to determine literacy per se; rather, the tests were applied selectively to weed out minority voters. Third, the VRA required that any change in voting practices be viewed and precleared by the appropriate officials, such as an attorney general or a special judicial panel, before it is implemented. Voting changes include changes in candidate requirements, voter eligibility, or voting practices themselves. The burden of proof is thus on the advocates of changes rather than on those who oppose them. Preclearance has even shaped efforts to draw congressional districts containing minority populations.

Judicial Changes

The Supreme Court has played a central and growing role in defining and expanding voting rights. Various landmark decisions—many of them during the 1950s and 1960s when Chief Justice Earl Warren presided over the Court—led the way for a liberalization of voting practices. At the same time, the Court has often served not as an instigator of change, but as a legitimator of the actions of other political elites who acted first.[14] Although it is true that the Court has often taken unpopular positions in favor of the rights of political minorities, a definitive ruling at the Supreme Court level is also seen as the final nail in the coffin of those challenging legislative and constitutional provisions. The Court has served as the graveyard for white primaries, poll taxes, and literacy tests.

A discriminatory tactic used in many southern locales was the "white primary" (see Chapter 5). Even if other forms of voter intimidation were eliminated, segregationists reasoned that they could still prevent black input into electoral outcomes by prohibiting black participation in primary elections, which nominate party candidates. Segregationists also reasoned that, because the Democratic Party was dominant in the "Solid South" during this time period, keeping blacks out of the Democratic primary would lead effectively to the election of a white Democrat in the fall general election.

In 1923 Texas passed a law that barred blacks from Democratic primaries. Four years later, the Supreme Court ruled in *Nixon v. Herndon* (1927) that the white primary violated the Constitution's "equal protection" clause: "We find it unnecessary to consider the Fifteenth Amendment, because it seems to us hard to imagine a more direct and obvious infringement of the Fourteenth." Proponents of the white primary worked to find a way around the Court, but *Smith v. Allwright* (1944) addressed the matter by integrating the primary with other aspects of the electoral process in Texas. Other decisions

> ## BOX 3-2
> ## QUESTIONS FROM ALABAMA LITERACY TESTS CIRCA 1965
>
> Before enactment of the Voting Rights Act of 1965, many states applied literacy tests or used other discriminatory practices. Some Alabama residents were required to pass such a test to register to vote. What follows are a few of the questions used in parts B and C of the test.
>
> - In what year did the Congress gain the right to prohibit the migration of persons to the states?
>
> - The power of granting patents, that is, over securing to inventors the exclusive right to their discoveries, is given to the Congress for the purpose of _____.
>
> - At what time of day on January 20 each four years does the term of the president of the United States end?
>
> - Can you be imprisoned, under Alabama law, for a debt?
>
> - A person appointed to the U.S. Supreme Court is appointed for a term of _____.
>
> - When the Constitution was approved by the original colonies, how many states had to ratify it in order for it to be in effect?
>
> - The Constitution limits the size of the District of Columbia to _____.
>
> *Source:* Civil Rights Movement Veterans, www.crmvet.org/info/litques.pdf.

Two centuries of change have eliminated most barriers to suffrage. The electorate has expanded from a small group of wealthy elites to nearly every American eighteen years or older. Today, just two groups lack full voting rights: noncitizens and felons. There is little support for extending voting rights to noncitizens, but felons' (and ex-felons') rights are more controversial. Of those who view voting as a privilege as well as a right, many find it reasonable to revoke that privilege when a person commits a crime. In the early Republic, restrictions on felons and ex-felons were constitutional and often were written into governing documents at the time of statehood. In all, twenty-one of the first thirty-four states had some form of crime-based voting restriction enshrined in their constitutions. As social changes, particularly those related to immigration, took place, such constitutional restrictions slowly fell by the wayside. They were replaced, many years later, by statutory limitations. As Box 3-3 suggests, suffrage for felons remains a difficult issue. Whether one believes that those convicted of a crime should be permitted to vote while in prison or even after their release depends in part on whether voting is seen as a privilege or a right.

How Are Legislative Districts Defined?

As noted at the outset of this chapter, restrictions on suffrage take two forms: direct and indirect. Most of the direct barriers related to race, sex, and residency have been eliminated, and so suffrage is nearly universal in this sense. One indirect barrier—how voters are corralled into districts—remains, however, and it is as important as the right to vote itself.

Whereas suffrage laws have direct effects on voting rights, both apportionment and districting have important indirect effects on suffrage. Apportionment is the process of distributing House seats among the states. (The distribution of Senate seats is specified in the Constitution—two per state.) After the apportionment of districts, states with more than one seat must then draw lines to create districts. In other words, apportionment distributes seats *across* states, and districting distributes seats *within* them. By favoring some kinds of candidates over others or weighing the votes of some citizens more heavily than others, a district map can effectively disenfranchise people by diluting their votes. Unlike laws that directly govern suffrage, which have clear consequences and rarely involve trade-offs, there is no set of "impartial" districts. After describing the processes by which district lines are drawn by state officials over time, this section will review the many controversies that districting invokes.

Any scheme for drawing district boundaries will grant one particular party, candidate, region, or kind of voter an advantage. Some criteria—whether equal populations,

such as *Terry v. Adams* (1953) went further, but Texas Democrats managed to resist complete integration until the Voting Rights Act.

Poll taxes were originally used along with a property requirement to screen out voters who were not financially independent. Later, poll taxes were used to discriminate against blacks and other poor people. Although the taxes were often modest, they were cumulative, and so missing a few elections could result in a sizable fee. The Twenty-fourth Amendment was supposed to end poll taxes, but that goal was only realized in *Harper v. Virginia State Board of Elections* (1966) when the Court found in favor of a voter alleging that the state's poll tax violated the Fourteenth Amendment. The Court also backed the Voting Rights Act's broader attack on discriminatory "tests and devices." *South Carolina v. Katzenbach* (1966) upheld the ban on poll taxes everywhere and also attacked literacy tests in the South. *Oregon v. Mitchell* (1970) upheld the act's ban on literacy tests in states outside the South.

BOX 3-3

DEBATE THE ISSUES: SHOULD FELONS AND EX-FELONS BE ALLOWED TO VOTE?

In November 2000, Massachusetts voters were given an opportunity to decide whether incarcerated felons should continue to have the right to vote. At the time, the Bay State was one of a few states that still permitted prisoners to take part in elections. Ballot Question 2 asked voters to amend the state constitution to prohibit inmates from voting in state and federal elections. Voters easily passed the measure by a two-to-one margin.

Today, forty-eight states and the District of Columbia prohibit current inmates from voting. Just over half of the states also disenfranchise those on parole or probation. Seven states impose a waiting period of several years once an inmate has been released before restoring voting rights. Another six states permanently disenfranchise ex-felons. The Sentencing Project (2003) estimates that roughly four million Americans are unable to vote because of felony-related restrictions.

Because incarceration rates vary tremendously across demographic groups, restricting felons and ex-felons from voting disproportionately harms some strata of society, particularly African American men. Litigation sponsored by various civil rights and civil liberties groups is presently in the judicial pipeline in an attempt to remove these barriers.

Source: The Sentencing Project.

---

district compactness, representation of minorities, competitiveness, or historical continuity—can be sought only by sacrificing other criteria. Since the 1960s, the courts have elevated the criterion of numerically equal populations over others in judging the legality of legislative districts. Racial considerations have been more ambiguous. As for historical inertia and compactness, the courts and those drawing district lines are continually negotiating the extent to which these concerns should be violated to provide reasonable opportunities for minority groups to have a say in the outcome.

Apportionment

Since 1911, 435 House seats have been apportioned among the states, and each state is guaranteed at least one House district. As mandated in the Constitution, reapportionment occurs every ten years, after the national census. Aside from recent intervention by courts, this is the only point at which the federal government influences the drawing of district lines. It is perhaps surprising that what

seems to be a rather mechanical process has been the subject of heavy political debate. In retrospect, however, it appears that even today's intense partisan wrangling over redistricting is tame by historical standards.

Early Practices

Because the Constitution is remarkably silent about most election practices, the federal government has had to issue many of the election guidelines in use today—a process that has taken 150 years. Article I, Section 4, of the Constitution states that "[t]he Times, Places and Manner of holding Elections for Senators and Representatives, shall be prescribed in each State by the Legislature thereof; but the Congress may at any time by Law make or alter such Regulations, except as to the Places of chusing Senators." Indeed, when the First Congress sat in 1789, the states were using a variety of practices. Five states had House districts of unequal size; six states elected members at-large; and two states used a hybrid system.

Idiosyncratic state procedures continued well into the 1800s. Some districts elected multiple members to the House and a few states experimented with at-large districts that could overlap with smaller districts within the state. For over a century, the House grew in size along with the American population as states were added. By the time the Apportionment Act of 1842 was passed, seven out of the twenty-six states still used at-large ("general ticket") elections. Because the act had little effect, it was quickly discarded and the general ticket system continued in states with small populations. Where districts were used, the timing and content of redistricting were quite irregular. For example, states often undertook redistricting more than once between censuses. Erik J. Engstrom notes that Ohio redistricted seven times between 1878 and 1892.[15] And the kinds of districts drawn varied. The "one person, one vote" standard was decades away, providing plenty of maneuvering room for a majority party hoping to strengthen its hold on state government.

The Census

The Constitution requires that an "actual enumeration" of the population be conducted every ten years. The census has become a mammoth operation, and one subject to serious political debate. At great expense, the government manages to collect data on nearly the entire population. In 2000 it was estimated to have missed as many as 4 million out of roughly 285 million people for a net "undercount" of about 1.2 percent. The undercount falls disproportionately on minority groups—mainly blacks, Latinos, and recent immigrants. Most politicians believe that these undercounted groups favor the Democratic Party. The only way to fix the undercount is to augment the hard count with statistical sampling. Democrats pushed for sampling to improve the 2000 census. Republicans countered that any move away from a literal count of the population would only provide room for partisan manipulation of the data and would violate the Constitution. The Supreme Court had already ruled that sampling could not be used for apportionment, but suggested that employing it for districting might be acceptable. In early 2001, the George W. Bush administration announced that it would not allow imputed data from the sampling procedure to be used in redistricting. (Congress could have overridden the decision had the Republican majority not agreed that sampling is undesirable.)

Beyond the count itself, there are long-standing disagreements about how to allocate House seats to the states. According to the Constitution, each state "shall have at least one representative," and the remainder are to be distributed by population. But there is no obvious way to do this so that each state receives one or more whole seats (not a fraction of a seat). For example, after the 2000 Census Rhode Island's population translated into 1.6 seats. Some methods would have given the state just one seat, while others—including the method actually in use—would have given it two. The difference has to do with how fractions are rounded. The current procedure, known as Hamilton-Hill, was adopted in 1941. It uses a particular rounding formula that some argue favors the smallest states.[16]

Malapportionment

When districts have unequal populations, malapportionment is said to be the cause. This situation violates the idea of equal representation of all voters. For much of U.S. history, the House suffered from severe malapportionment. In some states, the population of one congressional district would be many times larger than those of the neighboring districts. This situation changed with the "Reapportionment Revolution" of the 1960s, but malapportionment did not vanish. For example, after the 2000 census the largest district in Montana contained 900,000 people, whereas the largest district in Wyoming contained just 494,000 people, a ratio of almost two to one. This is an extreme example, but it illustrates that what malapportionment remains in the House exists across states rather than within them. In the Senate, malapportionment is much more serious. The average Californian now has 1/66th the representation of a Wyoming resident.

Court Emphasis on Equal Population

The 1960s saw the courts—particularly the Supreme Court—initiate what became known as the Reapportionment Revolution. Until that time, the courts had viewed districting issues as political matters outside their jurisdiction. In *Colgrove v. Green* (1946) the Court declared that districting issues were the responsibility of the legislative branch. To wade into districting battles, they argued, "would cut very deep into the very being of Congress. Courts ought not to enter this political thicket."[17] The Warren Court would change all that by issuing a series of decisions establishing the principle of "one person, one vote."

A critical step was taken when the Court agreed that apportionment was a justiciable issue. Several Tennessee residents alleged that the state's legislative districts did not adhere to existing law and did not change over time to accommodate shifts in population. In *Baker v. Carr* (1962), the Court agreed that the equal protection clause of the Fourteenth Amendment put such issues legitimately under judicial purview. Here the Court reversed its earlier claim that representational rights are not merely "political questions." The "allegations of a denial of equal protection present a justiciable constitutional cause of action" being as it is "within the reach of judicial protection under the Fourteenth Amendment."[18]

In the early 1960s, several Alabama voters challenged the apportionment of the state legislature. At the time, each county was given at least one representative, but this system effectively gave urban voters less representation. The Court ruled in *Reynolds v. Sims* (1964) that equal representation is the "bedrock of our political system." The justices concluded, "Legislators represent people, not trees or acres. Legislators are elected by voters, not farms or cities or economic interests."[19] The ruling recognized that unequal representation is a violation of the Fourteenth Amendment and may jeopardize the right of suffrage. To settle the matter, the Court alluded to its earlier decision in *Colgrove*: "We were cautioned about the dangers of entering into political thickets and mathematical quagmires. Our answer is this: a denial of constitutionally protected rights demands judicial protection." *Reynolds* thus took the step made possible by *Baker* in making "one person, one vote" the law of the land.

The Reapportionment Revolution brought about by the Court had several immediate consequences. It reduced the Republican advantage in districts outside the South, increased the incumbent advantage, and made courts important players in districting decisions.[20] And by focusing so narrowly on malapportionment, it left the door open for other kinds of districting mischief. As the next section on districting describes, later decisions clarified the Court's view that population equality is the most important criterion in a districting plan. *Karcher v. Daggett* (1983) required states to make districts mathematically equal unless otherwise justified by a "legitimate state objective." In this New Jersey case, the court struck down a plan in which districts varied by only a fraction of a percent. Small differences in district populations might be tolerable, the Court suggested, but New Jersey showed no evidence of a "good-faith effort to achieve population equality." For congressional districts at least, nothing but strict equality would be tolerated.[21]

Districting

After the apportionment of districts, the electoral responsibility shifts from the federal government to each state government, which must draw lines to create districts if the state has more than one House seat. The difficulty and controversy associated with a state's districting effort depend on several factors. Maine, to take an easy case, has a relatively homogeneous population of 1.3 million, relatively few sectional disputes, and only two House districts to create. Since the 1960 census, it has essentially maintained the same two districts, one in the south and the other made up of the larger north. By contrast, California's 33 million people must be divided into fifty-three districts of equal population. Those drawing district lines must not only maintain some continuity and contiguity in districts, but also take into account party control and the racial and ethnic considerations arising from a diverse and rapidly evolving population. In yet another contrast, some states in the Midwest and Northeast are losing population and therefore must lose seats, an unpleasant fact that often forces incumbents from office.

Drawing district lines in a state with more than just a few seats is an amazingly complex undertaking that can be done in an almost infinite number of ways. Determining who has the power to assume that task is thus quite important.

Who Draws the Lines?

States use several different procedures for congressional redistricting. The most common practice is to make state legislators responsible in some way. The National Conference of State Legislatures reports that as of 2000 forty-four of the fifty states placed redistricting powers primarily in the hands of legislatures (and governors) rather than commissions. Yet often the state legislature works with a commission specifically charged with redistricting duties. When the commission does not have the final say, as is in the case in most states, partisan politics becomes a determining factor. Highly partisan districting plans are often put into place when a single party holds the governorship and both chambers of the legislature, because they need not consult the opposition.

Today, nearly half of states use a commission of some kind, although these commissions vary in their authority and independence from the state legislature. In many of these states, members of the commission are selected by public officials, if not composed of public officials themselves. For example, the Ohio redistricting commission consists of the governor, auditor, secretary of state, and two other members chosen by each of the major political parties. The commission is thus overtly partisan because its members are all high-profile Democrats or Republicans. The commission has until October after the census year to complete its work.

The system used in Iowa takes redistricting out of the hands of politicians. The independent Legislative Service Bureau, which has authority for redistricting, is supposed to use only population data in going about its task; it is not given access to data on partisanship, race, ethnicity, or other "political" criteria. The bureau may submit up to

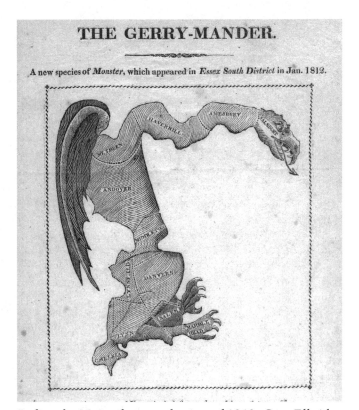

Before the Massachusetts election of 1812, Gov. Elbridge Gerry signed a bill redrawing the state senatorial districts so that his party, the Democratic-Republicans, would be likely to win more seats than their actual numbers warranted. One of the new districts looked like a salamander and was quickly dubbed a "gerrymander," a term that continues to be used to describe a redistricting plan designed to benefit one party. Source: Library of Congress

three plans to the state legislature for approval, only the last of which is amendable. Should no plan be adopted, the Iowa Supreme Court takes control. The Iowa approach is unique, however, because partisanship plays a leading role in most states' redistricting efforts.

Gerrymandering

Redistricting will always be controversial, because no plan is impartial in the sense of perfectly balancing all interests and values. In fact, any plan that favors one group or criterion will inevitably shortchange or violate other groups or criteria. For example, a plan designed to maintain contiguous districts will sacrifice partisan interests. One that provides for districts of equal population opens the door to "gerrymandering." And districts that are favorable to incumbents dampen electoral competition. As noted earlier, the Supreme Court has elevated some criteria above others. In the 1960s, it ruled that almost any malapportionment in congressional districting is intolerable. In the 1990s, it suggested that districts drawn primarily on the basis of race are questionable. Maintaining contiguity and keeping communities intact have some value, but the Court has mostly avoided issues of partisan and incumbent-based gerrymandering.

The term *gerrymandering* originated with an editorial cartoon that appeared in the *Boston Gazette* in the early 1800s (see photo). The cartoon depicts a district north of Boston as a kind of salamander, adding a head and wings to the district silhouette. The district had been proposed by Massachusetts governor Elbridge Gerry—thus the name gerrymander. Gerry's idea was to draw a district in a way that would maximize his party's chances of victory. Use of the term *gerrymandering* therefore suggests an intentional effort to configure districts to benefit one interest over another. Districts might be drawn to favor particular parties, racial and ethnic groups, demographic and occupational classes, and even incumbents and challengers. Every district will give some kinds of voters more power than others, but gerrymandering is distinguished as an intentional effort at electoral bias.

The many ways to gerrymander all depend on line drawers' abilities to predict how various groups will vote. The degree of uncertainty about voting choices varies across groups. The black vote might be predictable in many locations, but the "farm vote" is probably less predictable, and the "women's vote" is even more difficult to characterize. In addition, the geographic concentration of a group makes it easier for it to be part of a gerrymander. For example, Latinos' living patterns are relatively segregated, but women's are not. And even though a group might technically constitute a majority within a district, that advantage can be squandered if there are turnout disparities across groups. The effects of gerrymanders are thus not so easily detected. Moreover, efforts to favor one political party in one state will be offset by efforts to favor the other political party in another state. It has been suggested, for example, that the 1980 round of redistricting advantaged Democrats in California where they were in control of the process, but it favored the Republicans in charge in Indiana and other states, for a modest net effect nationwide.

The degree to which gerrymandering works to engineer outcomes has as much to do with how candidates and party elites strategize as it does with voters' preferences. New district lines generally threaten incumbents, making them more vulnerable and less likely to run for reelection. Carefully drawn districts can also affect the types of new candidates who run. For example, a well-qualified black candidate is unlikely to emerge in a conservative, mostly white district because his or her chances of victory would be low. Thus the "demands" of voters within districts, at least as they are understood by elites, affect the "supply" of candidates who appeal to those voters—a kind of self-fulfilling prophecy.[22]

Packing and Cracking

The purpose of a gerrymander is often to weaken the power of a group to elect a candidate of its liking. Vote dilution is generally accomplished in two ways—by packing or by cracking. The example used here to illustrate these two strategies is a Democratic gerrymander designed to harm Republican candidates. To undertake "packing," Democrats would try to corral most of the Republicans into one or two districts, perhaps by connecting disparate Republican strongholds. This strategy would give the opposition Republicans strong chances of victory in a small number of places in exchange for poor chances in the rest of the state.

The alternative strategy would be "cracking" the Republican vote by spreading Republican voters thinly across many districts, thereby giving the opposition Republicans fewer votes than they would need to ensure victory. Districts that heavily favor one party are likely to attract stronger candidates from that party, effectively disenfranchising voters from the other party. In summary, packing concentrates the opposition, and cracking spreads it out. Although cracking is often considered synonymous with vote dilution, packing can dilute votes as well by weakening a group's power in surrounding districts.

The Supreme Court has done its best to stay out of matters it deems to be "political" rather than legal, but it seems only a matter of time until partisan gerrymanders are subject to Court review. The Court resisted entering disputes over apportionment until equal protection claims pushed justices into the "political thicket" in the 1960s. And in one case, *Davis v. Bandemer* (1986), it has already pointed to the possibility that partisan gerrymandering cases might be justiciable. *Bandemer* sets up the possibility of future rulings the way *Baker* did for *Reynolds*. The ruling in *Vieth v. Jubelirer* (2004) indicated that the Court would not quickly enter the political thicket to stop partisan gerrymandering. In a split decision, justices refused to declare a Pennsylvania plan unconstitutional, because the Court lacked a solution to what was viewed as a political not a legal problem.

Majority-Minority Districts

Majority-minority districts are produced when redistricters pack minority populations. In a majority-minority district, a traditionally underrepresented minority group has become a mathematical majority. After the 1990 census, Democrats made a concerted effort to create districts in the South where black votes would constitute a solid majority. Because black voters strongly favor the Democratic Party, the assumption was that a majority-minority district would guarantee that Democrats would win the seats. Thus a racial gerrymander is effectively a partisan one. The 1990 round of redistricting was a watershed for three reasons. First, Democrats, who had more interest in electing black candidates, still controlled many state legislatures and districting commissions in the South. Second, whites had moved increasingly to the Republican Party, making it more difficult for Democrats to win without black support. Third, most observers sensed that many majority-minority districts could still be drawn.

By 2000 these conditions had changed. After the 1992 elections the number of African Americans in the House jumped from twenty-five to thirty-eight (all but one of them Democrats), a total that would not change much over the following decade. Republicans gained control of many state legislatures, which eased the pressure to create majority-minority districts. But many observers believed that the potential for creating more majority-minority districts was nearly tapped by the early 1990s anyway.

Even more interesting is that some Democrats now view the creation of such districts as counterproductive. By concentrating many blacks in a single district, surrounding districts become even more Republican than they might be otherwise. Some have even argued that racial packing by Democrats is partially responsible for the Republican takeover of Congress in 1994. There is evidence to support this "paradox of representation." [23] Although creating some heavily black districts increases the number of (Democratic) African Americans in office, it does so at the expense of creating a Republican majority with a different agenda. Others have suggested that Democrats can be elected—and blacks adequately represented—in districts with traditional white majorities.[24] But even beyond these potentially self-defeating moves by Democrats, there is another reason why blacks and other minority groups have not been elected more often since 1992: the courts have rendered many majority-minority districts unconstitutional.

Republicans challenged several majority-minority districts in the 1990s, and the Supreme Court agreed in several cases that such districts were unsustainable. The legal origins for these decisions appear in *Thornburg v. Gingles* (1986), which concerned the constitutionality of three multimember districts (districts where more than one candidate is elected) in North Carolina and whether minority votes were being diluted. The decision established a three-pronged test for determining whether racialized voting existed to the extent that a redistricting plan had to be judged unfair: (1) the minority group must be large enough to form a district majority; (2) the minority group must be politically cohesive; and (3) the white vote must be strong enough to defeat the minority group's candidate.[25] This three-pronged standard, which places the burden of proof clearly on the minority group alleging vote dilution, has been used to evaluate many districting plans ever since. *Gingles* would go on to shape legal and political debates over racial gerrymandering in the 1990s.

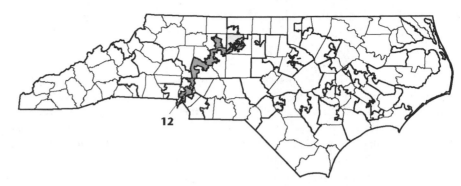

House redistricting in some states after the 1990 census sought to create so-called majority-minority districts that were likely to elect minority candidates, usually African Americans. These efforts resulted in such unusually shaped districts as this one created along Interstate 85 in North Carolina. In a series of rulings, the Supreme Court put limits on the use of race as a dominant factor in drawing districts. Source: Congressional Quarterly

A key court decision after the 1990 round of redistricting concerned the new twelfth House district in North Carolina (see illustration). Before the 1992 elections, politicians undertook intense efforts to create majority-minority districts in the Tar Heel state. Indeed, after almost a hundred years without a single black member of Congress, two were elected from North Carolina that year. An initial plan to create just one majority-minority district was rejected during the preclearance stage. A revised map proposed two such districts, one of which was the twelfth.

The unusual shape of the twelfth district reflects the ingenuity used to connect small pockets of black voters along Interstate 85. The district was challenged by five white North Carolinians on the grounds that it violated their civil rights under the Fourteenth Amendment. Although a federal district court rejected their claim, the Supreme Court disagreed in a 5–4 decision. In *Shaw v. Reno* (1993) the Court came down in opposition to majority-minority districts like these. Although the decision granted white residents the right to sue in cases only when they believed their voting rights were denied, *Shaw* was widely seen as a strike against racial gerrymandering. Justice Sandra Day O'Connor stated for the Court, "[W]e believe that reapportionment is one area in which appearances *do* matter. A reapportionment plan that includes in one district people who belong to the same race, but who are otherwise widely separated by geographical and political boundaries, and who may have little in common with one another but the color of their skin, bears an uncomfortable resemblance to political apartheid." [26]

Those drawing district lines were now required to react to a complicated set of mandates, and equal population was to be maintained at all costs. Legislation encouraged efforts to represent minority voters adequately, but the Court was setting limits on these efforts. Race can be a consideration, but efforts should not focus solely on race at the expense of "traditional districting principles such as compactness, contiguity, and respect for political subdivisions." Two years later, the Court strengthened the message by striking down two Georgia districts in *Miller v. Johnson* (1995). Shortly thereafter, in *Bush v. Vera* (1996), the Court threw out three Texas districts drawn after the 1990 census—two black majority, one Hispanic majority—because race was a predominant factor in the redistricting, overriding race-neutral principles.

Districting practices seem to be complicated in two ways. First, the drawing of district lines is in many states a demanding task that requires balancing the competing goals of partisan advantage, minority representation, compactness, and historical consistency, while avoiding even the smallest violations of the "one person, one vote" principle. A political party, interest group, or other participant is almost certainly going to be unhappy with the final map, and, increasingly, the courts have become the venue for airing such grievances. The multiplicity of goals and participants all but ensures that districting will be difficult in many states. Second, unlike direct limits on suffrage, districting systems have indirect and often misunderstood effects on the right to vote. Banning a group from voting, or throwing up hurdles to that process, has rather obvious effects. This is true whether the disenfranchisement is written in law or merely a practice of intimidation or favoritism. Districts have more subtle consequences for voting rights, because they do not literally disenfranchise any particular voter. But those who draw district lines may intentionally or unintentionally favor some voters over others by encouraging particular candidates or a particular party, race, or ideological stripe to run. Aside from felons and noncitizens, the electorate has slowly expanded to include nearly every adult American. This reality draws even more attention to how the drawing of legislative districts shapes voting rights.

Notes

1. Thanks are extended to Marni Ezra for comments on this chapter and to Michael Kang for excellent research assistance and criticism.

2. Alexander Keyssar, *The Right to Vote: The Contested History of Democracy in the United States* (New York: Basic Books, 2000); Jerrold G. Rusk, *A Statistical History of the American Electorate* (Washington, D.C.: CQ Press, 2001).

3. In this chapter, the term *elite* refers to influential policy makers, including politicians and local notables.

4. Keyssar, *Right to Vote*.

5. Eleanor Flexnor, *Century of Struggle: The Woman's Rights Movement in the United States* (Cambridge, Mass.: Harvard University Press, 1975); Keyssar, *Right to Vote*; Aileen S. Kraditor, *The Ideas of the Woman Suffrage Movement, 1890–1920* (New York: Norton, 1981).

6. Keyssar, *Right to Vote*.

7. Rusk, *Statistical History of the American Electorate*.

8. Richard Bensel, *The American Ballot Box in the Mid-Nineteenth Century: Law, Identity, and the Polling Place* (New York: Cambridge University Press, 2004).

9. Frances Fox Piven and Richard A. Cloward, *Why Americans Don't Vote* (New York: Pantheon Books, 1988); G. Bingham Powell Jr., "American Voter Turnout in Comparative Perspective," *American Political Science Review* 80 (March 1986): 17–43.

10. Raymond E. Wolfinger and Steven J. Rosenstone, *Who Votes?* (New Haven, Conn.: Yale University Press, 1980).

11. Keyssar, *Right to Vote*; Piven and Cloward, *Why Americans Don't Vote*.

12. Wolfinger and Rosenstone, *Who Votes?*; J. Morgan Kousser, *The Shaping of Southern Politics* (New Haven, Conn.: Yale University Press, 1974).

13. Stephen Knack, "Does 'Motor Voter' Work? Evidence from State-Level Data," *Journal of Politics* 57 (August 1995): 796–811.

14. Gerald N. Rosenberg, *The Hollow Hope: Can Courts Bring about Social Change?* (Chicago: University of Chicago Press, 1993).

15. Erik J. Engstrom, "Stacking the States, Stacking the House: The Partisan Consequences of Congressional Redistricting in the 19th Century," paper presented at the annual meeting of the Midwest Political Science Association, Chicago, 2003.

16. Michel L. Balinski and H. Peyton Young, *Fair Representation: Meeting the Ideal of One Man, One Vote,* 2d ed. (Washington, D.C.: Brookings, 2001).

17. *Colgrove v. Green,* 328 U.S. 459 (1946).

18. *Baker v. Carr,* 369 U.S. 186 (1962).

19. *Reynolds v. Sims,* 377 U.S. 533 (1964).

20. Gary W. Cox and Jonathan N. Katz, *Elbridge Gerry's Salamander: The Electoral Consequences of the Reapportionment Revolution* (New York: Cambridge University Press, 2002).

21. *Karcher v. Daggett,* 462 U.S. 725 (1983).

22. David T. Canon, *Race, Redistricting, and Representation: The Unintended Consequences of Black Majority Districts* (Chicago: University of Chicago Press, 1999).

23. Charles Cameron, David Epstein, and Sharyn O'Halloran, "Do Majority-Minority Districts Maximize Substantive Black Representation in Congress?" *American Political Science Review* 90 (December 1996): 794–812; David Lublin, *The Paradox of Representation* (Princeton, N.J.: Princeton University Press, 1999).

24. Carol M. Swain, *Black Faces, Black Interests: The Representation of African Americans in Congress* (Cambridge, Mass.: Harvard University Press, 1998).

25. Bernard Grofman, "Expert Witness Testimony and the Evolution of Voting Rights Case Law," in *Controversies in Minority Voting: The Voting Rights Act in Perspective,* ed. Bernard Grofman and Chandler Davidson, 197–229 (Washington, D.C.: Brookings, 1992).

26. *Shaw v. Reno,* 509 U.S. 630 (1993).

Suggested Readings

Balinski, Michel L., and H. Peyton Young. *Fair Representation: Meeting the Ideal of One Man, One Vote.* 2d ed. Washington, D.C.: Brookings, 2001.

Bensel, Richard. *The American Ballot Box in the Mid-Nineteenth Century: Law, Identity, and the Polling Place.* New York: Cambridge University Press, 2004.

Cameron, Charles, David Epstein, and Sharyn O'Halloran. "Do Majority-Minority Districts Maximize Substantive Black Representation in Congress?" *American Political Science Review* 90 (December 1996): 794–812.

Canon, David T. *Race, Redistricting, and Representation: The Unintended Consequences of Black Majority Districts.* Chicago: University of Chicago Press, 1999.

Cox, Gary W., and Jonathan N. Katz. *Elbridge Gerry's Salamander: The Electoral Consequences of the Reapportionment Revolution.* New York: Cambridge University Press, 2002.

Engstrom, Erik J. "Stacking the States, Stacking the House: The Partisan Consequences of Congressional Redistricting in the 19th Century." Paper presented at the annual meeting of the Midwest Political Science Association, Chicago, 2003.

Flexnor, Eleanor. *Century of Struggle: The Woman's Rights Movement in the United States.* Cambridge, Mass.: Harvard University Press, 1975.

Grofman, Bernard. "Expert Witness Testimony and the Evolution of Voting Rights Case Law." In *Controversies in Minority Voting: The Voting Rights Act in Perspective,* edited by Bernard Grofman and Chandler Davidson, 197–229. Washington, D.C.: Brookings, 1992.

Keyssar, Alexander. *The Right to Vote: The Contested History of Democracy in the United States.* New York: Basic Books, 2000.

Knack, Stephen. "Does 'Motor Voter' Work? Evidence from State-Level Data." *Journal of Politics* 57 (August 1995): 796–811.

Kousser, J. Morgan. *The Shaping of Southern Politics.* New Haven, Conn.: Yale University Press, 1974.

Kraditor, Aileen S. *The Ideas of the Woman Suffrage Movement, 1890–1920.* New York: Norton, 1981.

Lublin, David. *The Paradox of Representation.* Princeton, N.J.: Princeton University Press, 1999.

Piven, Frances Fox, and Richard A. Cloward. *Why Americans Don't Vote.* New York: Pantheon Books, 1988.

Powell, G. Bingham, Jr. "American Voter Turnout in Comparative Perspective." *American Political Science Review* 80 (March 1986): 17–43.

Rosenberg, Gerald N. *The Hollow Hope: Can Courts Bring about Social Change?* Chicago: University of Chicago Press, 1993.

Rusk, Jerrold G. *A Statistical History of the American Electorate.* Washington, D.C.: CQ Press, 2001.

The Sentencing Project. "Felony Disenfranchisement Laws in the United States." *The Sentencing Project,* September 26, 2003. www.sentencingproject.org/pdfs/1046.pdf.

Swain, Carol M. *Black Faces, Black Interests: The Representation of African Americans in Congress.* Cambridge, Mass.: Harvard University Press, 1998.

Wolfinger, Raymond E., and Steven J. Rosenstone. *Who Votes?* New Haven, Conn.: Yale University Press, 1980.

CHAPTER 4

Voting and Ballots

David C. Kimball

For many Americans, the 2000 presidential election served as an eye-opening primer on the once mundane aspects of election administration such as voting equipment, hanging chad, ballot designs, absentee votes, and recount procedures. In the critical state of Florida, where Republican George W. Bush defeated Democrat Al Gore by 537 votes, more than 175,000 ballots failed to record a vote for president. In addition, county election boards in Florida initially rejected a large number of absentee ballots from overseas voters, many in the military, because they were not properly signed or postmarked.[1] The disposition of the unrecorded presidential votes and absentee ballots in Florida stoked a month-long controversy, which finally ended when the U.S. Supreme Court, in *Bush v. Gore,* stopped any further recount of votes in Florida.

After the 2000 election controversy, state and local election officials reexamined their voting procedures. Meanwhile, several blue-ribbon commissions, government investigators, and professional associations proposed election reforms designed to modernize election administration in the United States.[2] In 2002 Congress passed, and President Bush signed, the Help America Vote Act (HAVA), which requires states to upgrade several aspects of election administration and includes federal funding to help pay for the reforms. Most states then passed their own election reform laws to comply with HAVA and to make other changes in election procedures. The close presidential election in 2004, with its disputes about rules for provisional ballots, long voting lines in some places, and voting machine breakdowns, kept the spotlight on voting procedures.[3] Indeed, these procedures merit closer scrutiny because of the frequency with which Americans use elections to select government officials and make laws.

This chapter examines several aspects of election administration in the United States, including the structure and schedule of elections, the different methods used to cast votes, and several ballot features. It describes how the decentralized nature of election administration in the United States has created a collage of voting methods, ballots, and other election procedures that vary substantially from one county or town to the next. Because political parties and candidates are acutely aware that voting methods and procedures can influence voters and affect election results, voting rules and procedures often figure in campaign strategies. Furthermore, interested parties sometimes try to change voting rules and procedures to gain an electoral advantage. The chapter concludes with a review of recent and upcoming changes in election administration, including the possibility of voting by Internet.

Legal Control over Voting Procedures

The U.S. Constitution gives Congress the authority to regulate "the times, places, and manner" of congressional elections (Article I, Section 4). In addition, the Supreme Court has interpreted Article II of the Constitution to give Congress the authority to regulate presidential primaries and general elections.[4] The equal protection clause of the Fourteenth Amendment to the Constitution also gives the federal government extensive legal authority to regulate elections and protect voting rights. However, the responsibility for election administration has largely been delegated to the states, which have assumed primary responsibility for developing and enforcing their own election laws and practices.

The states, in turn, have delegated important aspects of election administration to local governments. Many election decisions, such as choosing and buying voting equipment, designing and printing ballots, counting ballots, hiring and training poll workers, drawing precinct boundaries, and selecting locations for polling places, are usually made by county clerks or local election boards. In eight states, city or township officials administer elections. In the remaining states, county officials administer elections. The recent passage of HAVA and election reform legislation at the state level strengthens state and federal oversight of election procedures. However, many important decisions in conducting elections will continue to be made at the local level.

Structure and Schedule of Elections

Anthony King, a respected British observer of American politics, has said, "In a meaningful sense, America is about the holding of elections." [5] The United States is unique in terms of the frequency of elections and the length of the ballot. Americans elect more government officials than any other country in the world. By one estimate, the United States has over half a million elected positions.[6]

One can get a sense of the prevalence of elections in the United States by comparing the election schedule in St. Louis, Missouri, to the election schedule in Toronto, Ontario, for the period 2001–2004 (Table 4-1). St. Louis held fifteen elections during that period, and Toronto had only five. Although Canada's parliamentary form of government does not separately elect an executive (as in the United States), this disparity is fairly typical. Most American cities have an election calendar resembling that of St. Louis, while most foreign countries have an election schedule like Toronto's. A closer look at the table reveals the sources of frequent U.S. elections. Many candidates in the United States must win two elections to take office: the primary election held to choose each political party's nominee and the general election held to determine the officeholder. In addition, the division of government authority between different geographic levels means that American voters elect many state and local officials that are not elected in other counties. Finally, special elections are held to replace officials who leave office (from retirement or death, for example) before the end of an elected term (by-elections are held for the same purpose in Canada).

As required by federal law, general elections for president and Congress are held on the first Tuesday following the first Monday in November of even-numbered years. The selection in the 1840s of the month of November reflects the nation's agricultural heritage. By early November, the fall harvest was over and the weather was still mild enough for people to travel to polling places. Tuesday was likely selected as a voting day by the process of elimination. Sunday, as a day of worship and rest, was out of the question, as were Saturday and Monday because some rural voters needed at least a day to trek to the polls. The complicated wording of the law also prevents an election on November 1, which is All Saints' Day, a holy day particularly for Catholics.[7] Most state and local elections are also held on Tuesdays (for some examples, see Table 4-1). Thus, even though most established democratic nations hold elections on Sunday, most U.S. elections are held on a workday. Because researchers have found that voter turnout is higher when elections are held on Sunday,[8] some reformers in the United States have proposed moving elections to the weekend or making election day a national holiday as a way to boost turnout.[9] To minimize election costs, states and local governments could schedule their elections at the same time as federal contests. However, such an arrangement would join the electoral fortunes of candidates from the same party. Candidates at the top of the ballot, especially presidential candidates, can have "coattails." For example, if a presidential candidate wins in a landslide, other candidates from the president's party may be swept into offices at the state and local level. Candidates for lower-level offices thus have a strong interest in having high-quality candidates from their party running for the contests at the top of the ballot.

With the move toward primary elections and the growth of a candidate-centered campaign system (see Chapter 2), many politicians at the state and local levels realize they have less control than before over party nominations for the top contests. As a result, many have decided to separate their elections from the federal contests. For example, most states now hold gubernatorial elections during the midterm congressional elections, when the presidential race is not on the ballot. Only eleven states hold gubernatorial elections at the same time as the presidential election, and five states hold gubernatorial elections in odd-numbered years when there are no federal or statewide contests on the ballot. Most local elections (such as in St. Louis) also are held in odd-numbered years. As Marjorie Randon Hershey and Paul Allen Beck have observed, "This practice of insulating elected officials from one another limits the possibilities for coattail effects and has also worked to reduce the cohesiveness of the party in government." [10]

American voters go to the polls at different times to choose officials for executive and legislative positions at the national, state, and local levels—positions that are often appointed in other countries—but U.S. elections do not end there. Several state and local governments have provisions for recall elections, in which voters may attempt to remove a public official before the end of the official's term (see Chapter 26 for a description of this process). A recent example was the election in October 2003 in which Republican Arnold Schwarzenegger replaced Democrat Gray Davis as governor of California. The California election was, however, unique, because most recall elections are held at the local level (for another example, note the March 4, 2003, election in Table 4-1).

Many states and localities also use elections to decide matters of public policy through ballot initiatives and referenda (see Chapter 26). Ballot initiatives are laws or constitutional amendments proposed by citizens who collected the number of signatures required to have the measures placed on the ballot. Referenda are laws or constitutional amendments proposed by a state legislature or city council and placed on the ballot for voter approval. The number of statewide ballot initiatives has increased dramatically in the last twenty years, from approximately two hundred in the 1970s to almost four hundred in the 1990s.[11] Many states also elect judges in some fashion. In

Table 4-1 Comparison of Elections in St. Louis, Missouri, and Toronto, Ontario (Canada), 2001–2004

Date and type of election	Items on the ballot
St. Louis, Missouri	
Tuesday, March 6, 2001 Primary election	Mayor, comptroller, Board of Aldermen (15 of 28 wards)
Tuesday, April 3, 2001 General election	Mayor, comptroller, Board of Aldermen (15 wards), Board of Education, two city ballot initiatives
Tuesday, August 7, 2001 Special election	State representative (district 67)
Tuesday, Dec. 11, 2001 Special election	State senator (district 3)
Tuesday, Feb. 5, 2002 Special election	State senator (district 5)
Tuesday, March 5, 2002 Special election	State representative (district 66)
Tuesday, March 26, 2002 Special election	State representative (district 58)
Tuesday, June 4, 2002 Special election	Board of Aldermen (ward 23)
Tuesday, August 6, 2002 Primary election	U.S. senator, U.S. representative, state auditor, state senator, state representative, circuit clerk, recorder of deeds, license collector, collector of revenue, president of Board of Alderman, Board of Aldermen (ward 22), two statewide ballot initiatives, three city charter amendments
Tuesday, November 5, 2002 General election	U.S. senator, U.S. representative, state auditor, state senator, state representative, circuit clerk, recorder of deeds, license collector, collector of revenue, president of Board of Alderman, seventeen judge retentions, four state constitutional amendments, state constitutional convention, one statewide ballot initiative, three city charter amendments, two city ballot initiatives
Tuesday, March 4, 2003 Primary election	President of Board of Aldermen, Board of Aldermen (fourteen wards), recall proposition for Board of Aldermen (ward 21)
Tuesday, April 8, 2003 General election	President of Board of Aldermen, Board of Aldermen (fourteen wards), Board of Education
Tuesday, February 3, 2004 Primary election	U.S. president
Tuesday, August 3, 2004 Primary election	U.S. senator, U.S. representative, governor, lieutenant governor, secretary of state, state attorney general, state treasurer, state senator, state representative, circuit court judge
Tuesday, November 2, 2004 General election	President, U.S. senator, U.S. representative, governor, lieutenant governor, secretary of state, attorney general, treasurer, state senator, state representative, circuit court judge
Toronto, Ontario (Canada)	
Thursday, September 20, 2001 By-election	Toronto City Councillors (one seat)
Monday, March 18, 2002 By-election	Toronto School Board (one seat)
Thursday, October 2, 2003 Provincial elections	Legislative Assembly of Province of Ontario (one representative elected from each district)
Monday, November 10, 2003 City elections	Mayor, city councillors (one councillor elected from each ward); Toronto School Board (one trustee elected from each ward)
Monday, June 28, 2004 Parliamentary elections	Canadian Parliament

Sources: Missouri: St. Louis Board of Elections, stlouis.missouri.org/citygov/electionbd/index.html; Missouri Secretary of State, www.sos.mo.gov/elections/. Toronto: Toronto Elections, www.toronto.ca/elections/index.htm; Elections Ontario, www.electionsontario.on.ca.

some states, candidates run for judge in partisan or non-partisan elections. In some other states, judges are initially appointed by the governor, but later they must run in retention elections, where they face no opponent but voters must decide whether they should remain on the bench for another term.

Putting so many government positions and issues to a popular vote makes for not only frequent elections, but also lengthy ballots. In heavily populated urban areas, which often have many judicial contests and ballot initiatives, the ballot can be especially long. For example, in the election held on November 5, 2002, voters in St. Louis faced thirty-eight items on the ballot, including ballot initiatives, judicial retention elections, and contests for federal, state, and local offices (Table 4-1). Such lengthy ballots can induce fatigue, causing voters to abstain from the contests near the bottom of the ballot. In this phenomenon called "ballot roll-off," it is not unusual for 30 percent of voters to skip contests at the bottom of a lengthy ballot.[12]

Voting Methods and Equipment

Frequent elections and lengthy ballots also place burdens on state and local election officials, who must administer voting procedures. Because of the diversity of local jurisdictions in the United States, voters cast ballots in several different ways. Only eight states require a single voting method for all jurisdictions within the state, and several more states are moving toward a uniform voting method in response to the Help America Vote Act. The other states allow counties and cities to choose their own voting equipment, but most of these states allow local jurisdictions to use only voting equipment certified by the state. Thus in most states voting equipment varies from one local jurisdiction to the next.

Voting methods are undergoing substantial changes in the United States. Slightly more than fourteen million voters cast ballots on new voting equipment in the 2002 general elections, and another twenty million voted on new equipment in 2004. Increasing numbers of voters are casting their ballots before election day via absentee ballots or early voting. The federal government and some state and local governments have even begun to explore Internet voting. In addition, as mandated by HAVA, every state allowed provisional voting in 2004 for people who believed they were registered but whose names were not on the voter lists at their polling places. Over 1.6 million provisional ballots were cast in the 2004 presidential election, of which almost 1.1 million were accepted as valid ballots.[13]

Voting methods vary in their usability, in the degree to which they help voters to avoid mistakes, and in their accessibility to voters with disabilities. Roughly two million voters (almost one in every fifty who cast a ballot) failed to record a valid choice for president in the 2000 elections. These unrecorded votes were the result of "undervotes" (where voters make no selection) and "overvotes" (where too many selections are recorded). Unrecorded votes are more common with certain types of voting equipment such as punch card ballots.

Voting at the Polls

Generally, five different methods of voting are used in the United States: paper ballots, lever machines, punch card ballots, optical scan ballots, and direct recording electronic (DRE) machines. Within each of these general categories, some further distinctions can be made. Table 4-2 shows the number of counties and the number of voters using each type of voting equipment in the 2002 and 2004 national elections. In a small number of counties, not all ballots are cast using the same technology. Counties with mixed voting systems tend to be in states in which voting equipment decisions are made at the municipal or township level. Some counties in the process of switching to a new voting system may test the new equipment in some precincts while using the old equipment in the remaining precincts.

The oldest voting method in the United States is the paper ballot, which lists candidates and initiative choices. Voters simply use a pen or pencil to check the box next to the candidate of their choice. After the polls close, the ballots are counted by hand. Because of the time required to count ballots by hand, paper ballots are used only in small, rural counties. In recent U.S. elections, only 1 percent of the votes were cast on old-fashioned paper ballots.

Lever voting machines, the oldest type of automated voting equipment, were developed in the 1890s. The entire ballot is displayed on a hulking metal device that is taller than some voters. To vote, the voter flips the small lever next to each candidate or initiative preferred. When finished, the voter pulls a large lever at the side of the machine, which records the votes on counters in the back of the machine. After the polls close, votes are tabulated from the counters. Lever voting machines are no longer manufactured, but they are still used in some heavily populated areas in a handful of states. HAVA encourages states to replace these gawky machines. Indeed, if states accept federal funds to upgrade voting equipment, they must replace lever machines by 2006. The use of lever voting machines declined in recent years, because some jurisdictions have already replaced them with newer voting equipment (Table 4-2).

The punch card ballot, developed in the 1960s, is used in two types of voting systems. The system most favored is the Votomatic, in which the voter receives a card with several numbered and pre-scored holes (or "chad") that pop out when the center of the perforation is punched with a stylus (a pointed instrument). To "mark" the ballot, the voter inserts the punch card into a slot behind a booklet listing all of the ballot options, and then uses a stylus to punch out the hole in the card corresponding to

Table 4-2 Voting Methods, 2002 and 2004 National Elections

Method	Number of counties		Number of voters (millions)	
	2002	2004	2002	2004
Punch card—Votomatic	436 (13.9%)	317 (10.1%)	15.4 (19.2%)	14.4 (11.7%)
Punch card—Datavote	26 (0.8%)	14 (0.4%)	1.6 (2.0%)	0.6 (0.5%)
Lever machine	292 (9.3%)	239 (7.6%)	10.4 (13.0%)	14.9 (12.1%)
Paper ballot	297 (9.4%)	289 (9.2%)	0.75 (0.9%)	1.0 (0.8%)
Older DRE (full-face)	321 (10.2%)	309 (9.8%)	9.3 (11.6%)	13.4 (10.8%)
Newer DRE (touch-screen)	224 (7.1%)	361 (11.5%)	7.9 (9.8%)	21.5 (17.4%)
Optical scan—central count	837 (26.6%)	823 (26.1%)	9.8 (12.2%)	17.6 (14.3%)
Optical scan—precinct count	615 (19.5%)	711 (22.6%)	21.3 (26.5%)	35.5 (28.8%)
Mixed	100 (3.2%)	85 (2.6%)	3.7 (4.6%)	4.5 (3.6%)

Source: State and local election officials.
Note: DRE = direct recording electronic.

the preferred candidate. A less common punch card method is the Datavote, in which offices and candidates are printed directly on the punch card and the voter punches out the hole next to the chosen candidate. In both the Votomatic and Datavote systems, votes are counted by running the ballots through a machine that records where the holes are punched in each card.

Because of their low cost and because they could be counted quickly, punch card ballots had, by the 1980s, become the most popular voting method in the United States. More recently, however, election officials have become aware of problems associated with punch card ballots. For example, when Votomatic cards are punched, the voter cannot immediately verify that the chad have been removed. As a result, if the voter inadvertently punches out the wrong chad or does not use enough force to punch the chad out completely, his or her choice may not be counted correctly. In addition, sometimes the punch card is not aligned properly with the ballot booklet so that the candidates' names and holes on the punch card do not correspond properly. Several studies indicate that Votomatic punch cards produce rates of unrecorded votes higher than those of any other voting method.[14]

This voting system was a source of controversy during the recount of presidential votes in Florida in 2000. Many of the unrecorded votes in the presidential contest in Florida were cast on punch card ballots. Because the chad were not punched out completely in some punch

card ballots, election officials struggled to determine which punch card ballots should count as valid votes for president. HAVA requires states to replace the punch card ballots by 2006 if they accept federal funding for the effort. In response to the Florida controversy and many studies highlighting problems with punch cards, the use of punch cards declined substantially between 2000 and 2004. However, roughly 15 million voters still cast ballots on punch cards in the 2004 elections.

When election officials replace older voting methods, they switch to optical scan systems or electronic machines. Optical scan systems are similar in format to standardized tests. Candidates and initiative options are listed on a piece of paper, and voters simply darken an oval or arrow next to their choice. Ballots are counted by feeding them into a computerized scanner (sometimes called a "mark-sense" device) that determines where the ballots have been marked. Optical scan systems vary, depending on where ballots are counted: at a central location (such as the county courthouse) or at the voting precinct. One advantage of the precinct-count optical scan systems is that they give voters a chance to discover and correct mistakes (such as overvotes). When the voter inserts the ballot into the scanner at the precinct, the scanner spits the ballot out if there is an apparent mistake. The voter can then correct the ballot. The central-count systems, even though less expensive because they do not require a scanner for each precinct, do not have such an error-correction feature.

By the 1980s, punch card ballots were the most popular voting method in the United States. However, many of the unrecorded votes in the 2000 presidential contest in Florida were cast on such ballots. The chad on numerous ballots were not punched out completely, and election officials, including Joseph Robert Rosenberg, struggled to determine which should count as valid votes. Source: Rona Wise/EPA/Landov

Studies indicate that unrecorded votes are substantially lower in counties using precinct-count optical scan systems.[15] Optical scan voting systems have become the most commonly used voting method in the United States.

The direct recording electronic (DRE) voting machine, the newest voting method, is a computer, and the candidates and initiative options appear on the computer screen. Voters touch the screen or push a button next to their choice, much like they do on a bank's automatic teller machine (ATM). Votes are directly counted and stored on a disk, tape, or smart card inside the computer, but in most models there is no paper ballot to serve as backup. Older DRE voting machines, which were often designed to mimic lever machines, present the entire full-faced ballot at once and typically use a push-button interface.[16] The newer generation of DRE voting machines typically use a touch-screen interface (see photo, page 58) and allow voters to scroll through the offices and issues on the ballot (much like the Votomatic punch card bal-

lots). DRE voting machines do not allow overvotes, and the newer touch-screen voting machines let voters review their votes to make sure they are correct.

DRE voting machines, especially the newer touch-screen models, have become increasingly popular since 2000. The new technology allows votes to be cast and counted quickly. In addition, DRE machines are the preferred voting technology for voters with disabilities, because they can often be configured to allow people with disabilities to cast their ballots in secret—that is, without assistance. The growing concerns, however, about the security of electronic voting systems have fueled an intense debate about their suitability (see Box 4-1).

In contrast to the variety of voting methods available in the United States, the nation lacks uniform laws and standards for counting and recounting votes. At no time was this clearer than in the aftermath of the 2000 presidential election in Florida. At the time of the election, Florida did not have a clear and uniform definition of what counts as a valid vote and thus no uniform standard for conducting a recount. In counting and recounting ballots, some Florida counties pronounced the same kinds of ballots valid that other counties rejected (for example, overseas absentee ballots without a postmark, punch card ballots with chads hanging from the card, and optical scan ballots in which voters darkened the oval next to a candidate's name but then wrote the same candidate's name on the write-in line). The absence of uniform laws and standards in Florida was a primary reason why the U.S. Supreme Court in *Bush v. Gore* halted the state's ballot recount. Citing the equal protection clause of the Fourteenth Amendment to the Constitution, the Court decided that the different recount standards and procedures in Florida counties prevented voters from being treated equally. After the 2000 election, a survey of laws in other states found that many did not have well-defined provisions for recounts or clear definitions of valid votes.[17] HAVA requires states to have uniform provisions for counting and recounting votes, and most states have recently passed laws to comply.

Voting before Election Day

Ongoing changes in voting technology have obscured another development in voting processes: the practice of voting at a local polling place (such as a school, library, or courthouse) is gradually being replaced by other means of voting. One study estimates that 14 percent of ballots were cast outside of polling places in the 2000 presidential election, a notable increase from just 4 percent in 1972.[18] Approximately 22 percent of votes were cast before election day in the 2004 presidential election.[19] Indeed, in the last twenty years many states have made it far easier for voters to cast a ballot before election day.

Increased access to absentee ballots is one way in which preelection voting has become more common. These ballots are completed by voters and returned to election officials before election day, usually by mail. Traditionally,

Direct recording electronic (DRE) voting machines work much like an automatic teller machine (ATM). Voters touch the screen or push a button next to their candidate choice. Votes are directly counted and stored electronically inside the computer, but the absence of a paper ballot to serve as a backup has raised issues of accuracy and fraud. Source: Diebold Voting Systems

voters have had to meet certain conditions to get an absentee ballot. For example, voters with a disability or people working out of town on election day would usually qualify for an absentee ballot, although accepted reasons have varied from state to state. Recently, however, many states have removed all restrictions on absentee voting. Twenty-four states now allow unrestricted, "no-excuse" absentee voting. In the late 1990s, Oregon went a step further and switched entirely to a vote-by-mail system, thereby eliminating voting at polling places and sparing voters from having to request an absentee or mail-in ballot. Several states, mostly in the West, allow localities to hold vote-by-mail elections, and some have done so for local initiatives.

At the same time, several states have adopted procedures for early voting—a procedure that was first introduced in Texas. In participating states, early voting stations are usually located at election board offices or in high-traffic areas, such as malls or supermarkets, up to a few weeks before election day. Voters simply show up at an early voting station, sign in, verify their registration, and cast a ballot just as they would at a polling place on election day. Currently, thirty-five states have early voting procedures. Overall, a majority of states now allow all registered voters some way of casting a ballot before election day.

BOX 4-1
DRE VOTING MACHINE CONTROVERSY

A growing number of computer scientists and elected officials are concerned about the security of direct recording electronic (DRE) voting machines. In particular, they worry that the computer technology of DRE machines might malfunction or could be programmed or hacked to record or count votes in a way that would falsify voters' ballot choices. For example, roughly 4,400 votes were lost during the 2004 election in Carteret County, North Carolina, because the touch-screen voting machines ran out of memory to store the electronic ballots.[1] Because DRE machines produce no paper ballot, voters cannot be certain that their votes are recorded properly. Critics of the system advocate modifying DRE voting machines to print a paper ballot that voters can review and approve

(often called a "voter-verified audit trail").[2]

On the other side, many DRE machine manufacturers, other election officials, other experts, and advocates for civil rights and the disabled argue that security concerns about DRE voting machines are exaggerated and outweighed by the benefits of the new technology. For example, the state of Georgia substantially reduced the number of unrecorded votes in major elections after switching to new touch-screen voting machines in every county. Groups representing voters with disabilities argue that the paper trail will eliminate their ability to cast a ballot in secret.[3] Election officials worry about the added cost and burden on poll workers if ballot printers are installed on the DRE voting machines currently in use.

1. Mark Johnson, "Backup System Wanted to Prevent Repeat of Carteret Lost-Vote Fiasco," *Charlotte Observer,* February 10, 2005.

2. For more information on this side of the argument, see the Verified Voting Web site, www.verifiedvoting .org/, maintained by David Dill, a professor of computer science at Stanford University and one of the leading proponents of the voter-verified audit trail.

3. For more information on this side of the argument, see the Web site of the American Association of People with Disabilities (www .aapd-dc.org/dvpmain/votemachines/ dvpvotmachines.html), one of the advocates for DRE voting machines. In the meantime, manufacturers are developing new DRE voting machines that do include a paper trail.

BOX 4-2

EARLY VOTING AND UNRESTRICTED ABSENTEE VOTING

The rise in unrestricted absentee voting and early voting is a boon for candidates with a financial and organizational advantage over their opponents. For example, in the San Francisco mayor's runoff election in 2003, Democratic candidate Gavin Newsom outspent his opponent, Green Party candidate Matt Gonzalez, by a ten-to-one margin, and part of that spending advantage went into a vigorous absentee voting drive (in California roughly 30 percent of votes are cast by absentee ballot). In the end, Newsom received almost twice as many absentee votes as Gonzalez, which allowed him to overcome a stronger turnout for Gonzalez on election day. Newsom won the mayoral election with 53 percent of the total votes cast.

In the 2002 gubernatorial election in Kansas, Democratic candidate Kathleen Sebelius broke the state record for campaign expenditures in a statewide race by raising roughly $4 million and spending twice as much as her chief opponent, Republican Tim Shallenburger. Sebelius was aided by the fact that she faced no opponent in the Democratic primary, while Shallenburger had to win a divisive GOP primary to enter the general election. The financial advantage allowed Sebelius to start airing television ads in July, two months before Shallenburger, thus establishing a positive image for Sebelius among early voters. As a two-term state insurance commissioner, Sebelius had already developed a strong political organization, and she used that organization to target early voters as part of her campaign's get-out-the-vote drive in 2002. Her success at capturing 65 percent of the early votes helped to propel her to a victory in which she received 54 percent of all votes cast.

Sources: Rachel Gordon, Bill Wallace, and John Wildermuth, "Donated Dollars Nourish Contest: Newsom Outraises Gonzalez by Factor of 10 in Mayor's Race," *San Francisco Chronicle,* December 2, 2003; Scott Rothschild, "Sebelius Shatters Spending Record," *Lawrence Journal-World,* October 29, 2002; Kansas Secretary of State; San Francisco Department of Elections.

The move toward early voting and relaxed absentee voting is driven in part by their convenience and popularity with voters. In several western states, roughly one-third of votes are cast by absentee ballot. In Texas and Tennessee, two states with well-established early voting procedures, over one-third of ballots are cast before election day. Some officials believe that early voting and unrestricted absentee voting will increase voter turnout.[20] As more voters cast absentee and early ballots, election officials also hope to reduce the costs associated with staffing polling places.

That said, not everyone is in favor of early voting. Some critics argue that voting on election day is an important civic ritual, and that allowing people to vote in advance at their convenience will undermine the nation's sense of community and national unity.[21] Most studies also indicate that early and unrestricted absentee voting produces at best only a slight increase in voter turnout. Yet the political parties and candidates have increasingly incorporated absentee and early voting into their campaign efforts (see Box 4-2), and the combination of relaxed absentee voting and party mobilization has boosted voter turnout in some states.[22] Opponents also argue that increased early and absentee voting may have unintended effects on voters and campaigns. For example, some voters may cast their ballots before a late-breaking campaign event changes their mind about their preferred candidates. Finally, critics argue that absentee voting by mail is susceptible to fraud. Unlike voting at polling places and early voting stations, mail-in absentee ballots are completed without the supervision of election officials. Thus it is harder for election officials to ensure that the registered voter who requests an absentee ballot is the person who actually casts the ballot. Some fear that absentee voters may be coerced or unduly influenced by campaign loyalists, because election officials are not present to ensure that absentee ballots are completed in private. Indeed, several recent election fraud cases in the United States have involved efforts to manipulate absentee voting. For example, Orlando, Florida, mayor Buddy Dyer narrowly won reelection in 2004 with the help of a wave of absentee votes. However, a year later Dyer was indicted on charges of election law violations related to the collection of absentee votes in the mayoral election.[23] All these criticisms, however, have not prevented attempts by election officials to expand the opportunities for voters to cast their ballots before election day.

The Future: Internet Voting?

The current debates about DRE voting machines and absentee voting are a prelude to future debates about Internet voting. Enthusiasts point to the rapidly growing presence of computers and the Internet in American society and their belief that Internet voting will revolutionize elections in the near future. The arguments in favor of Internet voting run along these lines. First, Internet voting would make voting easier, because every computer with online access would become a polling place. Second, voters could cast their ballot in the comfort of their own home, and perhaps do so after browsing Web sites to learn more about the candidates and issues on the ballot. Third, Internet voting would help certain groups (such as voters with disabilities and military personnel) that face obstacles with current voting methods, and advances in wireless technology may make it easier for people in remote locations to vote. Finally, Internet voting would increase voter participation among younger Americans. Young adults turn out to vote at very low rates, but they are more comfortable with Internet technology than older Americans. Adherents see Internet voting as nothing less than a means of revitalizing electoral democracy in the United States.[24]

Detractors disagree; they believe Internet voting may undermine American democracy. One of the main concerns is the security of online voting. If computer hackers and viruses can cripple Web sites and computer networks, then Internet voting could be susceptible to large-scale manipulation. Moreover, there are no mechanisms to guarantee that ballots are actually being cast by the voters who are entitled to cast them and to prevent voter fraud and intimidation. Another concern is that low-income and minority groups do not enjoy the same access to computers and high-speed Internet connections as wealthy white Americans. Thus Internet voting may exacerbate socioeconomic disparities in voting and political representation. Finally, critics of Internet voting worry that if the traditional ritual of voting at a polling place is replaced by methods that allow people to vote at home (or early or absentee), community life will decline.[25]

Despite these concerns, Internet voting has already been tested. The Defense Department has been conducting pilot studies of Internet voting for American citizens living overseas; the Arizona Democratic Party used Internet voting for its presidential primary election in 2000; and the Michigan Democratic Party used Internet voting for its presidential caucuses in 2004. In addition, several groups and organizations, including professional associations, labor unions, and corporations, have conducted internal elections over the Internet. Finally, other countries, such as Britain, have experimented with Internet voting in elections. Meanwhile, a growing number of scholars, election officials, and other experts are exploring ways to address concerns about security and computer access to make Internet voting feasible.[26]

Ballot Features

The absence of uniformity in American election procedures extends beyond voting methods and equipment to the design and layout of actual ballots. The one thing almost all elections have in common is the use of some type of secret ballot. For most of the nineteenth century, each political party printed and distributed its own ballot that listed only its slate of candidates. Voters then brought their preferred party ballot to the polling place and placed it in the ballot box. Because each party's ballot was different in shape and color, votes could not be cast secretly; the observers on hand could determine how a person voted. This practice fostered vote buying and voter intimidation and discouraged ticket splitting (voting for candidates of different parties for different offices).

Beginning in the late 1800s, the Progressive movement sought to reform the corrupt party system by, among other things, replacing party-printed ballots with a single government-printed ballot that listed all candidates and was cast by the voter in secret. The new secret ballot, called the Australian ballot after the nation that invented the practice, made it easier for voters to cast a split ticket and reduced party control over elections.[27] More important, the Australian ballot ushered in an era in which state and local governments administered elections.

Beyond secrecy, however, U.S. ballots have almost nothing in common. The fact that local governments administer elections ensures that ballots vary widely in almost every element of their appearance, in the manner in which candidates and offices are listed, in the presence of party symbols and cues, and in ballot instructions. But the features of a ballot are not without consequences for the political parties, the candidates, and the voters, all of whom have certain goals in mind when it comes to ballot layout.

The Parties' Goal: Getting Help from the Ballot

Even though political parties lost direct control of the balloting process with adoption of the Australian ballot, some ballot features do highlight the parties. When the Australian ballot was first adopted, many states opted to use a "party column" format that lists each party's candidates in a single column, making it easier for voters to identify each party slate. This kind of format, which is still being used in some states (see photo, page 61), often includes a straight-party option, which allows voters to vote for all of the candidates of one party by simply marking a box under the party name or symbol. The party column format therefore tends to encourage straight-party voting.[28]

In recent years, many states and counties have switched to an office-bloc format that groups candidates by the office they are seeking (see photo, page 62). The move toward the office-bloc format was accelerated when punch card and optical scan balloting became popular, and today the vast majority of Americans cast their votes on office-bloc ballots. Office-bloc ballots label a candidate's party affiliation, but these ballots vary greatly in appearance (compare the first office-bloc ballot with the second on page 63).[29] Because party slates are less obvious in office-bloc ballots than in party column ballots, the office-bloc ballot tends to encourage ticket splitting.

The party column format, which appeared with the adoption of the Australian ballot, was still in use in the 2002 election in West Virginia as seen in this ballot from Barbour County. This format makes it easier for voters to identify each party slate.

Some office-bloc ballots offer a straight-party option, which enhances party loyalty (see photo). Without a straight-party option, voters using an office-bloc ballot have to mark each office separately, which reduces the chances they will follow party labels. Currently, only seventeen states have a straight-party ballot option, down from twenty-eight states that had such a ballot device in the 1960s.

Political parties and candidates tend to believe that the configuration of the ballot can influence election results. Campaigns incorporate ballot features into their electoral strategy, and heated partisan disputes can erupt over attempts to change ballot features. For example, in an ef-

fort to capitalize on the popularity of President Bill Clinton, Illinois Democrats used the straight-party option in their coordinated campaign in the 1996 general elections. The party produced pamphlets and campaign advertisements that prominently featured a "Punch 10" slogan (the ballot line for a straight Democratic Party ticket). The campaign was credited for helping to defeat some GOP incumbents in the Chicago area and allowing Democrats to regain control of the state house of representatives.[30] In response, in a lame-duck session one day before Democrats were scheduled to assume control of the house, Republican lawmakers passed legislation removing the straight-party option from Illinois ballots over the vehement objections of Democrats.

Legislative battles over the straight-party option and the prominence of partisan cues on the ballot are common in the United States and follow a familiar pattern. Typically, the political party that holds the edge in voter registration prefers a ballot that includes a straight-party option and party column format. A ballot that prominently features party labels facilitates a coordinated party campaign, as the Illinois example shows, and helps the stronger party to maintain its advantage in the voting booth. By contrast, the weaker political party typically prefers the office-bloc format without a straight-party option. The weaker party also prefers inconspicuous party labels. A ballot that forces voters to consider individual candidates rather than party labels increases the chances that the weaker party will gain support from the stronger party's voters.

The Candidates' Goal: Getting on the Ballot and Achieving Top Billing

In addition to partisan designs on the ballot's appearance, candidates have their own twin goals: gaining access to the ballot and, if possible, being listed before all other candidates running for the same office. Ballot access is one of the indicators that major political parties have skewed election laws to their own advantage. For Democratic and Republican candidates, getting listed on the general election ballot is automatic, because most states grant automatic ballot access to parties that received a certain number of votes in the previous election. By contrast, most states require independent and minor-party candidates to gather thousands of petition signatures to qualify for the ballot, often with deadlines several months before election day.[31]

Like other election features, ballot access requirements vary considerably from state to state. The diversity is evident in the number of presidential candidates who make it onto the ballots. In the 2004 election, few if any minor-party candidates for president qualified for the ballot in states with the most burdensome ballot access provisions. For example, Oklahoma required 51,781 signatures for a third-party candidate for president to qualify for the ballot in 2004 (over 2 percent of the state's registered voters,

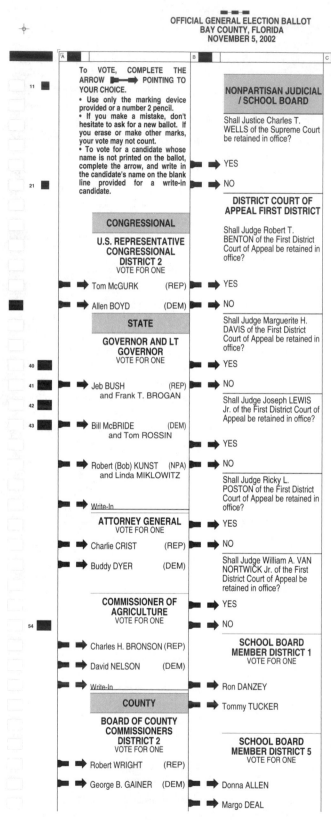

Political party labels and the party slates of candidates are less obvious on an office bloc ballot than on a party column ballot. The vast majority of Americans cast their votes on office-bloc ballots similar to this one from Bay County, Florida.

the highest rate in the country)—no third-party presidential candidates made it onto the ballot in Oklahoma.[32] In states with the least demanding ballot access requirements, as many as eight minor-party candidates for president were listed on the ballot. In Colorado, which only required a thousand signatures to qualify a third-party candidate for president in 2004, nine independent or third-party presidential candidates were listed on the ballot along with George W. Bush and John Kerry.[33]

Because the number of signatures required for third-party candidates is usually a percentage of the votes cast in a recent election, the most populous states tend to require the most signatures to qualify for the ballot. Most states require independent or minor-party presidential candidates to gather at least two thousand signatures, although in the last fifteen years several states have reduced ballot access requirements.[34]

The various ballot access rules present a special burden for independent and minor-party candidates running for president. For example, independent candidate H. Ross Perot spent $18 million and collected 5.5 million petition signatures to qualify for a spot on the ballot in every state in the 1992 presidential election.[35] In 2000 Green Party presidential candidate Ralph Nader filed lawsuits in at least eight states to challenge their ballot access laws. Nader lost most of those court cases and was not listed on the ballot in seven states. In 2004 Democrats worried that Nader might take votes from Sen. John Kerry and throw the presidential election to President Bush. Thus they aggressively challenged the Nader campaign's petition signatures in several states, and Nader failed to qualify for a place on the ballot in sixteen states in 2004. The reality, then, is that major-party presidential candidates are able to devote their financial and staff resources directly to campaign-related activities (such as advertising and voter mobilization), whereas independent and minor-party candidates must spend substantial resources simply to get their names listed on the ballot.

Once a candidate qualifies for the ballot, he or she would prefer to be listed first among candidates running for the same office. The psychological evidence is abundant that people are biased toward selecting the first choices in a list, but in some cases voting is no different (see Box 4-3). Controlled studies indicate that candidates listed first on the ballot can receive a modest boost in votes, particularly in nonpartisan contests such as judicial elections and races for sheriff, open-seat races, and races that receive very little media coverage.[36]

Because such studies document candidate name order effects, it might make sense for election officials to rotate the order of names on the ballot so no candidate gains an advantage from the first spot. Only twelve states currently have provisions for rotating the order of the candidates for at least some races on the ballot.[37] Overall, there are almost as many procedures for listing candidates on the ballot as there are states. For example, some states list

OFFICIAL GENERAL ELECTION BALLOT

| A | DALLAS COUNTY | B | STATE OF IOWA | C | NOVEMBER 5, 2002 |

INSTRUCTIONS TO VOTER
1. TO VOTE YOU MUST BLACKEN THE OVAL (⬬) COMPLETELY.
To write in a name, you must blacken the oval (⬬) to the left of the line provided, and write the name in the space provided for that purpose.
2. USE ONLY THE PENCIL PROVIDED.
3. DO NOT CROSS OUT. If you change your mind exchange your ballot for a new one.
4. AFTER VOTING, insert ballot in the secrecy sleeve so that the Precinct Official's initials appear at the bottom. DO NOT FOLD THE BALLOT.
5. STRAIGHT PARTY VOTING
To vote for every candidate of one party blacken the oval (⬬) to the left of the party name. Not all parties have nominated candidates for all offices. Marking a straight party vote does not include votes for nonpartisan offices, judges or questions.
6. WHERE TO FIND THE JUDGES: The judicial ballot is ON THE OTHER SIDE OF THIS BALLOT, BEGINNING IN THE SECOND COLUMN.

OFFICIAL BALLOT

Carol Bayum Dawson
Commissioner of Elections
Dallas County, Iowa

STRAIGHT PARTY TICKET
○ DEMOCRATIC PARTY
○ REPUBLICAN PARTY
○ IOWA GREEN PARTY
○ LIBERTARIAN PARTY

OTHER POLITICAL ORGANIZATIONS
The following organizations have nominated candidates only for one office.
ONE EARTH PARTY

FEDERAL OFFICES

FOR UNITED STATES SENATOR
Vote For No More Than One
○ TOM HARKIN — DEMOCRATIC
○ GREG GANSKE — REPUBLICAN
○ TIMOTHY A. HARTHAN — IOWA GREEN
○ RICHARD J. MOORE — LIBERTARIAN
○ ___ Write-In Vote, If Any

FOR UNITED STATES REPRESENTATIVE – 4TH DISTRICT
Vote For No More Than One
○ JOHN NORRIS — DEMOCRATIC
○ TOM LATHAM — REPUBLICAN
○ JIM HENNAGER — ONE EARTH

STATE OFFICES

FOR GOVERNOR AND LIEUTENANT GOVERNOR
Vote For No More Than One Team
○ TOM VILSACK / SALLY PEDERSON — DEMOCRATIC
○ DOUG GROSS / DEBI DURHAM — REPUBLICAN
○ JAY ROBINSON / HOLLY JANE HART — IOWA GREEN
○ CLYDE CLEVELAND / RICHARD CAMPAGNA — LIBERTARIAN
○ ___ Write-In Vote for Governor, If Any
○ ___ Write-In Vote for Lieutenant Governor, If Any

FOR SECRETARY OF STATE
Vote For No More Than One
○ CHET CULVER — DEMOCRATIC
○ MIKE HARTWIG — REPUBLICAN
○ DON ARENZ — IOWA GREEN
○ SYLVIA SANDERS OLSON — LIBERTARIAN
○ ___ Write-In Vote, If Any

FOR AUDITOR OF STATE
Vote For No More Than One
○ PATRICK J. DELUHERY — DEMOCRATIC
○ DAVID A. VAUDT — REPUBLICAN
○ CHRISTY ANN WELTY — LIBERTARIAN
○ ___ Write-In Vote, If Any

FOR TREASURER OF STATE
Vote For No More Than One
○ MICHAEL L. FITZGERALD — DEMOCRATIC
○ MATT WHITAKER — REPUBLICAN
○ TIM HIRD — LIBERTARIAN
○ ___ Write-In Vote, If Any

FOR SECRETARY OF AGRICULTURE
Vote For No More Than One
○ PATTY JUDGE — DEMOCRATIC
○ JOHN ASKEW — REPUBLICAN
○ BRIAN RUSSELL DEPEW — IOWA GREEN
○ FRITZ GROSZKRUGER — LIBERTARIAN
○ RONALD TIGNER — NOMINATED BY PETITION
○ ___ Write-In Vote, If Any

FOR ATTORNEY GENERAL
Vote For No More Than One

FOR STATE SENATOR 37TH DISTRICT
Vote For No More Than One
○ BILL FINK — DEMOCRATIC
○ DOUG SHULL — REPUBLICAN
○ BRAD L. NORDSTROM — NOMINATED BY PETITION
○ ___ Write-In Vote, If Any

FOR STATE REPRESENTATIVE 73RD DISTRICT
Vote For No More Than One
○ KATHRYN M. RUSSELL — DEMOCRATIC
○ JODI TYMESON — REPUBLICAN
○ ___ Write-In Vote, If Any

COUNTY OFFICES

FOR BOARD OF SUPERVISORS DISTRICT 1
Vote For No More Than One
○ MARVIN SHIRLEY — DEMOCRATIC
○ BRAD GOLIGHTLY — REPUBLICAN
○ ___ Write-In Vote, If Any

FOR BOARD OF SUPERVISORS DISTRICT 3
Vote For No More Than One
○ DAVID W. FORRET — DEMOCRATIC
○ KIM E. CHAPMAN — REPUBLICAN
○ ___ Write-In Vote, If Any

FOR COUNTY TREASURER
Vote For No More Than One
○ DARRELL BAUMAN — REPUBLICAN
○ ___ Write-In Vote, If Any

FOR COUNTY RECORDER
Vote For No More Than One
○ CAROL CINDY HOL — DEMOCRATIC
○ ___ Write-In Vote, If Any

FOR COUNTY ATTORNEY
Vote For No More Than One
○ WAYNE M. REISETTER — DEMOCRATIC
○ ___ Write-In Vote, If Any

SAMPLE BALLOT — Dawn County Auditor

An office-bloc ballot with a straight-party option, like the one shown here from Dallas County, Iowa, makes it easier to vote for a party slate and bypass individual contests on the ballot.

with an exceedingly close presidential contest to fuel the ballot counting controversy in Florida. For example, recently relaxed ballot access laws enabled ten candidates to qualify for the 2000 presidential contest in Florida, and county election officials struggled to find ways to fit ten names on the ballot. In Palm Beach County, a Democratic election director used a "butterfly" design for the presidential race on the county's punch card ballots (see photo, page 64). On a butterfly ballot, candidates are listed on two facing pages, and the punch holes are situated between the two pages. In the 2000 presidential contest, Al Gore's name was listed second on the left-hand page, but to select Gore, Palm Beach voters had to punch the third hole on the ballot (the second hole corresponded with a vote for Pat Buchanan, the first candidate listed on the right-hand page).

Pat Buchanan received an unusually large share of the votes in Palm Beach County, strongly suggesting that voters who preferred Gore mistakenly cast votes for Buchanan.[39] In addition, an unusually large number of voters in Palm Beach County (over nineteen thousand) mistakenly voted for more than one presidential candidate (that is, cast overvotes), thereby voiding their choice for president. It appears that by listing candidates in two columns, the butterfly ballot gave voters the incorrect impression that they were supposed to select a candidate from each column. But this problem was not limited to Palm Beach County. Eighteen other Florida counties listed the presidential candidates in multiple columns, and the vast majority of presidential overvotes in Florida (over 120,000) were cast in those counties.[40] By contrast, the remaining forty-eight Florida counties that listed the presidential candidates in a single column had relatively few overvotes or other voting errors. George W. Bush carried Florida in 2000 by only 537 votes, so ballot design may have influenced the outcome of the election.

States and counties vary considerably in several other ballot features that may affect a voter's ability to cast an error-free ballot. For example, ballots may include party mascots (such as a donkey for Democrats and an elephant for Republicans); the candidate's occupation, nickname, or place of residence (county or town); or identification of the incumbent candidate running for each office.[41] Other sources of variation are the location and

candidates in alphabetical order by their last names, while others place candidates in the same order as their party's share of the vote in the last gubernatorial election.[38] Still others list candidates in the order in which they file candidacy papers.

The Voters' Goal: Understanding How to Cast a Correct Ballot

For voters, the main concern is a ballot design that minimizes confusion and voting errors. The 2000 presidential election brought attention to one confusing ballot feature and sparked interest in other aspects of ballot design. Various election methods and procedures combined

---

BOX 4-3
BALLOT ORDER RESULTS

Political observers in Missouri were initially stunned at the results of the Republican primary contest for state auditor in 2002. Al Hanson, something of a political gadfly who had been convicted of financial fraud, handily defeated Jay Kanzler, the candidate recruited by party leaders and endorsed by every major GOP official in the state. Upon closer inspection, this contest appears to be a textbook case of ballot name order effects. Under Missouri law, in primary elections candidates are listed in the order in which they sub-

mit candidacy papers. In the GOP primary for state auditor, Hanson filed first. In addition, the primary contest for state auditor garnered almost no media coverage. The Democratic incumbent was favored to win reelection as state auditor, and political reporting was heavily tilted toward a very competitive U.S. Senate contest. The three largest newspapers in the state ran a grand total of three articles on the Republican primary for state auditor, and only one article emphasized Hanson's felony conviction. Thus only the most attentive

voters had any information about the two primary candidates for auditor. Moreover, there was no incumbent, and there were no party labels in the primary contest. Al Hanson was listed first on the ballot in every Missouri county, and he won handily in every county.

Sources: Missouri Secretary of State; Virginia Young, "Felon Upsets GOP's Pick in State Auditor Primary; Hanson Served 9 Months in Prison for Fraud," *St. Louis Post-Dispatch,* August 7, 2002, A1.

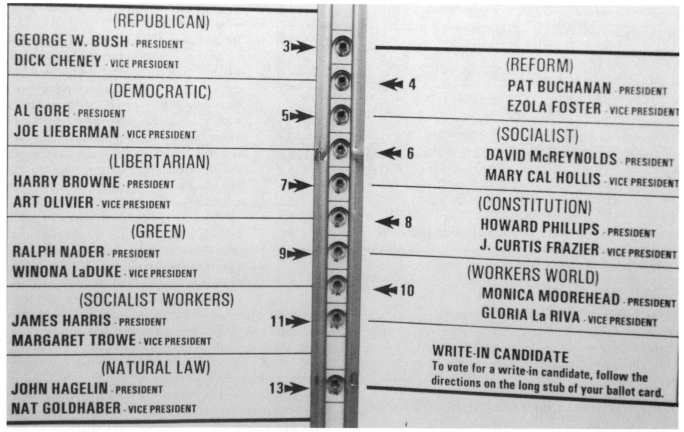

In the 2000 presidential election, voters in Democratic stronghold Palm Beach County, Florida, used a "butterfly" ballot. Democratic candidate Al Gore's name was listed second on the left-hand page, but to select Gore, voters had to punch the third hole on the ballot (the second hole corresponded with a vote for Reform Party candidate Pat Buchanan, the first candidate listed on the right-hand page). Buchanan's strong showing in the county fueled the debate over ballot design and the outcome of the election. Source: AP Wide World Photo

content of ballot instructions, as well font types and sizes. A recent study of seven states found that ballot instructions ranged from a third-grade reading level to a college reading level.[42]

Some ballot features help to reduce voting errors. For example, unrecorded votes are less common in counties where ballot instructions are written at a low reading level and are located in the top left-hand corner, just above the first office.[43] In addition, ballot features that facilitate straight-party voting, such as the party column format and the straight-ticket option, seem to reduce the frequency of unrecorded votes.[44] In some places, election officials have begun to consult with graphic design experts to help create ballots that simplify the voting process.

Conclusion

This chapter describes some of the laws and administrative procedures that shape the way votes are cast in the United States. Because state and local officials bear the responsibility for most election administration decisions, the U.S. electoral system is a patchwork of voting methods, electoral choices, ballot features, and other election procedures. As an illustration of this point, Table 4-3 lists seven election features described in this chapter and identifies each state in which the feature is used. It is difficult to find two states with the same combination of these seven elements.

The nationwide reexamination of election rules and procedures that followed the 2000 presidential election, the Help America Vote Act of 2002, and recent technological advances will likely produce more uniformity in voting methods and procedures and a reduction in the current diversity of voting technologies (see Table 4-2). As local election officials continue to replace punch card ballots and lever voting machines, the vast majority of voters in the United States will find themselves voting on optical scan ballots or computerized voting machines. The degree to which Internet voting will be incorporated into American elections remains to be seen.

HAVA will bring some uniformity to other aspects of election administration, particularly within states. The act attempts to place the responsibility for implementing election reforms on state election officials. It requires states to create computerized voter registration systems, and it calls for certain first-time voters to present photo identification. HAVA also requires improved voting instructions at polling places, access to polling places for

Table 4-3 Use of Election Features, by State

State	Recall statewide officials	Statewide initiative	Uniform voting equipment	Early voting	Unrestricted absentee voting	Straight-party option	Rotation of name order
Alabama	X					X	
Alaska		X	X	X	X		
Arizona	X	X	X[a]	X	X		X
Arkansas		X		X			X
California	X	X		X	X		X
Colorado	X	X		X	X		
Connecticut			X				
Delaware			X				
District of Columbia	X		X	X			
Florida		X		X	X		
Georgia	X		X	X			
Hawaii			X	X	X		
Idaho	X	X		X	X		X
Illinois		X		X			
Indiana				X		X	
Iowa				X	X	X	X
Kansas	X			X	X		X
Kentucky				X		X	
Louisiana	X			X			

(Table continues on next page)

(continued)
Table 4-3

State	Recall statewide officials	Statewide initiative	Uniform voting equipment	Early voting	Unrestricted absentee voting	Straight-party option	Rotation of name order
Maine		X		X	X		
Maryland			X				
Massachusetts		X		X			
Michigan	X	X				X	X
Minnesota	X			X			X
Mississippi		X					
Missouri		X				X	
Montana	X	X		X	X		X
Nebraska		X		X	X		X
Nevada	X	X	X	X	X		
New Hampshire						X	
New Jersey	X						
New Mexico				X	X	X	
New York			X				
North Carolina				X	X	X	
North Dakota	X	X		X	X		X
Ohio		X					X
Oklahoma		X	X	X	X	X	
Oregon	X	X	X^a	^b	X		
Pennsylvania						X	
Rhode Island	X		X			X	
South Carolina						X	
South Dakota		X		X	X		
Tennessee				X			
Texas				X		X	
Utah		X		X	X	X	
Vermont				X	X		
Virginia				X			
Washington	X	X			X		
West Virginia				X		X	
Wisconsin	X			X	X	X	
Wyoming		X		X	X		

Sources: National Conference of State Legislatures, "Overview of Recall Provisions," August 13, 2003, www.ncsl.org/programs/ legman/elect/recallprovision.htm (accessed December 9, 2003); Initiative and Referendum Institute at the University of Southern California, "Information on the Statewide Initiative Process in the United States," www.iandrinstitute.com/statewide_i&r.htm (accessed March 22, 2005); Election Reform Information Project and the Constitution Project, "Election Preview 2004: What's Changed, What Hasn't and Why," October 2004, www.electionline.org/site/docs/pdf/2004.Election.Preview.Final.Report .Update1.pdf (accessed December 21, 2004); Jon A. Krosnick, Joanne M. Miller, and Michael P. Tichy, "An Unrecognized Need for Ballot Reform: The Effects of Candidate Name Order on Election Outcomes," in *Rethinking the Vote: The Politics and Prospects of American Election Reform,* edited by Ann N. Crigler and Marion R. Just, 51–74 (New York: Oxford University Press, 2004).

Note: Table shows election features in place in the 2004 presidential election.

[a] Arizona and Oregon adopted statewide optical scan balloting for the 2004 general election, although not every county used the same model.
[b] Oregon has statewide mail-in balloting (no in-person voting).

voters with disabilities, and provisional voting procedures for voters whose registration status is in dispute. As states pass legislation and develop plans to comply with HAVA, they are likely to impose more uniform election procedures within their borders. However, because states have differed widely in how they have implemented HAVA and because many aspects of election administration are unaffected by HAVA, U.S. elections will continue to be marked by diverse rules and procedures. For example, in 2004 there were major disputes in several states over the rules on provisional voting. Seventeen states counted provisional ballots that were cast at the wrong voting precinct, whereas most other states rejected such ballots. Furthermore, even the procedures for handling provisional votes varied within some states.[45]

A theme of this chapter is that election laws and procedures are not neutral. They seem to help some candidates and political parties and work against others, thanks often to the state legislatures that tinker with election rules. Election administration in the United States tends to disadvantage minor parties, raising barriers to their participation in electoral politics. In addition, the electoral rules of the game impose constraints on campaign decisions and provide strategic opportunities. Candidates and parties that ignore the strategic aspect of election rules do so at their peril.

Notes

1. R. Michael Alvarez and Thad E. Hall, *Point, Click, and Vote: The Future of Internet Voting* (Washington, D.C.: Brookings, 2004).

2. Many of the election reform reports can be viewed and downloaded from the Web site of the Washington State's secretary of state, www.secstate.wa.gov/elections/reform_reports .aspx. Lillian Civili provided research assistance for this chapter.

3. Election Reform Information Project, "Election Reform Briefing 9: The 2004 Election," December 2004, www.electionline.org.

4. Trevor Potter and Marianne Holt Viray, "Federal Election Authority: Jurisdiction and Mandates," in *Rethinking the Vote: The Politics and Prospects of American Election Reform,* ed. Ann N. Crigler and Marion R. Just (New York: Oxford University Press, 2004), 102–116.

5. Anthony King, *Running Scared: Why America's Politicians Campaign Too Much and Govern Too Little* (New York: Free Press, 1997), 3.

6. Ronald Keith Gaddie, *Born to Run: Origins of the Political Career* (Lanham, Md.: Rowman and Littlefield, 2004), 1.

7. Robert L. Dudley and Alan R. Gitelson, American Elections: The Rules Matter (New York: Longman, 2002); Martin P. Wattenberg, *Where Have All the Voters Gone?* (Cambridge, Mass.: Harvard University Press, 2002).

8. Mark N. Franklin, "Electoral Participation," in *Controversies in Voting Behavior,* 4th ed., ed. Richard G. Niemi and Herbert F. Weisberg (Washington, D.C.: CQ Press, 2001), 83–99.

9. Wattenberg, *Where Have All the Voters Gone?* 169–173.

10. Marjorie Randon Hershey and Paul Allen Beck, *Party Politics in America,* 10th ed. (New York: Longman, 2003), 207.

11. Initiative and Referendum Institute, *Initiative Usage by Decade (1901–2000)* (Los Angeles: University of Southern California, 2004), http://iandrinstitute.com; Thomas E. Cronin, *Direct Democracy: The Politics of Initiative, Referendum, and Recall* (Cambridge, Mass.: Harvard University Press, 1999).

12. Walter Dean Burnham, "The Changing Shape of the American Political Universe," *American Political Science Review* 59 (March 1965): 7–28; Jack L. Walker, "Ballot Forms and Voter Fatigue: An Analysis of the Office Block and Party Column Ballots," *Midwest Journal of Political Science* 10 (November 1966): 448–463.

13. Election Reform Information Project, "Solution or Problem? Provisional Ballots in 2004," March 2005, www.electionline.org.

14. Caltech/MIT Voting Technology Project, *Voting: What Is, What Could Be* (Pasadena: California Institute of Technology, 2001), www.vote.caltech.edu/Reports/index.html; David C. Kimball, Chris T. Owens, and Katherine M. Keeney, "Unrecorded Votes and Election Reform," *Spectrum: The Journal of State Government* 76 (winter 2003): 34–37; Stephen Knack and Martha Kropf, "Voided Ballots in the 1996 Presidential Election: A County-Level Analysis," *Journal of Politics* 65 (August 2003): 881–897.

15. Kimball, Owens, and Keeney, "Unrecorded Votes and Election Reform."

16. Caltech/MIT Voting Technology Project, *Voting.*

17. Election Reform Information Project and the Constitution Project, "2002 Annual Report: What's Changed, What Hasn't and Why," October 22, 2002, www.electionline.org.

18. Caltech/MIT Voting Project, *Voting.*

19. The 2004 National Election Study, Advance Release, January 31, 2005, University of Michigan, Center for Political Studies, Ann Arbor, www.umich.edu/~nes (accessed April 23, 2005).

20. Phil Keisling, "Vote by Mail: Is It Good for Democracy? A Pro-Perspective," *Campaigns and Elections* (May 1996): 47.

21. Norman Ornstein, "Vote by Mail: Is It Good for Democracy? An 'Anti'-Perspective," *Campaigns and Elections* (May 1996): 47.

22. J. Eric Oliver, "The Effects of Eligibility Restrictions and Party Activity on Absentee Voting and Overall Turnout," *American Journal of Political Science* 40 (May 1996): 498–513.

23. *St. Petersburg Times,* "Orlando Mayor Dyer Is Indicted," March 12, 2005.

24. Alvarez and Hall, *Point, Click, and Vote.*

25. Ibid.

26. Ibid.

27. Jerrold G. Rusk, "The Effect of the Australian Ballot Reform on Split Ticket Voting: 1876–1908," *American Political Science Review* 64 (December 1970): 1220–1238.

28. Ibid.

29. Richard G. Niemi and Paul S. Herrnson, "Beyond the Butterfly: The Complexity of U.S. Ballots," *Perspectives on Politics* 1 (June 2003): 317–326.

30. James H. Lewis, D. Garth Taylor, and Paul Kleppner, *Metro Chicago Political Atlas '97–98* (Springfield, Ill.: Institute for Public Affairs, 1997).

31. Richard Winger, "More Choice Please! Why U.S. Ballot Access Laws Are Discriminatory and How Independent Parties and Candidates Challenge Them," in *Democracy's Moment,* ed. Ronald Hayduk and Kevin Mattson, 45–59 (Lanham, Md.: Rowman and Littlefield, 2002); Paul Allen Beck, *Party Politics in America,* 8th ed. (New York: Longman, 1997).

32. Richard Winger, "2004 Ballot Status for President," *Ballot Access News,* October 3, 2004, 5.

33. Ibid.

34. Winger, *More Choice, Please!*

35. Beck, *Party Politics in America.*

36. Jon A. Krosnick, Joanne M. Miller, and Michael P. Tichy, "An Unrecognized Need for Ballot Reform: The Effects of Candidate Name Order on Election Outcomes," in *Rethinking the Vote: The Politics and Prospects of American Election Reform,* ed. Ann N. Crigler and Marion R. Just (New York: Oxford University Press, 2004), 51–54.

37. Ibid.

38. The previous governor's contest determines the candidate order in Florida, which meant that George W. Bush was listed first on every Florida ballot in the 2000 presidential election. In 2004 President Bush was again listed first on every ballot in Florida.

39. Jonathan N. Wand, Kenneth W. Shotts, Jasjeet S. Sekhon, Walter R. Mebane Jr., Michael C. Herron, and Henry E. Brady, "The Butterfly Did It: The Aberrant Vote for Buchanan in Palm Beach County, Florida," *American Political Science Review* 95 (December 2001): 793–810.

40. Kimball, Owens, and Keeney, "Unrecorded Votes and Election Reform."

41. Niemi and Herrnson, "Beyond the Butterfly."

42. Kimball, Owens, and Keeney. "Unrecorded Votes and Election Reform."

43. David Kimball and Martha Kropf, "Ballot Design and Unrecorded Votes in the 2002 Midterm Election," paper presented at the annual meeting of the American Political Science Association, August 28–31, 2003, Philadelphia.

44. Jack L. Walker, "Ballot Forms and Voter Fatigue: An Analysis of the Office Block and Party Column Ballots," *Midwest Journal of Political Science* 10 (November 1966): 448–463; Kimball, Owens, and Keeney, "Unrecorded Votes and Election Reform."

45. Election Reform Information Project, "Solution or Problem? Provisional Ballots in 2004," Washington, D.C.

Suggested Readings

Alvarez, R. Michael, and Thad E. Hall. *Point, Click, and Vote: The Future of Internet Voting.* Washington, D.C.: Brookings, 2004.

Beck, Paul Allen. *Party Politics in America.* 8th ed. New York: Longman, 1997.

Burnham, Walter Dean. "The Changing Shape of the American Political Universe." *American Political Science Review* 59 (March 1965): 7–28.

Caltech/MIT Voting Technology Project. *Voting: What Is, What Could Be.* Pasadena: California Institute of Technology, 2001.

Cronin, Thomas E. *Direct Democracy: The Politics of Initiative, Referendum, and Recall.* Cambridge, Mass.: Harvard University Press, 1999.

Dudley, Robert L., and Alan R. Gitelson. *American Elections: The Rules Matter.* New York: Longman, 2002.

Election Reform Information Project. *Solution or Problem? Provisional Ballots in 2004.* March 2005. www.electionline .org.

Election Reform Information Project and the Constitution Project. *2002 Annual Report: What's Changed, What Hasn't and Why.* October 22, 2002. www.electionline.org.

———. *Election Preview 2004: What's Changed, What Hasn't and Why.* October 2004. www.electionline.org.

Franklin, Mark N. "Electoral Participation." In *Controversies in Voting Behavior,* 4th ed., edited by Richard G. Niemi and Herbert F. Weisberg, 83–99. Washington, D.C.: CQ Press, 2001.

Gaddie, Ronald Keith. *Born to Run: Origins of the Political Career.* Lanham, Md.: Rowman and Littlefield, 2004.

Hershey, Marjorie Randon, and Paul Allen Beck. *Party Politics in America.* 10th ed. New York: Longman, 2003.

Initiative and Referendum Institute. *Initiative Usage by Decade (1901–2000).* Los Angeles: University of Southern California, 2004. http://iandrinstitute.com.

Keisling, Phil. "Vote by Mail: Is It Good for Democracy? A Pro-Perspective." *Campaigns and Elections* (May 1996): 47.

Kimball, David C., and Martha Kropf. "Ballot Design and Unrecorded Votes in the 2002 Midterm Election." Paper presented at the annual meeting of the American Political Science Association, Philadelphia, August 28–31, 2003.

Kimball, David C., Chris T. Owens, and Katherine M. Keeney. "Unrecorded Votes and Election Reform." *Spectrum: The Journal of State Government* 76 (winter 2003): 34–37.

King, Anthony. *Running Scared: Why America's Politicians Campaign Too Much and Govern Too Little.* New York: Free Press, 1997.

Knack, Stephen, and Martha Kropf. "Voided Ballots in the 1996 Presidential Election: A County-Level Analysis." *Journal of Politics* 65 (August 2003): 881–897.

Krosnick, Jon A., Joanne M. Miller, and Michael P. Tichy. "An Unrecognized Need for Ballot Reform: The Effects of Candidate Name Order on Election Outcomes." In *Rethinking the Vote: The Politics and Prospects of American Election*

Reform, edited by Ann N. Crigler and Marion R. Just, 51–54. New York: Oxford University Press, 2004.

Niemi, Richard G., and Paul S. Herrnson. "Beyond the Butterfly: The Complexity of U.S. Ballots." *Perspectives on Politics* 1 (June 2003): 317–326.

Oliver, J. Eric. "The Effects of Eligibility Restrictions and Party Activity on Absentee Voting and Overall Turnout." *American Journal of Political Science* 40 (May 1996): 498–513.

Ornstein, Norman. "Vote by Mail: Is It Good for Democracy? An 'Anti'-Perspective." *Campaigns and Elections* (May 1996): 47.

Potter, Trevor, and Marianne Holt Viray. "Federal Election Authority: Jurisdiction and Mandates." In *Rethinking the Vote: The Politics and Prospects of American Election Reform,* edited by Ann N. Crigler and Marion R. Just, 102–116. New York: Oxford University Press, 2004.

Rusk, Jerrold G. "The Effect of the Australian Ballot Reform on Split Ticket Voting: 1876–1908." *American Political Science Review* 64 (December 1970): 1220–1238.

Schier, Steven E. *You Call This an Election? America's Peculiar Democracy.* Washington, D.C.: Georgetown University Press, 2003.

Walker, Jack L. "Ballot Forms and Voter Fatigue: An Analysis of the Office Block and Party Column Ballots." *Midwest Journal of Political Science* 10 (November 1966): 448–463.

Wand, Jonathan N., Kenneth W. Shotts, Jasjeet S. Sekhon, Walter R. Mebane Jr., Michael C. Herron, and Henry E. Brady. "The Butterfly Did It: The Aberrant Vote for Buchanan in Palm Beach County, Florida." *American Political Science Review* 95 (December 2001): 793–810.

Wattenberg, Martin P. *Where Have All the Voters Gone?* Cambridge, Mass.: Harvard University Press, 2002.

Wayne, Stephen J. *Is This Any Way to Run a Democratic Election?* 2d ed. Boston: Houghton Mifflin, 2003.

Winger, Richard. "More Choice Please! Why U.S. Ballot Access Laws Are Discriminatory and How Independent Parties and Candidates Challenge Them." In *Democracy's Moment,* edited by Ronald Hayduk and Kevin Mattson, 45–59. Lanham, Md.: Rowman and Littlefield, 2002.

CHAPTER 5

Nomination Politics: Primary Laws and Party Rules

Marni Ezra

In the United States, the voters, not party elites, select the parties' nominees for most statewide and national offices. Unlike in most other democracies where party leaders choose their own nominees at party conventions, voters in the United States retain this power at the polls in the form of primary elections. The U.S. electoral system is unique in two ways: the amount of power it gives to its voters and the lack of control that political parties have over the candidates who run under their party labels.

In some European democracies, such as Germany, Italy, Portugal, and Spain, rank-and-file voters cast their ballots only for a political party, not for any particular candidate. These countries use a closed list system, which means that parties determine the order of candidate names on a list of all possible nominees. Depending on the percentage of the vote received by the political party in the general election, candidates closest to the top of the list become elected officials.

Other democracies, such as Finland, Luxembourg, and Switzerland, use open lists—that is, voters decide which candidates on the list are elected. However, the range of choices that voters have in these democracies, even the open list nations, does not equal the power given to voters in the United States when they select their party's nominees in primary elections. Even in open list elections, the political party chooses the candidates who are on the list. In the United States, the political parties may encourage or discourage candidates from running for the nomination, but their influence can be easily ignored by a candidate who has built a rapport with district voters or who has the resources to fund his or her own campaign without party help.

Although its method of nomination is unique today, the United States in its earlier years used a system similar to that of many other European democracies. U.S. political parties had more power a century ago, when they more closely controlled the nomination process and minimized the input of average voters. Over the past century, however, nomination politics in the United States has been transformed from a system in which party elites retained power to one in which voters reign supreme. The next section explores these historical changes.

The History and Development of the Nominating Process

The evolution of nomination politics in the United States has been complex, and the nominating process has changed dramatically over the last two centuries. It has evolved from the congressional/legislative caucus, the party's method of nomination until 1824, to the party convention, which served as the dominant method of nomination until the early 1900s, to the primary, which gradually gained strength through the 1900s and has remained the most popular method of nominating candidates for public office since the 1970s. In addition to changing over time, nomination procedures have varied by state within each time period, because, constitutionally, states retain the right to govern their own elections. The result is a system that allows states wide latitude and variation in their nomination rules. Because each state's nomination system has different characteristics, the process is not an easy one to study. It is possible, however, to explore how these characteristics developed and how they differ across states; interesting comparisons across offices and within the same office across states can be drawn as well.

In the nation's first two presidential elections, there was little question about who would represent the parties. But once President George Washington retired in 1797, posturing for and disagreement over the parties' nominations increased. The first congressional caucuses appeared in 1800 to select the presidential nominees, John Adams and Thomas Jefferson, in secret proceedings.[1] Caucuses were held by the parties again in 1804, but no longer in secret. Through 1824, legislative caucuses determined who received the parties' nominations in both congressional and presidential elections. A caucus consisted of members of Congress (or state legislators if they were selecting the nominees for state offices), who joined together to select and support their party's presidential and vice-presidential nominees. Yet the caucus was derided and labeled "King Caucus" by its opponents, because it acted like a ruling clique. Although the caucus had its detractors, it had strengths as a method of nomination. It utilized knowledgeable leaders, was representative of all states, and its members were able to gather easily in their place of business, the U.S. Capitol.

After the election of 1812, criticism of the caucus increased, but it continued to function. Most popular meetings at the time condemned the nominations made by the caucuses as "a flagrant usurpation of the rights of the people." [2] The caucus was also criticized for excluding party officials from around the nation—rather, it centered its power in Washington, D.C. These two factors played a key role in its downfall. The debate over the existence of the caucus lasted for three days in February 1824 and finally King Caucus was no longer.

The period until the 1830s also saw party members of state legislatures meeting in caucuses to nominate candidates for state office, U.S. Congress, and presidential electors. Party leaders from around the state participated in the decision-making process. In some states, the decline of the caucus system and the transition to the party convention occurred earlier than at the national level. In fact, its removal in some states served as an impetus to rid the nation of the congressional nominating caucus at the national level. Once the reign of the congressional caucus ended at the federal level, the remaining state legislative caucuses gradually fell out of favor as well.

Soon after 1824, county conventions began to choose delegates to represent the locality at the state convention. The state convention, in turn, chose delegates to the national convention, which selected the presidential and vice-presidential nominees. By the 1830s, national party conventions had overtaken the caucus as the dominant method of nomination. Power shifted away from the "Washington Community," and party elites from around the nation gained stature in the nominating debate. [3] Because the president was able to acquire a base of support outside of Congress, the power to select presidential nominees shifted to the state and local politicians chosen by the state and local parties to attend the parties' national conventions. [4]

These state and local politicians focused more on local issues and patronage than on a broad national agenda. Their rise in stature changed the type of nominee who could appeal to such interests. The rise of conventions stemmed from Andrew Jackson's loss to John Quincy Adams in the 1824 presidential race. When no candidate received a majority of the electoral vote in the four-way race, the election was thrown into the House of Representatives and Adams, a member of Congress, used his party alliances to emerge victorious. In response, Jackson sought to create a nominating process that would enable an outsider to win, and he recognized that successful candidates were more typically the ones who brokered deals and offered patronage the most effectively.

The nominating convention was the answer. Until the early twentieth century, conventions were characterized by intense bargaining over delegates, whose support for a particular nominee was at times offered up in exchange for patronage, such as jobs or government funds. The conventions themselves were brokered, and nominees negotiated among small numbers of party elites. Nominees were not anointed as they were under the caucus system, nor were nominees chosen early in the election cycle as they are today. Much of the selection process was undertaken during the convention, although the groundwork was laid and commitments of delegate support were made before the opening gavel.

Through the nineteenth century, the convention prevailed. Toward the end of the nineteenth century, calls for more direct popular control over party nominations began to take root. The party convention, as the method of nomination, simply failed to involve the rank-and-file membership in the party's decision-making process. Indeed, no machinery was in place to ensure that the delegates to the party conventions were representing the wishes of the parties' members, and delegates were chosen not by popular election but by state and local party

The Republicans' second nominating convention was convened in 1860 in Chicago's Wigwam, a wooden building constructed in only six weeks. The delegates took three ballots to choose Abraham Lincoln of Illinois over William H. Seward of New York. Source: *Library of Congress*

bosses. Moreover, state laws did not regulate the nominating process; instead, individual political parties determined the nominating rules.

In his efforts to strengthen the executive, President Woodrow Wilson proposed changes in the presidential nominating process. He argued that conventions produced a "leaderless government" that was "frequently beholden to the bosses and the machines" that controlled the nominating process.[5] In response, Wilson proposed to Congress a system of direct national primaries. With party organizations removed from the selection process, candidates would have to appeal directly to voters, which would facilitate change in social policy.

Changes in party nominating practices developed simultaneously across the nation, but advanced for different reasons in the North and the South. The alternative to the party convention was the direct primary, in which all members of a political party would be able to vote directly for the candidates of their choice. The political party activists were effectively removed as the middlemen between the candidates and the voters. Although the impetus for primary elections originated with Progressives in the North, in the South the impetus was the desire to end one-party domination.[6]

In the North, primaries received the needed push from Progressives, who were fighting for a variety of reform policies in the late 1800s and early 1900s that would result in a more open government system free of party bosses, patronage, and political pressure. Progressives pointed to the widespread abuses that took place under the convention system, including bribery, disorder, and manipulation.[7] One of the most prominent Progressives of the era, Robert M. La Follette of Wisconsin, said this about the nominating process in his autobiography: "Put aside the caucus and convention. They have been and will continue to be prostituted to the service of corrupt organizations. They answer no purpose further than to give respectable form to political robbery. Abolish the caucus and the convention. Go back to the first principles of democracy; go back to the people. Substitute for both the caucus and the convention a primary election . . . where the citizen may cast his vote directly to nominate the candidate of the party with which he affiliates."[8]

Progressives, then, supported primaries as a way of bringing voting directly to the people and, in turn, thwarting party bosses and the machines that had accumulated too much power and prevented Progressive candidates from gaining electoral support. The primary acted to undermine the power of entrenched party leadership, especially in the states dominated by a single party. As for the Progressive movement itself, it took root in the northern states, but it failed to strike a responsive chord among southerners.

In many southern states, one party, the Democratic, dominated politics after the Civil War. Typically in these states, the winner of the dominant party's nomination won the office being contested, because the minority party, regardless of its candidate, lacked the electoral support to win a majority of the votes. When party nominees were chosen by elites at party conventions, voters in one-party states were left without a real choice in the general election. In essence, both the majority and minority party voters lost the power of the vote, because their decision-making power was transferred to party elites.

Direct primaries developed the fastest in those states in which one party dominated the political system. They returned to the majority party's voters the electoral choices they had lost under the convention system, and they restored some form of popular government.

In addition to giving voters direct access to the nomination of their politicians, primaries in the South ensured the continued political domination of the Democratic Party by settling its battles prior to the general election. As two scholars saw it, "The major purpose and effect of the primaries in many southern states was to guarantee Democratic control of southern politics. Democratic leaders believed that public primaries would legitimate the nominees, settle intra-party differences before the general election, and greatly reduce the power of opposition voters."[9] It was clear that political battles would be fought in the Democratic primary, effectively removing the political voice of minority party voters.

Although primaries in the North and South developed for different reasons, primary nominating systems developed rapidly in both regions. Between 1880 and 1890, numerous states passed a variety of primary regulations, though most of the laws were optional and applied only to specified jurisdictions within a state. Because states continued to refuse to pay the costs of these primaries, they remained governed and paid for by the political parties. As long as party nominations stayed in the hands of the parties, each particular state's party would govern the rules and regulations of its own nominations, and the parties had wide latitude in doing so. They did not need to comply with any uniform federal government rules, such as those governing today's presidential nominations.

In the 1890s, states switched from individual party-printed ballots (which made the voter's choice clear to poll watchers) to a system in which a single government-printed ballot listed all candidates and was cast by the voter in secret (see Chapter 4). The new secret ballot (called the Australian ballot after the nation that invented the practice) made it easier for voters to cast a split ticket and reduced party control over elections. More important, the Australian ballot ushered in an era in which state and local governments administered elections. Parties were given legal recognition, because the government did not want to encumber voters with long lists of minor parties on the ballot. But only the major parties receiving a certain percentage of the previous election's voters were allowed to appear on the ballot. In exchange for their privileged position, these parties had to abide by certain laws governing the nomination of candidates.

By 1899, two-thirds of states had enacted some kind of direct primary law. No state, however, had passed a mandatory statewide act. As the nineteenth century drew to a close, the days of optional primary laws were numbered, and states began to establish minimum mandatory regulations over primary elections and, in exchange, the government paid for and printed primary ballots.[10] In addition, mandatory, statewide primary laws were accepted rapidly, and the regulated convention became eclipsed by the direct primary.

Wisconsin, a Progressive stronghold, passed the first compulsory, comprehensive primary law in 1902 (it went into effect in 1903). Many other states quickly followed suit. By 1917, thirty-two of the forty-four direct primary states had mandatory, legally regulated direct primaries covering all nominations for statewide office. By 1924 all eleven southern states had enacted some form of statewide direct primary laws. The end of World War II saw all but two states using the direct primary. Primaries were funded with public money and were held on a fixed date, but the date varied by state. As for conventions, even after many states abandoned the convention as a method of selecting state-level offices, it continued to be the method used to select presidential candidates. It was not until later in the century that conventions no longer played a substantial role in the presidential nominating process.

After World War II, two developments emerged in the use of the direct primary. First, the direct primary expanded to the two holdout states, Rhode Island (1947) and Connecticut (1955). Second, the use of preprimary endorsing conventions by the parties gained popularity. Today, primary elections are used by all fifty states to nominate candidates in statewide races. For presidential nominations in 2004, caucuses were used by both parties in twelve states (plus the District of Columbia) and primaries were used by both parties in thirty states. Eight states had different methods of selection for each of the two major parties (see Table 5-1).[11]

It is important to differentiate the caucus/convention used in today's presidential nominating process from the legislative/congressional caucus used during the early part of the nineteenth century. Caucuses in the modern era are a method of selecting delegates, but participation and nominee selection are carried out by ordinary voters (though typically a small number of voters because of low voter turnout). In the congressional caucus of the early 1800s, members of the legislature or Congress selected nominees.

Primaries as Tools of Exclusion

Although the direct primary was instituted in all fifty states for statewide nominations by the middle of the 1900s, through the 1960s primary elections were used to exclude particular citizens, typically minorities, from voting for their party's candidates. To exclude minorities, political parties declared their primary elections part of the internal workings of a private organization, and so they were able to structure the rules of their own elections. Four main tactics were used to prevent minorities from voting in primary elections: the white primary, the poll tax, the grandfather clause, and the literacy test. These exclusionary tactics have been declared unconstitutional by the courts and are no longer used today.

White Primary

From Reconstruction through the mid-twentieth century, politics was the exclusive domain of the Democratic Party in the South. As noted earlier, because an overwhelming majority of southern voters were Democrats, the general election was far less important than the Democratic primary. With no real Republican opposition, whoever won the Democratic primary won the general election.

By declaring its primary an internal election in a private organization, the Democratic Party was able to choose which of its members could participate. It chose to disenfranchise African American voters and thereby eliminate their political power. When the legality of this system was challenged in the courts, it produced conflicting legal decisions. For example, in 1924 Lawrence A. Nixon, a black physician in Texas, challenged a 1923 state law that barred African Americans from voting in the Democratic primary, and his case reached the Supreme Court in 1927 with help from the National Association for the Advancement of Color People (NAACP). The Court unanimously declared in *Nixon v. Herndon* that the statute was unconstitutional, because it violated the equal protection clause of the Fourteenth Amendment. However, the Court did not discourage or prevent a political party from privately preventing African Americans from voting.

In 1944 the case of *Smith v. Allwright* came before the Supreme Court. Lonnie E. Smith, a black man from Texas, was denied the vote by a white election official, S. S. Allwright. The NAACP fought the case to the Supreme Court, which ruled that a racially exclusive primary violated the Fifteenth Amendment, which guarantees that "the right of citizens to vote shall not be denied or abridged by the United States or by any State on account of race, color, or previous condition of servitude." Primary elections that deny entry to persons for any reasons other than political party registration no longer exist in the United States.

Poll Tax

Poll taxes were imposed in thirty-five states in 1962, and in the South they were mainly intended to exclude African Americans from voting. A poll tax is a requirement to pay a small amount of money in order to vote. But many poor sharecroppers throughout the South, who were almost exclusively black, could not afford to pay the poll tax and so were essentially disenfranchised. The Twenty-fourth

Amendment, ratified in 1964, eliminated the tax, when it stated: "The right of citizens of the United States to vote in any primary or other election for President or Vice President, for electors for President or Vice President, or for Senator or Representative in Congress, shall not be denied or abridged by the United States or any State by reason of failure to pay any poll tax or other tax."

Grandfather Clause

Grandfather clauses were yet another means of denying the descendents of slaves the right to vote. These clauses, which were statutory or constitutional devices, were enacted by seven southern states between 1895 and 1910. They provided that persons who had the right to vote before 1866, or their lineal dependents, would be exempt from educational, property, or tax requirements for voting. These clauses were also a way to keep poor, uneducated whites from going to the polls. Because former slaves were unable to vote prior to 1870, the year the Fifteenth Amendment was adopted, these clauses were effective in preventing them from voting.

In 1915 the Supreme Court struck down the use of grandfather clauses, ruling that they violated the Fifteenth Amendment's guarantee of equal voting rights. In the case of *Guinn v. United States,* the Supreme Court declared unconstitutional an Oklahoma law denying the right to vote to any citizen whose ancestors had not been enfranchised in 1866. Although the Court declared grandfather clauses unconstitutional, it upheld the right of states to require a literacy test.

Literacy Test

Before passage of the 1965 Voting Rights Act, many southern states used a lengthy voter registration process to deny African Americans the right to vote. Part of that process was a literacy test that consisted of a lengthy list of questions administered selectively by the registrars. Although standard statewide registration procedures were in place, individual registrars had enormous discretion in applying various procedures based on race. A white person needed to answer only a small number of very simple questions, whereas a black person could answer all of them correctly and still be deemed unfit to vote. After a would-be potential voter took the test, a panel of registrars decided whether the applicant passed. The tests were therefore used as a tool of exclusion and inequality. (For an example of a literacy test see Box 3-2 in Chapter 3, which provides more details about these forms of exclusion.)

Many tools were thus used through the 1960s to exclude particular citizens, mostly African Americans, from voting in primary elections. These laws influenced the types of candidates who could run for office and certainly the types of candidates who could win. Even though the tactics described here are no longer legal or used to prevent participation in primary elections, African American vot-

ers continue to have low levels of participation in primary elections in the United States.

The Modern Presidential Nominating System

Different states have different rules for the presidential nominating process, because it is governed by the fifty different state legislatures and by political parties in each state. State nominating procedures vary dramatically by type of nominating system, the nominating schedule, the way in which delegates are selected, and the way in which delegates are rewarded. The following sections detail the ways in which this process differs across the states and political parties.

Types of Nominating Systems

Each state party must decide whether its presidential candidates will compete for the nomination in a primary or a caucus. The goals of primaries and caucuses are the same: they are both elections in which candidates within the same party compete to represent their party in the general election. And they both allocate delegates to candidates based on the candidates' shares of the vote. The processes, however, differ substantially.

The primary election, which is used more widely than the caucus, is the type of election that most Americans learn about in their high school civics courses. In a primary, a voter goes into a voting booth and casts a ballot for a candidate. The process is quick, private, and typically free of coercion. Primary voters are likely to have had little personal interaction with the presidential nominees. Candidates in most primary states rely on the mass media to get their messages to voters, and voters rely on these avenues for basic information about the candidates. Candidates and their surrogates cannot possibly meet personally with all or most voters, because many states hold their primaries on the same date.

A caucus differs significantly from a primary and is much more complex. Most Americans, unless they live in one of the states (about twenty for the 2004 presidential nominating season) that still use the caucus system for at least one of the parties, have never learned about the caucus process (see Table 5-1 for a list of which states used caucuses or primaries as presidential nominating methods in 2004). A caucus is a meeting of party members for the main purpose of nominating candidates. Other purposes include collecting dues, scheduling party events, and electing party officers. Instead of filling out a single ballot as voters do in a primary election, caucuses use a multitiered system that typically begins at the precinct level or local level, where voters openly declare their support for a party candidate. At the local level (the first-round caucus), caucuses are typically held in a school gymnasium or

Table 5-1 State Methods for Choosing Democratic and Republican National Convention Delegates, 2004

	Republicans	Democrats		Republicans	Democrats
Alabama	Open primary	Open primary	Montana	Open primary	Open primary
Alaska	Caucus	Caucus	Nebraska	Open primary	Open primary
Arizona	Caucus	Open primary	Nevada	Caucus	Caucus
Arkansas	Open primary	Open primary	New Hampshire	Closed primary	Closed primary
California	Closed primary	Closed primary	New Jersey	Closed primary	Closed primary
Colorado	Caucus	Caucus	New Mexico	Closed primary	Caucus
Connecticut	Closed primary	Closed primary	New York	Closed primary	Closed primary
Delaware	Caucus	Closed primary	North Carolina	Closed primary	Closed primary
District of Columbia	Caucus	Caucus	North Dakota	Caucus	Caucus
Florida	Closed primary	Closed primary	Ohio	Open primary	Open primary
Georgia	Open primary	Open primary	Oklahoma	Closed primary	Closed primary
Hawaii	Caucus	Caucus	Oregon	Closed primary	Closed primary
Idaho	Open primary	Caucus	Pennsylvania	Closed primary	Closed primary
Illinois	Open primary	Open primary	Rhode Island	Open primary	Open primary
Indiana	Open primary	Open primary	South Carolina	Open primary	Caucus
Iowa	Caucus	Caucus	South Dakota	Closed primary	Closed primary
Kansas	Caucus	Caucus	Tennessee	Open primary	Open primary
Kentucky	Closed primary	Closed primary	Texas	Open primary/ caucus	Open primary
Louisiana	Open primary	Open primary			
Maine	Caucus	Caucus	Utah	Caucus	Open primary
Maryland	Closed primary	Closed primary	Vermont	Open primary	Open primary
Massachusetts	Open primary	Open primary	Virginia	Open primary	Caucus
Michigan	Caucus[a]	Caucus	Washington	Caucus	Caucus
Minnesota	Caucus	Caucus	West Virginia	Closed primary	Closed primary
Mississippi	Open primary	Open primary	Wisconsin	Open primary	Open primary
Missouri	Open primary	Open primary	Wyoming	Caucus	Caucus

Sources: Rhodes Cook, *Race for the Presidency 2004* (Washington, D.C.: CQ Press, 2004), viii–ix; Project Vote Smart, "State Primary Dates," www.vote-smart.org/election_ president_state_primary_dates.php (accessed April 28, 2005); The Green Papers, "State by State Summary: 2004 Presidential Primaries, Caucuses, and Conventions," www.thegreenpapers.com/P04/events .phtml?format=alphabetical (accessed April 28, 2005).

Note: The term *caucus* is also used to indicate states that use party conventions or committees to choose delegates. In a "closed" primary, only registered members of a party may vote in that party's primary. Independents (those not registered with either major party) are not permitted to vote in either major party's primary. In an "open" primary, any voter—regardless of party registration—may vote in the primary of either major party (but not both). Independents may vote in either major party's primary. In 2004 a few states used "modified" open or closed primaries in which, generally, registered voters in the party plus unaffiliated (or independent) voters may participate. In these systems, there are usually provisions that automatically make an independent a registered member of the party holding the primary.

[a] Michigan's nominating event is called a caucus but is really a party-run primary.

other large public gathering place. Campaign representatives meet with voters for the purpose of swaying as many of them as possible. Because caucuses last several hours, only the most dedicated and enthusiastic party voters attend. Although voter turnout is low, caucus attendees are more likely to meet either a candidate or a member of the candidate's campaign during the process. Candidates with organization and time, but not necessarily the mass media coverage they would receive in a primary, are more successful in this venue. Once the local-level caucus is complete, the delegates who are selected advance to the next level of caucus, typically at the county level. Once the delegates are selected at the county level, they advance to the congressional district level and then to the state level. The levels are not the same for all states, but many states follow this pattern.

Types of Delegates and State Delegate Allocation

Candidates seeking the presidential nomination of their party run in a series of primaries and caucuses in each of the fifty states. In the process, they accumulate delegates, individuals who represent their state party at the party's national convention. Delegates are typically individuals who have shown loyalty to their political party through activism, voluntarism, financial contribution, or elective office. The Democratic Party allocates its delegates in a complex fashion. In 2004, 3,520 of the 4,322 Democratic delegates to the national convention were pledged to a particular candidate; the remaining delegates were free to change their pledges at any time. Pledged delegates are allocated among the fifty states based on three factors: (1) the state's Democratic votes for president in the last three elections, (2) the state's electoral vote relative to the national electoral vote, and (3) an add-on for party leaders and elected officials equal to 15 percent of the pledged delegates, called PLEOs or party leader and elected officials. Table 5-2 lists the number of delegates allocated by the Democrats and Republicans to the fifty states and the District of Columbia in 2004.

About 20 percent of Democratic Party's 4,322 delegates are unpledged. These so-called superdelegates are state members of the Democratic National Committee, distinguished party leaders, Democratic governors, Democratic members of the U.S. House and Senate, and add-on unpledged delegates.

The Republican Party allocates its 2,509 delegates to the party's convention in a simpler manner. Through the 2004 election, each state received a base allocation and a bonus allocation. The base allocation gave each state six delegates plus three delegates for each congressional district in the state (see Table 5-2). The bonus allocation was calculated according to three factors. First, if the GOP won the presidential vote in that state in the previous election, the state received a bonus of 4.5 delegates plus 60 percent of its number of electoral votes. Second, the state received extra delegates for each of its GOP elected officials. And, third, the state received additional delegates as the date of the primary or caucus moved to a point later in the election cycle. This system was intended to dissuade states from front-loading their primary elections. The Republican Party rewarded states that have later primary elections to encourage a more deliberative nomination process.

In 2004, however, this system of delegate allocation changed. The Republican Party eliminated its system of allocating bonus delegates and instead reserved seats at the convention for superdelegates made up only of members of the Republican National Committee. It is unclear whether the new system will remain in place or whether the Republican Party will revert back to the previous system.

Pledged delegates typically vote for the candidate to whom they are pledged at the party convention, but no law forces them to do so. Democratic rules state that "delegates elected to the national convention pledged to a presidential candidate shall in good conscience reflect the sentiments of those who elected them." Republican rules about delegate behavior are so varied that they are difficult to categorize. In some states, Republican delegates are bound through the first ballot; in other states they must wait until a second or third ballot; and in still others they must wait until the candidate officially releases them.

Candidate Delegate Allocation

Once delegates have been allocated, each state must decide how it will divide delegates among primary and caucus contestants. The first major distinction in delegate allocation is between the Democratic and Republican Parties. Democrats use a nationwide proportionality rule for allocating pledged delegates. A candidate must receive a minimum threshold of 15 percent of the primary or caucus vote (either statewide or in any particular congressional district) to receive any of that state's delegates. Once that threshold is reached, candidates are awarded delegates according to the percentage of the vote each won.

The Republican allocation varies greatly across the country, because the Republican Party gives the state parties wide latitude in determining the way in which delegates are selected—that is, guidelines from the national party are kept to a minimum. Republican delegates fall into two categories: congressional and at-large. Each set of delegates can be allocated differently, though typically states allocate them in the same manner. Six allocation methods are used by the Republican Party: winner-take-all (state), winner-take-all (state/congressional district), winner-take-all or proportional, direct election, proportional, and no formal system. In the winner-take-all system, the candidate who receives the most votes in each congressional district wins that district's delegates, and the candidate who gets the most votes statewide wins all of the at-large delegates. In the winner-take-all or proportional system, if a candidate receives a majority of the vote, the winner-take-all system is used; otherwise, delegates are allocated proportionally. In a direct election, voters cast their ballots directly for delegates. In a proportional system, delegates are divided to reflect the primary vote. Finally, some states have no formal system; delegates run as individuals and are not officially allocated to the candidates. Twenty-one states have a winner-take-all system, nine have a proportional system, five have a mixed system, and thirteen have a system of direct election. In the remainder of states, either there is no formal system or the state allocates its districts by caucus.

Nominating Schedule

With more and more states vying for influence in the nominating process, primaries occur earlier and earlier in the election cycle. The act of moving the date of the primaries and caucuses earlier in the election year is called front-loading. Because more than two-thirds of delegates are selected by the end of March, presidential candidates have little time to lose. They must move quickly from one

Table 5-2 Delegate Allocation by State, 2004

State	Democrats	Republicans	State	Democrats	Republicans
Alabama	62 (1.4%)	48 (1.9%)	Nevada	32 (0.7)	33 (1.3)
Alaska	18 (0.4)	29 (1.2)	New Hampshire	27 (0.6)	32 (1.3)
Arizona	64 (1.5)	52 (2.1)	New Jersey	129 (3.0)	52 (2.1)
Arkansas	47 (1.1)	35 (1.4)	New Mexico	37 (0.9)	24 (1.0)
California	440 (10.2)	173 (6.9)	New York	285 (6.6)	102 (4.1)
Colorado	63 (1.5)	50 (2.0)	North Carolina	107 (2.5)	67 (2.7)
Connecticut	62 (1.4)	30 (1.2)	North Dakota	22 (0.5)	26 (1.0)
Delaware	23 (0.5)	18 (0.7)	Ohio	159 (3.7)	91 (3.6)
District of Columbia	39 (0.9)	19 (0.8)	Oklahoma	47 (1.1)	41 (1.6)
Florida	201 (4.7)	112 (4.5)	Oregon	58 (1.4)	31 (1.2)
Georgia	102 (2.3)	69 (2.8)	Pennsylvania	178 (4.1)	75 (3.0)
Hawaii	29 (0.7)	20 (0.8)	Rhode Island	32 (0.7)	21 (0.8)
Idaho	23 (0.5)	32 (1.3)	South Carolina	55 (1.3)	46 (1.8)
Illinois	186 (4.3)	73 (2.9)	South Dakota	21 (0.5)	27 (1.1)
Indiana	81 (1.9)	55 (2.2)	Tennessee	85 (2.0)	55 (2.2)
Iowa	56 (1.3)	32 (1.3)	Texas	233 (5.4)	138 (5.5)
Kansas	41 (0.9)	39 (1.6)	Utah	29 (0.7)	36 (1.4)
Kentucky	56 (1.3)	46 (1.8)	Vermont	22 (0.5)	18 (0.7)
Louisiana	72 (1.7)	45 (1.8)	Virginia	96 (2.3)	64 (2.6)
Maine	35 (0.8)	21 (0.8)	Washington	95 (2.2)	41 (1.6)
Maryland	99 (2.3)	39 (1.6)	West Virginia	39 (0.9)	30 (1.2)
Massachusetts	121 (2.8)	44 (1.8)	Wisconsin	87 (2.0)	40 (1.6)
Michigan	154 (3.6)	61 (2.4)	Wyoming	19 (0.4)	28 (1.1)
Minnesota	86 (2.0)	41 (1.6)	Total for fifty states and District of Columbia	4,236	2,459
Mississippi	41 (0.9)	38 (1.5)			
Missouri	88 (2.0)	57 (2.3)	Total (including U.S. territories)	4,322	2,509
Montana	21 (0.5)	28 (1.1)			
Nebraska	31 (0.7)	35 (1.4)			

Sources: Democrats: Democratic National Committee Office of Party Affairs and Delegate Selection, "2004 Democratic National Convention–Delegate/Alternate Allocation," December 18 2003, www.democrats.org/pdfs/delegate_selection/delegate_allocation.pdf (accessed April 25, 2005). Republicans: Republican National Committee Counsel's Office, "2004 Delegate Allocation," December 19, 2003, www.gop.com/Images/COADelegateSheet.pdf (accessed April 25, 2005).

Note: Table shows number and percentage of total delegates.

primary contest to the next, with no break for strategizing, fund-raising, or rest.

A state's position on the primary calendar is more important than its size. Although New Hampshire and Iowa yield a small percentage of delegates to the parties' conventions, they receive a disproportionate amount of media attention because of their early placement. In recognition of this phenomenon, states vying for increased media coverage and heightened influence in the selection process have been inching their primaries forward over the past decade.

Both political parties have attempted to slow the fast pace of the presidential nominating process by awarding bonus delegates to states with later primaries and informally pressuring states to hold their primaries back. In

2000 both major party nominations were effectively over on March 7, further depressing voter turnout in states that held their primary elections after this date. In 2004 Senator Kerry had enough delegates on March 11 to clinch the nomination, equaling Al Gore's performance in 2000. The Democratic Party states in its rules that "no meetings, caucuses, conventions or primaries which constitute the first determining state in the presidential nomination process may be held prior to the first Tuesday in February or after the second Tuesday in June."

No longer is a candidate confident that the nomination is his or hers after a win in New Hampshire or Iowa. Once these early contests are over, the candidates are awarded delegates based on the percentage of the primary

Eight Democratic presidential candidates square off in Albuquerque, New Mexico, in January 2004 in the first debate leading up to the Iowa caucus and the New Hampshire primary. Source: Rick Scibelli/EPA/Landov

vote they won. The candidates then face a national grouping of primaries, one held soon after and the other the first week in March, in which large states such as New York, Ohio, and California hold their elections. Many southern states hold their primaries on Super Tuesday, which falls in the second week of March. By the end of the Super Tuesday primaries, the nominating process is essentially over.

Many people have called for changes in the presidential nominating process. Some have advocated a rotating regional primary system, in which four regional primaries would be held in March, April, May, and June. The order of the regions would rotate, thereby giving each region a chance to have greater influence on the process. Others have called for an inverted pyramid plan, which would group states by population; the states with the smallest populations would hold their primaries first. There also have been calls for a national primary in which all states would hold their primary election on the same date, slightly later in the election cycle, thus giving candidates more time to visit a larger number of states. So far, however, none of these plans has been approved by either political party.

Financing of Presidential Nominations

Public financing of presidential elections was approved as part of the 1971 Federal Election Campaign Act (FECA). Since the law took effect in 1976, a large majority of presidential candidates have taken advantage of the public funds it provides. The FECA and its public financing provision were passed for many reasons, one of which was to reduce the role of private contributions in presidential elections. Because of the enormous cost of presidential elections and the large amount of time required to raise this money, the public financing provision was passed to eliminate the appearance of corruption and to allow presidential candidates more time for campaigning and less time for fund-raising.

The presidential nomination is funded through a combination of public money in the form of matching funds and private donations (campaign finance is discussed in detail in Chapter 6). To qualify for public matching funds, a presidential candidate must raise at least $5,000 in contributions in increments of $250 or less from individuals in at least twenty states. Candidates continue to receive matching funds if they garner at least 10 percent of the vote cast in two consecutive primaries. But once a candidate's percentage of the vote falls below 10 percent for two consecutive primaries, the public funding ends until the candidate receives at least 20 percent of the vote in a later primary.

In the 2004 election, candidates were eligible for up to $18.7 million in primary matching funds. To receive matching funds, candidates must limit their campaign spending of both public and private funds to $45 million for all primaries. They must also limit spending in each state to $740,000, or to a specified amount based on the state's voting-age population, whichever is greater. Candidates are allowed an extra $4 million in legal and accounting spending above the cap, but they must limit their personal spending to $50,000.

Through the 2004 presidential nomination, most candidates accepted public financing. In 2000 nine of eleven presidential candidates accepted matching funds, which cost the program $61 million. Prior to 2000, only three candidates opted out of public financing, and each was independently wealthy. George W. Bush declined public funding during the 2000 primaries and did so again in 2004, along with the Democratic nominee, John Kerry. Candidates who refuse public matching funds during the primaries assume that they can raise far more than the government will permit, giving them a strategic advantage over their opponents.

Party Conventions

Today, the national party conventions are conducted in full view of the media and so are designed to put the best face on the political parties and their presidential nominees for the American public. They are held in presidential election years; the party holding the White House conducts its convention in August, and the party out of office holds its convention in July. Nominees are selected and well known before the summer conventions, because the delegates needed to secure the nomination are typically locked up by the end of March. There is no bargaining on the convention floor; conventions are no longer used to select candidates, but rather to send them off with full fanfare and the support of their political party.

As noted earlier, in the twentieth century conventions were used as tools to select presidential nominees. They were brokered, and competing candidates fought for a majority of delegates on the convention floor, using bargaining and promises of patronage to delegates who would lend their support. Candidates did not accumulate enough delegates by running in primary elections as they do today, and delegates were not always bound to the candidate—they could defect at the convention. Few states used primary elections in which the candidates controlled the selection of delegates.

As primary elections became a more popular way of selecting delegates and were adopted by more states, party control over presidential nominees declined. No longer were party leaders selecting nominees or controlling convention delegates. With the onset and rise of primary elections, presidential candidates appealed directly to voters, and the delegates selected were loyal to a specific candidate rather than to the party.

The last time a presidential candidate won the nomination without competing in primary elections was in 1968; the candidate was Hubert H. Humphrey, the Democratic presidential nominee. Although he won only 2 percent of the primary votes, he won 67 percent of the vote at

Attendees at the 1952 Republican National Convention in Chicago participated in what might prove to be the last convention in which uncertainty existed over who would win a party's presidential nomination. War hero Dwight D. Eisenhower finally prevailed over Ohio senator Robert Taft and went on to win the general election in a landslide over the Democratic candidate, Gov. Adlai Stevenson of Illinois. Source: Library of Congress

the Democratic national convention. Upset by the way in which the nomination was conducted, with little representation of women and minorities, many Democratic supporters protested Humphrey's nomination, and the legitimacy of the convention was thrown into question. Since the 1972 effort by Democrat George McGovern to unseat the Republican incumbent, Richard Nixon, every major-party nominee has been the candidate who received the highest percentage of the vote in the primary elections. McGovern received only 25 percent of the primary vote and 57 percent of the convention vote.

Nominating Systems for U.S. House and Senate Seats

Because the U.S. Constitution grants states the power to decide the "times, places and manner of holding elections for Senators and Representatives," election rules vary dramatically among the states. They differ in the type of nomination system used, whether the nomination is open to both parties or limited to only one party's registered voters, the date on which the nomination occurs, the power of the political parties in endorsing candidates, and whether a successful candidate must achieve a simple plurality or needs a majority of voters, perhaps by means of a runoff election. The majority of states instituted their primary systems at about the same time, but their laws differ in many respects. U.S. House and Senate elections are considered federal elections, subject to regulations under federal law. However, House and Senate *primaries* are regulated by state law, with the exception of campaign finance, which is regulated by federal law. The legal authority for deciding the type and date of primary elections, endorsement, and runoff procedures resides with the states and is greatly affected by the strength of political parties in each state.

Types of Primaries

Depending on the amount of control that a political party wants to exert on its nomination system, a state can employ two different types of primaries, closed and open.

Closed primaries allow only voters who are registered in advance with one of the two major parties to vote in the primary election. The voter's partisan affiliation is recorded and made part of official election records. Because the closed primary allows only party voters to influence its nomination, it represents greater control by the political party. Some states allow voters to change their party registration only before the primary nominees officially declare their candidacies, while other states allow voters to change their registration right up to the day of the election. For example, New York requires voters to declare or change their affiliation at least one year before the primary election; New Hampshire requires a declaration only ten days before the primary.

Open primaries allow voters to choose the primary in which they wish to vote on the day of the election without preregistering with either of the two major parties. States with open primaries use one of two forms: in the first, voters declare publicly in which party's primary they will vote, and in the second, no record is kept of the voter's partisan affiliation. In open primaries, voters do not need to preregister with one party, but they must select one party for the purpose of the primary election. In an open primary, the political parties exercise less control over their nominees, because it is possible that voters from the opposite party may change the results of an election. There is little evidence, however, that strategic crossover voting actually occurs. Prior to 2000, a third type of primary, the *blanket primary*, was in place in Alaska, California, and Washington, until it was struck down by the Supreme Court. The blanket primary allowed voters to cast a ballot for any candidate in any party on the same day, regardless of the voter's own party affiliation. For example, a voter could have chosen to participate in the Democratic primary for governor and the Republican primary for Senate. In March 1994, California voters adopted Proposition 198, which replaced California's closed primary with a blanket primary. California's Democratic and Republican Parties promptly challenged the new law in court by saying that the rules and desires of the political parties were in conflict with the law. By a vote of 7–2, the Supreme Court ruled in 2000 in *California Democratic Party v. Jones* that the law "was forcing political parties to associate with those who do not share their beliefs." [12] California now uses a "modified" closed primary system that permits unaffiliated ("decline to state") voters to participate in a primary election if authorized by an individual party's rules.

From 1975 to 1997, Louisiana had a *nonpartisan primary* in which candidates of all parties participated in a single primary election that took place prior to the uniform federal election day. If a candidate won the nonpartisan primary with more than 50 percent of the vote, he or she was declared the winner of the office and there was no general election. The candidate who won with less than 50 percent had to face the candidate with the second highest vote share in a runoff general election held on federal election day. In 1997 the U.S. Supreme Court, ruling in the case of *Foster v. Love,* unanimously agreed to strike down this primary system. The Court stated that the nonpartisan primary violated federal law, because when the primary is won by greater than 50 percent there is no election on election day and the U.S. Constitution states that all federal general elections will take place on the first Tuesday after the first Monday in November. Louisiana still conducts a so-called open primary, and the top two vote-getters, regardless of party affiliation, advance to the general election.

Although important in terms of campaign strategy, the type of primary held has little impact on the results of elections or voter turnout. There is evidence, however, that different types of primaries can produce different types of candidates. More moderate candidates are more likely to be elected in districts that have open primary systems, because candidates must consider voters who do not register as members of their party. Thus candidates elected from districts in open primary states may more closely represent the average voter in their districts. Candidates from states with closed primaries are more likely to be pulled to either the right or the left by the party loyalists who are more likely to vote in primary elections, especially in years where no other major offices are on the ballot.

Dates of Primaries

States have extremely different practices when selecting primary election dates. Congressional primaries typically cover a seven-month time span from early March to early October. California holds its congressional primaries in March; Minnesota holds its congressional primaries

Janet Reno, who served as attorney general in President Bill Clinton's administration, concedes the 2002 Florida Democratic gubernatorial primary election to Bill McBride. Source: Marc Serota/Reuters/Landov

in September. Some states such as Maryland and Ohio have switched to a system in which their congressional and presidential primaries are held on the same date, while other states hold their presidential primaries early in the election cycle and hold their congressional primaries at a later date.

The placement of the primary in the election cycle is important to different aspects of a candidate's campaign. Among other things, it affects the timing of announcing a candidacy and the timing of setting up a campaign headquarters and launching the campaign. It also affects when the candidate's general election campaign can begin. If the primary date is late and the primaries in a district are very competitive, a candidate may not know who his or her general election opponent will be for quite a while.

The date of the primary may also have an impact on a candidate's ability to raise and spend money. If the primary is late in the cycle, challengers may lack the legitimacy to receive campaign contributions before they have established themselves as the primary nominee. Furthermore, candidates with late primaries may spend a large

proportion of their money on the primary and find themselves with very little time to raise more money for the general election. When the general election occurs only six weeks after the primary, as it does in some states, the winning candidate in a close primary probably will have used virtually all of his or her funds in the primary, and so will have little time to raise enough money before the general election. This situation arose in Maryland's Eighth Congressional District in the 2002 U.S. House election. Democrat Chris Van Hollen faced a four-way, competitive primary. He spent all of his money, over $1 million, on the nomination and exhausted all of his resources. After winning the primary, he had only six weeks to raise more funds before the general election. Meanwhile, he had to turn to the Democratic Party to purchase his airtime in advance, because he could not afford to do so immediately.[13]

It is possible, however, that late primaries give relatively unknown challengers an advantage. During the extended period leading up to the primary, such challengers may receive the publicity needed to get their name out to voters while the voters are paying attention. Unknown candidates do not usually receive a great deal of publicity from early primaries, and voters are less likely to absorb the information even if the candidates do receive the publicity.

Rules also vary as to whether a congressional primary can be held on the same day as the presidential primary, dramatically altering turnout expectations. In the 2004 elections, twenty states held their congressional and presidential primaries on the same dates, twenty held them on different dates, and eleven relied on caucuses for presidential nominations.[14] When a congressional primary and presidential primary are held on the same day, turnout is significantly higher than in those states in which the congressional and presidential primaries are held on different days. If one party has a competitive presidential nomination, voters of this party are drawn to the polls.

Endorsement Procedures

Even though direct primaries are used in all fifty states for congressional nominations and about two-thirds of states (for one party or the other) for presidential nominations, political party activists did not easily cede their nominating power to the rank and file. In many states, parties attempt to control the nominating process through a system of formal or informal endorsement procedures, which restrict how candidates can get on the ballot. Party activists prefer to have preprimary endorsing conventions, because the conventions enable the activists to retain more control over which candidates are placed on the ballot. Some states have no endorsement systems at all, while others have legally mandated endorsements that strongly affect a candidate's chance of becoming the party's nominee.

In those states that have endorsement systems, the preprimary party endorsement rules and norms vary greatly from state to state. Currently, thirteen states use either legal or informal endorsement procedures at preprimary party nominating conventions. Eight of these states have legal party endorsement provisions, which make it easier for endorsed candidates to get access to the ballot as long as they receive a minimum vote at the party convention. If a party formally endorses a candidate, that candidate could be given preference over other candidates in access to and a position on the primary election ballot. Those candidates who do not get endorsed or meet other requirements can be denied ballot access. Candidates who receive informal endorsements have no advantage in getting on the ballot and improving their ballot position, but they may receive other advantages such as financial and political support from the party.

The eight states that have legal endorsement provisions vary considerably. Connecticut, a state with strong political parties and two-party competition, has long had in place the "challenge primary," in which endorsed party candidates are given access to the primary ballot and unendorsed candidates are denied access. When the endorsed party candidates are on the primary election ballot, they are free of intraparty challenges in the primary because of the challenge rule, which states that "if no person other than a party-endorsed candidate has received at least fifteen percent of the votes of the delegates or if within the time specified, no candidacy for nomination by a political party to the office has been filed by or on behalf of a person other than a party-endorsed candidate, no primary shall be held by the party for the office and the party-endorsed candidate for the office shall be deemed to have been lawfully chosen as the nominee of the party for the office." Similarly in Utah, only endorsed candidates can obtain access to the primary ballot, although the party must endorse two candidates unless one obtains 70 percent of the party convention vote.

In Colorado, candidates who receive certificates of designation by the state assembly—that is, they are approved by a 30 percent vote of the assembly—are placed on the ballot first. Candidates who do not receive certificates of designation can gain access to the ballot through the petition process, but the names of petition candidates will appear below those of candidates designated by the party. Candidates defeated in the primary election are barred by law from running in the general election, even as write-in candidates.

Like Colorado, the five other states with legal party endorsement procedures give ballot access to unendorsed candidates through the use of the petition. Endorsed candidates face a variety of advantages, including top positioning on the ballot, as well as the legitimacy of being the official party nominee.

Runoff Elections: The "Second Primary"

Some state laws require that the winning candidate in a primary receive a majority (more than 50 percent) of the vote. In a primary election with more than two candi-

dates, it is possible that the winning candidate will receive less than 50 percent of the vote. When this occurs, states that require a candidate to receive a majority of the vote will hold a runoff election between the two candidates who receive the most votes. Runoffs are typically held a few weeks after the primary election. The winner of the runoff becomes the party nominee.

Seventeen states have experimented with runoff elections, and they are presently used in nine states.[15] Runoffs were instituted for a variety of reasons. First, in one-party states in which there is intense competition in the dominant party's primary election, the winner may only receive a small fraction of the primary vote. Runoffs have become more common, because they prevent extreme candidates from winning the party's nomination by gaining support from a small portion of the electorate. Second, the runoff system allows the winner to receive a majority of the dominant party's vote, thus gaining increased party legitimacy. Third, in the South if two white candidates split the vote and an African American won, a runoff ensured a white nominee.

Although it is not entirely obvious what impact runoff elections may have on candidates, it does appear that runoffs may harm them. For example, if one party's candidate endures a runoff while the other party's does not, the candidate with the runoff will be forced to delay concentrating on the general election and will have to expend resources to win the runoff. Incumbents rarely face a runoff election unless they are in deep trouble. Challengers who already face a mountain of difficulties in winning elective office may face additional difficulties if they face a runoff, because they may emerge from the runoff sapped of resources with little time to revive their campaigns.

Conclusion

Winning a party's nomination is the first major hurdle that a candidate must overcome in the quest for political office. Sometimes, this hurdle is one that can be easily surmounted, which is usually true for incumbents in the U.S. House of Representatives. However, other candidates may face difficult nomination battles, which can set the stage, either positively or negatively, for the rest of their campaigns. State rules, among other factors, play a role in determining the level of competition that a candidate will face.

Since the emergence of direct primary legislation, states have generally controlled the rules and regulations governing their primary elections. These differences make the process complex for both candidates and students who need to understand the laws of all fifty states. The variation among states and the amount of control given to voters in the nomination process make the U.S. nomination process unique.

Notes

1. The appearance of the first congressional caucus has been the subject of debate. Some say the first official congressional caucus was held in 1804. See M. Ostrogorski, "The Rise and Fall of the Nominating Caucus, Legislative and Congressional," *American Historical Review* 5 (December 1899): 253–283; and James Sterling Young, *The Washington Community, 1800–1828* (New York: Columbia University Press, 1986).

2. Ostrogorski, "Rise and Fall of the Nominating Caucus, Legislative and Congressional."

3. Young, *Washington Community.*

4. James W. Ceaser, *Presidential Selection* (Princeton, N.J.: Princeton University Press, 1979), 148–149.

5. Ibid., 173.

6. Although it appears that direct primaries were instituted in the South to give voters a choice and to end one-party domination, Democrats in the South encouraged the establishment of the direct primary to entrench one-party domination. Because Republican candidates had no chance of winning a general election in many southern states, it was considered a waste of time to run in the Republican primary. Instead, direct primary legislation assured that the real battles for elective office would occur in the Democratic Party's primary election. In essence, then, the Democratic primary replaced the general election as the most competitive and important election for office.

7. V. O. Key, *American State Politics* (New York: Knopf, 1956), 96.

8. Ellen Tourelle, ed., *The Political Philosophy of Robert M. La Follette as Revealed in His Speeches and Writings* (Madison, Wis.: Robert M. La Follette Co., 1920), 197–198.

9. Malcolm E. Jewell and David M. Olson, *Political Parties and Elections in American States,* 3d ed. (Chicago: Dorsey Press, 1988), 87.

10. C. E. Merriman and Louise Overaker, *Primary Elections* (Chicago: University of Chicago Press, 1928).

11. Three southern states—Alabama, South Carolina, and Virginia—allow parties to choose whether their candidates are nominated by primary or convention. Only Virginia occasionally exercises this option for congressional nominations.

12. *California Democratic Party v. Jones,* 530 U.S. 567 (2000).

13. "Partisanship Trumps Incumbency in Maryland's 8th District," in *Running on Empty? Campaign Discourse in Congressional Elections,* ed. L. Sandy Maisel and Darrell West (Lanham, Md.: Rowman and Littlefield, 2004).

14. These numbers add up to fifty-one because they include the District of Columbia.

15. The states are Alabama, Arkansas, Florida, Georgia, Louisiana, Mississippi, Oklahoma, South Dakota, and Texas.

Suggested Readings

Ceaser, James W. *Presidential Selection.* Princeton, N.J.: Princeton University Press, 1979.

Galderisi, Peter F., Marni Ezra, and Michael Lyons, eds. *Congressional Primaries and the Politics of Representation.* Lanham, Md.: Rowman and Littlefield, 2001.

Jewell, Malcolm E. *Parties and Primaries: Nominating State Governors.* New York: Praeger, 1984.

Jewell, Malcolm E., and David M. Olson. *Political Parties and Elections in American States.* 3d ed. Chicago: Dorsey Press, 1988.

Mayer, William G., and Andrew E. Busch. *The Front-Loading Problem in Presidential Nominations.* Washington, D.C.: Brookings, 2004.

Merriman, C. E., and Louise Overaker. *Primary Elections.* Chicago: University of Chicago Press, 1928.

Ostrogorski, M. "The Rise and Fall of the Nominating Caucus, Legislative and Congressional." *American Historical Review* 5 (December 1899): 253–283.

Stone, Walter J., Lonna Rae Atkeson, and Ronald B. Rapoport. "Turning On or Turning Off? Mobilization and Demobilization Effects of Participation in Presidential Nomination Campaigns." *American Journal of Political Science* 36, no. 3 (1992): 665–691.

Young, James Sterling. *The Washington Community, 1800–1828.* New York: Columbia University Press, 1986.

CHAPTER 6

An Overview of Campaign Finance Law

Anthony Corrado

Money is an essential component of political campaigns. It is the crucial resource that provides candidates with the means of acquiring the goods and services needed to conduct campaigns for office and communicate their views to the electorate. The vitality of a democratic political system thus depends on an effective system of campaign finance. Without such a system, candidates, parties, and political organizations would not be able to garner the resources needed to conduct the types of competitive and robust campaigns that constitute the core of a democratic electoral process.

Yet this need for campaign money also poses a threat to democratic governance. Because candidates and party organizations have to solicit contributions to finance electoral activities, there is always a risk that financial considerations will influence their decisions in office or lead to special privileges or policy benefits in exchange for campaign dollars. The rules governing campaign finance are therefore designed to achieve two basic objectives: first, to ensure that participants in election contests have an opportunity to garner the resources needed to wage a viable campaign, and, second, to safeguard the political process from any corrupt practices or the appearance of impropriety or favoritism that can accompany campaign contributions. Fulfilling these objectives has proven to be a challenging task in view of the dynamic changes that characterize the flow of money in political campaigns. As a result, campaign finance reform has been a recurrent issue in American politics.

Since the early days of the Republic, citizens and politicians have expressed suspicion and cynicism about the influence of money on the political process and its effects on the character of U.S. democracy. This popular outlook in many ways reflects the continuing struggle to reconcile basic notions of political liberty and equality, such as the right of free speech and the principle of one person, one vote, with the unequal distribution of economic resources inherent in a capitalistic economic system. These economic disparities inevitably raise questions about the influence of money in the political system, because they give rise to various forms of political inequality. The need to raise private funds has fueled public speculation and distrust about the corruptive effect or undue influence of money on candidates' actions and the integrity of their decisions once in office. It also raises concerns about the equality of citizen participation, because some citizens are able or willing to contribute more of their own resources than others to the candidates or parties they support, thereby increasing their role in a campaign. Candidates able to rely on their own wealth or capable of raising large sums of money often enjoy a substantial financial advantage over less well-funded opponents, which leads to questions about the fairness of the electoral process and the importance of money in determining who runs for—and wins—elective office. The need to raise money can also undermine the quality of representation in government, because candidates may have to spend more time raising money to meet the growing financial demands of campaigns and therefore less time serving constituents or working on government policy issues.

Although the problems associated with campaign finance have been a subject of public debate for much of the nation's history, the issue has rarely provoked major public interest. Consequently, campaign finance reform has always been a vexing legislative problem. With little electoral pressure or public outcry for reform, incumbent legislators have shown little interest in changing a system under which they have benefited and successfully captured office. For the most part, major laws have been adopted only in response to scandals or other controversies that created windows of opportunity for legislative action. These laws typically made incremental changes in the regulations or left some aspects of campaign funding untouched, as legislators struggled to balance the idea of "cleaning up politics" with the fundamental principles of freedom of speech, freedom of association, and federalism. New regulations often gave rise to innovations or unintended consequences that allowed or encouraged circumvention of the rules. Reform thus generated demands for further reform and a desire for more comprehensive approaches to the regulation of campaign funding. This general pattern has been evident for the last century and continues to this day.

This chapter traces the evolution of campaign finance regulation from the earliest federal efforts in the mid-nineteenth century to the adoption of the Bipartisan Campaign Reform Act (BCRA) in 2002. It highlights the changing financial practices that have emerged over time and details the various regulatory approaches that have been adopted to address emerging problems and issues. In doing so, it indicates the complexities and difficulties involved in attempting to regulate such a dynamic component of political campaigns.

Regulation in the Era of Patronage Politics

The methods of financing political campaigns did not become a matter of public controversy until the 1830s. Before that time, the candidates typically provided most of the money needed for campaigns, often with the assistance of friends or relatives or with some assistance from the party organizations that were beginning to develop. Most commonly, the party assistance took the form of support from highly partisan newspapers that were owned or financed by partisan supporters.

The Rise of "Assessments"

The rise of party politics and the expansion of the franchise that accompanied the advent of Jacksonian democracy created a need for another means of financing campaigns, because the political process was gradually opening up to those who could not rely on personal or family wealth to seek elective office. These candidates had to raise funds from others or rely on the parties to pay for their campaigns. In response to this development, the parties and candidates began to raise money by imposing "assessments" on government workers and other patronage appointees, who were expected to donate a small portion of their salaries to finance election campaigns and other political activities. These assessments were the first organized system of campaign finance.

By the mid-1830s, some members of Congress, including Federalist senator Daniel Webster from Massachusetts, began to attack the practice of assessments, arguing that this partisan activity constituted an abuse of government service and a threat to the freedom of elections. In 1837 Rep. John Bell, a Whig from Tennessee, introduced a bill to prohibit assessments. His proposal is probably the first piece of campaign finance–related legislation at the federal level. Two years later, the issue became a matter of public controversy, when a House committee investigating the misappropriation of funds at a New York customhouse uncovered evidence of assessments imposed on customs employees by the Democratic Party's Tammany organization, the political machine that controlled New York City elections throughout most of the nineteenth century. The investigation revived proposals to

ban assessments on government workers, including an 1839 Whig proposal introduced in the Senate that would have made it illegal for a federal officer to "pay or advance" any money toward the "election of any public functionary, whether of the General or State Government." [1] Although the bill did not engender extensive debate, some members voiced opposition to it by claiming that the proposal would serve as a gag law that would violate the freedom of speech. Neither party, however, wanted to see assessments banned, and Congress failed to pass the restriction.

After the Civil War, Congress finally took a small step against the assessment of government workers. An 1867 act that set forth the naval appropriations for fiscal year 1868 included a provision that prohibited the solicitation of political contributions from government workers employed at navy yards by any officer or employee of the government. This restriction, which is considered the first provision of federal law related to campaign finance, had little effect on party funding, because it was not applicable to most federal patronage appointees and placed no restrictions on nonfederal appointees. In the years after its adoption, Republicans controlled the White House and continued to raise campaign money from officeholders and appointees.

The charges of corruption and incompetence in President Ulysses S. Grant's administration finally led to reform of the assessments system. By 1872 liberal Republicans were expressing outrage over the corruption in government and began to denounce the use of money gained by assessments and argue for civil service reform. Republican candidates hoping to succeed Grant took up the cause of reform in an effort to separate themselves from the tarnished president. When President Rutherford B. Hayes took office in 1877, he issued an executive order the same year that barred the assessment of government workers for political purposes. This reform became a permanent feature of government with the passage of the Pendleton Civil Service Act of 1883 and similar state laws. The Pendleton Act restrained the influence of the spoils system in the selection of government workers by creating a class of federal employees who had to qualify for positions through competitive examinations.[2] The act also prohibited the solicitation of contributions from these employees, thus protecting them from forced campaign assessments.

The Gilded Age

With the adoption of the civil service law, candidates and parties began to shift the burden of campaign fund-raising to corporate sources, especially the new industrial giants in oil, railroads, steel, and finance, which had major stakes in the outcomes of government regulatory decisions. Business leaders and the corporations they led were a source of campaign money before the 1880s, but in the years that followed candidates and party leaders increasingly sought large sums from them to finance the growing costs of presidential and congressional campaigns. Money from corporate sources, led by donations from major industrialists, filled party coffers, and some corporations were reportedly making donations to national party committees of $50,000 or more. By the turn of the century, Mark Hanna, the Republican Party boss who organized the presidential campaigns of William McKinley in 1896 and 1900, had established a formal system for soliciting gifts from Wall Street companies. He asked each to "pay according to its stake in the general prosperity of the country and according to its special interest in a region in which a large amount of expensive canvassing had to be done." [3] This emphasis on corporate fund-raising produced the revenues needed to meet rising campaign expenditures. Those expenditures totaled at least $3 million in each of McKinley's presidential campaigns, or more than twice the amount Benjamin Harrison spent in his victorious White House campaign in 1888 and three times the amount Hayes spent in 1876.[4]

Progressive politicians and muckraking journalists responded to these developments by highlighting the abuses in the system and demanding reform. They claimed that corporate donations, as well as continued assessments of candidates and non–civil service workers, were corrupting the political process by providing donors with special privileges and favorable legislation. They decried the lack of public reporting of campaign finances and argued that rising costs were increasing the importance of money in political campaigns. Finally, they demanded regulation, which led to reform at both the state and national levels.

Reform began in the states, where legislatures reacted to public criticism by adopting corrupt practices laws. These statutes were modeled on an act adopted in England in 1883, which defined corrupt practices and illegal payments, placed restrictions on campaign spending, and required public reporting of campaign expenditures. In 1890 New York became the first state to adopt a corrupt practices law, and by 1905 twenty states had enacted similar statutes (but four of these states later repealed their laws). Although the specific provisions varied, the state regulations had some common features. For one thing, they defined corrupt and illegal financial practices, including betting on elections, bribery or undue influence, promises of government positions or employment in exchange for contributions, and "treating," which was the practice of providing cigars, liquor, or other goods to prospective voters. For another, they required candidates to establish a unified account for campaign disbursements and to attest to a report of the amount spent in a campaign (usually filed after the election). The laws also typically sought to limit the amount spent on campaigns, either by establishing a ceiling based on the number of voters in a district or state, or a limit based on a percentage (usually 5–10 percent) of the salary of the office

sought. Five states also took the additional step of prohibiting corporate contributions.

The efforts in the states created pressure for similar reforms at the federal level, but Congress did not act until a controversy erupted over the financing of the 1904 presidential race and brought attention to the issue. During the campaign, Alton Parker, the Democratic Party's presidential nominee, alleged that corporations were providing contributions to President Theodore Roosevelt to gain influence with the administration. Roosevelt, a Republican, denied the charges, but in investigations conducted after the election several major companies did admit to making contributions to the Republican Party during the 1904 campaign. The investigations turned up little evidence of any wrongdoing by the president, however. The most damaging evidence was produced by an investigation by the New York state legislature in 1905 into the business practices of New York insurance companies. The investigation revealed that one of those companies had made a $48,000 contribution from an undisclosed account to the Republican National Committee for the 1904 campaign. Although there was no evidence of any quid pro quo in exchange for this gift, the revelation attracted substantial media attention and heightened concerns about the role of corporate contributions in federal elections.

President Roosevelt responded to the controversy by including a call for campaign finance reform in his annual messages in 1905, 1906, and 1907. The president called for a ban on corporate contributions and disclosure of campaign contributions and expenditures as means of safeguarding the electoral process from bribery and corruption. He also voiced support for public financing of campaigns as a way to reduce the influence of private contributions—an idea first raised in the Congress by Rep. William Bourke Cochran, a Tammany Hall Democrat, in 1904. But beyond these pronouncements, Roosevelt did not actively fight for reform and never pressured Congress to pass a particular proposal.

Tillman Act and Federal Corrupt Practices Act of 1910

Reform was spurred by a growing number of politicians, who joined Progressive reformers and journalists in promoting this cause. Various civic organizations, such as the National Publicity Law Organization (NPLO), also began lobbying for restrictions on campaign contributions and public disclosure of political spending. They were finally successful in changing federal law in 1907, when Democratic senator Benjamin "Pitchfork Ben" Tillman of South Carolina persuaded the Senate to take up a bill banning corporate giving in federal elections. Eager to appease advocates of reform and improve the public image of their party, Republicans supported the proposal, which passed easily in both houses, although not before the language was changed to exempt state-chartered corporations active in state and local elections. The Tillman

Act made it unlawful for any corporation or national bank to make a contribution in connection with any federal election. The ban was the first major federal restriction on campaign funding and became a cornerstone of federal campaign finance law. This prohibition has been reaffirmed in every major subsequent federal statute, including the Federal Election Campaign Act (FECA) of 1974 and, more recently, the Bipartisan Campaign Reform Act of 2002.

Adoption of the Tillman Act failed to quell the cries for reform. Most important, advocates of regulation continued to press for disclosure rules and restrictions on campaign spending. Prior to the 1910 elections, the Republican majority in Congress took an additional step by passing a bill initiated by the NPLO to establish the first federal disclosure rules. The law, entitled the Federal Corrupt Practices Act but more commonly known as the Publicity Act of 1910, was a minor step. It only required party committees "operating in two or more states" to issue a postelection report of contributions and expenditures made in connection with House races. It thus only imposed a disclosure requirement on the national party committees and federal congressional campaign committees; candidate committees and state party organizations were not included.

The next year the Democrats, who gained control of the House and picked up seats in the Senate in the 1910 contests, pushed for changes in the Publicity Act to include preelection reporting. Because Democrats were typically outspent by Republicans, they hoped to get financial information released before the election, so that campaign spending could be used as a campaign issue. The Republicans attempted to kill the bill by adding provisions affecting primary elections that they expected to be unacceptable to southern Democrats, but the move backfired. Instead of defeating the bill, the provisions were adopted as part of the Publicity Act Amendments of 1911. This law extended disclosure to Senate campaigns and required campaign committees to report their finances both before and after an election and in both primary contests and general elections. More important, the law established the first federal campaign spending limits, restricting expenditures in a House campaign to a total of $5,000 and in a Senate campaign to the lesser sum of $10,000 or the amount established by state law.

Federal regulations were in place for only a few election cycles before the need for additional reform became necessary. The spending limits established by the 1911 law were a matter of controversy soon after their adoption and were challenged in court after the 1918 Senate race in Michigan. In that race, Truman Newberry, a Michigan Republican who defeated Henry Ford in a fiercely contested Senate primary, was convicted of violating the expenditure limit. His campaign committee reported spending close to $180,000 in the primary, or almost a hundred times the amount permitted under Michigan law. Newberry challenged his conviction, arguing that Congress had no authority to regulate primaries because they were not part of the formal election process. In 1921 the Supreme Court ruled in *Newberry v. United States* that the congressional authority to regulate elections did not extend to party primaries and nominating activities, and thus struck down the primary spending limit. This narrow interpretation of congressional authority stood until 1941, when in *United States v. Classic,* a case involving election fraud in a Democratic House primary in Louisiana, the Court ruled that Congress did have the authority to regulate primaries and party nominating processes wherever state law made them part of the election process and wherever they effectively determined the outcome of the general election. But Congress did not fully assert its authority to regulate the financing of primary elections until the early 1970s, when it adopted the Federal Election Campaign Act.

Federal Corrupt Practices Act of 1925

Soon after the Court's decision in *Newberry,* the Teapot Dome scandal focused public attention once again on the potentially corruptive effects of large contributions. The scandal did not involve contributions to a candidate or the financing of an election campaign; it revolved instead around gifts made by oil developers in a nonelection year to the federal officials responsible for granting oil leases. Nevertheless, the scandal spurred renewed pressure for measures to protect the political system against corruption, which induced Congress to pass the Federal Corrupt Practices Act of 1925. This law provided the basic regulations governing campaign finance until adoption of the Federal Election Campaign Act in the 1970s.

The 1925 act followed the approach set forth in earlier legislation, although it omitted regulations for primary elections to conform to the ruling in *Newberry.* The law strengthened disclosure rules to try to encompass the financial activity that led to the Teapot Dome scandal; it required all multistate political committees, as well as House and Senate candidates, to file quarterly reports that included all contributions of $100 or more, even in nonelection years. Although the law maintained limits on spending, it loosened these restrictions, increasing the ceiling for a Senate candidate to $25,000 and for a House candidate to $5,000, unless state law set a lower limit.

Despite its more extensive disclosure requirements, the Federal Corrupt Practices Act had little effect on the flow of money in political campaigns. The spending limits were easily skirted through the creation of multiple political committees to support a particular candidate. Each of these committees could then technically comply with the spending limit established for a particular contest, even though the total amount spent greatly exceeded the ceiling provided in the law. These numerous organizations also facilitated evasion of disclosure requirements, because a donor could give less than $100 to each committee without any reporting obligation, or give larger sums to a number of committees, thereby obscuring the total given in support of any candidate. The law also lacked adequate enforcement provisions. It made no provision for the publication of reports, did not establish standard formats for reporting, and did not even stipulate the penalties for committees that failed to comply. The reports that were filed with the clerk of the House or the secretary of the Senate were difficult to access and usually destroyed after two years.

The inefficacy of the 1925 law is demonstrated by the lack of enforcement that characterized its history. Only two candidates, Republicans William Vare of Pennsylvania and Frank Smith of Illinois, were ever excluded from office, both in 1927, for violating expenditure limits, and no other candidates were punished under the act during its next forty-five years of operation. The act also proved incapable of regulating organized political groups, such as the Anti-Saloon League, which were active in politics during the Prohibition era. In 1928 Bishop James Cannon, leader of the Anti-Saloon League effort in Virginia, which opposed Democrat Alfred E. Smith of New York in the 1928 presidential race, was prosecuted for failing to report contributions and expenditures made against Smith. The enforcement proceeding led to a lawsuit challenging Congress's authority to regulate campaign finance. The issue was resolved by the Supreme Court in 1934 in *Burroughs v. United States*. In this decision, the Court again upheld Congress's authority to regulate campaign money, based in part on the argument that the free use of money in elections is a cause of concern and that Congress has the power to pass appropriate legislation to safeguard elections from the "improper use of money to influence the result." [5] Even though the courts upheld Congress's authority, Cannon was not convicted of conspiring to violate the law. The law was therefore left in a weakened position, and organized groups continued to operate outside of it.

Despite the weaknesses of the Federal Corrupt Practices Act, its adoption encouraged the states to adopt or strengthen their campaign finance statutes. By the beginning of World War II, every state had at least some sort of statute on the books, and a trend toward increasingly stringent regulation was evident.[6] All states made it unlawful to give a bribe in connection with elections; twenty-four prohibited the promise of an appointment by a candidate to secure votes; and twenty-one prohibited the solicitation of funds for political purposes from various classes of public employees. Reflecting the direction of federal regulation, all but nine states established ceilings on candidate expenditures, and, of the nine that did not, four specified the types of expenditures that could be made legally. Thirty-six states banned corporate contributions, but only two (Massachusetts and Nebraska) placed any restriction on individual contributions. Most states did require candidates to file a statement of receipts and expenditures, but only thirty-six imposed this requirement on party committees. Like the federal law, however, these state laws were poorly enforced or easily evaded. Thus they failed to resolve concerns about the undue influence of money in the electoral process.

Prelude to the Modern Era

Congress did not return to the issue of campaign finance until the success of President Franklin D. Roosevelt's New Deal coalition led conservative Democrats and staunch Republicans to seek additional reforms. This impulse for reform emerged in response to two developments: the hiring of workers under the New Deal's public works programs and the rise of labor unions as major sources of political contributions.

Although the government positions covered by the 1883 Pendleton Act had expanded since its adoption, many of the tens of thousands of workers added to public payrolls during the New Deal were not subject to the civil service restrictions. Conservative members of Congress who opposed the New Deal became increasingly concerned about the political activities that could be conducted by these employees and passed the Clean Politics Act, also known as the Hatch Act for its sponsor, Sen. Carl Hatch, a Democrat from New Mexico. The 1939 Hatch Act prohibited political activity by federal workers who were not constrained by the civil service rules. It also prohibited the solicitation of political contributions from government relief workers.

In 1940 Congress strengthened these prohibitions by amending the Hatch Act to include limits on individual contributions and expenditures. The revisions imposed a limit of $5,000 per year on individual contributions to national candidates or national party committees and a limit of $3 million per year on the total amount that a multistate party committee could raise or spend. The impetus behind these changes was a desire to reduce the resources the Roosevelt-controlled party organization and his major supporters could use to intervene in elections against New Deal opponents. But, like the earlier regulations, the law was limited in its effects by the failure to restrict contributions to multiple committees, the fact that the law was not applicable to the finances of independent nonparty organizations, and the lack of an effective enforcement authority. By the 1940 election, both parties were exceeding the new spending limit.

New Deal Years and Labor Unions

The major change in political finance during the New Deal years was the rise of labor unions as a political force and source of campaign funding. Labor unions supported Roosevelt in part through large contributions from their treasury funds, which primarily consisted of members' dues payments. Republicans joined with conservative southern Democrats to reduce labor's influence by passing the War Labor Disputes Act of 1943 over President Roosevelt's veto. The act included a provision that extended the Tillman Act's prohibition on corporate contributions in federal elections to labor union donations. More specifically, the act prohibited labor unions from using treasury funds to make political contributions to federal candidates. The law began as a temporary restriction, because it was passed as a "war measure." But Congress made the prohibition permanent when Republicans assumed the majority after the 1946 election and passed the Labor-Management Relations Act, more commonly known as the Taft-Hartley legislation, over President Harry S. Truman's veto. This act also strengthened the bans on corporate and labor donations by making it unlawful for any corporation or labor union to spend treasury funds in connection with a federal election. The law thus sought to ensure that labor unions or corporations could not circumvent the ban on giving by simply spending money directly in support of a candidate.

Unions responded to the prohibition on treasury fund contributions by organizing auxiliary committees for the purposes of engaging in election activity. These committees, which came to be known as political action committees (PACs), collected funds from union members apart from their dues and used these monies to make contributions to candidates and finance other types of political activity, such as voter education efforts and get-out-the-vote drives. The first committee of this sort was established by the Congress of Industrial Organizations in 1943 and became the model for similar PACs. By 1956 seventeen national labor PACs were active in federal elections, contributing more than $2 million to candidates. By 1968 the number had doubled, with thirty-seven labor PACs spending more than $7 million.[7] Business and professional groups did not immediately follow labor's tactics, but by the early 1960s groups such as the American Medical Association and National Association of Manufacturers had formed committees of their own.

Rise of Candidate-Centered Campaigns

The major changes in postwar campaign finance, however, were the result of changing styles of political campaigning. Although party organizations continued to be an important source of revenue and support, their strength began to decline, and campaigns became increasingly candidate-centered. Candidates for federal office placed greater reliance on their own campaign organizations and monies raised independent of party organizations. Meanwhile, television and radio became important means of political communication, which increased the cost of seeking elective office. These rising costs were met primarily by relying on large donors as a principal source of campaign revenue.

The changes taking place in political finance were evident by the early 1960s and rekindled the policy debate on campaign funding. President John F. Kennedy reflected the rising concern in his decision to form a Commission on Campaign Costs in 1962 to explore means of strengthening regulation to control the influence of big donors. The commission offered recommendations for a comprehensive program of reforms, including full disclosure of candidate and party monies, the creation of an independent commission to publicize data, tax incentives for small donors, and public subsidies for presidential candidates. But the only legislative changes came in 1966 in response to press reports criticizing the activities of the Democratic "Presidents Club," a group whose members consisted of donors of $1,000 or more, and to the censure of Democratic senator Thomas J. Dodd of Connecticut for using his political funds for personal purposes. Also in 1966, Sen. Russell Long, a Democrat from Louisiana, sponsored a proposal (a rider to the Foreign Investors Tax Act) to provide public subsidies to political parties to help pay the costs of presidential campaigns. A checkoff on federal income tax forms would allow taxpayers to allocate $1 to a party for this purpose. The plan, however, was never implemented. In 1967 Congress essentially repealed the law by voting to postpone its implementation until certain guidelines were established. These rules were never drafted, but the plan was revised and adopted a few years later as part of the Revenue Act of 1971.

Regulation under the FECA

During the 1960s, campaign spending continued to rise dramatically. In 1956 total federal campaign spending was an estimated $155 million, about $10 million of which was used for television and radio advertising. By 1968 overall spending had nearly doubled to $300 million, and media expenditures approached $60 million.[8] Democrats were particularly concerned about rising costs, because the party was often struggling with postelection debts, as opposed to the Republicans who had developed a broader base of small donors who gave the party a substantial financial advantage. This gap was especially apparent in the 1968 presidential race—the Republicans and their nominee, Richard Nixon, spent twice as much as the Democrats and their nominee, Vice President Hubert H. Humphrey. This pattern increased support for reform among Democratic legislators, some of whom also began to worry about the prospect of wealthy challengers who could spend their own money to defeat incumbents in expensive, media-based campaigns. The trends also spurred the development of a coalition of public interest groups led by Common Cause that began to lobby actively for campaign finance reform. This combination of factors and motives led to a new reform movement.

Birth of the FECA

Before the 1972 election, Congress passed some incremental measures to curb rising expenditures and address some of the inadequacies of the antiquated regulatory scheme. These changes were encompassed in the Federal Election Campaign Act of 1971, which was signed by President Nixon in 1972. This reform combined two different regulatory approaches. First, it sought to restrain the role of money by establishing a limit on the amount federal candidates could contribute personally to their own campaigns and by placing a ceiling on the amount a candidate could spend on media. Specifically, a presidential candidate was limited to $50,000 in personal contributions, a Senate candidate to $35,000, and a House candidate to $25,000. Presidential candidates were limited to less than $6 million in media spending, with lower limits for Senate and House candidates. Second, the act strengthened financial reporting and disclosure requirements by mandating that every candidate or political committee active in a federal campaign file quarterly reports of receipts and expenditures and that these reports be made available for public inspection.

The 1971 act may have helped to restrict media spending in the 1972 election, but it did little to slow the surge in overall campaign spending, which received even greater attention as a result of the improved disclosure rules. Reports filed under the new rules indicated that spending in the 1972 presidential race continued to soar; the two contenders spent more than $100 million in the general election contest, compared with less than half that amount in the race only four years earlier. President Nixon's reelection campaign spent more than twice the amount his campaign had spent in 1968, while the campaign of his Democratic opponent, George McGovern, spent four times as much as Humphrey's campaign in 1968. Yet McGovern was still outspent by a two-to-one margin. This jump in expenditures suggested to some that more extensive controls were needed; to others, it suggested the futility in attempting to restrict the flow of money in an electoral system characterized by an expanding electorate, new technologies, and a growing reliance on broadcast communications as a principal means of communicating messages to the electorate. But before the law could be tested in another election, the Watergate scandal captured public attention and generated demands for more comprehensive reform.

The Watergate scandal and subsequent investigations into the financial activities of Nixon's 1972 reelection campaign produced a watershed in the regulation of campaign finance. The investigations exposed financial abuses and improprieties, including illegal corporate contributions, donations that exceeded federal limits, and the existence of undisclosed slush funds that held millions of dollars. These inquiries also detailed allegations that contributors had "bought" ambassadorial appointments, gained legislative favors, and received other special privileges in exchange for campaign gifts. The national uproar spurred by the scandal caused Congress to undertake a complete overhaul of the rules governing campaign funding.

Federal Election Campaign Act of 1974

The Federal Election Campaign Act of 1974, which technically was a set of amendments to the 1971 act, stands as the most comprehensive campaign finance reform package ever adopted by Congress.[9] The law strengthened disclosure rules and contribution limits, established aggregate spending ceilings for all federal campaigns, and created a new regulatory agency, the Federal Election Commission (FEC), to administer and enforce the law. It also created an innovative public funding program for presidential candidates. In short, it erected a new regulatory structure for federal election campaigns.

The 1974 act was designed to achieve various objectives. Among other things, it sought to safeguard the electoral process against corruption by exposing campaign finance to public scrutiny and strictly limiting the role of private donors in the financing of campaigns. The law was also designed to equalize financial participation among donors by eliminating the large "fat cat" donors who had become an important source of campaign money and by shifting the emphasis to a broad base of small contributors. It also sought to create a more equitable and competitive electoral process by limiting the amounts candidates were able to spend. And finally, it attempted to reduce the role of private funding and the emphasis on fund-raising in the race for the White House by providing candidates with the option to use public subsidies.

Under the terms of the FECA, an individual was allowed to contribute no more than $1,000 per candidate for any primary, runoff, or general election and could not exceed $25,000 in annual aggregate contributions to all federal candidates and political committees. Donations by PACs were limited to $5,000 per election for each candidate, with no aggregate limit. Independent expenditures made on behalf of a candidate were limited to $1,000 a year, and cash donations in excess of $100 were prohibited. The law also retained the limits adopted in 1971 on personal contributions by candidates and the earlier prohibitions against corporate and labor union contributions.

Media spending limits were replaced with stringent limits on total campaign expenditures that were applied to all federal candidates. Under the new provisions, Senate candidates could spend no more than the greater amount of $100,000 or $0.08 times the voting-age population of the state in a primary election, and no more than the greater amount of $150,000 or $0.12 times the voting-age population in a general election. House candidates in multidistrict states were limited to total expenditures of $70,000 for each primary and general election. Those in states with a single representative were subject to the ceilings established for Senate candidates.

Presidential candidates were restricted to spending $10 million in a nomination campaign and $20 million in a general election. The amount they could spend in a state primary election was also limited to no more than twice the sum that a Senate candidate in that state could spend. All of these ceilings were indexed to reflect increases in the Consumer Price Index, and candidates were allowed to spend up to an additional 20 percent of the spending limit on fund-raising. This latter provision was instituted in recognition of the fund-raising burden placed on candidates by the contribution limits imposed by the act, which required that they finance their campaigns through small contributions.

The amendments also set limits on the amounts national party committees could expend in behalf of candidates. These organizations were allowed to spend no more than $10,000 per candidate in House general elections; the greater amount of $20,000 or $0.02 times the voting-age population for each candidate in Senate general elections; and $0.02 times the voting-age population (approximately $2.9 million) for their presidential candidate. The amount a party committee could spend on its national nominating convention was also restricted. Each of the major parties (defined as a party whose presidential candidate received more than 25 percent of the popular vote in the previous election) was limited to $2 million in convention expenditures, and a minor party (defined as a party whose presidential candidate received between 5 and 25 percent of the popular vote in the previous election) was limited to lesser amounts.

The reforms also sought to provide a meaningful enforcement mechanism by creating the Federal Election Commission, a six-member, full-time, bipartisan agency responsible for administering election laws and implementing the public financing program. This agency was empowered to receive all campaign reports, promulgate rules and regulations, make special and regular reports to Congress and the president, conduct audits and investigations, subpoena witnesses and information, and seek civil injunctions to ensure compliance with the law. To assist the commission in its task, Congress tightened the FECA's disclosure and reporting requirements. The most important provision in this regard was a requirement that each candidate certify one central campaign committee through which all contributions and expenditures had to be reported.

The most innovative aspect of the 1974 law was the creation of an optional program of full public financing for presidential general election campaigns and a voluntary system of public matching subsidies for presidential primary campaigns. It thus brought into being the first program of public campaign finance at the national level, actuating an idea that had been offered from time to time since the turn of the century. The subsidy was adopted to reduce the fund-raising pressures on presidential candidates and to encourage them to solicit small donations, which would serve to broaden citizen financial participation in presidential campaigns.

Under the terms of this public funding program, the presidential nominees of the major parties could receive the full amount authorized by the spending limit ($20 million) if they agreed to refrain from raising any additional private money. Qualified minor-party or independent candidates could receive a proportional share of the subsidy, with the size of the subsidy based on the proportion of the presidential vote their party received in the previous election—a proportion calculated in comparison with the average vote of the major parties. New parties and minor parties could also qualify for postelection funds on the same proportional basis, if their percentage of the vote in the current presidential election entitled them to a larger subsidy than the grant generated by their vote in the previous election.

In the primary election, presidential candidates were eligible for public matching funds if they fulfilled certain fund-raising requirements. To qualify, a candidate had to raise at least $5,000 in contributions of $250 or less in at least twenty states. Eligible candidates would then receive public monies on a dollar-for-dollar basis for the first $250 contributed by an individual, provided that the contribution was received after January 1 of the year before the election year. The maximum amount a candidate could receive in such payments was half of the spending limit, or $5 million under the original terms of the act. In addition, national party committees were given the option of financing their nominating conventions with public funds. Major parties could receive the entire amount authorized by the spending limit ($2 million); minor parties were eligible for lesser amounts based on their proportion of the vote in the previous election.

This program was funded through a checkoff on federal income tax forms established by the Revenue Act of 1971. This act, which was adopted before the 1974 FECA, revived the tax checkoff and public funding plan that had been adopted in 1966 but was never implemented. It provided a voluntary tax checkoff provision on individual federal income tax returns to allow individuals to designate $1 of their tax payments (or $2 for married couples filing jointly) to the Presidential Election Campaign Fund, a separate account maintained by the U.S. Treasury. In 1993 the amount rose to $3 for an individual or $6 for joint filers.

The Revenue Act also provided a federal income tax credit or tax deduction for small contributions to political candidates at all levels of government and to some political committees, including those associated with national party organizations. Like the matching funds program, it was designed to promote broad-based participation in campaign financing. These tax provisions were amended several times. The tax credit for political contributions was increased to $25 on an individual return and $50 on a joint return by the Tariff Schedules Amendments

BOX 6-1
PUBLIC FINANCING OF PRESIDENTIAL CAMPAIGNS
Daniel Oakes

Public financing of presidential campaigns represents an effort to reduce the influence of private donations and increase the importance of small donations in campaigns and to make elections more competitive. Through the 1974 Federal Election Campaign Act, Congress established a voluntary system of public financing for the presidential campaigns. Funds are raised through a voluntary tax whereby individuals may designate $3 and persons filing jointly may designate $6 to the system by checking a box on their tax forms. The legislation provides for three forms of financial assistance: (1) matching funds during the primaries, (2) subsidies for the national conventions, and (3) full financing of the general election campaigns. Candidates are free to participate in either or both of the primary and general election systems. In recent years, however, candidates have begun to refuse primary matching funds, while continuing to use general election financing. Both major parties accept convention subsidies,

yet the regulation of such funds is minimal and the intention of the legislation is circumvented. Effective public financing requires leverage to induce participation and sufficient corresponding regulations to change the way campaigns are run.

Primary Matching Funds
The voluntary program offers qualified primary candidates matching funds on the first $250 of every private donation. To be eligible, a candidate must agree to weighted spending limits in each state and an overall spending ceiling amounting to roughly $50 million in 2004. Also, a candidate may self-finance only up to $50,000 and must raise $5,000 in twenty states in $250 increments. In addition, a candidate must receive at least 10 percent of the vote in the two previous primaries in which his or her name appeared on the ballot. Failure to do so will deny a candidate eligibility, which can only be regained by receiving 20 percent in a later primary. Third party candidates, as well as those from new parties, are also

eligible, even if their nominations are secured without primaries or caucuses.

Recently, major-party nominees have opted out of public matching funds for the primaries. In 2000 and 2004, Republican George W. Bush refused matching funds, as did Democrats Howard Dean and John Kerry in 2004. The reason for nonparticipation is largely strategic—candidates are capable of raising money beyond the system's spending limits. In 2000 Bush raised $94 million, exceeding the system's cap of $45.6 million. In 2004 Bush raised $274 million and Kerry raised $249.5 million, both exceeding the public cap of $50.4 million. In addition, the front-loading of primaries has effectively lengthened the general election campaign, because the two likely nominees emerge well before the convention. This longer campaign requires additional funds. Conceivably, public financing could cripple a presumptive nominee, who, bound by spending limits, would be unable to spend new resources until

---

of 1975, and doubled again by the Revenue Act of 1978. The latter act also eliminated the tax deduction, leaving only the credit as an incentive for small donors. This credit was eventually repealed as part of the Reagan administration's tax reform effort in 1986.

Buckley v. Valeo

The FECA's regulatory scheme, as conceived by Congress, was never implemented. Before the act went into effect, most of its provisions were challenged by plaintiffs, who argued that the law violated the First Amendment's guarantee of free speech. In *Buckley v. Valeo* (1976), the U.S. Supreme Court addressed the issues raised by this group of legal challenges, and in doing so it set forth a framework for analysis that has guided regulatory efforts in this area ever since.[10] *Buckley* thus stands as the most important judicial opinion ever issued on campaign finance.

In *Buckley*, the Supreme Court held that the regulation of campaign money did entail an infringement on politi-

cal speech, because only by spending money on media could candidates communicate their views to the electorate. Consequently, only a state interest would justify regulation in this area. In the view of the Court, the interest that justified regulation was the need to prevent corruption or the appearance of corruption in the political process. But it specifically rejected the claim that there was also a rationale for regulation in the need to equalize the relative ability of individuals or groups to influence the outcome of elections. The Court found this desire to pursue greater equity by restricting some expenditures and activities of some individuals and groups to enhance the voices and activities of others to be "wholly foreign" to the First Amendment.

The Court also ruled that any consideration of the free speech implications of regulation had to distinguish between contributions and expenditures. Contributions could be regulated more broadly, because they convey support for a candidate or party, but not the reasons be-after the nominating convention. Candidates are also wary of state spending limits, which can hamstring candidates in crucial states.

Financing of Nominating Conventions

Major parties are eligible for national convention subsidies, which amounted to $14.9 million in 2004; minor parties receive partial subsidization in proportion to their previous vote percentage. Public funding, however, is not the only source of convention funding. Although corporations are banned from providing unlimited soft money to national parties, they are free to give unlimited donations to convention host committees for nonpartisan convention assistance. The size of these unlimited donations has steadily increased, from $8.4 million in 1992 to $103.5 million in 2004. Both parties accept convention subsidization, because it effectively amounts to free money with few strings attached.

Financing of the General Election Campaign

A separate system established by the FECA governs public financing of the general election. Major-party candidates are eligible for full general election financing. Minor-party candidates are eligible for partial subsidization proportional to the party's share of the popular vote in the most recent election. Major parties are defined as those receiving more than 25 percent of the vote in the previous election; minor-party candidates received more than 5 percent but less than 25 percent. The base level of full funding was set at $20 million in 1974 and has been subsequently adjusted for inflation, amounting to $74.6 million in 2004. There are no state spending limits. Candidates accepting public funds for the general election are limited to using only those funds, with the exception of spending related to general election legal, accounting, and compliance costs, which amounted to $11.3 million for Kerry and $17.7 million for Bush in 2004. Since the law's conception, every major-party candidate has utilized the general election program. General election candidates choose public financing over independent fundraising, believing the decision makes their campaign more competitive.

The Effectiveness of Public Financing

Effective public financing of elections requires leverage to induce participation. Leverage is created by making public financing systems more attractive than independent financing; thus participation becomes a strategic imperative. Candidates voluntarily accept general election funding, and parties accept convention subsidization, because it is more appealing than nonparticipation. Candidates opt out of primary matching funds, because they are more competitive through independent fund-raising.

The three presidential public financing systems therefore vary in their effectiveness. The primary matching fund system risks becoming irrelevant through nonparticipation. Indeed, its future is now in question. Convention subsidies pale in comparison with private donations to the parties. As a result, the intended effect of such subsidies—the elimination of private influence—is weakened at best. General election funding, however, induces both participation and alters the way campaigns are run. Whether the public financing of presidential elections improves campaigns remains the subject of debate.

---

hind such support. Yet contributions could not be limited to such an extent that the restrictions on giving would "starve" campaigns or block the basic signal of donor support. Expenditures, however, must be treated differently; they represent monies controlled or expended directly by a spender expressly to support or oppose a candidate. Restrictions on expenditures should therefore be subject to greater constitutional scrutiny, because such restrictions limit both the quantity and quality of speech.

Finally, the Court noted that regulations should be tailored narrowly to provide those participating in elections with clear but not overly broad rules. Congress had crafted the FECA to attempt to encompass all monies raised and spent "in connection with" federal elections or "for the purpose of influencing" federal elections. To the Court, these constructions were too vague and broad. In their place, the Court argued that regulation should be limited to activity that "expressly advocates" the election or defeat of a candidate. In a footnote to the opinion, the Court suggested that such activities would include communications that incorporate such words as "vote for," "elect," or "defeat." This example became known as the "magic words" test, and it was adopted as the standard for determining express advocacy in the majority of federal court decisions issued after *Buckley.*

Based on this doctrinal framework, the Court upheld in *Buckley* some key components of the FECA, but it struck down others. The Court upheld contribution limits and disclosure requirements, noting their role in safeguarding against corruption. But it struck down the spending ceilings and limits on independent expenditures, which substantially weakened the potential efficacy of the act. The Court ruled that spending limits were allowable only if they were accepted voluntarily as a condition for receiving public funding. It further held that limits on personal contributions by candidates to their own campaigns were unconstitutional under the First Amendment, unless a candidate had accepted public funding. Finally, the decision struck down the original method of appointing members of the FEC. Under the 1974 legislation, the president, the Speaker of the House, and the president pro tempore of the Senate each appointed two of the six commissioners. The Court ruled that this method violated the separation of powers, because four of the six members were appointed by Congress but exercised executive powers. As a result, the FEC was prohibited from enforcing the law until it was reconstituted under a constitutional appointment process.

A New Regime

Congress, now forced to modify the law to accommodate the Court's ruling before it could be applied in the 1976 election, did so by quickly passing another set of amendments to the FECA in the midst of the election. These regulations essentially followed the Court's guidelines: they limited contributions and thus restricted the supply of money, but they did not limit expenditures, or the demand for money.

Congress took advantage of this opportunity to establish additional contribution limits. New restrictions were placed on the amount an individual could give to a PAC ($5,000 per year) or a national party committee ($20,000 per year) under federal law, and these types of gifts were made subject to the aggregate ceiling of $25,000 per year that was imposed on individual donors under the 1974 reforms. The amount a PAC could donate to a national party committee was set at $15,000 a year, and the Democratic and Republican Senatorial Campaign Committees were restricted to $17,500 in contributions to a federal candidate. The law thus folded party contributions into the scheme of contribution limits so that individuals could not circumvent the law by giving money through the parties. It further sought to reduce the opportunities to avoid the law by stipulating that all PACs created by a company or international union would be treated as a single committee for the purpose of determining compliance with contribution limits.

The 1976 law also changed the method of appointing members of the Federal Election Commission. Instead of giving the president, Speaker of the House, and president pro tempore of the Senate two appointments apiece, with a requirement that appointees be of different parties and be approved by the Senate, the new rules called for the appointment of all six members by the president, subject to Senate confirmation. This process avoided the separation of powers issue raised by the Court in *Buckley* against the original procedure.

The amendments improved the FEC's enforcement powers by granting it the exclusive authority to prosecute civil violations of the law and jurisdiction over violations previously covered only in the criminal code. But at the same time it placed checks on the commission's ability to act by requiring an affirmative vote of four members to issue regulations and initiate civil actions, by restricting

the commission's advisory decisions to specific fact situations, and by giving Congress the power to disapprove proposed regulations.

Despite its shaky start, the FECA regulatory approach represented a major advancement over the patchwork of largely ineffective regulations it replaced. The disclosure and reporting requirements dramatically improved public access to financial information and regulators' ability to enforce the law. The contribution ceilings eliminated the large gifts that had tainted the process in 1972. Public financing quickly gained widespread acceptance among the candidates, and small contributions became a staple of presidential campaign financing.

But the new regime was not without its critics. Candidates and political committees complained that the law's detailed reporting requirements forced them to engage in unnecessary and burdensome paperwork, which increased their administrative costs. State and local party leaders contended that the law reduced the level of spending on traditional party-building activities (such as voter registration and mobilization programs) and discouraged grass-roots volunteer efforts. Because parties were limited in the amounts they could spend on behalf of candidates, party committees were not allowed to spend unlimited amounts on federal campaign paraphernalia or on get-out-the-vote drives in support of federal candidates. Instead, party leaders had to look to the presidential campaigns for the funding for some of these activities. But the presidential candidates were limited in the amounts they could spend under the public funding program, and both major-party candidates opted to concentrate their resources on media advertising rather than grass-roots political activities. Consequently, party leaders argued that the new rules undermined efforts to build party support.

FECA Amendments of 1979

The initial experience with the FECA in 1976 thus led to a call for further adjustments, and Congress again modified the law before the 1980 election. To ensure quick passage, the reform effort focused on revisions acceptable to both houses of Congress. The FECA amendments of 1979 included changes that eased some of the restrictions of the law and expanded the role of party funding in federal elections. To enhance the role of political parties and address the concerns voiced by party leaders based on the experience of the 1976 election, the law relaxed some restrictions on party spending. Specifically, it exempted certain types of party-related activity, such as grass-roots volunteer activities and voter registration and turnout programs, from the coordinated expenditure ceilings imposed on party spending in federal elections. The new rules allowed party committees to spend unlimited amounts of the money raised under federal contribution limits on voter registration and get-out-the-vote activities, provided such activities were primarily conducted on behalf of the party's presidential nominee. These committees were also allowed to spend unlimited amounts of regulated money on materials related to grass-roots or volunteer activities (such as buttons, bumper stickers, posters, and brochures), provided the funds used were not drawn from contributions designated for a particular candidate. The rules specified, however, that this exemption did not apply to any monies spent on public political advertising.

Congress also increased the amount provided to party committees for presidential nominating conventions under the public funding program. In 1974 the base amount available to a party from the public funding program to pay for convention expenses had been set at $2 million, plus a cost of living adjustment. The base amount was raised to $3 million in 1979. Congress increased the amount again in 1984, when it passed a bill that raised the convention subsidy to $4 million.

Finally, the 1979 amendments weakened the enforcement capability of the FEC by stripping the agency of its authority to conduct random audits—the FEC had been given this authority to ensure effective enforcement of the law. After the 1976 election, the agency had undertaken random audits of 10 percent of House and Senate candidates. Those audits generally exposed minor but embarrassing inaccuracies in the reports filed by many incumbents, but the concern about being audited was enough to convince Congress to reduce the FEC's efficacy.

Encouraged by the FECA, state reformers followed Congress's lead and passed further reforms at the state level. About two-thirds of the states enacted major new campaign finance laws after passage of the 1979 FECA amendments.[11] These laws were principally designed to address rising campaign costs and the growth of PAC funding. They also sought to strengthen the relatively lax regulations that existed in many states at the time the FECA was adopted. By 1980 most states had some form of disclosure requirement, but many placed no limit on contributions. Corporate contributions were prohibited in thirty-three states, but only twenty-two put any limits on individual contributions, while sixteen restricted contributions by PACs. By 1996 thirty-eight states had limits on individual gifts, forty-two restricted corporate donations, thirty-six limited labor contributions, and thirty-two limited PACs. Many of the states that already had contribution limits lowered these ceilings during this period of reform.

States also experimented with public funding programs as a means of reducing the emphasis on fund-raising and the role of private money in election campaigns. The number of states with some form of public subsidy for candidates or parties grew from four in 1974 to nineteen in 1984. In most states, the funding for these subsidies came from a checkoff on state tax forms or a provision that allowed citizens to add a dollar amount to their taxes for allocation to the public funding program. These programs, however, failed to generate substantial sums of money or provide benefits substantial enough to induce extensive participation from candidates. As a result, these programs had little effect in curbing private money or enhancing the competitiveness of elections.

How Well Did the FECA Work?

The FECA strengthened the regulation of campaign money, but it did not accomplish all of its objectives. The new law did significantly improve the disclosure of campaign finances and eliminated large donations to candidates. Candidates shifted the emphasis of their fund-raising efforts to the solicitation of smaller donors. The public funding system worked as anticipated, at least in the first few elections under the new system, and received broad candidate support, including participation by every presidential nominee.

But with Senate and House races freed of spending restraints, congressional campaign costs continued to rise, from about $115 million in 1976 to $450 million in 1986. Most of this money was raised by incumbents, who tended to outspend their opponents by sizable margins. Their financial advantage stemmed in part from their success in garnering contributions from PACs, which proliferated in the years after the FECA.

The growth of the role of PACs in the financing of federal campaigns was the most notable direct consequence of the FECA. The law allowed groups and organizations to form such committees, thereby acknowledging a 1972 Supreme Court decision in *Pipefitters v. United States* that affirmed the right of unions to form PACs as long as member contributions were voluntary and the funds were maintained in an account separate from dues money. Accordingly, from 1974 to 1986 the number of PACs registered with the FEC rose from 1,146 to 4,157. PAC contributions to federal candidates rose from about $12 million to $105 million.[12] Although there were many reasons for this growth, the FECA regulations were certainly a major factor. The FEC also encouraged PAC formation when, in a 1975 regulatory ruling involving Sun Oil Company, the agency approved the formation of PACs by corporations and declared that corporate funds could be used to pay the administrative and overhead costs of such a committee. By 1986 there were four times as many corporate PACs as labor PACs.

Rising costs and the role of PAC funding thrust congressional elections into the fray of reform efforts from the mid-1980s to the mid-1990s. Advocates of reform argued that PAC contributions were being used to buy legislative influence and to give incumbents an unfair financial advantage. Reformers thus supported restrictions on the amount congressional candidates could receive from PACs and proposals to provide candidates with some form of public subsidy, either in the form of free or reduced-cost broadcast time or free mailing privileges. These proposals, however, deeply divided Congress, leading to filibusters and other legislative machinations that stymied any major change in the campaign finance system.

While the focus of the reform debate was centered on candidate spending and PAC giving, new financial practices evolved that posed even greater threats to the integrity of the system. The most important of these—the advent of "soft money" and the rise of candidate-specific issue advocacy advertising—eventually raised new regulatory challenges and changed the terms of the legislative debate.

Soon after the FECA took effect, presidential campaigns and party organizations began to seek ways to circumvent the expenditure limits that accompanied public funding. Among the tactics they pursued was aggressive exploitation of the exemption in the law that allowed unlimited spending on party grass-roots and party-building activities. Because presidential candidates were limited in the amounts they could spend, they looked to the parties to assume a greater responsibility for voter identification and turnout efforts. In that way, the candidates could reserve more of their limited public funds to pay for advertising. This strategy became increasingly effective because of regulatory decisions made by the FEC.

The 1979 FECA amendments loosened the restrictions on party spending by allowing parties to spend unlimited amounts on party-building efforts. But the law did not alter the restrictions on contributions; the parties were still required to pay for these activities with monies that came from contributions limited by the FECA, which became known as "hard money." But just as Congress was easing the restrictions on spending, the FEC was issuing regulatory decisions that loosened the restraints on contributions. The commission ruled that party committees could accept and spend monies from contributions not subject to the FECA's limits to pay administrative costs, costs associated solely with state and local elections, and expenses incurred for other nonfederal, election-related activities. The commission also ruled that parties could use monies not subject to federal contribution limits, which became known as "soft money," to pay for the share of voter identification and turnout efforts that reflected the state or local portion of these costs, as long as it was done on some reasonable basis. In 1991, as a result of legal challenges filed by Common Cause against soft money finances, the FEC standardized the use of soft money by establishing allocation formulas for the use of hard and soft money by party organizations to reflect the fact that "joint activities," such as voter turnout drives, affected federal and nonfederal elections. These rulings in effect sanctioned the use of unregulated monies in connection with federal elections, and thus they encouraged national party organizations to take advantage of soft money financing.

By the end of the 1980s, party soft money had become a major component of national campaign expenditures, with each party spending tens of millions of dollars on activities that could influence the outcome of federal elections. Most of this money was raised through unlimited contributions from corporations, labor unions, and wealthy individuals willing to give large contributions of up to $100,000 or more. Advocates of campaign finance reform decried the practice, arguing that it made a mockery of contribution limits and rendered the expenditure limits of the presidential public funding system meaningless. But Congress took no action to address this new form of funding. As a result, national party committees raised increasingly large sums of soft money. Soft money receipts grew from $86 million in 1992 to close to $260 million in 1996 to almost $500 million in 2000. This growth in unregulated contributions resurrected concerns about the corruptive effects of large contributions in the political process and the role of elected officials in the solicitation of such contributions.

One of the factors that led to the surge in soft money financing in the late 1990s was the discovery of new ways to spend these funds. Beginning in the 1996 election cycle, parties began to move beyond voter mobilization and grass-roots activities and use these funds to pay for broadcast advertising campaigns. These campaigns were designed to exploit the distinction made in *Buckley* and its progeny between "express advocacy" communications that were subject to federal regulation and "issue advocacy" communications that were not. The parties interpreted this distinction to mean that any communication that did not include the specific terms of express advocacy, such as "vote for" or "elect," could be financed in part with soft money. In 1996 the parties spent tens of millions of dollars on issue ads featuring federal candidates, and particularly in support of their presidential nominees. Because no regulatory action was taken to discourage this practice after the election, parties placed even greater emphasis on this tactic in 2000, spending more than $100 million on issue advertisements that featured federal candidates. This new financial tactic changed the ways in which federal campaigns were financed, because a significant portion of the monies spent to elect federal candidates now came from unlimited contributions, especially in the key battleground elections that were the focus of party activity.

Reforming the Reforms: The Bipartisan Campaign Reform Act

The growth of soft money and issue advocacy convinced many advocates of reform that the FECA regulatory structure had essentially become meaningless and that bold changes in the system were once again necessary. As in the past, this demand for change was supported by financial controversies and scandals that were associated with the soft money phenomenon. The unprecedented financial activities in the 1996 election and news reports linking preferential political access to soft money gifts

Members of the prominent public interest group Common Cause rally outside the Capitol in March 2002, before the Senate vote on the Bipartisan Campaign Reform Act. Source: Common Cause

fueled a major controversy over party fund-raising tactics in the aftermath of the 1996 election. Congress, the Department of Justice, and the FEC all launched investigations into party fund-raising efforts, with the most prominent inquiries conducted by a Senate investigating committee led by Tennessee Republican Fred Thompson. The Thompson Committee revealed that the Democratic Party had received millions of dollars in contributions from illegal and questionable sources, and the party responded by returning about $3 million in questionable contributions to donors. The inquiries also led the White House to release documents indicating that President Bill Clinton had attended more than a hundred coffee klatches at the White House with major contributors and that Vice President Al Gore had been soliciting contributions for the party from his office, including gifts of $50,000 or more. These disclosures, as well as other revelations about the role of federal officeholders in the solicitation of soft money gifts, once again placed campaign finance reform on the congressional agenda.

The Reform Debate

The reform debate in the wake of the 1996 election was notably different from the debates that had taken place over the last ten years. Instead of focusing on congressional elections and public subsidies, reformers now concentrated on party fund-raising and the activities of organized groups, with an emphasis on mechanisms to close the soft money and issue advocacy loopholes. The debate centered on a proposal developed under the leadership of Senators John McCain, an Arizona Republican,

and Russell Feingold, a Wisconsin Democrat, that sought to ban soft money in federal elections and create a new standard for election communications that would restrict the use of unregulated monies for candidate-specific broadcast advertisements.[13]

Three successive Congresses considered the McCain-Feingold plan, which received majority support in both the House and Senate in legislative deliberations characterized by a variety of unusual procedural steps. But the plan was defeated several times, because advocates were unable to amass the sixty votes needed to defeat a filibuster in the Senate. Finally, in early 2002 the bill received the sixty votes needed to overcome a filibuster, aided by a pro-reform political environment created by the bankruptcy of the Enron Corporation, a giant energy company, and subsequent questions about the influence of the corporation's political contributions on legislative and administrative actions that benefited the company. In March 2002, President George W. Bush signed the bill, entitled the Bipartisan Campaign Reform Act, into law.

The BCRA Provisions

The BCRA consists of a set of complicated provisions designed to ensure that monies spent on federal election–related activity comes from regulated sources.[14] The current federal contribution and spending regulations under the BCRA are listed in Table 6-1. One of the central pillars of the act is a ban on soft money. The law prohibits federal officials and candidates, as well as national party leaders and their agents, from soliciting, receiving, spending, or transferring any funds that are not subject to federal contribution limits and reporting requirements. In an effort to discourage circumvention of this ban, the law also regulates fund-raising by federal officeholders and candidates and national party committees for political organizations that conduct activities related to federal elections. In particular, the rules generally prohibit federal officials from raising unrestricted contributions for organized groups or state and local political parties, although they do provide an exemption for federal officeholders seeking state or local office and allow federal officials to appear as speakers or featured guests at state or local party fund-raisers that may be raising monies subject to state rather than federal law.

In addition to banning soft money at the national level, the BCRA has more explicit rules about the types of state and local party activity that have to be financed with federally regulated funds. The act sets forth a new

Table 6-1 Federal Contribution and Spending Regulations under the Bipartisan Campaign Reform Act of 2002

Donor or Spender (Recipient)	Federal candidates	National party committees	State party committees (federal accounts)	Federal PACs (non-connected and segregated funds)	Coordinated expenditures (coordinated with candidate)	Independent expenditures/express advocacy (not coordinated with candidate)	Electioneering communications	"Levin" accounts
Individuals [a] (excluding foreign nationals without greencards)	$2,000 per election [b]; $37,500 per cycle	$25,000 per year; $57,500 per cycle	$10,000 per year; $37,500 per cycle	$5,000 per year; $37,500 per cycle	$2,000 per election (considered contributions); $37,500 per cycle	Unlimited, but must be disclosed to the FEC	Unlimited, but must be disclosed to the FEC	Whatever state law permits, up to $10,000
National party committees	Senate candidates $35,000 per election; presidential and House candidates $5,000 per election	Unlimited transfers of funds to other party committees	Unlimited transfers of funds to other party committees	$5,000 per year	See spending formulas for types of candidates[c-e] coordinated expenditures are in addition to contributions	Unlimited (except to presidential candidates)[f]; Must be disclosed	Unlimited, but must be disclosed	Prohibited
State party committees (federal accounts)	$5,000 per election	Unlimited transfers of funds to other party committees	Unlimited transfers of funds to other party committees	$5,000 per year	Pres. candidates $5,000 per election (are contributions); Senate candidate (see formula[d]); House candidate (see formula[e]) (for House and Senate, in addition to contributions)	Unlimited, but must be disclosed	Unlimited, but must be disclosed	Prohibited
PACs (multicandidate PACs)	$5,000 per year	$15,000 per year	$5,000 per year	$5,000 per year	$5,000 per year (are contributions)	Unlimited, but must be disclosed	Unlimited, but must be disclosed	Whatever state law permits, up to $10,000
PACs (nonmulticandidate PACs)	$2,000 per year	$25,000 per year	$10,000 per year	$5,000 per year	$2,000 per election (considered contributions)	Unlimited, but must be disclosed	Unlimited, but must be disclosed	Whatever state law permits, up to $10,000

Corporations and unions	Prohibited	Prohibited	Prohibited	Prohibited (but may pay administrative costs of connected PACs)	Prohibited	Prohibited	Prohibited	Whatever state law permits, up to $10,000
Section 527 organizations not registered with FEC	Prohibited	Prohibited	Prohibited	Prohibited	Prohibited if incorporated	Prohibited if incorporated	Prohibited if incorporated. If not incorporated, unlimited so long as using only funds contributed by individuals and disclosed to the FEC if over $10,000	Whatever state law permits, up to $10,000
Section 501(c)(4)s and (c)(6)s	Prohibited	Prohibited	Prohibited	Prohibited	Prohibited	Prohibited, except for qualifying 501 (c)(4) MCFL corporations	Prohibited, except for qualifying 501 (c)(4) MCFL corporations	Whatever state law permits, up to $10,000

Source: Campaign Legal Center, *The Campaign Finance Guide* (Washington, D.C.: Campaign Legal Center, 2004), www.campaignfinanceguide.org.

Note: MCFL refers to the Supreme Court case *FEC v. Massachusetts Citizens for Life, Inc.*, 479 U.S. 238 (1986).

[a] Individuals are subject to a $95,000 per two-year election cycle aggregate limit. Of that limit, a $57,500 limit is placed on federal noncandidate contributions, including no more than $37,500 to political action committees (PACs) and state and local parties' federal accounts, and a $37,500 limit on federal candidate contributions.

[b] With the "millionaire's provision," the contribution limits are increased (tripled to $6,000 for a House candidate and up to $12,000 for a Senate candidate). Where applicable, any amount over $2,000 does not apply against the individual's aggregate contribution limit.

[c] Coordinated expenditure limits for national party committees to presidential candidates are limited to $.02 × U.S. voting-age population × the cost of living adjustment. For 2004, this figure was $16.2 million.

[d] Coordinated expenditure limits for party committees (both national and state) to senatorial candidates are limited to the greater of $20,000 or $.02 × voting-age population of the state × the cost of living adjustment. Coordinated expenditure limit increases when the "millionaire's provision" is triggered.

[e] Coordinated expenditure limits for party committees (both national and state) to House candidates are limited to $10,000 × the cost of living adjustment, which for 2004 was $37,310. Coordinated expenditure limit increases when the "millionaire's provision" is triggered.

[f] A national party committee cannot make independent expenditures for its presidential candidate if it is also designated as the authorized committee of its presidential candidate.

Republican senator John McCain of Arizona (left) and Democratic senator Russell Feingold of Wisconsin (center) discuss their campaign finance bill in March 2001. Source: Scott Ferrell/Congressional Quarterly

definition of federal election activity that includes voter registration drives conducted in the last 120 days of an election, voter identification and turnout programs conducted in years when a federal candidate is on the ballot, and advertising that promotes, supports, attacks, or opposes a candidate for federal office. Such activities must be financed with hard money.

Acknowledging the traditional role of parties in the political process, the law also includes some provisions designed to ease the financial burdens that parties are likely to experience as a result of the loss of soft money funding. Most notably, the BCRA increases the contribution limits in effect under the FECA to allow individuals to give more to party organizations. The law also increases the aggregate amount an individual donor may contribute to candidates, parties, and PACs under federal law to $95,000 per election cycle, nearly double the FECA's aggregate ceiling of $25,000 per calendar year (the equivalent of $50,000 per election cycle). Within this aggregate limit, the statute provides a sublimit of $57,500 every two years in aggregate contributions to parties and PACs (though no more than $37,500 of this amount may be given to entities other than national party committees). Thus a donor who chooses to do so may contribute up to $57,500 every two years to party committees. As for contributions by individuals to specific party committees, the BCRA raises the annual limit on contributions to a national party committee from $20,000 to $25,000 and the allowable amount to a state party committee under federal law from $5,000 to $10,000. The law also raises the amount an individual may contribute to a federal candi-

date from $1,000 per election to $2,000 per election, and it increases the combined amount a national party committee and senatorial committee may give to a Senate candidate to $35,000, double the $17,500 allowed by the FECA. All of these contribution ceilings, except for the $10,000 state party committee limit, are indexed for inflation. But the changes were limited to individual donations. The law made no changes in the amounts an individual may contribute to a PAC or in the sum a PAC may contribute to a party committee or another PAC.

The new law also provides some leeway to state and local parties to spend nonfederal (soft money) funds in certain circumstances. Some members of Congress voiced concern during the debates on the legislation that a ban on soft money would reduce the role of parties in registering and turning out voters. To address this concern, the law includes a provision authored by Sen. Carl Levin, a Michigan Democrat, that allows state and local committees to use a combination of federal and nonfederal funds to pay for generic voter registration drives conducted more than 120 days before a general election and to finance generic voter registration and turnout drives that do not mention a federal candidate. These types of activities can be financed with a combination of hard money and "Levin Amendment monies" that can be raised in amounts of up to $10,000 per donor, if permitted by state law. In an effort to ensure that the availability of Levin funds did not become a major loophole in the soft money ban, Congress placed restrictions on the use of these funds. Most important, all federal and nonfederal funds used in association with activities exempted under this provision must be raised by the state or local committee that spends them. Monies transferred from national committees or other state committees may not be used for this purpose. Furthermore, no Levin funds may be used to finance activities that refer to a federal candidate or to pay for broadcast, cable, or satellite communications, unless the message solely refers to state or local candidates.

The other central pillar of the BCRA is a revised conception of "electioneering communications," designed to address the lack of regulation on candidate-specific issue advocacy advertisements. The law expands the realm of regulated political communications beyond the "magic words" doctrine that the Supreme Court suggested in *Buckley* to encompass advertisements that are targeted at federal candidates but do not use specific words of express advocacy. Accordingly, the law establishes a new regulatory standard for express advocacy by defining "electioneering communications" as any broadcast, cable, or satellite communications that refer to a clearly identified federal candidate, that are made within thirty days of a primary election or sixty days of a general election, and that target the electorate of the candidate. The law also contains an alternative definition that includes any broadcast, cable, or satellite communication that promotes or supports, or attacks or opposes, a federal candidate (regardless of whether it expressly advocates a vote for or against a candidate) and is suggestive of no other plausible meaning other than an exhortation to vote for or against a candidate.

Any electioneering communication that meets the law's new standard for express advocacy can be financed only with monies allowed under federal contribution limits. In most cases, this means that no corporate or labor union money can be used to pay for such communications. Groups organized as tax-exempt public issue advocacy organizations under the tax code, however, would be able to receive and spend unlimited amounts on advertising, so long as the funding consists solely of contributions from individuals. Otherwise, political committees and other organized groups are still able to advertise for or against candidates—with no restriction on the amounts they can spend—but they have to use funds subject to federal limits. Corporations or labor unions therefore must use PAC monies rather than treasury funds. The new rules also strengthen the disclosure requirements for electioneering communications by requiring that any spender, including individuals or unincorporated associations, disclose expenditures in excess of a total of $10,000 and any contributions of more than $1,000.

The BCRA is designed primarily to restore the regulatory structure intended by the FECA, but one major provision departs markedly from previous reform measures. The law includes a "millionaire's provision," which eases contribution limits for candidates facing self-financed opponents. The presidential candidacies of independent H. Ross Perot in 1992 and 1996 and of Republican Steve Forbes in 1996 and 2000 had highlighted the ability of some people to run for office simply by spending millions of dollars from their personal wealth. In the 1990s, some high-profile Senate and House races also featured self-financed candidates who spent large sums of their own money to contest open seats or take on incumbents. The fear of having to face such a free-spending opponent led to congressional support for a rule that would make it easier to raise money against such an opponent. Accordingly, the BCRA sets forth a complicated set of formulas that would trigger higher contribution limits and higher levels of party support for candidates facing self-financed challengers. Depending on the amount spent by the self-funded candidate, contribution limits could be increased to up to $12,000 per donor in Senate races and $6,000 per donor in House races. In both Senate and House

races, the limits on the amounts party committees could spend in coordination with a candidate also would increase in response to spending by a self-funded opponent.

Challenges to the BCRA

As soon as the BCRA was adopted, it was challenged in court by a broad array of plaintiffs, including Republican senator Mitch McConnell of Kentucky, the chief legislative opponent of the law; the party committees; and the American Civil Liberties Union, the National Rifle Association, and the National Association of Broadcasters. Anticipating a legal challenge, the congressional sponsors of the statute had included a provision that placed litigation on an extraordinary "fast-track" process that led to a Supreme Court decision before the start of the 2004 election year. In December 2003, a divided high court issued its ruling in *McConnell v. Federal Election Commission* in which a majority upheld the major provisions of the law.[15] Following the doctrinal framework established in *Buckley,* the Court reaffirmed the constitutional interest in safeguarding the political process from corruption or the appearance of corruption, and in doing so it articulated a broad understanding of this interest, noting that it did not simply entail quid pro quo exchanges for contributions, but also "undue influence on an officeholder's judgment, and the appearance of such influence." The Court concluded that large soft money contributions can corrupt or create such an appearance and thus upheld the ban on soft money. It further noted that regulation to prevent circumvention of contribution limits was also justified to prevent corruption or its appearance and upheld the restrictions on the use of soft money by nonfederal party committees for federal election activity, as defined under the law, to ensure that state parties did not become conduits for unregulated monies. The Court relied on this anticircumvention rationale as well to uphold the prohibition on the use of soft money to finance public communications that promote or attack federal candidates.

As for the BCRA's definition of "electioneering communications" and revised conception of what constitutes express advocacy broadcast advertising subject to federal regulation, the Court's majority acknowledged that the new standard was developed by Congress after the "magic words" standard developed in the aftermath of *Buckley* had failed. The Court noted that the means of distinguishing between express and issue advocacy was a matter of statutory law rather than strict constitutional rule, and it found the BCRA rules tailored narrowly enough to withstand constitutional scrutiny. The Court did, however, leave an opening for subsequent legal challenges if a plaintiff could show that the new rules had a chilling effect on political speech based on the application of new regulations. The more stringent disclosure requirements were also upheld.

That said, the Court struck down provisions of the law that would have prohibited contributions from minors,

Rep. Roscoe Bartlett, Republican from Maryland, introduces the First Amendment Restoration Act in September 2004. The campaign reform legislation would repeal a provision of the McCain-Feingold campaign law that banned non–PAC-funded issue advocacy and other such references to federal candidates in ads within thirty days of a primary election or sixty days of a general election. Source: Roger L. Wollenberger/UPI/Landov

and it forced party committees to choose whether to support candidates with limited coordinated expenditures or unlimited independent expenditures at the time of a candidate's nomination. It rendered no opinion on the constitutionality of the "millionaire's provision," noting that the plaintiffs lacked standing to bring such a challenge. The Court did leave open the possibility that a challenge could be brought in the future if a plaintiff could demonstrate harm. In short, instead of accepting only parts of Congress's reform package, as it did in *Buckley,* the Court essentially left the regulatory plan intact. This outcome reflected in part the care the congressional sponsors had taken to limit legislative changes to incremental reforms that could be accommodated within the *Buckley* framework. Although the plaintiffs contended that the new rules were too broad and vague to be upheld on the basis of prior court rulings, a majority of the Court was willing to show deference to Congress and in large part reflected the view that the BCRA required no major shift from prior doctrine. It thus affirmed the beginning of another stage in the quest to control the influence of money in American politics.

Conclusion

For more than a century, Congress and state legislatures have been adopting measures to limit the influence of money in election campaigns. The enduring character of

this issue reflects the inherent difficulty in attempting to regulate a dynamic process such as the flow of money in the political process. Political campaigns are continually adapting to changes in the broader political environment and developing new methods of funding, which means that any laws must be revised from time to time to account for changing practices and the consequences of reform, both intended and unintended. This task has proved to be a particularly vexing one for legislators because of the often competing goals and values on which campaign finance laws are based and the need to reconcile fundamental principles, including the right of free speech, economic liberties, the integrity of representative government, and the ideal of political equality. Diverse ideological perspectives on the relative importance of different principles and objectives result in different perspectives on the scope of regulation and the basic purposes that regulation should seek to achieve, which constrains the process of reaching agreement on campaign finance laws. Policy views are also influenced by partisan and practical considerations that often reflect the distinctive patterns of funding that characterize the electioneering efforts of incumbents and challengers, Democrats and Republicans, and party and nonparty organizations. As a result, most efforts at reform usually culminate in additional calls for reform.

Adoption of the BCRA is therefore unlikely to differ from previous reform efforts. Although passage of the law is considered by advocates of reform to constitute an important step in improving the system, many also argue that more needs to be done. In particular, advocates of further regulation note that the BCRA failed to address the problems of the presidential public funding system. Presidential campaign finance is beset by major problems, including spending limits that are no longer adequate to accommodate the costs of presidential primary campaigns, timetables that no longer conform to the practical realities of presidential contests, and deteriorating finances that threaten the fiscal health of the subsidy program. The inadequacies of the system were largely responsible for the decision by George W. Bush to opt out of the public funding program during the 2000 and 2004 primaries, a move that was followed by some of the leading Democratic contenders in 2004. The prospect of diminished candidate participation in the future has led some reformers to call for a revamping of the public funding program. But others contend that the experience of the presidential system points to the failure of public spending and the idea of expenditure limits, and thus they call for an end to the program altogether.

Similarly, many reformers argue that enforcement of the law must be improved if an effective regulatory system is ever to be achieved, and they call for fundamental reform of the FEC. Almost since its inception, the commission has consisted of three Democrats and three Republicans, who are appointed in a process in which one party defers to the other in the support of nominations. As a result, the commission is divided along partisan lines that often make it difficult to gain the four votes needed for regulatory action and especially hard to secure support for regulatory steps opposed by the major parties. These problems have led some legislators to call for a restructuring of the commission and an expansion of its enforcement authority.

Still others argue that recent legislation has done little to curb rising campaign costs or the emphasis on fundraising in campaigns. These advocates continue to push for free or reduced-cost television time for candidates or other forms of public subsidy. Some argue that the influence of money in the political process will not be fully addressed until a system of full public funding is created for political campaigns. These observers point to the public

funding programs adopted in the late 1990s in Maine and Arizona as models for other states and Congress to follow. In these two states, "clean election laws" provide full public subsidies to candidates who raise a small number of small donations, agree to raise no additional private money, and accept strict spending limits. Others, however, contend that even such comprehensive approaches as full public funding will fail to stem the flow of money in the electoral system and will simply encourage a shift of monies to undisclosed and unregulated sources, including political organizations that are not subject to campaign finance rules. This argument and the experience with unintended consequences under past regulations have led some observers to conclude that the only workable system is one in which the flow of money is left largely unregulated, subject only to public disclosure and reporting requirements.

The efforts of the last century to restrict campaign monies have created a more participatory and transparent system of political finance. But they did not resolve the myriad issues associated with the role of private funding in a representative electoral system. Campaign finance reform will thus continue to be a matter of public debate for the foreseeable future.

Notes

1. Quoted in Robert E. Mutch, *Campaigns, Congress, and Courts: The Making of Federal Campaign Finance Law* (New York: Praeger, 1988), xvi. Also see Robert E. Mutch, "The First Federal Campaign Finance Bills," in *Money and Politics,* ed. Paula Baker (University Park: Pennsylvania State University Press, 2002).

2. The phrase "spoils system" was coined by a U.S. senator in 1832 to justify the practice of discharging the federal workers of the party defeated in a presidential election and replacing them with followers of the victorious party.

3. Herbert Croly, *Marcus Alonzo Hanna: His Life and Work* (New York: Macmillan, 1912), 325.

4. For estimates of presidential campaign spending in elections before 1976, see Herbert E. Alexander, *Financing Politics,* 4th ed. (Washington, D.C.: CQ Press, 1992).

5. *Burroughs v. United States,* 290 U.S. 534 (1934).

6. For a summary of state campaign finance laws prior to World War II, see S. Sydney Minault, *Corrupt Practices Legislation in the 48 States* (Chicago: Council of State Governments, 1942).

7. Joseph E. Cantor, "Political Spending by Organized Labor: Background and Current Issues," Congressional Research Service Report, 96-484 GOV, May 29, 1996, 1–2.

8. Congressional Quarterly, *Dollar Politics* (Washington, D.C.: CQ Press, 1982), 8; and Alexander, *Financing Politics,* 11.

9. For background on the FECA and its subsequent amendments, see Federal Election Commission, *Legislative History of*

Federal Election Campaign Act Amendments of 1974 (Washington, D.C.: Government Printing Office, 1977), and *Legislative History of Federal Election Campaign Act Amendments of 1976* (Washington, D.C.: Government Printing Office, 1977). Frank J. Sorauf provides a thoughtful assessment of the FECA and its effects in *Money in American Elections* (Glenview, Ill.: Scott, Foresman, 1988), and in *Inside Campaign Finance* (New Haven, Conn.: Yale University Press, 1992).

10. *Buckley v. Valeo,* 424 U.S. 1 (1976).

11. This discussion of state campaign finance laws is based on the analysis in Michael J. Malbin and Thomas L. Gais, *The Day after Reform: Sobering Campaign Finance Lessons from the American States* (Albany, N.Y.: Rockefeller Institute Press, 1998), 14–23.

12. Sorauf, *Money in American Elections,* 78–79.

13. The legislative debate over the McCain-Feingold bill is recounted in Diana Dwyre and Victoria A. Farrar-Myers, *Legislative Labyrinth: Congress and Campaign Finance Reform* (Washington, D.C.: CQ Press, 2001).

14. For summaries of the provisions of the BCRA, see Campaign Legal Center, *The Campaign Finance Guide* (Washington, D.C.: Campaign Legal Center, 2004), www.campaign financeguide.org. For a discussion of the law's provisions, see Robert F. Bauer, *More Soft Money Hard Law* (Washington, D.C.: Perkins Coie, 2004); and Michael J. Malbin, ed., *Life after Reform* (Lanham, Md.: Rowman and Littlefield, 2003).

15. *McConnell v. Federal Election Commission,* 124 S. Ct. 644–648 (2003).

Suggested Readings

Alexander, Herbert E. *Financing Politics*. 4th ed. Washington, D.C.: CQ Press, 1992.

Baker, Paula, ed. *Money and Politics*. University Park: Pennsylvania State University Press, 2002.

Bauer, Robert F. *More Soft Money Hard Law*. Washington, D.C.: Perkins Coie, 2004.

Corrado, Anthony. *Campaign Finance Reform*. New York: Century Foundation Press, 2000.

Corrado, Anthony, Thomas E. Mann, Daniel Ortiz, Trevor Potter, and Frank Sorauf, eds.*Campaign Finance Reform: A Sourcebook*. Washington, D.C.: Brookings, 1997.

Dwyre, Diana, and Victoria A. Farrar-Myers. *Legislative Labyrinth: Congress and Campaign Finance Reform*. Washington, D.C.: CQ Press, 2001.

Fox, George L. "Corrupt Practices and Elections Laws in the United States since 1890." *Proceedings of the American Political Science Association* 2 (1905): 171–186.

Heard, Alexander. *The Costs of Democracy*. Chapel Hill: University of North Carolina Press, 1960.

Magleby, David B. *Financing the 2000 Election*. Washington, D.C.: Brookings, 2002.

Malbin, Michael J., and Thomas L. Gais. *The Day after Reform: Sobering Campaign Finance Lessons from the American States*. Albany: Rockefeller Institute Press, 1998.

Minault, S. Sydney. *Corrupt Practices Legislation in the 48 States*. Chicago: Council of State Governments, 1942.

Mutch, Robert E. *Campaigns, Congress, and Courts: The Making of Federal Campaign Finance Law*. New York: Praeger, 1988.

Overacker, Louise. *Money in Elections*. New York: Macmillan, 1932.

Pollock, James K., Jr. *Party Campaign Funds*. New York: Knopf, 1926.

Shannon, Jasper B. *Money and Politics*. New York: Random House, 1959.

Sorauf, Frank J. *Inside Campaign Finance*. New Haven, Conn.: Yale University Press, 1992.

———. *Money in American Elections*. Glenview, Ill.: Scott, Foresman, 1988.

Thompson, Joel A., and Gary F. Moncrief. *Campaign Finance in State Legislative Elections*. Washington, D.C.: CQ Press, 1998.

PART III
Voters and Voting

CHAPTER 7

Overview of the Electorate and Party Identification

Peter F. Galderisi

Voter turnout in the United States, by both international and U.S. historical standards, is extremely low. In almost all U.S. elections, including the relatively high-turnout presidential election of 2004, those who do not vote exceed the proportion of those who vote for the winning candidate. If politicians believe in representing the concerns, views, and aspirations of all citizens, then any differences between voters and nonvoters would be of little consequence.[1] Yet if those concerns, views, and aspirations are different, then politicians, acting strategically to win election or reelection, may cater disproportionately to those who do vote. The fact, for example, that older Americans are both more likely to vote and constitute an ever-growing proportion of the voting-age population may explain why the political leaders of both parties have for decades danced around the question of Social Security solvency and are now both competing to provide the best prescription drug benefit programs for the elderly, regardless of the cost. Meanwhile, public college tuitions (paid for by mainly young students and their middle-aged parents) continue to increase in states facing severe budgetary constraints.

Starting from the premise that politicians have an electoral incentive to cater to those who participate regularly in elections, this chapter describes the different demographics, ideologies, and issue concerns of voters and nonvoters. In particular, it reveals and tracks the changing nature of partisanship. Partisans, after all, represent the core constituency of most candidates. Their support is usually needed to win a party's nomination, and their votes are the single most important determinant of general election outcomes.[2]

Defining the Electorate

In the United States, defining the electorate is complicated. The electorate may refer broadly to those who are qualified by citizenship and age to participate in elections or to that subset who formally register to vote. Some journalists and academic scholars limit their definition further to those who participate in politics on a regular

basis.[3] This chapter starts with the broadest definition of *electorate* and discusses the legal circumstances that have broadened or restricted entry into the voting process. Chapter 8 discusses the conditions under which members of the legally eligible electorate decide whether to exercise their franchise and how.

The chief legal impediment to voting is the availability of the franchise (the right to vote). That right has changed substantially since the writing of the U.S. Constitution in 1787. Although the rules of enfranchisement have always been predominantly a function of state governments, constitutional amendments now extend the franchise nationally to all citizens age eighteen and over (Twenty-sixth Amendment, 1971) and without regard for race (Fifteenth Amendment, 1870), gender (Nineteenth Amendment, 1920), or ability to pay a poll tax (Twenty-fourth Amendment, 1964). In addition, citizens of the nation's capital have, since ratification of the Twenty-third Amendment in 1961, been granted the right to vote, but only for presidential electors (see Chapter 3 for a full discussion of changes in suffrage over time). One major exception to these rules is that almost all states limit the franchise of convicted felons—some while they are incarcerated, some while on parole, and some permanently. This felon exclusion is no small matter, because it falls disproportionately on black males. According to the chief advocate for reform, the Sentencing Project, roughly 13 percent of black males are denied the right to vote because of a felony conviction, and they represent over one-third of all disenfranchised voters. In some states, most notably in the South, the rate of black male disenfranchisement reaches 25 percent, and that figure could reach as high as 40 percent in the future.[4]

Having the right to vote does not end with the legal definition of the franchise. All states, with the exception of North Dakota, require some form of formal registration before a voter is legally able to vote.[5] States vary in terms of their requirements for registration, but some U.S. Supreme Court decisions and national laws, particularly the National Voter Registration Act of 1993 (NVRA), commonly called the Motor Voter law, have added some uniformity to the states' individual legal requirements. Since 1972, court decisions have generally limited a state's residency requirement to no more than thirty days. The NVRA, among other actions, prohibits a state from removing or purging citizens from voter registration lists after a period of nonvoting, thus removing the need for the occasional voter to reregister.

Although registration laws have been progressively liberalized by national or state action, with many states allowing registration at shopping malls, by mail, when obtaining a driver's license, or on the day of the election, registration laws still pose a cost that many citizens are not willing or able to bear. Moving from one state to another requires not only re-registration (a circumstance not common throughout the world) but also familiarizing oneself with the local tone and often distinct style of politics. Even moving within a state can prevent someone from voting, at least for local elections.

The legal definition of *electorate* is even more limited when it comes to primary elections and caucuses—nomination contests used to select who will represent each party in the general election. As discussed in more detail in Chapter 5, in states with closed primary laws the "electorate" is limited to those who, by formal registration or other, less stringent means, have listed themselves as a member of the party in whose nominating process they wish to participate. Under the strictest of closed primary rules, voters who indicated they were not affiliated with any party when they registered to vote are eliminated from the potential voting pool. They are thus unable to help choose those candidates—Republicans or Democrats—with the only real chance of winning the general election.

In contemporary U.S. elections, registration laws do seem to have a substantial impact on voter turnout. Steven J. Rosenstone and John Mark Hansen estimated that between 1960 and 1980 easement of voting requirements increased turnout by almost 2 percent. Voting turnout has also been consistently high in those states with the easiest registration requirements, such as in Minnesota where eligible citizens can register at the polling place on election day. It has been estimated that if all states matched the laws of these least restrictive states, turnout would increase nationwide by as much as 9 percent.[6] Yet voting turnout is low by both international and U.S. historical standards, a fact that cannot be explained exclusively by registration requirements and other legal barriers. If that were the case, voting turnout should have risen with enactment of the Motor Voter law. Instead, voting turnout declined after the law was passed in 1993. Similarly, in the 1920s the addition of millions of women to the eligibility rolls did not immediately translate into votes, with the result that voter turnout was even lower than it is now. Having the means to vote must therefore be accompanied by sufficient motive. The same is true with other forms of participation, perhaps even more so. Having the ability to write, for example, does not guarantee that an individual will correspond with his member of Congress.

Voters and Nonvoters: Two Different Groups?

As detailed in Chapter 8, certain types of people—because of the perceived importance of issues, an attachment to a political party and its philosophy, the attractiveness of candidates, the perceived closeness of the vote, or a traditional obligation to democratic processes—are more likely to vote and engage in other forms of political participation than others. This chapter takes a look at how these differences affect the demographic profiles of voters and nonvoters to determine whether the differences might project a biased image and set of concerns to candidates assessing their electoral strategies and fortunes (see Box 7-1).

Demographic Differences

Table 7-1 lists the education, age, income, race, marital status, religion, and other demographics of voters and

---

BOX 7-1

READING DEMOGRAPHIC PROFILES: A QUICK GUIDE

Demographic profiles of the electorate do not directly indicate causality. After all, voting does not cause one to be older or to obtain certain racial characteristics. Rather, such profiles indicate the potential relevance of each group of voters—that is, who is more likely to be heard—to everyone, from the candidate on down, concerned with the next election.

That relevance is a function of both the likelihood that a member of a group will vote and the proportionate size of the group within the total potential electorate. A certain group—for example, men and women over age seventy with advanced degrees—may be very likely to vote (perhaps 90 percent do), but if that group constitutes only 1 percent of the eligible electorate, its potential impact on the outcome of an election, and the attention it receives from politicians, will be slight except under the most competitive of circumstances (members of the group are heavily concentrated in particular "battleground" districts and states, or their intensity of participation, including contributing time and money to campaigns, is much greater than the norm). A proportionately large but nonparticipating group, such as young people or the poor, would not be of immediate electoral consequence, but it might be a viable group from which to mobilize future voters. Groups that are both proportionately large and likely to participate, such as older citizens, should carry the greatest immediate electoral weight.

Table 7-1 Voters and Nonvoters by Demographic Category: 2000 Current Population Survey (CPS) and 2000 and 2004 National Election Studies (NES) (percent)

	2000 CPS		2000 NES		2004 NES	
	Voters	Nonvoters	Voters	Nonvoters	Voters	Nonvoters
< High school degree	9.2	21.7	9.6	28.8	10.0	28.6
High school degree	29.5	39.3	30.3	40.8	29.3	38.9
Some college	30.1	25.8	29.7	24.1	29.6	24.6
Bachelor's degree or higher	31.2	13.3	30.4	6.3	31.1	7.9
Age						
18–25	8.9	22.5	10.8	23.7	10.7	23.7
26–35	15.5	21.0	15.5	23.3	16.2	18.6
36–55	42.8	35.7	41.4	34.0	39.8	33.2
56–70	19.9	11.9	20.1	10.7	21.5	13.8
Over 70	12.9	8.9	12.3	8.4	11.8	10.7
Working class	NA	NA	42.7	63.0	42.3	63.9
Middle class	NA	NA	42.0	30.9	40.9	28.2
Upper middle/upper class	NA	NA	15.3	6.1	16.8	7.9
Annual income						
Under $15,000	10.2	20.8	10.1	25.9	9.0	21.7
$15,000–$34,999	22.7	30.0	26.5	28.4	16.4	29.1
$35,000–$49,999	16.6	16.5	15.5	20.3	13.6	10.7
$50,000–$74,999[a]	21.8	16.5	26.4	15.6	23.9	13.1
$75,000 and over	28.7	16.1	21.5	9.7	37.1	25.4
Union household	NA	NA	16.7	13.2	20.9	12.3
Nonunion household	NA	NA	83.3	86.8	79.1	87.7
Male	46.5	49.3	44.8	39.0	48.3	53.0
Female	53.5	50.7	55.2	61.0	51.7	47.0
White	85.8	82.3	79.0[b]	73.5	75.8	62.9
Black	11.7	13.0	11.7	11.4	14.1	20.3
Hispanic	5.4	9.6	4.3	9.3	5.5	11.2
Asian	1.8	3.5	NA	NA	NA	NA
Married/widowed	71.8	53.1	69.7	51.4	66.8	54.0
Divorced/separated	10.8	14.6	10.4	14.8	12.2	12.7
Never married/partnered	17.3	32.3	19.9	33.8	21.0	33.3
Practicing Protestant	NA	NA	33.5	18.4	28.6	22.1
Practicing Catholic	NA	NA	23.1	12.8	18.0	18.6
Practicing Jew[c]	NA	NA	1.5	0.7	2.6	0.4
Practicing other	NA	NA	14.7	20.3	18.7	17.0
Does not attend any religious service	NA	NA	27.0	47.8	32.1	41.9

Sources: Current Population Survey, 2000, http://www.bls.census.gov/cps/cpsmain.htm; National Election Studies, 2000 and 2004, Center for Political Studies, University of Michigan, Ann Arbor, www.umich.edu/~nes/.

Note: NA = not applicable for study or numbers too low to be meaningful. Entries represent the proportion of voters and nonvoters with the listed demographics. Percentages should be read down columns. For example, in the CPS survey 9.2 percent of those who claimed to have voted never completed high school. Percentages do not necessarily add up to 100 because CPS racial/ethnic categories overlap, because not all NES race/ethnic categories are listed, and because of standard rounding error. For NES demographic data, those who refused to specify a category or responded "Don't know" were excluded.

[a] In 2004 NES categories changed to $50,000–$79,999 and $80,000 and over.
[b] Self-designation. Categories refer to those who only specified one answer.
[c] Case size is very small, but the proportion for this and other tables is in line with other evidence.

A student at the University of California at Los Angeles (UCLA) votes in her residence hall on election day 2004. According to the 2004 NES survey, young citizens and older citizens were more likely to affiliate with the Democratic Party, whereas middle-aged Americans are more likely to be Republicans. Source: Fred Prouser/Reuters/ Landov

were still evident. In 2004 voters were 31.4 percentage points more likely than nonvoters to be interested in following the campaign. Voters also were more likely to watch television programs about the campaign, to read about the campaign in a newspaper, and to listen to political talk radio. They were also more likely to have viewed election information on the Internet, which by 2004 had become a major medium of campaign news and commentary. Interest in the 2004 elections explains part of these differences. Voters were more likely to care about both the presidential and U.S. House elections, and they seemed more knowledgeable about politics— that is, they were more likely to know the names of prominent government officials.

If politicians pay more attention to those who participate, they are attending to an active electorate that is clearly more politically concerned and knowledgeable than the general populace. Moreover, interest and knowledge carry over to other forms of political activity. For example, voters are more likely than nonvoters to intervene personally in the campaign. During the 2004 election season, they were more likely than nonvoters to discuss politics and more likely to try to influence others (Table 7-2). Although the number of cases is a bit too small to report, the data do indicate that voters were also more likely to contribute to candidates and parties, to go to rallies or public meetings, and to display buttons, bumper stickers, or signs. Voters also were more likely to participate in other political and community activities—that is, to contact public officials, to attend community meetings, to work on community issues, to do volunteer work, and to join an organization. Prior surveys indicate that those who vote were also more likely to feel it was their civic responsibility to serve on a jury, perhaps indicative of a civic culture that both fosters and is fostered by participation and within which voting is just one type of activity.[10]

Ideological and Issue Differences

In 2004 (as in other recent studies), when asked to think about their overall ideological perspective, voters were slightly more likely to identify themselves as conservatives than were nonvoters (Table 7-3). Compared with nonvoters, voters also were more likely to hold conservative positions on many issues, particularly economic ones. They were more likely to favor less government with fewer services and less likely to believe that government should guarantee jobs and provide medical insurance.[11]

The pattern becomes more complicated when it comes to race, the environment, defense, and social issues. In the 2004 election, voters were more likely than nonvoters to

nonvoters, according to the Current Population Survey (CPS) and the National Election Studies (NES), which are described in Box 7-2. Some demographic differences are apparent between the two groups. For example, the CPS sample reveals that in 2000 better-educated individuals made up 31.2 percent of the voting population, but only 13.3 percent of nonvoters. Similarly, those with the least education constituted less than a tenth of voters, but over a fifth of nonvoters. Eighteen- to twenty-five year-olds made up over 22 percent of nonvoters, but less than 10 percent of voters.[7] Almost a third of voters are over fifty-five compared with only 20.8 percent of nonvoters. Finally, voters tend to also be disproportionately white (although this gap has been sharply reduced since the 1960s), non-Hispanic, religious attendees, and married.[8]

Participatory Differences

Voting is not the only means of expressing political preferences; it is part of a cluster of civic activities undertaken by the active electorate.[9] Those who vote are more likely to familiarize themselves with the election and to participate civically in other significant ways (Table 7-2). Between the 2000 and 2004 elections, campaign interest and involvement generally increased for both voters and nonvoters. Yet major differences between the two groups

BOX 7-2
CURRENT POPULATION SURVEY AND NATIONAL ELECTION STUDIES

Modern analysis of the electorate relies heavily on survey research. Two studies that social scientists and others turn to for factual information about voting behavior are the Current Population Survey (CPS): Voting and Registration Supplement and the National Election Studies (NES). Each study has its own strengths and limitations.

The CPS (www.bls.census.gov/cps/cpsmain.htm) is a monthly survey of households conducted by the U.S. Census Bureau for the Bureau of Labor Statistics. The survey, which has been conducted since the 1940s, provides a comprehensive body of data on the labor force, employment, unemployment, and persons not in the labor force. CPS data are used by policy makers and legislators as important indicators of the U.S. economic situation and for planning and evaluating many government programs. They are also used by the press, students, academics, and the general public.

Questions on voting and registration by various demographic and socioeconomic characteristics are posed to respondents in November of congressional and presidential election years and are included in the CPS Voting and Registration Supplement. Like all full or partial U.S. Census files, the supplement has a much larger sample size (almost 135,000 in 2000) than do most academic surveys. That size allows researchers to break the sample down into smaller and smaller demographic subgroups and still have a fairly accurate representation of each of those groups.

Most census questions revolve around geographic, economic, and social characteristics and are used to track changes in these characteristics. The Voting and Registration Supplement contains only a handful of questions about voter turnout and registration. Unlike many political surveys, the CPS does not include questions on partisanship, issues, government trust, or candidate evaluations and preferences.

For a more systematic examination of U.S. elections, most scholars turn to the National Election Studies (www.umich.edu/~nes/), which date back to 1948 and were formally established as a national resource for data by the U.S. National Science Foundation in 1977. The NES, which is located at the University of Michigan, has become the standard database for studying U.S. elections. The studies include a wider range of subject areas related to campaigns and elections, including social and political issues, campaign activity, candidate evaluation and preference, and demographics. The NES conducts in-person and telephone surveys of the U.S. electorate in presidential and midterm election years, often interviews potential voters both before and after an election, and sometimes tracks respondents over a series of elections. More important, NES researchers interview both voters and nonvoters, a distinction that exit polls cannot match.

Like the CPS, standard exit polls use much larger samples than the 1,000–2,000 range used in the NES, but because of time constraints as people rush from the polls to home or to work, they can ask only a handful of both demographic and political questions.

---

oppose preferential hiring policies but less likely to favor decreasing immigration. Voters were marginally more likely than nonvoters to find jobs more important than environmental protection, but also slightly more likely to find environmental regulations more important than jobs. And voters were more likely than nonvoters to support the costs of intervention in Iraq and Afghanistan, but also slightly more likely to both favor and oppose increases in defense spending. Also in 2004 voters were more likely than nonvoters to both favor and oppose investing Social Security funds in the stock market. They were less likely to support the total abolition of abortion rights, slightly less likely to favor school vouchers (using taxpayers' money to subsidize private, often religious, school tuition), but marginally more likely to oppose gay marriage or civil unions. On many issues, nonvoters were less likely than voters to have developed clear opinions, so voters could actually have higher proportions on both sides of some issues.

However, these figures represent general attitudes, not how deeply they are held or whether they influence a person's vote. On certain issues, those espousing one side might be more likely to use that issue as a cue in deciding how to vote. For example, although voters and nonvoters differed little in 2004 on the issue of gun control, in most circumstances those who oppose gun control are more likely to vote on the basis of that opposition than those who favor gun regulation but who might vote based on their views on other, often economic issues. Politicians seem to be well aware of these differences in issue intensity or salience.

Voters are also more partisan and less independent than nonvoters. In the 2004 election, voters were only marginally less likely than nonvoters to be Democrats, but much more likely than nonvoters to be Republicans, with the difference attributed to the increased prevalence of independents in the nonvoting column. Most important from the perspective of campaigns, strong partisans

Table 7-2 Participatory Differences between Voters and Nonvoters: National Election Study 2004 (percent)

	Voters	Nonvoters
Interested in following campaigns	47.7	16.3
Watched programs about campaign	88.7	77.1
Read about campaign in newspaper	70.0	49.0
Listened to political talk radio	49.0	24.9
Saw election information on the Internet	67.2	49.6
Cared about presidential election outcome	93.1	64.9
Cared about congressional election outcome	75.7	49.0
Knew name of House Speaker	11.2	3.6
Knew name of Vice President	90.5	65.1
Knew name of Supreme Court chief justice	33.3	10.7
Discussed politics with others	86.1	58.0
Tried to influence others	53.8	28.6
Contacted public officials	22.5	8.7
Attended community meetings	31.3	11.5
Worked on community issues	31.4	13.9
Did volunteer work	45.7	21.8
Is a member of an organization	45.6	21.8

Source: National Election Study, 2004, Center for Political Studies, University of Michigan, Ann Arbor, www.umich.edu/~nes/.

Note: Entries represent the percentage of voters and nonvoters who participated in the listed activity, expressed a high level of interest or concern, or knew the names of public officials.

(the core constituency for most candidates) are much more likely to show up in the voting electorate.

Partisanship

The formal definition of a *partisan* differs across nations. In some democracies, party members are required to formally affiliate, pay dues, and carry cards defining their membership. Few such requirements exist in the United States. Formal party registration is required only to vote in the nomination contests of the parties in those states that limit participation to the parties' own members. Most states, however, either allow those without a pre-registered affiliation to vote, or allow voters to express their partisanship at the time and place of the nomination contest (in order to determine in which party's nomination contest they may participate). Even in those states with closed nominating processes, participants often have an opportunity to change their party registration before the contest actually takes place.

In the absence of a uniform national legal definition in the United States, *partisanship* can be most easily defined as a feeling of individual attachment to, or a psychological identification with, a party even without a formal membership or voting record.[12] Much like racial, ethnic, or religious identification, partisanship is also defined by what one is not. A partisan defines himself or herself not only by identification with others of like mind, but also by opposition to those in the opposing party. The stronger these two components, the stronger should be one's sense of partisanship. The definition of partisan attachment can vary, particularly in a political system that historically has decentralized voting rules, party rules, and partisan ideology. Different people may identify themselves as, for example, a Democrat without agreeing on the meaning of that term, and they may not even feel "less of a Democrat" if they occasionally vote for a candidate of the opposition party. Attitudes and behavior, however, cannot be totally different for those groups that share the same partisan identification.

Has Partisanship Declined?

Many scholars and journalists have argued that the public's acceptance of party labels and sense of partisan identification have declined. But any attempt to judge the merits of that argument must be prefaced with an

Table 7-3 Ideological and Issue Differences between Voters and Nonvoters: National Election Study, 2004 (percent)

	Voters	Nonvoters
Conservative	58.7	54.4
Moderate	5.7	7.5
Liberal	35.6	38.1
Better off with less government	45.9	27.5
Government should do more	52.1	70.5
Fewer services from government	23.5	11.9
More services from government	40.6	47.4
Each person should get ahead on own	45.2	34.5
Guarantee jobs and living standard	28.5	38.1
Increase defense spending	49.1	45.2
Decrease defense spending	16.8	12.7
Oppose stricter gun control	44.5	43.4
Favor stricter gun control	55.2	54.6
Oppose preferential hiring/promotion for blacks	79.7	67.6
Favor preferential hiring/promotion for blacks	15.9	24.1
Favor decreasing immigration	44.7	55.0
Oppose decreasing immigration	53.7	43.4
Environment more important than jobs	39.6	34.1
Jobs more important than environment	23.0	21.4
Prefer private medical insurance	33.6	24.2
Prefer government medical insurance	41.2	46.4
Favor investing Social Security funds	45.3	35.7
Oppose investing Social Security funds	26.1	19.8
Afghan war worth cost	71.5	64.0
Afghan war not worth cost	27.3	32.8
Iraq war worth cost	41.7	34.7
Iraq war not worth cost	56.5	60.2
Abortion should never be allowed	12.1	20.6
Women should always have the right	37.1	30.8
Favor school vouchers	29.2	34.4
Oppose school vouchers	67.2	61.6
Not allow gay marriage	60.1	58.5
Allow gay marriage or civil union	34.9	37.5
Democrat	47.5	49.6
Independent	6.2	22.0
Republican	46.3	28.5
Strong partisan	38.5	15.4

Source: National Election Study, 2004, Center for Political Studies, University of Michigan, Ann Arbor, www.umich.edu/~nes/.

Note: Entries represent percentages of voters and nonvoters who aligned themselves with the listed ideological/issue preference. Percentages should be read down columns. Those who stated no position (don't know/haven't thought much about it) or a neutral position on each issue were included in calculating the percentages. Thus the paired (read down) percentages may fall short of 100 percent (especially for nonvoters). The ideology and party listings are only for those who chose one of the listed categories.

BOX 7-3
WHAT IF NONVOTERS TURNED OUT TO VOTE?

Many scholars argue that in most presidential elections the winning candidate would have done even better had nonvoters participated, regardless of any partisan, ideological, or issue predispositions those nonvoters might have had. Being more weakly involved and less informed about politics, nonvoters would, in most circumstances, follow the lead of the majority of those who normally vote.[1] This "bandwagon effect" would be greatest in elections in which one candidate won by a landslide, because the more politically attractive of the candidates would have an even stronger pull on that portion of the electorate with limited long-term attachment to the political process generally.

Others argue that, if sufficiently mobilized, nonvoters would likely follow the lead of those voters who share their characteristics and concerns rather than that of the majority of those who vote.[2] Working-class citizens, for example, would develop a greater sense of class consciousness,

and would carry that heightened consciousness over to more class-based rather than "follow-the-leader" voting behavior, benefiting the Democratic Party and its candidates.

Perhaps the best conceptual compromise is one that argues that even if the victorious party and candidate did not change, the issues they address, or the way in which they address them, might. This argument is especially true in the U.S. winner-take-all system, which makes third party voting fairly inconsequential, thus at least theoretically causing parties and candidates to merge toward the position of the median general election voter.

The reality is that overall changes in turnout, even if they do produce different partisan breakdowns in the electorate, would not necessarily change the partisan balance of power in presidential or congressional contests. Because of the U.S. system of winner-take-all, single-member districting, sizable changes might be needed in many districts (for state legislatures and the U.S.

House of Representatives) and states (for governor, senator, and presidential electors) to produce a partisan change in victory. Only in those "battleground" states and districts where the two parties are highly competitive would an influx of different-minded traditional nonvoters affect the actual outcome. If a sizable number of nonvoters with different attitudes and partisan preferences came to the polls, however, elections might at least become more exciting, perhaps more competitive, and thus a harbinger of greater future turnout.

1. See, for example, John R. Petrocik, "Voting Turnout and Electoral Preference: The Anomalous Reagan Elections," in *Elections in America*, ed. Kay Lehman Schlozman (Boston: Allen and Unwin, 1987), 239–259. Also see James DeNardo. "Turnout and the Vote: The Joke's on the Democrats," *American Political Science Review* 74 (1980): 406–420.

2. For a review of this argument, see Thomas E. Patterson, *The Vanishing Voter: Public Involvement in an Age of Uncertainty* (New York: Knopf, 2002).

---

understanding of how partisanship is measured. The most commonly used measure, employed in the NES, is derived from a response to two questions. In the first question, survey respondents are asked whether they consider themselves to be a Democrat, an independent (those who responded "apolitical" are included here), or a Republican. If a partisan, they are queried about the strength of their partisanship (strong or weak). If an independent, they are asked whether they are more likely to lean toward one of the two major parties, or if they consider themselves to be pure independents.

The growth in the proportion of all independents (pure and leaning combined) has been rather pronounced (Figure 7-1).[13] During the 1952 presidential election season, about one-quarter of all national survey respondents listed themselves as independents. By 2000 that proportion had increased to almost 42 percent. In addition, the proportion of independents has continually exceeded the proportion of Republicans since 1966 and rather regularly the proportion of Democrats since 1988. Much of that increase occurred in the late 1960s and 1970s, and it

has been attributed mainly to the growing disaffection among younger people with the political system during that time.[14] Moreover, the magnitude of this shift was heightened by the fact that this younger generation became a proportionately larger segment of the eligible electorate. It was, after all, the "baby boom" generation, whose numbers were supplemented by the enfranchisement of eighteen- to twenty-year-olds after the ratification in 1971 of the Twenty-sixth Amendment.

The growth of partisan independence is important, particularly for voting turnout—independents are generally less likely than partisans to vote. The magnitude of that growth, however, may have been overstated. In many ways, "independent leaners" tend to behave more like partisans than pure independents. When they vote, they tend to cast their ballots for the candidates of the party with which, when pressed, they affiliate. Indeed, for them independence may be more rhetorical than behavioral. If these leaners are categorized as partisans, as many scholars believe they should be (and as they are listed in the tables), a somewhat different picture of partisan decline emerges.

Figure 7-1 Partisan Identification: Partisans Excluding Leaders, National Election Studies, 1952–2004

Percent of electorate

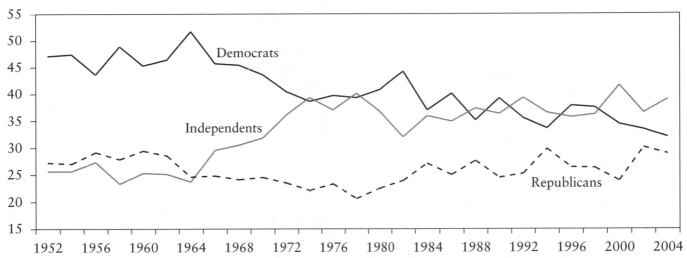

Sources: National Election Studies, Center for Political Studies, University of Michigan, Ann Arbor, www.umich.edu/~nes/.

Note: Included here are all respondents, even those who were not interviewed postelection. Leaners are Independents who consider themselves closer to one party.

Figure 7-2 Partisan Identification: Partisans Including Leaders, National Election Studies, 1952–2004

Percent of electorate

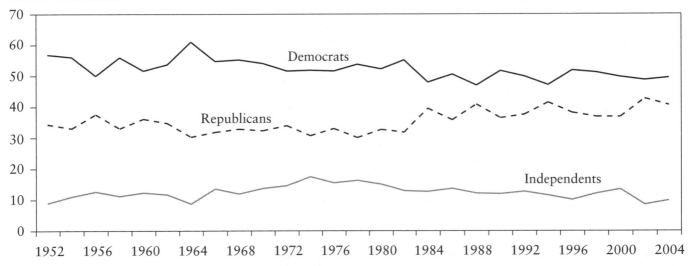

Sources: National Election Studies, Center for Political Studies, University of Michigan, Ann Arbor, www.umich.edu/~nes/.

Note: Included here are all respondents, even those who were not interviewed postelection. Leaners are Independents who consider themselves closer to one party.

The increase in the proportion of these "pure independents" has not been very dramatic at all. That proportion averaged 10.9 per cent from 1952 to 1960, increased to an average of 15.5 percent in the 1970s, only to settle down in the last decade to roughly 1950s levels (Figure 7-2).

The pattern is not static, however. Although the proportion of actual independence might not have increased

as dramatically as some have stated, a marked change in the *partisan balance* within the electorate has indeed occurred in the last half-century. In the 1950s and early 1960s, the proportion of Democrats (counting leaners or not) far exceeded the proportion who classified themselves as Republicans. By the mid-1990s, those proportions converged to near parity between the parties, with some surveys indicating slight Republican dominance in some election years. Republicans have also generally been more likely to vote and more likely to be loyal to their party's candidates when voting. Consequently, Democratic control of both the presidency and both houses of Congress has become more the exception than the norm.

The Group Basis of Partisanship

Just as demographic differences help to explain turnout (Chapter 8), they also help to explain one's choice of political party. Parties have always been defined by the types of people who join and support them. In turn, each party represents ideological and issue perspectives that appeal to different groups at different times with different intensities.

One of the most obvious patterns of differences is based on class. As Table 7-4 illustrates, self-defined working-class men and women are the most likely to identify with the Democratic Party, upper-class individuals are predominantly Republicans, with middle-class respondents split fairly evenly between the two. Similar differences exist among income categories, with the poorest segment most disproportionately Democrats. Democrats outnumber Republicans in every education category, but most disproportionately among those who never graduated from high school.

Partisan affiliation is also a function of age, but not in a strictly linear fashion. Both the youngest (under thirty-five) and oldest (over seventy) citizens are the most likely to be Democrats.[15] Women are more likely than men to affiliate with the Democratic Party, a long-term trend called the gender gap. Those from labor union households are more likely to be Democrats than are their nonunion counterparts. Practicing Protestants are the most likely to classify themselves as Republicans. The most consistently Democratic groups have been blacks and Jews. Finally, political analysts have recently taken note of the relationship between marital status and partisanship, with married individuals being the least likely to affiliate with the Democrats (even less so if only married people with children are counted).

Partially defined by group differences, partisan choice is also a function of ideological and issue positions. Individuals will choose parties whose issue positions are closer to their own. Selected variables that play an important role in partisan affiliation are listed in Table 7-5. Self-identified liberals are overwhelmingly Democrats; conservatives are overwhelmingly Republican (with strong liberals and strong conservatives most different in their partisan choices). Those who prefer more government, more services, job guarantees, less defense spending, stricter gun control, preferential hiring, increased immigration, environmental protections, government-sponsored medical insurance, and standard Social Security funding are decidedly Democrats. Those who prefer less government, fewer services, individual initiative, greater defense spend-

Democratic senator Hillary Rodham Clinton of New York encourages women to get out and vote in the 2004 election. Recent census surveys report that women are more likely than men to vote. Source: Reuters/Jon Way/Landov

ing, maintaining existing or easing gun controls, jobs over the environment, private medical insurance, and private investment of Social Security funds are more likely to affiliate with the Republicans. On current issues of national security—issues that might shape immediate but not long-term partisan attachments—opponents of the wars in Afghanistan and Iraq are overwhelmingly Democrats; those who support those conflicts are mainly Republicans.

On those issues with religious overtones, the electorate is also divided. Those who favor a woman's total right to choose whether to have a child and who support gay marriages or civil unions are decidedly Democrats. Those who oppose abortion under any circumstances and oppose gay marriages are more likely to define themselves as Republicans. On some issues, the electorate is fairly evenly split between the two parties (oppose preferential hiring, favor decreasing immigration, favor school vouchers). And on most every issue, a sizable minority is often found in the opposition camp. These issues, at least at the national level, can complicate the strategies of candidates (particularly, it seems, Democrats), a point that is addressed again later in this chapter.

Democratic and Republican Constituencies

A quick review of the profiles of Democrats and Republicans provides some insight into the strategic constraints of each party's candidates and campaigns, at least at the national level.[16] Recall that the profiles combine both the

Table 7-4 Demographics and Partisan Identity: National Election Study, 2004 (percent)

	Democrat	Independent	Republican
All	48.0	9.9	42.2
< High school degree	53.4	18.9	27.7
High school degree	46.4	11.7	41.9
Some college	46.5	8.7	44.8
Bachelor's degree or higher	48.7	4.0	47.3
Age			
18–25	56.9	9.7	33.3
26–35	55.9	7.3	36.7
36–55	41.9	10.4	47.6
56–70	42.2	11.7	46.1
Over 70	55.4	9.1	35.5
Working class	51.2	12.8	36.0
Middle class	47.9	6.1	46.1
Upper class	37.7	6.6	55.6
Annual income			
Under $15,000	52.4	18.5	29.0
$15,000–$34,999	54.2	9.5	36.3
$35,000–$49,999	52.6	7.4	40.0
$50,000–$79,999	43.5	8.1	48.4
$79,999 and over	43.5	9.6	46.9
Union household	55.3	11.2	33.5
Nonunion household	46.4	9.4	44.2
Male	44.3	10.6	45.1
Female	51.5	9.2	39.3
White	40.7	8.4	50.9
Black	79.3	12.8	7.9
Hispanic	57.1	14.3	28.6
Married/widowed	42.6	9.9	47.5
Divorced/separated	55.3	8.3	36.4
Never married	58.2	10.8	31.1
Practicing Protestant	37.9	8.1	54.0
Practicing Catholic	43.9	14.3	41.8
Practicing Jew	81.0	0.0	19.0
Practicing other	54.5	10.5	35.1
Does not attend any religious service	52.2	9.4	38.4

Source: National Election Study, 2004, Center for Political Studies, University of Michigan, Ann Arbor, www.umich.edu/~nes/.

Note: Entries represent the proportion within each demographic group that classifies itself as a Democrat, independent, or Republican. Percentages should be read across rows. Apoliticals are included in the independent category. For consistency in this and all succeeding tables, only those voters and nonvoters interviewed after the election (and therefore included in Tables 7-1–7-3) are included.

tendency for one group to affiliate with a particular party (Tables 7-4 and 7-5) and the size of that group within the electorate. They also indicate the base or natural constituency of a party's strength, the issues that the parties and their candidates are most likely to use to appeal to that base (particularly during primary seasons), and the

issues that they try to avoid or can use as wedges to split support for the opposition party.

Democrats are more likely than Republicans to have limited educations and incomes, and thus the Democratic Party's constituency is more likely to be self-defined members of the working class (Table 7-6). Democrats are

Table 7-5 Ideology, Issues, and Partisan Identity: National Election Study, 2004 (percent)

	Democrat	Independent	Republican
Conservative	28.9	8.1	63.0
Moderate	42.6	13.1	44.3
Liberal	78.7	7.8	13.4
Better off with less government	32.6	8.5	58.9
Government should do more	59.2	10.8	30.0
Fewer services from government	20.3	7.4	72.4
More services from government	62.0	10.7	27.3
Each person should get ahead on own	29.7	8.8	61.6
Guarantee jobs and living standard	65.4	12.8	21.7
Increase defense spending	30.3	9.0	60.7
Decrease defense spending	72.8	10.1	17.2
Oppose stricter gun control	35.3	8.4	56.3
Favor stricter gun control	58.5	10.1	31.4
Oppose preferential hiring/promotion for blacks	41.2	9.8	49.0
Favor preferential hiring/promotion for blacks	74.3	7.5	18.2
Favor decreasing immigration	44.4	12.0	43.6
Favor increasing immigration	61.0	5.0	34.0
Jobs more important than environment	28.9	11.3	59.8
Environment more important than jobs	58.9	8.2	32.9
Prefer private medical insurance	27.2	8.3	64.5
Prefer government medical insurance	62.4	10.2	27.3
Favor investing Social Security funds	33.0	7.3	59.8
Oppose investing Social Security funds	68.1	10.5	21.4
Afghan war worth cost	37.0	8.6	54.4
Afghan war not worth cost	74.8	11.4	13.8
Iraq war worth cost	16.3	7.1	76.6
Iraq war not worth cost	70.5	10.8	18.7
Abortion should never be allowed	36.7	11.6	51.7
Woman should always have the right	59.5	10.2	30.3
Favor school vouchers	45.0	8.5	46.5
Oppose school vouchers	51.0	8.8	40.2
Not allow gay marriage	38.7	8.9	52.4
Allow gay marriage or civil union	63.4	11.3	25.3

Source: National Election Study, 2004, Center for Political Studies, University of Michigan, Ann Arbor, www.umich.edu/~nes/.

Note: Entries represent proportion within each ideological and issue group that classifies itself as Democrat, independent, or Republican. Percentages should be read across rows. Middle or neutral categories of issues have been omitted. Only those voters and nonvoters interviewed after the election are included.

more likely to come from union households than are Republicans, but the proportion of voters who hold union jobs has decreased greatly within the last several decades. Democrats are also more likely than Republicans to be females, and they are less likely to be married and to be practicing Protestants. Finally, the Democratic Party is much more dependent on the affiliation of blacks, particularly in states where they constitute a sizable proportion of the electorate.

Republicans, overwhelmingly conservative, are much more consistent in their overall ideological perspective, while Democrats, decidedly liberal, are nevertheless more

Table 7-6   Demographic Differences between Democrats and Republicans: National Election Study, 2004 (percent)

	Democrat	Republican
< High school degree	15.6	9.3
High school degree	30.5	31.4
Some college	27.5	30.2
Bachelor's degree or higher	26.3	29.1
Age		
18–25	16.3	10.8
26–35	19.6	14.7
36–55	33.5	43.3
56–70	17.3	21.4
Over 70	13.3	9.7
Working class	50.9	40.2
Middle class	37.4	40.4
Upper class	11.7	19.4
Annual income		
Under $5,000	13.1	8.2
$15,000–$34,999	22.0	16.7
$35,000–$49,999	14.3	12.4
$50,000–$79,999	19.6	24.7
$79,999 and over	31.0	38.0
Union household	21.7	15.0
Nonunion household	78.3	85.0
Male	45.7	52.9
Female	54.3	47.1
White	62.0	87.4
Black	26.0	2.9
Hispanic	8.0	4.5
Married/widowed	56.5	71.6
Divorced/separated	14.5	10.8
Never married/partnered	29.0	17.6
Practicing Protestant	21.6	34.8
Practicing Catholic	16.6	17.8
Practicing Jew	3.4	0.9
Practicing other	20.8	15.1
Does not attend any religious service	37.7	31.4

Source: National Election Study, 2004, Center for Political Studies, University of Michigan, Ann Arbor, www.umich.edu/~nes/.

Note: Entries represent proportion of Democrats and Republicans with listed demographic attributes. Percentages should be read down columns. Not all race/ethnic categories are included. Only those voters and non-voters interviewed after the election are included.

ronment, medical insurance, and abortion rights. Republicans are more likely to be supportive of both the Afghan and Iraq wars, with the latter presenting a rather dramatic polarization of party constituencies, perhaps attributable to the direct association of these conflicts with a Republican president.

On most issues, the views of a sizable constituency within each party are at odds with those commonly held by their fellow partisans. In certain elections, the salience of one or more of these issues, often called *wedge issues,* can serve as a short-term force to change the partisan outcome in favor of one party. When these issues take over the agenda of discourse and permanently shift the partisan loyalties of a sizable group of the electorate, however, the potential for a long-term, partisan realignment occurs.

Partisan Change and Realignment

Partisanship explains most electoral behavior, but it is not the only explanation. Campaigns can alter the partisan balance in districts and states by strengthening voters' sense of attachment to their chosen party and weakening the attachment of the opposition, differentially influencing both turnout and loyalty in the process. More short-term influences on the vote also exist, particularly on the decisions of independents. The importance of certain issues, the salience of the contest, the perceived competitiveness of the race, and even the political attractiveness of candidates can help to explain proportionately minor changes from normally expected electoral outcomes in any given election.

When these short-term effects produce outcomes dramatically different from those expected—say, the election of a Republican president in spite of the electorate's overwhelming identification with the Democratic Party—the outcome is commonly called a *deviating election.* In other words, the outcome deviates temporarily from the partisan baseline or normal vote visible in the most recent elections. The successful presidential candidacy of Republican Dwight D. Eisenhower in 1952 is one example. In a deviating election, a disproportionately large number of members of one party, together with a large majority of independents, are temporarily induced to vote for the minority party's candidate. This result, however, is temporary. Democrats, at least in terms of affiliation, remain

ideologically diverse (Table 7-7).[17] Republicans are also more likely to have more consistent (and conservative) positions on government job guarantees, defense spending, preferential hiring, privatizing Social Security, and gay marriages. Democrats are more consistent (and liberal) on the benefits of government, gun control, the envi-

Table 7-7 Ideological and Issue Differences between Democrats and Republicans: National Election Study, 2004 (percent)

	Democrat	Republican
Conservative	35.0	82.7
Moderate	5.5	6.2
Liberal	59.5	11.1
Better off with less government	28.2	57.8
Government should do more	69.8	40.2
Fewer services from government	8.7	35.5
More services from government	55.1	27.8
Each person should get ahead on own	26.2	61.9
Guarantee jobs and living standard	42.5	16.0
Increase defense spending	30.8	70.0
Decrease defense spending	24.4	6.5
Oppose stricter gun control	32.5	58.9
Favor stricter gun control	66.9	40.9
Oppose preferential hiring/promotion for blacks	66.2	89.1
Favor preferential hiring/promotion for blacks	27.8	7.7
Favor decreasing immigration	43.5	48.5
Favor increasing immigration	12.1	7.7
Jobs more important than environment	13.7	32.3
Environment more important than jobs	47.4	30.1
Prefer private medical insurance	17.7	47.5
Prefer government medical insurance	55.8	27.7
Favor investing Social Security funds	29.8	61.4
Oppose investing Social Security funds	34.7	12.4
Afghan war worth cost	53.8	90.1
Afghan war not worth cost	44.2	9.3
Iraq war worth cost	13.7	73.1
Iraq war not worth cost	83.8	25.3
Abortion should never be allowed	10.7	17.2
Woman should always have the right	44.1	25.6
Favor school vouchers	28.4	33.3
Oppose school vouchers	70.2	62.8
Not allow gay marriage	48.3	74.2
Allow gay marriage or civil union	47.1	21.3

Source: National Election Study, 2004, Center for Political Studies, University of Michigan, Ann Arbor, www.umich.edu/~nes/.

Note: Entries represent percentage of Democrats and Republicans who aligned themselves with the listed ideological/issue preference. Those who stated no position (don't know/haven't thought much about it) or a neutral position on each issue were included in calculating the percentages. Thus the paired (read down) percentages may fall short of 100 percent. Only those voters and nonvoters interviewed after the election are included.

Democrats; Republicans remain Republicans; and the proportional balance between the two is hardly altered, if at all. When the result is more long-lasting—when it is repeated across consecutive elections, across different offices—and is combined with a dramatic change in the proportion of voters who side with each party, who those individuals are, and what the parties stand for, it is said that the country has entered a period of *realignment*.[18]

Realignment is partially but not totally defined by a change in the partisan balance of power. A long-term change in the numerical balance of partisan power can occur in several ways without, by the definition used here, causing a partisan realignment. The issues that the parties debate and the sides they take can remain unaltered. The proportion of individuals within each subgroup who affiliate with each party can remain the same. But if the proportionate size of that subgroup within the entire electorate increases, so will the success of the party that group has always supported. For ex-

A T-shirt appealing specifically to Hispanic voters hangs in the headquarters of Howard Dean, who was seeking the 2004 Democratic presidential nomination. The T-shirt says "Enough! Go for Dean." Cuban Americans are overwhelmingly Republican in their preferences and are more likely to vote than other Hispanic groups, who tend to vote Democratic. Source: Jason Reed/Reuters/Landov

ample, if wealthy citizens are more likely to be Republican because of that party's views on tax policy, and if the country becomes more affluent over, say, a generation, then the electorate would gradually become more Republican. It is not that wealthy people are acting differently; rather, there are proportionately more wealthy people.

Other demographic changes can similarly affect the numerical partisan balance over time. For example, differential birthrates among racial, religious, and ethnic groups can gradually alter the proportionate numbers of potential supporters for each party. Differential in-migration can do the same. It is not coincidental, for example, that politicians from both parties are very concerned about the partisan direction and participation of an ever-growing Hispanic population. Changes in the proportionate size of class and economic sectors can also alter the partisan balance. For example, even if individual union members still supported the Democratic Party as much as they did a half-century ago (which they do not), the long-term decline in union membership would by itself still have an adverse effect on the electoral success of this party, which long has depended on union support.

These demographic shifts reinforce the need to study party profiles. The proportionate size of a group within a party's constituency, and therefore the attention paid to it, can increase or decrease without a single member of that group deciding to change his or her party affiliation. The likelihood of support from within each group (like

those shown in Tables 7-4 and 7-5) could remain unchanged. But if the proportionate size of a very supportive group within the entire electorate grew, the party they supported would directly benefit. In turn, groups that are losing their proportionate advantage within the party would either receive less attention, or they might increase their activism to maintain their failing political influence.

Long-term subtle shifts in the partisan balance that occur without changes in the policy stances that divide the parties can have significant long-term policy consequences, both locally and nationally. Losers can become winners and reverse the policy initiatives of previous partisan regimes, or the majority can be reinforced, thus offering a mandate for greater change in the same direction. Realignments, however, are not merely shifts in the numerical balance of partisan power. Rather, a realignment is by definition a change in the *definition of partisan conflict*. It is a change in the *types* of players on each side of the partisan divide, not just a change in their numbers. This change of types is also associated with a change of policy agenda— that is, the issues the parties debate and the sides they take. It is therefore also a change in the reasons types of voters align and vote as they do. Policy does not change only because losers might become winners, but rather because the winners espouse a new set of policy objectives more consistent with a newly coalesced and differently constituted electoral majority. The ascendancy of the Democratic Party in the 1930s, for example, resulted from its adoption and the Republican Party's rejection of a pro–working-class, federal government–sponsored initiative that would take care of individuals displaced by the severe economic decline known as the Great Depression. This collection of New Deal programs did attract some disillusioned Republicans, but, even more important, it gained the overwhelming support of the great many people who, sensing the old partisan battles between Democrats and Republicans to be irrelevant, had never before voted.

In reality, though, this distinction between long-term demographic and realigning change is not as clear-cut as presented. Differential migration, mobility, sector growth, and the like may create societal tensions that promote political reevaluation. The disproportionate growth of one ethnic group, either by birthrate or immigration, usually brings up political discussions of immigration and race policy not previously high on the agenda of partisan politics (as it did in the 1850s, 1890s, and 1990s). The decline of the agricultural sector intensified demands for, as well as resistance to, policies geared toward protecting that sector (1890s). At the same time, the rapid growth of the industrial sector focused concerns on the social (1890s, 1930s) and, more recently, the environmental externalities of that growth. And increased wealth in society has led a newly formed desire to address postindustrial quality of life issues that were not part of the original partisan discourse. As the proportional strength of each segment of each party's coalition is altered by any one of these forces, pressure is placed on party leaders to redirect their policy agenda or risk losing elections.

All this said, changes in the partisan balance in the electorate, realigning or not, do not automatically translate into immediate changes in the partisan balance in government. The pace of that change can be either delayed or enhanced by the peculiarities of winner-take-all, single-member districting. For example, a 10 percent shift from one party to another will not change the winning party in districts or states where one party traditionally enjoys a 25 percent advantage. Conversely, changes in partisan vote counts can be magnified if properly allocated. For example, a 10 percent shift in very competitive districts or states can result in a complete and long-lasting change in the partisan outcome in all such districts. Between the time just prior to the start of the New Deal realignment and the time it reached its fruition (1928–1936), the Democratic percentage of the two-party vote increased by less than 15 percent (a not insignificant amount). The increase in the proportion of House seats held by Democrats, however, increased by 39 percent.

The End of Realignment?

Some scholars consider the concept of realignment to be no longer useful in a discussion of partisan change in the

twentieth century.[19] Most Americans do not vote on a regular basis, and, these scholars argue, Americans have become totally disenchanted with the electoral process generally. Although voting turnout increased in the 1930s and again somewhat in the 1960s and in 2004, the level of turnout has never reached that of the nineteenth century, the heyday of partisan politics. The level of independence, however measured, seems rather permanent, as the very concept of partisan politics becomes increasingly weaker for even that segment of the population that continues to vote. The evidence for these scholars, therefore, seems to point toward a continuing and irreversible *dealignment* from, or abandonment of, partisan politics and, consequently, a lessening of voter turnout generally.

Yet the contours of a post–New Deal realignment, perhaps within a reduced active electorate, did occur over a period of time. By the 1960s, the Democratic Party was no longer quite the party of Franklin D. Roosevelt. The Democratic Party of FDR's day was strongly dependent on the votes of white southerners (few blacks voted and many who did voted Republican), union members, evangelical Protestants (mainly in the South), Catholics, and Jews. By the 1960s, Democratic support had declined in all but the last group. Union membership began to decline precipitously, and the remaining members were no longer so likely to support Democratic candidacies, thereby decreasing in two ways the proportionate strength of union members within the Democratic Party's profile. Southern victories were becoming scarcer and more dependent on the votes of a newly mobilized black electorate. In 1952 over three-fourths of deep and border state southerners were expressing affiliation with the Democratic Party, making the South the most Democratic of regions. A half-century later, the South (particularly the states of the Old Confederacy) had become, along with the Mountain West, the least Democratic.

With the exception of the mobilization of southern blacks, which tapered off after the initial successes of the 1960s and 1970s, Democratic gains have been restricted to Hispanics; northern, upper-class whites; and, particularly after 1990, women.[20] Class distinctions, particularly when measured by income, continue to divide the parties but to a diminished extent. Further support for the GOP comes from those associated with the Christian Right, a support that cuts across economic, age, and gender lines. By 1994 a majority of white evangelicals were identifying themselves as Republican and voting in larger numbers than ever before, becoming, according to John C. Green, the GOP's single largest constituency whose power was advanced by their activism.[21] Coupled with diminished support for Democratic candidacies among Catholics, the pro-Republican movement of evangelical Protestants has dramatically altered the religious cleavages across which the parties divide. Ironically, perhaps the most interesting feature of these changes is that the states recently won most consistently by Republican presidential candidates (classified as the "red states" by the news media) closely match the states captured by Democratic Party candidate and Christian fundamentalist William Jennings Bryan in 1896.

In all likelihood, the social base of the New Deal coalition did not dissipate in the late 1960s because long-term Democrats had changed their minds about the benefits of Social Security, unemployment compensation, or the minimum wage (all central features of the New Deal policy agenda), although a small proportion may have. Rather, the movement away from the Democratic Party had more to do with a rejection of what many viewed as the new central focus of the party: civil rights and civil liberties for groups, particularly minorities—a concern not normally associated with the New Deal coalition. Civil rights had long been considered a Republican issue. The post–Civil War movement of blacks to the industrial cities of the North, a demographic change, did, however, help to promote a more sympathetic view of civil rights by at least northern Democrats, but, like influxes of foreign immigrants in the past, that movement spurred a reaction from many urban, working-class whites who had formed the core constituency of the New Deal coalition.

Old habits die hard, however, and the swing toward the Republican Party did take some time, aided by the gradual replacement of a cohort that came to political maturity during the depression and New Deal, assisted by economic changes that made New Deal objectives less salient, and promoted by the Democratic Party's inclusion of women, gays, and other minority groups under its civil rights umbrella. The Democrats of the 1930s fought for government protection of the working class. The Democrats of the 1960s extended that protection to the nonworking poor and into noneconomic areas. The Democratic Party became the party of regulation (much like the progressive wing of the Republican Party had been in the 1920s). Some of this regulatory bent, like job safety, was a natural extension of its New Deal origins. But other aspects of this trend moved beyond the pro–working-class mentality of the previous realignment to government protection of individual rights for minorities, support for abortion rights, and protection for the environment. It is

perhaps this last, postindustrial dimension of conflict that has fundamentally changed the basic policy orientation of the old Democratic Party, for this orientation conflicts in many ways with its pro-worker core. Most important, after the 1960s realignment, the Democratic Party became the party less likely to promote states' rights over national sovereignty, a change that fundamentally altered that party's century and a half philosophical commitment to that cause and perhaps forever changed its standing in the states of the South and the noncoastal West.

All in all, the result is a predominantly two-party system that is now highly competitive at the national level, that is categorized by a social base of party division quite unlike that existing in the 1930s, and that is dominated by issues different from those prominent during the New Deal. By the late 1960s, the Democrats were still considered the majority party, but the demographic and issue basis of the party was dramatically altered. Parties and partisanship are still extremely important in understanding the contours of electoral politics. Who those partisans are and what the parties stand for have, however, changed fairly dramatically since the launching of the New Deal.

Conclusion

Voters and nonvoters are two fairly distinct groups that differ demographically, philosophically, and by the nature and level of their participation in the political process. Voters are much more likely to be drawn from the ranks of partisans. Depending on how it is measured, the level of partisanship may not have declined much since the 1960s. The two parties, however, currently do represent constituencies that are fairly distinct from each other, and distinct from those they represented a half-century ago. The sizable proportion of the eligible electorate that does not vote is perhaps permanently dealigned from traditional partisan politics. If elected officials follow the lead of those who vote, they will find themselves catering to a group of citizens that is not exactly representative of the entire U.S. adult population.

Notes

1. In the long run, low participation rates may diminish the trust that nonvoting citizens have in their government and its leaders. Participation breeds consent, and a citizen is less likely to feel attached or committed to a system in which he or she does not take an active part.

2. For an excellent treatment of electoral strategies and constituencies, see Daniel M. Shea and Michael J. Burton, *Campaign Craft: The Strategy, Tactics, and Art of Political Campaign Management*, rev. ed. (Westport, Conn.: Praeger, 2001).

3. Different pollsters often use different definitions when sampling the potential "electorate." Generally, the more re-

strictive the definition, the more accurate is the prediction. Also because Republicans are more likely to vote than Democrats, more restrictive samples usually produce higher predicted margins for Republican candidates.

4. The Sentencing Project, "Losing the Vote: The Impact of Felony Disenfranchisement Laws in the United States," October 1998, www.sentencingproject.org/pdfs/9080.pdf (accessed January 24, 2005).

5. North Dakota actually has no formal registration, but one must, if challenged, provide proof of citizenship and residency.

6. Steven J. Rosenstone and John Mark Hansen, *Mobilization, Participation, and Democracy in America* (New York: Macmillan, 1993).

7. Much has been written about the increased turnout of young people in 2004. Indeed, preliminary evidence indicates that younger citizens were more likely to vote in 2004 than in recent previous elections. However, increases in turnout were also seen in other age groups. As a proportion of the voting/nonvoting electorates, therefore, the figures for this younger group remained fairly constant.

8. Part of this is a function of age. Younger people are the least likely to be married, but the relationship, somewhat diminished, still exits among older age cohorts.

9. Although the major causal connection is that interest and knowledge make one more likely to vote, one can argue that participation in the voting process may, in future contests, make individuals even more likely to be concerned about, read about, and discuss the electoral campaign. The causal pattern may therefore be somewhat reciprocal.

10. For a useful, modern, and readable treatment of this sense of civic culture, see Robert D. Putnam, *Bowling Alone: The Collapse and Revival of American Community* (New York: Simon and Schuster, 2000).

11. Consider the question of whether the United States would be better off with less or more government. A majority of both voters and nonvoters support the liberal position of more government, but the proportion of voters who did so in 2004 was much lower (52.1 percent to 70.5 percent). Voters are almost evenly split on the issue; nonvoters are overwhelmingly pro-government. On this issue, as an example, voters are not more conservative than they are liberal—they are just more conservative than nonvoters.

12. As the authors of *The American Voter* describe it, partisanship is an "affective orientation to an important group-object in his environment"—Angus Campbell, Philip E. Converse, Warren E. Miller, and Donald E. Stokes, eds., *The American Voter,* (New York: Wiley, 1960), 121. Most discussions of voting turnout, choice, and partisanship owe much to this seminal analysis of early NES data.

13. In both figures and all subsequent tables, those who classified themselves as "apolitical" are treated as independents. Those few who, even when pressed, refused to comment on the question are eliminated from the results.

14. Warren E. Miller, "Party Identification and the Electorate at the Start of the Twenty-First Century," in *The Parties Respond: Changes in American Parties and Campaigns,* 4th ed., ed. L. Sandy Maisel (Boulder, Colo.: Westview Press, 2002), 79–98.

15. The relative importance of young people to the Democratic Party is a fairly new phenomenon. Other data also indicate a rather dramatic shift to the Democratic column and away from independence among the youngest portion of the electorate. Whether this is a short-term phenomenon related to the candidates and issues of 2004 or a long-term, generational adjustment of party support remains to be seen.

16. The electorate may not be so split at the local or even state level. However, because of the nature of modern technology and campaign communications, even candidates for local office often have difficulty isolating themselves from their party's national image.

17. These figures include all respondents, regardless of whether they voted. Limiting the analysis to only those who voted, or, especially, only those who voted for their party's presidential candidate, would most likely increase several of the differences seen here and in Tables 7.4–7.6. As an example (see Table 7.7), 59.5 percent of all Democratic identifiers are liberal, and 82.7 percent of all Republicans are conservative. Among only those who voted, the figures increase to 64.4 percent and 85.4 percent, respectively. And for those whose presidential vote was consistent with their identification, the figures are, respectively, 68.8 percent and 86.5 percent. If presidential candidates look only at their voting constituency, then they see an even greater ideological division than exists in the partisan electorate at large. (Chapter 8 discusses why people vote the way they do, a discussion that includes partisan identification.) In addition, because "wedge issues" are used to attract individuals from the opposition party (and these may change from election to election), a listing of the demographics and views of all "partisans" has been deemed important.

18. Three of the standard and readable earlier works on realignment are E. E. Schattschneider, *The Semi-Sovereign People: A Realist's View of Democracy in America* (New York: Holt, Rinehart and Winston, 1960); Walter Dean Burnham, *Critical Elections and the Mainsprings of American Politics* (New York: Norton, 1970); James L. Sundquist, *Dynamics of the Party System: Alignment and Realignment of Political Parties in the United States,* rev. ed. (Washington, D.C.: Brookings, 1983).

19. For a discussion of this "end of realignment" thesis, see the essays in Byron Shafer's *The End of Realignment? Interpreting American Electoral Eras* (Madison: University of Wisconsin Press, 1991), particularly the works by Joel Silbey and Carl E. Ladd. Also see David Mayhew, *Electoral Realignments: A Critique of an American Genre* (New Haven, Conn.: Yale University Press, 2002).

20. Yet women are no more likely to be Democratic now than they were in 1960. See Karen M. Kaufmann and John R. Petrocik, "The Changing Politics of American Men: Understanding the Sources of the Gender Gap," *American Journal of Political Science* 43 (1999): 864–887. Hispanic refers to several different ethnic groups, not all of whom vote or participate in the same way. Cuban Americans, for example, are overwhelmingly Republican in their preferences and are more likely to vote than other "Hispanic" groups with decidedly Democratic preferences. Although it may be an injustice to individuals with differing cultural characteristics to combine them into one category, the limitations of small sample sizes force analysts to create such combinations. Too few "Cuban Americans," "Mexican Americans," "Puerto Ricans," and others exist in the NES surveys to be able to investigate their behavior separately.

21. John C. Green, "The Christian Right and the 1994 Election: An Overview," in *God at the Grassroots: The Christian Right in the 1994 Elections,* ed. Mark J. Rozell and Clyde Wilcox (Lanham, Md.: Rowman and Littlefield, 1995), 1–18.

Suggested Readings

Abramowitz, Alan. *Voice of the People: Elections and Voting in the U.S.* Boston: McGraw-Hill, 2004.

Beck, Paul Allen. "A Tale of Two Electorates: The Changing American Party Coalitions, 1952–2000." In *The State of the Parties: The Changing Role of Contemporary American*

Parties, 4th ed., edited by John C. Green and Rick Farmer, 38–53. Lanham, Md.: Rowman and Littlefield, 2003.

Burnham, Walter Dean. *Critical Elections and the Mainsprings of American Politics.* New York: Norton, 1970.

Campbell, Angus, Philip E. Converse, Warren E. Miller, and Donald E. Stokes. *The American Voter.* New York: Wiley, 1960.

Campbell, Angus, Philip E. Converse, Warren E. Miller, and Donald E. Stokes, eds. *Elections and the Political Order.* New York: Wiley, 1967.

Carmines, Edward G., and James A. Stimson. *Issue Evolution.* Princeton, N.J.: Princeton University Press, 1989.

DeNardo, James. "Turnout and the Vote: The Joke's on the Democrats." *American Political Science Review* 74 (1980): 406–420.

Flanigan, William H., and Nancy H. Zingale. *Political Behavior of the American Electorate.* 10th ed. Washington, D.C.: CQ Press, 2002.

Green, Donald, Bradley Palmquist, and Eric Schickler. *Partisan Hearts and Minds: Political Parties and the Social Identities of Voters.* New Haven, Conn.: Yale University Press, 2002.

Green, John C. "The Christian Right and the 1994 Election: An Overview." In *God at the Grassroots: The Christian Right in the 1994 Elections,* edited by Mark J. Rozell and Clyde Wilcox, 1–18. Lanham, Md.: Rowman and Littlefield, 1995.

Kaufmann, Karen M., and John R. Petrocik. "The Changing Politics of American Men: Understanding the Sources of the Gender Gap." *American Journal of Political Science* 43 (1999): 864–887.

Keith, Bruce E., David B. Magleby, Candice J. Nelson, Elizabeth Orr, Mark C. Westlye, and Raymond E. Wolfinger. *The Myth of the Independent Voter.* Berkeley: University of California Press, 1992.

Layman, Geoffrey. *The Great Divide: Religious and Cultural Conflict in American Party Politics.* New York: Columbia University Press, 2001.

Mayhew, David. *Electoral Realignments: A Critique of an American Genre.* New Haven, Conn.: Yale University Press, 2002.

Miller, Warren E. "Party Identification and the Electorate at the Start of the Twenty-First Century." In *The Parties Respond: Changes in American Parties and Campaigns,* 4th ed., edited by L. Sandy Maisel, 79–98. Boulder, Colo.: Westview Press, 2002.

Nie, Norman H., Sidney Verba, and John R. Petrocik. *The Changing American Voter.* Cambridge, Mass.: Harvard University Press, 1976.

Patterson, Thomas E. *The Vanishing Voter: Public Involvement in an Age of Uncertainty.* New York: Knopf, 2002.

Petrocik, John R. *Party Coalitions: Realignments and the Decline of the New Deal Party System.* Chicago: University of Chicago Press, 1981.

———. "Voting Turnout and Electoral Preference: The Anomalous Reagan Elections." In *Elections in America,* edited by Kay Lehman Schlozman, 239–259. Boston: Allen and Unwin, 1987.

Putnam, Robert D. *Bowling Alone: The Collapse and Revival of American Community* (New York: Simon and Schuster, 2000).

Rosenstone, Steven J., and John Mark Hansen. *Mobilization, Participation, and Democracy in America.* New York: Macmillan, 1993.

Schattschneider, E. E. *The Semi-Sovereign People: A Realist's View of Democracy in America.* New York: Holt, Rinehart and Winston, 1960.

Shafer, Byron E., ed. *The End of Realignment? Interpreting American Electoral Eras.* Madison: University of Wisconsin Press, 1991.

Shea, Daniel M., and Michael J. Burton. *Campaign Craft: The Strategy, Tactics, and Art of Political Campaign Management.* Rev. ed. Westport, Conn.: Praeger, 2001.

Stonecash, Jeffrey M. *Class and Party in American Politics.* Boulder, Colo.: Westview Press, 2000.

Sundquist, James L. *Dynamics of the Party System. Alignment and Realignment of Political Parties in the United States.* Rev. ed. Washington, D.C.: Brookings, 1983.

Wattenberg, Martin P. *The Decline of American Political Parties, 1952–1984.* Cambridge, Mass.: Harvard University Press, 1986.

White, John Kenneth. *The Values Divide: American Politics and Culture in Transition.* New York: Chatham House, 2003.

White, John Kenneth, and Daniel M. Shea. *New Party Politics: From Jefferson and Hamilton to the Information Age.* 2d ed. Belmont, Calif.: Wadsworth/Thomson Learning, 2004.

CHAPTER 8

Voter Turnout and Vote Choice

David E. Campbell

U.S. elections are shaped by two central questions: Who votes? And for whom do they vote? More specifically, why do some people turn out to vote while others do not? And, once voters are at the polls, what influences the choices they make? This chapter, which proceeds from the premise that both of these questions are equally important in seeking to understand elections in the United States, looks at individual voters and what drives their decisions.

Why people show up at the polls and what they do upon getting there has been the subject of much research. This chapter thus surveys and synthesizes two vast research literatures: first the literature on voter turnout and then that on vote choice. A comparison of U.S. voters with those in other nations is followed by an examination of trends in turnout within the United States. From there, the decision to vote is examined as a function of the characteristics of individuals, institutions, and elections, respectively. The chapter then turns to examining vote choice. As with turnout, the factors affecting vote choice are layered; they include candidates (and the campaigns they run), the characteristics of individual voters, and the features of specific elections.

Who Votes?

Discussions of voter turnout in the United States generally center on the fact that voter participation among Americans is low by international standards (that is, when America is compared with other nations) and low by historical standards (that is, when Americans today are compared with Americans of the past). Thus throughout the research literature on voter turnout in America, one often finds as a subtext the question of why turnout is not higher.

International Comparisons

When compared with that of other industrialized democracies, voter turnout in the United States is low. As displayed in Figure 8-1, voter turnout in U.S. presidential elections is lower than the turnout for comparable na-

tional elections in every country listed, with notable exception of Switzerland. Why do so many citizens of the United States choose to stay home on election day?

Anyone looking at voter turnout should keep a careful eye on what is being counted. Sometimes, voter turnout in the United States is reported as the percentage of *registered voters* who turned up at the polls. When comparing the United States with other nations, this is a mistake. In most other countries, voter registration is the responsibility of the government, and thus virtually every citizen ends up on the registration rolls. In the United States, registering to vote is the responsibility of each citizen; in 2000 roughly a third of Americans who were eligible had not registered to vote. Thus for anyone comparing turnout across nations, the most valid statistic for the United States is the percentage of the total voting-age population (VAP) who turned out to vote—a group that includes everyone who meets the legal criteria to vote, whether registered or not. Calculating voter participation as the percentage of registered voters who cast ballots overstates the level of turnout in the United States. Unfortunately, when reporting on turnout in U.S. elections most journalists rely on the level of participation among registered voters, not the VAP. Consequently, news reports usually inflate the real level of turnout.

A second way in which the level of turnout in the United States can be distorted is by focusing only on national elections. Americans vote in far more elections than the citizens of virtually every other democratic nation. Over a single four-year period, elections are held at many different levels of government. Indeed, in many states even members of the judicial branch are elected (see Chapter 25), and in still more states voters are also regularly asked to vote on numerous ballot initiatives (see Chapter 26). In addition, most states hold primary elections in which voters indicate their choices for the nominees for multiple offices, from the presidency on down (see Chapter 5). Further adding to the number of elections, many states have moved to holding gubernatorial elections in odd-numbered years, when there are no elections for national office. By contrast, most other nations—even federal states such as Canada and Germany—hold far fewer

Figure 8-1 Voter Turnout Worldwide

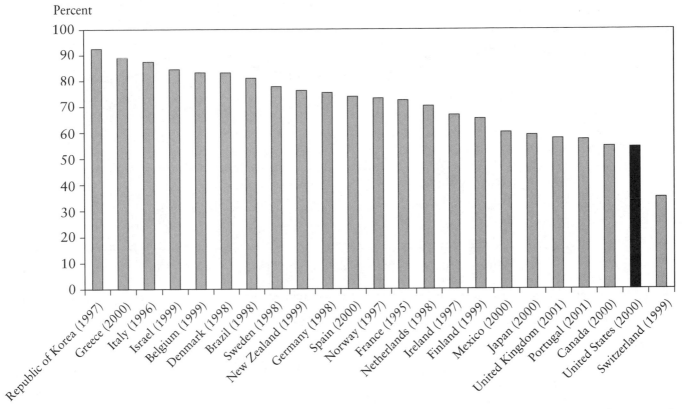

Source: International Institute for Democracy and Electoral Assistance, www.idea.int/vt/survey/voter_turnout2.cfm (accessed March 28, 2005).

elections than the United States. The frequency of U.S. elections keeps turnout in any one election down, because there is generally an inverse relationship between the number of elections in which voters can participate and the number of voters participating in any given election. In this respect, the United States resembles Switzerland, another nation with low voter participation. Both nations hold a large number of elections, and both nations have low rates of turnout.

America's rate of turnout in Figure 8-1 is actually the upper bound of voter participation, because the turnout in state and local elections is even lower than in presidential contests. Voter turnout varies widely according to the type of election; the lower an election's prominence, the lower the turnout on election day. Turnout in state and local elections, which receive limited attention in the news media compared with the races for federal offices, is thus even lower than in federal elections. Because Americans have so many opportunities to vote, perhaps the most valid comparison with the citizens of other nations is not turnout in any single election, even a presidential contest, but rather the percentage who turn out at least once in a four- or five-year period. By this standard, Americans' turnout is not so low when making international comparisons.

Voter Turnout across Time

Much has been written about whether voter turnout has declined over the last forty or so years.[1] Political scientists generally agree that voter turnout has dropped since 1960. Turnout in the heated 1960 presidential race between Democrat John F. Kennedy and Republican Richard Nixon was 64 percent, compared with only 54 percent in the equally close election of 2000, but climbing to 60 percent in the 2004 contest (like all turnout figures reported in this chapter, these figures refer to the voting-eligible population).

For many years, it appeared as though overall turnout in presidential elections was declining. More recent evidence, however, suggests that it has held more or less steady since 1972. This revised thinking returns to the earlier point about the importance of keeping one's eye on what is being counted. Political scientists Michael P. McDonald and Samuel L. Popkin recalculated turnout figures in the post–Vietnam War period, taking into account the fact that the U.S. Census Bureau's count of the VAP was including an increasing number of people who were not actually eligible to vote: felons (in some states) and noncitizens.[2] In other words, the VAP was actually smaller than it appeared, making turnout seem lower than

Figure 8-2 Voter Turnout in U.S. Presidential Elections, 1952–2004

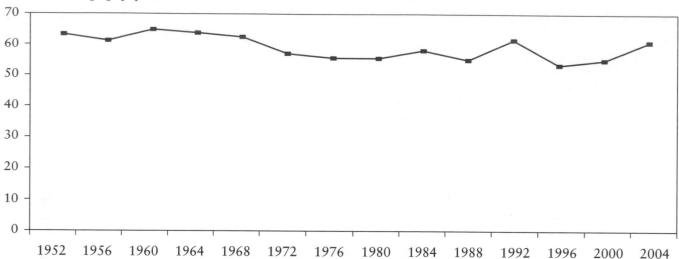

Percent of voting-age population

Source: United States Election Project, http://elections.gmu.edu/voter_turnout.htm (accessed March 28, 2005). Note that this figure reports voter turnout as a percentage of the eligible population, as calculated by Michael McDonald and Samuel Popkin in "The Myth of the Vanishing Voter," *American Political Science Review* 95, no. 4 (2002): 963–974.

it really was. After the necessary adjustments to the VAP, there is still a drop in turnout from 1960 to 1972, but voting rates have remained quite stable since 1972. Figure 8-2 displays the corrected trend in presidential election turnout and makes clear that, with the exception of 1992, turnout has hovered at about half of the eligible electorate. Interestingly, even in the intense 2004 presidential election in which much attention was paid to voter mobilization efforts, turnout still fell slightly short of the level in 1992, when third party candidate H. Ross Perot's bid for the presidency drew many new voters to the polls.

In short, then, voter turnout in the United States is lower than in most other democratic nations, and, with some notable exceptions, it has followed a general pattern of decline over the last forty years. This decline has occurred in spite of increasing levels of education within the electorate—education is an enormously important factor in whether people turn out to vote. Even if turnout held steady in the wake of such dramatic increases in education among Americans, it would be fair to characterize the trend as a net loss, because turnout could be expected to rise substantially. These trends provide a backdrop for the first of the two basic questions posed at the outset of this chapter: who actually turns out to vote? The answer is that three sets of characteristics lead some people to turn out and others to stay home: individual characteristics, the characteristics of the formal institutions within a political jurisdiction, and the characteristics of particular elections.

Characteristics of Individual Voters

Much has been written about why certain groups of people are more likely to vote than others (also see Chap-

ter 7). Knowing which subgroups of the population are more likely to vote is important in understanding the electoral process as well as what motivates politicians, political parties, and interest groups—all of whom target and mobilize particular individuals based on their propensity to vote. Of all of the factors examined over time, the one that has received the most attention is education.

Education

Of the individual-level factors that affect whether someone votes, education has the largest, most consistent impact. Yet, even though the effect of education is universally recognized, the explanation for that effect is a matter of ongoing debate. One view is that education equips people with the cognitive ability to wade through the sea of information that characterizes the U.S. electoral system, thereby increasing their engagement in the political process. Similarly, more education is thought to enhance one's awareness of voting as a social norm.

An alternative perspective on why education increases voter turnout is simply that more education leads to higher social status—sometimes called the "sorting model," because education sorts people by social status.[3] The sorting model suggests why a general increase in Americans' level of education would not lead to an increase in turnout. If that model is correct, what matters is not a person's absolute level of education, but that level *relative to others*. Because far fewer Americans attended college fifty years ago than today, having a college degree conferred more social status then than it does now. Thus, according to the sorting model, college graduates fifty years ago were much more likely to vote than college graduates today. If education levels are rising, there is no reason to expect an overall increase in voter turnout. The final verdict is still out on the effects of absolute versus relative levels of education, but a judicious assessment would seem to be that education has an impact on turnout through both processes.

Gender and Race

Because of their political salience, gender and race have also been the subject of much scrutiny, although the impact of each pales in comparison to education. The differences in voter turnout between men and women and between blacks and whites are relatively small. Although men consistently have a slightly higher rate of participation than women in political acts other than voting, women have a similarly small edge in voter turnout. Likewise, African Americans are slightly less likely to vote than are whites, but once differences in socioeconomic status are taken into account, blacks and whites participate at about the same rate. Latino and Asian Americans, however, are substantially less likely to vote than are other Americans, even when accounting for differences in socioeconomic status.

Religious Involvement

Like education, attendance at religious services has a relatively large influence on voter turnout. The more often people attend church, the more likely they are to vote. Churchgoers tend to be embedded in a social network of other church members, which facilitates political mobilization. In general, people with more extensive social networks, or a greater degree of what is often called "social connectedness," are more likely to vote, because they are more likely to be mobilized into political action by friends and acquaintances who share their political preferences.

Mobility

People tend to have more social connections the longer they live in the same place. At times, residency requirements for voter registration keep new move-ins from voting, although the U.S. Supreme Court has sharply limited the length of such requirements to no more than fifty days. Residency requirements aside, being new to a community also means less familiarity with local issues and candidates, which further dampens turnout. In short, the more often people move, the less likely they are to vote.

Age

Young people are particularly likely to move frequently, especially students residing temporarily in a community to attend college. And, compared with the rest of the population, young people are less likely to be married, have kids, and own homes—all factors leading to deeper roots in a community and thus a greater likelihood of turning out to vote. Given this demographic profile, it is perhaps not surprising that young people have a low rate of voter turnout. According to a preliminary postelection estimate by the Center for Information and Research on

Following passage of the Voting Rights Act of 1965, civil rights groups such as the National Association for the Advancement of Colored People created and distributed posters encouraging African Americans to exercise their voting rights. Source: The National Association for the Advancement of Colored People

Civic Learning and Engagement, only 42 percent of eighteen- to twenty-four-year-olds turned out in the 2004 presidential election, compared with 60 percent of the general population.

The fact that young people are less likely than their elders to vote is partly attributable to a life cycle effect. In other words, young people are less likely to vote simply because of their age, but, as they age, they become more likely to turn out. The natural progression of the life cycle does not appear to account fully for the low turnout rates among young people, although, compared with people of the same age in past decades, today's youth are far less likely to vote. As a generational cohort, people born in the 1960s and later are unusually

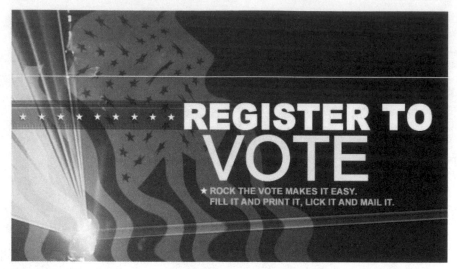

Rock the Vote is a non-profit, non-partisan organization founded in 1990 with the goal of increasing youth voter turnout. The organization, which incorporates youth culture and entertainment into its efforts, coordinates voter registration drives, get-out-the-vote events, and voter education efforts. Source: Rock the Vote

disconnected from political involvement of all types. Today's young people will undoubtedly increase their level of voter turnout as they age, but they are starting at a much lower point than their parents and grandparents, and thus at the current trajectory it does not appear that they will catch up to previous generations. Many explanations have been offered for young people's disconnection from the electoral process, including a de-emphasis on civic education in America's schools, a relative absence of voter mobilization efforts among the young, and candidates who do not address issues of relevance to young voters. These explanations are neither mutually exclusive nor totally exhaustive, and undoubtedly others apply as well. Whatever the explanation(s), young voters remain a potentially rich challenge for political candidates. Any candidate who is able to bring young people to the polls will reap substantial electoral rewards.

Efficacy

In addition to the demographic factors known to affect who votes are the psychological factors. One studied widely by political scientists is the sense of efficacy, internal and external. Internal efficacy is a belief that one personally can bring about political change, whereas external efficacy refers to the perceived fairness of the political system in general. It is not surprising that the groups that vote at the highest rates generally have the highest rates of both internal and external efficacy. However, differences in efficacy do not by themselves *explain* differences in turnout, because a whole array of factors affect whether people turn out to vote. Women generally have a slightly lower level of political efficacy than men, although upon

accounting for a broad array of factors influencing the vote they turn out at slightly higher rates. Likewise, African Americans are less efficacious than whites, but when other factors are taken into account they actually have a higher level of turnout. These examples are a reminder that it is important not to place too much significance on any one factor as influencing voter participation without considering other influences as well. When compared with other factors known to affect turnout, internal and external efficacy have relatively modest effects.

Trust

A second psychological factor that has been the subject of much scholarly attention is a person's level of trust, which, like efficacy, takes two forms. One is a person's degree of trust in other people; the other is trust in government. It is not immediately obvious how trust in government would be related to turnout. If voters are spurred by a desire to ride herd on a government they view as suspicious, then lower trust should lead to a higher likelihood of voting. But if voting is viewed an act that expresses the voter's allegiance to the system of governance (and nonvoting expresses disaffection with that system), the opposite might be true: greater trust translates into a greater likelihood of voting. At first glance, there may appear to be a strong case in favor of the second hypothesis, because trust in government has declined sharply over roughly the same period in which voter turnout has fallen. Yet closer analysis reveals that there is actually very little connection between trust in government and voter turnout in either direction. Voters are neither more nor less trusting of their government than nonvoters.

Duty

Civic duty is almost universally recognized as an important psychological factor in explaining the vote. When Americans are asked why they participate in various civic and political activities, most say they feel it is their duty, a civic obligation. It is difficult to explain why voters who have no sense of duty would take the trouble to turn out, given the infinitesimal chance that their vote will sway the outcome of an election. Any voter undertaking a simple cost-benefit analysis would probably conclude that voting entails more costs (such as the time to register and then to travel to the polls) than benefits, and thus would stay home on election day.

Recognition of the importance of a sense of civic obligation does raise the question of why some people have a greater sense of duty than others. Scholars have long recognized the importance of civic duty as an explanation for voting, but they have conducted relatively little research into its origins. A promising area of research is thus the study of how civic norms develop in one's youth, both at home and in school.

This section has skimmed the surface of some of the demographic and psychological factors known to affect voter turnout. An individual's characteristics, however, are not the whole story. It is not only who people are but where they live that shape their political participation. Men and women who have the same characteristics but reside in places with different electoral institutions have different levels of turnout. For that reason, the complete story of turnout requires a look at institutional factors as well.

Institutional Factors

The laws, policies, and customs that define the electoral environment provide both incentives and disincentives to vote. All else being equal, the more difficult a state makes it to register and vote, the lower is its level of voter turnout. Historically, some barriers to registration such as poll taxes and literacy tests (see Chapters 3 and 5) were blatantly designed to suppress turnout among African Americans and other minorities. Eventually, however, these obstacles were eliminated by means of Supreme Court rulings, federal legislation, and constitutional amendments. Other barriers are not necessarily motivated by racial animus, but they serve to restrict turnout nonetheless. These include the hours during which the registrar's office is open and the length of time one must live in a community before being eligible to vote (known as the closing date). States also vary in their policies on "purging" the voter rolls—that is, removing registered voters from the official roll if they have not voted over a certain period of time. In their seminal book on voter turnout *Who Votes?* Raymond E. Wolfinger and Steven J. Rosenstone estimated the impact of various registration laws and practices on voter turnout. Writing about laws in place in the early 1970s, they simulated what would happen to turnout if every state adopted what were at the time the most permissive provisions for voter registration: (1) eliminating the closing date; (2) keeping registrar's offices open for the regular forty-hour work week, in the evening, and on Saturdays; and (3) liberalizing absentee voting.[4] Wolfinger and Rosenstone predicted that if every state adopted these registration reforms, aggregate turnout would rise by about nine percentage points. Since they made their prediction, the unmistakable trend has been a steep discount in the costs associated with voting. In many respects, registration today is even easier than they simulated, providing a rare opportunity to put a political science prediction to the test.

The most dramatic reduction in the costs associated with voter registration nationwide came in 1993 with enactment of the National Voter Registration Act (NVRA), more popularly known as the "Motor Voter" law. This act represents the most significant change in the laws governing voter registration since the Voting Right Act of the civil rights era. Its "Motor Voter" moniker derives from the fact that the NVRA requires states to link voter registration with renewal of a driver's license. Although this provision is the law's best known, the law also includes other substantial changes to how voters are registered. States must allow voter registration not only at the department of motor vehicles, but also at welfare and unemployment offices and military recruitment centers. In addition, the NVRA introduced universal mail registration and restrictions on removing voters from the registration rolls for not having voted.

Rather than standardizing voter registration across the United States, the NVRA is really a minimum threshold for registration requirements. States can, if they choose, make registration even easier than mandated by Congress, and many do. In fact, states could avoid implementing the NVRA's mandates by adopting election day registration, an option chosen by Idaho, New Hampshire, and Wyoming after passage of the NVRA, and by three other states earlier, in the 1970s, not including North Dakota, which does not require any voter registration. Of the barriers to registration imposed on the U.S. electorate, the closing date for registration has often been singled out as having a particularly dampening impact on turnout. What has been the impact of election day registration? The experience of states who have adopted it suggests that it increases turnout by four or five percentage points, a substantial but not overwhelming boost.

Many states have also made voting easier by loosening the requirements for absentee voting by mail. Eleven states permit absentee voting without any restrictions. Although it was once true that people requested an absentee ballot because they were *unable* to go to the polls on election day, today's voters are increasingly requesting absentee ballots so that they can *avoid* appearing at the polls. In Washington State, for example, the chairman of the House committee on overseeing election laws calculates that 68 percent of voters are voting by mail. Even though it represents a significant reduction in the costs of voting, liberalized absentee voting has little or no independent effect on turnout. It appears to increase turnout only when political parties incorporate efforts to encourage absentee voting into their mobilization tactics. Because the parties seek to mobilize their own supporters and such partisans are more likely than nonpartisans to vote in the first place, the ironic result of these reforms is that absentee voters are largely people who would have turned out to vote anyway.

There does, however, seem to be an uptick in turnout when voters have no option but to cast their ballots through the mail. For example, all-mail elections in the 1970s increased municipal election turnout in California,

Oregon, and Washington, although at least some of the turnout gain stemmed from the novelty effect of mail balloting. Oregon is the best state in which to examine the impact of voting by mail without any novelty effect, because it has been conducting statewide elections of one sort or another through the mail since 1981. Close analysis of the Oregon experience suggests that, like absentee balloting, voting by mail enhances turnout, but this increase is more the result of retaining previous voters than mobilizing new ones.

The debate over the Motor Voter law and other reforms designed to increase turnout has generally hinged on whether one party over another would benefit from the changes. Generally, Republicans have been concerned that newly mobilized voters would favor the Democrats. Over the decade since Motor Voter was enacted, however, there has been no evidence that it has favored the Democrats or Republicans. The same applies to similar reforms, such as voting by mail. How can it be that lowering barriers to registration does not have a large impact on the outcome of an election? The answer lies in the fact that relaxing registration requirements does not raise turnout by anything approximating 100 percent, but rather leads to only modest gains in voter participation. The gains that do occur are concentrated among the population groups who are disproportionately affected by the barriers in the first place. The two groups most affected by the current obstacles to registration are the young and the mobile (categories that obviously overlap). Because neither group has a particular partisan profile, increasing their turnout does not appreciably shift the results of an election toward the Democrats or the Republicans. Yet it does have the potential to alter the political landscape by benefiting third party and independent candidates. For example, the 1998 election of former professional wrestler Jesse Ventura as governor of Minnesota has been widely attributed to that state's system of election day registration. Many Minnesotans who had not previously registered to vote, presumably because they did not feel represented by either of the major parties, were pulled to the polls by Ventura as he surged in the closing weeks of that campaign. Similarly, as noted earlier, voter turnout nationwide spiked in 1992 when third party presidential candidate Ross Perot made a serious run for the White House. In light of this increased support for third party candidates, perhaps Republicans are right to be concerned about the electoral consequences of expanding the electorate (even if for a different reason than they generally articulate). Similarly, perhaps Democrats should not be so sanguine about any electoral gains resulting from increased turnout.

Features of Specific Elections

The features of specific elections also greatly influence whether an individual goes to the polls. If an election is highly salient and voters are mobilized, they are more likely to respond by going to the polls. For example, people are more likely to vote in presidential elections than midterm elections because of the higher profile of the office being contested and the greater media coverage received by presidential candidates. The media are also more likely to devote coverage to races characterized by scandal or that are otherwise anomalous.

One important factor that increases the salience, and thus the media coverage, of an election is how close the outcome appears to be. Close elections can spark higher turnout, in part because people are more likely to head to the polls when they believe that their vote may make a difference in the outcome of the election. However, a close election in and of itself apparently has only a minimal impact on turnout. For example, turnout in the presidential elections of 1996 and 2000—the first an overwhelming victory for the winner and the second the closest in American history—differed by only one percentage point (an increase). The relatively small increase in turnout between 1996 and 2000 suggests that, even though the closeness of an election may be enough to motivate some voters to head to the polls, many more need the extra push that comes from get-out-the-vote efforts by parties and other groups, as evidenced by the contrast between the 2000 and 2004 elections. The 2004 election was similar to the 2000 contest in that it was close. There was a huge difference, however, in the efforts at voter mobilization among supporters of both the Republicans and Democrats. The 2004 election saw more efforts directed at turning out the vote, and voter participation rose accordingly. Voter mobilization is highly targeted, and thus most likely is found in states and congressional districts when and where elections are close. Although turnout rose nationwide by roughly six percentage points in the 2004 election, areas in which targeted mobilization efforts were conducted had much greater increases in voter participation. For example, the state of South Dakota saw a rise of ten percentage points from 2000 to 2004 because of a highly competitive Senate race.

It has been demonstrated that people are more likely to vote when they have been mobilized by a campaign (see Chapter 19 for a more detailed discussion of voter mobilization). When a campaign worker contacts a voter and asks for his or her vote, the likelihood of voting increases substantially. One interesting aspect of voter turnout is not whether someone votes but when they vote. People may vote in one election and not another, and central to understanding when someone votes is mobilization.

Voter mobilization is a blend of time-worn practices and state-of-the-art technology. Until recently, the trend was to replace old-fashioned volunteer labor with technology. Automated telephone calls began to replace doorstep conversations with a local party worker about why the voter should turn out for a particular candidate. Technology's gains in the quantity of contacts, however, came at the expense of their quality. Extensive research

Voters form a line outside a polling station in Alexandria, Virginia, on November 2, 2004. Polls indicated a virtual deadlock between President George W. Bush and Democratic nominee Sen. John Kerry, and turnout in the general election was about 60 percent, higher than usual. Close elections often, but not always, result in higher turnout, because voters sense that their votes can make a difference. Source: Reuters/Gregg Newton/Landov

has found that "robo-calls," as they are called, have no measurable impact on voter turnout. Neither, apparently, do e-mail messages. Face-to-face politicking has the greatest impact on voter turnout, boosting the likelihood of voting by, in some cases, almost ten percentage points.[5]

In recent elections, the parties seem to have recognized the virtues of old-fashioned door knocking and other forms of personalized contacts. Although automated calls continue, often using voices of political celebrities, both parties do appear to have stepped up efforts to mobilize voters through face-to-face interactions. The current trend is for technology to enhance, not replace, old-fashioned shoe-leather politicking. In the past, the party's precinct captains knew everyone in a neighborhood and used that information to personalize appeals to turn out. Today, the information that was once idiosyncratically collected by local party volunteers with deep roots in their communities has been replaced by massive databases containing information about tens of millions of voters. Yet the objective remains the same—providing campaign volunteers with personalized information about each voter.

Parties are not the only organizations mobilizing voters during an election. Interest groups, most of which are closely aligned with one party, also work to get their supporters to the polls. Interest groups can engage in mobilization in at least three ways. The most overt method is through the explicit endorsement of a candidate, which is generally the practice of organizations such as labor unions, the National Rifle Association, and NARAL Pro-Choice America. Upon providing an endorsement, these organizations often use their organizational resources to locate and mobilize supporters. However, to preserve their tax-exempt status, many other organizations do not formally endorse particular candidates. Instead, they engage in "voter education" efforts that fall short of an official endorsement but essentially operate as an endorsement by another name. Indeed, the voter guides they often produce comparing candidates are anything but subtle. Yet another strategy is to engage in voter registration drives. Again, these drives are technically nonpartisan, but they generally target areas in which the newly registered voters are more likely to support one party over another.

People concerned about the overall level of turnout in the United States should recognize that, although parties and their allied groups play an essential role in getting people to the polls, they are not in the business of enhancing the general level of voter turnout; they are in the business of winning elections. Specifically, party operatives seek to maximize the votes for their side, and they have only finite resources to do so. Therefore, they focus on mobilizing those people most likely to support their party and candidate. In those states that have party registration, the parties home in on people who have registered under their partisan label. They also mobilize people who are most likely to turn out—that is, those who voted in the past. The result of these entirely rational mobilization strategies is huge efforts expended to turn out the votes of those people already the most likely to vote, thereby perpetuating a vicious circle. One example is young voters. They are the least likely to have registered to vote, let alone register under a party label, and to have voted in a previous election. In addition, they move frequently and so are difficult to track from one election to the next. Consequently, young people are unlikely to be the target of electoral mobilization in any given election. The situation is a classic catch-22. Why don't more young people vote? Because they are not mobilized. Why are they not mobilized? Because few of them vote.

Presidential campaigns are very selective about their mobilization efforts. They are largely confined to the "battleground" states, where the presidential vote tally is expected to be tight. Visits by the presidential candidates, television, radio, and billboard advertising, as well as get-out-the-vote drives, are all limited to states deemed competitive. Wide swaths of the country are, therefore, essentially shut out of the excitement accompanying the spectacle of presidential campaigning and given little encouragement to turn out.

Voter turnout is only half the story, however. Elections are not simply about who casts ballots; they are also about for whom those ballots are cast.

Who Votes for Whom?

Once individuals decide that they are going to vote, how do they make their vote choice? Although the airwaves are rife with politicians making conflicting promises and claims and with interest group–sponsored advertisements and endorsements, one would think that voters have an enormous amount of information. But, in fact, many voters lack the critical information they need to make informed decisions about the candidates who are running for office. Instead, voters rely on cues, such as incumbency and political party, to help them choose among the candidates. The following sections describe how individuals go about making their vote choice.

Candidate and Campaign Factors

The most significant candidate-specific factor influencing an election is incumbency. According to one rule of thumb, the higher the profile of an election, the fewer advantages incumbency brings. Incumbent senators are thus reelected at a much lower rate than incumbents in the House of Representatives. Further up the ballot, Gerald R. Ford, Jimmy Carter, and George Bush can attest that the institutional advantages afforded an incumbent president hardly ensure reelection.

Incumbency is important in low-profile elections for many reasons, but especially because it builds name recognition among voters. There is an old saying in politics, "You can't beat somebody with nobody," which means "You can't beat somebody voters know with somebody they don't know." Incumbents take this adage seriously and have implemented numerous institutional perquisites they can use to make themselves better known to their constituents. For example, the franking privilege allows members of Congress to send free mail to constituents boasting of their accomplishments, with only a few restrictions around election time. Incumbents also devote considerable resources to constituent service, which promotes beneficial, word of mouth advertising. Because most legislators work mainly out of the media spotlight, these efforts are the primary way in which they can raise their name recognition. It is often difficult for challengers to overcome this advantage in name recognition, even with an expensive blitz of advertising.

Their familiarity to voters is not the only advantage held by incumbents. Increasingly, current officeholders are receiving job protection through the redistricting process. Low turnout is an unintended effect of the increasingly common practice of legislators drawing congressional districts to favor incumbents—a process known as gerrymandering.

None of this is to say, however, that incumbents can become complacent about keeping their jobs. Politics is inherently volatile, and so incumbents typically need to be vigilant if they want to stay in office. Just because incumbents rarely lose elections, they cannot risk falling out of touch with their constituents. On the contrary, they keep winning because they are attuned to voters' opinions. When officeholders take positions or cast votes that are out of step with their constituents' preferences, they risk a strong challenge in the next election. Often such a challenge will come from within the incumbent's party during the primary, which can be damaging even if the incumbent survives. Winning a hotly contested primary is, then, usually a pyrrhic victory, leading to a weakened position in the general election. Likewise, a scandal can undo an incumbent's advantages, because an embattled officeholder will often draw a strong field of opposition.

Yet, barring a sharp deviation from their constituents' preferences or a scandal, well-entrenched incumbents usually face only token opposition. The conventional wisdom that current officeholders have such a big electoral advantage leads to a self-perpetuating cycle. As long as incumbents continue to stand for reelection, quality candidates choose to forego challenging them, biding their time until an election without an incumbent. What determines a challenger's "quality"? Generally, political experience is helpful. Having held, or at least run for, office in the past boosts name recognition, seasons a candidate for the rigors and exposure of the campaign trail, and provides a network of past donors. But experience should not be overrated, because it is neither necessary nor sufficient for victory at the polls. One archetypal strategy for a campaign consists of running as an outsider who has never held elective office against an incumbent portrayed as aloof and out of touch. An outsider strategy is especially effective in years when the electorate is in an anti-incumbent mood, although the extent to which such a mood is fostered by the use of outsider strategies remains an open question.

In many cases, money is a substitute for experience, because more and more political candidates are independently wealthy. With enough money, candidates can purchase advertising to increase name recognition, thereby minimizing the impact of not having held office. Wealthy candidates can also circumvent the need to ask others for checks by simply writing their own. Like experience, though, having a lot of money does not guarantee victory at the polls. The electoral field is strewn with the failed campaigns of wealthy candidates such as Steve Forbes (onetime Republican presidential candidate), Michael Huffington (onetime Republican senatorial candidate in California), and Blair Hull (onetime Democratic senatorial candidate in Illinois). Each spent tens of millions of dollars in a losing effort (and Forbes did it twice).

Although the quality of the candidate is important, so is the quality of the campaign itself—that is, the way in which it is run. In races for the highest offices, particularly the presidency, campaigns are always run by teams of highly experienced, well-compensated political professionals. Professionalized campaigns make extensive use of polls and focus groups, produce a stream of press releases, prepare detailed policy statements, and conduct detailed research on their opponents. Because at the top echelons of American politics the staff on both sides have roughly the same level of expertise and experience, any advantages gained by modern campaign techniques tend to cancel each other out. In races for lower offices, however, there is greater disparity in the quality of the campaign operations. Being perceived as a serious candidate can mean the difference between raising enough money to hire an experienced staff and having to make do with inexperienced campaign management on the cheap.

Campaign management has become such an industry in part because U.S. election campaigns, compared with those in other nations, are unusually centered on candidates rather than parties. Nevertheless, the importance of the parties should not be dismissed. After all, virtually all candidates are affiliated with one of America's two major parties, although the degree to which candidates emphasize that party label depends on where they are running. A Republican running in Massachusetts (a heavily Democratic state) is likely to downplay his or her party label, as is a Democrat running in Utah (a heavily Republican state). Deft candidates can win office even when they represent the minority party in an area by responding to the local ideological climate. Thus Republicans can win elections in Massachusetts, but only by veering to the left, and Democrats can win in Utah by running to the right. Even though a handful of current members of Congress did manage to win office by representing the local minority party, such ideological maneuvering was far more common in the past, when there was wide ideological variation within the parties; the notion of a liberal Republican and a conservative Democrat was quite familiar. Now such labels are rare. One of the most dramatic changes in the American political landscape over the last generation has been the ideological polarization of the parties.

The polarization of the parties, however, has not changed the fundamentals of winning the most votes in a general election. Whether an incumbent or a challenger, essentially every candidate is compelled to follow the same basic strategy to win office—head to the center (the location of most voters along the continuum from the most conservative to most liberal), thereby illustrating the "median voter theorem." Yet if this is true why was there such partisan rancor in the streets, the media, and the courts during the weeks after the 2000 presidential election in which the winner of Florida's electoral vote was in doubt? Because candidates George W. Bush and Al Gore were both centrists, should voters not have concluded that there was little difference between them, and thus it did not matter much who actually took office? The answer is that although both presidential candidates went to great lengths to appear as centrists, each was nevertheless a bona fide partisan, as was clear to anyone who followed their campaigns to win the nomination of their respective parties.

During their campaigns to become their party's nominee, both Bush and Gore had to win the votes of ideological outliers within their parties. The primary elections used by the political parties to determine their nominees generally have a relatively low turnout, which means they attract only the most passionate of a party's supporters, who tend to hold ideologically extreme views. Here, then, is a perfect illustration of the principle that elections are shaped by whoever turns out to vote in them, because winning the nomination for office often requires adopting issue positions that satisfy the ideological extremists within a party. Candidates thus face two countervailing forces—the pull toward the ideological center in order to win the general election after the push toward the ideological extremes in order to win their party's nomination. This is a delicate balancing act, because stepping too far from the median voter in the general election is a recipe for electoral defeat. For example, onetime presidential candidates Barry Goldwater and George McGovern were perceived by voters to be out of the political mainstream, and both suffered ignominious defeats at the hands of a more moderate opponent—Goldwater, a Republican, lost to President Lyndon Johnson in 1964 and McGovern, a Democrat, was defeated by President Richard Nixon in 1972.

Candidates thus face the challenge of shifting their ideological positioning between the primary and the general election. Too dramatic a shift leads to charges of "flip-flopping." Such accusations are part and parcel of American political rhetoric, but in reality few candidates ever change their position on an issue in the course of a single campaign. In fact, candidates generally signal their placement on the ideological spectrum less by the specific positions they take and more by the issues they choose to emphasize. During primary campaigns, candidates are more likely to stress issues near and dear to the hearts of party activists, shifting to issues of greater interest to the mass electorate in the general election campaign. Abortion is the quintessential example. Activists in both parties have clear, and thus sharply polarized, preferences on the issue, but because of this very divisiveness candidates in general election campaigns try to steer clear of it. General election campaigns are thus often less about candidates debating the merits of one policy position over another and more about emphasizing the issues their party is thought to "own." Republican candidates, for example, like to talk about national security (an issue that generally favors their party), while Democrats prefer to shift the conversation to popular social programs such as Social Security (traditionally a Democratic strength).

Many successful candidates "neutralize" an issue by focusing on a policy area the opposing party is thought to own. Bill Clinton, for example, singled out law and order issues for priority in his 1992 and 1996 presidential campaigns and promised to reform welfare, traditionally two Republican issues. Similarly, George W. Bush made education, long a Democratic strength, a signature issue of both of his campaigns for the presidency. These two successful presidential candidates also demonstrate the delicate balance between appealing to the median voter while appeasing the party's base. Although Clinton promised to "end welfare as we know it," he left vague just what would emerge in its stead. His supporters on the left envisioned an expanded welfare program, while conservatives heard in his words a promise to promote work requirements and time limits for welfare. Similarly, Bush's description of himself as a "compassionate conservative" was fruitfully ambiguous. In the primaries, he talked up the conservative half of his slogan, while in the general election he focused on the compassionate half.

Individual-Level Factors

Candidates and the campaigns they run are an essential part of understanding the electoral process, but equally essential are the predispositions voters bring to each election.

Party Identification

Far and away, the most important of the predispositions voters bring to the polls is partisan allegiance. Also known as party identification, this allegiance is defined as a psychological attachment to either the Democratic or Republican Party, operating as an enduring social identity.[6]

One reason that party identification has become such a fixture in the study of U.S. politics is that ideology has historically been a poor predictor of the way Americans vote. When individual-level survey research was first conducted on a large scale to predict the vote in the 1950s, the Democratic and Republican Parties had substantial conservative and liberal wings, respectively. But times have changed; the last two decades or so have seen the parties become more ideologically cohesive, and thus polarized. One consequence is that ideology now has a larger impact on the vote than historically was the case. It also means that, by past standards, partisanship among voters is quite high.[7]

Perhaps the most useful way of understanding the influence of party identification is to think of it as a "standing decision." [8] In the absence of other criteria, voters will rely on their long-standing partisan preference when casting their ballots. Moreover, like incumbency, all else being equal the significance of party identification is inversely proportional to the salience of an election. Although plenty of voters cross party lines in a presidential election, such crossovers are less common in low-profile races, such as that for state legislature.

Religion

Early researchers considered party identification analogous to religious affiliation—a product of childhood socialization that rarely changes over a lifetime.[9] Given that analogy, it is appropriate that religion now rivals party identification as a factor influencing how people vote. That religion affects the vote is, historically, nothing new. What is new is the way in which religion has an effect. In the past, voters were divided by denomination—for example, Catholics were Democrats, and Protestants were Republicans. Today, however, bigger differences are found within, rather than across, denominations. Voters are defined less by their *denomination* and more by their level of *devotion*. With only a few exceptions, attending church more frequently, or otherwise demonstrating a greater level of religious commitment, corresponds with voting Republican. For example, conventional wisdom holds that evangelical Christians are a reliable constituency of the GOP. In reality, though, evangelicals, when taken as a whole, are neither more nor less likely to vote Republican than nonevangelicals. Evangelicals who attend church frequently, however, are extremely reliable Republican supporters. The same pattern is observed for Catholics and mainline Protestants—greater participation in religious activities leads to a higher likelihood of voting Republican, although neither group reaches the same level of GOP support as found among evangelicals.[10]

Race

One notable exception to the connection between devotion and the vote is found among African Americans. Notwithstanding their high levels of religious involvement, African Americans almost monolithically vote Democratic—although this support is defined more by race than religion. Within the African American community, the political role of churches is more a matter of influencing voter turnout than vote choice. Latinos, who as a group are also characterized by a high degree of religious involvement, are neither as Republican as religiously committed whites nor as Democratic as African Americans. Although Latinos generally favor Democrats, this support is far from uniform across different subgroups within the Latino population. Cuban Americans, for example, are predominantly Republican supporters. Latinos are thus thought to be "in play" when the parties compete for votes, and, because of the high growth rate of the Latino population, the parties are likely to devote even more efforts to winning over this bloc of voters.

Gender

In addition to the religious and racial gaps between Democrats and Republicans, there is also the much-discussed gender gap. Women are much more likely to identify with and thus vote for Democrats than are men. When tracked over time, however, this gap stems less from women swelling the ranks of the Democratic Party and more from men leaving that party. Yet for all the discussion of the gender gap, the "marriage gap" is actually larger. Married people, especially married women, are far more likely to vote Republican than their single counterparts.

Income

Religion, race, and gender speak to differences between the parties on "cultural" issues, but pocketbook issues matter as well. Along with voters' perceptions of the economy—discussed at length later in this chapter—socioeconomic status remains a significant factor affecting how people vote. Even though many Democrats are wealthy and many Republicans are found among the working class, Republicans have a higher average socioeconomic status than Democrats.

Age

A voter's age is also related to the vote. In general, the voting patterns of generational cohorts differ, owing largely to the era in which each group was politically socialized. Voters over the age of sixty-five, who came of age during the ascendancy of Franklin D. Roosevelt's New Deal coalition, are more likely to identify with the Democratic Party than the Republican Party. Reflecting the polarized partisan environment of today, voters under thirty do not have a distinctive preference for one party over another.

Information

Even though political analysts often divide the electorate into demographic groups, demography and even ideology are not political destiny. Groups do tend to lean toward one party over the other, but within those groups there is often much variation. Americans generally pay little attention to public affairs, and, as a consequence, their opinions often do not correspond to the political landscape as defined by close observers of politics. The seeming ideological incoherence of Americans' opinions has long troubled many students of politics. An alternative view, however, is that even though many voters do not have an ideological framework within which to structure their opinions, they are, nevertheless, far from politically naïve. Voters, according to this view, act rationally by economizing on the information they need to gather in order to make sense of their political world. They use information shortcuts, or what psychologists call "heuristics," to infer politically relevant information about candidates. A party label is an important heuristic, but often symbolic gestures also can impart a lot of information to voters about a candidate.[11] Such symbols are especially important during primary campaigns, when all of the candidates are of the same party, thus negating the party label

as a source of information. One example is the information communicated to voters in a single comment by George W. Bush during a debate with the other candidates competing for the 2000 Republican presidential nomination. When asked to name his favorite political philosopher, Bush responded, "Christ, because he changed my heart." In light of the religious divide in the electorate described earlier, any voter who heard that statement did not need to read Bush's campaign's position papers to infer that a Bush administration would be socially conservative. Modern campaigns are often a battle over the symbols with which candidates are associated—and a small, even subtle, symbol can often impart a lot of information.

External Factors

Neither candidates nor voters operate in a vacuum during an election campaign. For all of the orchestration that accompanies modern campaigning, external factors beyond the control of a campaign often define the course of an election. The most important of these include war, the economy, and the type of election in which the candidate is running (midterm or presidential).

War

Voters care about whether the nation is at war or at peace. Presidential approval predictably skyrockets when American troops are committed abroad. A military campaign is hardly a guarantee of electoral success, however. Under normal conditions, voters pay little attention to foreign affairs, but mounting American casualties do trouble them and thus eat into a president's support. Democrat Lyndon B. Johnson routed Republican Barry Goldwater in the 1964 election, only to pull out of the 1968 contest because of the growing unpopularity of the Vietnam War. By contrast, George W. Bush won reelection in 2004 notwithstanding the controversial military engagement in Iraq. Although the war faced significant opposition both at home and abroad, it was still supported by a majority of Americans. Even unquestionably successful military efforts, though, also do not guarantee victory at the polls. The example of the senior George Bush demonstrates the transitory effect of even an overwhelming military victory. After record approval ratings on the heels of the first Gulf War in 1990, President Bush found that the afterglow quickly faded as voters turned their attention to the sour economy, leading to Bush's defeat in 1992 by Democrat Bill Clinton.

Economy

As suggested by George Bush's experience, the economy rivals war for influence on the vote. The state of the economy well before an election has long been recognized as an important indicator of how Americans will cast their ballots, particularly in presidential elections. Presumably, the fact that elections are shaped by the state of the economy does not come as a surprise to even the most casual observer of American politics. Candidates for public office, especially at the presidential level, regularly focus on economic conditions, epitomized by the informal slogan of Bill Clinton's 1992 campaign, "It's the economy, stupid." During the 1992 presidential election season, Clinton, with that slogan in mind, successfully capitalized on a relatively weak economy. Similarly, in 1980 Ronald Reagan turned to the camera during a televised debate with Jimmy Carter and asked voters, "Are you better off now than you were four years ago?" (when Carter's term began). At a time of high inflation and unemployment, few Americans could answer yes. Both Clinton and Reagan were drawing on the fact that voters generally vote *retro*spectively rather than *pro*spectively.[12] For all the promises candidates make about the good times that will roll under their future policies, elections (particularly presidential ones) are largely referenda on the state of the economy. Furthermore, the evaluation of the economy need not be limited to a voter's own wallet, but also can include its effect on the economic well-being of others. For example, voters with jobs may still punish an incumbent for a high unemployment rate. Casting a ballot on the basis of national conditions in this way is known as sociotropic voting.

Coattails

Even campaigns for offices below the presidential level have to be concerned with existing national conditions, because those races can be affected by the fate of the incumbent president during presidential election years. Historically, candidates who are members of the same party as the winning presidential candidate have been able to ride into office on the president's "coattails." Examples are the many Democratic members of Congress who rode on President Lyndon Johnson's coattails in the 1964 elections; likewise, many Republicans entered Congress upon Ronald Reagan's initial election to office in 1980. In more recent elections, presidential coattails have seemed shorter, because neither Bill Clinton nor George W. Bush was accompanied by a comparable congressional cohort upon winning the White House. From the perspective of a candidate running in a particular district or state, whether to embrace a presidential candidate, even of the same party, requires a careful calculation of the electoral consequences. In areas in which the president or presidential candidate is popular, local candidates are eager to showcase their connection to the person at the top of the ticket. Conversely, a common party label notwithstanding, local candidates will studiously avoid any association with an unpopular presidential candidate.

Midterm Elections

The shortening of the presidential coattails reflects in part the increasingly independent presidential and congressional elections. The decoupling of the two types of elections also means that voters are less likely than they once

were to use midterm elections to "send a message" to the president. The conventional wisdom, based on every race but one (1934) from the Civil War to 1994, had long held that the president's party loses seats in the midterm election. In both 1998 and 2002, however, the parties bucked the trend. In 1998 Democrats picked up five seats in the House with Bill Clinton in the White House, while in 2002 Republicans gained four with George W. Bush as president. In 2002 the GOP also gained a seat in the Senate to become the majority party.

One common explanation for the apparent end of the predictable midterm loss for the president's party is that idiosyncratically local issues are dominating races for the House and Senate. Yet local issues have long loomed large in such races. Indeed, the long-term trend has been toward greater nationalization of campaigns. For example, in the 1994 midterm elections House Republicans, under the leadership of Newt Gingrich of Georgia, explicitly adopted a national election strategy. Republican candidates promoted their Contract with America, made up of campaign promises for all GOP House members. Because a similar strategy has not reappeared since 1994, many casual observers have suggested that the nationalization of congressional elections was a flash in the pan, discarded as was Gingrich himself. In truth, congressional campaigns for candidates of both parties continue to be subject to nationalizing forces, although they are more subtle than efforts like the Contract with America. The central committees of the parties are actively recruiting congressional candidates, dispensing advice on campaign strategy, assisting with advertising, and so on. Taken together, these functions of operatives in the parties' headquarters have served to homogenize congressional campaigns nationwide. All politics may be local, but congressional campaigns generally have a national flavor to them.

Whether a presidential candidate's coattails are long or short, races in presidential and midterm years provide very different electoral environments, a fact that candidates ignore at their peril. Most significantly, turnout is substantially higher in presidential years, suggesting that the midterm electorate is skewed toward the most dedicated voters. Thus congressional voting has become increasingly partisan—both a cause and an effect of the increasing polarization of the two parties. (Voting in congressional elections remains less partisan than in presidential contests only because congressional incumbents, especially in the House, have such a huge electoral advantage, as discussed earlier.)

Conclusion

This discussion of how differing levels of turnout affect midterm and presidential elections has brought this chapter full circle, because it serves as a reminder that U.S.

elections are as much about who casts a ballot as for whom the ballot is cast. The question *Who votes?* goes hand in hand with *Who votes for whom?* For the purposes of empirical analysis, it is often useful to think of these decisions as distinct, but in reality they are inextricably linked. Thus any campaign strategist needs to worry not only about turning out the vote, but also about how those who turn out are going to vote once they get to the polls. Anyone who neglects who votes runs a serious risk of seeing the supporters of his or her candidate stay home on election day. And anyone who neglects who votes for whom runs the risk of helping the supporters of his or her opponent get to the polls. The secret to electoral success is to pay equal attention to both. Likewise, the secret to understanding U.S. elections is to treat both as equally important.

Notes

1. Robert D. Putnam, *Bowling Alone: The Collapse and Revival of American Community* (New York: Simon and Schuster, 2000); Martin P. Wattenberg, *Where Have All the Voters Gone?* (Cambridge, Mass.: Harvard University Press, 2002); Thomas E. Patterson, *The Vanishing Voter: Public Involvement in an Age of Uncertainty* (New York: Knopf, 2002).

2. Michael P. McDonald and Samuel L. Popkin, "The Myth of the Vanishing Voter," *American Political Science Review* 95, no. 4 (2001): 963–974.

3. Norman H. Nie, Jane Junn, and Kenneth Stehlik-Berry, *Education and Democratic Citizenship in America* (Chicago: University of Chicago Press, 1996).

4. Raymond E. Wolfinger and Steven J. Rosenstone, *Who Votes?* (New Haven, Conn.: Yale University Press, 1980).

5. Donald P. Green and Alan S. Gerber, *Get Out the Vote! How to Increase Voter Turnout* (Washington, D.C.: Brookings, 2004).

6. Donald Green, Bradley Palmquist, and Eric Shickler, *Partisan Hearts and Minds: Political Parties and the Social Identities of Voters* (New Haven, Conn.: Yale University Press, 2002).

7. Larry M. Bartels, "Partisanship and Voting Behavior, 1952–1996," *American Journal of Political Science* 44, no. 1 (2000): 35–50.

8. V. O. Key, *The Responsible Electorate: Rationality in Presidential Voting, 1936–1960* (Cambridge, Mass.: Belknap Press of Harvard University Press, 1966).

9. Angus Campbell, Philip E. Converse, Warren E. Miller, and Donald E. Stokes, *The American Voter* (New York: Wiley, 1960).

10. Geoffrey Layman, *The Great Divide: Religious and Cultural Conflict in American Party Politics* (New York: Columbia University Press, 2001).

11. Samuel L. Popkin, *The Reasoning Voter: Communication and Persuasion in Presidential Campaigns*, 2d ed. (Chicago: University of Chicago Press, 1994).

12. Morris P. Fiorina, *Retrospective Voting in American National Elections* (New Haven, Conn.: Yale University Press, 1981).

Bartels, Larry M. "Partisanship and Voting Behavior, 1952–1996." *American Journal of Political Science* 44, no. 1 (2000): 35–50.

Campbell, Angus, Philip E. Converse, Warren E. Miller, and Donald E. Stokes. *The American Voter*. New York: John Wiley, 1960.

Fiorina, Morris P. *Retrospective Voting in American National Elections*. New Haven, Conn.: Yale University Press, 1981.

Green, Donald P., and Alan S. Gerber. *Get Out the Vote! How to Increase Voter Turnout*. Washington, D.C.: Brookings, 2004.

Green, Donald, Bradley Palmquist, and Eric Shickler. *Partisan Hearts and Minds: Political Parties and the Social Identities of Voters*. New Haven, Conn.: Yale University Press, 2002.

Key, V. O. *The Responsible Electorate: Rationality in Presidential Voting, 1936–1960*. Cambridge, Mass.: Belknap Press of Harvard University Press, 1966.

Layman, Geoffrey. *The Great Divide: Religious and Cultural Conflict in American Party Politics*. New York: Columbia University Press, 2001.

McDonald, Michael P., and Samuel L. Popkin. "The Myth of the Vanishing Voter." *American Political Science Review* 95, no. 4 (2002): 963–974.

Nie, Norman H., Jane Junn, and Kenneth Stehlik-Berry. *Education and Democratic Citizenship in America*. Chicago: University of Chicago Press, 1996.

Patterson, Thomas E. *The Vanishing Voter: Public Involvement in an Age of Uncertainty*. New York: Knopf, 2002.

Popkin, Samuel. *The Reasoning Voter: Communication and Persuasion in Presidential Campaigns*. 2d ed. Chicago: University of Chicago Press, 1994.

Putnam, Robert D. *Bowling Alone: The Collapse and Revival of American Community*. New York: Simon and Schuster, 2000.

Wattenberg, Martin P. *Where Have All the Voters Gone?* Cambridge, Mass: Harvard University Press, 2002.

Wolfinger, Raymond E., and Steven J. Rosenstone. *Who Votes?* New Haven, Conn.: Yale University Press, 1980.

Suggested Readings

Ansolabehere, Stephen, and Shanto Iyengar. *Going Negative: How Political Advertisements Shrink and Polarize the Electorate*. New York: Free Press, 1995.

PART IV
The Players

CHAPTER 9

The Candidates

Cherie D. Maestas and Cynthia R. Rugeley

The health of American democracy depends on the willingness of citizens to run for office. Campaigns cannot take place without candidates, and voters cannot make choices about political leadership unless they are presented with meaningful options during the campaign process. The quality of those choices depends, most fundamentally, on the qualities of the men and women who choose to become candidates for office.

U.S. voters regularly elect thousands of local, state, and national public officeholders. In America's candidate-centered electoral system, the decision to run is in the hands of those Americans able to meet the minimum requirements for any given office. Often, the formal requirements are minimal, and so literally thousands or millions are eligible to seek elective office. However, the vast majority of eligible citizens have no interest in running, and only a few eligible citizens ever become candidates. Who are the men and women who willingly subject themselves to the rigors of campaigning? Why do they choose to run while others choose to sit on the sidelines? And are they "average citizens," or do they differ substantially in income, occupation, race, or other characteristics? The answers to these questions are important, because the quality and content of campaigns that citizens evaluate when electing public leaders are directly related to candidates' backgrounds, resources, skills, and abilities.

Becoming a Candidate

The path to becoming a candidate varies tremendously for each person, but the first step on that path must begin with the formation of political career ambitions. Ambition for political office stems from a combination of personal characteristics or goals and the structure of opportunities to win local, state, or federal office. This section explores the factors that shape ambitions for office and traces the more well-worn career paths of legislators and executives. It concludes by looking at the more unusual career paths followed by political amateurs (see Box 9-1 for examples of two contrasting career paths).

Ambition for Office

Ambition is defined as "an eager or strong desire to achieve something, such as fame or power," [1] and it is a precondition for becoming a candidate. A lack of ambition will keep even the best potential candidates out of the ring, whereas strong ambitions can prompt individuals to run, even when the odds are against them. But where does ambition for political office come from? Studies of the political elite—such as party leaders, community leaders, officeholders, and candidates—over the years have offered some ideas about political ambition, but no consensus. The three commonly cited sources of ambition for office are psychological factors, socialization into the political system, and the opportunity structure of the political career ladder. The latter can be thought of as "strategic" ambition, because it focuses on how the political system creates costs and incentives that shape the decisions of possible candidates for office.

Sociopsychological Bases of Ambition

Congressional scholar Linda Fowler has reviewed some early studies on ambition and found that scholars focused on the emergence of candidates as a class-based phenomenon and as a function of personality traits. Studies of candidate personalities sought to identify particular traits, such as power needs or authoritarian tendencies, thought to prompt ambitions for public office. Contemporary literature, however, questions the existence of a distinct "leadership personality." Instead, politics and public office satisfy a range of psychological needs, and those needs or interests differ across individuals.[2]

At the same time, people who are likely to emerge as candidates do have common characteristics. A personal attraction to public life stimulates individuals to become involved in politics. Indeed, men and women who have specific policy interests, or a desire to shape government choices, are more likely to consider a political career than those who lack such interests. Conversely, citizens who choose politics as a career generally feel a duty to serve the public in some capacity. Many of those who seek and hold public office simply enjoy politics as a vocation. A survey of potential candidates for the U.S. House of

BOX 9-1
TRADITIONAL AND NONTRADITIONAL POLITICAL CAREER PATHS: TWO EXAMPLES

A Traditional Career Path,
Sen. Bob Graham, D-Fla.

Bob Graham's election to the U.S. Senate in 1986 was just one more step in a long career in politics.

Graham was socialized into politics early in life. His father served as both a state senator and a gubernatorial candidate in Florida. Through his family, Graham met party and political leaders and worked for vice-presidential nominee Lyndon B. Johnson at the 1960 Democratic National Convention.

Graham first ran for and won elective office in 1967. He served in the Florida House until 1971, when he was elected to the Florida Senate. From there, he ran for the governor's office and held that post from 1979 to 1987. At the end of his term as governor, Graham sought a U.S. Senate seat and won handily. His bids for reelection to the Senate were also successful. Graham ran for the Democratic presidential nomination in 2004, but dropped out of the race after five months. He retired from the Senate in 2005.

A Nontraditional Career Path,
Sen. Bill Bradley, D-N.J.

Bill Bradley won a seat in the U.S. Senate in 1978 with no prior political experience, but with perhaps as much fame as any member of the upper chamber.

Bradley was a basketball star during his college days at Princeton University, and later he enjoyed a Hall of Fame career with the New York Knicks. In 1964 he served as captain of the U.S. Olympic basketball team that won the gold medal in Tokyo. In between leaving Princeton and becoming a professional, Bradley attended Oxford University on a Rhodes Scholarship.

Bradley's only work in government was interning for a congressman during the summer before his graduation from Princeton. In 1978 Bradley ran for the U.S. Senate, defeating Republican Jeffrey Bell, who had unseated incumbent Republican Clifford Case in the primary. Bradley served four terms in the Senate before leaving to run unsuccessfully for the Democratic presidential nomination in 2000.

Sources: CQ's Politics in America, 1988, the 100th Congress (Washington, D.C.: Congressional Quarterly, 1988); *CQ's Politics in America, 2004, the 108th Congress* (Washington, D.C.: CQ Press, 2004).

Table 9-1 Potential U.S. House Candidates' Reasons for Involvement in Politics

| Importance of . . . | Percentage listing reason as "important" or "extremely important" | |
	Officeholders	Nonofficeholders
Influencing public policy	93	93
Concern about a particular issue	53	61
Interest in serving public	90	84
Advancing political career	14	23
Making social contacts	6	11
Making business contacts	5	15
Excitement of politics	42	42
Smallest number of cases	940	194

Source: Candidate Emergence Study, 1998.

Note: The survey asked potential U.S. House candidates, such as city and state officeholders and prominent private citizens, in two hundred House districts to indicate the importance of each of the reasons shown in the table to their current involvement in politics. Answer choices ranged from "extremely unimportant" (−3) to "extremely important" (+3), but shown in the table is the percentage of those who responded "important" or "extremely important." The percentage shown for each line item is the percentage of the total response to that item.

Although 1,201 people responded to the survey, not all respondents answered every question. "Smallest number of cases" indicates the fewest number of responses to each line item for the full battery of items.

Representatives in 1998 revealed a range of reasons for their involvement in politics (see Table 9-1).[3] Although the vast majority cited public service and policy goals as important, a small percentage also admitted to more pedestrian, self-interested reasons, such as making business or social contacts.

So, why do some citizens develop a strong interest in public service while others do not? Early socialization, mentorship, and recruitment play an important role. Family socialization to politics is perhaps most central to the formation of ambition. In other cases, educators and educational experiences prompt an awareness and interest in politics. Family and cultural background offer young children a varied exposure to politics. The children of community, business, and political leaders are likely to have greater contact with the political world because of parental involvement in politics, and they are more likely to view public service as an appropriate and desirable career. Parental activity in politics is often a major predictor of a child's future participation, including candidacy. This type of socialization is evident in some of America's

prominent political families such as the Kennedys of Massachusetts, who produced a long list of public servants, ranging from local officials to President John F. Kennedy. Likewise, the Bush family has, so far, produced two presidents, a U.S. senator, and a governor of Florida. Indeed, the fact that socialization often occurs in certain types of families and is more common among elite families has led scholars to view ambition as an elite phenomenon.

Strategic Ambition

Although the sociopsychological aspects of ambition are important, equally if not more important is the "strategic" aspect of ambition. Historian Joseph A. Schlesinger has pointed out that ambition is directly related to the opportunities one has to win office.[4] Few people develop ambitions for the unattainable. Rather, they tend to develop ambitions for offices that they have a reasonable expectation of winning. The strategic aspects of ambition and candidacies relate not so much to the interests, backgrounds, and personalities of candidates, but to the environment in which candidates find themselves and how that environment shapes the chances of winning and the costs of obtaining office. These factors will be discussed in detail later in this chapter.

Ambitions for office differ across individuals and across the life cycle of a political career. Schlesinger identifies three types of ambition that lead people to become candidates for office: *discrete ambition*—the ambition to hold a seat for a short time and then return to private life; *static ambition*—the desire to hold a single office for a long-term career; and *progressive ambition*—the desire to move up the political career ladder to obtain higher office. Although all three types of ambition prompt the emergence of political candidates, the second and third lead to repeat candidacies. Younger candidates and lower-level officeholders are more likely to be ambitious for higher office than older potential candidates or those who already hold a high-ranking political office. A combination of personal political goals, experiences holding office, and assessments of the opportunity to move to higher office serves to shape the type of ambition a person holds at each stage of his or her political career.

The Political Opportunity Structure and Career Paths

The formation of static or progressive ambition is closely related to the political opportunities that prospective candidates see before them. Although the American political career ladder is not rigid or impermeable, the arrangement of local and state political offices are roughly hierarchical, with local and state legislative offices seen as less prestigious or rewarding than statewide or national political offices. In most states, the size of constituency increases as an officeholder moves from local to state and from state to national office. Similarly, the complexity and breadth of policy problems increase as one moves from local to national office. As a result, office resources, prestige, power, and salary all tend to increase as well. Taken together, these differences make some offices more attractive than others and prompt progressive ambition among lower officeholders.

The hierarchy of offices is important, because it creates a career "ladder" for politicians that channels ambitions and competition for office in a predictable way. Serving in lower offices helps officeholders to decide whether they enjoy public service as a career, allows prospective candidates to build a political record and a constituent base, and helps them to develop the skills to run a competitive campaign for higher office. At the same time, it is important to note the surprising openness of the political system to candidate entry at any level. Harold D. Lasswell once described the career path as "a tangle of ladders, ropes and runways that attract people from other activities at various stages of the process, and lead others to a dead end or a drop."[5] This chapter, then, defines a common path through which candidates progress to higher offices, but in doing it certainly does not define the only path.

The "Legislative Path"

Generally, the pinnacle of a legislative career is the U.S. Senate, although many politicians end their career with long service in the U.S. House. Candidates for national office perform best on the campaign trail when they have an established record of legislative service, a strong constituent base, campaign skills, and ample financial resources. Because experience pays off for candidates by increasing their vote share and odds of success, most U.S. House and Senate members have experience in legislative service. Well over half of House members came to office after serving in their state legislature, and over half of senators served first in the U.S. House. Some senators also served first as governors of their states. Because both the offices of U.S. senator and governor are statewide, governors who are subjected to term limits can capitalize on their success and public support to move on to national office. Thus even though the political system certainly allows amateurs—often celebrities or wealthy citizens—to enter directly at the national level, most candidates move up through lower office ranks. It is therefore possible to identify a career ladder that typically begins at the local elective office or at the state legislature level and extends to the U.S. House and Senate.

Career ladders differ within each state, however, in part because of the differences in the professionalism of the state legislatures. State legislatures range in professionalism from the part-time, low-paying "amateur" bodies in states such as Alabama or New Hampshire, to the full-time, high-paying professional legislatures in states such as California or Wisconsin. Professionalism affects career ladders in two ways. First, political novices have an easier time jump-starting their careers in nonprofessional legislatures than in professional ones. In an amateur body,

the less rigorous competition for office and the fewer resources usually needed to win office allow more inexperienced candidates to gain office. Second, legislative professionalism shapes the ability of candidates to move up the political career ladder. Candidates for professional legislatures often employ a professional campaign staff, create a media-oriented campaign, and raise and spend a substantial amount of money. Candidates for nonprofessional legislatures rely on volunteer staff, run low-visibility campaigns, and raise little money. Actual numbers give a sense of the difference: in 2002 candidates for the California state assembly raised an average of $295,000, whereas candidates for Wyoming's nonprofessional legislature raised an average of less than $5,000.[6] In addition to differences in campaign experience, legislators in professional institutions have access to more resources to build a loyal constituency. Professional legislatures also typically offer their members staff support, money to fund a district office, and some limited mailing privileges—resources that can be used to secure a member's existing seat as well as to prepare a base for moving up.

At the same time, the attractiveness of a lower office can stifle the desire of prospective candidates to seek a higher office. Lower offices that offer a full-time legislative career, high salaries, and ample opportunities for involvement in shaping policies are attractive venues for long-term careers. As such, professional legislatures may become a stopping point rather than a rung to higher office. Or, to put it differently, the opportunity structure encourages static rather than progressive ambition. In-depth interviews with state legislators in New York revealed that many prefer a long-term career at the state level to making a risky run for a U.S. House seat.[7]

Perhaps the most significant change to the legislative career path in recent years is the advent of term limits. Term limits fundamentally alter the calculus of ambition by denying candidates the ability to exercise static ambition. The results of term limit laws have not yet been fully realized, and attempts to study the effects of these laws on the career path of legislators have produced mixed results. In some states, the career ladder is turned upside down as term-limited state senators move down the ladder to the state assembly. In other states, term-limited legislators move to local or statewide elective positions. Because U.S. House seats can be so difficult to win, the advent of term limits does not uniformly or clearly increase the number of candidates for the U.S. House. Instead, state legislators seem to look for other outlets in which to serve while waiting for a clear opportunity for a national office.

The "Executive Path"

The executive path is similar to the legislative path in that it begins at the local level and ends with the most prestigious national office—president of the United States. However, the executive path is less clearly marked than the legislative path. Some take a path through state legislative office into statewide office and then seek the governor's office. Others move through local positions into statewide office. A small percentage come to statewide office as amateurs. In one sense, it is not surprising to find candidates from many different backgrounds emerging to run for statewide executive posts, including the gubernatorial seat. Most state executive offices are subject to term limits and therefore present more frequent opportunities for candidates to run in open-seat contests. Candidates are much more likely to win an open-seat race than a race against a popular incumbent, and political novices as well as experienced politicians are aware of this fact. As a result, the primary fields for state executive posts are often crowded with candidates from many walks of life.

Candidates for president of the United States are defined by two sets of standards—the requirements detailed in the U.S. Constitution and the more informal requirements of candidacy of the voting public. The constitutional requirements to serve as president reflect some of the early goals of the founders. The president must be a native-born citizen, a fourteen-year resident of the United States, and at least thirty-five years of age. Those requirements ensure that the executive is free of foreign influence and of a mature age.

In practice, the American public has expected its candidates to be professional and capable of meeting the rigorous demands of the presidency. American voters tend to look for a candidate with a record of experience in positions of public trust and with a demonstrated ability to perform well during a long and often arduous political campaign. Presidential candidates must be able to reach out and inspire large audiences, and apparently they must possess what Bruce Buchanan has described as an "old-fashioned morality." [8] Democratic senators Gary Hart of Colorado and Edward M. Kennedy of Massachusetts both fell short of that test during their runs for the presidential nomination when allegations arose about marital infidelities and other questionable personal behavior. Bill Clinton's election in 1992 and his reelection in 1996 amid allegations of extramarital affairs raised questions about whether the public today is becoming more forgiving of moral transgressions. Recent elections seem to bear this out, because questions about George W. Bush's alleged drug use and National Guard service were not central issues in the minds of voters who elected him to office.

Studies of presidential campaigns since the twentieth century have identified three dominant career paths of nominees.[9] Until 1960, governors dominated the nominating process. Members of Congress, judges, military heroes, and business leaders occasionally emerged as nominees, but governors were the primary recipients of the party nominations. Theodore Roosevelt, Woodrow Wilson, and Franklin D. Roosevelt all stepped up from being governors to serving in the White House. The second phase emerged between 1960 and 1972 when nominees

4.ᵗʰ May 1840,

Published by J.S.Horton, corner Baltimore and South St.
Baltimore, Md.

Whig candidate William Henry Harrison capitalized on his background as a war hero to win the presidential election of 1840. Many U.S. presidents have used military service as a stepping-stone to the White House.
Source: Library of Congress

were primarily former U.S. senators. Included among the ranks of former U.S. senators were Presidents Kennedy, Lyndon B. Johnson, and Richard Nixon and nominees Barry Goldwater, Hubert H. Humphrey, George McGovern, and Walter F. Mondale.[10]

Since 1976, presidential nominees have once again tended to be state governors. Presidents Jimmy Carter, Ronald Reagan, Bill Clinton, and George W. Bush all served as governors, as did Democratic nominee Michael S. Dukakis. Presidents George Bush, Lyndon Johnson, Richard Nixon, and Gerald R. Ford and Democratic nominees Al Gore, Hubert Humphrey, and Walter Mondale are all recent examples of presidential nominees who sought promotion from the vice presidency. Candidates lacking elected office experience have stressed other executive qualifications. H. Ross Perot and Steve Forbes emphasized their business backgrounds, and President

Dwight D. Eisenhower and 2004 Democratic candidate Wesley Clark emphasized their experiences as military generals.

Recent presidents and nominees have had mixed occupational backgrounds. Although it is still common to see governors and senators on the candidate lists, it is also more common for the path from amateur to the White House to be quite short. For George W. Bush, Ronald Reagan, and Bill Clinton, the gubernatorial posts in their states were their first and only political positions prior to running for president.

The Roads Less Traveled—Paths for Amateurs

In recent years, more and more amateurs have jumped directly into the political arena for high-level office rather than working their way up the political ladder from local office. Two of the notable political amateurs are basketball star Bill Bradley, who won a seat in the U.S. Senate in 1978 with no prior political experience, and movie star and body builder Arnold Schwarzenegger, who won California's gubernatorial recall election in 2003. Neither had ever held elective office, but both saw an opportunity to convert past experiences and visibility into political careers. Celebrities are only one category of amateurs who throw their hats in the ring for public office each year. Amateurs can range from a local janitor (one ran in several elections for a U.S. House seat in Texas) to highly credible, well-funded, and respected local business leaders. What makes these individuals run?

David T. Canon, in his study of political amateurs, identifies three types of amateurs who run for office: the *ambitious amateur,* who behaves much like an experienced, progressively ambitious politician when weighing the choice to run; the *policy amateur,* who runs to further a cause or bring visibility to an issue; and the *hopeless (or experience-seeking) amateur,* who runs with little or no hope of winning.[11] The decision process for those in the first two categories is "rational" in the sense that the goals and reasons for running are clear. It is less clear why those in the latter category run. Some may simply misjudge the political environment. Others may run as a favor to party leaders so that a name appears on the ballot beside the party label. Still others may run as a lark. The distinction between hopeless amateurs and ambitious amateurs is the realistic chances of winning a seat. The ambitious amateur emerges when chances are optimal, such as when an incumbent retires. The hopeless amateur steps into the ring despite overwhelming odds against winning.

What makes some amateurs more successful than others? A variety of factors shape the prospects of all candidates, and amateurs are no different. Wealth, visibility, a knack for organization, and a tireless drive to succeed are the necessary ingredients of a strong campaign. Amateurs who are independently wealthy often have an advantage, because they can purchase any visibility that they lack.

For example, investment banker Jon S. Corzine spent $60 million of his own money to win an open New Jersey U.S. Senate seat in 2000. In nearby New York City, media mogul Michael Bloomberg dipped into his own pocket in 2001 to the tune of $79 million to finance his successful effort to replace retiring mayor Rudolf Giuliani. By the same token, many high-profile wealthy candidates have been defeated. In Texas, Laredo businessman and lawyer Tony Sanchez spent $60 million of his personal wealth on a losing bid for governor, while businessman and publisher Steve Forbes spent $30 million of his own money on his short-lived 1996 presidential campaign. Money, although it helps, does not guarantee a victory.

The decline of political party influence in elections and the growing importance of the news media have contributed to a trend in which Americans turn toward celebrity candidates and "political legacy" candidates from famous political families (for more on the media's role in political campaigns, see Chapter 13). Darrell M. West and John M. Orman in their book *Celebrity Politics* argue that the media now emphasize Hollywood-style gossip and scandal in political coverage to the detriment of traditional politicians and parties, changing the political system into a "celebrity regime."[12] At the same time, they point out that these celebrity outsiders might represent a way to revitalize American politics, because they might seem more credible to voters who have become cynical about a government that works backroom deals with other politicians. Celebrities are familiar faces to voters, but they come from outside the political arena many Americans have come to distrust.

Finally, an important but often overlooked class of "amateur" candidates are the unelected politicians—that is, those who move through the ranks of appointive offices or work in the halls of state and national political institutions. Service in the political party or as staffers to legislators or executives brings possible candidates into contact with the campaigns and helps them to develop the skills they need to run their own campaign. Moreover, legislative aides develop policy expertise in areas relevant to constituents in their district or state, and they gain insights into the needs and opinions of constituents. It is not surprising to find that in the 108th Congress (2003–2004), seventy of the House and Senate members had previously served as congressional aides.

The Decision to Enter a Race

A prospective candidate with ambitions for a particular political office must decide when to enter the race to win that office. The decision is often challenging, because potential candidates must make guesstimates about the costs of running and their chances of success. Political elites may actively encourage individuals to run, but the final decision rests with the candidates who must commit their own resources to risky races. Factors that influence the decision include their assessments of the district, the incumbent, national political or economic shifts, the personal and monetary costs of running, and their own willingness to meet the requirements of state and federal election laws.

Emergence versus Recruitment

Several decades ago, scholars and political observers believed candidacies were filled by party recruitment. As party leaders worked their way up through the ranks of party positions, they identified potential candidates from among loyal party members. Because various party organizations—primarily local party machines—held the power to choose party nominees, they had the power to handpick and groom individuals to become officeholders. Dedication to the party agenda and loyalty to party leaders were important qualifications.

In recent decades, however, the concept of candidate "recruitment" has given way to candidate "emergence." With the advent of primary elections to nominate candidates for office, party leaders lost the power to handpick and groom nominees (for a discussion of the changes in nominating procedures and their impact, see Chapter 5). Now, prospective candidates act as "self-starters" in choosing when and where to run for office. To win nomination, candidates must develop a campaign team, raise money, formulate a message, and get that message to voters. In most states, the party stays out of this process, at least in a public sense, to avoid visibly backing a loser. Prospective candidates recognize the limited role of the party organization in the nominating phase, and thus they first look to their own skills and resources when deciding whether to enter a race.

Yet even in a candidate-centered era, the party still plays some role in the emergence of candidates (also see Chapter 11 on political parties). Party leaders often talk to and encourage individuals to run for office and promise support in the event that those candidates secure the nomination. At times, the party may actively discourage candidates from running to prevent a divisive primary that might hurt party fortunes in the general election. Party encouragement sends important signals to candidates about likely support in the general election and about the chances a district is winnable. Potential candidates for national office are most influenced by the efforts of the national party organizations, the Democratic and Republican National Committees, and the Democratic and Republican campaign committees that serve candidates for the House and Senate. Because national parties ration their resources to focus on the most competitive and winnable districts, contact by the national party sends an important message about a prospective candidate's prospects for winning. State and local party organizations can also encourage candidates for national of-

fice, but are most influential in encouraging candidates for state and local offices.

What types of candidates are the parties likely to target when they contact people about running for office? It depends, in part, on the office and in part on the electoral context. In national, state, or local races expected to be competitive, parties target the strongest possible candidates they can find—preferably ones with previous experience running a professional campaign team. If experienced candidates are unavailable or unwilling to run, parties might look to local "celebrities" or community and business leaders. Noncompetitive or incumbent-held districts present the greatest challenge in finding party candidates. In these districts, the opposition candidate is likely to be a sacrificial lamb, who only serves as a name with the party label. In these situations, parties seek anyone willing to put his or her name on the ballot, provided that the person will not embarrass the party. Often, however, parties find it difficult to lead anyone to slaughter.

Strategic Choices

Regardless of background or experience, all prospective candidates face the same decision: should I run now, or should I wait? The decision to run rests heavily on potential candidates' assessments of their chances of winning weighed against the costs of running. Those costs are not only financial, but also personal—time away from family or careers, as well as the heavy toll an aggressive campaign can take on a candidate and a candidate's family. Even incumbents must go through the decision process of weighing their chances, skills, and resources against those of their prospective challengers and against the costs of running. In this sense, the decision for incumbents is roughly identical to that of nonincumbents. The difference between the two is that incumbents make their assessments in full knowledge that they have fared well in past elections and that they have control over substantial resources to reinforce their chances of winning in the future.

Rules of the Game

State and national laws that define the "rules of the game"—such as those dealing with candidate eligibility requirements, nominating procedures, campaign finance laws—affect both the chances of winning and the costs of running.

In the realm of *eligibility laws,* candidates for state and local offices must adhere to state guidelines for eligibility and must officially "file" to be a candidate for office. National candidates must meet constitutional requirements as well as state filing requirements. Those seeking to become a candidate must fill out paperwork showing that they meet the minimum requirements to run, and they must pay a fee or demonstrate support for their candidacy by submitting a petition signed by registered voters (the required number of signatures varies from state to state). The minimum requirements often include age and

Table 9-2 Age and Residency Requirements for Major-Party Candidates in Four States

| State | Governor | | State assembly | |
	Age	Citizenship/residency	Age	Citizenship/residency
California	No requirement	U.S. citizen Registered to vote in state	No requirement	U.S. citizen Registered to vote in assembly district
Florida	Thirty	Resident of state seven years Registered to vote	Twenty-one	Resident of state two years Resident of district
Indiana	Thirty	Resident of state five years	Twenty-one	Resident of state two years Resident of district one year
Oklahoma	Thirty-one	Qualified elector in state ten years	Twenty-one	Resident of district six months Registered to vote in district

Source: State election codes of each state, accessed through official state Web sites.

Table 9-3 Filing Fee Requirements for Major-Party Candidates in Four States (2004 filing deadline)

| State (deadlines) | Governor | | U.S. House | | State assembly | |
	Filing fee	Petition	Filing fee	Petition	Filing fee	Petition
California (December 10)	2 percent of salary	10,000 in lieu of fee	1 percent of salary	3,000 in lieu of fee	1 percent of salary	1,500 in lieu of fee
Florida (May 7, federal and judicial candidates; July 16, all others)	6 percent of salary	1 percent of total registered voters in state in lieu of fee	6 percent of salary	1 percent of total registered voters in district in lieu of fee	6 percent of salary	1 percent of total registered voters in district in lieu of fee
Indiana (February 20)	None	4,500, (500 from each U.S. House district)	None	None	None	None
Oklahoma (June 23)	$1,500	None	$750	None	$200	None

Source: State election codes of each state, accessed through official state Web sites.

residency restrictions, as well as status as a registered voter (see Table 9-2).

All paperwork and fees must be submitted by the filing deadline set by each state. Filing deadlines range from as much as a year before the general election to as little as a few months (see Table 9-3 for the filing deadlines and requirements for candidacy for various offices in four states). Earlier filing deadlines place a heavier burden on candidates—particularly challengers to incumbents—because they make the campaign season longer, forcing candidates to make decisions about running under greater uncertainty about political conditions at the time of the general election. High fees or petition requirements tend to discourage candidates who have no chance of winning or who plan to run for personal rather than strategic reasons. Notably, the cost of filing increases with the prestige of office, with statewide and national offices at the top of the fee structure.

As for the *nomination rules*, each state and party has its own rules for securing a party nomination (see Chapter 5 for specific details). The "openness" of the primary system and the timing of the primary or caucus affect the calculus of prospective candidates as they consider running. States with a closed nominating process that limits participation to party members will attract candidates who appeal to the traditional party base. Nominating systems that are more open attract candidates who are "outsiders" or centrists—that is, who can mobilize a broad base of support within and beyond the party base. The timing of the nomination matters, because it defines the length of the campaign season and, consequently, the costs. An early primary means a long, grueling, and typically more costly campaign season. However, a long period between a divisive primary and the general election can give a candidate time to recover and refill the financial coffers.

The system of nominating presidential candidates is a process unlike that for any other office (also see Chapter 20 on presidential campaigns). Presidential hopefuls must win the nomination in many individual state primaries or caucuses over a period that runs from January to July of the election year. Candidates must crisscross the country, trying to find a message that appeals to voters from diverse backgrounds with different needs and concerns. They must contend with all types of nominating systems, from party caucuses that attract the party faithful in Iowa to the open primaries in Minnesota that attract voters from both parties. Different nominating procedures call for different candidate strategies, including, at times, different types of campaign messages. This process favors candidates who are moderate rather than extreme and candidates who can develop platforms that appeal to the broadest constituencies.

Although the process of campaigning in different states at different times and to different audiences is challenging, the dynamics and sequencing of nomination contests also create opportunities. Unknown or maverick candidates can gain name recognition, media attention, and momentum from early primaries or caucuses. Indeed, in recent years some surprise finishes in the earliest caucuses and primaries stimulated interest and money for candidates who had been dubbed "unlikely." Early successes in primary elections extended the campaign lives of religious leader Pat Robertson in 1988, Republican challenger Pat Buchanan in 1992, and Sen. John McCain in 2000. Early victories by Governors Ronald Reagan in 1980 and Bill Clinton in 1992 helped to showcase their talents as candidates and build momentum for their campaigns. Candidates who are not well known or who are outsiders to the party may place great weight on the first few nomination contests in deciding whether to run. Without victories or at least strong second-place showings in early contests, their chances are virtually nil.

Other key rules and laws revolve around district boundaries and campaign finance. National candidates are subject to national campaign finance laws administered by the Federal Election Commission (FEC). The limits and constraints placed on candidates' fund-raising and spending shape their chances of success (for specific details on campaign finance laws, see Chapter 6). Efforts

to build name recognition in the district and to get a candidate's message out to voters cost money. The more money required to run a successful campaign, the more state and national laws governing campaign finance will influence candidate decisions. Restrictive fund-raising practices fall most heavily on those candidates challenging incumbents. Incumbents already enjoy high name recognition and free media attention—resources a challenger must purchase to compete effectively.

District boundaries play a central role in shaping the decisions of legislative candidates, because the boundaries most directly determine the chances that a candidate from one party or the other can win office. Redistricting is usually carried out once per decade, after the decennial census when House seats are reapportioned. In most states, the legislature defines the boundaries for state legislative seats and for U.S. House seats. The process is highly political, because it determines how competitive seats will be for members of each party. When states draw boundaries that create single-party districts, prospective candidates from the favored party are likely to far outnumber those from the "out" party. Often, changes to district boundaries strongly favor incumbents from the party that controls the state legislature. By contrast, incumbents from the party out of power often suffer in the redistricting process when the districts drawn are less secure for the incumbents or even eliminated. It is not surprising to see a surge in strategic "retirements" among incumbents after redistricting. Such a development opens up opportunities for nonincumbents to win and entices strong potential candidates to run.

Not surprisingly, redistricting can become quite acrimonious. In Texas, for example, statewide offices and the legislature had been dominated by Democrats since Reconstruction (1866–1877), but beginning in 1994 and culminating with the 2002 elections, Republicans captured all statewide offices and gained control of both chambers of the legislature. They then proceeded to argue that the political makeup of the state demanded that the GOP also hold a majority of U.S. House seats—at that point, Democrats held a 17–15 majority. In 2003, and therefore in a break with the custom of redistricting after the decennial census, the GOP-led and -dominated legislature proposed a bill that would redraw congressional boundaries to favor Republicans. Democrats responded by engaging in a parliamentary maneuver aimed at derailing Republican efforts. Fifty-one Democrats in the Texas House fled to Ardmore, Oklahoma, thereby breaking the quorum needed to bring up a bill in the 150-member House. Although House Speaker Tom Craddick dispatched Texas state troopers to Oklahoma to retrieve the House members, a Texas district court determined that neither the Texas Speaker of the House nor Texas state police had jurisdiction in other states. The legislature therefore adjourned its regular session with redistricting still on the table. When Texas governor Rick Perry called lawmakers into a special session, eleven Senate Democrats bolted, traveling to Albuquerque, New Mexico, to wait out the thirty-day session. This time, the Texas Supreme Court ruled that the state had no authority to force the lawmakers back to Texas. The Democrats' tactic forced state leaders to end the special session without a bill. After Perry called yet another special session, one wayward Democrat returned, the Senate rules on quorums were changed, and the redistricting bill sought by Republicans was approved.

Although Texas represents an extreme example of a bitter redistricting battle, the partisan stakes in all states are high when boundaries are redrawn. Each party's ability to convince strong candidates to run depends in part on its ability to convince prospective candidates that a race is winnable—and that depends at least in part on the placement of district boundaries.

Factors Influencing the Chances of Winning

The rules of the game for each office in each state underlie the political climate in which a candidate must run. However, the decision to enter a race depends on how a candidate views or deals with a host of factors that affect the chances of winning a particular race, including the possible opponent(s) in the primary and general election, the characteristics of the electoral arena, national and local political conditions, and financial support.

Perhaps the most important factor that prospective candidates consider is the strength and quality of their *likely opponents*. Because winning any office involves winning both the nomination and the general election, potential candidates must assess the strength of opponents in each stage. As noted earlier, district or electoral structure plays an important role here. Districts that favor one party are likely to attract strong candidates from the favored party and repel candidates from the party out of favor.

Similarly, prospective challengers must assess whether the incumbent will run in the race. Because incumbent reelection rates for many offices are well over 90 percent, most challengers think twice before stepping into the ring with one. Indeed, an incumbent-held seat attracts the weakest pool of candidates. Interestingly, inexperienced politicians are more likely than experienced challengers to choose to run against incumbents, even though their chances are lower. Experienced politicians generally prefer to wait for an open seat, particularly if they hold a desirable political office to begin with. Inexperienced politicians may have the best chance at winning the seat when they face no nomination challenge and can concentrate efforts on the general election. Indeed, many "hopeless amateurs" have been swept into office unexpectedly by a strong national tide.

Open-seat races attract the strongest field of candidates from both parties. Thus the chances of winning the general election may increase dramatically in the absence of an incumbent, but the prospects of winning the nomination often fade because the "best and brightest" seek the party nomination. Nevertheless, open seats generally offer nonincumbent candidates the best overall chance of winning an election and typically draw a large, high-quality field of candidates. For example, Texas congressman Larry Combest rarely faced challengers for his U.S. House seat during his tenure, and, when he did, they were only token candidates with little funding or chance of winning. However, when Combest stepped aside in 2002, a broad array of well-funded and viable candidates stepped forward, including business and community leaders and experienced state legislators hoping to move up. Most districts have an ample supply of possible candidates, but they rarely appear until conditions are favorable.

In conjunction with assessing the field of challengers, prospective candidates for office must evaluate the *electoral arena* in which the campaign battle will be waged. For state or local offices, the electoral arena may be quite small, encompassing only a few thousand voters. Most House candidates must assess the qualities of a district that has more than 600,000 citizens. Because each U.S. senator represents an entire state, anyone eyeing a Senate seat must gauge an even larger and more diverse population. Finally, those considering a run for the presidency must assess their own ability to appeal to a geographically and politically diverse landscape that encompasses all fifty states. The larger and more diverse the population, the more difficult it becomes for potential candidates to assess district characteristics and formulate a message that appeals to all. Larger, more diverse populations also are more expensive to reach and convince. Yet, on the upside, the prestige of the office grows with the size of the district.

Overall, the task of assessing the landscape is similar for all candidates, no matter the size of the district. They must determine the partisan leanings and policy preferences of constituents, the existing support for candidates or incumbents, and the chances that a new candidate could attract support. Some districts or states lean heavily toward one party. In these situations, the most important race, or competition, occurs during the nomination phase, because the general election phase just serves to rubberstamp the nominee. In heavily partisan districts, candidates from the weaker party may be reluctant to squander their resources and political capital on a run that is unlikely to be successful. But districts evenly matched between parties draw strong candidates from both.

A key part of assessing electoral conditions is determining how *national economic and political conditions* will affect likely voters. For prospective U.S. House and Senate candidates, this assessment often includes gauging the state of the national and local economy and the prevailing views of the president and his administration and forming a set of expectations about those views months in advance of an election. Potential candidates for state and local offices also study state and local economic conditions and whether approval of the governor is a possibility. When conditions favor members of their party, candidates-in-waiting are more likely to jump into the race. Popular presidents and governors can help candidates from their party ride their "coattails" into office by mobilizing party voters. When the economy is failing or when top party leaders are embroiled in scandal, potential candidates may decide to wait for a more favorable year rather than see their efforts scuttled by high opposition turnout.

Prospective Democratic candidates at all levels of government, but particularly congressional candidates, faced this dilemma in 1998 when President Clinton's marital infidelities became public knowledge. The scandal surfaced during a time that many high-quality candidates were considering whether to run for office. For Democrats, choosing to run meant having to defend the president and the party against charges of immorality. Many potential candidates feared that the negative views of Clinton would cost them votes and assessed their chances of winning as lower. As a result, some decided not to run. By contrast, Republicans became more optimistic about their chances, because they saw themselves as having a clear "moral" advantage and an additional weapon in their arsenal to help them attract votes. Although, ultimately, the scandal did not harm the general election outcomes of Democratic candidates who did choose to run, the party might have fared even better had the scandal not deterred some high-quality office seekers. At the same time, some Republicans—particularly those in competitive districts—felt a backlash from the Clinton scandal and performed more poorly than expected. Although potential candidates for office often factor in national conditions when considering a run, the outcome of those conditions can be unpredictable.

Finally, prospective candidates must assess *prospective supporters*—that is, the likelihood of obtaining support from local, state, and national party leaders; interest groups; community leaders; and, of course, family and friends. Interestingly, family and friends are the most important to potential candidates, because they become the inner circle the candidate relies on for emotional support during the campaign and political career. Indeed, few will run if family and close friends are vehemently opposed.

Potential candidates seek the support of key interest groups or industries that will contribute money directly through their political action committees (PACs), solicit and coordinate contributions from their members, and mobilize voters in behalf of the candidates (also see Chapter 12 on the role of interest groups in campaigns). Prospective candidates who have received commitments of support from important interests in and beyond their district tend to believe they have a better chance of winning the election than those who have no expectations of support. According to the seminal work by scholars Gary C. Jacobson and Samuel Kernell, interest group support for potential candidates tends to expand and contract with the national economic and political tides.[13] Candidates from the party favored by national political tides, such as Republican candidates during the conservative

movement of the 1990s, are more likely to receive support, and stronger candidates tend to emerge as a result. Interest group support of candidates magnifies and extends the effect of national political moods by increasing the odds that the favored party will win office.

Because prospective candidates view party support as central to their chances of winning, they base their decision to run partly on expectations of support from their party. Local party support is almost guaranteed to the party nominee. However, state and national party leaders are often more selective and, therefore, more influential. Party leaders direct the bulk of their resources toward the most winnable districts. This strategy sends important signals to interest groups and candidates in these target races, but it leaves candidates in less favorable races with the party label but little else in the way of support.

Costs of Running

Even if the conditions are favorable, the costs of running may seem so daunting that promising candidates decide not to run. Indeed, for most prospective candidates the tangible and intangible costs of mounting a campaign may outstrip the expected benefits of office, leading them to stay on the sidelines rather than run.

Tangible Costs of Running

The tangible costs include all those typically incurred by a campaign in running a campaign office and hiring campaign staff, creating and airing campaign ads, paying travel expenses, and employing political consultants to help develop and sell the campaign message. The type of campaign and associated expense vary greatly, depending on the office sought. District size, quality of opponents, and the level of professionalism of the office are the most central factors in the costs of campaigning. Candidates for offices with small districts—perhaps mayor of a small township or legislator in a state with small districts—may not need an expensive, professional campaign organization. Instead, they can rely on family and friends as their "staff" and use low-cost materials or door-to-door canvassing for advertising rather than the broadcast media. By contrast, campaigns for high-profile state offices or national offices such as a U.S. House seat typically require hundreds of thousands of dollars or more, and competitive Senate campaigns or gubernatorial campaigns typically run into the millions. As the expense of mounting a credible campaign increases, the number of candidates willing to run declines substantially. Candidates who are independently wealthy naturally have an advantage over others, because they can "self-fund" their campaigns until they gain enough momentum and name recognition to seek outside backers, but money alone does not guarantee success.

Intangible Costs

Equal to if not more important than the tangible costs of running a campaign are the intangible costs associated

BOX 9-2
A DAY ON THE ROAD IN SOUTH DAKOTA . . .

In 2004 Democrat Stephanie Herseth of South Dakota ran in a special election for a seat in the U.S. House of Representatives. What follows is the actual campaign schedule prepared by her staff for May 28, 2004. The special election, which Herseth won, was held on June 1.

Stephanie Herseth (center) with campaign workers
Source: Steven Dahlmeier

Stephanie Herseth for South Dakota
The "YEP" Tour
May 28, 2004

USE THIS INFO FOR CANDIDATE BRIEFING MEMO/EVENT PLANNING
INTERNAL USE ONLY – DO NOT DISTRIBUTE

9:30 to 10: 30 am CONFIRMED	Pierre Event	
	Location:	Pier 347
	Address:	347 South Pierre Street
	Phone:	605-xxx-xxxx
	Advance:	Nick and Elizabeth
	Contact:	Christy, Manager
	Crowd-building:	Jason Schulte, 605-xxx-xxxx/ Pam
	Press:	Russ and Angie
	Invitees:	Hughes County Dem and GOP IDs for SMH

***Elizabeth get Subway for the RV passengers for lunch

11:00 am	Depart Pierre for St. Francis (115 miles)

1:00 pm CONFIRMED	Meet Tribal Chair Colombe in Mission	
	Location:	Maverick Hotel
	Address:	Mission
	Phone:	605-xxx-xxxx
	Contact:	Charlie Colombe, President
	Staff:	Ira Taken Alive

**The Chairman will ride with SMH in the RV to the graduation in order to give her an update on what is happening with the tribe, community, etc.

2:00 to 4:00 pm CONFIRMED	Speak at St. Francis Indian School Graduation – Rosebud	
	Location:	St. Francis Indian School
	Address:	St. Francis
	Phone:	605-xxx-xxxx
	Contact:	Jean Miller
	Press:	Russ Levsen
	Briefing Materials:	Ira Taken Alive
	Advance:	Ira and Machaela
4:00 pm	Travel St. Francis to Pine Ridge (102 miles) (You will gain an hour)	
5:00 to 6:15 pm CONFIRMED	Pine Ridge Rally	
	Location:	Billy Mills Hall
	Address:	Pine Ridge
	Phone:	605-xxx-xxxx
	Advance:	Ira and Machaela
	Contact:	Jesse Clausen 605-xxx-xxxx
	Crowd-building:	Ira Taken Alive
	Press:	Russ and Angie
	Invitees:	Shannon County Dem and GOP IDs for SMH
	***Ira get Taco John's for the passengers on the RV; SMH likes the Taco Bravo Meal	
6:30–7:30 pm	Travel Pine Ridge to Kyle	
7:15 to 8:30 pm CONFIRMED	Kyle Event	
	Location:	Little Wound School
	Address:	Kyle
	Phone:	605-xxx-xxxx
	Advance:	Ira and Machaela
	Contact:	Beverly Tuttle
	Crowd-building:	Ira Taken Alive
	Press:	Russ and Angie
8:30 to 12:30 pm	Travel Kyle to Pierre (200 miles) (You will lose an hour)	

Source: Herseth for Congress; edited by Stephen K. Medvic

Note: The schedule has been edited to remove phone numbers and other personal information. The name of the campaign tour is based on a campaign ad in which Ms. Herseth's grandfather, a former governor of South Dakota, repeatedly says "Yep" to her issue positions. SMH refers to the candidate, Stephanie Herseth. Ira Taken Alive is native vote director, Herseth for Congress.

with running for office. Candidates must spend long days on the road with little or no time to spend with family and close friends. Indeed, a candidate's day can be grueling, often starting before dawn and ending well after most people retire for the night (see Box 9-2). Meanwhile, candidates must endure constant media scrutiny and attacks on their character, past behavior, and political positions; deal with a variety of staff and consultants; make numerous "risky" decisions about campaign direction and strategy; and continually raise money to keep the process going. For many men and women, these intangible costs are overwhelming, and so they are unwilling to subject themselves to the process, regardless of their prospects for winning.

Candidate Characteristics

The decision process used by candidates in deciding whether to run for office favors certain types of candidates. Some minority groups tend to view their chances of winning as low and choose not to run. Others lack contact with the type of socialization processes that encourage ambition. Still others see the costs of running as especially daunting. As a result, state and federal offices throughout the country continue to reflect poorly the demographic makeup of the American public. Much of this situation can be attributed to the slow emergence of women and minorities as candidates for elected office at all levels. Recent elections have seen more women and more nonwhite candidates seek office, but their numbers in the candidate pool lag far behind their percentages in the population, and the opportunity for greater diversity in public office remains unfulfilled. This section focuses on the backgrounds of candidates for national offices, but similar patterns appear in state and local offices as well.

Presidential Backgrounds

Throughout the history of the presidency, candidates for the office have largely fulfilled what author Clinton Rossiter described as an "unwritten law." Candidates, he wrote, are white, male, Christian, and of Northern European stock.[14] In the decades since Rossiter's work, presidential candidates have begun to diverge from that tradition. Although women and African American candidates have not won major-party nominations, they have launched serious campaigns. Jessie Jackson, an African American with strong roots in the civil rights movement, sought the Democratic nomination for president in 1984 and 1988. In 1988 he won about 1,200 delegates, not enough for the nomination but enough to make him a serious candidate. Gen. Colin Powell, also an African American, was courted by officials in both major parties to consider a candidacy in 1996 and is still mentioned frequently as a potential candidate, a sign that barriers to African American candidates may be coming down. Elizabeth Dole, a former cabinet secretary and president of the American Red Cross, was a Republican candidate for president in 2000.

People outside the Protestant denomination are also emerging as serious candidates. Sen. Joseph I. Lieberman, who is Jewish, was nominated for vice president on the Democratic ticket in 2000 and sought the presidency in 2004. Senators John F. Kennedy in 1960 and John Kerry in 2004, both Catholics, won the Democratic Party nominations for president, and Kennedy was elected after openly confronting questions about his religious views.

But Rossiter's model is mostly intact, and it remains a fact that only white men have served as president and have been nominated by major parties for the position. Furthermore, Rossiter's assertion of a candidate of Northern European stock remains largely unchallenged. Michael S. Dukakis, the Democratic nominee in 1988 and who is of Greek ancestry, remains the only major-party candidate not of Northern European heritage. In addition, the country seems to favor candidates living in more traditional family situations. Only two bachelors—James Buchanan and Grover Cleveland—have been elected president (but Cleveland married while in office).

The key to expanding the demographic background of presidents is increasing the diversity of officeholders in state and other federal offices. Doing so begins when more nontraditional candidates make the decision to seek these public offices.

Congressional Candidate Backgrounds

Although congressional races are attracting more women and minorities as candidates, the numbers are still far from reflecting the makeup of the American public. In 1981, 5 percent of House members were either African American or Hispanic, and the Senate had no African American or Hispanic members. In the 108th Congress, the Senate continued to lack African American members, but 9 percent of House members were African American (see Table 9-4). In 2004 one African American—Barack Obama of Illinois—was elected to serve in the Senate (see Table 9-5). Women have fared only slightly better. In the 109th Congress, 14 percent of the Senate is women and 15 percent of the House—far fewer, proportionally, than the 51 percent of women in the population.

The lack of diversity in Congress begins with a lack of diversity in the candidate pool. In 2002 about 3 percent of Senate candidates and 14 percent of House candidates were nonwhite, compared with 30 percent of the population as a whole. However, this is an improvement over earlier years. The Voting Rights Act of 1982 required states with minority voters to draw electoral districts that ensured these voters would be represented in the U.S. House of Representatives, state legislatures, and other elected bodies. The act and court interpretations of the act have increased the emergence of minority candidates, particularly in the House. African American and Hispanic candidates are seeking election from districts that are made up largely of minority populations, and they are doing quite well in those elections.

Candidates for Congress are also older than the general population. About half of the candidates for Congress in 2002 were fifty-five years of age or older, and the average age in Congress increased to its highest level after the 2004 elections. Yet this age group makes up only about 20 percent of the population as a whole.

The domination of the election process by older candidates is attributable to the experience needed to run a competitive campaign for public office, as well as the length of the career path to higher office. Middle-aged or older men and women have acquired the political or business success necessary to win elective office. They also are more likely to have the financial resources that would allow them to put their occupations aside for the period of time necessary to seek elective office. Finally, as discussed earlier, the path to Congress and ultimately to the U.S. Senate often winds its way through lower elected positions. Older candidates are more likely to have generated the political experience and associations that will assist in a campaign for Congress.

Women are also underrepresented in the candidate pool. Historically, America's political system has been characterized by sex role stereotyping that has prevented women from competing as candidates for public office. Even though many of the roadblocks that have kept women from elective office are coming down, women are often waiting until they are older to run for elective office, and some studies suggest that they hold fewer ambitions than men for highly professional state and national offices. In part, this tendency stems from family responsi-

Table 9-4 Characteristics of Congressional Candidates and Members, 2002 (percent)

		House		Senate	
	General population	General election candidates	Members	General election candidates	Members
Race and ethnicity					
Native American	0%	0%	0%	0%	1%
Asian	4	2	1	0	1
Hispanic	12	6	5	1.5	0
African American	12	7	9	1.5	0
White	70	86	86	97	95
Other	3	0	0	0	3
Gender					
Male	49	84	86	84	86
Female	51	16	14	16	14
Age					
Under 25	34	0	0	0	0
25–39	22	11	7	6	2
40–54	21	46	47	34	26
55–74	15	41	44	55	65
75 and older	6	2	2	5	7
Occupation					
Agricultural or blue-collar workers	30	4	3	5	4
Business or banking	4	22	20	18	19
Clergy or social work	1	1	0	5	2
Education	4	10	11	6	1
Entertainer, actor, writer, or artist	1	1	1	0	0
Law	1	23	27	37	53
Medicine	3	4	3	3	3
Military or veteran	0	1	0	0	0
Politics or public service	3	25	31	22	15
Other white-collar professionals	20	7	3	5	3
Outside workforce	33	2	0	0	0
Unidentified, not politics	0	0	0	0	0
Total (N)	281,400,000	1,472	435	67	100

Sources: General population: U.S. Department of Commerce, Bureau of the Census, *Statistical Abstract of the United States* (Washington, D.C.: Government Printing Office, 2001), 13, 14, 19, 380–384. House candidates and members: Paul S. Herrnson, *Congressional Elections: Campaigning at Home and in Washington,* 4th ed. (Washington, D.C.: CQ Press, 2004), 57–62. Senate candidates and members: authors compiled information from several sources, including various issues of *CQ Weekly,* newspaper stories, and candidates' Web sites.

Note: Figures include all 2002 major-party House and Senate candidates and all members of the 108th Congress, including independents. 0% = less than 0.5% in some cases. Some columns do not add to 100 percent because of rounding.

bilities. Women remain the primary caretakers in most families, making it difficult for them to take time to campaign. It also stems in part from early socialization. Women only recently began entering many of the fields such as law and business that are training grounds for those entering the political arena.

Although the percentage of women holding elected office is well below the percentage of women in the population, the participation of women in all levels of government continues to grow. In 1980 only one woman sat in the U.S. Senate; in 2005 there were fourteen. Likewise, in

the U.S. House of Representatives, women held sixty-five seats in 2005 compared with sixteen in 1980. Yet in spite of the growing numbers, the proportion of women in Congress does not come close to the proportion in the U.S. population.

Finally, the occupation of those who seek elected office, and those who attain it, is significantly different from that of the general population. A very small percentage of the American public lists law as its profession. However, more than a third of U.S. Senate candidates and more than half of U.S. senators have a legal background. Other

Table 9-5 Selected Characteristics, 109th Congress (2005–2007)

	House	Senate
Average age	55	60.4
Number of minorities and women		
African Americans	40	1
Hispanics	23	2
Asians	2	0
American Indian	1	0
Women	65	14
Previous occupation		
Public service/politics	209	45
Law	178	64
Education	91	13
Agriculture	29	5
Blue-collar	9	3

Source: Gregory Giroux, "A Touch of Gray on Capitol Hill," *CQ Weekly,* January 31, 2005.

occupations, such as agricultural or blue-collar worker, are substantially underrepresented in the House and the Senate when compared with their representation in the general population.

The difference in the occupations of candidates and members of Congress is also reflected in the presence of higher-income candidates and members of the two chambers. Almost half of the new members of Congress elected in 2002 were millionaires. Of the sixty-three first-term members of the House and the Senate, twenty-seven or 44 percent, were millionaires.[15]

Minor-Party Candidates

The discussion of candidacies to this point has focused on major-party candidates, because most "viable" candidates choose to run under one of the major-party labels. Indeed, the single-member district, winner-take-all electoral system in the United States clearly favors major-party candidacies. Major-party candidates who have met the filing requirements in their states and won their party's nomination have automatic ballot access for the general election. Major-party presidential nominees automatically gain access to the ballot in all fifty states. Independent and third party candidates, however, must file for access to the general election ballot. Requirements vary by state, and some states require much higher fees or a greater number of petition signatures for minor-party candidates than other states. Ballot access is particularly challenging for minor-party presidential candidates; they must file paperwork and meet eligibility requirements in each of the fifty states to compete. Finally, third party presidential candidates rarely meet the requirements to receive federal matching funds for their campaigns, further hampering their efforts.

Other problems associated with running as a minor-party or independent candidate are capturing serious attention from the media, gaining access to candidate debate forums, and convincing voters that they are not "wasting" a vote. Nevertheless, some independent candidates have made a credible showing at the polls and even been successful. Ross Perot garnered a substantial 19 percent of the general election vote in 1992 and spawned a brief but strong third party movement. In 1998 professional wrestler Jesse "the Body" Ventura's surprise win in the governor's race in Minnesota stunned his major-party opponents and most of the rest of the political world. Nevertheless, examples such as these are the exception rather than the rule. Most candidates with serious ambitions to hold office run under a major-party label to ensure they maximize their chances of winning.

If not to win, why do people become minor-party or independent candidates? For most, their goals are related to the gains they hope to make through campaigning. They are trying to gain visibility for particular issues or ideologies, or they are aiming to demonstrate to major-party candidates that a pool of voters in their area cares about particular issues or stances. Their cost expectations are often different than those of major-party candidates as well, because they do not run a full-blown campaign for office. Instead, they rely on ideologically driven volunteers and nontraditional outlets for their messages. Arguably, these candidates have served as spoilers in elections. In 2000 Democrats complained bitterly that Ralph Nader's emergence as a third party candidate robbed them of votes in key electoral states and ultimately cost them the election. Nader sought the presidency again in 2004, but had less of an impact on the outcome of the race. He appeared on the ballot in fewer states, and his vote did not affect the outcome of the race between Bush and Kerry. In short, the decision calculus is quite different for minor-party and independent candidates and is more strongly driven by ideological ambitions than strategic ambitions.

Running for Office

No matter how daunting the process seems, or how unfavorable the odds, during each election cycle thousands of people decide that the time to run is now. The decision process outlined in this chapter has important implications for the types of campaigns to which citizens are exposed. Chapters 14–25 of this volume provide an in-depth look at the process of campaigning in general as well as campaigns for specific offices. It is therefore useful to wrap up this discussion of candidates by thinking about the type of races and campaigns produced by the candidate emergence process. The most common types of races at the state and national levels are the incumbent versus no challenger or the incumbent versus weak challenger, in which a poorly funded candidate—often a political novice—runs against a sitting incumbent.

Incumbent versus Weak Challenger

The advantages that incumbents have from holding office—visibility, resources to provide constituent and district services, and resources to bring office activities to the attention of constituents—increase their odds of winning reelection and make it likely they will run for office. Incumbents wage an ongoing campaign while in office to ensure the continued support of voters and to discourage strong potential challengers. For most incumbent officeholders the strategy works, and they face only token opposition.

This type of race is perhaps the worst situation for voters, because the challenger is unlikely to wage a campaign that captures the attention of the media or the voters. In these types of races, the challengers may have very little money or support from outside interests, and so they are unable to field campaigns. They simply appear as names on the ballot. The campaigns of inexperienced and weak challengers are difficult to categorize, because the goals and reasons for running are so varied. Some run for personal reasons, such as seeking name recognition in their communities. They may run extensive yard sign and bumper sticker campaigns with little real content. Others may run as a favor to party leaders, so that a name appears with the party label on the ballot. These candidates may not campaign at all. Still others run to gain visibility for a particular issue or to force an incumbent to address a particular issue. These candidates may secure funding from special interests to run a single-issue campaign. Low-profile or limited-issue races do little to stimulate citizen interest in politics or hold incumbents accountable for their action, because challengers lack the resources and ability to bring their messages to voters.

Incumbent versus Strong Challenger

In this kind of race, an experienced or well-known and well-funded challenger senses vulnerability in the incumbent because of missteps while in office or because district conditions are favorable, such as a competitively drawn district or a closely balanced state. Incumbents are still able to bring all their resources and skills to bear in their efforts to retain their seats, but in this kind of race they are facing well-funded, often experienced politicians who hope to unseat them. The same electoral and incumbent factors that convince prospective candidates that they have a viable chance of winning also stimulate support from interest groups and party leaders, further enhancing the prospects of strong challengers. Candidates who have already sought and won elected offices are among the strongest challengers to incumbents, because they come to the table with some understanding of how to run a winning campaign, and they may already have developed financial and constituency support through their previous offices. These candidates, with their records of governing and service, are the best positioned to develop and bring their messages to voters.

Many of the strongest inexperienced challengers are wealthy in their own right, or they are well known. Such challengers can use these resources to jump-start their campaigns during the primary process and gain credibility from a strong showing. Inexperienced challengers often play the "outsider" card to emphasize their advantages over entrenched incumbents or other experienced challengers. As a result, an increasing number of celebrity or wealthy "outsiders" have performed well against incumbents, because they can generate the type of name recognition and buy the campaign management that puts them on par with experienced politicians. Either way, the presence of a strong challenger produces a race that allows voters to be aware of both candidates and their messages.

Open-Seat Races

In an open-seat race, challengers from both major parties face off in the general election. These kinds of races occur most often in executive offices that have term limits. And with the advent of term limits in state legislative elections, these types of races will become more prevalent. Open-seat challengers vying for national, statewide, and professional state legislative offices are likely to have past experience and a large pool of resources. Because primary competition is typically strong in open-seat contests, both candidates may come to the general election with the experience of a hard-fought nomination behind them. But, as noted earlier, open-seat races are also most likely to attract experienced politicians hoping to move to higher office. Similarly, they will attract the strongest and most strategic of candidates from the amateur pool. Citizens, then, are likely to see a vigorous campaign and debate between the parties in open-seat races. When the open-seat district is strongly dominated by one party, the most important competition will occur in the primary election.

Conclusion

For most potential candidates, the strategic decision process of weighing the chances of winning against the costs of running leads to their nonemergence as a candidate rather than their emergence. The chances of unseating an incumbent in most offices are low, and laws governing campaigns and elections typically favor incumbents. A possible challenger to an incumbent must be willing to take on an uphill battle or wait until the incumbent decides to leave. Because the challenger's prospects are often dismal, a portion of elective officers go unchallenged each cycle. Many others draw only token challenges from candidates who lack the strength or resources to run a competitive or visible race against the incumbent. Moreover, the bias toward incumbency limits the ability of citizens to hold incumbents accountable while in office and slows change in the type of candidates holding office. Private sector gains for minorities and women do not translate as easily to public office, and changes in the representation of minority and female constituents are slow to come.

Notes

1. *American Heritage Dictionary of the English Language,* 4th ed. (Boston: Houghton Mifflin, 2000).

2. This section draws from the excellent review of the psychological and sociological perspectives on ambition by Linda L. Fowler, *Candidates, Congress, and the American Democracy* (Ann Arbor: University of Michigan Press, 1993), 41–60.

3. Data are drawn from the 1998 Candidate Emergence Study, a survey of potential candidates for the U.S. House in 1998. Details of the study can be found at http://ces.iga.ucdavis.edu/.

4. Joseph A. Schlesinger, *Ambition and Politics: Political Careers in the United States* (Chicago: Rand McNally, 1966).

5. Harold D. Lasswell, *Psychopathology and Politics* (Chicago: University of Chicago Press, 1930), 303.

6. Data on campaign finance are drawn from the Web site of the Center for Responsive Politics, http://opensecrets.org.

7. Linda L. Fowler and Robert D. McClure, *Political Ambition: Who Decides to Run for Congress?* (New Haven, Conn.: Yale University Press, 1989).

8. Bruce Buchanan, "The President and the Nominating Process," in *The Presidency and the Political System,* 5th ed., ed. Michael Nelson (Washington, D.C.: CQ Press, 1998).

9. Charles C. Euchner, John Anthony Maltese, and Michael Nelson, "The Electoral Process," in *Guide to the Presidency,* 3d ed., ed. Michael Nelson (Washington, D.C.: CQ Press, 2002).

10. Of those listed, Johnson, Nixon, Humphrey, and Mondale served as vice president prior to receiving the nomination.

11. David T. Canon, *Actors, Athletes, and Astronauts: Political Amateurs in the United States Congress* (Chapel Hill: University of North Carolina Press, 1990).

12. Darrell M. West and John M. Orman, *Celebrity Politics* (Upper Saddle River, N.J.: Prentice Hall, 2003).

13. Gary C. Jacobson and Samuel Kernell, *Strategy and Choice in Congressional Elections* (New Haven, Conn.: Yale University Press, 1981).

14. Clinton Rossiter, *The American Presidency* (New York: Harcourt Press, 1956).

15. Associated Press, "Nearly Half of Congressional Freshmen Are Millionaires," *USA Today,* December 24, 2002.

Suggested Readings

Barber, James David. *The Lawmakers: Recruitment and Adaptation to Legislative Life.* New Haven, Conn.: Yale University Press, 1965.

———. *Presidential Character.* Englewood Cliffs, N.J.: Prentice Hall, 1988.

Berkman, Michael, and James Eisenstein. "State Legislators as Congressional Candidates: The Effects of Prior Experience on Legislative Recruitment and Fundraising." *Political Research Quarterly* 52 (September 1999): 481–498.

Buchanan, Bruce. "The President and the Nominating Process." In *The Presidency and the Political System,* 5th ed., ed. Michael Nelson. Washington, D.C.: CQ Press, 1998.

Canon, David T. *Actors, Athletes, and Astronauts: Political Amateurs in the United States Congress.* Chapel Hill: University of North Carolina Press, 1990.

Carey, John M., Richard G. Niemi, and Lynda W. Powell. *Term Limits in State Legislatures.* Ann Arbor: University of Michigan Press, 2000.

Carroll, Susan J. *Women as Candidates in American Politics.* 2d ed. Bloomington: Indiana University Press, 1994.

Center for American Women and Politics. "Women in the U.S. Congress 1917–2003." Eagleton Institute of Politics. Rutgers, N.J.: Rutgers University, 2003.

Edwards, George C., III, and Stephen J. Wayne. *Presidential Leadership.* 6th ed. Belmont, Calif.: Thomson Wadsworth, 2003.

Ehrenhalt, Alan. *United States of Ambition: Politicians, Power, and the Pursuit of Office.* New York: Times Books, 1991.

Fowler, Linda L. *Candidates, Congress, and the American Democracy.* Ann Arbor: University of Michigan Press, 1993.

Fowler, Linda L., and Robert D. McClure. *Political Ambition: Who Decides to Run for Congress?* New Haven, Conn.: Yale University Press, 1989.

Francis, Wane L., and Lawrence W. Kenny. *Up the Political Ladder: Career Paths in U.S. Politics.* Thousand Oaks, Calif.: Sage Publications, 2000.

Gaddie, Ronald Keith. *Born to Run: Origins of the Political Career.* Lanham, Md.: Rowman and Littlefield, 2004.

Giroux, Gregory L. "A Touch of Gray on Capitol Hill." *CQ Weekly,* January 31, 2005.

Herrnson, Paul S. *Congressional Elections: Campaigning at Home and in Washington.* 4th ed. Washington, D.C.: CQ Press, 2004.

———. *Party Campaigning in the 1980s.* Cambridge, Mass.: Harvard University Press, 1988.

Jacobson, Gary C., and Samuel Kernell. *Strategy and Choice in Congressional Elections.* New Haven, Conn.: Yale University Press, 1981.

Kazee, Thomas, ed. *Who Runs for Congress? Ambition, Context, and Candidate Emergence.* Washington, D.C.: CQ Press, 1994.

Kazee, Thomas, and Mary Thornberry. "Where's the Party? Congressional Candidate Recruitment and American Party Organizations." *Western Political Quarterly* 43 (1990): 61–80.

Maisel, L. Sandy. *From Obscurity to Oblivion: Running in the Congressional Primary.* Knoxville: University of Tennessee Press, 1982.

Mann, Thomas, and Raymond Wolfinger. "Candidates and Parties in Congressional Elections." *American Political Science Review* 74 (1980): 617–632.

Matthews, Donald. *The Social Backgrounds of Political Decision Makers.* New York: Doubleday, 1954.

Moncrief, Gary F., Peverill Squire, and Malcolm Jewell. *Who Runs for the Legislature?* Upper Saddle River, N.J.: Prentice Hall, 2001.

Moncrief, Gary F., and Joel A. Thompson. *Changing Patterns in State Legislative Careers.* Ann Arbor: University of Michigan Press, 1992.

Rossiter, Clinton. *The American Presidency.* New York: Harcourt Press, 1956.

Schlesinger, Joseph A. *Ambition and Politics: Political Careers in the United States.* Chicago: Rand McNally, 1966.

Squire, Peverill. "Member Career Opportunities and the Internal Organization of Legislatures." *Journal of Politics* 50 (1988): 726–744.

Stone, Walter J., and L. Sandy Maisel. "The Not-So-Simple Calculus of Winning: Potential U.S. House Candidates' Nomination and General Election Prospects." *Journal of Politics* 65 (November 2003): 951–977.

Weko, Thomas, and John Aldrich. "The Presidency and the Election Campaign: Framing the Choices in 1996." In *The Presidency and the Political System,* 5th ed., ed. Michael Nelson. Washington, D.C.: CQ Press, 1998.

West, Darrell M., and John M. Orman. *Celebrity Politics.* Englewood Cliffs, N.J.: Prentice Hall, 2002.

CHAPTER 10

Campaign Organization and Political Consultants

Stephen K. Medvic

A campaign's organization is the foundation on which all its efforts will be built. The work done by members of a campaign organization is rarely glamorous, but it is essential for an effective operation. Although a strong organization will not guarantee success, it would be difficult for a candidate in a competitive election to do well without a dependable campaign team.

This chapter discusses the campaign organization as it has developed over time, with special emphasis on organizations in the candidate-centered era—that is, the era in which campaigns revolve around candidates rather than political parties. It will describe the typical campaign organization and the functions performed by various members of that organization. Professional political consultants, in particular, will receive considerable attention because of the prominent role they play in contemporary campaigns.

From Party-Based to Candidate-Centered Campaign Organizations

Campaigning has changed dramatically in the more than two hundred years since elections were first held under the U.S. Constitution (see Chapter 2). In those early electoral contests, candidates relied heavily on the parties to conduct campaigns, and the parties did so largely by committee. With only a few exceptions, campaigns were managed by a group of party leaders. Furthermore, even at the presidential level there was no concept of a national campaign. Party leaders in the various states organized the parties' efforts at the local level on behalf of their presidential and congressional nominees. Thus until at least 1824, campaigns were run according to what might be called a state-centered group management model.[1]

As the United States became more democratic in the mid-1820s, the campaign activities of the parties became more sophisticated. Not only were the two major parties (the Democratic-Republicans and National Republicans) organizing at the grass-roots level, but they also were be-

ginning to package their candidates using evocative symbolism and to appeal to voters through entertainment such as rallies and torchlight parades.[2] Throughout the country, political entrepreneurs such as Martin Van Buren of New York, John Easton of Tennessee, and Thomas Hart Benton of Missouri were making names for themselves as party strategists. Yet presidential campaigns were handled not by a single manager but by a party committee. By this point, however, presidential campaigns had become national affairs. Indeed, the first national nominating convention was held in 1831—by the Anti-Masons—and the first permanent national party committee—the Democratic National Committee—was established in 1848. The result was a nation-centered group management model that was used by presidential campaigns until around 1860.[3]

In his fascinating history of the activities of presidential candidates, Gil Troy notes that candidates began stumping for themselves at the congressional and state legislative levels as early as the 1830s. It was not until the late nineteenth century, however, that presidential candidates would do the same.[4] To that point, presidential candidates refrained from "running" for office, which was considered undignified. Instead, they "stood" for office, allowing party activists to make the case for their candidacy. In addition, by the 1880s individual campaign managers increasingly controlled the campaigns on behalf of presidential candidates, and those campaigns were also becoming more national in scope. The most famous such manager was Republican Mark Hanna of Ohio. Hanna and other campaign managers handled presidential campaigns from their posts as chairs of the national parties. Until the 1930s, then, candidates at all levels relied heavily on the party apparatus to run their campaigns, and thus the partisan campaign manager model held sway.[5]

In the 1930s, first in California and then throughout the country, candidates began to build their own campaign organizations headed by campaign managers who were not connected to a party organization and may not, in fact, even have had an allegiance to a party. The prototypical example of an operative who fit this independent campaign manager model was Campaigns Inc., a California campaign management firm established by Clem Whitaker and Leone Baxter.[6] In all the campaigns they handled, Whitaker and Baxter had complete control of the organization; they not only directed the day-to-day operations, but also made all of the strategic decisions. Few campaigns were as hierarchical as those run by Whitaker and Baxter, but in most campaigns the manager was the administrative, and to some extent the decision-making, center of the organization. And in all cases, the managers were independent of the party apparatus. In 1952 the presidential campaigns of both parties' nominees were, for the first time, run by personal campaign organizations headed by managers who were not the party chairs.[7]

By the 1960s, a new breed of campaign operative—the political consultant—had emerged. A political consultant is a "campaign professional who is engaged primarily in the provision of advice and services (such as polling, media creation and production, and direct-mail fundraising) to candidates, their campaigns, and other political committees."[8] The primary difference between a consultant and a manager was that the manager handled the day-to-day operations of one campaign at a time, while the consultant periodically dispensed advice and services for numerous campaigns per election cycle, often from afar. All campaigns had a manager who oversaw campaign organizations that were relatively similar to those of an earlier era. Only well-funded campaigns, however, could afford to use consultants. In those that did, consultants began to creep up the organizational charts of campaigns to eventually share a place with managers at the top.

One response to the developments in campaigns by the 1980s and 1990s, most notably dramatic changes in the complexity of communications technology, was the replacement of the generalist consultants from the early years by specialists. Unlike the generalists, who were knowledgeable about all facets of a campaign, specialists were experts in particular niches within a campaign. Today, competitive campaigns employ multiple consultants to handle various campaign functions. These consultants, like the professional campaign managers that preceded them, are independent of party organizations (though parties also employ consultants to handle those aspects of a campaign for which the party is responsible). Most consultants work only for candidates of one party, but a few have been known to work both sides of the aisle.

Political parties still play an important role in campaigns, but they no longer constitute the candidates' campaign organizations. As such, they do not directly control a candidate's efforts to get elected. That task falls to the personal campaign organizations that candidates build and to the high-priced consultants brought in to direct the campaign.

Campaign Organization

Campaign organizations have thus changed over time, from entirely party-based entities to largely candidate-centered ones. Today, candidates build organizations around their own personal and professional connections. Parties may suggest particular individuals, including party-approved consultants, and may even provide people to serve in particular staff positions, but candidates are largely responsible for piecing together the structure that will design and implement a strategy for electing the candidate (see Figure 10-1).

The Campaign Committee

At the heart of a campaign organization is the candidate's campaign committee (sometimes referred to as the steering committee). This committee is responsible for the activities undertaken by the campaign to get the candidate elected. Campaign communications, for example, are said to be "paid for by" the candidate's campaign committee. These committees are made up of men and women who serve as volunteers and who are well known in the community, represent some part of the community that will be important to the campaign, or have experience working on campaigns in the area. Committee members do not actually carry out the campaign activities, but they are asked to give advice and to occasionally undertake specific tasks such as organizing a fund-raiser or assisting in securing a particular endorsement.

Campaign committees usually meet regularly, so that the candidate or campaign manager can keep the members apprised of important developments in the campaign. Regularly held meetings also allow committee members to give the campaign feedback on its performance. Ideally, campaigns make decisions based on systematic evidence of what is working and what is not. Nevertheless, anecdotal accounts of the campaign's operations can be useful if particular impressions are widespread. If nothing else, soliciting committee input allows the members to feel as though they are contributing to the effort, which is likely to make them dedicate themselves all the more to the campaign and the candidate. Incidentally, particularly big news or a breaking scandal might prompt an emergency meeting of the committee, so that members are not embarrassed by first hearing the news from someone else or through the news media.

The size of a campaign committee depends on the scope of the campaign. Nevertheless, all campaign committees have a chair, at least two vice chairs, and a treasurer, as well as members who are selected on the basis of some strategic importance. For example, a committee for a congressional candidate may seek to include members representing each state legislative district within the larger congressional district. People who are able to raise

Figure 10-1 Organizational Chart, Richard Burr, R-N.C., U.S. Senate Campaign, 2004

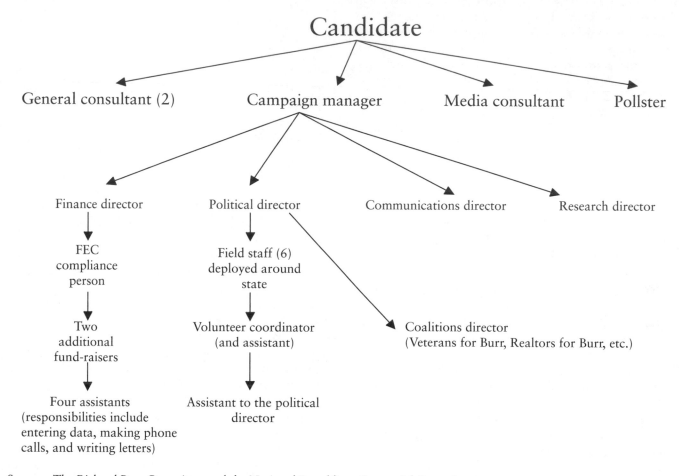

Sources: The Richard Burr Committee and the National Republican Senatorial Committee.

Note: FEC = Federal Election Commission. This chart is typical of large-scale campaigns and indicates a hierarchy of at least three levels (the influence of each is represented by various font sizes). The arrows denote lines of communication and authority.

a considerable amount of money or who are at least well connected to potential sources of campaign contributions also will be asked to serve on the campaign committee. In addition, some committee members will represent groups that the campaign views as integral to its electoral coalition. For example, most committees will have members from the business community and from particularly important policy areas such as education, health care, or public safety. Additional members may reflect the ideological predilections of the candidate, including, for example, social conservatives or antitax advocates on the right and labor or environmental activists on the left.

Larger campaigns may also form additional committees that serve specific functions. A separate finance committee, for example, may be established to assist with fund-raising for the campaign. An individual who is particularly effective at raising money would serve as chair of the committee, and the campaign's treasurer would be a committee member. Large campaigns might also set up a series of advisory committees made up of people who

are knowledgeable about (and well known in) particular areas of public policy. These committees would serve as mini–think tanks for the candidate, advising him or her on various policy alternatives and perhaps even helping to write white papers on specific proposals to be released by the campaign. Regional committees might also be formed in statewide and presidential campaigns to delegate some responsibility and create efficient lines of communication, as well as to indicate a campaign's commitment to various geographic areas. Presidential campaigns establish campaign committees in all the states and the District of Columbia. Senate or gubernatorial campaigns will have committees in major regions and cities throughout their states.

Finally, campaigns often create what could be called constituency or outreach committees. These committees are designed to court groups that the campaign is targeting heavily, especially when the groups have not traditionally backed the candidate's party. In the broadest sense, a campaign might form a committee made up of members of the opposite party. Republican candidate Smith, for example, might form a "Democrats for Smith" committee to indicate that he or she has bipartisan support. It is also common for such committees to appeal to interests aligned with the other party but that are vital to electoral success. In the 2001 Virginia gubernatorial campaign, Democrat Mark Warner established a "Sportsmen for Warner" committee in order to counteract perceptions of the Democratic Party (and thus the Democratic candidate) as antigun. This committee was credited, in part, with helping to convince the National Rifle Association to withhold an endorsement in the campaign, thereby helping Warner to neutralize a potentially damaging issue. In reality, many outreach committees are little more than names that appear on letterhead and bumper stickers (though the media are increasingly exposing such committees). However, when outreach committees consist of real members who genuinely back the candidate, they can send a powerful signal to voters that the candidate's appeal to particular segments of the community is sincere. They also can serve beneficially as advisory committees to help the candidate navigate unfamiliar issues.

All candidates have a small inner circle of friends and family who serve as a "kitchen cabinet" or informal committee that offers advice and support. These committees have no formal organization, and the confidants rarely meet as a group. But a handful of trusted individuals can be extremely valuable to a candidate when key decisions are required or when the candidate simply needs encouragement in the dog days of a campaign.

Campaign Staff

Members of the campaign committee may serve in a voluntary capacity, but the daily operation of a campaign requires a paid staff. The size of the staff, like the size of the campaign committee, depends on the complexity of the campaign. Nevertheless, certain campaign activities are essential in campaigns of all sizes and someone on the staff will be responsible for carrying out those activities.[9]

The Campaign Manager

All campaigns need a campaign manager. This chief administrator of the campaign is responsible for running the operation on a day-to-day basis and so, unlike political consultants, is present in the campaign (either traveling with the candidate or working at headquarters) every day.

No staff member works more closely with the candidate than the campaign manager. For this reason, candidates often rely on someone they know personally to fill this role. Just as often, however, party officials or activists or some other adviser to the candidate will recommend a manager who has experience and a successful track record. If the candidate did not know the manager before the campaign, great care must be taken to ensure a good working relationship between the two. The manager must be trusted to give the candidate frank advice but also to carry out the candidate's wishes even when he or she disagrees. Campaign managers are expected to put the candidates' interests above their own.

In small campaigns, the manager is literally responsible for everything that happens in the campaign, including campaign logistics such as scheduling candidate appearances, organizing press conferences, and placing advertising in newspapers and on radio and television, as well as cultivating ties to key interest groups. In addition, the manager will often be in charge of organizing volunteers and directing their activities, from stuffing envelopes to canvassing precincts. The manager might even have to order campaign materials, such as yard signs and bumper stickers, as well as office supplies. In larger campaigns, most of these things are delegated to other staff members.

Regardless of the size of the campaign, one of the manager's primary jobs is staff motivation and relations. In the course of a campaign, moments of success and failure will produce peaks and valleys in staff attitudes. Managers must ensure that campaign workers avoid feeling too dejected in times of trouble or too elated when victory seems within reach. The goal is to keep the staff enthusiastic but focused on the tasks at hand. The manager also must ensure that staff members, including outside consultants, work well together. Staffers with different opinions about how the campaign should be run can cause friction in a campaign in a variety of ways. Personality clashes also can contribute to tension in the organization. Occasionally, conflict within a campaign will lead to a change in staff (see Box 10-1). Nevertheless, a manager with legitimacy in the campaign—based either on close ties to the candidate or on personal experience and skill, or both—will have an easier time controlling staff quarrels than one without such legitimacy. Of course, a winning campaign always suffers from less discord than one not doing as well.

In all campaigns, the campaign manager is ultimately responsible for implementing the campaign strategy, a task that requires a combination of political instinct and effective resource allocation. The extent to which the manager also helps to develop strategy depends on the manager's talents, his or her relationship with the candidate, and the size of the campaign. Generally speaking, the manager is most likely to be involved in the creation of campaign strategy in very small and very large campaigns. Campaigns for local offices often cannot afford high-priced consultants, and so the campaign's inner circle, which usually includes the manager, will plan the campaign. In presidential campaigns, the manager will often be a political consultant who has been hired to run the daily operation but who also serves as the chief strategist. Joe Trippi famously played this role for Democrat Howard Dean's presidential campaign in 2004, just as James Carville did for Bill Clinton in 1992. In mid-level races such as congressional campaigns, the manager will often serve as a tactician, because outside consultants are

---

BOX 10-1
STAFF SHAKE-UPS
Kristyn Miller

Although problems in a campaign can arise for a number of reasons, candidates often react in a similar way—they shake up their campaign organization. Staff shake-ups, involving the firing or "resignation" of staff members, typically occur whenever things are not going well for a candidate. Although it is intended to give the campaign a new direction, staff reshuffling is rarely effective at fixing the problems plaguing the campaign.

Occasionally, shake-ups stem from unethical behavior or politically damaging actions. For example, in his 1996 U.S. Senate bid John Warner of Virginia fired his media consultant, Greg Stevens, when it was discovered that Stevens had manipulated a photograph of Warner's opponent for a television ad. Likewise, John Sasso, campaign manager for Democratic presidential candidate Michael Dukakis, resigned in October 1987 after news broke that the Dukakis staff had sabotaged a rival candidate. Sasso leaked a video of Democratic senator Joe Biden of Delaware, one of Dukakis's rivals for the Democratic nomination, in which Biden seemed to be plagiarizing a speech. The video apparently derailed Biden's campaign and raised questions about the tactics of the Dukakis campaign. In such situations, the offending staffer is forced to resign or must be fired to indicate the candidate's intolerance of unethical behavior.

Far more common than these scandal shake-ups, however, is staff reshuffling because of candidate frustration over the direction of his or her campaign. The 2004 presidential race included several such shake-ups. In November 2003, with his candidacy in trouble, John Kerry got rid of his campaign manager, Jim Jordan, in response to both internal disputes and discontent from donors and supporters. Mary Beth Cahill, a political operative with experience in numerous Democratic campaigns, replaced Jordan. After the shake-up, Kerry went on to win the Democratic nomination. In September 2004, facing a double-digit deficit in the polls and chafing to gear up for the homestretch, Kerry initiated another round of shake-ups. In the midst of a downward slide in the polls spurred on by attack ads by a veterans group attacking Kerry's Vietnam War record, the Kerry campaign brought in new hands, many of them advisers to former president Bill Clinton, shortly after the September Republican National Convention. By October, the race for the White House had tightened.

The Kerry examples illustrate how hard it is to know whether shake-ups are effective. The success of Kerry's campaign in the Democratic nominating process cannot be attributed solely to the reshuffling that occurred in November 2003. One significant factor was the collapse of the campaign of former Vermont governor Howard Dean after a

series of controversial comments Dean made in the months leading up to the Iowa caucuses and the obsessive coverage of the "Dean scream" after his loss in those caucuses. In addition, the first presidential debate probably figured heavily in Kerry's turnaround in the fall of 2004. Within days of his convincing victory in the debate against the Republican incumbent, George W. Bush, the polls began to show an increase in Kerry's support. It is therefore almost impossible to attribute a candidate's success or failure to one event, and, as Kerry's shake-ups demonstrate, multiple factors contribute to the success or failure of the candidate.

In fact, candidates who have shake-ups typically lose—for example, Republican presidential nominee Robert J. Dole in 1996 and Democratic presidential nominee Al Gore in 2000. Most often, shake-ups are a symptom of a broader problem; candidates are losing before they alter their campaign organizations, and, most times, they are behind for reasons other than their staff. The problems within a campaign are not usually the result of decision making by one or two people. Rather, a faltering campaign may find itself unable to raise enough money, to resonate with voters, or to establish solid organizations in key states. In the end, it is the candidate who wins or loses the election, and staffing is likely to make a difference only if the race is close. Yet even then the impact is not assured.

---

expected to create the strategy (this situation is described more fully later in this chapter). Thus in these mid-level races, the manager's job is to carry out the plan, even though some managers, again depending on personal ability and connections to the candidate, will have input into the strategic decision making. Even in races in which consultants are primarily responsible for developing strategy, managers will typically be present in strategic development meetings if for no other reason than to fully understand the approach and be better able to implement it.

Professional political consultants are significant members of a campaign's staff (and their role is discussed at length in the rest of this chapter). Unlike the campaign manager, consultants are not always present in the day-to-day business (with the exception of those who might manage a presidential campaign). They dispense their advice and services at various times, and are therefore able to work for different candidates at the same time. Indeed, some consultants work on campaigns at various levels, for several offices, and in multiple states in the same election cycle. Because consultants are sometimes thought to have little knowledge of local political culture, their advice may cause dissension within the campaign. Furthermore, full-time staffers may resent consultants' large salaries but part-time presence. Nevertheless, their knowledge and skill are extremely valuable, especially for candidates who are disadvantaged, such as challengers.

Other Staffers

In addition to the campaign manager and outside consultants, a finance director is typically hired to oversee the campaign's fund-raising effort. If the campaign has a finance committee, this person will work closely with the chair of that committee or may even serve as the chair (but, as noted earlier, that role is typically voluntary and is reserved for a well-known and well-connected member of the community). Even though fund-raising consultants are often hired to create events or to produce direct mail to raise money, the finance director coordinates the entire endeavor and attempts to ensure that fund-raising goals are met. The director also will work closely with the campaign's treasurer to manage the campaign's budget. The treasurer, who is usually a volunteer, is responsible for the campaign's financial records and for complying with campaign finance laws. His or her signature is required for any purchase the campaign makes.

Larger campaigns employ a political director to serve as a liaison with interest groups. One of the most crucial responsibilities of the political director is to court key voting blocs and organized interest groups to gain their support and endorsements. In very large campaigns, coordinators for specific groups might also be hired, but they would answer directly to the political director. The political director also helps to establish constituency committees, should they serve a strategic purpose in the campaign.

In a campaign that covers a large geographic area, a field director is hired to organize the campaign activities on the ground in various parts of the electoral district. The district or precinct coordinators who report to the field director (and who may or may not be paid staff) organize smaller geographic areas within the campaign. The primary responsibility of the field operation is voter mobilization on election day. This effort begins early in the campaign with door-to-door and telephone canvassing designed to identify the candidate preferences of voters. Those identified as undecided will be the targets of persuasive campaign communications. Those initially identified as supporters of the candidate, as well as those who eventually indicate a preference for the candidate, will be contacted with get-out-the-vote (GOTV) messages near election day.

Although the campaign's message is crafted by a team of strategists, many of whom will be paid consultants, the integration of the message into all aspects of the campaign is supervised by a communications director. Every time the campaign communicates publicly, it should convey a consistent message. Advertising and direct mail, speeches, press conferences, the campaign Web site, and all other forms of communication must be coordinated to reinforce that message. It is the communications director's job to see that this happens. He or she also spends a considerable amount of time interacting with reporters and editors, because very few voters receive campaign communications that are not filtered through the media. Finally, the communications director often oversees event planning—or advance work—for the campaign, though in larger campaigns a separate staffer is assigned to this task. In preparing for campaign events, staff must choose venues, test sound systems, maximize crowd size, prepare stage backdrops (or "wallpaper"), and placate local politicians to convey the image (if not the reality) of a well-oiled campaign machine. Because they communicate something important to journalists and voters, campaign events fall under the purview of the communications director.

Although much of a communications director's job entails media relations, the press secretary conducts the day-to-day interaction with the media. Perhaps the most visible member of the campaign staff, the press secretary is the spokesperson for the campaign. An important part of that job is cultivating a good relationship with journalists, which requires gaining the trust of the reporters covering the campaign and establishing credibility with them. The press secretary is also responsible for arranging interviews with the candidate and answering journalists' questions when the candidate is not available (or when the campaign would prefer that the candidate not face the media). Reporters pride themselves on not succumbing to campaigns' attempts to manipulate coverage, but a good press secretary can influence journalists in subtle ways. When the spokesperson is successful, the campaign's message will be reinforced in the media's coverage of the race.

Reliable information on both the issues and the candidates is critical in modern campaigns. A campaign decision based on unreliable information is likely to create trouble for a candidate at some point in the campaign. Potential problems include the development of a misguided strategy and media exposure of inaccurate statements. A research director is often hired to conduct this research, along with perhaps a professional consultant who specializes in "opposition research"—that is, collecting information about the opponent, ranging from voting records and past public statements to details of personal matters such as finances and family life. So that the campaign can utilize efficiently the mountains of research produced, the research director is also responsible for organizing the information on issues and the candidates' records and creating briefing books for the candidate.

BOX 10-2
THE RISE OF THE PERMANENT CAMPAIGN

In recent years, political observers have begun to notice an aspect of American politics sometimes called the "permanent campaign." Typically, the term refers to the fact that electoral campaigns are in perpetual motion—that is, candidates, including elected officials running for reelection, are continually looking ahead to the next election and are regularly engaged in activities designed to help them win that election.

This nonstop campaigning is not especially new to American politics. But what seems to have changed is the intensity of the effort. Raising money, in particular, is an endless activity. Although permanent campaigning principally applies to high-profile races such as those for the presidency, U.S. Senate, competitive U.S. House seats, and governorships, it is increasingly pursued by candidates in state legislative races and in big-city mayoral races. In addition to raising money, candidates feel pressured to maintain a ubiquitous presence in their districts and states and to stay abreast of their constituents' opinions. All of this, of course, requires staff assistance.

At the federal level, and in most states, legislative or executive staffers are prohibited from explicitly campaigning while working in the office of an elected official.[1] Consequently, when election time rolls around some staffers usually take a leave of absence from the office to work on the campaign. But the line between the legislative or executive office and the campaign staff is not as clear as the law suggests. To begin with, many official decisions by legislators and their staffs are made with electoral ramifications in mind. Furthermore, legislative staffers often have responsibilities, such as drafting speeches, that have both official and campaign functions. And then staffers who move to the campaign maintain a circle of associates that includes those still in the elected official's office, and they are likely to share information when meeting informally over lunch or drinks. Staffers who move back and forth between the office and the campaign also have a keen understanding of how official business and campaign organizations operate, and so they draw from this knowledge in both of their capacities.

The ambiguous role of staffers points directly to a second, and more unique, sense of the term *permanent campaign*—namely, the blurring of the line between campaigning and governing. This blurring is captured not only in the revolving door between official offices and campaign organizations, but also in the use of political consultants as if they are on retainer. Consultants are increasingly employed to provide services—polling, fund-raising, strategic advice—even when the campaign is not in full swing.

The use of campaign tactics to govern was first explicitly addressed in a memo from pollster Patrick Cadell to President-elect Jimmy Carter in December 1976. In the memo, Cadell suggested that "governing with public approval requires a continuing political campaign."[2] Since then, each White House staff has made a conscious effort to manage the president's image as they would a presidential candidate's. The tactics employed in doing so include polling to help establish priorities within the president's agenda and to frame arguments in defense of his initiatives; techniques to "earn" positive media coverage of the president's performance; and constant fund-raising not only for one's own campaign war chest but also for the party's efforts to promote the president's agenda. In addition to these tactics, paid advertising has become part of the process of governing. Interest groups and parties now routinely purchase airtime in an attempt to influence public opinion on matters before Congress. Perhaps the most famous example of this approach is the "Harry and Louise" ads run by the insurance industry against Bill Clinton's health care plan in 1993. Those ads, in which a married couple worries about what the Clinton plan will mean for their health coverage, were widely credited with helping to scuttle the president's reform.

The White House has not entirely jumped on this advertising bandwagon, though the Democratic National Committee did run ads in the summer of 1995 attacking Speaker of the House Newt Gingrich and presumptive Republican presidential nominee Robert J. Dole. These "issue ads" were obviously intended to weaken Dole for the 1996 campaign, but they also directly addressed legislative issues such as the budget battles under way at the time.

The line between running for office and running the country has thus been blurred, if not entirely erased. As a result, the offices of elected officials will increasingly resemble campaign organizations, generating a great deal of controversy along the way.

1. Technically, campaign work by congressional staffers must be done "outside the congressional office, on their own time, and without using any congressional office resources" (www.house.gov/ethics/m _Campaign_Work_Staff.html#_ftn1).

2. Memo, Patrick Cadell to President Jimmy Carter, December 10, 1976, Press Office: Jody Powell, Box 4, Folder "Memoranda—Pat Cadell 12/10/76–12/21/76," Jimmy Carter Library and Museum, Atlanta.

As for other staff members, some campaigns employ a full-time scheduler to keep track of the candidate's meetings, appearances, and other appointments. An office manager is also useful for keeping the campaign headquarters organized and operating smoothly. Other staff members usually perform these functions if the campaign cannot afford to pay additional full-time staff members. And volunteers can often successfully perform other vital tasks. For example, a local attorney who is supportive of the candidate might offer legal advice for free.

Decision Making in Campaigns

Although the responsibility in campaign organizations is rather clearly demarcated, decision making in campaigns is actually quite chaotic. One scholar who has studied campaign organizations closely noted, "If there is any single rule that dominates political decision making it is this: *decisions are made by whoever happens to be in the room at the time.*" [10] That is certainly true for tactical decisions—on a day-to-day basis questions about exactly how to implement the campaign strategy are left to various members of the staff to settle. However, larger strategic decisions are made at the top levels of the campaign, and input into those decisions comes from only a handful of people, including the candidate, key political consultants, and perhaps a few close advisers.

Staff members are often uncomfortable with the chaos that reigns in campaigns. For that reason, those setting up campaigns tend to try to organize them in such a way as to control all aspects of the decision-making process. This approach to campaign organization, called the comprehensive model, requires "a hierarchical structure" with "functional specialization, unbroken lines of authority, and complete internal communication." [11] In a comprehensive campaign, staff members know their roles and carry out their tasks as expected. Clem Whitaker and Leone Baxter utilized this model in all the campaigns they handled. The 1964 Goldwater presidential campaign also attempted to implement the comprehensive model. Few other campaigns have been fully comprehensive, because it is both unrealistic and counterproductive.

Most campaigns adhere to an incremental model of organization, particularly the professional as opposed to the more amateur ("personalized") campaigns.[12] In incremental campaigns, authority is dispersed throughout the organization, and "decisions are coordinated through mutual adjustment, an endless process of bargaining and compromise." [13] This process tends to produce a range of ideas from various members of the staff about how the campaign should proceed at any given point in time. Although this approach seems to be a recipe for inertia, incremental campaigns are dynamic and creative and appear to be more successful than comprehensive campaigns.[14]

Political Consultants

Regardless of how a campaign organization functions, the central players in that organization are likely to be professional political consultants. Today, nearly all competitive campaigns for offices above the most local level hire such consultants to advise their campaigns in one capacity or another. Evidence suggests that these consultants are effective in helping their candidates garner more of the vote than they might otherwise get without professional advice. This section describes the role and effects of consultants in campaigns, beginning with a brief examination of the development of the consulting industry.

The Development of Political Consulting

As noted at the beginning of this chapter, professional political consultants began to appear in elections as early as the 1930s.[15] Perhaps not coincidentally, they did so in California, a state notorious at the time for weak party organizations. Although Alan Ware has correctly noted that independent consultants could have developed alongside strong parties—just as the British railway system developed in the nineteenth century while the canal system continued to function effectively—it so happens that consultants emerged to fill a void in campaign management.[16] Without effective party organizations to help with various aspects of campaigning—especially communications activities—candidates turned to political entrepreneurs from the world of public relations (itself a new industry in the 1930s).

Early in the development of the political consulting industry, Campaigns, Inc., the firm of Whitaker and Baxter, served as the model for professionally managed campaigns. Its success at winning nearly all of the campaigns it handled[17] suggested that the "new style" of politics was superior to the more traditional ways of running campaigns. Traditional campaigns relied heavily on voter mobilization and partisan appeals; in new-style campaigns, appeals were candidate-based and poll-tested and disseminated via the mass media.[18]

In the 1960s, political consulting became "a nationwide service industry that reached all electoral levels." [19] By the 1970s, professionalized campaigns were commonplace, and the candidate-centered nature of campaigns was the norm. Rather than depend on political parties to mount a campaign, candidates across the United States were building their own organizations. The result was that candidates were far more independent of party structures than they had been in the past (although, to be sure, American political parties have never been able to ensure ideological cohesion among all their candidates).

Until the late 1960s or 1970s, consultants were experts in campaigning generally. These generalists knew a bit about all facets of campaigns, but were particularly skillful at creating campaign strategy. Yet during this period campaigns were not technologically complex. As television became a more important campaign tool and as polling began to gain credibility (and sophistication), candidates began to need experts in these particular areas of campaigning. Thus specialists in advertising and polling began to appear in campaigns.

Today, consultants specialize not only in media (including broadcast advertising and direct mail) and polling, but also in fund-raising, research, and voter mobilization. And some vendors supply technical services and products, often in very specific niches.[20] For example, one of the latest developments in consulting is the emergence of a cadre of vendors who are experts in the political use of the Internet. Their services include Internet fund-raising, Web site design and maintenance, online issue and opposition research, and computer-based electronic communication such as managing e-mail lists, distributing press releases, coordinating volunteers, and organizing voter mobilization. *Campaigns and Elections,* the trade magazine for the consulting industry, now has a regular section on Internet campaigning, which includes a directory of consultants who offer Internet services.

The highly specialized consultants that advise contemporary campaigns learn their trade in various ways. Most begin with some formal connection to a political party. Many have served as staffers for one of the party committees, either at the state or at the national or congressional level. There, they probably either worked on the party's general campaign efforts for all of its candidates or lent a hand to a specific campaign (at the candidate's expense). As staffers for individual campaigns, they often coordinate the candidate's field operation, using the party committee's knowledge of the political terrain throughout the country and its ability to maintain vast amounts of information about voters. Party staffers also are occasionally sent in to manage an entire campaign, although this situation often causes conflict because the party person lacks familiarity with the local context. At any rate, once they have gained adequate experience (and built a sufficient potential client base), these party operatives leave the staff and join or open a political consulting firm. They are likely to maintain a positive relationship with the parties, but these consultants will work autonomously, occasionally sacrificing party discipline for the electoral benefits of candidate independence.

Other operatives begin their careers as consultants by either moving into politics from other fields (for example, corporate or nonprofit public relations, academic public opinion research, or commercial advertising) or simply hanging out a shingle and declaring themselves political consultants. The "hanging out a shingle" career path is taken rarely, because it is difficult to build a network of clients without the entrée parties provide. The same is true of the path of entering politics from other fields, although that path is taken a bit more often than the one of independent political consultant. (Interestingly, political consultants often pick up nonpolitical work, particularly corporate accounts, between election cycles. Thus consultant movement between the realm of politics and the world of business is fairly common, raising at least normative concerns about the connection between the two.) Finally, those seeking to become political consultants can attend one of a handful of university graduate programs in campaign management. These programs provide both the theory and practice of campaigning and help graduates find jobs either in particular campaigns or with party committees.

Types of Consultants

As noted earlier, consultants now specialize in a variety of aspects of campaigning. The most common specialties include polling, advertising (or "media"), direct mail, and fund-raising. Some generalists are still at work in campaigns, but there are certainly fewer of them now than there were four decades ago. As one might guess, generalists provide all-purpose advice to candidates on how to organize and run their campaigns. In particular, generalists are skilled at developing campaign strategy. Thus they are often hired in the early stages of a campaign and consulted only occasionally throughout the remainder of it. Generalists are most likely to work on large-scale campaigns, where the staff is relatively big and the campaign can afford to hire someone who provides advice but no product (such as a poll or an advertisement).

No serious candidate would throw his or her hat into the ring today without hiring a pollster. In high-profile races, such as those for president, U.S. Senate, or governor, candidates usually hire pollsters *before* entering the race so they have some idea of the likelihood of success should they decide to run. It is often more cost-effective to pay for a national or statewide poll and not run than to spend millions on an effort that was doomed from the beginning.

Should the potential candidate become an actual candidate, the pollster's job is to provide a roadmap to victory (see Chapter 16). Early polling helps the campaign to determine the mood of the electorate and the voters' policy priorities. The ultimate goal of a campaign strategy is to link the candidate's agenda to the voters' preferences. This is done by identifying issues that are salient to the voters and on which there is agreement between the positions of the candidate and the voters. Polling can also reveal the most positive personal traits of the candidate. The campaign's message will, then, ultimately emphasize those issues and candidate qualities that polling suggests will be most effective. Meanwhile, throughout the campaign polling will test the resonance of the message and, through the use of tracking polls, the effects of individual campaign tactics such as running a specific advertisement.

*A brochure
from Democratic
political consultant
Dale Emmons
emphasizes
Kentucky themes,
his childhood, and
his track record in
winning elections.*
Source: Emmons
and Co., Inc.

Because of the central role played by polling, especially in crafting campaign strategy and message, a pollster often serves as the chief strategist in a campaign. Generalists initially played this role, and media consultants eventually took it over, but today pollsters are viewed as having a scientific (as opposed to intuitive) basis for their strategic decisions. Armed with data, pollsters can show how the "numbers" react to various moves by the campaign. The result is campaigns that are precise in their targeted messages but that, as media consultants are quick to point out, too often lack emotion.

Media consultants traffic in emotional appeals. Although their product is not devoid of rational content (that is, issues), they argue that effective advertising must tap voters' passions. They, therefore, have the tricky job of balancing simultaneous appeals to the heart and mind (see Chapter 17). Whereas pollsters employ the tools of social science, media consultants are artists, relying heavily on creativity and intuition. They are expected to use the analysis provided by pollsters in crafting their spots, but their skill lies in translating arguments into gut reactions.

The media consultant is responsible for the most public aspect of the campaign. Few voters will actually see the candidate in person during the course of the campaign, but thousands will get impressions of him or her via television and radio. Indeed, some research suggests that voters learn more about the candidates from advertising than from the news media.[21] Media consultants do not simply produce ads about their own candidate; they also try to create impressions about the opponent. Although negative ads, whether "pure attack" or "contrast" ads, have more issue content than positive, or "pure advocacy,"

ads,[22] voters claim to find ads aimed at opponents distasteful. As a result, media consultants get much of the blame for the perception that campaigns are less civil than they once were. Putting aside the fact that there never was a golden age of campaign civility, media consultants should not have to shoulder the responsibility for voters' squeamishness and disdain for politics. That said, there are plenty of examples of media consultants appealing to the public's baser instincts.

In addition to creating and producing campaign spots, some media consultants "place" ads—that is, they purchase time on television and radio stations to air the ads in return for between 10 and 15 percent of the total ad buy. Ultimately, it is the media buyer's responsibility to ensure that the candidate's spots air at the most opportune times and reach the largest number of viewers at the lowest possible cost. Consultants who handle media placement must be familiar with the viewing patterns of various demographic groups and must take advantage of the increasing opportunities to target the campaign's ads to those groups of voters deemed essential to the candidate's election.

Media consultants are not the only operatives responsible for communicating directly with the voters. Direct-mail specialists also produce persuasive appeals intended for potential voters. In fact, more money is spent on direct mail in campaigns at all levels than on broadcast advertising. Because mail is less public than television advertising, much of it flies under the radar of the news media. Campaigns thus mount some of the most negative appeals through the mail. But whether positive or negative, direct-mail pieces are often the most creative communications in a campaign. This is by necessity; so that it is not thrown away with the junk mail, campaign mail must catch the attention of the recipient. It is the also the direct-mail consultant's job to target the brochures effectively. Using specialized computer software, they can precisely target mail to voters based on a range of individual characteristics. For example, voters who are members of unions will receive brochures that explain the candidate's position on labor issues, while voters interested in health care will receive campaign mail outlining the candidate's views on, for example, Medicare reform. This targeting is so precise that voters living next door to one another can receive different mail from the same campaign.

Fund-raising is a critical element of any campaign. Even though much of the fund-raising is done by committee, consultants are often hired to bring in the cutting-edge tactics needed to raise even more money. These consultants usually specialize in either event fund-raising or direct-mail fund-raising. Fund-raising events may take the form of a small gathering in someone's home or a larger dinner or concert. Direct-mail fund-raisers differ from their persuasive counterparts in that their appeals are based primarily on text (in the form of a letter) and use fewer images. Like persuasion mail, however, fund-raising mail is often most successful when negative. Nothing raises money like reminding the would-be donor of the horrible consequences of the opponent's victory. Finally, as noted earlier, candidates are also increasingly raising money via the Internet and thus are depending on the services of specialists in Internet fund-raising.

Of the countless other campaign specialists, some handle only initiative and referendum, rather than candidate, campaigns. Others are experts in opposition research or in obtaining "earned" or free media coverage. Because of the increasing importance of voter mobilization, some consultants specialize in get-out-the-vote efforts. Finally, some consultants simply provide services such as Web site maintenance or products such as budgeting software. As modern campaigns become ever more complex, the number of different types of consultants is sure to grow.

Consultants: How Big an Impact?

How much of an impact do consultants actually have on elections? Even though the news media, and the candidates themselves, seem to think consultants are electoral magicians, their effect on the outcome of elections is probably limited. Most factors that determine who wins and loses elections are beyond the control of campaigns, making it unlikely that even the best consultants could influence the outcome in the vast majority of races. For one thing, few elections, especially for legislative seats, are actually competitive, in large part because districts are drawn to give one party an overwhelming majority. In addition, incumbents enjoy such an advantage in elections that few challengers can mount serious threats to them.

Senior White House political adviser Karl Rove grins during a phone conversation on election day, November 2, 2004. Rove is given much of the credit for the successful 2000 election and 2004 reelection of George W. Bush. Source: Shawn Thew/EPA/Landov

Nevertheless, the evidence suggests that candidates at some sort of electoral disadvantage gain a higher share of the vote with the assistance of a professional consultant than without it.[23] That is particularly true for challengers.

In theory, consultants bring a storehouse of knowledge to campaigns based on their experience. This "social learning" argument suggests that consultants gain valuable expertise—skills and knowledge—as they work on dozens or hundreds of campaigns.[24] They learn not only how campaigns function, but also what strategies and tactics are likely to work in various situations. In short, they develop models of how successful campaigns are run. These models are particularly useful for novice candidates. Even though celebrity consultants such as James Carville or Karl Rove, the "architect" of George W. Bush's victories in 2000 and 2004, might be especially crafty, this explanation of consultant influence implies that, by and large, consultants bring similar sets of talents to campaigns.

In the public's mind, a political consultant is little more than a hired gun, someone who will work for candidates of either party and any ideology as long as they can pay. The truth is that most consultants work for candidates of only one party. They are, in fact, loyal partisans. But that does not mean that they toe the party line. When given a choice between advancing the party's agenda or winning an election for a client, the consultant will always side with the client. Those goals are not, however mutually exclusive—that is, sometimes advancing the party's agenda will help a candidate to win; at other times the candidate can win without running away from his or her party. But there are certainly times when, to be successful, candidates will have to distance themselves from the party. In those cases, consultants are likely to advise the candidate to be independent.

Political consultants and their parties are, then, potentially at odds with one another. To the extent that they are, consultants might have the effect in campaigns of weakening the political parties. Indeed, some scholars suggest that once consultants arrived on the scene, they usurped some of the traditional responsibilities of the parties, making it difficult for parties to regain the strength they once had. Others believe the strength of parties is unrelated to the existence of political consultants. In fact, consultants and parties have come to a division of labor and a peaceful coexistence.[25] Because parties are well equipped to handle certain aspects of campaigns, such as voter mobilization, and consultants are better at others, such as advertising, a mutually beneficial relationship has developed. Evidence of this relationship is the lists kept by the parties of consultants who are approved for candidate use and the fact that parties actually hire some consultants directly to oversee the party committees' own polling and advertising as well as the development of a general campaign strategy.

If consultants' impact on election outcomes and on the parties is less dramatic than often assumed, perhaps their influence on the tone and substance of campaigns is significant.[26] The media, in particular, seem to think that consultants are the root of all campaign evil. But could it be that they have selective amnesia about much earlier campaigns? This is not the place to document the often vile behavior of candidates and parties throughout U.S. history, but it should be pointed out that long before the emergence of political consultants campaigns were marred by scurrilous accusations, dirty tricks, and fraudulent activities that amounted to attempts to steal elections. To be sure, modern-day consultants have done little to improve the conduct of campaigns. In fact, their practices may even raise unique concerns about campaign ethics, and their monopoly on technical expertise within a given campaign, for example, may make them unaccountable for their behavior. Ultimately, however, they seek to win elections as vigorously as party operatives of a bygone era. They collectively share some of the blame for contemptible campaign activity, but there is plenty to go around, and none of the actors involved in the process—candidates, journalists, parties, interest groups, and even voters—are exempt.[27]

Political consulting in the United States may be having another impact as well—the export of professional campaigning to democracies around the world.[28] Political systems—especially party and electoral systems—differ significantly from country to country, and various characteristics of those systems directly affect the way campaigns are run.[29] Nevertheless, there is some evidence of the "Americanization" of campaigning in other countries, including an increasing number of poll-driven campaigns that rely more heavily on negative advertising than in the past.[30] Some scholars attribute these changes to the modernization of campaign practices generally rather than a specifically American influence.[31] It is true, however, that some high-profile American consultants have worked in campaigns abroad in recent years. For example, Democratic and Republican consultants worked for the prime ministerial candidates of both major parties in Israel in 1999 and 2001. American consultants also play a significant role in an international network of campaign professionals.

Whether the influence of consultants is good or bad for a political system, they are likely to remain a permanent part of campaign organizations for the foreseeable future. Those organizations, in turn, are the central nervous systems of campaigns. Indeed, to speak of "the campaign" is, in many ways, to speak of the campaign organization and its members, including both paid staff and volunteers.

Notes

1. Stephen K. Medvic, "Is There a Spin Doctor in the House? The Impact of Political Consultants in Congressional Campaigns," Ph.D. diss., Purdue University, 1997, 22.

2. Robert J. Dinkin, *Campaigning in America: A History of Election Practices* (Westport, Conn.: Greenwood Press, 1989).

3. Medvic, "Is There a Spin Doctor in the House?" 28.

4. Gil Troy, *See How They Ran: The Changing Role of the Presidential Candidate* (Cambridge, Mass.: Harvard University Press, 1996), 40. Troy points out that the first presidential candidate to stump for himself was Gen. Winfield Scott, a Whig, in 1852.

5. Medvic, "Is There a Spin Doctor in the House?" 32.

6. Ibid., 40.

7. V. O. Key Jr., *Politics, Parties, and Pressure Groups* (New York: Crowell, 1958), 502–503.

8. Larry J. Sabato, *The Rise of Political Consultants: New Ways of Winning Elections* (New York: Basic Books, 1981), 8.

9. Larry Powell and Joseph Cowart, *Political Campaign Communication: Inside and Out* (Boston: Allyn and Bacon, 2003), 93–99.

10. Xandra Kayden, *Campaign Organization* (Lexington, Mass.: D. C. Heath, 1978), 11 (emphasis in original).

11. Karl A. Lamb and Paul A. Smith, *Campaign Decision-Making: The Presidential Election of 1964* (Belmont, Calif.: Wadsworth, 1968), 21.

12. Kayden, *Campaign Organization*, 9–10.

13. Lamb and Smith, *Campaign Decision-Making*, 29.

14. Ibid., 212–215.

15. Robert J. Pitchell, "The Influence of Professional Campaign Management Firms in Partisan Elections in California," *Western Political Quarterly* 11 (1958): 278–300.

16. Alan Ware, *The Breakdown of Democratic Party Organization, 1940–1980* (Oxford: Clarendon Press, 1988), 10; Sabato, *Rise of Political Consultants*.

17. Dan Nimmo, *The Political Persuaders: The Techniques of Modern Election Campaigns* (Englewood Cliffs, N.J.: Prentice Hall, 1970).

18. Robert Agranoff, "Introduction," in *The New Style of Election Campaigns*, ed. Robert Agranoff (Boston: Holbrook Press, 1972); Paolo Mancini and David L. Swanson, "Politics, Media, and Modern Democracy: Introduction," in *Politics, Media, and Modern Democracy*, ed. David L. Swanson and Paolo Mancini (Westport, Conn.: Praeger, 1996).

19. Nimmo, *Political Persuaders*, 37.

20. Dennis W. Johnson, "The Business of Political Consulting," in *Campaign Warriors: Political Consultants in Elections*, ed. James A. Thurber and Candice J. Nelson (Washington, D.C.: Brookings, 2000).

21. Thomas E. Patterson and Robert D. McClure, *The Unseeing Eye: The Myth of Television Power in National Politics* (New York: Putnam's, 1976).

22. Kathleen Hall Jamieson, Paul Waldman, and Susan Sherr, "Eliminate the Negative? Categories of Analysis for Political Advertisements," in *Crowded Airwaves: Campaign Advertising in Elections*, ed. James A. Thurber, Candice J. Nelson, and David A. Dulio (Washington, D.C.: Brookings, 2000).

23. Stephen K. Medvic, "The Effectiveness of the Political Consultant as a Campaign Resource," *PS: Political Science and Politics* 31 (1998): 150–154; Stephen K. Medvic, "Professionalization in Congressional Campaigns," in *Campaign Warriors: Political Consultants in Elections*, ed. James A. Thurber and Candice J. Nelson (Washington, D.C.: Brookings, 2000); Stephen K. Medvic, *Political Consultants in U.S. Congressional Elections* (Columbus: Ohio State University Press, 2001); Stephen K. Medvic and Silvo Lenart. "The Influence of Political Consultants in the 1992 Congressional Elections," *Legislative Studies Quarterly* 22 (1997): 61–77; Paul S. Herrnson, "Hired Guns and House Races: Campaign Professionals in House Elections," in *Campaign Warriors: Political Consultants in Elections*, ed. James A. Thurber and Candice J. Nelson (Washington, D.C.: Brookings, 2000); David A. Dulio, *For Better or Worse: How Political Consultants Are Changing Elections in the United States* (Albany: State University of New York Press, 2004).

24. Marjorie Randon Hershey, *Running for Office: The Political Education of Campaigners* (Chatham, N.J.: Chatham House, 1984).

25. Robin Kolodny, "Electoral Partnerships: Political Consultants and Political Parties," in *Campaign Warriors: Political Consultants in Elections*, ed. James A. Thurber and Candice J. Nelson (Washington, D.C.: Brookings, 2000).

26. See Candice J. Nelson, Stephen K. Medvic, and David A. Dulio, "Hired Guns or Gatekeepers of Democracy?" in *Shades of Gray: Perspectives on Campaign Ethics*, ed. Candice J. Nelson, David A. Dulio, and Stephen K. Medvic (Washington, D.C.: Brookings, 2002).

27. Ibid.

28. David A. Farrell, "Political Consultancy Overseas: The Internationalization of Campaign Consultancy," *PS: Political Science and Politics* 30 (1998): 171–176.

29. Fritz Plasser, with Gunda Plasser, *Global Political Campaigning: A Worldwide Analysis of Campaign Professionals and Their Practices* (Westport, Conn.: Praeger, 2002).

30. Shaun Bowler and David M. Farrell, "The Internationalization of Campaign Consultancy," in *Campaign Warriors: Political Consultants in Elections*, ed. James A. Thurber and Candice J. Nelson (Washington, D.C.: Brookings, 2000), 154.

31. Paolo Mancini, "New Frontiers in Political Professionalism," *Political Communication* 16 (1999): 231–246.

Suggested Readings

Agranoff, Robert. "Introduction." In *The New Style of Election Campaigns*, edited by Robert Agranoff. Boston: Holbrook Press, 1972.

Dinkin, Robert J. *Campaigning in America: A History of Election Practices.* Westport, Conn.: Greenwood Press, 1989.

Dulio, David A. *For Better or Worse: How Political Consultants Are Changing Elections in the United States.* Albany: State University of New York Press, 2004.

Farrell, David A. "Political Consultancy Overseas: The Internationalization of Campaign Consultancy." *PS: Political Science and Politics* 30 (1998): 171–176.

Hershey, Marjorie Randon. *Running for Office: The Political Education of Campaigners.* Chatham, N.J.: Chatham House, 1984.

Jamieson, Kathleen Hall, Paul Waldman, and Susan Sherr. "Eliminate the Negative? Categories of Analysis for Political Advertisements." In *Crowded Airwaves: Campaign Advertising in Elections*, edited by James A. Thurber, Candice J. Nelson, and David A. Dulio. Washington, D.C.: Brookings, 2000.

Kayden, Xandra. *Campaign Organization.* Lexington, Mass: D. C. Heath, 1978.

Key, V. O., Jr. *Politics, Parties, and Pressure Groups.* New York: Crowell, 1958.

Lamb, Karl A., and Paul A. Smith. *Campaign Decision-Making: The Presidential Election of 1964.* Belmont, Calif.: Wadsworth, 1968.

Mancini, Paolo. "New Frontiers in Political Professionalism." *Political Communication* 16 (1999): 231–246.

Mancini, Paolo, and David L. Swanson. "Politics, Media, and Modern Democracy: Introduction." In *Politics, Media, and*

Modern Democracy, edited by David L. Swanson and Paolo Mancini. Westport, Conn.: Praeger, 1996.

Medvic, Stephen K. "Is There a Spin Doctor in the House? The Impact of Political Consultants in Congressional Campaigns." Ph.D. diss., Purdue University, 1997.

————. *Political Consultants in U.S. Congressional Elections.* Columbus: Ohio State University Press, 2001.

————. "The Effectiveness of the Political Consultant as a Campaign Resource." *PS: Political Science and Politics* 31 (1998): 150–154.

Medvic, Stephen K., and Silvo Lenart. "The Influence of Political Consultants in the 1992 Congressional Elections." *Legislative Studies Quarterly* 22 (1997): 61–77.

Nelson, Candice J., David A. Dulio, and Stephen K. Medvic, eds. *Shades of Gray: Perspectives on Campaign Ethics.* Washington, D.C.: Brookings, 2002.

Nimmo, Dan. *The Political Persuaders: The Techniques of Modern Election Campaigns.* Englewood Cliffs, N.J.: Prentice Hall, 1970.

Pitchell, Robert J. "The Influence of Professional Campaign Management Firms in Partisan Elections in California." *Western Political Quarterly* 11 (1958): 278–300.

Plasser, Fritz, with Gunda Plasser. *Global Political Campaigning: A Worldwide Analysis of Campaign Professionals and Their Practices.* Westport, Conn.: Praeger, 2002.

Powell, Larry, and Joseph Cowart. *Political Campaign Communication: Inside and Out.* Boston: Allyn and Bacon, 2003.

Sabato, Larry J. *The Rise of Political Consultants: New Ways of Winning Elections.* New York: Basic Books, 1981.

Thurber, James A., and Candice J. Nelson, eds. *Campaign Warriors: Political Consultants in Elections.* Washington, D.C.: Brookings, 2000.

Troy, Gil. *See How They Ran: The Changing Role of the Presidential Candidate.* Cambridge, Mass.: Harvard University Press, 1996.

Ware, Alan. *The Breakdown of Democratic Party Organization, 1940–1980.* Oxford: Clarendon Press, 1988.

CHAPTER 11

Political Parties

Raymond J. La Raja

Political parties boast a colorful past in American campaigns. They have provided the political themes and personalities that give meaning and texture to the nation's politics. Although contemporary party organizations occupy a less prominent role in political campaigns than they did a century ago, the party label continues to be a vital signpost for candidates and voters alike. Since the 1970s, reinvigorated Democratic and Republican organizations have reemerged as important players in U.S. politics by adapting to the candidate-centered aspects of modern political campaigns. This chapter presents an overview of the party's role in campaigns and, in doing so, explains the electoral relevance of the party organization.

Campaigns have always been about organizing resources to help elect candidates. Traditionally, both in the United States and abroad, political parties have been at the center of this task. Parties recruit and nominate candidates, craft and advertise campaign themes, and mobilize citizens to vote. The desire of party leaders to control government by running a team of candidates for office is a linchpin of genuine democracy. By means of the competition between two or more parties, voters have choices at the ballot box and may hold leaders accountable.

Much has changed for political parties since Lord Bryce, an acute foreign observer of U.S. politics, declared almost ninety years ago that "party is king." [1] Bryce was referring to the heyday of party organizations in the post–Civil War era, frequently referred to as the Golden Era of parties (see illustration on page 177). During this period, parties organized all aspects of campaigning, from handpicking candidates for each level of office to "treating" partisan voters to entertainment and drinks on election day. [2] The Golden Era was a period of strong "party bosses," who dominated the proverbial smoke-filled rooms and made political decisions that enriched their friends and patrons. The desire of party leaders to control government as a means of doling out government jobs and contracts to loyal supporters gave them a strong incentive to win elections by campaigning on broad-based issues and mobilizing large blocs of voters. The happy consequence of party self-interest was robust com-

petition for office and widespread turnout among average citizens.

Even though elections stirred citizens, generating high levels of turnout, the dark side of party organizations and "bossism" could not be ignored as government's role expanded in the economic life of the nation. An emerging reform movement, buttressed by muckraking journalism, exposed the rising tide of party patronage, political favors, and illegal practices, including vote fraud. Reformers sought to end the corruption of the party bosses and the power of the machine. The Pendleton Act of 1883, which made it illegal for parties to dun the salaries of government employees, marked an early salvo in the battle to loosen the grip of the boss. From this point forward, a series of reforms championed by the Progressives—advocates of a government managed by nonpartisan experts—attacked the spoils system and the power of the party leaders. To undermine the rich vein of patronage in government offices and to improve government efficiency, reformers concentrated on developing a professional civil service branch by instituting merit examinations and making it difficult for a new administration to dismiss government employees easily when it took office.

One of the Progressive reforms most effective at weakening the power of party leaders was the institution of the direct primary (discussed later in this chapter and in Chapter 5), which allowed voters to select the party nominees for the general election. Under a primary system, potential candidates could seek support directly from voters rather than party leaders. This reform and others weakened the power of party bosses by taking away critical resources and changing the rules so that the party had fewer spoils to distribute to loyalists.

Broader changes in society were also undermining the importance of party organizations in campaigns. The greater mobility of citizens weakened ties to local parties, and national issues rose to prominence with the onset of world wars and economic depressions. Increasingly, the federal government played a larger role in public affairs, giving national leaders more prominence at the expense of local leaders. Technological changes also made tradi-

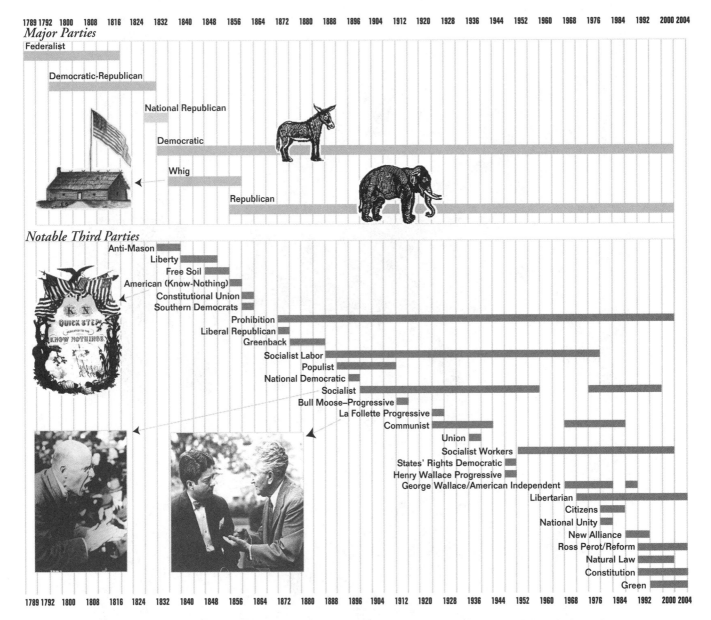

Source: *Congressional Quarterly's Guide to U.S. Elections*, 5th ed., Vol. 1 (Washington, D.C.: CQ Press, 2006). Updates provided by Rhodes Cook.

Note: Throughout U.S. history there have been more than 1,500 political parties. For this chart Congressional Quarterly editors have selected those parties that achieved national significance during presidential election years. The spaces between the rules on this chart indicate the election year only. For example, the Constitutional Union Party and the Southern Democrats were in existence for the 1860 election only and were gone by 1864. Similarly, the Green Party first fielded a presidential candidate in 1996.

tional forms of party organizing in campaigns obsolete. As the economy changed from one based on labor to capital resources, so did political campaigns. Candidates did not need party foot soldiers to attract voters when they could raise money and hire consultants to help them take their campaigns directly to the electorate through advertising. Changes in campaign finance laws and political strategies allowed candidates to create personal financial and electoral constituencies.

After World War II, the parties seemed even more irrelevant. By the 1970s, books and articles by prominent political observers, entitled *The Party's Over* and *Where's the Party?* called into question basic assumptions about the importance of political parties in U.S. political campaigns. It was an era of candidate-centered elections in which the parties played a minimal campaign role. As the end of the century approached, however, scholars noted that party organizations seemed to be growing in strength, even as

Cartoonist Thomas Nast created the enduring symbols of the two major parties: the Democratic donkey and the Republican elephant. Source: Library of Congress

the partisan attachments of voters weakened.[3] The strategic environment had changed, making party organizations relevant again. Rising campaign costs, intensive use of communications technology, and sharpened competition for control of government gave candidates a reason to seek the collective benefits of strong organizations.[4]

Political parties now operate in an era of political campaigning in which noncandidate groups are actively raising and spending money in elections. Yet the parties' influence is not as pervasive as it was during the Golden Era, especially because party organizations have lost the ability to control nominations. Instead, party renewal is tied to providing candidates with campaign services and coordinating resources to win elections. Since the 1970s, party organizations have expanded their fund-raising, hired professional staff, and enlarged the range of services they provide to candidates. The 2002 changes in the federal campaign finance laws altered the strategic terrain considerably and created uncertainties for all campaign actors in the 2004 election, but the parties appeared poised to exploit new opportunities and maintain an important presence in campaigns.

The next section of this chapter describes how U.S. political parties are organized in a system of government with separation of powers and federalism. Later sections describe how party organizations engage in traditional campaign functions, such as recruiting and nominating candidates, holding conventions, and helping candidates to win elections. In particular, they focus on the highly decentralized presidential nominating process in the states, which culminates in the national party conventions held every four years during the summer preceding the presidential election.

Party Organizations

In contrast to typical bureaucratic organizations such as corporations and the military, power in political parties has traditionally flowed from the bottom to the top. During the parties' formative period in the nineteenth century, a nonhierarchical relationship among the levels of a party grew out of the constitutional features of separation of powers and strong federalism. Before the rise of the large welfare state during the New Deal era, most sources of government contracts, jobs, and power were below the federal level. Party committees typically mushroomed around the numerous local elective offices, starting at the local "ward" level—typically, a neighborhood—and extending to the higher levels, which included city, county, congressional, state, and national committees. Typically, the local parties controlled critical campaign resources such as access to the ballot, patronage, and the grass-roots workers recruited to mobilize voters. In the last quarter-century, however, the national and

state committees have accumulated power, largely through their control of the political funds that can be used to support party activities locally. Even though influence has shifted noticeably toward the higher levels of the party, where it is easier to raise campaign funds, the relative autonomy of each party unit is a political tradition that continues.

One advantage of the decentralized character of parties is that it allows them to hold together citizens of diverse political cultures under one party label. A Democrat in Massachusetts, for example, may have more in common on the political issues with a Republican from his state than with a Democrat from Mississippi. Local autonomy, then, has forced party subgroups to bargain and cooperate in their choices of candidates and campaign activities. For most of U.S. history, localism was so strong that the national parties rarely had a stable presence in Washington—few party adherents in the states felt committed to sustaining such an operation. However, the shared goal of electing the party's presidential candidate provided the incentive to create a loose national structure that bound together party elements. The national convention is the fixture that holds the parties in the state together. In order to select the presidential nominee for the general election, the two major parties hold a national convention every four years. The national conventions are the plenary meetings of the major national committees, which include delegates from the parties in all fifty states and U.S. territories. These conventions of delegates provide the authority and the legitimacy for the permanent national organizations of the two major parties, the Democratic National Committee (DNC) and the Republican National Committee (RNC). Today, the national committees have an enduring presence in U.S. politics through their respective large headquarters in Washington, where their staffs engage mostly in fund-raising and campaign work.

A foreign observer might be surprised at how few third party organizations exist in the United States. The most successful third party campaigns have usually centered on the personalities of their candidates, such as H. Ross Perot's presidential campaigns in 1992 and 1996, or the successful gubernatorial campaign of former professional wrestler Jesse Ventura of Minnesota. The Green Party has made significant efforts to organize activists in neighborhood communities, and the Libertarian Party runs candidates in many local contests. Typically, however, when an election ends there is rarely an effective effort to sustain an ongoing party organization. Third parties face intimidating challenges. Election laws in the states make it difficult for third party candidates to get on the ballot, and raising money is never easy for campaigns that are unlikely to win. More critically, good candidates rarely want to risk running on the third-party ticket in an electoral system where two parties dominate the simple plurality voting system. In addition to these institutional obstacles, third parties are prone to factional disputes, because they

Presidential candidate Ralph Nader shows off a campaign poster during a 2004 press conference. The poster contrasts the antiwar stance of the independent ticket of Nader and vice-presidential running mate Peter Miguel Camejo with those of the candidates for the two major parties. Source: Ezio Peterson/UPI/Landov

usually attract an eclectic mix of activists who are disillusioned with the major parties. For example, the Reform Party established by Perot almost disintegrated before it could nominate a presidential candidate at its national meeting in 2000, because delegates had vastly different views on the mission and values of the party.

National Committees

Until fairly recently, the national committees were virtually nonexistent outside of the period from the nominating convention through the general election. They were something like circus performers, appearing every four years for the express purpose of nominating the presidential candidate, after which they folded their tents and their skeletal organizations disappeared, or they shrank to a few administrative staff. Year-round national party headquarters did not appear until 1918 for the GOP and 1928 for the Democrats, and even these had an air of impermanence to them.[5] For example, the Democrats operated out of Washington's Watergate office-hotel complex during the 1972 election, which became famous after the break-in by Republican operatives working for the reelection of President Richard Nixon. Through the middle of the twentieth century, the national committees were frequently on the brink of insolvency, having to ask the wealthier state parties to contribute funds for upkeep of the national operation.[6]

The state parties typically exerted significant control over presidential elections, because they operated under state elections laws, which were under the influence of

local party leaders. Indeed, national organizations appeared to do little more than coordinate the transfer of funds from the wealthy state parties and donors to parties in states where the race was expected to be close. These local and state parties would then carry out the campaign by advertising the presidential candidate and mobilizing voters. Because of the separated system of government and intensely local character of congressional elections, local party officials had little incentive to link the electoral destinies of the party's presidential and congressional candidates with a centralized, national party apparatus.

Permanent Organization

The national party structure has changed dramatically in just the last three decades. Both major national committees now own large, permanent headquarters in Washington, and money flows from the national committees to lower party levels. Unlike their counterparts in Europe, U.S. national parties are not mass-based organizations with dues-paying members. Instead, the parties receive voluntary contributions from a relatively small but dedicated constituency of upper-income partisans and operate much like large campaign consulting firms. The funds pay for a professional staff, which, working out of headquarters, helps the party to win elections throughout the nation. In 2000 the RNC employed a staff of about 250, and the DNC had about 150 staff members on the payroll.[7]

The national committees now set a standard among U.S. party organizations for providing campaign services to candidates. The RNC and DNC work primarily to help elect their presidential nominees, though they also participate in legislative elections at the federal and state levels and gubernatorial contests. These organizations help candidates with fund-raising, voter files, issue research, and various kinds of campaign advice and training. They also help to coordinate the activities of other party organizations and allied interest groups. Although it would be inaccurate to say the national committees stand atop a hierarchy, the RNC and DNC function at the center of an extended party network that includes affiliated party committees in Congress and the states, as well as the political committees of candidates and partisan interest groups.

The extraordinary emergence of a strong national party organization reflects changes in the strategic environment that puts a premium on raising cash to pay for expensive media, polling, and voter contact technologies. After a disastrous election for the Republicans in 1964, the RNC adapted to the capital-intensive campaigns by taking advantage of fund-raising laws, developing technical expertise to raise money, and supporting a fledgling network of activists and party committees in areas of nascent Republican strength, especially the South. A central reason for the RNC's success was its ability to develop a strong and independent financial base through mass mailing solicitations. Over time, the RNC has established a massive list of small donors who support the party, and so it no longer has to rely on the largesse of state parties to fund its activities. The DNC has imitated the Republican successes, but it lags behind the RNC in both fund raising and the provision of services. It is likely that the Republican advantage with donors is a structural advantage of being the party favored by upper-income voters. More Republicans than Democrats can afford to make regular political contributions.

Officially, the staff of each party organization is responsible to its respective RNC or DNC permanent governing body, which includes representatives of all fifty state organizations and U.S. territories. Traditionally, the national committees included one committeeman and committeewoman from each state, as well as ex officio members such as elected officials and interest group leaders. In 1974, however, in an effort to widen participation and to gain greater organizational legitimacy among partisan activists, the Democrats broke with this custom by having membership reflect populations and partisan support in the states. Today, the RNC maintains a confederative character and nurtures an organizational culture that is businesslike in contrast to the more fluid practices and deliberative arrangements of the DNC.[8] For example, the DNC has established caucus groups within the party structure that may represent women, minorities, and young activists in organizational decision making.

Party Chairs

In practice, the governing body has little to do with day-to-day operations of national committees; each is led and supervised by a party chair and the chair's professional staff. Most members of the national committees are busy with the affairs of their local and state parties. Even the smaller executive committees of the party leave discretion to the party chair, who acts like the chief executive officer of a sprawling company. The chair tries to set tone for the organization and give strategic direction to party adherents, even though other levels of the party organization have significant autonomy in conducting campaigns. More specifically, the chair is chiefly responsible for fund raising, putting together a national campaign infrastructure, and spurring state organizations to organize voter mobilization programs. In carrying out these tasks, the chair must be a good politician, adept at working with diverse factions within the party.

In the past, the chair was chosen by the presidential nominee—the de facto national party leader—and then ratified by the national committee at the convention. Since the 1980s, however, the lengthening of presidential campaigns and concern about maintaining party unity in the general election have led to a change: the presiding chair going into the convention serves out his or her term.

The chair whose party controls the White House tends to have less power than the out-party chair. For the party in power, most political decisions are made by political staff in the White House, and the chair is responsible for implementation rather than party leadership. Indeed, the chair serves at the pleasure of the president and can be easily removed. In 1994, for example, David Wilhelm was ousted from the DNC because the Republicans triumphed decisively in the midterm elections. More recently, in 2001, the RNC chair, Virginia governor James Gilmore, was forced out of his RNC office after only one year because he resisted White House control.[9]

Starting in the Jacksonian era, when the spoils system emerged through the New Deal, the chair of the winning party had the enviable task of coordinating federal patronage appointments among the state delegations. Today, however, the in-party chair concentrates largely on raising money, mediating among party factions, and preparing the campaign groundwork for the next presidential election. The White House may call frequently on the national organizations to conduct polls and organize events that help to sustain the president's popularity. The chair of the out party usually assumes a more prominent public profile than the chair of the in party, because the out party lacks a leader in the executive branch.

Yet that leader may not be the same one that served the party during the election. As noted earlier, after an electoral loss the chair is usually a magnet for dissatisfaction among party activists and frequently is replaced. A struggle ensues over appointing a new chair, and the pick may indicate the strength of a faction within the party. A prodigious fund-raiser, Terry McAuliffe, continued as DNC chair after Al Gore's defeat in 2000, suggesting the continued influence of his original patrons, the Clintons.

The chair faces a daunting task after an electoral defeat—healing old wounds, paying debts, raising new money, inspiring party activists around the country, and building the infrastructure for the next campaign. According to party scholar John F. Bibby, there are traditionally two styles of party chair. The *speaking chair* acts as spokesperson for the party, trying to generate publicity for the party's causes and candidates, and pointing out the faults of the opposition. The style increasingly favored today, however, is the *organizational chair* such as Ronald H. Brown (DNC chair, 1989–1993) or Lee Atwater (RNC chair, 1989–1991). Such chairs manage professional staff, attend party meetings throughout the country, and participate intimately in planning campaign strategies. The decline of the chair as spokesperson is related to the ever greater public visibility of party leaders in Congress, who appear on television regularly. DNC chair McAuliffe appeared to balance these two roles, initially acting as the vocal partisan by criticizing the outcome of the 2000 election in Florida and the policies of the George W. Bush administration. However, as the 2004 election approached and presidential candidates emerged, McAuliffe moved into the background, concentrating more on fund-raising and working with allied interest group organizations. At first blush, the selection of former presidential candidate Howard Dean as DNC chair after the 2004 election suggests that the Democrats wanted an ideological spokesperson for the party. However, Dean's elevation may have resulted primarily from the desire of Democratic activists for organizational reforms to help the party compete more effectively with Republicans. State party leaders supported Dean, a former governor of Vermont, because he promised to invest in local organizational building.

Congressional Campaign Committees

After the Civil War, members of Congress established campaign committees that focused exclusively on their electoral needs and priorities, which frequently differed from those of the presidential candidates. The four Capitol Hill committees are the Democratic Congressional Campaign Committee (DCCC), the National Republican Congressional Committee (NRCC), the Democratic Senatorial Campaign Committee (DSCC), and the National Republican Senatorial Committee (NRSC). These committees focus primarily on helping their members to get reelected to Congress, but they also try to recruit challengers to compete against the opposing party. Typically, these committees, which are run and operated by members of Congress, have been fiercely independent of the national committees, although they have cooperated in presidential campaigns more frequently during the past decade.

Like the national committees, the Hill committees have become more institutionalized and service-oriented in recent decades. Higher revenues from fund-raising have helped the congressional committees to augment the professional staffers who assist candidates with new technologies and campaign advice. These committees also provide data on voters and research on opponents. Most important, they help candidates to raise money by hosting fund-raising events, providing contributor lists, and directing political action committees (PACs) their way (see Chapters 12 and 15). Campaign finance laws permit the Hill committees to make contributions to candidates, though these rarely exceed a small fraction of the total amount of candidate receipts. The parties also help candidates by spending money on their behalf in key races—called "coordinated expenditures"—for advertisements or voter mobilization efforts. Because the central goal of these committees is to pursue or maintain majorities in Congress, they allocate resources efficiently by concentrating money where it will make the most difference—in races that appear close.

State and Local Parties

Each state has a Republican and a Democratic state central committee. Like the national committees, many of these organizations adapted to modern campaigns by professionalizing and providing services to candidates. State parties face considerable variation in the political environment across the country; their levels of partisan competition, resources, and electoral laws diverge widely. In some states, the parties confront stiff competition from candidates and PACs when raising money. And the states face high turnover in the party leadership, because most state party chairs serve as volunteers. However, many of these organizations have grown substantially in ways similar to the growth of the national committees.

In many states, party members in the legislature have developed formidable campaign operations called legislative campaign committees. These organizations are akin to the congressional campaign committees, because they serve the needs of legislative candidates. They have emerged in states with professional legislatures where holding office is an attractive job and where competition tends to be strong. Legislative campaign committees direct their efforts toward recruiting candidates to run for office and helping them to raise money. Because of the premium these committees put on raising money and deploying sophisticated media technologies, they tend to weaken other aspects of parties because they ignore grassroots work and local party building.[10]

Among local committees in counties and towns, there is even greater variation in style and substance. It is sometimes difficult to fill leadership positions, and many committees are inactive, particularly during the off-election season. The relative weakness of local committees is a drastic change from when local organizations were among the most active in campaigns. As in previous eras, however, the biggest value of local organizations for candidates is canvassing voters and getting them to the polls. Some organizations do a fairly good job rousing volunteers and generating excitement for the campaign. There is some evidence that strong local organizations can make a difference in winning elections and building public support for parties.[11]

Political Party Activity in Campaigns

Although campaigns focus on the candidates rather than party-based themes, parties have the organizational muscle to influence the outcome of campaigns. They are part of a constellation of "outside" actors that increasingly are entering the fray in the most competitive races. Since the 1980s, the strategic environment has changed in ways that make the party more relevant than during the previous period when candidates could run their campaigns without help. Increasing competition for partisan control of Congress has raised the stakes for all members, putting a premium on collective action that helps the party maintain or win control of the government. The rising cost of campaigns and the technical requirements for winning increase the incentives for candidates to seek help from outside groups such as parties. In presidential races, the front-loading of the primary campaigns (discussed later in this chapter), in which a party nominee emerges well before the national convention, puts a premium on early organizing by political parties. Because of the limits on candidate fund-raising in presidential and other races, the political parties have stepped into the breach to help their nominees, exploiting campaign finance laws to engage in independent, parallel, and coordinated campaigns with their candidates. The rest of this chapter proceeds through the stages of the process in which parties can make a difference in campaigns.

Recruitment

The parties can play an important role shaping a potential candidate's decision to run for elective office. Because the parties have an incentive to contest as many elections as possible, they actively seek candidates to run for office—and especially those who they think are likely to win.[12] The ideal candidate has name recognition among potential voters and some campaign experience, and knows how to raise money. To the chagrin of many party leaders, some of the best candidates often choose to stay out of the race when the party's prospects seem poor. It is difficult to convince good candidates to run, because they tend to be strategic about entering a contest.[13] They frequently hold lower levels of office or have successful careers in the private sector that they do not want to give up unless the odds of winning are good. For this reason, they wait until good opportunities present themselves. Typically, this strategy means avoiding races against incumbents who are hard to beat or waiting for an open seat. They also consider whether an anti-incumbent attitude is pervading public opinion or whether the political climate favors their party.[14]

One way in which party officials recruit candidates is to simply ask them to run. According to a study of possible candidates, the frequency of party contacts with candidates can make a difference in a candidate's decision to run.[15] The parties may also induce potential candidates by offering to support them with money and services in the general election. At the national level, the parties hold briefings for PACs, encouraging them to invest in key races highlighted by party analysts. The parties also host fund-raising events where they introduce candidates to PAC leaders. Party-based professionals provide training sessions to help potential candidates organize campaigns, give advice on the technical aspects of campaigns such as campaign finance rules, and recommend campaign consultants. In these ways, the party acts as a central clearinghouse that helps candidates to connect with party activists, allied groups, and donors. In the past several elections, some interest groups have been behaving more like parties, trying to recruit like-minded candidates and shape who emerges from primaries (see Chapter 12). These groups include EMILY's List, a liberal group that

supports pro-choice women, and the Club for Growth, a conservative pro-business group.

The party groups most active in recruitment are the congressional campaign committees, state organizations, and legislative campaign committees. These groups have an incentive to contest elections to pursue majorities in the legislature. They focus on the marginal districts where the outcome is uncertain and the odds of success are the best. The parties thus ignore many districts where they believe there is little chance they can pick up a seat. The decision by parties to ignore anything but the most tightly contested races tends to dry up resources in districts not considered in play and may further dampen competition.

Although few parties endorse or contribute to candidates in the primaries, they may try to clear the field by discouraging other possible candidates from running. For example, in the 2002 Senate election in Minnesota leaders of the Republican Party actively discouraged entrants in the primary as a way of helping the party-preferred candidate, Norm Coleman, former mayor of Minneapolis. Coleman eventually won the seat. Occasionally, parties help a favored candidate through preprimary endorsements. In seven states (Colorado, Connecticut, New Mexico, New York, North Dakota, Rhode Island, and Utah), state law provides for preprimary endorsement by party conventions.[16] Candidates who receive a certain percentage of votes from delegates at a party convention are automatically placed on the primary ballot. Candidates who are not endorsed by party delegates may still get on the ballot if they file a petition with the appropriate state election officers (usually the secretary of state). In ten other states, party rules allow for endorsements that do not guarantee placement on the ballot, but send a signal to others about party favorites. The evidence about whether party endorsements matter in the outcome of primary elections is mixed. Between 1960 and 1980, endorsed gubernatorial candidates won at least 80 percent of the time in states with endorsement procedures, but this percentage dropped to 53 percent between 1982 and 1998.[17] The nonendorsed candidate can excel through high name recognition or the support of allied interest groups and alternative party factions.

Fund-Raising and Finances

Today, political parties are prodigious fund-raisers compared with those of the candidate-centered era of the 1960s and 1970s. When Congress passed the Federal Election Campaign Act (FECA) in the early 1970s to address the problems of regulating money in politics, it did not seem overly concerned about the role that parties might play in the future financing of campaigns.[18] Instead, reformers took aim at the individual and interest group contributors to candidates, establishing contribution limits and clear disclosure guidelines. The political parties benefited from relatively generous rules on the size and source of contributions. Candidates could accept only $1,000 per election from individual donors, whereas

Figure 11-1 National Party Hard Money Receipts, 1976–2004

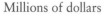
Millions of dollars

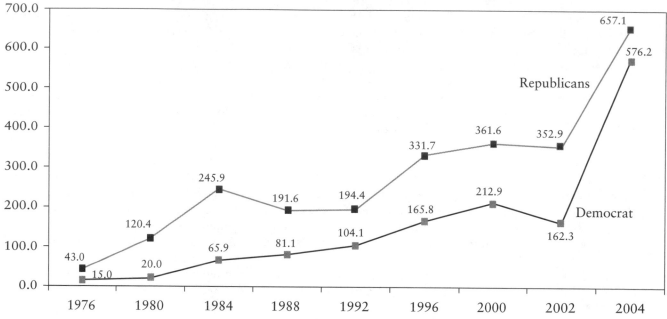

Source: Federal Election Commission.

the national party committees could accept contributions up to $20,000 per year. Because parties operate in both federal and state campaigns, the Federal Election Commission (FEC) also allowed them to raise and spend funds under state guidelines, so long as the money was used in state elections, or to build the organization and promote party-based messages. These funds, which became infamously known as "soft money," were later banned from federal election activities by the 2002 Bipartisan Campaign Reform Act, or BCRA (see Chapter 6).

In contrast to an earlier era when the national parties relied on state organizations for funds, the RNC and DNC developed independent financial bases under the FECA. Republicans were the first to take advantage of the rules to institutionalize political contributions to parties. Under the guidance of RNC chair Bill Brock (1977–1981), the Republicans developed formidable mailing lists of partisan donors, who routinely gave "hard money" or federally regulated contributions. Democrats did not begin to imitate the RNC until about 1984 under DNC chair Charles Manatt. In the three decades since the FECA was implemented, party fund-raising has grown substantially (see Figure 11-1). The Republican national committees increased their hard money receipts from $43.0 million in 1976 to $361.6 million in 2000. The Democrats increased their receipts from just $15.0 million to $212.9 million during the same period.

In the early years of the FECA, the parties raised some soft money to defray the basic costs for office buildings,

administrative activities, and volunteer activities. Provisions in the FECA allowed parties to perform these basic "party-building" functions with funds that did not conform to federal limits on the source and size of contributions. Increasingly, however, party officials used it in ways that appeared to cross over into direct electioneering. For example, the DCCC, led by Rep. Tony Coelho of California in the 1980s, began supplementing hard money contributions and coordinated expenditures with party soft money that could be used to mobilize voters. Coelho maintained that these soft money expenditures were directed toward contacting voters—a genuine party-building activity. In reality, however, these funds were intended to help the House candidates in the districts win their elections. Coelho was determined that the Democrats would go toe to toe with the Republicans, who controlled more hard money.

As soft money began to be used for television "issue ads," its strategic value increased and the parties sought more of it. Soft money (nonfederal) receipts grew substantially in the 1990s, and parties spent them on advertisements that avoided electioneering phrases that directly called for the election or defeat of a federal candidate. In avoiding the electioneering phrases, the party could claim these television ads supported generic party building rather than support for federal candidates. The party argument, however, was weakened by the fact that these advertisements heavily targeted closely contested federal elections. Within a decade, the combined national party soft money funds increased more than fivefold, from $86 million in 1992 to almost $500 million in the 2000 election.

The 2002 BCRA attempts to address end runs around federal law by placing tougher restrictions on political parties (see Chapter 6 for details). The national party committees may no longer raise and spend soft money. The state parties may use soft money in nonfederal campaigns and for grass-roots mobilization during federal campaigns so long as the size of the contribution does not exceed $10,000. To compensate for the loss of soft money, the limits on individual hard money contributions to national parties were raised from $20,000 to $25,000 per year and the limits on contributions to state parties were increased from $5,000 to $10,000.

The changes in federal campaign finance law have important implications for how parties will engage in future elections. In the short term, Democrats are especially vulnerable because a much larger percentage of their total funds came from soft money donations. In 2004 both parties expanded their pool of hard money contributors significantly, which was one of the intents of the new law. Democrats, however, continue to lag slightly behind Republicans in raising hard money contributions; in 2004 Democratic committees raised $747 million compared with a Republican total of $840 million. Remarkably, the DNC raised as much money ($394 million) as the RNC ($392 million)—something that has only rarely occurred in their long history of competition. Both parties benefited from the expected closeness of the presidential contest, the passions aroused by the war in Iraq, and the expanded use of the Internet to increase the number of party donors. In anticipation of being outspent by Republicans, several Democratic quasi-party groups—called "527" organizations because of how they are defined in the U.S. Tax Code—formed well in advance of the presidential primaries to raise soft money in lieu of the parties. Republican partisans were not as quick to exploit this strategy, but they also developed similar organizations in the months leading up to election day. These groups, with names such as America Coming Together (supporting Democrats) and Leadership Forum (supporting Republicans), are run by former party operatives and leaders of allied interest groups such as labor unions. These partisan groups spent heavily on issue ads and voter mobilization in targeted areas.

The Nominating Process

In most democracies, party leaders choose who will run for office, but U.S. political parties typically nominate candidates through a unique institution called the direct primary (see Chapter 5 for details). In a direct primary, the electorate goes to the polls to choose which candidates will bear the party label in the general election. The candidate who wins a plurality earns the opportunity to appear on the ballot on election day. The fact that the nominating process is removed from the party organization in the United States has important implications for how campaigns are waged and the degree to which political parties influence the behavior of candidates.

In spite of recent court decisions that give the parties greater discretion in setting nominating rules, the institution of the direct primary weakens U.S. party organizations. Before the advent of primaries, the power to bestow the party label in an election gave organizational leaders at the local level the capacity to influence the behavior of officeholders and candidates. Under the British party system, for example, the party organization may refuse to nominate a candidate who appears disloyal to party leaders. In the United States, however, it is easier to be a party maverick, because the party does not directly control the electoral destiny of candidates running with the party label. American candidates have benefited from changes in the strategic environment that allow them to organize their own election campaigns, even when the party is unwilling to support them. Rather than rely on the labor of party workers, candidates can raise money on their own to build a personal organization and pay for campaign services from consultants (see Chapter 10). By organizing and winning the party primary on their own, candidates have the campaign infrastructure in place to contest the general election, which makes the party organization less important.

Even though the direct primary is a popular institution because it appears to give voters more choices in elections, it occasionally creates dilemmas for parties beyond the fact that it weakens the organization. For example, because candidates are largely self-recruited, there is always the chance that a weak or unattractive candidate could win the nomination. Some candidates gain the nomination by appealing to a small but intensely passionate segment of the electorate. Because voter turnout tends to be low in primaries, such candidates have a good chance of winning, even though they are unappealing to the wider electorate. Primaries may also sharpen the factional disputes within the party. A hard-fought party primary can be divisive for activists who support different candidacies and thereby undermine party efforts to win the general election. The primary campaigns also expose candidate weaknesses that can be used against the candidate in the general election. Finally, hard-fought primaries force party candidates to spend a lot of campaign funds that might otherwise be used to challenge the opposing party candidates in the general election.

Presidential Nominations

The U.S. Constitution describes how the president is to be elected, but it does not mention how to nominate presidential candidates. The U.S. political parties have assumed this task through a highly decentralized, varied, and open process. Technically, the party's presidential nominee is selected by party delegates at a national convention several months prior to the general election. But how the delegates themselves are chosen is the key to understanding the selection of presidential candidates. Each state has developed its own method of picking party delegates (see Chapter 5 for greater detail).

Broadly speaking, delegates to the national convention can be chosen in two ways. The first is through the party caucus or convention process, and the second is through a presidential primary. The Democrats are unique in using a third class of delegates, called superdelegates, who are automatically invited to the national conventions by virtue of their official positions in the party as appointed members of the organization or elected members of government. The method of delegate selection in each state depends on state laws and the statutes regulating political parties. In states that are silent on such matters, the party creates internal rules for the process.

In the caucus system, local party members choose delegates to pass to the next level of party. This process repeats itself until delegates reach the state convention. Subsequently, the state party sends these delegates to the national convention. In the past, at each selection stage party leaders influenced who would be chosen to attend the next level of caucus, just as they influenced nominations to other offices. These delegates would take their cues from party leaders, who typically rewarded delegates for their loyalty. Party leaders who controlled delegate votes used them in the bargaining process at the convention. Today, however, most delegates affiliate early in the process with a particular candidate, and then they move through the various caucus stages committed to the same candidate.

In contrast to the caucus system, presidential primaries use a popular vote to determine which delegates will attend the national convention. Potential delegates are listed on a slate sponsored by a presidential candidate. The votes cast for the Democratic candidate in the primary election translate into a proportional share of "pledged" delegates from his or her slate. For Republican candidates, the winner of the plurality in most states receives all the delegate votes. A candidate who accumulates enough delegates in this fashion is virtually assured of the nomination on the first ballot at the convention.

Beginning in the 1970s, the presidential nominating process for both parties emphasized primaries over the caucus system. The reasons behind this were complex, but the decisive factor was a decision by national Democratic leaders to adopt the recommendations by various party-sponsored commissions that the state party rules for selecting delegates be changed. At the time, there was strong sentiment for opening up the process to a broader group of partisans as a way of increasing the legitimacy of the party organization. Many of the rules were adopted and enforced by the DNC, compelling party leaders in the states to accept a primary system for nominating the party's presidential candidate. When state legislatures—mostly controlled by Democrats—chose to revise their

statutes, they frequently implemented the same rules for Democrats and Republicans; thus the number of Republican primaries increased as well. In 1968 only seventeen states used primaries to select convention delegates; about forty states used them in 2004.

Over the past three decades, many states have moved their primaries to earlier in the campaign season to maximize their influence on the selection of presidential candidates. This "front-loading" of primaries tends to generate momentum behind one candidate early in the primary cycle, giving the leader a big enough delegate lead to become the nominee several months before the convention. In response, many of the states that hold primaries later in the season may cancel their presidential primaries to save money. When this happens, the parties switch to traditional caucus meetings to choose delegates to the national convention.

It matters strategically whether a primary is closed or open. Closed primaries, which permit only voters registered with the party, tend to help candidates from the more ideologically extreme wings of the party, because strong partisans tend to vote in these elections. Open primaries, which allow all voters to participate, tend to widen the mix of voters, even attracting those registered with the opposite party. The openness tends to help party moderates and mavericks, because these elections dilute the voice of strong partisans, who favor candidates standing firmly for the ideological principles of the party. A good example of this difference was displayed in the 2000 Republican primaries. The more conservative candidate, Texas governor George W. Bush, lost in states that held open primaries in 2000, such as New Hampshire and Michigan, to Arizona senator John McCain, whose bipartisan call for campaign finance reform earned him credibility with independent voters. In states that held closed primaries such as California, Colorado, and South Carolina, Bush beat McCain handily because nonpartisans were excluded from voting.

The candidate-centered nature of the nominating process, which emphasizes primaries, has turned delegate loyalty to the candidates rather than party leaders. Success in the nominating process is now associated with having a strong personal organization made up of dedicated activists who campaign in primary states or overrun local party caucuses to push for a preferred candidate. As a result of these changes, delegates at the national party convention tend to reflect the preferences of party activists committed to particular issues and candidates rather than those of party professionals whose chief purpose is to win elections.

The parties thus appear to be more polarized along ideological lines than in previous generations. Because of the premium placed on mobilizing factions to win primaries, party candidates have diminished incentives to forge coalitions early in the nominating process.[19] Indeed, candidates may win the nomination through partisan voters who are considerably more ideological than the typical voter, which may lead to problems winning the general election. A good example of this was the ill-fated campaign of the 1972 Democratic presidential candidate, George McGovern. In 1984 Democratic leaders tried to remedy the problems created by the primary system by creating the category of superdelegates, who would remain unpledged to a particular candidate going into a convention. As elected officials, they are usually interested chiefly in winning the election, and so they are ready to cast their votes in favor of the most promising candidate. Superdelegates matter, however, only under the unusual circumstance of a "brokered" convention in which no candidate secures a majority of pledged delegates prior to the convention.

National Conventions

Traditionally, the national convention was where the party nominated its presidential candidate. In recent decades, however, each party has settled on its presidential nomination several months before its convention, which is held during the summer preceding the November election. As described earlier, the widespread use of state primaries, in which voters select the party nominees, has made the conventions practically irrelevant for choosing the presidential candidates. In the past, nominations were contested inside the convention hall among party delegates from the states. Today, the convention is a venue to advertise the campaign of the party nominee and unify activists to support the nominee's campaign. Bibby aptly calls the convention a "coronation" of the party candidate who has won the greatest support among the party electorate.[20]

The demise of the convention as a place to choose the nominee is fairly recent. Through much of the nineteenth century, party conventions were outsized party gatherings where delegates from different states bargained over who would be the presidential candidate. The delegates usually did not pledge themselves to any particular candidate before the start of the convention. Once at the convention, different party factions would campaign informally on behalf of their favorite. As the convention proceeded, delegates from a state would cast ballots on successive roll calls until one candidate received a majority. Usually, local party leaders had significant control over the delegation from their state and influenced how individual ballots were cast. These leaders would use their control over delegations to negotiate with other party leaders over selecting the nominee.

In those days, conventions were often contentious, raucous affairs, and frequently the selection process took several ballots before a nominee was named. In one extreme example, in 1924 Democrats considered 103 ballots at their convention in New York City before a majority settled on John W. Davis as the party nominee.[21] Today, the party nominee is almost always chosen on the first ballot because convention delegates are merely ratifying the decision generated by the preconvention campaigns in state primaries and caucuses.

Purpose and Goals of Conventions

The most important purpose of the party convention is to introduce the presidential candidate to a large television audience.[22] During the four days of a convention, the political parties produce an extended infomercial about the nominee for the American public. A parade of political well-knowns deliver rousing speeches, and television cameras capture the fanfare of party traditions and the enthusiasm of delegates, culminating in a prime-time acceptance speech by the presidential candidate on the final evening. Thus the parties have transformed their conventions from deliberative bodies fed by spontaneous outbursts of loyalty and invective to a Hollywood-style production with scripted scenes and characters.

Traditionalists may lament that present-day national party conventions appear to be empty vessels, bereft of decision-making power. But an alternative perspective is that these quadrennial gatherings of political luminaries and loyalists give shape and substance to a party system that at other times seems to be fifty separate state party systems and congeries of factional interests. The national party convention is one of the few times—usually the only time in four years—in which all elements of the party are brought together in one place. The convention is the clearest manifestation that the various party committees at the local, state, and national levels form an integrated whole.

The coming together of party members at the national convention is also an important signal for voters to begin paying attention to the presidential contest. Except for strong partisans, most voters are uninterested in the preconvention presidential campaigns, especially now that those campaigns have lengthened to almost two years before the general election. The flourish surrounding the convention is a bugle call to voters that the official campaign is under way. The display of party symbols and history at the convention reminds voters of partisan leanings and spawns a recurring four-year cycle in which the electorate polarizes more starkly into two major camps until election day.

Because the conventions may be the first time that most voters take a close look at the presidential candidates, the parties want the voters to receive a favorable impression. The nominee's campaign advisers work closely with the national party staff to craft a theatrical and compelling presentation for the television audience. This is an opportunity for the candidate to set the themes for the campaign and burnish an image perhaps bruised by a grueling year of fighting for the nomination with fellow partisans. For the party out of power or in open contests, it is likely that the nomination battle has been fiercely contested. The candidate must recover from being the recipient of negative advertising, mudslinging, and slanderous rumors.

On top of the wounds inflicted by fellow partisans are the thrusts taken from the opposing party even before the convention begins. As a front-runner emerges from one party, the opposing party already has that candidate in its sights, ready to air advertisements that target perceived weaknesses of the candidate. The risks of attack are greater for a nominee facing an incumbent party. Typically, the incumbent does not face a difficult nomination and so has unspent money that can be used to harass the opposition. A good example of this strategy emerged during the 1996 contest when the Clinton campaign chose to use party-sponsored advertisements to set the campaign issue agenda and define the presumed Republican nominee, Sen. Robert J. Dole of Kansas, in the worst possible light.

The convention is also an opportunity for the candidates to set the record straight. More than any other time during the campaign, they are able to present themselves in an environment that is relatively free of hostile rhetoric from the opposition. For at least four days, the candidate and fellow partisans have a soapbox from which they can trumpet how they stand for light and reason, while the opposition reflects darkness and folly. Because of this extraordinary period of one-sided grandstanding, candidates usually receive a significant bump in the polls at the close of the convention.

The convention is also an opportunity for the party to unite factions that supported different candidates. Whoever wins wants the help of all activists in the general election. A wise party nominee goes out of his or her way to make amends with losers, generate feelings of goodwill, and rally party adherents against the opposition. One way to do this is through the various convention meetings, particularly in discussions about the party platform, which is a statement of party philosophy. The nominee shows magnanimity by agreeing to issue "planks" in the party platform put forward by leaders of other factions, or by allowing changes in the party organizational rules that might benefit a particular faction at a future nominating convention. Providing good time slots for speeches by losing candidates is also a symbolic gesture of reconciliation, especially if the losing candidate shows enthusiastic support for the nominee. In this way, the convention is a mechanism to rebuild the party coalition and lay the groundwork for the final months of the general election.

Choosing the Host City and Convention Date

Given the symbolic importance of the convention and the party's desire to avoid glitches in presenting its best face, the national party chooses the host city carefully. Not long after the election year convention, a committee representing the party's national committee begins its search, reviewing proposals from several cities that want to host the next gathering. Municipal officials, civic boosters, and

local businesses understand that conventions are good public advertising for a city and bring in lots of cash for the local economy. The political parties consider several factors when choosing a convention site, but the willingness of a city to subsidize much of the convention is paramount.[23] The cash or services offered by a city are usually raised from local businesses and large corporations that expect to profit from the week-long visit by thousands of delegates, alternative delegates, families, friends, convention personnel, and representatives from the domestic and international news media, as well as protestors. At the very least, the host city must have sufficient hotel rooms, reliable transportation, and a good convention hall. In 2004 Boston officials estimated convention visitors for the Democratic gathering at 35,000, while New York City, the site of the Republican convention, estimated 50,000 visitors, not including the hundreds of thousands of demonstrators who converged on Manhattan.[24]

In addition to private money solicited by the host city, each major party receives roughly $15 million in federal subsidies to run the convention (state and local governments also chip in). The subsidy program began under the Federal Election Campaign Act of 1971 as a way of lessening reliance on private funds that may corrupt the party and its candidates. However, in 2004 these federal public funds covered only 17 percent of the costs of running these events, which grew into megamedia productions, with expenditures of roughly $100 million for Republicans and $72 million for Democrats.[25]

Private donors also underwrite the costs of conventions. In 2000 private donors accounted for $56 million in funding for both conventions, or 35 percent of total funding (state and local governments accounted for an additional $37 million, on top of the federal subsidy). In 2004 private sources accounted for more than 80 percent of funding. Among the large donors were corporations such as Microsoft, Coca-Cola, and Bristol-Meyers Squibb, as well as wealthy individuals. The infusion of private money from interest groups has raised concerns about the corrupting effect it may have on officeholders and party leaders. Corporate sponsors and other well-heeled donors get prime boxes at the conventions and host numerous wine and cheese affairs for mingling with party and elected officials. The access for large convention donors gives at least the appearance of impropriety, and it suggests that the public subsidy program is no longer achieving its goal of lessening party reliance on wealthy donors. The Bipartisan Campaign Reform Act of 2002 banned unrestricted contributions for elections, but it is silent on funds for political conventions (see Chapter 6). The Federal Election Commission ruled that the host committees—the city-based entities directly responsible for organizing the party convention—may continue to receive and spend corporate and labor treasury funds and unlimited funds from individuals to defray expenses for party conventions. Federal candidates and officeholders may raise these funds without limit, even though they are barred from doing so for political parties.[26]

Aside from pledges from host committees to provide adequate funding, the parties consider certain political factors in choosing the convention location. Advertising the presidential nominee from a particular city sends a message to particular voters and emphasizes relevant campaign themes. In 1988, for example, both parties held conventions in the South where they believed the most important battles of the general election would take place. For the 2004 election, the DNC and RNC were interested in New York City, the site of the September 11, 2001, terrorist attacks and a symbol of national resilience and pride. New York mayor Michael Bloomberg made a bid to get both party conventions and won the RNC. The Democrats chose Boston after heavy lobbying from Mayor Thomas M. Menino, who pledged the city host committee would commit almost $40 million to making the convention a success.[27]

Finally, the timing of the convention has become a strategic decision related to campaign finance rules and special events on the public calendar. In the past, conventions were held from midsummer through August, with the out party going first. In 2004 the Democrats held their convention in July, and the RNC declared it would shift its convention to the first week of September in order to avoid competing with the August Olympics. Skeptics believe the RNC wanted its gathering to coincide with the anniversary of the September 11 terrorist attacks, as a reminder to voters of President Bush's assertive response. The president's reelection campaign also may have wanted to take advantage of the campaign finance laws that release public funds for the party nominees *after* the convention (see Chapters 6, 15, and 20). The president chose to forgo public funding for the extended nominating season and raised record-breaking amounts of donations, even though he faced no opposition within the party. His campaign calculated that the closer the date of the convention was to election day, the more time Bush would have to spend his private funds in the campaign before he was committed to using only public money. The Democrats running Sen. John Kerry's campaign were so concerned about being forced to use only public money starting in July—five weeks before the Bush campaign— that they briefly flirted with the idea of having Kerry not accept the Democratic nomination at the convention and put off formal acceptance until later in the summer.

Participants and Activities

Convention delegates have always been unrepresentative of rank-and-file voters and the general population—they tend to be more affluent, better educated, and more ideological.[28] Researchers have shown that upper-status groups have the resources such as time, money, and skills to participate in politics, and convention delegates reflect this pattern.[29]

Although delegates have little decision-making power over the party nominee, their presence is important for the success of the convention. For one thing, delegates set the tone for a gathering that is largely about creating a positive media image. Delegates appear as extras on the television screen, displaying their ardor for the party, its symbols, and its leaders.[30] The news media capture the comings and goings of delegates, creating a distinct impression of who belongs to the party for viewers at home. In subtle ways, these impressions contribute to the party message and may affect the willingness of voters to associate with the party in the November election. Delegates also send political messages by displays of enthusiasm for particular party symbols and speeches. In 1984, for example, the convention crowd cheered Democratic nominee Walter F. Mondale for having the courage to say he would raise taxes. Many viewers at home, though, had a different reaction.

The composition of delegates at the convention is also a rough barometer of the state of the party coalitions. Both major parties contain influential factions that seek to push each party and its candidates in one or more directions. In some ways, the ideological preferences of delegates reflect the balance of power at a given moment in time, although it is always possible for intense minority factions to have significant influence on a party's policies and its candidates. The party's candidate must be mindful of building support among activists of different factions, because motivated delegates will return home to work on the frontline of campaigns on behalf of the nominee.

Beyond the opportunity it presents for organizational housekeeping, such as approving the platform and organizing committees for future party work, the convention serves, as noted earlier, as a four-day advertising event for the party and its nominee. Any disagreements among delegates over making rules and platforms are buried as much as possible before the national television audience, so that it has the perception of the party as a happy, united family. However, the tamping down of party disputes and the preconvention selection of the nominee have only served to make the convention less newsworthy. As a result, the major networks now air only one hour of convention coverage each evening rather than the gavel-to-gavel coverage commonplace from the 1960s through the 1980s.

The parties have responded to the media schedule by arranging for the best speakers to appear during prime time and shifting to a visual format conducive to television. To accommodate the concentrated pace of television viewers, convention organizers show many video clips rather than live coverage of meetings or speeches. Both parties also air a dramatized biographical video of the nominee. Professional media consultants script the performances down to the smallest details: arranging clusters of delegates close to cameras, designing handheld signs, and prompting cheers from the crowd. Gone are the sweaty affairs of the past, with delegates fanning themselves, sleeves rolled up, perhaps looking bored or exasperated. Even with the recent stylistic changes, the television audience for conventions has been declining over the years. In 1960 the conventions had an average 28.6 percent share of U.S. households and the networks broadcast an average of 27.4 hours of convention coverage. By contrast, in 2000 the conventions managed only an average 14.6 percent share of U.S. households over only an average 5.25 hours of total coverage.[31]

Aside from the climactic speech by the nominee, the other source of excitement is the choice of vice-presidential nominee.[32] Traditionally, this decision is reserved for the presidential candidate. It is a purely strategic one, made with the goal of placing someone on the ticket who will help the party nominee win the presidency. The conventional wisdom is that the presidential nominee needs to balance the ticket. In practice, this means finding a partner who shores up the potential liabilities of the presidential candidate. In 2000 George W. Bush, considered an intellectual "lightweight" among political elites, chose experienced Washington insider Dick Cheney. Earlier, in 1988, the first president Bush selected as his running mate Sen. Dan Quayle, a Midwest conservative who would compensate for the perception of Bush as a northeastern moderate. On the Democratic side, Walter Mondale, who was viewed by some as old hash, tried to look bold by choosing as his running mate former U.S. representative Geraldine A. Ferraro of New York, the first woman to share the ticket. Similarly, in 2000 Al Gore chose Sen. Joseph I. Lieberman of Connecticut to join him on the ticket, the first Jewish vice-presidential candidate. The strategic imperative is to satisfy as many factions within the party as possible, while broadening the ticket's appeal to the electorate. The choice of vice president demonstrates a willingness to compromise and build coalitions rather than maintain policy purity.

The high point of the convention is the acceptance speech by the party's presidential nominee. It is here where viewers get their best glimpse of the candidate. The candidate has the difficult task of inspiring the partisans who will be the foot soldiers of the campaign, while looking presidential, which means appearing above the political fray. The best speeches deliver both partisan punch and soaring rhetoric that taps into national pride and history. The closing of the speech is met with the release of balloons and the gathering of families on stage. With a standing ovation from delegates, pumping music, and raining confetti, the nominee is sent off to launch the campaign.

The Party Platform

Even though conventions are less about party business than advertising the anointed candidate, delegates still have some administrative chores to perform when they arrive. Party rituals include seating the delegates, hearing reports from the convention committees, presenting the platform, and listening to countless speeches from party notables. All this occurs before the official balloting for the presidential nomination. Through much of the week, a festive atmosphere of camaraderie pervades the hall, with numerous social gatherings sponsored by different state delegations.

The delegate activity that receives the most attention is conducted by the committee that drafts the party platform. Frequently, the party platform is a source of infighting, particularly because the selection of the nominee is no longer in play. In fact, the closer the delegate counts for different candidates, the more likely there will be fighting among factions for placement of a preferred "plank" in the party platform.[33] Since the early 1980s, when conservative Christian groups began to become more active in Republican organizations, the party has fought intensely over whether an antiabortion plank should be included in the party statement. Democrats tend to have battles over issues such as affirmative action, free trade, and other policies that divide the centrists from the more liberal wings of the party. Supporters of the winning candidate may have a greater influence in shaping the party platform, but they frequently make concessions to losing factions as a way to unify the party for the general election.[34]

Some observers believe that the parties differ little on policy issues, but a substantive review of the platforms suggests otherwise. The two parties show clear divisions on taxes, trade, education, and a host of other issues (see Box 11-1). Meanwhile, not only do the statements in the platforms attract and energize partisans during the campaign, but they also frequently are enacted if the party wins.

The General Election Campaign

U.S. elections have entered a post–candidate-centered era in which outside organizations engage intensively in selected campaigns. Although candidates and their staff continue to dominate the campaign process, they no longer have full control of the resources and messages associated with their campaigns. Other groups, including political parties, weigh in with television ads, direct mail, and voter mobilization. The stakes for winning elections are too high for outside groups to allow the contest to be waged solely by the two major candidates, particularly when the outcome is uncertain. Political parties have proven adept at marshaling resources and targeting them in the closest races.

Candidate committees remain the locus for managing individual campaigns, but parties play three important roles: broker, coordinator, and investor. As brokers, political parties link candidates with valuable campaign services. Candidates may not be able to afford the premium services offered by consultants, but parties can buy such services in bulk and parcel them out to candidates at lower rates. For example, the parties might conduct frequent

BOX 11-1
PARTY PLATFORM COMPARISON
Sarah Steward

For all of the fanfare and revelry of the national conventions organized by the major political parties in the United States, there is often surprisingly little discussion of the actual work that is conducted behind the scenes during those conventions, including the writing of the party's official platform. By the end of the 2004 Democratic and Republican conventions, both parties had distilled the disparate interests and competing beliefs of their membership into documents that outlined the principles that would guide the parties in going forward.

These documents are clearly critical and quite telling to the extent that they delineate the official position of the parties across the spectrum of political issues. It is, therefore, surprising that they receive scant coverage in the news media and rarely any attention from the average citizen.

It is instructive to examine each platform as a whole and get a sense of the overarching themes that the parties seek to embrace. Those themes are reflected in the 2004 platform titles: "Strong at Home, Respected in the World" (Democrats) and "A Safer World and a More Hopeful America" (Republicans). Also revealing is the rhetoric used by the parties on both sides of a particular issue. The platform comparisons that follow attempt to do just that by selecting one issue and then examining how each party approaches it. These platforms are in no way binding for party members, but they offer a rare glimpse into the consensus about particular issues that has developed within parties. And such issue-based comparisons sometimes reveal starkly different perspectives on the best way to handle a particular issue. For example, the parties differ sharply on the best way to reform the tax code to benefit the American economy. The comparisons also illustrate how politicians use rhetoric to frame an issue in a way that is favorable to their cause. A clear example of this practice is seen in the debate over abortion. Both parties avoid the "for" or "against" label by framing the debate so that they are both "for" something—Republicans for the sanctity of life, Democrats for a woman's right to choose. Such rhetorical maneuvers are the hallmark of political life, and it is instructive to see that their roots grow as deep as the parties' platforms.

These comparisons are not meant to be comprehensive or contextualized. In all cases, the best effort was made to select the passage most salient to the issue at hand to place in contrast with the same from the opposing party. Parties often have much to say on any given issue, and anyone seeking a more thorough understanding of a party's stance on a particular issue should read the relevant section of the platform in its entirety.

2004 Democratic and Republican Platforms

Foreign Policy

Democrats

John Kerry, John Edwards and the Democratic Party believe in a better, stronger America—an America that is respected, not just feared, and an America that listens and leads. . . . [W]e believe in an America that people around the world admire, because they know we cherish not just our freedom, but theirs. Not just our democracy, but their hope for it. Not just our peace and security, but the world's. We believe in an America that cherishes freedom, safeguards our people, forges alliances, and commands respect. That is the America we are going to build. Our overriding goals are the same as ever: to protect our people and our way of life; and to help build a safer, more peaceful, more prosperous, more democratic world. Today, we face three great challenges above all others—first, to win the global war against terror; second, to stop the spread of nuclear, biological and chemical weapons; and third, to promote democracy and freedom around the world, starting with a peaceful and stable Iraq. To meet these challenges, we need a new national security policy guided by four new imperatives: First, America must launch and lead a new era of alliances for the post–September 11 world. Second, we must modernize the world's most powerful military to meet the new threats. Third, in addition to our military might, we must deploy all that is in America's arsenal—our diplomacy, our intelligence system, our economic power, and the appeal of our values and ideas. Fourth and finally, to safeguard our freedom and ensure our nation's future, we must end our dependence on Mideast oil.

Republicans

To protect our people, President Bush is leading America, staying on the offensive against threats within our own country. . . . [P]resident Bush recognized that to overcome the dangers of our time, America would have to take a new approach in the world. That approach is marked by a determination to challenge new threats, not ignore them, or simply wait for future tragedy—and by a renewed commitment to building a hopeful future in hopeless places, instead of allowing troubled regions to remain in despair and explode in violence. Before entering office, President Bush recognized that our age is

(Box continues on next page)

BOX 11-1 *(continued)*
PARTY PLATFORM COMPARISON

a time of opportunity for America—an opportunity to translate this moment of influence into decades of peace, prosperity, and liberty. That conviction is in the finest traditions of the Republican Party. As our platform said in 1984, during the height of Cold War confrontation: "The supreme purpose of our foreign policy must be to maintain our freedom in a peaceful international environment in which the United States and our allies and friends are secure against military threats, and democratic governments are flourishing in a world of increasing prosperity."

Health Care

Democrats

We will attack the health care crisis with a comprehensive approach. Our goal is straightforward: quality, affordable health coverage for all Americans to keep our families healthy, our businesses competitive, and our country strong. In President George Bush's America, drug company and HMO profits count for more than family and small business health costs. Health care costs increased four times as fast as wages in the last year alone. Prescription drug spending has more than doubled during the past five years. Nearly 82 million Americans went without health care coverage at some point in the last two years. And the President has done nothing to bring costs down or lift these burdens. The few small proposals he has offered would further divide our health system between one that is affordable for the healthy and wealthy, and one that is unaffordable for the elderly, the sick, and increasingly, for America's broad middle class. John Kerry, John Edwards and the Democratic Party believe in a better, stronger, healthier America. Our resolve to fix the health crisis is stronger than ever. In the wealthiest

country in the world, every expectant mother should get quality prenatal care; every child should get regular check-ups; every senior should be able to get safe, affordable prescription drugs; and no hard-working family should ever lose everything because illness strikes a loved one.

Republicans

Republicans recognize that health care is intrinsic to every family's economic comfort. Americans must have the security to know that the next illness will not wipe out their savings or drive them into debt. We appreciate the fact that market-based health care has given America the most advanced medical system in the world. Proposals discussed earlier, such as Health Savings Accounts and Association Health Plans, provide economic benefits while also making health care more consumer-driven and increasing access to high-quality, affordable health care. We reject any notion of government-run universal health care because we have seen evidence from around the world that government-run health care leads to inefficiencies, long waiting periods, and often substandard health care. And we applaud efforts by President Bush and the Republican Congress to reform the broken medical liability system that is raising health care costs and limiting patients' access to doctors—doctors who are being driven out of their practices by excessive medical liability costs. We support continued efforts to make health care more affordable, more accessible, and more consumer-driven.

Taxes

Democrats

First, we must restore our values to our tax code. We want a tax code that rewards work and creates wealth for more people, not a tax

code that hoards wealth for those who already have it. With the middle class under assault like never before, we simply cannot afford the massive Bush tax cuts for the very wealthiest. We should set taxes for families making more than $200,000 a year at the same level as in the late 1990s, a period of great prosperity when the wealthiest Americans thrived without special treatment. We will cut taxes for 98 percent of Americans and help families meet the economic challenges of their everyday lives. And we will oppose tax increases on middle class families, including those living abroad.

Republicans

George W. Bush ran for President on a promise of lower taxes, so that people could keep more of the income they earn. He fulfilled that pledge. The fundamental premise of tax relief is that everyone who pays income taxes should see their income taxes reduced. The President offered a plan to lower all tax rates. . . . [W]e believe that good government is based on a system of limited taxes and spending. Furthermore, we believe that the federal government should be limited and restricted to the functions mandated by the United States Constitution. The taxation system should not be used to redistribute wealth or fund ever-increasing entitlements and social programs.

Trade

Democrats

We will stand up for American workers and consumers by building on President Clinton's progress in including enforceable, internationally recognized labor and environmental standards in trade agreements. We will aggressively enforce our trade agreements with a real plan that includes a complete review of all existing agreements; immediate investigation into China's workers' rights abuses and currency manipulation; increased funding for efforts to protect workers' rights and stop child labor abuse; new reforms to protect the innovations of high-tech companies; and vigorous enforcement of U.S. trade laws. We will use all the tools we have to create new opportunities for American workers, farmers, and businesses, and break down barriers in key export markets. . . . [W]e will effectively enforce our trade laws protecting against dumping, illegal subsidies, and import surges that threaten American jobs. New trade agreements must protect internationally recognized workers' rights and environmental standards as vigorously as they now protect commercial concerns.

Republicans

Republicans know that a strong world economy enhances our national security by advancing prosperity and freedom in the rest of the world. Economic growth supported by free trade and free markets creates new jobs and higher incomes. It allows people to lift their lives out of poverty, spurs economic and legal reform, enhances the fight against corruption, and reinforces the habits of liberty. Under Republican leadership, the United States has fostered an environment of economic openness to capitalize on our country's greatest asset in the information age: a vital, innovative society that welcomes creative ideas and adapts to them. American companies continue to show the world innovative ways to improve productivity and redraw traditional business models.

Education

Democrats

John Kerry, John Edwards and the Democratic Party believe that a strong America begins at home with strong families, and that strong families need the best schools. We believe schools must teach fundamental skills like math and science, and fun-

damental values like citizenship and responsibility. We believe providing resources without reform is a waste of money, and reform without resources is a waste of time. And we believe politicians who expect students to learn responsibility should start by keeping their own promises.

Republicans

Public education, access for every child to an excellent education, is a foundation of a free, civil society. The children who enter schools today will leave as young adults, full of dreams for the future. . . . [E]very child deserves a first-rate education, because every child holds infinite potential, and we should give them every opportunity to reach it. We recognize that under the American Constitutional system, education is a state, local, and family responsibility, not a federal obligation. Since over 90 percent of public school funding is state and local, not federal, it is obvious that state and local governments must assume most of the responsibility to improve the schools, and the role of the federal government must be limited as we return control to parents, teachers, and local school boards.

Abortion

Democrats

We will defend the dignity of all Americans against those who would undermine it. Because we believe in the privacy and equality of women, we stand proudly for a woman's right to choose, consistent with *Roe v. Wade,* and regardless of her ability to pay. We stand firmly against Republican efforts to undermine that right. At the same time, we strongly support family planning and adoption incentives. Abortion should be safe, legal, and rare.

Republicans

As a country, we must keep our pledge to the first guarantee of the Declaration of Independence. That is why we say the unborn child has a fundamental individual right to life

which cannot be infringed. We support a human life amendment to the Constitution and we endorse legislation to make it clear that the Fourteenth Amendment's protections apply to unborn children. Our purpose is to have legislative and judicial protection of that right against those who perform abortions. We oppose using public revenues for abortion and will not fund organizations which advocate it. We support the appointment of judges who respect traditional family values and the sanctity of innocent human life.

Gun Control

Democrats

We will protect Americans' Second Amendment right to own firearms, and we will keep guns out of the hands of criminals and terrorists by fighting gun crime, reauthorizing the assault weapons ban, and closing the gun show loophole, as President Bush proposed and failed to do.

Republicans

Republicans and President Bush strongly support an individual right to own guns, which is explicitly protected by the Constitution's Second Amendment. Our Party honors the great American tradition of hunting and we applaud efforts by the Bush Administration to make more public lands available to hunters, to increase access to hunting clinics and safety programs for children and adults, and to improve opportunities for hunting for Americans with disabilities. We believe the Second Amendment and all of the rights guaranteed by it should enable law-abiding citizens throughout the country to own firearms in their homes for self-defense.

Social Security

Democrats

We are absolutely committed to preserving Social Security. It is a

(Box continues on next page)

BOX 11-1 *(continued)*
PARTY PLATFORM COMPARISON

compact across the generations that has helped tens of millions of Americans live their retirement years in dignity instead of poverty. Democrats believe in the progressive, guaranteed benefit that has ensured that seniors and people with disabilities receive a benefit not subject to the whims of the market or the economy. We oppose privatizing Social Security or raising the retirement age. We oppose reducing the benefits earned by workers just because they have also earned a benefit from certain public retirement plans. We will repeal discriminatory laws that penalize some retired workers and their families while allowing others to receive full benefits. Because the massive deficits under the Bush Administration have raided hundreds of billions of dollars from Social Security, the most important step we can take to strengthen Social Security is to restore fiscal responsibility. Social Security matters to all Americans, Democrats and Republicans, and strengthening Social Security should be a common cause.

Republicans

Social Security needs to be strengthened and enhanced for our children and grandchildren. . . . [P]ersonal retirement accounts must be the cornerstone of strengthening and enhancing Social Security. Each of today's workers should be free to di-

rect a portion of their payroll taxes to personal investments for their retirement. It is crucial that individuals be offered a variety of investment alternatives and that detailed information be provided to each participant to help them judge the risks and benefits of each plan. Today's financial markets offer a variety of investment options, including some that guarantee a rate of return higher than the current Social Security system with no risk to the investor.

Environment

Democrats

John Kerry, John Edwards and the Democratic Party believe in a stronger, safer, healthier America. A strong America depends on healthy families, and healthy families depend on fresh air, pure water, and clean neighborhoods. These are our commitments: we will make our air cleaner and our water purer. We will ensure our children can safely play in our neighborhoods, our families can enjoy our national parks, and our sportsmen can hunt and fish in our lakes and forests. We will foster a healthy economy and a healthy environment by promoting new technologies that create good jobs and improve our world. And we will work with our allies to achieve these goals and to protect the global environ-

ment, for this generation and future generations.

Republicans

Republicans know that economic prosperity is essential to environmental progress. That belief is supported by compelling historical evidence. For example, over the last 30 years, air pollution from the six major pollutants decreased substantially, even as our population grew, our energy consumption increased, and the economy expanded. . . . [R]epublicans are committed to meeting the challenge of long-term global climate change by relying on markets and new technologies to improve energy efficiency. These efforts will help reduce emissions over time while allowing the economy to grow. Our President and our Party strongly oppose the Kyoto Protocol and similar mandatory carbon emissions controls that harm economic growth and destroy American jobs.

Sources: "2004 Republican Party Platform: A Safer World and a More Hopeful America," www.gop.com/media/2004platform.pdf (accessed September 16, 2004); "Strong at Home, Respected in the World: The 2004 Democratic National Platform for America," www.democrats.org/pdfs/2004platform.pdf (accessed September 16, 2004).

national polls on issues or candidates that could be helpful to particular campaigns. The parties also have preferred lists of consultants that they recommend to their candidates. Finally, at various intervals the parties sponsor training seminars for candidates and their staff on how to manage campaigns, raise money, comply with campaign finance laws, and use voter data.

A second important party role in campaigns is coordinating the activities of various outside actors who seek to help candidates win. For federal races, the national parties use their financial leverage to convene lower levels of party and allied interest groups to develop coordi-

nated plans to mobilize voters. At briefings held at party headquarters in Washington and attended by important interest groups, party staff and consultants give presentations about key races, salient campaign issues, and the vulnerabilities of opponents. These briefings give groups important cues about where they should campaign and make contributions on behalf of candidates. Parties also introduce candidates to potential contributors through party-sponsored "meet and greets" in Washington and provide them with valuable donor lists.

Although congressional elections tend to be local affairs, the congressional campaign committees have sometimes encouraged candidates to focus on particular national themes and policies. For example, in the 1994 midterm election House Republicans developed the "Contract with America," a statement of ten policy goals Republican candidates promised to carry out if elected. National campaign themes and issues appear in many congressional districts, based on research developed by the campaign committees in Washington. Occasionally, candidates may take advantage of "cookie cutter" ads produced by the party committees, which provide an overarching issue framework across congressional races. But such ads are not always effective in local races. One example was the Republicans' "Operation Breakout" strategy in 1998, which emphasized partisan attacks on President Clinton. For the most part, congressional campaigns continue to focus on candidate character and locally relevant issues rather than party-based themes.

A third prominent role for parties is that of major investor by concentrating resources in targeted races. Party contributions of hard money to candidates make up a small portion of candidate funds, because parties can contribute only $5,000 per election. However, these party donations indicate to other donors that the party believes the candidate is worth helping, and they complement the party's invisible role in channeling donors to candidates through briefings and informal word of mouth. One side effect is that campaigns not targeted by the party receive few resources, either from the party or from those groups that follow the party's lead.

More important than party contributions are the funds that parties spend in parallel, independently, or coordinated with candidates (see Chapter 2). In these instances, candidate committees do not receive party funds. Instead, money is spent by the party and outside groups to influence the electorate directly. Party-sponsored teams of pollsters, consultants, media strategists, and voter contact experts devise campaign communications and mobilization strategies to appeal to voters in ways that help targeted candidates. Parallel, independent, and coordinated efforts are a result of the weakening of the Federal Election Campaign Act, which had established limits on the funds that parties could raise and spend in federal elections. The BCRA attempts to clarify the relationship between parties and candidates by crafting explicit guidelines about the ways in which a party can help its candidates indirectly. The activity most affected by the BCRA will be the parallel campaigns supported by party soft money.

Parallel spending refers to campaign activities conducted by the parties and outside groups that have been *semi*coordinated with the candidates. Typically, parties used a mix of hard and soft money to air "issue ads"—thinly disguised campaign commercials that avoid using electioneering words, even though they criticize or support targeted candidates. Although the parties occasionally have used generic advertisements early in presidential elections to establish campaign themes, issue ads became

a core campaign strategy for the Clinton reelection team in 1996. The DNC transferred soft money to state parties, where laws allowed them to spend more soft money than the national committees. Consultants to the national party crafted the ads, with input from the candidates, and selected where to place them. The state parties then bought the airtime from local networks with money they received via the national parties. The RNC and Republican state parties responded with their own soft money ads on behalf of their presidential candidate, Robert Dole. In 2004 the parties changed their strategies. With soft money banned at the national level, they emphasized independent spending that was paid for with hard money receipts. The Democrats increased their independent spending from just $2.3 million in 2000 to $176.5 million in 2004. Similarly, the Republican committees increased spending from $1.5 million to $88.0 million over the same period.[35] As mentioned earlier, partisans also established 527 organizations outside the party structure that could continue to spend soft money in political campaigns. In 2004 these groups spent more than $400 million in soft money, about $260 million more than in the 2000 election.[36]

In 2000 issue advertising by political parties spread to congressional campaigns and increased significantly in the presidential campaign. According to the Annenberg Public Policy Center, more than $500 million was spent on issue advertising in the seventy-five largest media markets in the 2000 campaign.[37] Typically, parties, along with interest groups, tend to air negative ads, while candidates try to stay above the fray by sponsoring positive ads about themselves. Under the BCRA, the political parties may no longer pay for issue ads with soft money and interest groups may not use soft money to air issue ads that identify a federal candidate thirty days before a primary or sixty days before the general election.

Now that parallel spending is more difficult under the BCRA, it is likely that parties will increase their independent campaigns, which are funded only by hard money and have no spending limits. In 1996 the U.S. Supreme Court ruled in *Colorado Republican Federal Campaign Committee v. FEC* that political parties, like other political committees, could spend unlimited amounts of legally raised money, so long as they did not coordinate this spending with candidates. Thus through independent spending, the parties have an opportunity to concentrate funds in key races, even though the lack of communication with candidates creates tactical problems. For example, the candidates do not always agree with the way the parties spend money to influence their campaigns and occasionally fear the party will air advertisements that do not resonate well with local voters.

Under the new campaign finance laws, the parties will continue their coordinated campaigns, which are the traditional grass-roots efforts to mobilize voters on behalf of the party ticket. The BCRA allows state and local parties to use some soft money mixed with hard money to identify and register voters and get them to the polls. The rules guiding national party activity are rather complex, and it is doubtful that the national organizations will assume the central role they once had as planners and patrons of this activity. In the past, national committees channeled soft and hard money to state and local committees, once these organizations submitted comprehensive mobilization plans. In future elections, state and local parties will likely take on greater responsibility for managing coordinated campaigns. The national parties, however, will continue to make coordinated *expenditures*, which include the goods and services they purchase on behalf of candidates (see Chapter 6). These expenditures, which are made in consultation with the candidates, are likely to grow under the BCRA, because the party can no longer use soft money to support federal candidates.

Conclusion

The next few elections will be a time of experimentation for parties under the new campaign finance law and within a changing electoral environment. The new rules banning soft money and limiting issue ads will surely change the relative influence of political parties, at least in the short term. Democrats, who have relied on soft money more than Republicans, must intensify their efforts to catch up with their rivals in raising hard money, a task that could be bolstered by fund-raising through the

Internet. Both parties have done rather well so far, exceeding the pace of hard money fund-raising in previous cycles. Nevertheless, in 2004 the fear that the Democrats would be outspent by the Republican committees and George W. Bush spurred the creation of 527 organizations able to influence elections by spending soft money for a variety of campaign activities (see Chapter 12). Surrogate party groups such as America Coming Together, run by former party staff and partisan activists, hoped to complement the efforts of party organizations to mobilize voters in behalf of the party ticket. In several instances, these groups appeared highly effective. One 527 group, the "Swift Boat Veterans for Truth," aired scathing ads about John Kerry's military record and cast doubts on his leadership. The Kerry campaign was forced to respond to these ads, which pushed them off their campaign message soon after the party convention.

Political parties will adapt to the new laws, campaign technologies, and electoral environments in ways that advance their primary goal of winning elections. As long as control over Congress is in play and presidential elections remain closely contested, partisans will have a strong incentive to organize resources collectively through the party apparatus to maximize electoral prospects. Traditionally, the party organization has served as the most efficient and accountable venue for partisans seeking control of government. Although elections will continue to center on the candidates' organizations and draw a mixed assortment of electioneering interest groups, nothing on the horizon suggests that political parties will be relegated to the sideline anytime soon.

Notes

1. James Bryce, *The American Commonwealth* (New York: Macmillan, 1916).

2. Glenn C. Altschuler and Stuart M. Blumin, *Rude Republic: Americans and Their Politics in the Nineteenth Century* (Princeton, N.J.: Princeton University Press, 2000).

3. Cornelius P. Cotter, James L. Gibson, John F. Bibby, and Robert J. Huckshorn, *Party Organizations in American Politics* (Pittsburgh: University of Pittsburgh Press, 1984).

4. Paul S. Herrnson, *Party Campaigning in the 1980s* (Cambridge, Mass.: Harvard University Press, 1988); John H. Aldrich, *Why Parties? The Origin and Transformation of Party Politics in America* (Chicago: University of Chicago Press, 1995).

5. Leon Epstein, *Political Parties in the American Mold* (Madison: University of Wisconsin Press, 1986).

6. Alexander Heard, *The Costs of Democracy* (Chapel Hill: University of North Carolina, 1960).

7. John F. Bibby, *Politics, Parties and Elections in America* (Belmont, Calif.: Wadsworth, 2003), 101.

8. Ibid.

9. Marjorie Randon Hershey and Paul A. Beck, *Party Politics in America*, 10th ed. (New York: Longman, 2003).

10. Daniel M. Shea, *Transforming Democracy: Legislative Campaign Committees and Political Parties* (Albany: State University of New York Press, 1995).

11 John J. Coleman, "Party Organizational Strength and Public Support for Parties," *American Journal of Political Science* 40 (1996): 805–824; John Frendreis and Alan R. Gitelson, "Local Parties in the 1990s: Spokes in a Candidate-Centered Wheel," in *The State of the Parties: The Changing Role of Contemporary American Parties*, 3d ed., ed. John C. Green and Daniel M. Shea (Lanham, Md.: Rowman and Littlefield, 1999), 135–153.

12. L. Sandy Maisel, Cherie Maestas, and Walter J. Stone, "The Party Role in Congressional Competition," in *The Parties Respond: Changes in American Parties and Campaigns*, 4th ed., ed. L. Sandy Maisel (Boulder, Colo.: Westview Press, 2002), 121–138.

13. Gary C. Jacobson and Samuel Kernell, *Strategy and Choice in Congressional Elections* (New Haven, Conn.: Yale University Press, 1983).

14. Paul S. Herrnson, *Congressional Elections: Campaigning at Home and in Washington*, 3d ed. (Washington, D.C.: CQ Press, 2000).

15. Maisel, Maestas, and Stone, "The Party Role in Congressional Competition."

16. Malcolm E. Jewell and Sarah M. Morehouse, *Political Parties and Elections in American States,* 4th ed. (Washington, D.C.: CQ Press, 2001).

17. Ibid.

18. Frank J. Sorauf, *Inside Campaign Finance: Myths and Realities* (New Haven, Conn.: Yale University, 1992).

19. Nelson W. Polsby, *Consequences of Party Reform* (New York: Oxford University Press, 1983).

20. Bibby, *Politics, Parties and Elections in America.*

21. Hershey and Beck, *Party Politics in America,* 193.

22. Nelson W. Polsby and Aaron Wildavsky, *Presidential Elections: Strategies and Structures of American Politics,* 10th ed. (New York: Chatham House, 2000).

23. Ibid. 128–129.

24. *Financial Times,* "Republican and Democratic Meetings: US City Hotels Hope for Boost from Party Conventions," July 10, 2004, U.S. ed., 3.

25. Federal Election Commission, "2004 Presidential Campaign Financial Activity Summarized," press release, February 3, 2005, www.fec.gov/press/press2005/20050203pressum/20050203pressum.html (accessed May 7, 2005).

26. See Part II, Federal Election Commission, 11 CFR Parts 104, 107, et al., "Public Financing of Presidential Candidates and Nominating Conventions; Final," *Federal Register* 68, no. 153 (August 8, 2003), www.fec.gov/pdf/nprm/public_financing/fr68n153p47385.pdf (accessed February 10, 2004).

27. The City of Boston expected roughly 35,000 people to attend the convention, including nearly 5,000 delegates, 15,000 members of the press, members of Congress, friends, and foreign dignitaries. About $100 million was expected to be spent by visitors on services such as hotel rooms, dinners, catered receptions, cab rides, and flower arrangements, with the remaining $50 million being spent by local companies and organizations. See Lizzie Andrews, "Money, History Put Boston over the Top," *The Hill,* November 5, 2003, 24. Also see Meredith O'Brien, "It's Their Party: DNC Demands Boost Cost of Convention, Paid for by Special Interests," Center for Public Integrity, July 12, 2004.

28. John S. Jackson, Nathan S. Bigelow, and John C. Green, "The State of Party Elites: National Conventions Delegates, 1992–2000," in *The State of the Parties: The Changing Role of Contemporary American Parties,* 4th ed., ed. John C. Green and Rick Farmer (Lanham, Md.: Rowman and Littlefield, 2003), 54–78.

29. Sidney Verba, Kay Lehman Schlozman, and Henry E. Brady, *Voice and Equality: Civic Voluntarism in American Politics* (Cambridge, Mass.: Harvard University Press, 1995).

30. Polsby and Wildavsky, *Presidential Elections,* 128–150.

31. Campaign Finance Institute, "Conventions and the Media," 2004, www.cfinst.org/eguide/partyconventions/background/media.html (accessed May 7, 2005).

32. In 2004 John Kerry selected North Carolina senator John Edwards to join the ticket several weeks *before* the convention. This departure from tradition may become more frequent given that the party nomination appears sewn up earlier in the process because of front-loading. Under these circumstances, the presumed nominee may choose to pick the vice-presidential nominee before the convention so that together they can combat attacks by the candidate of the opposing party early in the campaign.

33. Bibby, *Politics, Parties and Elections in America.*

34. L. Sandy Maisel, "The Platform Writing Process: Candidate-Centered Platforms in 1992," *Political Science Quarterly* 108 (1993–1994): 671–699.

35. Federal Election Commission, "2004 Presidential Campaign Financial Activity Summarized."

36. See Campaign Finance Institute, "New CFI Study of '527' Groups," press release, February 9, 2005, www.cfinst.org/pr/020905.html (accessed May 7, 2005).

37. Annenberg Public Policy Center, "Issue Advertising in the 1999–2000 Election Cycle," February 1, 2001, www.annenbergpublicpolicycenter.org/ISSUEADS/reports_previous.htm (accessed February 10, 2005).

Suggested Readings

Aldrich, John H. *Why Parties? The Origin and Transformation of Party Politics in America.* Chicago: University of Chicago Press, 1995.

Altschuler, Glenn C., and Stuart M. Blumin. *Rude Republic: Americans and Their Politics in the Nineteenth Century.* Princeton, N.J.: Princeton University Press, 2000.

Bibby, John F. *Politics, Parties and Elections in America.* Belmont, Calif.: Wadsworth Publishing, 2003.

Bryce, James. *The American Commonwealth.* New York: Macmillan, 1916.

Coleman, John J. "Party Organizational Strength and Public Support for Parties." *American Journal of Political Science* 40 (1996): 805–824.

Cotter, Cornelius P., James L. Gibson, John F. Bibby, and Robert J. Huckshorn. *Party Organizations in American Politics.* Pittsburgh: University of Pittsburgh Press, 1984.

Epstein, Leon. *Political Parties in the American Mold.* Madison: University of Wisconsin Press, 1986.

Frendreis, John, and Alan R. Gitelson. "Local Parties in the 1990s: Spokes in a Candidate-Centered Wheel." In *The State of the Parties: The Changing Role of Contemporary American Parties,* 3d ed., edited by John C. Green and Daniel M. Shea, 135–153. Lanham, Md.: Rowman and Littlefield, 1999.

Heard, Alexander. *The Costs of Democracy.* Chapel Hill: University of North Carolina Press, 1960.

Herrnson, Paul S. *Congressional Elections: Campaigning at Home and in Washington.* 4th ed. Washington, D.C.: CQ Press, 2004.

———. *Party Campaigning in the 1980s.* Cambridge, Mass.: Harvard University Press, 1988.

Hershey, Marjorie Randon, and Paul A. Beck. *Party Politics in America.* 10th ed. New York: Longman, 2003.

Jackson, John S., Nathan S. Bigelow, and John C. Green. "The State of Party Elites: National Convention Delegates, 1992–2000." In *The State of the Parties: The Changing Role of Contemporary American Parties,* 4th ed., edited by

John C. Green and Rick Farmer, 54–78. Lanham, Md.: Rowman and Littlefield, 2003.

Jacobson, Gary C., and Samuel Kernell. *Strategy and Choice in Congressional Elections*. New Haven, Conn.: Yale University Press, 1983.

Jewell, Malcolm E., and Sarah M. Morehouse. *Political Parties and Elections in American States*. 4th ed. Washington, D.C.: CQ Press, 2001.

Maisel, L. Sandy. "The Platform Writing Process: Candidate-Centered Platforms in 1992." *Political Science Quarterly* 108 (1993–1994): 671–699.

Maisel, L. Sandy, Cherie Maestas, and Walter J. Stone. "The Party Role in Congressional Competition." In *The Parties Respond: Changes in American Parties and Campaigns,* 4th ed., edited by L. Sandy Maisel, 121–138. Boulder, Colo.: Westview Press, 2002.

O'Brien, Meredith. "It's Their Party: DNC Demands Boost Cost of Convention, Paid for by Special Interests." Center for Public Integrity, July 12, 2004.

Polsby, Nelson W. *Consequences of Party Reform*. New York: Oxford University Press, 1983.

Polsby, Nelson W., and Aaron Wildavsky. *Presidential Elections: Strategies and Structures of American Politics*. 10th ed. New York: Chatham House, 2000.

Shea, Daniel M. *Transforming Democracy: Legislative Campaign Committees and Political Parties*. Albany: State University of New York Press, 1995.

Sorauf, Frank J. *Inside Campaign Finance: Myths and Realities*. New Haven, Conn.: Yale University, 1992.

Verba, Sidney, Kay Lehman Schlozman, and Henry E. Brady. *Voice and Equality: Civic Voluntarism in American Politics*. Cambridge, Mass.: Harvard University Press, 1995.

CHAPTER 12

Interest Groups

Peter L. Francia

Interest groups (also known as pressure groups or special interests) are associations of individuals who have shared concerns and seek to advance their interests through political activities. In the *Federalist Papers,* James Madison explained that interest groups are a natural by-product of people's pursuit of selfishly motivated interests. Madison hoped that he and the other framers of the Constitution had designed a government that would allow various interests to exist, but also to check one another so that no one group could control society.

Since the earliest days of the Republic, interest groups have had an important influence on U.S. politics and elections. In some of the very first elections, the leaders of agricultural and commercial groups played a significant role in determining which candidates appeared on the ballot, which candidates received press coverage, and even the voting patterns that determined electoral outcomes. The involvement of big business in political campaigns dates back to the mid-1800s, and it has played a significant role in federal elections since the late 1800s. William McKinley's presidential campaigns in 1896 and 1900 received millions of dollars from banks, railroads, corporations, and wealthy people representing business interests. This development concerned Progressive reformers, who charged that business contributions to candidates corrupted public officials. After allegations surfaced that corporations made large donations to President Theodore Roosevelt's 1904 presidential campaign in exchange for protection against trust-busting legislation, Congress took action and in 1907 passed the Tillman Act, which prohibited corporate contributions in federal elections.[1]

In later years, organized labor formed political action committees (PACs) to counter the influence of big business and provide a voice for workers in the political system. In the 1930s, the Congress of Industrial Organizations (CIO) formed Labor's Non-Partisan League (LNL), which played a significant role in the 1936 reelection of President Franklin D. Roosevelt. When the CIO merged with the American Federation of Labor (AFL) in 1955, the Committee on Political Education (COPE) became the electoral arm of the modern-day AFL-CIO.[2]

Links between money and politics were a target for editorial cartoonists even before Thomas Nast drew this lampoon in 1871. Source: Library of Congress

Other associations, such as those representing religious and ethnic groups, have also flourished through their participation in elections, although their financial and organizational efforts rarely match those of business and labor. As the twenty-first century begins, groups representing women, the elderly, and gun owners have become major players in the political arena as well, particularly in congressional elections. The growth of political organizations, their political strength, and the means by which they influence congressional elections have all been shaped by various developments, such as changes in campaign finance law and court rulings.

This chapter examines the development and functions of interest groups and the role they play in congressional elections. In doing so, it describes the different types of interest groups and their activities, including issue advocacy advertisements and voter mobilization efforts. The chapter also covers the political strategies of interest groups and their PACs, as well as the impact of interest groups' efforts on congressional policy making.

The Development and Functions of Interest Groups

Interest groups develop when a specific segment of the population feels its interests have been ignored or it has been victimized by circumstances that affect its social status, pocketbook, or both.[3] Some interest groups evolve in response to changes in society, such as technological advances that alter the economy. A "disturbance," such as a business cycle or war that alters the social "equilibrium," also may spur people to organize into groups.[4] An economic downturn, for example, may prompt workers to organize into a group to protect their interests. Groups also can arise from the efforts of leaders or entrepreneurs who identify a cause and provide selective benefits to potential members of the group.[5]

On February 19, 2004, Democratic presidential contender John Kerry greets supporters as he arrives to accept the endorsement of the AFL-CIO, which includes the American Federation of Teachers. Source: Scott Ferrell/Congressional Quarterly

Once formed, interest groups seek to represent the views of their members before government and to translate their social and economic interests into political power. In doing so, they rely on a variety of resources—financial, communication, and human, among others—to advance their cause. Financial resources are the contributions and expenditures that groups give candidates to assist them in their campaigns. Communication resources are typically expenditures on mass media advertising. Human resources are the organization's members and volunteers.

An interest group often delivers these resources through its PAC, which is the electoral arm of an organized interest. Interest groups form PACs to provide campaign contributions and services to federal, state, or local candidates in an attempt to influence election outcomes, public policy, or a combination of both. Many corporations, trade associations, and labor unions also have PACs. The software giant Microsoft has its Microsoft Corporation Political Action Committee; the National Automobile Dealers Association, a trade organization that represents the interests of automobile and truck dealerships, has its Dealers' Election Action Committee of the National Automobile Association; and the American Federation of Teachers, a labor union, has its American Federation of Teachers Committee on Political Education. Some PACs, such as EMILY's List (a group that pledges to elect Democratic women who are committed to protecting abortion rights) operate independently of any other group or organization and are called nonconnected PACs.

Interest groups have formed PACs over the years in response to various campaign finance laws and court rulings. The Federal Election Campaign Act (FECA), passed in 1971 and amended in 1974, allowed groups to establish a "multicandidate committee" that could raise money from at least fifty donors and spend it on at least five candidates for federal office. Interestingly, the term *political action committee* (or *PAC*) is not mentioned in any federal statute. Rather, it is a residual category that refers to a political committee other than a political party.

Because the FECA set a lower contribution limit for direct individual contributions to candidates than it did for PACs, PACs became a popular vehicle for people who wanted to influence congressional elections. PACs, which may contribute up to $5,000 each to a federal candidate in a general or primary election, are the second largest source of campaign funds, trailing only individuals. In 1975 the FEC ruled in an advisory opinion that the Sun Oil Company could pay for the overhead and solicitation costs of its PAC. This ruling freed the PAC to spend all the funds it collected from donors on federal elections.[6] The Supreme Court's 1976 decision in *Buckley v. Valeo* also allowed PACs to make unlimited "independent" expenditures, which are defined as monies spent without the knowledge or consent of a candidate. These developments all contributed to an explosion of PACs from the 1970s through the end of the century.

The Rise of Political Action Committees

From the mid-1970s to 2004, the number of PACs increased almost sevenfold—from 608 in 1974 to 4,184 by

Figure 12-1 Number of Political Action Committees, 1974–2004

Number of PACs

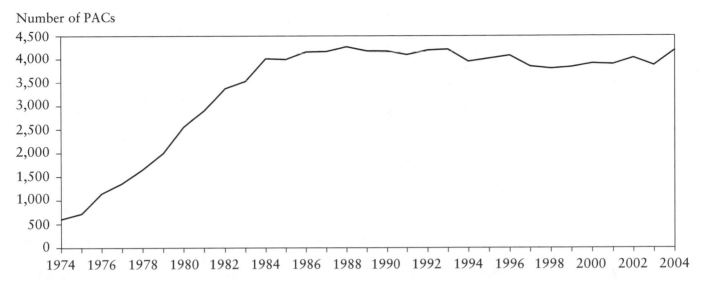

Note: All PAC counts reflect year-end totals.

Source: Federal Election Commission, "FEC Issues Semi-Annual Federal PAC Count," press release, January 25, 2005.

Figure 12-2 PAC Contributions to Congressional Candidates, 1974–2004

PAC contributions ($ millions)

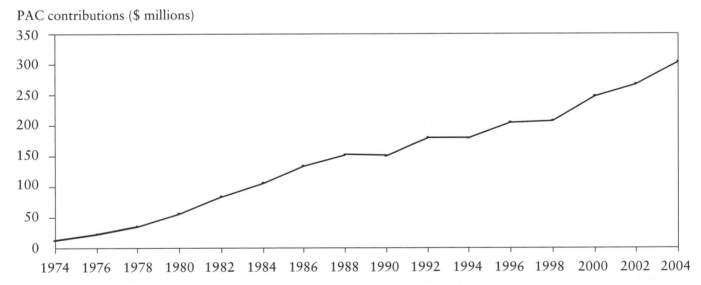

Sources: 2004: Center for Responsive Politics, www.opensecrets.org/overview/stats.asp?cycle=2004 (accessed May 8, 2005); 2002: Federal Election Commission (FEC), "PAC Activity Increases for 2002 Elections," press release, March 27, 2003; for 1978–2000 data: FEC, "PAC Activity Increases in 2000 Election Cycle," press release, May 31, 2001; for 1974–1976 data: Joseph E. Cantor, *Political Action Committees: Their Evolution and Growth and Their Implications for the Political System* (Washington, D.C.: Government Printing Office, 1986).

2004 (see Figure 12-1). The largest growth has come from corporate PACs—from 89 in 1974 to 1,622 in 2004. Likewise, nonconnected PACs—which include ideological and issue-oriented groups and which first formed in 1977—grew from 110 in 1977 to 1,223 in 2004.

PACs contributions to congressional elections have grown as well (see Figure 12-2). PACs gave $12.5 million in 1974, but by 2004 they were contributing more than $300 million to congressional candidates running for office. One of the largest single PAC contributors in most elections is the PAC of the National Association of Realtors (RPAC), which contributed almost $3.8 million to candidates during the 2004 campaign. As a whole, corporate PACs consistently account for the largest percentage of campaign contributions in congressional elections.[7]

PAC campaign expenditures typically total more than twice the amount that they contribute to candidates. In most elections, corporate PACs are the largest spenders, followed by nonconnected PACs, labor PACs, trade/health/membership PACs, corporations-without-stock PACs, and cooperative PACs. One of the single largest spenders in most congressional elections is EMILY's List, which disbursed $34 million to candidates in federal elections. EMILY's List has become a prolific fund-raiser, and it maximizes the money from its contributors by means of a process known as "bundling"—that is, it asks its members to make individual donations directly to female candidates, but it collects these checks and presents them physically to the candidates. This "bundling" technique allows EMILY's List to funnel additional money to the candidates it supports beyond the money it spends from its own coffers.[8]

As these examples and the broader patterns demonstrate, PACs have grown in number and have become major financial players in congressional elections. PAC money is important to candidates because it allows them to afford campaign professionals, such as pollsters, media consultants, and other campaign advisers. These specialists handle advertising, conduct polls, and manage the candidate's fund-raising effort (see Chapter 10). PAC contributions, particularly early ones, are often important in determining whether other financiers, such as party committees, will assist a candidate's campaign.[9]

Types of PACs

PACs represent a variety of policy interests that range from economic matters to social and ideological concerns. The National Beer Wholesalers Association, for example, represents more than 2,200 licensed independent beer wholesalers. Its PAC works to advance the economic interests of the beer industry. Like many PACs with business interests, the National Beer Wholesalers Association contributes to candidates of both political parties. In 2004 it gave roughly 76 percent of its contributions to Republicans and 24 percent to Democrats.[10] PACs contribute to candidates of both parties for access to candidates who are in a position to advance the interests of the organization. These "access PACs" contribute the lion's share of their funds to incumbents, particularly those on powerful congressional committees. Ideological PACs, by contrast, tend to contribute their funds almost entirely to candidates of only one political party. These ideological PACs include the National Committee for an Effective Congress (NCEC), which seeks to elect progressive Democrats to public office. On the other side of the aisle, the New Republican Majority Fund works to elect Republican candidates. Some PACs are focused exclusively on a single issue, such as NARAL Pro-Choice

America, which seeks to protect a woman's legal right to choose an abortion.

PACs, whatever their policy interests, fall into two broad types—connected and nonconnected. Connected PACs have a parent organization. They may solicit contributions only from their owners, employees, and members. Nonconnected PACs, by contrast, do not have a parent organization and are therefore free to solicit money from all citizens. However, nonconnected PACs must pay all of their expenses. A connected PAC can have its parent organization pay its utility, phone, postage, and even payroll expenses, but nonconnected PACs have no such luxury and must use the funds they raise to pay for all in-house and political expenses.

The major connected PACs are the corporate, labor, and trade/health/membership groups. Some of the top corporate spenders in federal elections include the United Parcel Service, Federal Express, Bank One, BellSouth, and SBC Communications. The major labor PACs are the Teamsters, Electrical Workers, American Federation of State, County, and Municipal Employees (AFSCME), Service Employees International Union (SEIU), and the National Education Association (NEA). Trade/health/membership PACs are led by those associated with the National Rifle Association (NRA), Association of Trial Lawyers of America, National Association of Realtors, and American Medical Association.[11]

The major nonconnected PACs include several groups that focus on abortion, such as pro-choice EMILY's List and the Pro-Life Campaign Committee. Nonconnected PACs also include so-called "leadership PACs." Most leadership PACs have been created by members of Congress, particularly those in leadership positions, or candidates for the presidency. ARMPAC, led by former House majority leader Dick Armey of Texas, spent more than $4.2 million in support of Republican candidates in 2002, which was the fifth highest total among nonconnected PACs.[12] Likewise, Americans for a Republican Majority, led by Tom DeLay who replaced Armey as House majority leader in the 108th Congress, was one of the top spenders among nonconnected PACs in 2004.[13]

Interest Group Activities and Resources

In addition to their campaign contributions and expenditures, political organizations influence elections by educating voters about the candidates and the issues. Interest groups often engage in high-profile advertising campaigns to provide citizens with the information they need to make informed decisions on election day. Interest groups disseminate their messages through the use of independent expenditures, mass media communications, grass-roots mobilization, and other campaign services. These resources have become increasingly important as political action committees and interest groups have responded to changes in the campaign environment. Interest groups also make endorsements, publish voter guides, and develop "hit lists" that specify candidates who have strongly opposed their group's agenda.

Independent Expenditures

Independent expenditures are monies spent by political committees or individuals without the candidate's knowledge or consent. There are no dollar limits on independent expenditures. In *Buckley v. Valeo* (1976), the Supreme Court stipulated that the First Amendment right of free speech entitles political committees and individuals to spend unlimited amounts of their own money in federal elections, provided that such spending is independent of the candidates' campaign organizations. Although there are no limits on independent expenditures, the law requires that they be disclosed to the Federal Election Commission.[14]

Independent expenditures usually include those for television or radio advertisements, although they do not qualify for the lowest unit charges given to candidates' campaign organizations. Independent expenditures also include other, less expensive means of communication, such as direct mail and mass telephone calls. A defining feature of independent expenditures is that they expressly call for the election or defeat of a federal candidate and that they must consist of funds raised within the parameters of federal campaign finance laws (see Chapter 6).

The groups most likely to allocate their resources on independent expenditures are trade/health/membership PACs, which often account for more than half of all independent expenditures in federal elections. Political organizations typically make independent expenditures in competitive races or to shape the issue agenda.[15]

Issue Advocacy Advertisements

Mass media advertisements have long been a popular weapon of choice for interest groups in elections. Issue advocacy advertisements were popular under the pre-BCRA regulations because they carefully avoided the definition of "express advocacy" and therefore escaped federal regulations. In *Buckley v. Valeo* (1976), the Supreme Court held that restrictions on the disclosure of contributions and expenditures applied only to express advocacy, which used "explicit words of advocacy of election or defeat." The Court typically has applied rather loose standards to what constitutes express advocacy. In *FEC v. Christian Action Network* (1992), the Court found that an ad using Bill Clinton's face, which morphed into black and white and stated that Clinton supported "militant homosexual" causes, was not express advocacy because it did not use the words "vote for" and "vote against."[16]

As a result of these rulings, interest groups began to rely increasingly on "issue advocacy" spots that carefully avoid the words "vote for" or "vote against." The ads, however, often appeared to be thinly veiled campaign ads. Indeed, many of the ads featured the likeness or image of a candidate and often attacked the candidate's position or voting record on a particular issue. Some ads even attacked a candidate's character. Indeed, the majority of the ads were negative.[17]

The rise of issue advocacy advertising began during the 1996 election. More than two dozen organizations, including political parties, labor unions, business groups, environmental groups, and pro-choice, pro-life, and other ideological groups, spent between $135 and $150 million on issue advocacy advertising—or roughly one-third of the amount that candidates spent on advertising in 1996. The ads sought to influence public opinion and the issue agenda of the election.[18]

The BCRA, however, has expanded regulation of political communications. Federal law now requires that organizations spend "hard money" (that is, regulated money) for broadcast communications that refer to a clearly identified candidate for federal office if they are made within thirty days of a primary or caucus or sixty days of a general election. In addition, federal law covers "targeted" advertisements, which are defined as federal candidate–specific communications that could be received by fifty thousand or more people in a congressional district or a state in which a candidate is running for the Senate. Nevertheless, federal regulators ruled in May 2004 that the use of "soft money" (that is, unregulated money) by a 527 or 501(c)(4) organization to promote or criticize a federal candidate does not violate the BCRA's ban on soft money.[19] As a result, issue advocacy advertisements have remained a viable weapon for interest groups in elections.

Interest groups use these advertisements to influence the issue agenda of the election in a manner that is beneficial to the candidate the group supports. Strategic organizations that support conservative candidates often try to focus the election on those issues traditionally thought by voters to be Republican strengths, such as crime, taxes, and defense. Likewise, strategic organizations that support progressive candidates often try to turn the election toward those issues traditionally favorable to Democrats, such as health care and education. Many groups also run issue advertisements simply to publicize their organization's agenda and issues, even when they may be harmful to the candidate it supports.

The rise of issue advocacy advertising has shifted much of the control that candidates once had over setting the issue agenda to political parties and outside interest groups. Candidates, sometimes to their dismay, can do little to prevent outside organizations from saturating the airwaves with issue ads that can influence the agenda and tenor of an election.

Issue advertisements also allow organizations to hide under ambiguous names. The pharmaceutical industry, for example, has sponsored issue ads under the name

Citizens for Better Medicine. Groups adopt this ploy when their organization is not popular in a district, or to give the false impression that they are a disinterested party when advocating a particular issue. For these many reasons, issue advocacy advertisements have been a major weapon of interest groups in recent elections.

Grass-Roots Mobilization

All interest groups need a stable, loyal, and participatory membership. Political organizations build political strength by attracting members. A political organization that can claim to represent the interests of millions is more likely to gain the ear of an elected official than one that represents thousands or fewer. Smaller-size groups can, however, often be as effective as larger groups if they have a committed and energized membership. Organizations that can readily dispatch a cadre of volunteers to assist campaigns with election activities, such as voter registration and get-out-the-vote drives, mail and literature drops, and telephone banks, can make a significant political impact.

Some organizations have members who are highly motivated and willing to engage in aggressive political action. The Sierra Club can call on some thirty thousand to engage in telephone and letter-writing campaigns.[20] Activists in a political organization participate in protests, demonstrations, and boycotts. Civil rights organizers in the 1950s and 1960s, anti-Vietnam protestors in the 1960s and 1970s, and the women's rights advocates in the 1970s made effective use of these techniques. The labor movement also has used civil disobedience effectively in bringing attention to its cause. For example, during the late 1970s Cesar Chavez and the United Farm Workers led a boycott of grapes and lettuce in California, and the effort succeeded in bringing public attention to the cause. Energized members are a critical resource to interest groups and provide them with much of their political leverage and influence.[21]

Indeed, grass-roots mobilization has been the primary weapon of organized labor. In the 1998 midterm election, the AFL-CIO set aside $18 million for a so-called "ground war," which was designed to help Democrats win back control of Congress.[22] In the final week of the 1998 election alone, the AFL-CIO sent seven million pieces of mail to union members urging them to vote, and union workers and volunteers made 14.5 million phone calls for the AFL-CIO and local unions combined.[23]

These efforts had impressive results. The AFL-CIO estimates that 6.5 million more voters from union households went to the polls in 1998 than in 1994.[24] Moreover, in 1998 the voter turnout of union households accounted for 23 percent of the electorate, despite the fact that union households are 17 percent of the voting population, and that turnout represented a major increase from 1994 when only 14 percent of the electorate came from union households.[25]

Even business groups, which are cash-rich and rely heavily on their financial resources, engage in grass-roots mobilization efforts. The National Federation of Independent Business (NFIB), for example, mailed 197,051 letters and recruited volunteers in 103 congressional districts in 1996.[26] In 1998 a coalition of business groups sent videotapes to top corporate executives urging them to contribute money to counteract the efforts of organized labor in the 1998 elections, and it announced plans to send literature to its members in 150 congressional districts.[27] Grass-roots mobilization is thus another critically important weapon in the arsenal of an interest group.

Endorsements

Interest groups primarily make political endorsements to persuade their members to vote for a particular candidate. These endorsements are distributed to members through various means, such as local meetings, monthly magazines, newsletters, or even the Internet. Local labor unions often announce their endorsements at a meeting with their members, while groups such as the Sierra Club issue their endorsements through their monthly magazines.

Many interest groups never formally endorse candidates, despite the fact that they may provide various candidates with contributions and other campaign assistance. A group's tax status may prevent it from issuing endorsements, but some organizations, even when their tax status does not prevent them from endorsing a candidate, prefer to be bipartisan and shy away from controversy. Corporate PACs, for example, often avoid issuing formal endorsements. They realize that the endorsement process can create controversy and alienate politicians, which is at odds with the access-oriented goals of many corporate PACs. Still other organizations, such as labor unions and many nonconnected PACs, almost always issue formal endorsements of political candidates. Thus the decision to issue an official endorsement is often linked to the overall strategies and goals of an interest group and its PAC.

When a controversial group issues an endorsement, it often becomes a significant matter. For example, the NRA, which supports the rights of citizens to own and operate firearms, regularly issues formal endorsements of political candidates. In many parts of the United States, particularly in the South, an NRA stamp of approval can benefit the endorsed candidate enormously. In many northeastern states, however, an NRA endorsement can mobilize the opposition.

Endorsements can also have another important effect: they can create cross pressures and splinter another group's membership. The NRA utilized this strategy effectively in the 2000 presidential election when it targeted gun owners who belonged to labor unions. The NRA campaign warned union members that the election of Democrat Al Gore would result in the loss of gun ownership rights. Union leaders had to counter the campaign with their own message, instructing union members that Al Gore would not take away their guns, but that Republican George W. Bush would take away their jobs.

Indeed, endorsements are more than trivial matters. Candidates often work very hard to secure endorsements from groups to help them mobilize potential supporters. In some instances, candidates even work to win endorsements from groups that traditionally support candidates from the opposing party. During the 2001 Virginia gubernatorial election, for example, Democrat Mark Warner actively courted the support of the NRA to help win the support of the many gun owners in Virginia. In states with high union membership, such as New York, Republican candidates frequently seek endorsements from organized labor, as Alfonse D'Amato did in 1998 when he won the endorsement of the Building and Construction Trades Council in his U.S. Senate contest against Democrat Charles Schumer.

Scorecards and Voter Guides

Many interest groups compile scorecards and voter guides that evaluate an incumbent candidate's support for a group's policy agenda. Sometimes, the scorecards look like a report card—for example, the NRA issues grades from A to F on a legislator's support for gun ownership. Other groups, such as the AFL-CIO's Committee on Political Education, grade legislators on a scale of 0 to 100. The scores are based on legislators' votes on the most important roll-call votes on labor issues each year. A score of 100 reflects 100 percent support from the legislator on the most important labor issues, whereas a score of 0 reflects no support. Some groups, such as the Christian Coalition, provide voter guides that present the candidates' positions on the group's primary issues of concern. These scorecards, ratings, and voter guides can play an important role in mobilizing the group's membership for the candidates who receive the best evaluations.

Yet scorecards, ratings, and voter guides also can mobilize the opposition. The liberal organization Americans for Democratic Action (ADA) has issued ratings of candidates since 1947. Conservative candidates are often able to mobilize their base of supporters against a candidate who receives a high rating from the ADA. Likewise, a high rating from organizations such as the NRA can mobilize gun control advocates, as occurred in 1996 in New York when Carolyn McCarthy defeated Republican incumbent Daniel Frisa for a seat in the U.S. House. McCarthy, whose husband was killed and whose son was left paralyzed by a gunman who opened fire on a Long Island train, campaigned on the issue of gun control and defeated Frisa, who had the backing of the NRA.

Hit Lists

Some interest groups target vulnerable candidates for defeat. The most well-known example of this is the League of Conservation Voters' "Dirty Dozen"—the legislators with the worst environmental records. Hit lists are often effective in removing members of Congress from office. During the 1980 election, many experts credited the NRA's hit list with the defeat of several prominent congressional Democrats who supported gun control measures. In 1996 the AFL-CIO targeted forty-five House Republicans for defeat, and it succeeded in removing eleven from office.[28]

In some instances, however, hit lists mobilize the opposition. Candidates who have been targeted for defeat by an interest group often use this information in their fund-raising solicitations. Progressive candidates are often quick to remind their supporters that conservative organizations have targeted them, such as the NRA or a right-to-life PAC. Likewise, conservative candidates often publicize to their supporters that they have been targeted by "big labor bosses" or "militant feminists."

Hit lists, however, are a less common practice than endorsements. The most obvious reason is that hit lists antagonize incumbents, which typically is the opposite goal of most interest groups. In addition, interest groups take a significant gamble in issuing their hit lists. Incumbents who survive a group's hit list are likely to become even more aggressive in working against the group's interests and concerns. Hit lists also are a form of negative campaigning that can attract criticism from the media and others involved in politics. Interest groups may even receive criticism from their own members when their tactics become too negative. Thus many interest groups avoid hit lists.

Other Campaign Services

PACs also assist candidates with various campaign services such as polling and issue research. The American Israel Public Affairs Committee (AIPAC), for example, provides candidates with research assistance on political issues affecting Israel. AIPAC contributes no cash to congressional candidates. Its primary political activity is to provide information about candidates to other PACs that support Israel.

Other groups provide strategic advice. The NCEC, for example, provides Democratic candidates with demographic profiles of their district, which campaigns can use to mobilize potential supporters and target swing voters.[29] Polling, issue research, fund-raising assistance, and strategic advice are thus important services that can help candidates supplement their own campaign organizations.

Recruitment

Not only do interest groups provide money and resources to candidates, they often recruit candidates themselves, either from their own memberships or beyond their memberships. Many interest groups work with promising legislators at the local level and then encourage them, when the circumstances appear to be optimal, to run for higher office. Several interest groups have made recruitment an important element of their political efforts. The AFL-CIO, for example, announced a program called "Goals 2000" that pledged to recruit at least two thousand union members to run for office by the year 2000. The NRA often receives suggestions for potential pro-gun candidates from its own members. And Christian conservative groups often recruit activists from evangelical churches to run for the local school board or for local, county, state, and federal offices.

The National Women's Political Caucus (NWPC) has developed one of the most sophisticated programs for identifying potentially strong candidates to recruit for office. It identifies districts likely to become open (open seats present the best opportunity to elect a new candidate to office), and then gives its state and local chapters a recruitment manual that describes how to identify women candidates who best fit the profile of a particular district. The state and local chapters proceed to identify promising candidates. Civil rights organizations also have sought to recruit minority candidates to run for public office, and with some success, as evidenced by the rising number of African Americans elected. Interest groups, therefore, can play an important role in increasing occupational, religious, gender, and racial diversity among the pool of candidates running for office.

Candidate Training

Interest groups perform another important function in the electoral process: they train candidates to run for office. Interest groups hold seminars and produce educational materials in the form of manuals, videotapes, and audiotapes that they then distribute in a variety of different ways. The NRA, for example, provides candidates with a videotape or an audiotape on how best to craft a winning campaign message on crime and gun ownership rights and how to respond to the arguments of gun control advocates. The NFIB provides candidates with a training videotape that illustrates how to produce a campaign advertisement that presents a favorable message for small businesses. The NFIB also invites candidates to visit its headquarters for one-on-one sessions in which candidates learn about the different ways in which to incorporate the concerns of small business owners into their campaigns.

The National Women's Political Caucus provides female candidates with a manual that instructs them to control their emotions, "especially anger or tears," and to avoid body language that might communicate a lack of confidence. The manual also warns female candidates to avoid drinking alcohol or smoking in public. In addition to addressing style and appearance, the NWPC instructs women to be prepared to answer questions on many issues to counter the stereotype that women can respond only to questions about health care and education.

Other groups conduct training seminars throughout the nation to help teach candidates how best to present their issues and concerns in a campaign. The AFL-CIO,

for example, sponsors the National Labor Political Training Center. The center aggressively recruits union volunteers for get-out-the-vote activities and political education efforts in competitive congressional districts.

Some interest groups have scaled back their training efforts and abandoned hosting their own campaign training seminars, because political parties have become the most reliable providers of campaign information. The national party organizations have become an excellent resource for candidates who need campaign planning, publicity, and precinct-level data for targeting different campaign messages. Interest groups such as the National Association of Realtors have abandoned their campaign seminars and now direct candidates in need of strategic assistance to party organizations or party-affiliated groups. Indeed, many interest groups now work together with party organizations to train candidates to run for office. They find that their efforts often supplement the strategic assistance that parties provide.[30]

Distributing Resources and the Tax Code

Although interest groups are able to offer a variety of different political resources at election time, tax laws play a significant role in how they are able to distribute these resources. Under the Internal Revenue Code, interest groups fall into three primary types of organizations—501(c)(3), 501(c)(4), and 527 committees (see Table 12-1 for examples)—although 501(c)(5) and 501(c)(6) groups also exist to a lesser extent.

Section 501(c)(3) of the tax code allows groups to qualify for tax-exempt status and receive tax-exempt contributions if their purpose is to promote the social welfare of the country. These groups can educate voters about political issues or encourage their participation in elections. However, all political activities must remain strictly *nonpartisan*. All 501(c)(3) groups, such as the Million Mom March Foundation, which supports stricter gun control laws, are also prohibited from lobbying Congress.

Many interest groups have tested the boundaries of their 501(c)(3) status. The Christian Coalition, for example, does not issue formal endorsements of candidates and therefore claims to be a nonpartisan organization. However, it does distribute an educational voter's guide that summarizes for evangelical Christians the candidates' positions on what are often controversial social and cultural issues such as abortion, school prayer, or the rights of homosexuals. Likewise, the League of Conservation Voters, another 501(c)(3) organization, publishes in its *Green Guide* profiles of where members of Congress stand on environmental matters.

Organizations designated as 501(c)(4) and 501(c)(3) are similar. The Internal Revenue Service (IRS) defines a 501(c)(4) organization as a group that is "operated exclu-

Table 12-1 Examples of Major 501(c)(3), 501(c)(4), and 527 Organizations

	Type of organization	Partisan leanings
National Resources Defense Council NRDC is an environmental group that supports the protection of wild life and wild places.	501(c)(3)	Democratic
Citizens United Citizens United is a conservative organization that supports limited government, freedom of enterprise, strong families, and national sovereignty and security.	501(c)(3)	Republican
Progressive Donor Network The Progressive Donor Network seeks to unite those who care about progressive politics by providing members with polling information and strategic analysis.	501(c)(4)	Democratic
Progress for America Progress for America is committed to mobilizing conservative voters and educating its members about the public policy positions of candidates for federal, state, and local office.	501(c)(4)	Republican
Americans Coming Together Americans Coming Together is dedicated to mobilizing millions of new and persuadable voters and electing progressive candidates to federal, state, and local office.	527	Democratic
Swift Boat Veterans and POWs for Truth Swift Boat Veterans and POWs for Truth, a group of former military officers and enlisted men who served in Vietnam, challenged Democratic presidential candidate John Kerry's claims about his service record in Vietnam.	527	Republican

Source: Eliza Newlin Carney, Peter H. Stone, and James A. Barnes, "New Rules of the Game," *National Journal* (December 20, 2003), 3803.

sively for the promotion of social welfare if it is primarily engaged in promoting in some way the common good and general welfare of the community." Unlike 501(c)(3) organizations, however, 501(c)(4) groups can engage in partisan political activities. They also can endorse candidates and sponsor their own PACs. Groups cannot qualify for 501 (c)(4) status if political activity is their primary purpose.

Officially, 527 organizations are defined as political committees, which distinguishes them from 501(c)(3) and 501(c)(4) groups. Political parties and candidate campaign committees, for example, are 527 groups. These groups are exempt from taxation, although contributions to these organizations, unlike those to 501(c)(3) groups, are not tax-deductible. A 527 group can accept unlimited donations and can spend its donations on issue advocacy advertisements and get-out-the-vote efforts. The League of Conservation Voters, which is a 501(c)(4) organization, also has a 527 committee that it uses to finance issue

advocacy advertisements. Since passage of the Bipartisan Campaign Reform Act, 527 organizations have become increasingly important, because they can collect soft money donations. Although the BCRA prohibits political parties from raising unlimited soft money donations, the law does not ban 527 organizations from accepting unlimited donations from unions, corporations, or wealthy individuals, or from spending their donations on issue advocacy advertisements and get-out-the-vote efforts.

During the 2004 election, several organizations invested heavily in 527 organizations. In total, 527 groups spent $405 million during the 2004 election—an increase of $254 million from 2002.[31] In some instances, groups affiliated with different interests came together to form broad coalitions. For example, America Coming Together (ACT) was composed of representatives of organized labor, environmental groups, and the women's movement. The organization, which received a $7.5 million gift from billionaire financier George Soros, spent $76 million to mobilize new and persuadable voters, primarily in battle-ground states, in an effort to defeat President George W. Bush and other Republican candidates in 2004. ACT played a significant role in voter mobilization efforts for America Votes, an umbrella organization made up of twenty-two progressive groups that served as a "traffic cop" to ensure that money and manpower were not wasted on duplicative campaign activities during the 2004 election.[32] MoveOn.org, another progressive 527 organization, was one of the most visible groups in the 2004 election. It spent more than $21 million and ran several advertisements on its Web site that some television networks refused to air.[33]

Conservative 527 organizations also were very active, outspending progressive groups by a more than three-to-one margin in the final three weeks of the 2004 election.[34] A group with one of the highest profiles, Swift Boat Veterans and POWs for Truth, spent more than $22 million.[35] This group drew attention for a series of controversial television advertisements that attacked Democratic presidential nominee John Kerry's Vietnam military service record. The advertisements were televised in only a few small markets, but the group effectively used its Web site to spread them throughout the nation. Some political pundits even credited the Swift Boat Veterans' anti-Kerry ads as a major factor in Bush's reelection in 2004. The Swift Boat Veterans advertisements, as well as those of other 527 organizations, were highly controversial during the course of the 2004 election, prompting campaign finance reformers to seek tighter restrictions of 527 organizations. Absent any changes in the law, however, it seems likely that 527 organizations will continue to thrive in the post-BCRA era.

PAC Strategies and Decision Making

In the 1970s, the majority of PACs relied on partisan or ideological strategies. PACs simply gave to candidates whose political positions and partisanship were consistent with their groups' goals. As one would expect, corporate PACs largely supported Republicans, and labor PACs contributed mainly to Democrats.

In the 1980s, however, corporate PACs began to adjust their strategies. With Democrats in control of the U.S. House of Representatives, business groups began to contribute more money to Democrats in an effort to gain access to the majority party. Indeed, after the Republicans' disappointing performance in the 1982 election, many business groups concluded that it was a lost cause to elect a Republican majority to Congress. As a result, business PAC contributions began shifting heavily toward Democrats, who seemed to have a lock on power in the House.[36]

In the Senate, corporate PACs responded to the change in power after the 1986 election, when control shifted from the Republicans to the Democrats. Many access-seeking PACs that had supported Republicans began giving to Democrats. In the 1994 election, however, Republicans won control of both chambers in Congress. This shift in power saw a huge increase in corporate PAC contributions to Republicans, who not only held power in Congress, but also supported a pro-business agenda.[37]

Access Strategies

Access PACs seek to gain access to members of Congress. In many instances, they even contribute to incumbents running unopposed for office, underscoring the point that these PACs view elections as an opportunity to create goodwill with those in power. Not surprisingly, access PACs are most generous to those who are in a position to advance or hinder their groups' ability to achieve goals—that is, party leaders, committee and subcommittee chairs, members of powerful committees such as Ways and Means, and senior members of Congress. Yet most access PACs adopt bipartisan strategies in an attempt to win favor with powerful and influential members of Congress from both sides of the aisle.[38]

Access PACs generally ignore challengers in elections, because challengers rarely defeat incumbents, making them an unattractive investment. Open-seat candidates, however, have a much better chance at winning. For that reason, access PACs are often willing to take a minor gamble on an open-seat candidate in an attempt to build a long and productive relationship with a future member of Congress.

Ideological Strategies

Not all PACs are motivated by access to legislators. As noted earlier, some PACs participate in the political process to influence the ideological composition of Congress. Those that follow ideological strategies, also referred to as electoral strategies, seek to maximize the number of House members who support the group's position on one or two highly charged policies, such as abortion rights or gun owner's rights, or on some broad political perspective, such as workers' rights or family values. These groups behave much like political parties; they view elections as their primary opportunity to affect the composition of the government and shape public policy. They typically contribute to candidates in close races, although in some instances they contribute to long-shot candidates in an attempt to attract attention to their issues. Attracting publicity is often important to a political organization, because it can rally supporters and increase political donations.

Ideological PACs almost never make cross-party contributions or assist a candidate who is unsympathetic to their interests, because most have taken firm positions on high-profile and controversial issues such as abortion. On the other side, few legislators are likely to change their positions on such issues because of a contribution or extensive lobbying from a group. Ideological PACs are uncompromising on their issues of concern and will sometimes even require candidates to fill out questionnaires or sign written pledges designating their unwavering support for the group's policy positions. For example, the group Americans for Tax Reform seeks a written pledge from all candidates that they will not raise taxes.

Even some business organizations follow ideological strategies. The Business-Industry PAC (BIPAC), for example, contributes money to candidates based on their ideological commitment to and support for a pro-business agenda. BIPAC gives predominantly to Republicans, because they are more likely than Democrats to support business interests. In the 1992 elections (before the Republicans won control of the House of Representatives in 1994), BIPAC gave 36 percent of its House contributions to pro-business challengers, compared with just 9 percent for other corporate PACs.[39] After the Republicans won a majority in Congress, BIPAC targeted its money to protect vulnerable freshmen Republicans.[40]

Mixed Strategies

The most common PAC strategies are a combination of ideological and access strategies. Using a "mixed" strategy, a group supports candidates who share its concerns or those who are in a position of power to influence legislation affecting the organization. PACs using mixed strategies are likely to contribute to challengers and open-seat candidates in competitive elections who support the policies of the group. They also are likely to give to those incumbents to whom access would be useful. In a competitive race with a challenger who strongly supports the PAC's positions and an incumbent who is in a powerful position, mixed PACs generally favor the incumbent, although it is not uncommon for these PACs to contribute to both candidates.

PAC Structure and Strategies

Several factors influence the strategies that PACs pursue. Indeed, the structure of a PAC is often important. Some PACs have a federated structure with affiliated groups across the nation. These PACs carefully consider the attitudes of their members when contributing to political candidates. By contrast, PACs affiliated with a single corporation or other entity have a less diverse membership that leads many of these groups to make decisions using a top-down organizational structure that relies heavily on elite decision making. Some groups follow a combination of strategies.

RPAC, which represents the interests of the real estate industry and is consistently one of the largest PAC contributors, has a specific set of considerations when it decides to contribute to a political candidate. It evaluates candidates based on their likelihood of waging a winning campaign and their positions on real estate issues. Incumbents who serve on committees that address real estate issues are also given special preference. Challengers and open-seat candidates are less likely to receive the support of RPAC. However, those who have already held office

are similarly judged based on their previous support of real estate issues.

Local RPAC representatives also interview nonincumbents and request that they complete a questionnaire on real estate issues. RPAC officials further consider candidates' ability to raise money and the strength of their campaign organizations. Those who have proven more adept at fund-raising are more likely to receive RPAC's support. RPAC's criteria are similar to those of other institutionalized PACs such as the PACs associated with AT&T, the American Medical Association, and the League of Conservation Voters.[41]

Smaller PACs that lack serious money and staff resources must rely on personal contacts with candidates and other Beltway insiders for their political information. Noninstitutionalized PACs typically lack any formal rules and procedures for making their contribution decisions, and so the leaders of these PACs have more flexibility in decision making than the leaders of more institutionalized PACs.

The Impact of Interest Groups

The reach and power of interest groups are felt widely in U.S. elections. Interest groups are able to shape issue agendas and provide candidates with the resources and services they need to wage stronger campaigns. The benefits that candidates derive from interest groups are thus clear. However, the benefits that interest groups derive from their participation in the political process are fraught with controversy.

Many Americans believe that interest groups use their resources to win favorable policies and legislation from the candidates they assist. Yet it is often difficult to discern a clear cause-and-effect relationship between campaign contributions and a legislator's support for the group's policies. The difficulty lies in the proverbial "chicken or the egg" dilemma. Do legislators support a group's policies because they received campaign contributions, or do interest groups provide contributions to legislators who are already predisposed to agree with the group's policy positions?

Studies that have attempted to unravel this question have arrived at conflicting results and conclusions. Some studies find that PAC contributions do not influence congressional roll call votes,[42] whereas others have reached the opposite conclusion, finding a correlation between contributions from interest groups and legislators' roll call votes.[43] Many researchers do agree, however, that the election assistance provided by interest groups gives them access to legislators. Indeed, contributions can increase the time that interest groups spend with legislators.[44] PAC money also can affect legislation before it reaches the floor for a vote in Congress, such as through amendments during committee markups.[45]

Thus interest groups' election activities have at least some influence on the legislative process. At a minimum, interest groups gain access to and time with legislators through their election assistance. At the most, interest groups actually win roll call votes and legislation favorable to their interests in exchange for the contributions and services they give candidates in elections.

Conclusion

Interest groups play a significant role in campaigns and elections; they contribute money to candidates, make independent expenditures, and provide campaign services. Corporate PACs and trade/health/membership PACs are the largest contributors to candidates, who are mainly incumbents or other likely winners. Nonconnected PACs, unlike most other PACs, are the most willing to invest in long-shot candidates, who are usually challengers. Labor organizations rarely can match the financial power of corporate PACs, although they compensate by providing candidates with volunteers and sponsoring voter mobilization drives. Increasingly, labor unions, ideological and issue-oriented groups, and even some business organizations are using issue advocacy advertisements or independent expenditures to influence the political agendas or the outcomes of elections. Other tools employed by some interest groups are scorecards, voter guides, and hit lists that evaluate where candidates stand on the groups' issues of concern.

The return that interest groups receive for their election efforts is not entirely clear. The considerable disagreement over whether PAC contributions directly affect roll call voting is accompanied by a greater consensus that interest groups gain access to politicians based on the amount of their contributions and the services they provide. There is virtually no argument, however, about the importance of interest groups in the electoral process. Some critics contend that wealthier interests subvert democracy by drowning out the voices of the groups that lack money and resources. More recent criticisms focus on the rise of issue advocacy advertisements and how interest groups have begun to drown out the voices of political parties and the candidates themselves. The recently passed Bipartisan Campaign Reform Act may exacerbate this development, as interest groups funnel their money through their own 527 organizations rather than through political parties, which can no longer accept soft money from interest groups. Although the effects of the BCRA are not yet known, interest groups appear likely to remain an increasingly important player in the electoral process.

Notes

1. Anthony Corrado, "Money and Politics: A History of Federal Campaign Finance Law," in *Campaign Finance Reform: A Sourcebook*, ed. Anthony Corrado, Thomas E. Mann, Daniel R. Ortiz, Trevor Potter, and Frank J. Sorauf (Washington, D.C.: Brookings, 1997), 25–35.

2. Philip Taft, *Organized Labor in American History* (New York: Harper and Row, 1964). Also see Robin Gerber, "Building to Win, Building to Last: AFL-CIO COPE Takes on the Republican Congress," in *After the Revolution: PACs, Lobbies, and the Republican Congress*, ed. Robert Biersack, Paul S. Herrnson, and Clyde Wilcox (Boston: Allyn and Bacon, 1999), 77–93.

3. Carol S. Greenwald, *Group Power: Lobbying and Public Policy* (New York: Praeger, 1977).

4. David B. Truman, *The Governmental Process* (New York: Knopf, 1951).

5. Robert H. Salisbury, "An Exchange Theory of Interest Groups," *Midwest Journal of Political Science* 13 (1969): 1–32.

6. Paul S. Herrnson, *Congressional Elections: Campaigning at Home and in Washington*, 4th ed. (Washington, D.C.: CQ Press, 2004).

7. Center for Responsive Politics, www.opensecrets.org/overview/stats.asp?cycle=2004 (accessed May 7, 2005).

8. Center for Responsive Politics, www.opensecrets.org/pacs/lookup2.asp?strid=C00193433&cycle=2004 (accessed May 7, 2005).

9. Robert Biersack, Paul S. Herrnson, and Clyde Wilcox, "Seeds for Success: Seed Money in Congressional Elections," *Legislative Studies Quarterly* 4 (1993): 535–551.

10. Center for Responsive Politics, www.opensecrets.org/pacs/lookup2.asp?strID=C00144766&cycle=2004 (accessed May 7, 2005).

11. Federal Election Commission, "PAC Activity Increases for 2002 Elections," FEC press release, March 27, 2003, www.fec.gov/press/press2003/2003news.html (accessed February 11, 2005).

12. Ibid.

13. Center for Responsive Politics, www.opensecrets.org/pacs/lookup2.asp?strID=C00292946&cycle=2004 (accessed May 8, 2005).

14. Frank J. Sorauf, "Political Action Committees," in *Campaign Finance Reform: A Sourcebook*, ed. Anthony Corrado, Thomas E. Mann, Daniel R. Ortiz, Trevor Potter, and Frank J. Sorauf (Washington, D.C.: Brookings, 1997), 121–129.

15. Federal Election Commission, "PAC Activity."

16. Trevor Potter, "Issue Advocacy and Express Advocacy: Introduction," in *Campaign Finance Reform: A Sourcebook*, ed. Anthony Corrado, Thomas E. Mann, Daniel R. Ortiz, Trevor Potter, and Frank J. Sorauf (Washington, D.C.: Brookings, 1997), 227–239.

17. David B. Magleby, "Interest-Group Election Ads," in *Outside Money: Soft Money and Issue Advocacy in the 1998 Congressional Elections*, ed. David B. Magleby (Lanham, Md.: Rowman and Littlefield, 2000), 41–61.

18. Deborah Beck, Paul Taylor, Jeffrey Stranger, and Douglas Rivlin, "Issue Advocacy Advertising during the 1996 Campaign," Annenberg Public Policy Center, University of Pennsylvania, 1997.

19. Thomas B. Edsall and Dan Balz, "GOP Backers Urged to Raise, Spend: FEC Ruling Clears Way for Groups 'Soft Money' Efforts," *Washington Post,* May 15, 2004, A11.

20. Ronald J. Hrebenar, *Interest Group Politics in America* (Armonk, N.Y.: M. E. Sharpe, 1997).

21. Philip A. Mundo, *Interest Groups: Cases and Characteristics* (Chicago: Nelson-Hall, 1992).

22. Aaron Bernstein and Richard S. Dunham, "Unions: Laboring Mightily to Avert a Nightmare in November," *Business Week,* October 19, 1998, 53.

23. Jill Lawrence and Jim Drinkard, "Getting Out the Vote," *USA Today,* October 29, 1998, 6A.

24. Donald Lambro, "AFL-CIO's Election Day Effort Paid Off Big for Democrats," *Washington Times,* November 5, 1998, A11.

25. Kevin Galvin, "Labor Claims Victory in Elections," Associated Press, November 4, 1998.

26. Paul S. Herrnson, "Parties and Interest Groups in Postreform Congressional Elections," in *Interest Group Politics* ed. Allan J. Cigler and Burdett Loomis (Washington, D.C.: CQ Press, 1998), 145–167.

27. Jonathan D. Salant, "Business Groups Prepare to Battle Labor Unions on Political Front," *Buffalo News,* April 14, 1998, 3E.

28. Mark J. Rozell and Clyde Wilcox, *Interest Groups in American Campaigns: The New Face of Electioneering* (Washington, D.C.: CQ Press, 1999).

29. Herrnson, *Congressional Elections.*

30. The sections on recruitment and candidate training draw mainly from Rozell and Wilcox, *Interest Groups in American Campaigns,* 1999.

31. Steve Weissman and Ruth Hassan, "BCRA and the 527 Groups," draft chapter, Campaign Finance Institute, George Washington University, Washington, D.C.

32. Thomas B. Edsall, "Money, Votes Pursued for Democrats," *Washington Post,* December 7, 2003, A8.

33. Center for Responsive Politics, www.opensecrets.org/527s/527cmtes.asp (accessed May 8, 2005).

34. Jeffrey H. Birnbaum and Thomas B. Edsall, "At the End, Pro-GOP '527s' Outspent Their Counterparts," *Washington Post,* November 6, 2004, A6.

35. Center for Responsive Politics, www.opensecrets.org/527s/527cmtes.asp (accessed May 8, 2005).

36. Theodore J. Eismeier and Philip H. Pollock III, *Business, Money, and the Rise of Corporate PACs in American Elections* (New York: Quorum Books, 1998).

37. Robert Biersack and Paul S. Herrnson, "Introduction," in *After the Revolution: PACs, Lobbies, and the Republican Congress,* ed. Robert Biersack, Paul S. Herrnson, and Clyde Wilcox (Boston: Allyn and Bacon, 1999), 1–17.

38. J. David Gopoian, "What Makes PACs Tick? An Analysis of the Allocation Patterns of Economic Interest Groups," *American Journal of Political Science* 28 (1984): 259–281.

39. Candice J. Nelson, "The Business-Industry PAC: Trying to Lead in an Uncertain Election Climate," in *Risky Business?*

PAC Decisionmaking in Congressional Elections, ed. Robert Biersack, Paul S. Herrnson, and Clyde Wilcox (Armonk, N.Y.: M. E. Sharpe, 1994), 29–38.

40. Candice J. Nelson and Robert Biersack, "BIPAC: Working to Keep a Pro-Business Congress," in *After the Revolution: PACs, Lobbies, and the Republican Congress,* ed. Robert Biersack, Paul S. Herrnson, and Clyde Wilcox (Boston: Allyn and Bacon, 1999), 36–45.

41. Herrnson, *Congressional Elections.*

42. John Wright, "PACs, Contributions, and Roll Calls: An Organizational Perspective," *American Political Science Review* 79 (1985): 400–414. Also see Diana Evans, "PAC Contributions and Roll-Call Voting: Conditional Power," in *Interest Group Politics,* ed. Allan Cigler and Burdett Loomis (Washington, D.C.: CQ Press, 1986), 114–132; Janet M. Grenzke, "PACs and the Congressional Supermarket: The Currency Is Complex," *American Journal of Political Science* 33 (1989): 1–24; and Gregory Wawro, "A Panel Probit Analysis of Campaign Contributions and Roll-Call Votes," *American Journal of Political Science* 45 (2001): 563–579.

43. James Kau and Paul H. Rubin, "The Impact of Labor Unions on the Passage of Economic Legislation," *Journal of Labor Research* 2 (1981): 133–145. Also see James Kau and Paul H. Rubin, *Congressmen, Constituents, and Contributors: Determinants of Roll-Call Votes* (Boston: Martinus Nijhoff, 1982); Gregory Saltzman, "Congressional Voting on Labor Issues: The Role of PACs," *Industrial and Labor Relations Review* 40 (1987): 163–179; and Richard Fleisher, "PAC Contributions and Congressional Voting on National Defense," *Legislative Studies Quarterly* 18 (1993): 391–409.

44. Laura I. Langbein, "Money and Access: Some Empirical Evidence," *Journal of Politics* 48 (1986): 1052–1062.

45. John Wright, *Interest Groups and Congress* (Boston: Allyn and Bacon, 1996).

Suggested Readings

Berry, Jeffrey M. *The Interest Group Society.* New York: Longman, 1997.

Eismeier, Theodore J., and Philip H. Pollock III. *Business, Money, and the Rise of Corporate PACs in American Elections.* New York: Quorum Books, 1988.

Greenwald, Carol S. *Group Power: Lobbying and Public Policy.* New York: Praeger, 1977.

Hrebenar, Ronald J. *Interest Group Politics in America.* Armonk, N.Y.: M. E. Sharpe, 1997.

Mundo, Philip A. *Interest Groups: Cases and Characteristics.* Chicago: Nelson-Hall Publishers, 1992.

Rozell, Mark J., and Clyde Wilcox. *Interest Groups in American Campaigns: The New Face of Electioneering.* Washington, D.C.: CQ Press, 1999.

Sabato, Larry J. *PAC Power.* New York: Norton, 1984.

Wright, John. *Interest Groups and Congress.* Boston: Allyn and Bacon, 1996.

CHAPTER 13

The Media

David A. Jones

It would be difficult to exaggerate the importance of the media in modern elections. Journalist and political analyst Walter Lippmann once pointed out that Americans rarely experience politics firsthand; rather, they develop "pictures in their heads," nearly all of which are provided by the media. At their core, elections are centered on a singular firsthand experience: individual voters going to the polls and casting votes. Yet for most voters, the campaign itself is experienced vicariously through a variety of media sources. For information about the candidates, voters rely much more on the media than on the campaigns themselves. And they view the media as the more credible source of information.[1]

The media fulfill a variety of vital functions during an election campaign. Not only are they the primary source of information about the candidates and their platforms, but they also serve as "watchdog," scrutinizing the campaigns and exposing any misdeeds. In addition, the media give the campaign discourse some structure by emphasizing certain issues and events over others.[2]

Critics believe the media are not always equipped or inclined to carry out these roles, particularly the one of providing information. Typical election news lacks adequate coverage of the candidates' policies and leadership abilities—information that citizens need to cast votes that are grounded in substantive knowledge. And election news has become increasingly negative, with cynical, self-serving motivations associated with nearly every move a candidate makes.[3] Rather than attract new voters to the political process, news coverage is so focused on political scandal, polls, and campaign strategy that people are turned off by both politicians and the media.[4] As for news priorities, elections have joined the growing list of serious public affairs, "hard news" topics that are being shunted aside by entertainment, personality-driven "soft news."[5]

This chapter examines the U.S. news media and the role they play in contemporary elections. It begins by reviewing how the news media have evolved over the past two centuries, and then analyzes the differences between various media outlets, old and new. This analysis is followed by an assessment of the state of election news coverage, with its focus on the "horse race," scandal, and other sensational aspects of politics. Finally, the chapter concludes with a look at how media messages may or may not have an impact on election results.

Evolution of the Media

The media have not always been such central, independent players in the electoral process. Rather, their power has ebbed and flowed in response to a variety of economic and social forces.[6] Until the 1840s, the major press outlets were sponsored by the two political parties. Thus during the election season, the Republican papers would report only the news that was favorable to their candidates while openly attacking the opponents. Federalist (and later Whig) papers would do the same. On both sides, the rhetoric and imagery more closely resembled modern TV attack ads than election news coverage. Yet the impact of the party press on elections was inhibited by the fact that, until the 1830s, newspaper reading was limited to the wealthy elites.

Newspaper audiences began to expand with the technological advances and economic changes that characterized the "commercial media" phase of the media's evolution, which ran from the 1840s until the 1920s. Fostered in part by advances in high-speed printing technology and literacy, mass-circulated "penny press" newspapers became widely available. The advent of the telegraph in the mid-1800s allowed reporters to instantly transmit news items that had previously been sent by mail. Eventually, the innovation led to the creation of the Associated Press, the nation's first wire service. Newspapers were now independent commercial entities, no longer reliant on the political parties for funds. With broader "mass" audiences to satisfy, most publishers began to shift their emphasis to the more sensational aspects of politics. By the turn of the century, *New York World* publisher Joseph Pulitzer and *San Francisco Examiner* publisher William Randolph Hearst were breaking circulation records with their tabloid-style newspapers, which became "the leading practitioners of yellow journalism."[7]

Journalism began to clean up its act and "professionalize" during the Progressive era and into the early twentieth century. It was not until then that journalists seriously attempted to cover politics *objectively*—that is, with an emphasis on fairness, balance, and neutrality rather than sensationalism and partisan favoritism. More reporters had college degrees, and many were graduates of the growing number of journalism schools. Commentary and editorializing were increasingly relegated to a separate editorial page, and the news pages featured more straight-facts reporting than before.

In the 1950s and 1960s, television emerged as the primary source of political news. Suddenly, the visual aspects of politics became paramount. After the first televised debate between presidential candidates in 1960, television viewers gave the victory to the more "telegenic" John F. Kennedy, the Democratic candidate, while radio listeners favored the Republican candidate, Richard Nixon. Presidential nominating conventions became television events.

Meanwhile, the nightly network news began to overtake radio and newspapers in popularity with the public, and it emerged as the primary source of information about politics for most Americans. Indeed, on some nights, more than half of the country's televisions were tuned into the *CBS Evening News with Walter Cronkite*. With Cronkite in the lead, the evening news programs brought vivid pictures of the Vietnam War into American living rooms. And in 1968, Americans watched when riots erupted outside the Democratic convention in Chicago while delegates shouted each other down inside the convention hall. A few years later, TV viewers tuned into live coverage of the Watergate hearings, culminating in the resignation of President Nixon in 1973 and the Democratic sweep of the congressional elections in 1974.

By this time, the media were perceived to be so powerful that scholars were using terms like "mass media election." [8] Perhaps leading the way were the *Washington Post* and two of its metro reporters, Bob Woodward and Carl Bernstein, who, by breaking the Watergate story, garnered a great deal of professional prestige. Indeed, journalism itself was now a prestigious profession. News organizations stepped up their investigative journalism efforts, producing more Watergate-type scandal stories. They also began to report unsavory details about politicians' personal lives, including charges of adultery, and to offer more interpretation and analysis rather than straight-facts reporting. Overall, negativity pervaded news coverage of elections, politicians, and public affairs in general.[9] This aggressive approach to covering politics contrasted sharply with the "lapdog journalism" practiced by previous generations of journalists, who were more likely to report what they were told by official sources.[10]

Today, negativity still pervades political news. News organizations continue to spend an inordinate amount of time covering scandal and the private lives of politicians.

What is different now is that news is available from so many more sources. Most Americans still retrieve their news from the traditional news organizations—daily newspapers, the nightly network news, local TV news, and the weekly news magazines such as *Time* and *Newsweek*. But the audiences for these sources have been declining for decades. For the networks, the decline stems in part from the widespread availability of cable television, which gives TV viewers a host of other programs to watch besides the news. Before cable, Americans who wanted to watch television during the early evening "news hour" had few choices other than either local or national news programs. Today, they can choose among dozens of entertainment programs that have no explicit public affairs content whatsoever. The network news and other traditional media are facing competition from "new media" sources of political communication: twenty-four-hour cable news programs on CNN, Fox News, and MSNBC; political talk shows on radio and television; and the hodgepodge of political communication that can now be found on the Internet. To a great extent, the traditional media outlets have responded to these competitive pressures by mimicking the new sources—thus the "taboloidization" of news and the rise of soft news.

Who Are the Media?

The current era of media fragmentation adds an extra element of confusion to the study of media and politics, so that when someone says he is studying "the media," it is not clear what media. Much of this chapter focuses on the role of journalistic news organizations. These organizations include both print (such as local daily newspapers) and traditional broadcast (network operations such as ABC, CBS, and NBC News), as well as the cable networks that broadcast news twenty-four hours a day, seven days a week (for example, MSNBC, CNN, and Fox News). This section also considers the impact of other "new" media such as political talk radio and comedy programs such as *The Daily Show with Jon Stewart*. Although these new media sources provide popular programming centered on public affairs, they operate under a fundamentally different set of norms and will be considered separately.

Unlike the major political institutions—the presidency, Congress, and the judiciary—nearly all U.S. news organizations are either privately owned corporations or are owned by huge multinational corporations. Advertising provides most of their revenue. Thus to varying degrees all but a handful of news organizations are motivated to deliver audiences to advertisers, even though, in theory, a wall still separates the advertising and editorial functions. Yet it would be a misleading oversimplification to suggest that the behavior of individual journalists is shaped solely—or even primarily—by the commercial considerations. "Profit" may not enter the consciousness of the individual reporter at all. Some are more interested in impressing fellow journalists and gaining professional prestige by undertaking serious public affairs journalism. But they also are motivated by the desire for people to read or watch their stories. This goal often leads to stories that are "soft" rather than "hard," sensational rather than straight, and simple rather than complicated.

Local versus National News

Although much of the existing media research has focused on the role of national news organizations, Americans get most of their news from their local daily newspaper and evening news. Unfortunately, except for a few reputable newspapers, these sources provide less news about politics and government than they once did, in part because TV news stations are staffed with so few reporters. But it is also true that election news is now toward the bottom of the list of priorities. For local TV news operations, the mantra is "if it bleeds, it leads." News shows attempt to grab the attention of viewers by leading off the broadcast with stories about violent criminal acts, tragic car accidents, and fires. These events receive even more attention if they can be covered live, as "breaking news," during the broadcast. Weather, traffic, and sports also consume a larger than ever share of the typical thirty-minute broadcast. Stories that are not local consume airtime as well. These "out-of-town feeds" largely consist of dramatic visual stories or generic health and technology reports that local stations buy from the networks or news services. What remains is little or no time or staff resources for coverage of local or state campaigns.[11]

Compared with their television counterparts, daily newspapers have larger reporting budgets and a much larger "news hole" for election news. During election season, many newspapers assign a cadre of reporters to cover particular state, local, and congressional campaigns. As for the presidential campaign, the papers rely on the national wire services for stories and assign local reporters to provide a local angle. Indeed, understaffed local television and radio news outlets frequently turn to newspaper articles for story ideas and reporting facts.

But the news operations at daily newspapers also are under pressure. Until the 1970s, most newspapers were small, private, "family-owned" operations. Now, four out of five newspapers are owned by national corporate chains. These chains—Gannett and Knight Ridder being the largest—demand profit margins that far exceed the expectations of the previous owners. This situation not only leads to staff cutbacks, but also puts more pressure on editors to "give the people what they want." According to the marketing research, what people want is more entertainment programming and less news about public affairs.

The decline in public news reporting by local media outlets poses particular problems during election season.

Although the national news outlets are devoting less airtime and fewer resources to election news than they once did, they still provide extensive coverage of presidential elections. They also provide some coverage of the high-profile Senate, House, and gubernatorial races, as well as broader stories analyzing nonpresidential elections from a national perspective. Examples of such stories are how the president's popularity might shape the congressional elections; where the national party organizations are spending their money; or how the results will shape party dynamics in Congress. Not surprisingly, unless it is competitive or controversial, voters are not going to find much news about their local congressional race, much less about other state and local candidates. The problem is exacerbated in large metropolitan areas that encompass multiple congressional or legislative districts, where any given news organization must subdivide its election news across several races.[12]

Television versus Print

Fundamental differences distinguish television from print sources. Television, as a visual medium, relies on dynamic video images to tell a story. If there are no compelling pictures, there rarely is a story—that is, it is bumped from the broadcast. Particularly on local TV, a premium is placed on stories that are conducive to live, "breaking news" coverage. Thus campaigns struggle to attract television coverage during the course of the campaign, and yet are inundated with cameras on election night when stations are eager to report live from their victory parties—after the votes are cast. By contrast, print sources need only still pictures, if any at all. Although newspapers and other print sources also favor dramatic stories that attract broad audiences, they are not constrained by the need for visuals.

There also is a striking difference between television and the print media in capacity for information. Factoring in commercials, the typical nightly television news broadcast is about twenty minutes long (the script for such a broadcast could easily fit on the front page of a typical newspaper). Newspapers and other print sources have a much larger news hole to fill. Thus even when election news does not make the front page, it is likely to find a place somewhere in the newspaper. On television, an election story might be bumped unless it entails live coverage and exciting visuals.

Does this mean print media are better sources of information? Clearly, newspapers and news magazine reports contain much more information than broadcast reports. And print stories require active information processing, whereas watching television is a relatively passive enterprise. Furthermore, the visual aspects of televised news reports may actually distract viewers from the information being provided in the script. Yet a growing number of studies cast television in a more favorable light. In 1992, although newspapers provided more coverage of policy issues, television offered proportionately as much information about candidates and where they stood.[13] Television also is associated with significant gains in knowledge among certain voters and about certain topics. Specifically, television seems remarkably effective when it comes to information about candidates. Perhaps that is because viewers can watch the candidates in action, which gives them a vivid sense of the candidate's personality and enhances the factual information the story provides. And television is an essential source of knowledge for two sectors of the population that do not actively seek out information about the election—young people and immigrants.[14]

The emergence of twenty-four-hour cable news outlets has helped to close the overall news hole gap between television and newspapers. CNN, Fox News, and MSNBC provide news every day, around the clock. Whereas local and nightly network news organizations are constrained by the thirty-minute time frame, the all-news networks have a huge news hole to fill. They do not, however, readily fill the hole with in-depth stories about the candidates and their issue positions. As commercial pressures have mounted, news about elections and other public affairs has been pushed aside to make room for more celebrity news and talk shows. And because the all-news networks cater to a national audience, they usually limit their coverage to the presidential and high-profile gubernatorial, Senate, and congressional elections. On balance, though, the advent of these organizations has resulted in a net gain in news coverage of elections.

How many Americans take advantage of these additional news outlets? Compared with the major network programming, cable news attracts small audiences—3.5 million homes versus the 20 million American homes that still tune in to the big three nightly network news. Despite CNN's reputation as the network Americans turn to when big stories break, its audiences are dwarfed by the numbers for NBC, CBS, and ABC. For example, on the evening of September 11, 2001, the three big cable news channels attracted a record 14 million households, whereas 80 million people tuned in to regular network coverage of the terrorist attacks on the United States.[15]

New Media

Like the cable news networks, the other "new media" that have emerged as alternate sources of public affairs programming also attract relatively small audiences, but then these niche audiences are specialized. Because audience members share common interests and preferences, many advertisers prefer them over the heterogeneous "masses" that tune in to traditional network programming or read large-circulation daily newspapers. Many of the political Web sites on the Internet, talk radio, and comedy programs such as *The Daily Show* owe their success to such audiences.

Internet

Initially, the Internet served primarily as an electronic means of delivering text-based information. Even today, the most popular Web sites are hosted by traditional news organizations such as CNN and the *Washington Post*. Although an increase in high-speed Internet connections is helping providers to overcome the technological constraints on providing video, most political sites rely primarily on text illustrated by still photos.

Internet news sources differ significantly from their traditional counterparts. For one thing, voters with Internet access can enjoy news on demand. If they want the latest news coming out of the Iowa caucuses, they can get it instantly by linking to the Web site of the *Des Moines Register* or any other news organization covering the event. For another, they can read the stories they want, when they want them. Although print sources also allow voters to pick and choose the stories that interest them, they cannot provide constant updates the way Internet-delivered sources do. And although cable news is accessible twenty-four hours a day and is updated regularly, viewers have no control over when the story is broadcast. They might have to wait minutes or even hours to get the update on Iowa.

In theory, the news hole is unlimited on the Internet. Big stories might dominate the home page, but there is also room for Internet-only features and coverage of more obscure topics. Many Web sites have taken advantage of the medium's multimedia, interactive capabilities, offering new forms of content that neither television nor print can provide. For example, washingtonpost.com maintains a special "Elections" section that contains links not only to all of the *Post*'s stories about the most recent national election, but also to full transcripts of candidate debates; an interactive map with information about key races in each state; and, during the nomination phase of the election, an interactive calendar listing state-by-state particulars of the presidential primaries and caucuses.

The Internet also serves as an outlet for news sources that are purely political in content. For example, Matt Drudge is the host of the *Drudge Report,* one of the most popular conservative political sites on the Web. During election season, his no-frills site is loaded with links to election stories from news organizations and other sources from across the globe. The biggest attention-grabber, however, are Drudge's "exclusive" stories, which often report tabloid-style political gossip that the traditional news outlets are reluctant to report. More conventional outlets are *Salon* and *Slate,* which serve up political commentary and news digests to relatively high-brow, left-leaning audiences. But these sources only scratch the surface. Because the basic set-up, transmission, and production costs are so low, anyone with the necessary equipment and know-how can provide "news" on the Web. The Internet is thus loaded with "blogs"—Web

BOX 13-1
SPOOFING THE NEWS

Is *The Daily Show with Jon Stewart* a legitimate source of news? Surveys show that college-age Americans get much of their information about public affairs from this and other late-night talk shows. But the jokes are not funny unless the viewer has at least some awareness of not only current events but also news operations. On one level, *The Daily Show* spoofs elected officials and the things they do. But it also offers a parody of the television news.

In its May 5, 2004, "Web-Only Headlines" that typify the program's brand of satire and spoof not only campaign strategizing but also the media's preoccupation with style over substance, *The Daily Show* commented on a front-page story in the *New York Times* about John Kerry's inability to find a campaign theme and then went on to add:

> Kerry's latest slogan—his sixth in 18 months— is "Together, we can build a stronger America," which was chosen after his original slogan— "I love puppies and rainbows"—was deemed too edgy and confrontational.

The "news" story continued with another reference to a *New York Times* report on Kerry's aides engaging in a lengthy debate over whether a heckler they planned to send to a Bush rally should be a person dressed as Pinocchio, a chicken, or a mule. Each character was meant to symbolize, respectively, the President's dishonesty, evasion of the draft, or stubbornness.

> Fortunately, cooler heads prevailed, and the staff was finally able to settle on a, relatively speaking, more sensible choice: Pinocchio the chicken mule.

As for viewers' awareness of the issues and political figures lampooned on late-night talk and comedy shows, a University of Pennsylvania/Annenberg study conducted during the 2004 campaign found that those who tuned into such programs, especially *The Daily Show,* are more likely than nonviewers to know the issue positions and backgrounds of presidential candidates.

Sources: Comedy Central, www.comedycentral.com /tv_shows/thedailyshowwithjonstewart, May 5, 2004; National Annenberg Election Survey, www .annenbergpublicpolicycenter.org/ naes/2004_03 _late-night-knowledge-2_9-21_pr.pdf, September 21, 2004.

about it. For decades, AM radio, in particular, has been home to talk shows that invite listeners to call in and share their views on the air. Today, though, advances in satellite communication and toll-free telephony, coupled with the weakening of the Fairness Doctrine (described later in this chapter), have fostered the rise of nationally syndicated programs such as the one hosted by Rush Limbaugh. At the peak of his popularity in the 1990s, Limbaugh claimed he was attracting twenty million listeners per week. Sean Hannity, Don Imus, and other hosts also attract large audiences.

Like Matt Drudge and other Internet sources, most talk show hosts are not trained journalists, and so do not consider themselves constrained by journalistic norms of objectivity, balance, and fairness. The point of their shows is to provide provocative, entertaining commentary on current events punctuated by calls from listeners, most of whom presumably agree with the views expressed by the host. Besides their penchant for provocative commentary, most of the top-rated shows share a decidedly conservative tenor in the views they express and the audiences they attract.[16] With host and audience members politically aligned, anecdotal evidence suggests that talk show hosts can be remarkably effective at reinforcing and mobilizing opinion. In fact, Limbaugh was once called the precinct captain of the Republican Party. When Republicans gained control of the House in 1994, House Speaker Newt Gingrich thanked Limbaugh for rallying the troops on election day. One first-term victor told Limbaugh, "Talk radio, with you in the lead, is what turned the tide." In a celebration held shortly after the election, she and her fellow new members expressed their gratitude by making Limbaugh an honorary member of the freshmen class of the 104th Congress. They also gave him a pin that read "Majority Maker," a label the host used on the air to tout his perceived ability to influence elections.[17]

Infotainment

Influential or not, talk radio and many other "new" forms of political communication blur the line between news and entertainment. Late-night comedy programs such as *Saturday Night Live* and the *Tonight Show* contain more political satire than they used to. And *The Daily Show* muddies the distinction even more. It is a spoof of the news; actors play the roles of anchors and correspondents, who provide parodied reports of actual news events (see Box 13-1). Clearly, these programs are geared more toward entertaining viewers than informing them. But survey evidence suggests that college-age voters rate such shows as important sources of information.

News Coverage of Elections

How do traditional news organizations cover elections? Which elements of the campaigns do they tend to feature?

logs—which are personal journals posted on the Web by "bloggers" for anyone to read. Jumping on the bandwagon, campaigns and other political organizations are posting their own blogs as a means of supplying information to supporters and potential supporters.

Political Talk Radio

Political talk radio is an old medium that uses new technology. Indeed, in terms of format there is nothing new

What is the nature of that coverage? In an ideal world, the news media would provide the information voters need to cast an informed vote. Election stories would focus on the candidates' issue positions and report facts about the candidate—such as personal histories and past political decisions—that would help voters to assess leadership qualities.

Horse Races, Scandals, Gaffes, and Endorsements

Yet, according to a multitude of observers, the media's attention is focused elsewhere. Although news organizations hardly ignore issue positions and leadership qualities, day-to-day election coverage tends to center on subjects that meet journalists' criteria for newsworthiness. To a journalist covering a campaign, "news" is often an event that stands out on one particular day. And the subject of the story must lend itself to straightforward reporting that attempts to be fair and objective. Better yet, the subject must entail some sort of conflict—preferably a direct confrontation between the candidates, although one-sided attacks are also newsworthy.

Stories about policy issues fall short on all three criteria, particularly the need for novelty. Once the campaign is under way, candidates rarely make major changes in their policy platforms. And if they do, they risk being portrayed as unprincipled. Driven by the need to be consistent, stay "on message," and avoid mistakes, candidates tend to stick with the same basic stump speech. That speech usually contains much of the information that voters need about the candidate's broad principles and his or her specific issue positions. But the reporters assigned to cover the campaign have heard the speech dozens and dozens of times. Once they have reported it once, it is no longer news.

What does change from day to day are the "horse race" aspects of the election: who is ahead and who is behind; the tactics and strategies being employed by both sides to improve their positions in the polls; competitive campaign events (such as debates) that pit one candidate against the other; and conflicts and confrontations between the candidates. These subjects get the lion's share of coverage. Not only do the horse race elements possess the novelty that static issues positions lack, but they also are relatively easy to prepare within the constraints of standard news-gathering practices. Professional norms dictate that reporters base their stories on hard facts; poll results, advertising campaigns, and campaign expenditures seem to fit that criterion. Late in the 1992 election, when the media began portraying President George Bush as a candidate in trouble, such stories were based on hard evidence: several polls

The Daily Show *host Jon Stewart and Democratic presidential hopeful Howard Dean prepare for an interview in January 2004. The show, on the cable channel Comedy Central, spoofs the news, but a University of Pennsylvania/Annenberg study found that its viewers are more likely to know the issue positions and backgrounds of presidential candidates than people who do not watch late-night comedy. Source: Reuters/Landov*

showing that Bush's popularity with the voters had slipped below Bill Clinton's after the party conventions (see Box 13-2).

Even horse race stories get pushed aside, though, when a scandal emerges. To many critics, the media seem to have an insatiable appetite for stories that involve a candidate who is embroiled in scandal. Even among mainstream news outlets, the hunger has grown. The pattern of news coverage that accompanies an emerging scandal is what Larry J. Sabato calls a media "feeding frenzy"—that is, "the press coverage attending any political event or circumstance where a critical mass of journalists leap to cover the same embarrassing or scandalous subject and pursue it intensely, often excessively, and sometimes uncontrollably." [18] Election campaigns, for all their emphasis on integrity and leadership, are an ideal context for the emergence of political scandals, as evidenced by the subjects of some of the most famous feeding frenzies: Bill Clinton's affair with Gennifer Flowers, which surfaced during the 1992 Democratic primaries; the mental health history of Thomas F. Eagleton, which emerged immediately after he was selected to be Democrat George McGovern's running mate in 1972; and Republican Richard Nixon's "secret fund" in 1952. In all of these cases, the intense media scrutiny had a serious impact on the dynamics of the election, with some candidates (Clinton and Nixon) more successful at parrying the charges than others (Eagleton).

BOX 13-2
MEDIA POLLS

It is no secret that election news coverage tends to focus on the "game" or horse race aspects of a campaign—who is ahead, who is behind, who has momentum, who is losing steam. So if elections are games, how do the media keep score? For the most part, they rely on poll results.

Election polls attempt to measure the opinions, behavior, and other relevant characteristics of the voting population by surveying a cross section of members (called a representative sample) of that population. Campaigns typically hire small political firms to conduct the polls used to guide strategic decision making, but many news organizations also do their own polls, frequently in collaboration with well-established, independent firms such as Gallup, Roper, and Harris.

The media use poll results to prepare news stories that not only estimate who is winning, but also attempt to explain *why*. So in addition to questions about voting intentions, a respectable media poll will include questions designed to tap into voters' views on particular issues, their issue priorities, and their general feelings about the candidates and their performance as elected officials. The poll also might record demographic characteristics such as gender, race, education, and income. Such questions can help the news organization analyze questions such as: To what extent is the president faring worse among voters who oppose the war in Iraq? Is there a "gender gap" in support for the Democratic versus the Republican candidate? To what extent are percep-

tions of the economy shaping voters' candidate preferences?

The quality of media polls, like all polls, varies. Some have better questions than others. Others do a better job of limiting their sample to voters who are likely to show up at the polls and therefore determine the results of the election. There also is the matter of sample size—the number of people who participate in the poll. The larger the sample size, the smaller is the sampling error, or, more accurately, the greater is the chance that the poll will gauge the views of the whole population. A respectable media poll will have a sample size of 900–1,000 respondents, which results in a margin of error of about three percentage points. Thus if a poll indicates that 43 percent of the sample plans to vote for candidate A, then between 40 and 46 percent of the voting population can be expected to do so. That may seem like a wide range until one considers that some media use polls that draw on samples as low as 400–500 respondents and have margins of error of about five percentage points. With a sampling error this high, a poll showing 43 percent support for candidate A could be very misleading, because actual support could be as low as 38 percent (43 minus 5) or as high as 48 percent (43 plus 5).

What follows are sample questions from a *USA Today*/CNN poll conducted by the Gallup Organization on May 7–9, 2004. About one thousand people participated in the poll, which is considered by professionals to be a respectable sample size.

- How much thought have you given to the upcoming election for president—quite a lot, or only a little?
- If Massachusetts Senator John Kerry were the Democratic Party's candidate and George W. Bush were the Republican Party's candidate, who would you be more likely to vote for: John Kerry, the Democrat, or George W. Bush, the Republican?
- Now suppose Ralph Nader runs as an independent candidate, who would you be most likely to vote for: Kerry, the Democrat, Bush, the Republican, or Nader, the independent?
- Do you approve or disapprove of the way George W. Bush is handling his job as president?
- In general, are you satisfied or dissatisfied with the way things are going in the United States at this time?
- Do you approve or disapprove of the way George W. Bush is handling:
  - The economy
  - The situation in Iraq
  - Terrorism
- Next, regardless of which presidential candidate you support, please tell me if you think John Kerry or George W. Bush would better handle each of the following issues.
  - The economy
  - The situation in Iraq
  - Terrorism
- All in all, do you think it was worth going to war in Iraq, or not?

Source: The Gallup Organization, 2004.

Although media coverage of political scandal is nothing new, the standards for what constitutes scandalous behavior have changed. Today, even the traditional news sources are willing to report stories about candidates' personal lives, even if the circumstances are tangential to the candidates' qualifications for office. Indeed, it was a *Miami*

Herald reporter who asked Gary Hart, a candidate for the Democratic presidential nomination in 1988, whether he was having an affair with Donna Rice—an event that many observers credit with opening the floodgates of mainstream media's intense scrutiny of politicians' personal lives. Any reluctance to report such charges may be

Sen. Thomas Eagleton listens to Democratic presidential nominee George McGovern announce that Eagleton is stepping aside as his vice-presidential running mate in 1972. Media scrutiny of Eagleton's mental health history eventually forced his departure from the ticket.
Source: AP Wide World Photos

overcome if the story is cleaned up by the "tabloid laundromat"—once tabloid sources break the story, mainstream outlets can claim they have no choice but to report on scandalous information that is now widely circulated in the public domain. This is exactly what happened to Clinton during the 1992 Democratic presidential primaries. The *Star,* a sensational supermarket tabloid, broke the news about Clinton's alleged affair with Gennifer Flowers. Once the story reached the public domain, it was fair game for the mainstream press, particularly if its coverage was framed in terms of how Clinton and his campaign team were responding to the allegations.

Candidates themselves may trigger a feeding frenzy when they make a glaring public gaffe. During the second debate of the 1976 election, President Gerald R. Ford ended a rambling answer to a foreign policy question by arguing there was "no Soviet dominance of Eastern Europe." Despite the mistake, polls taken immediately after the debate indicated that a plurality of voters thought Ford had won the event. But the media pounced on what came to be known as Ford's "Free Poland" gaffe. The media also pounced on Vice President Dan Quayle's "potato(e)" gaffe during the 1992 campaign. Quayle, participating in a spelling bee held at a grade school in New Jersey, mistakenly corrected a student who spelled *potato* without an *e*. In 2000 Vice President Al Gore spent much of the race fending off the effects of the public comments he made about inventing the Internet. More recently, news coverage of the 2004 Democratic nomination campaign

homed in on Howard Dean's remark that he wanted to be "the candidate for guys with Confederate flags on their pickup trucks." Dean's campaign then collapsed after the media feeding frenzy surrounding "The Scream"—a speech-ending rallying cry he delivered to supporters after a disappointing finish in the Iowa caucuses. On TV, the gesture came across as a demented, shrieking yowl. Broadcast news outlets played "The Scream" repeatedly for the next two days, late-night television comics had a field day, and countless Internet outlets posted manipulated versions of the video clip on the Web.

Not all gaffes and potentially scandalous events trigger a feeding frenzy. In 1996 the *Washington Post* killed a story that would have publicized allegations that Robert Dole had had an extramarital affair with a Washington, D.C., woman while serving in the Senate. This decision was made despite the objections of several *Post* reporters and editors, who argued that the allegations belied Dole's campaign attacks on Clinton's morality and character.[19] In the closing days of the 2000 election, reports that George W. Bush had been arrested in 1976 for driving under the influence of alcohol garnered widespread media attention, but the coverage never reached the level of "frenzy." Both investigations emerged in the elections' final days and weeks, perhaps making some editors and producers wary about breaking stories that might influence the results.

Editorial Endorsements

In the final days or weeks of the election, most newspapers use their editorial pages to endorse one candidate for each office, sometimes even for minor races. Historically, Republican candidates for president have received more endorsements than Democrats,[20] perhaps reflecting the conservative tendencies of newspaper owners and editors. When Bill Clinton obtained the majority of editorial endorsements in 1992, he was the first Democrat to do so since Lyndon B. Johnson in 1964.[21] In 2004 Kerry gained slightly more endorsements in part by picking up support from many of the newspapers who endorsed Bush over Gore in 2000.[22]

Do endorsements affect election results? According to one study, they seemed to help Clinton get more votes in 1992.[23] In 2004 the languishing candidacy of North Carolina senator John Edwards got a shot in the arm when he was endorsed by the *Des Moines Register,* which was followed by a surprising second-place finish in the Iowa caucuses. In elections below the presidential level, newspapers tend to give more coverage to candidates they endorse.[24] One recent study of U.S. Senate elections suggests that endorsements can actually shape voters' preferences through a two-step process. When a newspaper endorses a candidate, it tends to cover the endorsed candidate more favorably on the *news* pages. This "slanted" positive news coverage is associated, in turn, with more positive evaluations of the endorsed candidate among voters.[25]

BOX 13-3
MEDIA REPORTING OF CAMPAIGNS

The media's preoccupation with scandals, gaffes, and the horse race aspect of campaigns is a source of frustration for many scholars, voters, campaign professionals, and the candidates themselves. Critics also chafe at the tone of election coverage, especially as it has become more negative and cynical in its underlying assumptions about candidate's motives. During the "objective media" era that extended from the 1920s to the 1970s,[1] reporters tended to convey in a straightforward fashion what the candidates said and did on the campaign trail. But news organizations became more aggressive in the wake of the Vietnam War and the Watergate scandal. Both events damaged the credibility of official sources. The Watergate affair not only illustrated the importance of investigative journalism, but also glamorized the profession.

Negativity

Disillusionment with public officials and political candidates stemming from the Vietnam War and the Watergate scandal explain in part why election news coverage subsequently became more negative. Until the 1980 election, the presidential candidates of both parties received largely favorable news coverage. Today, candidates get primarily unfavorable coverage.[2] Even when coverage is not explicitly negative, news about the election is shaped by increasingly interpretive analysis. Rather than simply take candidates' statements or actions at face value, reporters might inject their own interpretation, which often portrays the subjects as self-serving cynics who are interested primarily in making political gains, not making good policy. So when House minority leader Richard A. Gephardt endorsed Al Gore for president in 1999, the lead paragraph in an Associated Press article speculated that the move was a "sign that top Democrats would like to settle the presidential nomination early and focus on winning in November 2000."[3] In the same article, Gore was described as "hoping to begin stepping out of President Clinton's shadow." His promise to promote more preventive health care practices was interpreted as "staking out territory in poll-tested health care issues" rather than a genuine effort to develop effective policy.

The reporter's assessment of Gore's motives is typical. Regardless of whether the candidate is announcing a new policy or firing the campaign's pollster, both are treated as strategic maneuvers geared toward winning the election. This tendency to associate political decisions with vote grubbing represents a shift in two ways: first, it reflects the trend toward more negativity overall, and, second, it embodies the willingness of the press to go beyond straightforward reporting. Minus the cynical analysis, the Gore story can be reduced to a few skeletal facts: Gephardt endorsed Gore, and Gore made a speech about health care that included a new emphasis on preventive measures.

Bias

Are GOP candidates treated particularly harshly? Republicans have ac-

---

Ad Watches

With all the attention paid to the strategic horse race aspects of elections, it is not surprising that news organizations also scrutinize the most expensive element of campaign operations: television advertising. Journalists cover campaign ads in part because they reveal so much about a campaign's messages, issue priorities, and strategic decision making. Ads also are the primary medium for attacks on the opposition, providing fodder for journalists eager to highlight the conflictual elements of the campaign.

Ad coverage also gives journalists an opportunity to fulfill their watchdog function. Through what are now called "ad watches," both print and news organizations set aside part of their news hole for lengthy critiques of individual TV ads. Ad watches strive to scrutinize the ad's major components: whether the factual information is accurate, whether the claims are misleading, and whether the combination of factual information and visual images invite truthful inferences. A televised ad watch usually entails replaying portions of the ad, followed by an assessment of the information, messages, and imagery. On CNN's ad watches, "FALSE" appears across the ad when the information is inaccurate. Newspaper ad watches of TV ads offer an even more detailed, sometimes line-by-line assessment, coupled with a display of some of the more relevant visual images.

Although press scrutiny of campaigns ads is nothing new, formalized ad watches did not fully emerge until after the 1988 presidential election. The Bush–Dukakis race was widely criticized for its focus on trivial issues, meaningless attacks, and consultant-driven manipulation. One of the news media's perceived contributions to this mess was their uncritical news coverage of campaign ads. Broadcast news organizations in particular were crit-

cused the media of having a pro-Democratic "liberal bias" since at least the 1960s, when Vice President Spiro Agnew called reporters "nattering nabobs of negativism." North Carolina Republican senator Jesse Helms made a career out of charging liberal bias, targeting in particular his hometown newspaper, the *Raleigh News and Observer*, and CBS anchor Dan Rather. The 1992 Bush campaign charged the media with favoring Bill Clinton—an attitude captured by the bumper sticker "Annoy the Media—Re-elect Bush." Four years later, Republican nominee Robert J. Dole lashed out at the media in the closing days of the campaign for their seemingly preferential treatment of Clinton. More recently, bias accusations have found their way into best-selling books by conservative commentator Ann Coulter and former CBS News reporter and producer Bernard Goldberg. Meanwhile, more and more Republican voters are beginning to agree that the media favor Democratic candidates.[4] Such suspicions seemed confirmed when CBS's 60 *Minutes Wednesday,* hosted by Dan Rather, broadcast a story in September 2004 suggesting that George W. Bush used political connections to avoid the draft and cut short his service in the National Guard. The documents supporting this assertion turned out to be fake, fueling accusations that Dan Rather and other CBS journalists were blinded by their determination to defeat Bush.

Survey research suggests that journalists do indeed lean to the left on some (but not all) issues and tend to vote for Democratic candidates. Yet there has been little scholarly research linking these views to consistently pro-Democratic election news coverage. Although big-city reporters lean to left, owners and editors tend to hold more conservative views, as do reporters for small-town newspapers. Because owners and editors hire the reporters, presumably they, as managers, are in the position to rein in those who stray too far from objectivity and the editorial leanings of their paper. Objectivity, fairness, and other professional norms also may keep reporters in check, as do the organizational environment and the day-to-day pressures of putting the paper to bed.

Part of what fuels the liberal bias charges is that, on occasion, news coverage does tend to favor one candidate over the other. Although all three major candidates in 1992 suffered from negative press treatment, Clinton's coverage was less negative than that of either George Bush or third party candidate H. Ross Perot.

But that discrepancy stemmed in part from the media's preoccupation with the horse race. Clinton enjoyed relatively positive press treatment, largely because he led in the polls from July through November. He beat expectations; he "won" at least two of the three debates; and his campaign was well run. By contrast, the horse race was not so kind to the incumbent. Linked with an economy that was slow to emerge from recession, the Bush campaign was seen as lackluster and ineffective. Bush lagged behind throughout the general election campaign, and his news coverage reflected that.

1. Darrell M. West, *The Rise and Fall of the Media Establishment* (New York: St. Martin's, 2001).

2. Thomas E. Patterson, *Out of Order* (New York: Vintage, 1994).

3. Ron Fournier, "In N.H., Gephardt Endorses Gore," Associated Press, March 15, 1999.

4. Stephen J. Farnsworth and S. Robert Lichter, *The Nightly News Nightmare: Network Television's Coverage of U.S. Presidential Elections, 1988–2000* (Lanham, Md.: Rowman and Littlefield, 2003).

---

icized for providing "free advertising" to the campaigns by replaying components of their ads without evaluating the ads' accuracy. The practice of replaying ads was not new: in 1964 all three network newscasts replayed the infamous "Daisy Ad" the day after it ran.[26] The ad ran only once, but the coverage and uproar spread the ad's anti-Goldwater messages to millions of viewers. In 1988 tawdry attack ads such as the "Willie Horton" spot were blamed for coarsening the debate, and the media were held partly responsible for failing to set the record straight.[27] By the time the 1992 election rolled around, both print and broadcast news sources made formal ad watches a prominent part of their election coverage.

It is not clear whether ad watches achieve their desired effect. One group of scholars found that ad watches can backfire—that is, by replaying portions of the ads and repeating their more inflammatory charges, they may benefit the candidate whose ad is being scrutinized.[28]

But follow-up research suggests that news organizations can lessen this problem by tweaking the format and strengthening their critique. If nothing else, audience members seem to remember seeing ad watches and value their contributions.[29] And campaigns are presumably more careful about the content of their ads, because they know they will be scrutinized.

Candidate Access to the Media

If candidates are frustrated by the coverage they are receiving, what can they do? They can buy advertising time, or they can employ some "free media" strategies designed to attract the attention of the news media (see Chapter 17). Yet it is nearly impossible to force news organizations to provide access. This is especially true of the print media. The courts have ruled consistently that newspapers and magazines are free to decide which candidates they will and will not cover. Only when candidates are

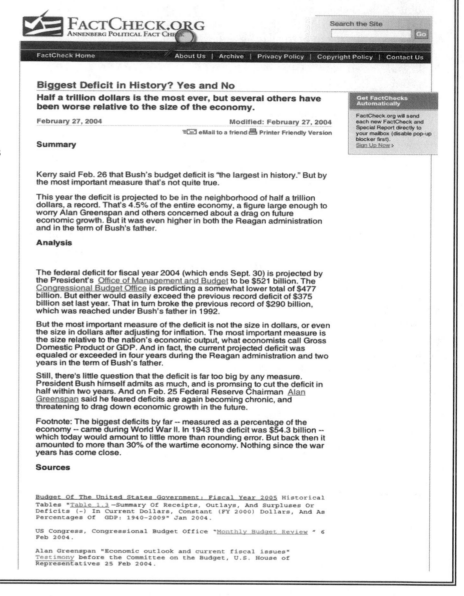

This unusually detailed ad watch at www.factcheck.org/article. aspx?docID =148# was prepared by the Annenberg Political Fact Check, which describes itself on its Web site as "a nonpartisan, nonprofit, 'consumer advocate' for voters that aims to reduce the level of deception and confusion in U.S. politics." Fact Check is a project of the Annenberg Public Policy Center of the University of Pennsylvania. Its ad watches are available on the Web site of PBS's *News Hour with Jim Lehrer* at election time.

Copyright 2004 Annenberg Public Policy Center of the University of Pennsylvania. Judgments expressed are those of FactCheck.org's staff, not the Annenberg Center.

Note: The tables have been deleted from the article. The full article is available at the URL above.

FACTCHECK.ORG
ANNENBERG POLITICAL FACT CHECK

Search the Site [   ] Go

FactCheck Home   About Us | Archive | Privacy Policy | Copyright Policy | Contact Us

Biggest Deficit in History? Yes and No

Half a trillion dollars is the most ever, but several others have been worse relative to the size of the economy.

February 27, 2004   Modified: February 27, 2004
                         eMail to a friend   Printer Friendly Version

Get FactChecks Automatically
FactCheck.org will send each new FactCheck and Special Report directly to your mailbox (disable pop-up blocker first).
Sign Up Now >

Summary

Kerry said Feb. 26 that Bush's budget deficit is "the largest in history." But by the most important measure that's not quite true.

This year the deficit is projected to be in the neighborhood of half a trillion dollars, a record. That's 4.5% of the entire economy, a figure large enough to worry Alan Greenspan and others concerned about a drag on future economic growth. But it was even higher in both the Reagan administration and in the term of Bush's father.

Analysis

The federal deficit for fiscal year 2004 (which ends Sept. 30) is projected by the President's Office of Management and Budget to be $521 billion. The Congressional Budget Office is predicting a somewhat lower total of $477 billion. But either would easily exceed the previous record deficit of $375 billion set last year. That in turn broke the previous record of $290 billion, which was reached under Bush's father in 1992.

But the most important measure of the deficit is not the size in dollars, or even the size in dollars after adjusting for inflation. The most important measure is the size relative to the nation's economic output, what economists call Gross Domestic Product or GDP. And in fact, the current projected deficit was equaled or exceeded in four years during the Reagan administration and two years in the term of Bush's father.

Still, there's little question that the deficit is far too big by any measure. President Bush himself admits as much, and is promising to cut the deficit in half within two years. And on Feb. 25 Federal Reserve Chairman Alan Greenspan said he feared deficits are again becoming chronic, and threatening to drag down economic growth in the future.

Footnote: The biggest deficits by far -- measured as a percentage of the economy -- came during World War II. In 1943 the deficit was $54.3 billion -- which today would amount to little more than rounding error. But back then it amounted to more than 30% of the wartime economy. Nothing since the war years has come close.

Sources

Budget Of The United States Government: Fiscal Year 2005 Historical Tables "Table 1.3 —Summary Of Receipts, Outlays, And Surpluses Or Deficits (-) In Current Dollars, Constant (FY 2000) Dollars, And As Percentages Of GDP: 1940-2009" Jan 2004.

US Congress, Congressional Budget Office "Monthly Budget Review " 6 Feb 2004.

Alan Greenspan "Economic outlook and current fiscal issues" Testimony before the Committee on the Budget, U.S. House of Representatives 25 Feb 2004.

---

deliberately slandered or libeled do they have legal recourse. So far, Internet sources and cable television outlets enjoy the same freedoms.[30]

The rules are stricter for broadcast television and radio. These outlets are regulated under the original and amended versions of Communications Act of 1934, which established the Federal Communications Commission (FCC). They are treated differently in part because the available broadcast spectrum contains a finite amount of space. Although cable technology effectively opens up the spectrum to an infinite number of channels, the basic rules are still in place, in part because the airwaves belong

to the public, not the broadcasters. Deregulatory trends and court decisions have weakened many of the provisions of these rules, but broadcasters who want the privilege of using the public airwaves still must abide by certain government regulations.

The rule most relevant to candidate access is the *equal time* provision. Under this rule, if a candidate buys or is given time on a television or radio station, other candidates running for the same office must be given an "equal opportunity" on that same station. News programs and talk shows are exempt from this provision. Unfortunately, many stations play it safe by not providing any access at all outside of news coverage, especially for state and local elections and when there are more than two candidates. This risk-avoidance strategy surfaces in surprising ways. In December 2003, all four NBC affiliates in Iowa decided against carrying an episode of *Saturday Night Live* because it was hosted by Al Sharpton, a candidate for the Democratic presidential nomination; apparently, the stations' lawyers feared they would be forced to give equal time to the other presidential candidates.

Even more controversial is the Fairness Doctrine, but that provision has been virtually dismantled. It required stations to provide "free airtime for the presentation of issues of public concern and the expression of opposing views whenever a highly controversial public issue, including the candidacy of a named official, was discussed on television." [31] Part of the Fairness Doctrine guaranteed candidates a *right of rebuttal* to personal attacks. After the landmark case *Red Lion Broadcasting Co. v. Federal Communications Commission* (1969), broadcasters were required to provide free airtime to individuals or groups who were attacked on their stations. But recent FCC rulings and court decisions have lead to a gradual erosion of this and other components of the Fairness Doctrine.

Frustration over media access, negative campaigning, and the quality of campaigns overall have fueled reform efforts. Among them is the call for "free airtime" to candidates during the final month or so before the election. The Alliance for Better Campaigns, for example, is calling for broadcasters to set aside at least two hours a week for debates, interviews, "candidate statements," and "other news or public affairs formats that provide for a discussion of issues by candidates . . . [and] ballot measures on the ballot in the forthcoming election." In a trial run during the 1996 election, all of the major networks except ABC set aside brief blocks of time for free, unfiltered statements from the candidates. The format was barebones, with candidates speaking directly to the camera about issues of their choosing. Although supporters lauded the noninflammatory, issue-oriented aspects of the experiment, critics objected to the drab production and absence of give-and-take and challenges to the candidates' statements. Since then, a handful of stations have been providing free airtime using various formats, and Congress has considered legislating the Alliance's proposals.

Media Effects

For campaigns, all of this would not matter much if media messages had no impact on the election. Indeed, for much of the twentieth century the lack of clear-cut evidence led to the conclusion that the media had only "minimal consequences" on how people voted. Beginning in the 1970s, however, mounting empirical evidence began to confirm what many political professionals have

suspected all along: the media can shape voters' issue priorities, attitudes, and sometimes their behavior.

Until the 1940s, it was widely assumed that the media that existed at the time—radio, newspapers, magazines—were quite powerful. Although there was no empirical research to support this assumption, the anecdotal evidence was persuasive. The first few decades of the twentieth century witnessed an explosion in the mass media. Radio emerged as a key source of news and entertainment; mass-circulation newspapers and magazines proliferated. Meanwhile, the apparent success of official government propagandists fueled the assumption that audiences were virtually defenseless against the onslaught of mass media messages. The media were everywhere, and their potential influence seemed massive.

Yet the scientific studies that followed suggested otherwise. According to research on elections in the 1940s and 1950s, any effects the media might have had were negated by the fact that most voters made up their minds before the campaigns began. News coverage thus had only "minimal consequences" for candidate preferences and vote choices, and the same was true for candidate speeches, advertising, and other campaign efforts. Instead of causing massive changes in opinion, the news media and campaign messages simply reinforced what voters already believed. If voters were influenced at all, the primary sources of persuasion were family members, community figures, and other "opinion leaders." Although media messages were pervasive, phenomena such as "selective exposure" inhibited their impact—that is, voters were picking and choosing information from the news based on whether it was in line with their existing views. Thus if a voter read a news story containing negative information about a candidate he or she supported, that part of the story was tuned out.

This "minimal consequences" theory held sway for decades, even though it ran counter to popular assumptions and professional intuition among campaign operatives. It cast doubt on the perceived importance of some of the more famous episodes in the media and politics. If voters had already made up their minds, did it really matter whether John Kennedy outperformed Richard Nixon in the 1960 debates? Why bother speculating about the effectiveness of Harry S. Truman's whistle-stop campaign? Or about the Dwight D. Eisenhower campaign's foray into television advertising?

The questions persisted in part because the media *seemed* to have a greater impact than thought. Indeed, as F. Christopher Arterton wrote in 1984, "When campaigners are asked about the importance of the media, most respond with disbelief that the question need be asked and an inability to convey adequately the perceived importance." [32] In recent years, media effects research has begun to catch up with intuition. For one thing, evidence mounted confirming the "agenda-setting" effect—that is, by focusing on certain issues and not others the media determine which policy items are at the top of the public's agenda. This effect helped to explain why environmental concerns gained prominence in the public despite a perceived lack of urgency among most politicians. Under the corresponding "priming" effect, these issue priorities become, in turn, the criteria by which voters evaluate government officials. Priming happens in part because most voters are not actively involved or interested in politics, making it difficult for them to process and synthesize the information needed to form opinions and take action. The media help to simplify the standards they employ to make decisions. By this logic, for example, the media could have had a major impact on the 1992 presidential election. On balance, news coverage hurt President Bush to the extent that it focused on economic issues, because voters evaluated the president's performance based on their perceptions of the economy, which was only beginning to emerge from recession.

A related phenomenon is the "framing" effect. This concept describes the process by which journalists organize, structure, and apply themes to political issues, and the corresponding effect of this behavior on the audience. Journalists adopt a variety of themes when covering elections. Some apply them to particular events, others to a candidate, and still others to a campaign as a whole. News stories covering a candidates' debate might be framed in terms of winners and losers; if so, noncommitted voters exposed to these stories may be more inclined to favor the winner over the loser. Overall, news coverage tends to frame the election in terms of a "game" with winners and losers, perhaps leading to opinion change that favors the candidate portrayed as the likely winner. Some researchers distinguish between "episodic" and "thematic framing." Usually, the media frame issues episodically—that is, they focus on specific events and individual cases. More desirable but less common is the use of a thematic frame, which provides a broader perspective by incorporating historical factors, policy-making dynamics, and collective outcomes. When the media frame a problem episodically, voters tend to blame the problem on the individuals depicted in the story. Thematic frames tend to encourage voters to attribute the problem to broader societal factors and blame government officials and institutions for failing to address them.[33] Accordingly, if the media were to employ the thematic frame more often, perhaps voters would demand more creative policy solutions from candidates running for office.

Evidence of even more dramatic effects began to emerge as researchers sorted out various methodological and theoretical challenges. Larry Bartels, blaming the persistence of minimal-effects findings on research design limitations and what scientists call "measurement error," made adjustments and found evidence of significant opinion change during the course of the 1980 presidential election.[34] John Zaller also homed in on methodological issues, finding that the media can have a "massive impact"

during elections when coverage clearly favors one candidate over another.[35]

Nomination campaigns have proven to be fertile ground for evidence of media effects. During presidential nomination campaigns, saturation coverage of the early primaries and caucuses provides "media momentum" to the candidates who do well or beat expectations.[36] Primary candidates who are portrayed by the media as beating expectations can benefit from increased campaign contributions, as can strongly favored candidates who are losing ground.[37] Front-runners and expectations beaters tend to get far more coverage than "hopeless" candidates, and the differences can be dramatic in a crowded field. Front-runners do not always benefit from more positive coverage, but voters are provided with far more information about them. And it rarely hurts to be portrayed as a likely winner.

Still, elections can be a tricky setting for identifying dramatic media effects. This difficulty stems from the media's usual success at meeting its goal of providing balanced coverage to all of the major candidates. As Zaller demonstrates, the media can foster opinion change when news coverage clearly favors one candidate over the other.[38] But that rarely happens.

Election Night

On election night, the media spotlight is brighter than ever. During their special election night coverage, the major networks and the cable news outlets begin to project winners and losers, based on exit polls, as polling places close across the country. Even local TV stations join in, with correspondents reporting live, on location, from campaign headquarters and victory parties across the viewing area. To the extent that the media have turned the election into a horse race, this is the finish line. And as in any horse race, the projections of winners and losers intensify even before the race is over.

In 2000 election night coverage was a disaster for the national broadcast media. The controversy centered on Florida. As in all other elections since 1980, the networks had pledged to refrain from projecting each state's electoral college results until the polls closed in that state. In most of Florida the polls closed at 7:00 p.m. EST. Fifty minutes later, the networks announced their projections based on the exit polls: Al Gore had beaten George Bush by a nose, which would be a major victory for the Democrats. The problem, however, was that polls were open for another ten minutes in the westernmost panhandle portion of the state, which unlike the rest of the state, is in the central time zone. Republicans charged that the early projections discouraged Bush supporters from going to the polls. On CBS, one commentator claimed that ten thousand Republicans had stayed home as a result.[39]

The Florida Panhandle controversy was overshadowed, however, by further media confusion over Florida. Once the vote tallying began, it appeared that the exit polls were wrong: Bush was pulling ahead in Florida. But rather than saying Florida was still "too close to call," the networks projected Bush would win. Before long, it became clear that Florida's twenty-five electoral college votes were enough to decide the election one way or another. When CBS News called Florida for Bush, anchor Dan Rather concluded: "Sip it, savor it . . . George Bush is the next president of the United States." [40] Later that night, Gore called Bush to concede the election. It turned out, though, that Florida was indeed too close to call—close enough to trigger an automatic recount of the ballots. Gore called Bush to retract his concession, and the networks retracted their projection of a Bush presidency. The "Florida recount" began.

Clearly, the networks were wrong both times. Early on election night, they had projected victory for Gore in a state that would have given him the presidency. Later, they gave Florida to Bush, who was then declared the overall winner. For the networks, it was among the most embarrassing episodes in their history of election coverage. As NBC anchor Tom Brokaw said, "We just don't have egg on our face. We have an omelet all over our suits." [41] Did their second projection fuel the assumption that Bush had won the election and that the recount was simply Gore's sore-loser effort to take it away from him? Gore and many of his supporters seemed to think so.

Election night projections have always been controversial. Most of the criticisms have reflected the Florida Panhandle concerns—that early projections will dampen turnout among supporters of the projected loser. But there is still little empirical evidence to support this notion. And other than the ten-minute Panhandle time gap and a handful of other slip-ups, the networks have honored their pledge to wait until the polls closed. If nothing else, Florida brought home the fallibility of exit polls. In 2002

the Voter News Service (VNS), which until recently conducted the exit polls for all the major news organizations, pulled the plug on its exit polling effort, citing unresolved technical issues (see Chapter 16).[42] Election night 2002 was thus remarkably bereft of projections. But in 2004 new problems emerged. Early exit polls collected midday showed Kerry leading Bush in Florida and Ohio, two states that experts agreed would determine the winner. Although the major television outlets honored their pledge to refrain from projecting the results until the polls closed, many popular Internet blogs projected a Kerry victory by late afternoon. But as the official vote counts rolled in that evening, it became clear that the early exit poll results were misleading and that Bush would carry both states, ensuring victory. This time it was the bloggers who had omelets on their clothes.

Conclusion

For at least fifty years now, the news media have played a powerful and sometimes pivotal role in U.S. elections. Even when they do not shape particular attitudes and voting behavior, their clout persists because they now serve as the primary communication link between candidates and voters. For the most part, this is a role they inherited unwittingly. And according to critics, many members of the news media are not equipped to fulfill their inherited responsibilities. The health of a democracy depends in part on a citizenry that is well-informed and engaged in public affairs. Many (if not most) professional journalists strive to facilitate these functions. But they also seek to gain professional prestige by writing compelling stories. And, more important, their behavior is bound to be affected by commercial pressures—that is, the need to deliver audiences to advertisers, the ones who help to pay the bills. To many observers, the end result is often less than satisfying.

Notes

1. Richard Joslyn, *Mass Media and Elections* (Reading, Mass.: Addison Wesley, 1984).

2. Kim Fridken Kahn and Patrick J. Kenney, "The Slant of the News: How Editorial Endorsements Influence Campaign Coverage and Citizens' Views of Candidates," *American Political Science Review* 96, no. 2 (2002): 381–394.

3. Thomas E. Patterson, *Out of Order* (New York: Vintage, 1994).

4. Darrell M. West, *The Rise and Fall of the Media Establishment* (New York: St. Martin's Press, 2001).

5. Thomas E. Patterson, *The Vanishing Voter: Public Involvement in an Age of Uncertainty* (New York: Knopf, 2002).

6. This section is based primarily on the analysis of West, *Rise and Fall of the Media Establishment*.

7. Ibid. 44. "Yellow journalism" is the phrase used to describe the sensationalistic, gossipy journalism of that era. A precursor of today's big-city tabloids, the style was characterized by splashy headlines and low-brow stories on gory murders and other crimes.

8. Ibid., 65.

9. Patterson, *Out of Order*.

10. Larry J. Sabato, *Feeding Frenzy: How Attack Journalism Has Transformed American Politics* (New York: Free Press, 1993).

11. Leonard Downie Jr. and Robert G. Kaiser, *The News about the News: American Journalism in Peril* (New York: Knopf, 2002).

12. Edie N. Goldenberg and Michael W. Traugott, "Mass Media in U.S. Congressional Elections," *Legislative Studies Quarterly* 12, no. 3 (1987): 317–339.

13. Marion Just, Ann Crigler, and Tami Buhr, "Voice, Substance, and Cynicism in Presidential Campaign Media," *Political Communication* 16 (1999): 25–44.

14. Steven Chaffee and Stacey Frank, "How Americans Get Political Information: Print Versus Broadcast News," *Annals of the American Academy of Political and Social Science* (July 1996): 48–58.

15. Downie and Kaiser, *News about the News*, 145.

16. Liberal talk radio has never caught on at the national level. Air America Radio, which describes itself as a "progressive talk radio network," hopes to change that. Launched in the spring of 2004, it broadcasts nationally syndicated talk shows, hosted by celebrities such as comedian Al Franken, actress Janeane Garofalo, and musician Steve Earle.

17. Katharine Q. Seelye, "Voters Disgusted with Politicians as Election Nears," *New York Times*, November 3, 1994, 1, 10.

18. Sabato, *Feeding Frenzy*, 6.

19. Downie and Kaiser, *News about the News*.

20. Doris A. Graber, *Mass Media and American Politics*, 6th ed. (Washington, D.C.: CQ Press, 2001).

21. Dean E. Alger, *The Media and Politics*, 2d ed. (Belmont, Calif.: Wadsworth, 1996).

22. Greg Mitchell, "Daily Endorsement Tally: Kerry Wins, Without a Recount," *Editor and Publisher*, November 5, 2004.

23. Paul Allen Beck, Russell J. Dalton, Steven Greene, and Robert Huckfeldt, "The Social Calculus of Voting: Interpersonal, Media, and Organizational Influences on Presidential Choices," *American Political Science Review* 96, no. 1 (2002): 57–73.

24. Graber, *Mass Media and American Politics*.

25. Kahn and Kenney, "Slant of the News."

26. The "Daisy Ad" may have been the first attack ad broadcast on television. Produced by President Lyndon Johnson's campaign, it aimed to highlight the perception that Republican candidate Barry Goldwater was eager to use nuclear weapons. The ad begins with an image of a little girl standing in the middle of a field plucking daisies as she counts "One . . . two . . . three . . ." The girl pauses and looks up. Meanwhile, an ominous-sounding male voice finishes the countdown. The ad then shifts to an image of a nuclear mushroom cloud and the sound of an explosion. It ends with the words "Vote for President Johnson on November 3," while an announcer says, "The stakes are too high for you to stay home."

27. Run on behalf of Vice President George Bush, the "Willie Horton" ad sought to portray Democratic candidate Michael Dukakis as soft on crime. It centered on the story of William Horton, a man convicted of being accessory to a murder, who was released on furlough from a Massachusetts prison. While on furlough, Horton held a couple hostage, stabbing the man and raping his fiancé. The ad implied that Dukakis was partly responsible, because he was governor at the time and it was his furlough program. But the truth was that Dukakis inherited the program from his Republican predecessor. Kathleen Hall Jamieson and Paul Waldman, *The Press Effect: Politicians, Journalists, and the Stories that Shape the Political World* (New York: Oxford University Press, 2003).

28. Stephen Ansolabehere and Shanto Iyengar, *Going Negative* (New York: Free Press, 1995).

29. Darrell M. West, *Air Wars: Television Advertising in Election Campaigns, 1952–2000*, 3d ed. (Washington, D.C.: CQ Press, 2001).

30. Graber, *Mass Media and American Politics*.

31. Ibid., 63–64.

32. F. Christopher Arterton, *Media Politics: The News Strategies of Presidential Campaigns* (Lexington, Mass.: Lexington Books, 1984), 8.

33. Shanto Iyengar, *Is Anyone Responsible?* (Chicago: University of Chicago Press, 1991).

34. Larry Bartels, "Messages Received: The Political Impact of Media Exposure," *American Political Science Review* 87 (1993): 267–285.

35. John Zaller, "The Myth of Massive Media Impact Revisited: New Support for a Discredited Idea," in *Political Persuasion and Attitude Change*, ed. Diana C. Mutz, Paul M. Sniderman, and Richard A. Brody (Ann Arbor: University of Michigan Press, 1996).

36. Gary R. Orren and Nelson W. Polsby, *Media and Momentum: The New Hampshire Primary and Nomination Politics* (Chatham, N.J.: Chatham House, 1987).

37. Diana C. Mutz, "Effects of Horse-Race Coverage on Campaign Coffers: Strategic Contributing in Presidential Primaries," *Journal of Politics* 57, no. 4 (1995): 1015–1042.

38. Zaller, "Myth of Massive Media Impact Revisited."

39. Patterson, *Vanishing Voter*.

40. Jamieson and Waldman, *Press Effect*, 80.

41. Ibid.

42. Disbanded after the 2002 election, VNS represented an attempt by the major TV networks and wire services to pool their news-gathering efforts on election day. A primary purpose of VNS was to share the huge costs and logistical difficulties associated with gathering vote totals nationwide, conducting exit polls involving tens of thousands of respondents, and analyzing the results so that news organizations could predict the winners. But it was partly blamed for fueling the erroneous projections made by the networks on election night 2000. This debacle led to a two-year overhaul of the VNS system. Yet on election day 2002, VNS announced that it was not ready—that it would not be able to provide exit poll data to its member news organizations for their election night coverage. See Thomas Guterbock and Robert P. Daves, "The Polls—Review Symposium Election Night 2000 in Perspective: Fluke or Normal Accident? Introduction to the Symposium," *Public Opinion Quarterly* (2003): 67. Two months later, VNS was dissolved. In its place, the networks and Associated Press formed the National Election Pool, which will rely on Edison Media Research and Mitofsky International to conduct its exit polls.

Suggested Readings

Alger, Dean E. *The Media and Politics*. 2d ed. Belmont, Calif.: Wadsworth, 1996.

Ansolabehere, Stephen, and Shanto Iyengar. *Going Negative*. New York: Free Press, 1995.

Arterton, F. Christopher. *Media Politics: The News Strategies of Presidential Campaigns*. Lexington, Mass.: Lexington Books, 1984.

Bartels, Larry. "Messages Received: The Political Impact of Media Exposure." *American Political Science Review* 87 (1993): 267–285.

Beck, Paul Allen, Russell J. Dalton, Steven Greene, and Robert Huckfeldt. "The Social Calculus of Voting: Interpersonal, Media, and Organizational Influences on Presidential Choices." *American Political Science Review* 96, no. 1 (2002): 57–73.

Chaffee, Steven, and Stacey Frank. "How Americans Get Political Information: Print Versus Broadcast News." *Annals of the American Academy of Political and Social Science* (July 1996): 48–58.

Dautrich, Kenneth, and Thomas H. Hartley. *How the News Media Fail American Voters: Causes, Consequences, and Remedies*. New York: Columbia University Press, 1999.

Downie, Leonard, Jr., and Robert G. Kaiser. *The News about the News: American Journalism in Peril*. New York: Knopf, 2002.

Farnsworth, Stephen J., and S. Robert Lichter. *The Nightly News Nightmare: Network Television's Coverage of U.S. Presidential Elections, 1988–2000*. Lanham, Md.: Rowman and Littlefield, 2003.

Goldenberg, Edie N., and Michael W. Traugott. "Mass Media in U.S. Congressional Elections." *Legislative Studies Quarterly* 12, no. 3 (1987): 317–339.

Graber, Doris A. *Mass Media and American Politics*. 6th ed. Washington, D.C.: CQ Press, 2001.

Guterbock, Thomas M., and Robert P. Daves. "The Polls— Review Symposium Election Night 2000 in Perspective: Fluke or Normal Accident? Introduction to the Symposium." *Public Opinion Quarterly* (2003): 67.

Iyengar, Shanto. *Is Anyone Responsible?* Chicago: University of Chicago Press, 1991.

Jamieson, Kathleen Hall, and Paul Waldman. *The Press Effect: Politicians, Journalists, and the Stories that Shape the Political World*. New York: Oxford University Press, 2003.

Joslyn, Richard. *Mass Media and Elections*. Reading, Mass.: Addison Wesley, 1984.

Just, Marion, Ann Crigler and Tami Buhr. "Voice, Substance, and Cynicism in Presidential Campaign Media." *Political Communication* 16 (1999): 25–44.

Kahn, Kim Fridken, and Patrick J. Kenney. "The Slant of the News: How Editorial Endorsements Influence Campaign Coverage and Citizens' Views of Candidates." *American Political Science Review* 96, no. 2 (2002): 381–394.

Mutz, Diana C. "Effects of Horse-Race Coverage on Campaign Coffers: Strategic Contributing in Presidential Primaries." *Journal of Politics* 57, no. 4 (1995): 1015–1042.

Orren, Gary R., and Nelson W. Polsby. *Media and Momentum: The New Hampshire Primary and Nomination Politics*. Chatham, N.J.: Chatham House, 1987.

Patterson, Thomas F. *Out of Order*. New York: Vintage, 1994.

———. *The Vanishing Voter: Public Involvement in an Age of Uncertainty*. New York: Knopf, 2002.

Sabato, Larry J. *Feeding Frenzy: How Attack Journalism has Transformed American Politics*. New York: Free Press, 1993.

Seelye, Katharine Q. "Voters Disgusted with Politicians as Election Nears." *New York Times*, November 3, 1994, 1, 10.

West, Darrell M. *Air Wars: Television Advertising in Election Campaigns, 1952–2000*. 3d ed. Washington, D.C.: CQ Press, 2001.

———. *The Rise and Fall of the Media Establishment*. New York: St. Martin's, 2001.

Zaller, John. "The Myth of Massive Media Impact Revisited: New Support for a Discredited Idea." In *Political Persuasion and Attitude Change*, edited by Diana C. Mutz, Paul M. Sniderman, and Richard A. Brody. Ann Arbor: University of Michigan Press, 1996.

PART V
Campaigning

CHAPTER 14

Strategic and Tactical Decisions in Campaigns

David A. Dulio

Any campaign manager or political consultant will ask two questions the day he or she steps into a candidate's campaign headquarters: How many days are there until election day? How many votes do we need to win? These fundamental pieces of information fit together with other essential campaign-related data to create a puzzle that is a campaign strategy. The easy part of a strategy is deciding what issues the candidate wants the campaign to be about, because all candidates have ideas about what they want to do after they are elected. The more difficult part is formulating a plan for winning the election. The strategy a campaign develops for reaching its goal of 50 percent plus one vote (the number of votes needed to win in a two-way race) on election day is a critical component of every campaign. This chapter examines the many aspects of campaign strategy in modern campaigns, including how strategy is defined, what goes into determining campaign strategy, and how strategy differs from tactics (not always an easy distinction to make).

A sound strategy is essential in modern campaigns, but it is not always very well understood. Some campaign professionals have defined strategy as Supreme Court justice Potter Stewart defined pornography in *Jacobellis v. Ohio* (1964): "I know it when I see it." Although it is sometimes difficult to understand, a campaign strategy is in general a game plan that defines the steps that will be taken in a campaign to reach the ultimate goal: victory. It answers two questions: Who will vote for the candidate? Why will they vote for the candidate? A campaign strategy is the same regardless of the level of campaign, whether a county commissioner's race or a presidential contest. It is decided well in advance of any announcement speech, fund-raiser, candidate debate, or television spot—that is, it is in place *before* the campaign begins; it is not something developed as the campaign progresses. In a similar fashion, a football coach and his assistants implement their game plan the week before the game; they would never leave the plan for how best to win the game until after kickoff or after halftime.

A campaign strategy is different from campaign tactics. Tactics are how a campaign executes the strategy it has defined. If a strategy is the long-term plan on how to achieve victory, tactics are the devices used to carry out the strategy. Although the concept of strategy is the same for all races, the tactics used to execute that strategy will likely differ. For example, a mayoral race in a small midwestern town and a U.S. Senate race in California may have similar strategies on how to win, but they will not use the same tactics to achieve victory. The mayoral race would likely rely on door-to-door campaigning and literature drops to communicate with voters, while the California Senate campaign would spread its message via television and radio commercials.

Most consultants agree that there are four principles to every campaign strategy.[1] First, there are three groups of potential voters in any campaign: those who support the candidate, those who support the opponent, and those who are undecided. Second, through research a campaign can identify the potential voters in a district or state who are in each of these categories. Third, a campaign does not need every single vote to win the election; it needs only to garner enough votes to give it the magic 50 percent plus one total (or in a three way race a simple plurality). And, fourth, campaign resources are allocated in a way that reflects the strategy that was designed. A campaign would be inefficient if it tried to get all the votes in the election; in fact, such a goal is impossible (unless the candidate is running unopposed), because some voters are going to vote for the other candidate no matter what. In addition, the number of days until election day will, in part, determine how the strategy is carried out—that is, it will help to determine which tactics are used to implement the strategy.

Constraints on Campaign Decision Making

To fully understand campaign strategy, one must consider the constraints that affect candidates, campaign managers, political consultants, and political parties in modern campaigning. The constraints include the rules governing U.S. elections; disengaged, apathetic, and cynical publics; the vagaries of media coverage; and funding levels. Failure to take these constraints into consideration may make the difference between winning and losing.

Electoral Rules

The first constraint is bigger than the campaign process itself; it is the system of electoral rules used in the United States. The U.S. single-member plurality (or first-past-the-post) system translates into a winner-take-all system in which the only candidate rewarded with a seat in government is the one who finishes first. In the United States, no value is placed on finishing second. Elections also are typically dominated by the two major parties, and therefore the vast majority of U.S. elections require the winning candidate to garner 50 percent of the vote plus one—a simple majority. Candidates, then, must devise a strategy that will result in a much greater number of votes than that sought by candidates in other systems, such as the multimember district or the proportional representation systems employed by many European nations. This reality can pose quite a challenge to candidates in many areas, because most candidates' supporters do not represent enough votes to achieve the magic 50 percent plus one figure. Thus they must attract the support of undecided voters or an opponent's supporters.

Disengaged, Apathetic, and Cynical Publics

The majority of citizens in the United States do not pay much attention to politics, and they are relatively uninformed about important political issues. This is an undisputed finding of voting studies, which report that voters fall far short of the minimum threshold of knowledge that classic theorists claimed they needed in order for democracy to work.[2]

There is no clearer evidence of Americans' lack of interest in campaign politics than the fact that only about half of all eligible Americans cast a ballot in presidential elections. That figure is even lower in years in which there is no presidential election and in "down-ballot" races for offices such as city council, school board, or mayor. Furthermore, only about one in ten Americans will actively campaign for a candidate, and even fewer people donate money to candidates' campaigns.

These factors are also important for those responsible for planning a campaign strategy. Because of the sheer number of votes that candidates have to amass to win elections under U.S. electoral rules and the fact that candidates have to fight through the clutter of present-day television with its varied program choices and advertisements, as well as the explosion of information on the Internet, candidates face a tough challenge on the path to election day. They not only have to compete with the hundreds of messages that people take in on a daily basis, but also must confront potential voters who say that they have lost interest in voting, do not have time to vote, or do not see any reason to vote.

Media Coverage

To some extent, a campaign needs the media if it is going to carry out its strategy successfully. Media coverage of campaign events, candidate speeches, and other campaign activities is defined by those in the business of campaigning as "earned media" (also known as "free media" because campaigns do not actually purchase this coverage). Newspaper or television coverage of a campaign event or speech given by the candidate spreads the message of a campaign to a wide variety of potential voters. Campaigns in general find it difficult to attract any coverage, because many media outlets simply do not cover campaigns in much detail or for extended periods of time. The traditional campaign season lasts from Labor Day through election day, but many campaigns, especially those for nonpresidential races, are covered only at the very end of the campaign period. Campaigns for the U.S. House of Representatives, state legislature, and races that are further down the ballot receive little if any attention in news broadcasts or newspapers. Indeed, the news media devote little coverage to state and local politics.

Even when the media do cover campaigns, their coverage is often shallow. Truly in-depth and issue-oriented stories about candidates and their opponents are few and far between. Rather, news stories about campaigns tend to feature the results of public opinion surveys, which can be reported quickly and are more easily understood by readers, listeners, or viewers. The media tend to cover a campaign as they would a sporting event, highlighting the "horse race" aspect of the race—who is ahead and who is behind rather than covering policy issues.[3] What do these trends in news coverage mean for campaign strategy? Candidates cannot rely upon the news media to spread campaign messages as much as they once did. This finding, however, is as much a tactical problem for campaigns as it is a strategic one.

Funding Levels

A final constraint on the strategic decision making in campaigns is the resources with which the campaign has to work. Not all campaigns are created equally. In the 2004 presidential race, President George W. Bush, who had no primary opponent, spent more than $220 million *before* Labor Day, while his opponent, Sen. John Kerry who was involved in a closely contested race for his party's nomination, spent almost $200 million during the primary season. In races for city council or school board, candidates may only spend a couple of thousand dollars out of their own pockets. The rest of the campaigns waged in the United States fall somewhere in between. Although it is true that campaigns for the presidency or school board could devise a similar strategy to win, these figures do have strategic implications.

How much money a campaign has to spend will greatly influence the type of strategy adopted. Campaigns flush with resources may decide to try to attract votes from all three sections of the electorate—the candidates' supporters, the opponents' supporters, and undecided voters—whereas campaigns with budgetary constraints may have only enough resources to focus on a very small segment of the electorate that contains a bare minimum of the potential voters needed to get the candidate over his or her vote target of 50 percent plus one. For example, during the summer of the 2000 presidential campaign Republican George W. Bush spent some time and money in California, a state that is traditionally a Democratic stronghold. Given the size of his budget, Bush was able to maintain this state longer than most previous Republican presidential campaigns—throughout the primary season and in the general election. That strategy forced Al Gore and the Democratic Party to spend valuable time and resources in California as well, rather than simply take it for granted.[4] Had the Bush campaign had greater budgetary constraints, it would not have had the same luxury; it would have had to focus only on toss-up states or those solidly in its column.

These strategic implications directly affect tactical decisions. The level of a campaign's budget drives the kinds of communications it is able to afford. Campaigns for presidency, U.S. Senate, and most governorships are waged on television, but only if the candidates can afford to purchase these media. Races for mayor, the state legislature, or county commissioner are waged on the ground, which requires relatively little spending. Campaigns with a lot of cash can use any kind of communication tactics they want—television ads, phone calls to potential voters, or sophisticated direct-mail campaigns, among others. Campaigns with fewer dollars in their coffers are limited to less expensive alternatives such as door-to-door campaigning and literature drops.

Deciding on a Campaign Strategy

Today, who decides what the strategy of a campaign will be is driven in part by the strength of the political parties in the United States. It is well documented that at one time the United States had a "party-centered" electoral system, but that has been replaced by what many have called a "candidate-centered" system, whose "seeds . . . were sown by the Constitution and election laws."[5] Federalism, different constituencies for different public offices, prescribed terms of office and timing of elections, single-member districts with a winner-take-all format, and a presidential rather than a parliamentary system all

encourage an electoral system that is candidate-centered. The decline of American political parties at the turn of the twentieth century encouraged candidates to develop their own campaign organizations, including a greater reliance on nonparty funding and professionals to fill the void left by the parties (see Chapter 2).

Strategic decisions in campaigns during the modern era are generally made inside the candidate's campaign organization (see Chapter 10). This situation is in stark contrast to the party machine era when the party organization set the strategy (as well as all other aspects of the campaign) for each of its candidates. Because campaign strategy is now devised and carried out by individual candidate organizations, these organizations, not the parties or the candidates themselves, coordinate the most important aspects of election campaigns. At least some scholars would argue that this is true of campaigns for high-level offices.[6] Others maintain that media, fund-raisers, and other consultants who provide specialized services really run the show in contemporary campaigns.[7] Nevertheless, some state and local contests still resemble those of yesteryear and are driven by the candidate and the candidate's spouse, close friends, and volunteers.

The importance of consultants in deciding the strategy of individual campaigns is also evident in some of the actions taken by the parties. First, both the Democrats and Republicans maintain lists of political consultants for recommendation to their candidates. These professionals, who are outside of the formal party structure, go into the individual campaign organizations and help direct the campaign. Second, the parties focus on only a few races every election cycle—usually those deemed to be the most competitive. Thus the parties have little if any role in deciding the strategic direction of the vast majority of campaigns around the nation.

However, state and national political parties still try in some cases to affect the strategic direction of candidates' campaigns: "Since the early 1980s, Democratic and Republican congressional leaders have produced lengthy issue handbooks, white papers, or 'talking points' for congressional candidates that focus on national issues and include instructions on how to use party rhetoric and statistics compiled in Washington to address local concerns."[8] One specific example of a national party trying to affect the direction of campaigns around the nation was the National Republican Congressional Committee's 1998 television campaign "Operation Breakout." It consisted of a series of television ads that focused on various issues, including the Clinton-Lewinsky scandal, and that aired in some of the most competitive districts in the country. These efforts were not appreciated by all the candidates running in those districts. One Republican Party staffer recalls: "I had a candidate who . . . openly disavowed what we were doing and called me . . . two and three times a day telling me to take the issue ads off [the air]. I told him I wasn't going to do that. I believed in what we were doing. He didn't win, but I think it was the right thing to do."

Research Drives Strategy

As noted earlier, under the rules the candidate who wins 50 percent plus one of the votes cast is elected.[9] This is fine in the abstract, but just how many votes does it take to get to the magic 50 percent plus one number? The answer varies by race. In a U.S. Senate, gubernatorial, or any other statewide campaign, the number of votes needed might be in the millions; in a campaign for the U.S. House of Representatives the number might be only 150,000; and in a state legislative race it might be only 25,000. The figures vary by region or competition. A Senate candidate in California must attract more votes than one in Rhode Island because of the difference in the size of the states' electorates. A candidate in a hotly contested U.S. House race in Michigan must receive more votes than an entrenched incumbent in Missouri, because the competitiveness of the race often affects the number of votes cast. The key to determining the number of votes necessary to win on election day is systematic research.

The process of researching the different elements that will lead to a sound campaign strategy is complex and multifaceted, requiring several different kinds of research. Professionals researching a district or state examine its demographic profile, electoral and vote history, and the attitudes and beliefs of its citizens, as well as the backgrounds of both their opponent and their own candidate.

Demographic Research
A close look at a district's or state's demographic elements, such as age, race, and ethnicity, helps those formulating the strategy to better understand the district or state as a whole. This is true for both the most sophisticated of federal campaigns and the most local of campaigns. In professionalized campaigns that hire consultants, most of the professionals come to the district or state from afar, and thus they need to gather a great deal of information about the area in which their campaign will be waged. For campaigns run by the candidate and the candidate's friends and family, this kind of research may be even more important, because even though the candidate's closest advisers may say they "know the district better than anyone," they do not know it in the same way that is revealed by a systematic analysis of the demographics of the district.

Research based on political demographics, such as race, age, and home ownership, is based on three fundamental assumptions: that the electorate is heterogeneous, that the heterogeneity can be used to divide the electorate into important analytic groups, and that those in similar demographic groups have shared concerns. A campaign that can identify the important issue differences among these groups has some clues about the policy differences and voting preferences among groups of potential voters. Even electorates that appear to be very homogeneous—a congressional district in Miami, Florida, for example, that has a large majority of potential voters with a Hispanic background—will have cross-cutting differences, such as voters of Cuban, Haitian, and Honduran descent. With this kind of information, campaign analysts can make important predictions about the groups' membership. For example, Cubans tend to vote Republican—a trend that dates back to the Bay of Pigs incident during President John F. Kennedy's administration. Other Hispanic groups have tended to vote Democratic. In another example, a high proportion of union households may encourage a candidate to push the issues of the minimum wage or workplace safety to the forefront of the campaign. In short, when a campaign is fully aware of the demographic profile of the electorate, it is able to target the right people with the right campaign message.[10]

Prior Electoral Performance
Research into the voting history of a district helps to answer the question of how many votes are needed to win. Such research relies on formulas appropriate to each type of race and campaign, but the same general idea holds for any type of campaign. The first piece of information sought by a professional campaigner is the number of registered voters and the number who actually go to the polls. These figures can help a campaign to gauge how many votes it needs to win.

A strategist working in a campaign in a congressional district in Ohio, for example, can safely assume that the district will have a population of about 650,000, roughly the average number of residents in all 435 congressional districts. However, the strategist would not conclude that his or her candidate needs 325,001 votes to win, because not everyone living in the district is eligible to vote in the election, and among those eligible not everyone who is registered is going to vote. Rather, the strategist would identify the number of registered voters and then project the number of people who will turn out in order to arrive at an estimate of the number of people who will vote. Once a campaign has a projected electorate, establishing the number of votes needed to achieve the magic 50 percent plus one figure is easy: simply take the number of persons expected to go to the polls, divide by two, and add one. In a multicandidate race, the task becomes more difficult, because the strategist must be able to gauge accurately the support for the other candidates in the race. In all races, however, the most successful campaigners will estimate the number of votes needed to win very conservatively. It is always better to estimate too high, hit that mark, and have more votes than needed than to estimate too low, reach that number, but fall short of victory.

Each of the figures just described is found by looking back at voter turnout and candidate performance. It is important to look back at the right election cycles and comparable campaigns. As noted earlier, a researcher working in a state legislative race in a presidential year would not examine a U.S. Senate campaign in a nonpresidential year when looking for vote history data. A good deal of political experience, expertise, and "feel" are required to know which races to use in the analysis.

Once the campaign estimates the number of votes needed to win, it needs to determine where the votes will come from. By examining concepts such as base vote, average party performance, soft partisan vote, and swing vote, the campaign can identify both where its most likely supporters are and how far those supporters will take the campaign toward its vote goal. The key concepts here are the base vote and the swing vote. Base partisans are those who will vote for a candidate of their party no matter who the candidate is. "Yellow dog Democrats" (from the saying "I'd vote for a yellow dog if he ran on the Democratic ticket") are just one example. The results of past elections will reveal how many votes fall into this category—that is, how many votes the campaign can count on getting without much effort. The voters who do not fall into the category of base vote for either party are the swing voters—that is, the voters who are up for grabs. In most campaigns, these are the voters who will decide the election.

Another significant aspect of vote history research is the geographic unit analyzed. In a presidential contest, the analysis may be done on a state basis; in a U.S. Senate or gubernatorial race it may be done on a county basis; and in a state legislative race it may be done on a precinct basis. Whatever the type of campaign, it will want to perform this kind of analysis on the smallest possible level. In doing so, it can begin to develop an idea of how to allocate its scarcest resources—money and time. Candidates will spend a lot of time and effort in areas that have large numbers of persuadable voters, because those areas represent a potentially abundant source of votes that can help the campaign to reach its vote goal. Candidates also will spend time and effort in areas in which their parties traditionally do well in order to firm up this support and, more important, to mobilize those voters on election day. However, most professional campaigners agree that it is a waste of time and money to try to pull votes from the opponent's base.

Strategically intelligent and efficient campaigns understand this concept and use it to make the most of their resources. Early in President Bill Clinton's 1996 reelection effort, two of the president's consultants, Mark Penn and Doug Schoen, used research to identify the prime groups in the electorate and to develop a strategic picture of the nation. This picture was used to decide where to air commercials and plan campaign visits. As a result, few resources were wasted. By contrast, Richard Nixon's 1960 campaign was a classic example of a vast wasted effort. Thanks to a campaign pledge to visit all fifty states, Nixon spent time in states that he should not have, including those that were solidly in his column and those he was sure to lose. After the election, his consultants probably looked back on the trips to less vote-fertile states as a part of the reason for his close defeat.

Research focused on the demographics of the electorate and the vote history of the district or state amounts to the "where" of campaign strategy in that it can help campaigns to identify the areas that are rich with supporters. The "why" and the "who" of campaign strategy are found in other kinds of research—specifically, opposition research and public opinion research.

Opposition and Candidate Research

Opposition research consists of examining an opponent's past in search of facts that can be used to highlight reasons why that candidate should not be elected to office. This type of research is often equated with "digging up dirt" on candidates. However, not all campaigns engage in this kind of activity. True opposition research focuses on things that the candidate has done or said as part of public life and elements of the candidate's life that could affect his or her ability to serve in office. This kind of information can be divided into four types of information: political, campaign finance, career, and personal.

Political information is generally only useful for candidates who are running against an opponent who has held elective office in the past; the campaign might investigate the opponent's prior voting record, absenteeism on the job, and other legislative activities, among other things. For example, the campaign communications (direct mailings, television commercials, or radio spots) of challengers today are often full of claims about their incumbent opponents, usually focusing on votes the opponents took that were detrimental to the district or state. During the 2004 Democratic presidential primary campaign, Howard Dean continually referred to his opponents' voting records on the invasion of Iraq. In November 2003, during the run-up to the primaries, the Dean campaign ran a television commercial in Iowa that attacked the U.S. House votes that fellow Democratic primary candidate Richard A. Gephardt cast on the Iraq war resolution. The ad said: "Dick Gephardt agrees to co-author the Iraq war resolution, giving George Bush the authority to go to war. A week later, with Gephardt's support, it passes Congress. Then, last month, Dick Gephardt votes to spend $87 billion more on Iraq." The ad clearly focuses on Gephardt's voting record, with the implication that Democrats should not support a candidate who voted to give President Bush authority to launch a war. Campaign ads that mention a legislative vote will also include the vote number and the date the vote was cast as supporting evidence. Campaigns that do not do so risk being accused of making up the information.

Campaign finance research is aimed at revealing any irregularities or violations of law in how candidates have raised the money needed to run their campaigns. When a campaign publicizes from whom its opponent has received contributions and whether some questionable characters are contributors, it may become a campaign issue. During Bill Clinton's 1996 reelection campaign, the Republican Party tried desperately to make a campaign issue out of how President Clinton and Vice President Gore raised money by arguing that they had "sold" and "rented out" the Lincoln Bedroom in the White House to "the highest bidder" and "fat cow contributors" and by pointing out how Gore had raised money from Buddhist monks. The implication was that these were inappropriate fund-raising activities for the president and vice president.

Campaigns also look closely at the opponents' prior careers and certain aspects of their personal lives. Candidates who have exaggerated certain aspects of their life experience (such as education, previous jobs, or military service) or who have had business dealings with suspicious individuals may find those questionable aspects hoisted before the electorate by their opponents. The same is true of candidates' personal problems, including any bankruptcies or failures to pay taxes. If a campaign uncovers this type of information about its opponent, it will likely argue that candidates who cannot keep their own fiscal houses in order cannot be trusted to look at the public's fiscal matters.

This kind of research is not limited just to the opponent. A good campaign will also thoroughly research its own candidate. No campaign should be unprepared for an attack launched by the opposition about something the candidate did in the past. Therefore, all campaigns should practice one strategic principle: know thyself. In this way, they are prepared for what the opposition uncovers in its own research.

Attitudinal Research

Research in modern campaigns goes beyond the hunt for information about both candidates, about the district or state, or about prior electoral trends. The polls that a campaign conducts lay the foundation for its theme and message (described later in this chapter). Polling allows a campaign to get a sense of what might be worrying the electorate and what issues are important in the district or state. Poll figures can help a campaign to learn who supports its candidate, who opposes its candidate, and the issues that can be used to attract persuadable voters. Polls also help the campaign to assess the mood of the electorate. In short, polling tells the campaign what groups in the electorate are likely to respond to the candidate's message and, based on the issues that are important, what groups should be targets of the candidate's message (such as women, white men, African Americans, "soccer moms," or "NASCAR dads").

Pulling the Research Together

Once the campaign has the raw materials for the "why," "where," and "who" of the strategy, it is likely to turn to specific analyses of this information to further its strategic planning. One of these analyses is commonly known as "SWOT"—Strengths, Weaknesses, Opportunities, and Threats. The information gleaned from the research is used to identify each element of SWOT.[11] For example, *strengths* consist of assets of the campaign and the candidate, including certain attributes of the candidate (such as incumbency, expertise in a certain issue area, or high name recognition among the electorate); major voting blocs in the electorate (such as African Americans, union members, or Christian conservatives); and financial resources. *Weaknesses* consist of any negative aspect of the candidate's public record—such as certain votes taken while in office, questionable business practices, or a failure to pay taxes—and an inability to raise money or attract significant support. *Opportunities* are outside factors that might prove to be beneficial to the campaign such as the state of the economy, prior voting trends in the electorate, or a mood among the electorate or a campaign issue that favors the candidate. For example, the state of the economy, the large budget deficits, and the less-than-ideal conditions in the Iraq war prior to the 2004 presidential election seemed to favor Democrat John Kerry, who had been critical of President Bush on each of these fronts. Kerry tried to use his military and foreign policy experience to his advantage during the campaign. *Threats* are the opposite of opportunities and include external factors that might be detrimental to the campaign. For example, the same factors that were opportunities for the Democratic candidates in 2004 could be classified as threats for the sitting president.

Messages and Themes

After a campaign has carried out the research that helps to define the campaign strategy, those involved in planning the strategy must determine how they are going to attract voters to their candidate. Convincing potential voters to cast a ballot for a candidate is not an easy task. Aside from all the constraints that campaigns face, voters can be tough sells, and most will not vote for a candidate without a sound reason. The campaign's theme and message are therefore crucial to its success. The difference between a campaign theme and a campaign message is subtle, and the two can be confused quite easily. Some campaign professionals will disagree with how others define *theme* and *message*. Sometimes, the two concepts are used interchangeably, or one person will define *theme* using the same words another uses to define *message*. Here, a campaign theme is understood to be what the campaign is generally about, and the message tells voters why a partic-

"It's the economy, stupid" was a phrase made famous by Bill Clinton's chief political strategist, James Carville (left). The sign hung on the wall of the Democratic presidential candidate's Little Rock, Arkansas, campaign office to keep everybody "on message" in the 1992 election. Source: AP Wide World Photos

also help a campaign to prepare for what may come from the opponent's campaign. By trying to anticipate the type of contrast the opponent will create, the campaign can plan how to respond or take a preemptive stand on a potentially thorny issue or problem.

Where do messages and themes come from? At their root, they come from the candidate and the candidate's stances on various issues. But from a practical standpoint, in the modern campaign it is the political professional who helps to craft a campaign's theme and message. A good deal of the process that leads to the development of the strategy, theme, and message of a campaign is research conducted through focus groups and survey research (see Chapter 16). Pollsters use surveys to gather information about the candidates' level of name identification and voters' approval/disapproval and likes/dislikes about certain candidates. Campaigns also use polls to determine which issues are the most salient to voters. Critics argue that the process contributes to poll-driven candidates. They claim that through survey research pollsters tell candidates what issue positions to take, and that candidates simply take a poll and regurgitate the attitudes and beliefs of a majority of the electorate. But, in fact, rather than telling candidates what side of an issue to be on or what position to take, polling acts as a type of agenda-setting tool. For example, a candidate might want to talk about six things during the campaign: the environment, Social Security, Medicare reform, taxes, foreign policy, and education. If polling data demonstrate that the electorate cares only about Social Security, taxes, and education but that the candidate has an advantage over the opponent only on Social Security and education, then those are the issues that will be featured in the campaign. In short, a sound message is a combination of voter desires, the candidate's strength, and the opponent's weaknesses.

The process of creating a theme and message involves emphasizing certain topics with the intention of reinforcing or changing the criteria that voters use for candidate evaluation.[13] A good campaign will focus on only one theme. Many incumbent officeholders choose a theme of "experience" or "stability" because such a theme shows voters that the officeholder has done a good job and deserves to serve another term. In his 2004 reelection campaign, George W. Bush adopted the theme "Steady Leadership in Times of Change" in an effort to tell Americans

ular candidate is the best choice.[12] A campaign theme might be "change," "experience," or "stay the course," such as when Ronald Reagan asked voters in 1980, "Are you better off today than you were four years ago?" It might also be an important issue area, such as when Bill Clinton's campaign informally declared in 1992, "It's the economy, stupid." If someone asks what the campaign theme is, the answer is "This campaign is about . . ." When someone asks what the message is, the answer is "You should vote for our candidate because . . ."

Research conducted suggests many campaigns and professional political consultants develop what is sometimes called a "message box." It amounts to a summary of who will say what about whom (see Box 14-1). Its quadrants list, respectively, what the candidate wants to say about the opponent, what the candidate wants to say about himself or herself, what the opponent is expected to say about the candidate, and what the opponent is expected to say about himself or herself. The box allows the campaign to begin to create a contrast between its candidate and the opponent. Contrast is central to any message, because elections are about the choices that voters make on election day. Detailing what the campaign wants to highlight about its candidate, as well as the opponent, helps to frame this choice for voters. A message box can

BOX 14-1

HYPOTHETICAL MESSAGE BOX, 2004 PRESIDENTIAL ELECTION

Amy Miller and Stephen K. Medvic

	Bush	Kerry
What **George W. Bush** says about . . .	• Strong leader • Resolute and confident • Dealing with national security crisis • Compassionate conservative	• Changes positions frequently • Cannot be trusted • Has voted against key defense measures • Liberal
What **John Kerry** says about . . .	• Stubborn • Has alienated friends and allies • Has weakened America • Has failed domestic policies	• War hero • Courageous • On "your" side • Will strengthen America

A campaign's message is crucial to its success. Above all else, it tells voters why a particular candidate should be elected. Therefore, the most important task for every campaign is to guarantee that voters remember the one phrase that distinguishes the candidate from the opponent. As such, the campaign's message should be clear, simple, believable, and reflected in absolutely everything the candidate does or says.

To construct the message, campaigns often create a message box. This box lays out what each candidate plans to say about himself or herself and the opponent. Because the message is such a fundamental part of the campaign's planning process, the message box is typically prepared early in the race. Ideally, it targets key voters, addresses a particularly important issue, and plays to the party's and the candidate's strengths. Thus creating the message box is a far more complicated task than it first appears and relies on a delicate mix of art and science.

Initially, the message box is used to collect pieces of salient information about the candidates. These will typically include personal characteristics, such as trustworthiness, but also can include contextual information (such as, "the economy is weak") and specific issue positions (such as, "supports universal health care"). The hypothetical message box shown here simulates the basic building blocks the campaign of Republican George W. Bush might have used early in 2004 to develop its message.

The messages produced about a candidate and opponent are based in part on polling that helps to reveal salient issues or candidate traits and the most effective way to emphasize that in the post-9/11 world (referring to the September 11, 2001, terrorist attacks on the United States) he, not his opponent, was the right choice for president. These themes have been consistently used over time. For example, in his 1864 reelection campaign President Abraham Lincoln said, "Don't change horses in the middle of the stream."

In choosing a theme, many challengers enjoy more flexibility, because they are not limited by a record from having already held office. A common theme for challengers is "change," because a challenger must give voters a reason to fire the incumbent and give someone else a chance to represent the district or state. For example, many challengers run for Congress by running against Congress. They tell voters that they are not like the other candidate in the race, who, as an incumbent, is "a Washington insider" no longer in touch with the voters. This message can work at any level, as Jimmy Carter illustrated in his 1976 presidential campaign when he successfully campaigned as the candidate who was from outside the Washington Beltway.

Having a single theme does not mean that a campaign has a single message. Indeed, campaigns often disseminate multiple messages, depending on both the issue and the audience. For example, if a Democratic candidate has determined that part of his strategy to achieve a winning coalition of voters is to solidify his base vote, which lives in an urban center, and to talk to swing voters, who are female and under the age of thirty five, these two different groups will likely get two different messages, but the theme will be the same. If the candidate is an incumbent,

them. A campaign can only guess at the opponent's message, but political consultants can anticipate the other side's strategy based on experience and a systematic reading of the political landscape. Messages must also capture the mood of the electorate, and this too requires a professional's expertise and intuition. The process of building a message box is therefore simultaneously scientific, predictive, and expressive.

Drawing on the hypothetical 2004 Bush message box, one can begin to identify the messages the Bush campaign might have crafted. Bush's message about himself would have emerged clearly from polling and consultant intuition—"President Bush is a strong, resolute leader in a time of crisis." Voters saw the president's strength to be his leadership in the war on terror. What Bush intended to say about his Democratic opponent, Sen. John Kerry, was, however, unclear early in the campaign. Bush might very well have attacked Kerry as one of the most liberal candidates ever to run for president. Yet Kerry's famous "subtlety" made him at least appear to flip-flop on issues over the course of his Senate career. For obvious reasons, then, Bush could not credibly claim that Kerry was both consistently very liberal and willing to take a number of positions on any given issue. Kerry himself would ultimately settle the matter for the Bush campaign when he told a group of supporters that he voted for $87 billion in funding for the Iraq war before voting against it. Thus the Bush message about Kerry would be "John Kerry is a flip-flopper who can't be trusted to protect America."

In planning for Kerry's message, the Bush camp might have anticipated some attacks. Kerry might have said that Bush was stubborn and thus would not admit to policy mistakes in Iraq and the economy. He might have charged Bush with incompetence in handling difficult issues. Or he might have simply criticized what he saw as the failures of Bush administration policies such as weakening of America's standing internationally and the economy, education, and the environment domestically. To adequately capture these various lines of attack, the Kerry message about Bush could have been "George Bush has ruined America's standing in the world and ignored problems at home."

Kerry also had various options in selecting his message about himself. He was likely to emphasize his war record and to make claims that he would keep America strong at home and abroad. But he also might sound a populist theme and remind voters of job losses over the course of Bush's first term, claiming that he was on the side of the average American, while Bush was too cozy with big business.

In this hypothetical example, the Bush campaign might have predicted that Kerry would do what campaigns often do in distinguishing themselves from their opponents—that is, he would contrast himself with Bush on the same criteria: "John Kerry is a war hero who will build a stronger America." Thus Bush would be said to be weakening the United States, while Kerry would claim to be strengthening the country (while reminding voters of Kerry's service in Vietnam and Bush's lack thereof). Similarly, Bush would present himself as resolute and Kerry as vacillating. Portraying oneself as the mirror image of one's opponent has the benefit of consistency and reinforces the issue or characteristic that one hopes will become central to the voter's decision.

In creating a message box, campaign planners have to put themselves in the shoes of their opponents and develop as realistic a message as possible regardless of how awkward it might be to confront their own candidates with that message. Because the message box is a planning document, it must closely reflect reality as it presents itself at the time. Real-world conditions may change the campaign's calculus, but a sound strategy based on an accurate message box is essential to a disciplined—and successful—campaign.

the theme might be "stay the course" or "experience." The message to the base might then focus on "continuing the fight for working families," while the message to women under thirty-five might concentrate on "keeping a woman's right to choose." The two messages are on very different issues, but they reinforce the same theme.

George W. Bush's campaign for president in 2000 provides a more concrete example. It is safe to say that the theme of the Bush campaign was "change." Nearly every issue that Bush brought up during the campaign emphasized how he would be different than the administration in place at the time. Bush called himself a "reformer with results" and touted his record as governor of Texas on taxes as well as social services, saying that he had brought change to the state capital. He also promised to "bring dignity back to the White House"—another issue altogether, but one still focused on change. Bush claimed as well that he was "going to change the tone in Washington" and be someone who could work with members of Congress from both sides of the aisle. The Bush campaign believed voters would respond to the theme of change after eight years of the Clinton administration, and it found issues on which Bush had an advantage over his opponent to make that case.

One final key aspect of a campaign theme and message is the idea of message discipline. According Mary Matalin, Republican strategist and former aide to Vice President Richard B. Cheney, "The absolute rule of message dissemination and message penetration is consistency and repetition. The principle is the same for political

During their 1956 reelection bid, President Dwight D. Eisenhower and Vice President Richard Nixon used the message "peace, prosperity, and progress" to focus voters' attention on the administration's role in ending the Korean War and bringing about a strong economy. Source: Dwight D. Eisenhower Library

campaigns or companies: Everyone says the same thing, over and over." [14] To cut through the clutter of information that fills potential voters' lives, candidates have to continually repeat their message so it penetrates the greatest number of potential voters' minds. In the 2000 election, Al Gore probably best optimized the practice of "message discipline." Almost every speech Gore gave or communication his campaign put out mentioned the "risky tax scheme" that his Republican opponent had cooked up or the "lock box" that Gore was going to use to save Social Security and Medicare. During the 2004 presidential primary campaign, Sen. John Edwards also proved to be quite adept at staying on message. In the series of debates with his Democratic rivals, Edwards seemed to try to answer each question briefly and then turn to segments of his stump speech to continue to hammer home the message he wanted potential voters to receive.

Yet sometimes candidates may decide that, strategically, it is in their best interest to remain vague about certain issues because it gives them the best chance to win. During his 1996 reelection campaign, Bill Clinton blurred the differences between him and his Republican rivals on issues that traditionally are Republican strongholds (taxes, crime, a balanced budget, and welfare reform, for example). By doing so, Clinton was able to take many of these issues off the table, if not co-opt the rhetoric for his own. One recent candidate also proved to be very adept at practicing strategic ambiguity. In his bid to be governor of California during the 2003 recall election, Arnold Schwarzenegger deliberately kept many of his statements on various issues unclear. For example, Schwarzenegger, who enjoyed a lead

in the polls early on, was not eager to detail his association with groups such as U.S. English, an organization whose goal is to establish English as the official language of the United States. In a state like California, which has a large Hispanic and Asian population, ties to groups such as U.S. English are clearly not beneficial to a candidate. Instead, Schwarzenegger traveled around the state, claiming that the recall election was a choice between "people and the politicians" and promising to return California to its glory days by rebuilding the state's troubled economy. "The choices are clear," he told a group of supporters in San Jose. "Do you want to go backwards with Gray Davis or do you want to go forward with Arnold?" The theme of the Schwarzenegger campaign was clearly "change," evidenced by his frequent promises to "clean up the mess in Sacramento" and his criticism of Gov. Gray Davis's handling of the state's fiscal problems, including a $38 billion deficit. However, the way in which he communicated the messages associated with this theme did, for the most part, lack detail. This strategy works only for some candidates, however. It is unlikely that candidates who are not as well known among the electorate and who do not have as high a standing in the preelection polls could adopt this kind of message as successfully as Schwarzenegger did.

Campaign Tactics

A campaign's tactics are the devices it uses to execute its strategy. Strategies may be similar from campaign to campaign, whatever the type, but the tactics employed to carry out those strategies will be very different, depending on the type of campaign. For example, strategists in a U.S. Senate campaign and a state auditor campaign in the same state may conclude that a successful campaign lies in winning a significant number of votes from one section of the state. However, the tactics the campaigns employ to reach that goal will likely be very different. Because of the differences in the two campaigns—the Senate campaign is likely to be very well funded and the auditor campaign is likely to have a small budget, to name only one—the Senate candidate will probably use television to spread his or her message, while the auditor candidate will probably have to rely on direct mail. Here the different tactics are communications-based: television versus direct mail. Other tactics on which candidates rely to communicate messages are persuasion phone calls, Web sites, speeches and rallies, and door-to-door canvassing.

One strategic component, with several different tactical approaches, of a campaign that all candidates would like to conquer is earned media—coverage of the campaign by reporters and other media outlets. For most campaigns, the local media are more important than the national press, because the local media more directly reach the very people who will go to the polls and cast ballots on election day. Developing a plan that will foster media coverage is difficult; many times reporters have to be convinced that the candidate's campaign is worth covering and will be considered newsworthy by the editor of the paper or producer of the evening news. The payoff for campaigns who do get reporters to pay attention to them is great in that it can be another avenue for the candidates to show message discipline and continue to talk about things that reinforce the themes of their campaigns and their messages. Different tactics can be used to implement an earned media strategy, such as press releases, campaign events, press conferences, and actualities (sending audio to a radio or television stations for use on the air). However, spreading a message through earned media can be risky because of the inherent trade-off that exists between control and expense. Although a campaign does not directly pay for the coverage it receives from a news account, it does relinquish control of the message in that report. For example, after the debate between Al Gore and George W. Bush during the 2000 presidential campaign, much of the coverage focused on Gore's body language and behavior during the debate. Rather than spreading the message of the campaign, the media focused on Gore's sighs of frustration and the manner in which he interrupted his opponent. *Saturday Night Live* even did a parody of the debate, which was the only exposure many Americans had to the candidates' debate performances.

Another tactic that many successful campaigns will engage in is the mobilization of voters, more commonly known as field operations or get-out-the-vote (GOTV) efforts. However, a campaign does not want to see all voters in a district or state go to the polls on election day—they want to see only their supporters show up. A strong GOTV effort will return to the research that was conducted at the beginning of the campaign so that the campaign can focus on the areas more populated with its supporters. If a campaign knows that one county in a congressional district has traditionally voted for the candidates of its party, and its research reveals that there is no reason to believe that this trend will change, the campaign might send a mailing to all registered voters of its party in that area or place reminder phone calls to individuals in that area. Political parties and organized interests also often offer services that facilitate voters (who are friendly to their agenda) getting to the polls. For example, they might offer older voters a ride to the polls and single parents child-care services. Labor unions in Michigan have gone one step further and negotiated a contract that calls for election day to be a paid day off for their members so they can vote. The enticements offered by today's GOTV drives differ greatly from those offered in the nation's earliest years, when candidates and parties tried to lure people to the polls by offering

them a lavish feast that often included as much liquor as they could drink.

Conclusion

Strategy is central to a winning campaign. Without it, the campaign has no direction and no plan as to how it will gather the number of votes needed to win. Creating the strategy is part science and part art. The science of strategy lies in the research conducted to gather the requisite information to form the strategy—the demographic makeup of the district or state, its voting history, information about the opponent and the candidate, and public opinion data. When aggregated, the results of the research paint a picture of the district or state in which the campaign is waged. At this point, the political expertise of the men and women running the campaign becomes critical. Those creating the strategy must be able to put the pieces of the puzzle together in such a way that the candidate has an opportunity to get the needed number of votes on election day. This is the art of campaign strategy. Decisions have to be made about what information from the opposition research and polling will be a part of the campaign's theme and message, and information from the demographic and vote history research has to be used to decide how to allocate the campaign's scarce resources.

Although the principles of strategy are the same in all campaigns, the tactics that a campaign adopts—that is, the activities that execute the strategy—will be different across most campaigns. For example, many campaigns for federal office use television advertisements to spread the campaign message, whereas lower-level races usually rely on less technically sophisticated communications tactics, such as door-to-door canvassing, literature drops, and mailings. This difference between campaigns stems largely from one of the constraints that candidates in down-ballot races have to deal with—the lack of large campaign budgets. Campaigns that raise a large amount of money can afford to do many different things both strategically and tactically. They can campaign across the entire district or state and can use any tactic they wish because they can afford it. Campaigns with smaller budgets, however, must be more careful and more efficient in both their tactical and strategic decisions.

One constant in all campaigns is that the candidates must fight through the clutter that surrounds potential voters. Many are uninterested in, disaffected by, or cynical about the election process, making the campaign strategy even more important. Campaigns have to find a way to connect with voters, convince them to vote for their candidate, and get them to the polls on election day. Only those campaigns that map out their strategy long before the campaign begins and develop a detailed plan for how to reach the magic 50-percent-plus-one vote number will have a real chance to win.

Notes

1. Joel Bradshaw, "Who Will Vote for You and Why: Designing Strategy and Theme," in *Campaigns and Elections American Style*, ed. James A. Thurber and Candice J. Nelson (Boulder, Colo.: Westview Press, 1995).

2. Angus Campbell, Phillip E. Converse, Warren E. Miller, and Donald E. Stokes, *The American Voter* (Chicago: University of Chicago Press, 1960).

3. Thomas E. Patterson, *Out of Order* (New York: Vintage, 1994).

4. Dave Boyer, "Buoyed Bush Seeks a California Coup; Gore Follows as Polls Show State in Play," *Washington Times*, October 31, 2000, A1; Donald Lambro, "Slow but Steady Gain in Polls Has Bush California Dreaming; Clinton Called In as Gore Camp Tries to Stop the Erosion," *Washington Times*, October 29, 2000, C3.

5. Paul S. Herrnson, *Congressional Elections: Campaigning at Home and in Washington*, 2d ed. (Washington, D.C.: CQ Press, 1998).

6. The rise of professional consultants to prominence in American elections has troubled some observers—see Larry J. Sabato, *The Rise of Political Consultants: New Ways of Winning Elections* (New York: Basic Books, 1981); Mark P. Petracca, "Political Consultants and Democratic Governance," *PS: Political Science and Politics* 22, no. 1 (1989), 11–14; David S. Broder, *The Party's Over: The Failure of Politics in America* (New York: Harper and Row, 1971); Dan Nimmo, *The Political Persuaders: The Techniques of Modern Election Campaigns* (Englewood Cliffs, N.J.: Prentice Hall, 1970); and Nicholas J. O'Shaughnessy, *The Phenomenon of Political Marketing* (New York: St. Martin's Press, 1990). However, some argue that consultants are actually in a position to help democratic elections. See David A. Dulio, *For Better or Worse? How Professional Political Consultants Are Changing Elections in the United States* (Albany: State University of New York Press, 2004); and Candice J. Nelson, Stephen K. Medvic, and David A. Dulio, "Political Consultants: Hired Guns or Gatekeepers of Democracy?" in *Shades of Grey: Perspectives on Campaign Ethics*, ed. Candice J. Nelson, Stephen K. Medivc, and David A. Dulio (Washington, D.C.: Brookings, 2002), 75–97.

7. Daniel M. Shea and Michael John Burton, *Campaign Craft: The Strategies, Tactics, and Art of Political Campaign Management* (Westport, Conn.: Praeger, 2001), 12.

8. Paul S. Herrnson, *Congressional Elections: Campaigning at Home and in Washington*, 4th ed. (Washington, D.C.: CQ Press, 2004).

9. Much of the information in this section is drawn from Shea and Burton, *Campaign Craft*, and Bradshaw, "Who Will Vote for You and Why." Unless otherwise noted, readers should consult these sources for more information on concepts presented here.

10. Shea and Burton, *Campaign Craft*.

11. Larry Powell and Joseph Cowart, *Political Campaign Communication Inside and Out* (Boston: Allyn and Bacon, 2003).

12. Thanks to longtime Republican strategist Carol Whitney for her advice on how to differentiate between theme and message.

13. Stephen K. Medvic, *Political Consultants in U.S. Congressional Elections* (Columbus: Ohio State University Press, 2001), 51.

14. Mary Matalin and James Carville, *All's Fair: Love, War, and Running for President* (New York: Random House and Simon and Schuster, 1994).

Suggested Readings

Baer, Denise. "Contemporary Strategy and Agenda Setting." In *Campaigns and Elections American Style*, edited by James A. Thurber and Candice J. Nelson. Boulder, Colo.: Westview Press, 1995.

Bradshaw, Joel. "Who Will Vote For You and Why: Designing Strategy and Theme." In *Campaigns and Elections American Style*, edited by James A. Thurber and Candice J. Nelson. Boulder, Colo.: Westview Press, 1995.

Covington, Cary R., Kent Kroeger, Glenn Richardson, and J. David Woodard. "Shaping a Candidate's Image in the Press: Ronald Reagan and the 1980 Presidential Election." *Political Research Quarterly* 46 (1993): 783–798.

Dulio, David A. *For Better or Worse? How Professional Political Consultants Are Changing Elections in the United States.* Albany: State University of New York Press, 2004.

Farrell, David M. "Campaign Strategies and Tactics." In *Comparing Democracies: Elections and Voting in Global Perspective*, edited by Lawrence LeDuc, Richard G. Niemi, and Pippa Norris. Thousand Oaks, Calif.: Sage Publications, 1996.

Faucheux, Ronald A. *Running for Office: The Strategies, Techniques and Messages Modern Political Candidates Need to Win Elections.* New York: M. Evans, 2002.

Herrnson, Paul S. *Congressional Elections: Campaigning at Home and in Washington.* 4th ed. Washington, D.C.: CQ Press, 2004.

———. *Party Campaigning in the 1980s.* Cambridge, Mass.: Harvard University Press, 1988.

Hrebnar, Ronald J., Matthew J. Burbank, and Robert C. Benedict. *Political Parties, Interest Groups, and Political Campaigns.* Boulder, Colo.: Westview Press, 1999.

Johnson, Dennis W. *No Place for Amateurs: How Political Consultants Are Reshaping American Democracy.* New York: Routledge, 2001.

Maisel, L. Sandy. *Parties and Elections in America: The Electoral Process.* 3d ed. Lanham, Md.: Rowman and Littlefield, 1999.

Matalin, Mary, and James Carville. *All's Fair: Love, War, and Running for President.* New York: Random House and Simon and Schuster, 1994.

Medvic, Stephen K. *Political Consultants in U.S. Congressional Elections.* Columbus: Ohio State University Press, 2001.

Menefee-Libey, David B. *The Triumph of Campaign-Centered Politics.* New York: Chatham House, 2000.

Nelson, Candice J., Stephen K. Medvic, and David A. Dulio. "Political Consultants: Hired Guns or Gatekeepers of Democracy?" In *Shades of Grey: Perspectives on Cam-*

paign Ethics, edited by Candice J. Nelson, Stephen K. Medvic, and David A. Dulio, 75–97. Washington, D.C.: Brookings, 2002.

Powell, Larry, and Joseph Cowart. *Political Campaign Communication Inside and Out.* Boston: Allyn and Bacon, 2003.

Powell, Larry, and J. T. Kitchens. "Analyzing Campaign Strategies: Contingencies, Assumptions and Techniques." *Southeastern Political Review* 14 (1986): 161–179.

Sabato, Larry J. *The Rise of Political Consultants: New Ways of Winning Elections.* New York: Basic Books, 1981.

Shea, Daniel M., and Michael John Burton. *Campaign Craft: The Strategies, Tactics, and Art of Political Campaign Management.* Westport, Conn.: Praeger, 2001.

Simon, Adam. *The Winning Message: Candidate Behavior, Campaign Discourse, and Democracy.* New York: Cambridge University Press, 2002.

Thurber, James A., ed. *The Battle for Congress: Consultants, Candidates, and Voters.* Washington, D.C: Brookings. 2001.

Thurber, James A., and Candice J. Nelson. *Campaigns and Elections American Style.* 2d ed. Boulder, Colo.: Westview Press, 2004.

———. *Campaign Warriors: Political Consultants in Elections.* Washington, D.C.: Brookings, 2000.

CHAPTER 15

Campaigning for Cash

Clyde Wilcox

In the United States, candidates for public office compete not only for votes, but also for the money needed to win those votes. They usually begin their campaign for cash before they actively seek to persuade voters, and most candidates continue fund-raising up until the final week of the election. In fact, those vying for office often spend as much time or more asking potential donors for money as they do asking potential voters for their votes. Scholars therefore frequently speak of parallel campaigns for money and for votes.

More broadly, U.S. candidates spend more time raising money than candidates in most other democracies. This is true for three reasons. First, U.S. candidates often compete in two distinct elections—one within the party and another between the nominees of the parties. Only a few other countries have party primaries to select candidates, and seldom are those primaries as contentious as those in the United States. Second, candidates in the United States must communicate more information to potential voters. In most other countries, all candidates within a party support a common party platform—that is, they "stand for" the party. In the United States, however, all candidates have their own issue positions that may differ from those of others in the party. Thus a Republican candidate for the U.S. House of Representatives from Vermont will need to carefully explain her position on the issues, distinguishing herself not only from the Democratic candidate but also from others in her party. Finally, in most other countries party leaders play the dominant role in fund raising and then distribute the funds to candidates. In the United States, party leaders help certain candidates in their fund-raising, but candidates are ultimately responsible for raising their own funds.

Candidates need to raise large sums of cash because communicating with potential voters is expensive. Even in modest local campaigns, candidates need money to travel around the constituency, to buy some yard signs and bumper stickers, and perhaps to hire some campaign workers. Most candidates also use some kind of mass media to get their message out—direct mail or phone contacts with potential voters, newspaper advertisements, cable TV ads, radio advertisements, even spots on broadcast television. To mount a sustained media campaign, candidates need to retain the services of professional consultants and a sizable paid campaign staff. In expensive election contests such as for the presidency or U.S. Senate, candidates often have a team of fund-raisers and spend millions of dollars or more on consultants, advertising, and other expenses.[1]

In the campaign for cash, certain types of candidates have clear advantages. Incumbents typically raise far more money than their challengers for many reasons. They are experienced campaigners who know how to go after cash. They have made friends in the donor community and have established ties to party officials and interest groups. Most important, they can influence public policy—something that their challengers can seldom do.

How Much Is Enough?

The amount of money a candidate must raise to compete in an election varies by the type of office. Americans elect public officials to a dazzling array of positions. At the national level, they elect presidents to represent the nation, senators to represent entire states, and members of the U.S. House of Representatives to represent congressional districts of approximately 600,000 voters. State governments include elected governors who represent the entire state, other state officials such as lieutenant governors and attorneys general, and state legislators who represent districts of varying sizes. In some states such as California, special elections can be called to remove elected officials between elections. In 2003 the voters of California replaced Gov. Gray Davis with Arnold Schwarzenegger, a well-known actor, in a special recall election. Some states also elect justices to their state supreme court. And then there are the tens of thousands of local governments in the United States with their elected mayors, city council members, county commissioners, school board members, sheriffs, dog catchers, prosecutors, and justices of the peace.

Presidential candidates must raise tens of millions of dollars or more in their primary election campaigns. In

New York State Attorney General Eliot Spitzer greets a supporter at a December 2004 campaign fund-raising luncheon for his bid for the 2006 Democratic nomination for governor. Because the U.S. electoral system includes both primary and general elections, candidates in the United States spend more time raising money than candidates in most other democracies.
Source: Mike Segar/Reuters/Landov

states, whereas Powhatan County has only seven thousand residents.

The costs of campaigns are also affected by the state and local political culture. In New Jersey, U.S. Senate races have recently centered on negative television advertising in huge quantities, forcing one winning Senate candidate to spend $63 million. By contrast, in Wisconsin there has long been a tradition of restraint in spending. Democratic senator William Proxmire, who retired in 1989, routinely raised less than $5,000 for his reelection bids, and he would return some of his unused funds to his donors after the campaign was finished. In 1998 incumbent Democratic senator Russell D. Feingold and his challenger, Rep. Mark Neumann, agreed to limit their direct campaign spending to less than $4 million and to limit how much money they could raise from political action committees (PACs) and other sources.[2]

The amount of money that candidates must raise depends as well on how much their opponents are prepared to spend. Candidates do not always need to outspend their opponents to win office, but they do need to spend enough to introduce themselves to voters, to frame campaign issues, and to counter their opponent's campaigns. Many U.S. elections are not competitive—indeed, many candidates for state and local government run unopposed. In these cases, incumbent candidates do not need to spend large sums, although some may choose to run vigorous campaigns to deter others from challenging them in the next election. The most expensive campaigns tend to be for open seats, when incumbents have retired. Because it is so difficult to defeat incumbent politicians, many ambitious politicians wait patiently for incumbents to retire and then run aggressively for the vacant seats. Because these seats are often "in play"—that is, they could be won by the nominee of either political party—many candidates enter the primary election to win their party's nomination.

In addition to the money that candidates raise and spend, parallel fund-raising campaigns are usually mounted by political parties and interest groups. In the 2000 presidential election, for example, the Democratic and Republican Parties aired many television commercials in critical states, and they mounted massive voter mobilization drives on behalf of their candidates. Interest groups were also quite active. Planned Parenthood spent more than $15 million on an ad campaign aimed at defeating George W. Bush, while the National Rifle Association (NRA) was mailing materials to coal miners in West

one unusual twist, George W. Bush's reelection campaign announced in 2003 a goal of raising more than $170 million for its campaign for the GOP nomination, despite the fact that Bush was unopposed within his party. Because this money would inevitably be spent to help Bush's chances in the general election, Democratic hopefuls were therefore required to raise not only the money they needed to compete with one another for the Democratic nomination, but also additional funds to compete with Bush before their party's convention. U.S. Senate candidates and gubernatorial candidates must raise anywhere from a few million to tens of millions of dollars. Some campaigns for local office may cost only a few hundred dollars.

The cost of elections depends on the size of the constituency. Although all senators represent entire states, some states like California have tens of millions of voters, while Wyoming has only a few hundred thousand—indeed, there are more hotel rooms in Los Angeles alone than there are voters in Wyoming. State legislative districts vary enormously in size, from California with its more than 400,000 residents per assembly seat to New Hampshire, with only 3,000 voters per district. Mayoral elections cost more in big cities like New York, where Michael Bloomberg spent some $70 million in 2002, than in small towns like Phillipi, West Virginia (population 3,132). County commissioners may represent constituencies of vastly different sizes, even within the same state. In Virginia, for example, Fairfax County has more than one million residents, making it larger than at least eleven

Supporters of President George W. Bush applaud his arrival at a 2004 Bush-Cheney fund-raiser in Washington, D.C. The campaign exceeded its $170 million target for the Republican nomination in the biggest presidential fund-raising drive in U.S. history. Source: Jason Reed/Reuters/Landov

Virginia urging them to "vote their jobs and their guns" by supporting Bush. Although this cash does not pass through candidates' campaign committees, interest groups are clearly important in the election and candidates frequently (though not always) encourage groups to mount these campaigns.[3]

Campaign Finance Regulations

Campaign finance is regulated in America, but not without ongoing controversy (see Chapter 6). The role of money in elections is a source of debate in most democracies, but in the United States campaign finance is especially controversial because of the clash of several important values—the need to control corruption versus the values of political equality and freedom of speech. Most Americans believe that large campaign contributions have the potential to corrupt politicians. If donors make very large contributions to candidates or parties, they are likely to expect to be listened to when they have an opinion on public policy. And if money buys access to government officials, then the voice of wealthy interests is amplified at the expense of those with fewer financial resources. Many scholars have argued that this extra "voice" for donors is undemocratic.[4]

If politicians do more than just listen to donors—if they also do favors for them—then corruption becomes a problem. Donors may want a policy maker to intercede with the bureaucracy in interpreting a law, or to put special provisions into laws that would benefit them. For ex-

ample, when congressional Republicans produced their compromise energy bill in November 2003, it contained special provisions that exempted one company that had given large sums to GOP candidates and party organizations from lawsuits over damages caused by its pollution. Such provisions are worth millions and even billions to corporations. Because politicians need money and individuals and groups need various policies from government, the temptations of corruption are significant. To control this kind of corruption and remove its temptation, many nations have limited the size of political contributions and also limited the amount that candidates and parties can spend. Indeed, some countries use public funds to partially or fully pay for campaigns.

Yet in the United States free speech is one of the most celebrated of the personal liberties, ensconced in the First Amendment to the Constitution. And elections are a time when free speech matters most, as candidates, parties, and interest groups try to persuade voters to back their agendas. In an election campaign, a candidate's right to free speech is meaningless without the funds to make that speech heard, and thus campaign funds play a vital role in the policy debates during the campaign. Some Americans believe that contributing or spending large amounts of money is equivalent to "shouting" a political message, yet giving money to a candidate is different in subtle and important ways from making a speech or volunteering for a campaign.

In the United States, campaigns for national office (president, Senate, and House of Representatives) are regulated by national laws that seek to balance these competing values. States regulate campaigns for state and local office, and local governments often have their own regulations. The resulting regulatory framework is so complicated that many candidates, and most party committees and interest groups, hire lawyers and accountants that specialize in that framework.

Federal Campaign Finance Law

In 1974 Congress passed amendments to the 1971 Federal Election Campaign Act (FECA) in reaction to the revelations of abuses by President Richard Nixon's reelection committee. The FECA established a comprehensive framework of campaign finance regulations. Its spending limits helped to reduce the demand for contributions, and its contribution limits helped to limit the competition to raise funds. Transparency was assured by a disclosure system that required candidates, parties, and interest groups to file reports detailing their contributions and spending. Finally, partial public funding was provided for presidential candidates.

Over the next two decades, each of these pillars of campaign finance regulation eroded. By the early twenty-first century, most analysts believed that the system of campaign finance regulations was badly flawed and needed to be reformed.

Contribution Limits

The FECA established limits on the amount that individuals could give to candidates, to political parties, and to the electoral arm of interest groups. Parties were limited in the amount they could give to candidates and also in the amount that they could spend in coordination with candidates to help their campaigns. Interest groups could not give or spend money from their treasuries to help candidates, but they could form political action committees to raise money from members of the group and then give that money to candidates or spend it in their behalf. Contributions from PACs to candidates, parties, and other PACs were limited in size, but PACs could spend unlimited amounts to independently advertise on behalf of a candidate, so long as they did not coordinate with the campaign.

In the late 1970s, Congress and the Federal Election Commission (FEC) established a new type of contribution—"soft money." [5] Soft money evaded contribution limits in two important ways. First, no limits were placed on the amount of soft money that an individual or group could give. Contributions of hundreds of thousands of dollars were not uncommon, and some groups gave millions. Second, interest groups could give money directly from their treasuries, not merely the money that they would raise from their PACs.[6] Soft money was eliminated in the Bipartisan Campaign Reform Act (BCRA) of 2002, but both political parties are currently scrambling for ways to channel these funds in new ways. In October 2004, corporate soft money donors began to give to nonprofit groups able to mobilize turnout to benefit one party or the other, perhaps signaling a new path for treasury funds into politics.

Transparency

The disclosure system of the federal government has been rightly called the greatest success in campaign finance regulation. Any federal candidate who raises a minimum threshold of money, as well as all party committees and all national PACs, are required to file regular reports with the Federal Election Commission listing their donors and their spending. Small contributions are not listed, because compiling a list of all small contributions would be a burden for campaigns and small contributions are thought to pose little danger of corruption. But all contributions of significant amounts—over $200—must be disclosed, along with the name, occupation, and address of the individual donor, or the name and address and identification number of the PAC or party committee.[7]

Despite these measures, in the 1980s and 1990s increasing amounts of money began to flow outside of the disclosure system. Groups seeking to mobilize voters without regard to political party were exempt from disclosing their activity, and they could in fact receive large tax-exempt contributions to finance this activity. Because the voter mobilization was nonpartisan, the law did not define it as electoral activity. But the requirement that contacts with potential voters be nonpartisan was easily evaded by groups that sought to help candidates of a particular party, because political consultants knew quite well which districts were predominantly Republican and which were mostly Democratic and could concentrate their activities in those districts. Groups could also seek to educate the voters in a nonpartisan manner and spend unlimited sums that were not disclosed to the FEC. In 1992 the Christian Coalition claimed to have distributed some forty million voter guides in conservative Christian churches across the nation. The Coalition worked closely with the George Bush campaign to develop and distribute these guides, but a district court ruled that its activity was not "coordinated" with the Bush campaign and thus could be done outside the disclosure system. The Coalition was not required to disclose who funded the voter guides, how much money was spent, or how it was spent.

More important, by the late 1990s many interest groups were engaged in "issue advocacy" advertising that did not directly ask voters to support or defeat a particular candidate, but made it clear which candidate the group preferred. For example, issue ads on behalf of Rep. Rick Lazio, the Republican candidate who opposed Hillary Rodham Clinton in the 2000 New York U.S. Senate race, extolled his virtues and finished by calling for voters to "let Rick know that you think that he is doing a good job." Because the ads did not directly ask voters to cast their ballots for the GOP candidate, they were not considered campaign ads and thus were exempt from the FECA disclosure requirement. Moreover, these issue ads could be financed by treasury funds and not through a PAC. Labor unions, issue groups, and even companies ran these ads in increasing numbers over time, although companies frequently did so through front organizations such as Citizens for Better Medicare, which largely represented the pharmaceutical companies. Other groups with misleading names also sprang up, and, unless journalists and citizens watch groups such as opensecrets.org and the Center for Public Integrity were able to track down the groups' financial sources, their spending was essentially anonymous. During the 2000 presidential primary in New York, a group called Republicans for Clean Air mounted an issue ad campaign attacking Sen. John McCain's record on the environment. Yet most environmental groups thought that George W. Bush's record as governor of Texas was at least as weak as that of McCain. It eventually turned out that the group was merely an organizational front for two wealthy Bush donors from Texas, neither of whom was known for his environmental activism. This incident and many earlier ones led over time to the erosion of the disclosure system, as more money was raised and spent in ways that were not transparent to voters.[8]

Public Financing

The FECA established partial public financing of the presidential nominating campaigns, conventions, and general election campaigns. Under the FECA provision, taxpayers check a box on their federal tax return if they wish to direct some of their income tax to a public fund to help finance elections. But, as described later in this section, candidates who accept public funds trade away their right to unlimited spending.

Candidates for their party's nomination for president can choose to receive public funds that match the first $250 of each donor's contribution to their campaign. Thus a contribution of $250 to Reform Party candidate Patrick J. Buchanan in 2000 would have been doubled by the federal match, but a contribution of $1,000 to Democratic candidate Al Gore would have been increased by only 25 percent, to $1,250. Candidates must receive a minimum percentage of the vote over time to remain eligible for these funds, and there is an overall limit to the amount a candidate can receive.

Both major parties receive a flat grant from the government that helps to pay for their conventions. This grant was originally intended to pay for most of the convention activity, although over time the parties have stretched the limits of the law to allow large amounts of private money to pour into the conventions.

Finally, each of the major-party presidential candidates receives a grant for the general election campaign. In 2000 each major-party nominee received approximately $68 million, in 2004 that figure increased to nearly $75 million. Minor parties that received at least 5 percent of the vote in the past presidential election can receive partial funding for their campaigns as well. In 1996 H. Ross Perot's Reform Party received matching funds, but Ralph Nader did not receive 5 percent of the vote in 2000 and thus the Green Party did not receive funds in 2004.

As noted earlier, candidates who accept public funds in the primaries give up their right to unlimited spending. Thus those who take matching funds in the primary elections must abide by a spending limit for all primaries and spending limits for each specific state. In practice, these limits are somewhat elastic, but they can pose a barrier for candidates in some instances. In 1996 Sen. Robert J. Dole accepted matching funds and spent all of his allowable funds competing with other GOP candidates for the presidential nomination. Thus he could not spend any more money until the Republican National Convention launched his general election campaign, although he did receive some soft money support from his party. By contrast, his opponent, President Bill Clinton, spent none of his public funds running against a Democratic candidate because he was unopposed, and so he was able to direct all his funds into his campaign against Dole.

In 2000 George W. Bush became the first candidate of a major political party to refuse matching funds in the primaries and therefore to avoid the spending limit associated with them. Bush raised more than $90 million for his primary elections, far more than any candidate in history. In the 2004 primaries, Bush raised more than twice as much as he had in the 2000 campaign, for a total of $261 million. In November 2003, Democrats Howard Dean and John Kerry announced that they too would refuse matching funds in order to avoid spending limits in the primaries. This move allowed Kerry, the Democratic nominee, to continue to raise substantial sums after the Democratic primaries were effectively over, but before the Democratic convention. Kerry raised more than $40 million by February 29, when he effectively clinched the Democratic nomination. He raised an additional $207 million before the convention.

Candidates can refuse matching funds in the general election as well, but to date no candidate has done so. Because political parties can spend money to help their presidential candidates, most nominees spend the public grant on their campaign and encourage donors who support them to give to the party. Yet it is likely that a major-party candidate could raise more money in the general election than the public grant, and it is possible that someday soon a candidate will refuse these funds as well.

Overall, then, by 2004 the matching fund program was beginning to crumble as serious candidates refused the public grant. Matching funds were also in trouble for a second reason, however. Over time, fewer Americans have checked the box to redirect their tax money, raising the specter that the matching fund would go bankrupt if several candidates qualified for the maximum grant. It is not clear why so few Americans now check the box on their tax form, although there is reason to believe that many incorrectly believe it will increase their tax bill.

The BCRA and Beyond

The Bipartisan Campaign Reform Act passed by Congress in 2002 changed many of the rules of fund-raising. The maximum contribution from individuals doubled to $2,000, but soft money contributions to the political parties are banned. Interest groups are permitted to spend treasury funds for issue ads, but these ads are banned within thirty days of a primary election and sixty days of a general election. During these final days of campaigns, groups can spend money to contact voters through the mail, by phone, in person, or through the Internet. It is too early to know how these new rules will affect fund raising by candidates, although experts predict that it will increase the influence of large donors and perhaps reinvigorate political action committees as an avenue for interest group activity.

State and Local Campaign Finance Laws

U.S. states are often known as the laboratories for public policy. As states adopt different laws affecting elections, others can study their effects and perhaps learn from these experiments. The states have engaged in a wide variety of experiments, but there has been little serious study of what works where and why. Some states offer public financing of elections, usually linked to some kind of spending limit. These public financing campaigns vary greatly in their generosity. Some states have strict contribution limits, but others have no limits at all. In Virginia, real estate developers often make very large contributions to candidates for governor. In some states, an interest group must establish a PAC to give money; in other states it can make contributions from its treasury. States also differ widely in their transparency, with some states insisting that most campaign activity be disclosed and others allowing broad exemptions to disclosure that cover a great portion of campaign activity. Local governments sometimes pass their own campaign finance laws. The city of Akron, Ohio, has experimented with quite strict contribution limits.

State and local campaign finance laws do not need to duplicate those of the national government, but they do need to meet standards established by the U.S. Supreme Court for protecting free speech. For example, spending limits for candidates can be established for only those who take public funding. So long as state and local laws do not violate the Constitution or a constitutionally valid national law, states are free to adopt whatever regulations they choose.

The Process of Fund-Raising

For most candidates for public office, fund-raising is the least enjoyable part of campaigning. Indeed, many people who have considered running for office have decided not to run after realizing how much money they would have to raise. Some incumbent politicians have retired in part because of the relentless and growing demands for campaign cash. The prospect of raising large sums is also daunting to most nonincumbents, who must ask everyone they know to contribute and then must try to introduce themselves to strangers and ask them for cash (see Box 15-1).

Candidates usually get help in their fund-raising. Nearly all campaigns hire accountants to keep track of the money and help them meet any disclosure or contribution limit laws that apply to their office. Most serious candidates for higher office have a fund-raising director—usually someone with experience in fund-raising and sometimes someone for whom raising campaign cash is a profession. Serious campaigns also form one or more finance committees, whose members are chosen based on their ability to raise funds from various constituencies. Candidates for national office receive advice and often assistance from their political parties in setting up their fund-raising operations and getting started.

Where does that money come from? For many challengers and open-seat candidates, some or perhaps most of the money comes out of their own pockets. Nonin-

cumbents must persuade potential donors that they are serious about running and that they have a real chance of winning. Many candidates invest large sums of their own money hiring consultants and doing some advertising that might convince others that they are viable. Democrat Jon Corzine of New Jersey invested nearly $60 million of his own money in his successful U.S. Senate campaign in 2000, and Ross Perot invested tens of millions of his own cash in his 1992 and 1996 losing bids for the presidency. Incumbents seldom have to spend their own money, because plenty of individuals and interest groups are willing to support them.

Most of the money in U.S. elections comes ultimately from individuals and from organizations, but the precise routing of that money depends on the laws in effect in the jurisdiction. To understand these sources of money, it is easiest to focus on national campaigns—for president, the Senate, and the House of Representatives. These campaigns are mostly financed by contributions from individuals, although individual contributions may pass through many hands before they are spent.

Individuals

Most Americans do not give to candidates for public office, and those who do usually make small contributions. More than 70 percent of those who gave to a presidential candidate in 2000, for example, gave less than $100—but only 600,000 people made these small contributions. Those donors who give more end up contributing a much larger share of all campaign funds. In 2000 less than one-third of all donors to George W. Bush gave maximum contributions, but they accounted for nearly three-quarters of all of Bush's campaign receipts. In 2004 Bush received more than three-quarters of his funding during the primary period in checks of $1,000 or more (the majority of which came in contributions of $2,000, the new legal limit). After March 2004 the Bush campaign mobilized a small giving campaign that raised significant sums.[9]

Most donors have given before and also give at least occasionally to all kinds of candidates and groups. The donor pool is not representative of the broader population. Nearly all donors are white, more than two-thirds are men, and most are quite wealthy. Many have incomes of more than $500,000 a year, and few have incomes at or below the median. A large majority of donors are members of business associations and professional groups, and very few are members of labor unions. Finally, most donors are middle-aged or older; very few are under thirty years of age.

Donors who give small contributions are less educated and much less wealthy than large donors. But even these donors of $25 and $50 are overwhelmingly white and male. Because individual contribution limits were not indexed to inflation under the FECA, candidates and parties have had to attract growing numbers of donors over the years, but the new donors look remarkably like the

BOX 15-1
A POLITICAL NEWCOMER RAISES CASH

David Madland

Steve Shannon knew he would have to raise a quarter of a million dollars if he wanted to have a chance to win a seat in the Virginia General Assembly in 2003. That is the amount he estimated it would take to communicate with the fifty thousand voters in his district, rent office space, pay staff, and do everything else a candidate needs to do to win in the Thirty-fifth House District, which is closely divided between Democrats and Republicans.

Shannon, a Democrat, was only thirty-two years old and had been in school for most of his life. He had received a bachelor's degree from Fairfield University in Connecticut, a law degree from the University of Virginia, and master's degree in public policy from Georgetown University. He did not have the money to finance his own campaign. And, because he had never run for office before, he did not have a pool of donors to rely on. So Shannon looked at what he had— friends and family—and formulated a plan to win the election. He started early and worked hard.

In February, ten months before the election, Shannon asked his parents and his wife's parents to throw him fund-raisers. He invited friends and family to both and asked them to contribute to his campaign. "At that point," Shannon explained, "people gave money, not because they were interested in my policies, but because they wanted to see me succeed because they liked me." With this start, Shannon began to branch out, asking his friends to host fund-raisers and invite their friends. After raising early money from his inner circle, Shannon was intent on proving two things to the powerful people watching his race: that he had the ability to raise money and that he was serious enough to ask his family and friends for money. "It is not easy asking grandma for $500," he reflected.

Next, Shannon branched out to former classmates and colleagues at

work. He invited graduate school classmates to inexpensive fund-raisers at barbeques or bars, and he sent mailings to classmates from college. He also asked a colleague at one of his former law firms to host a fund-raiser at the firm.

At this point, Shannon was spending 70 percent of his day fund raising. He had raised enough money to be seen as a credible candidate, but he still had a long way to go and he had tapped out his inner circle. The next step was cold calls to people he did not know. "Those were the toughest calls," Shannon recalled. He searched for people who had at one time served on the boards of organizations for which he volunteered. And he looked through public records for prospects. "For every seven calls, you can expect $125," Shannon learned. "But to raise a quarter of a million dollars, that is a lot of calls." In fact, it would require 14,000 phone calls if Shannon raised all his money this way. Although Shannon did not like making the calls, he refined his pitch and learned to ask for a specific amount of money; otherwise, the prospective donor might give less than Shannon's research indicated he or she could afford.

A few months before the election, Shannon began to work toward getting the endorsement of organizations such as the AFL-CIO, the U.S. Chamber of Commerce, and the Sierra Club. He filled out questionnaires and met with organization leaders. He wanted endorsements not only for the money the group could give directly, but also because once he had the endorsement, he could solicit money from the group's members. Shannon secured the endorsement of these organizations and a dozen others and then began asking for donations from key people in these organizations.

The Democratic Party did not get financially involved until the fall. According to Shannon, the party

wanted to wait to see which candidates were picking up traction and doing well in the polls. "It's sort of a Darwinian process," he observed. "The party is not a bank, they are just another donor." Indeed, it wrote Shannon a $15,000 check a few weeks before the election.

As election day neared, Shannon found himself spending far less time fund-raising than early in the campaign, but large sums of money began to flow in, and he raised 40 percent of the money in the last six weeks of the campaign. Because he had raised money successfully earlier in the campaign, large donors had a sense that Shannon was a viable candidate, and Shannon learned that "money begets money." As his race tightened in the last few weeks, checks continued to come in. He realized that "people like to back someone they think might be a winner." Interest groups also began to make phone calls to likely Democratic voters, encouraging them to turn out at the polls and support Shannon. They mailed letters as well to their members and to voters whom they thought might agree with their arguments.

By election day, Shannon's opponent had raised almost $220,000, and Shannon had raised over $260,000. Over half of his donors were people who gave less than $100, but larger donors accounted for almost 90 percent of the total funds raised. "If you want to run for office," Shannon counsels, "first figure out how much the race is going to cost and then figure out how you are going to raise the money."

On November 4, 2003, Shannon won election to Virginia's General Assembly with 52 percent of the vote. The governor of Virginia praised Shannon's effort as a "textbook way to run a great campaign."

Source: Steve Shannon, interview with David Madland, December 5, 2003.

old donors. This is not surprising, because the most likely contributors are the friends and neighbors of those who already give.[10]

Candidates who seek to raise money from individuals need to size up their own resources and the motives of donors. Some incumbent politicians have influence over the policy agenda or over the content of legislation. They can intercede with the bureaucracy on behalf of a donor or present their case to other policy makers. Some candidates have an ideological profile that is attractive to certain donors—a strong position on abortion, for example.

Individuals give money to candidates for a variety of reasons. Investors give to protect their businesses or to help secure special economic benefits from government. Ideologues give to help advance policies that do not benefit them economically, especially issues such as abortion, environmental protection, and downsizing the role of government. Intimates give because they enjoy the social contacts of contributing and because their friends ask. Successful fund-raisers match their candidates' resources to the motives of donors, tailoring their appeal so that it is most likely to work.[11]

Candidates and parties raise money from individuals in a variety of ways, but two methods are especially common. To raise larger contributions, campaigns put together networks of people who will ask their friends, business associates, and even their families to give to the candidate. These networks are structured like pyramids: a fund-raiser who pledges to raise $100,000 might contact ten associates who each pledge to raise $10,000, and they in turn ask some of their friends to raise $2,000. Requests for large contributions are often accompanied by invitations to dinners and other events where the candidate will speak and mingle with the crowd. This kind of fund-raising works especially well with investors and intimates.

Smaller contributions are frequently raised through impersonal mail solicitations (see Box 15-2). Candidates and parties mail letters to potential donors, asking for money to help pursue specific policies. Fund-raising letters are usually directed at ideologues, and they often contain inflammatory language aimed at convincing potential donors of the importance of their contribution. Direct-mail fund-raising is especially useful in presidential campaigns, because the amount of the contribution is doubled by the federal match. Candidates, parties, and interest groups often "prospect" for new donors by renting lists of likely contributors. A candidate who opposes gun control might rent the membership list of a pro-gun association, for example, or the subscription list of a hunting magazine. Prospecting mailings often lose money, but those who give can be solicited again and again and asked to give larger amounts.

Interest Groups

The PACs formed by interest groups can raise money from the groups' members and use that money to make contributions or occasionally independent expenditures to candidates running in federal elections. About four thousand PACs are registered with the FEC, but many of them are inactive, and many others raise and contribute small amounts. A small percentage of all PACs give the vast majority of contributions to candidates.

Because PACs are solicited for donations by all kinds of candidates, most of them develop rules to help them decide whom to support. They usually follow some combination of two strategies that correspond to the investors and ideologues among individual donors. Under the "access-oriented" strategy, PACs give to important members of Congress who have influence over the shape of public policy. Party leaders, committee chairs, issue leaders, and other key members of Congress receive far more money from access-oriented PACs than do ordinary members. PACs that seek access tend to give more money to candidates from the party that controls Congress and therefore sets the congressional agenda, but many access-oriented PACs give to both parties, both because they want friends when party control changes and because they want votes in committees and on the floor for their policies. These PACs do not direct their money to close elections; in fact, many give a large portion of their money to incumbents who face little, if any, opposition. Access-oriented PACs are often associated with large corporations that routinely have important business before Congress and that seek narrow provisions in legislation that will help their bottom line.[12]

"Ideological" PACs seek to change the composition of Congress. These PACs do not routinely give to party leaders or committee chairs, because these incumbents usually face little chance of defeat. Instead, they try to channel their money to races in which it might actually make a difference—that is, in the two dozen House races and handful of Senate races that are close in any given election. Ideological PACs often care about the policy views of the candidate at least as much as those of the candidate's party. The NRA gives to pro-gun Republicans but also supports pro-gun Democrats, for example, and NARAL Pro-Choice America gives to pro-choice Republicans as well as to pro-choice Democrats.

Some PACs are creative in their approach to elections. EMILY's List is a pro-choice PAC that supports Democratic women candidates. The acronym EMILY ("Early Money Is Like Yeast") is significant. In the same way that yeast is the ingredient that makes bread rise, early money is the ingredient that allows women's campaigns to rise (or perhaps to raise more bread). Members of EMILY's List promise to contribute to two candidates endorsed by the organization. By bundling together the contributions of thousands of members, EMILY's List is able to channel far more money to candidates than it could through a regular PAC contribution.

PACs are not the only way in which interest groups can participate in elections. Groups can spend their

BOX 15-2
INTERNET FUND-RAISING
Carin Larson

Fund-raising dinners for elite contributors and direct-mail solicitations to smaller donors are traditional methods of fund-raising. But many candidates are now seeking to raise money with a mouse and a modem. In 2004 nearly 75 million Americans at one point turned to the Internet for political news and information. To tap these online constituencies, candidates are creating official campaign Web sites, which also allow them to recruit support in a much less expensive and perhaps more effective way than mail solicitations or face-to-face meetings. According to Michael Cornfield, research director at the Institute for Politics, Democracy and the Internet, "The Internet streamlines the fund-raising process, and [online] contributions can spike after the [candidate] appears favorably in the news." [1]

Internet fund-raising is often used best by candidates who are outside the traditional party networks. Minnesota gubernatorial candidate Jesse Ventura demonstrated the ability of the Internet to raise money in the late 1990s, and Arizona senator John McCain showed that the Internet can raise a lot of money when he ran for the GOP presidential nomination in 2000.

The Internet as a fund-raising tool received much political and media buzz during the 2004 Democratic presidential primaries. Instead of relying on wealthy donors to fund their campaigns, candidates relied on the smaller, but numerous, contributions from individuals online. Former Vermont governor and Democratic presidential candidate Howard Dean took Internet fund-raising to new heights in 2004, and, largely through his online efforts, he managed to out-raise his Democratic competitors in the year before the start of the primaries. During the first quarter of his campaign, almost half of his funds were raised via the Internet, making Dean the first candidate to rely on the Internet so heavily from the start.

Many of Dean's supporters found one another through Internet forums such as www.meetup.com. Indeed, Dean's Internet efforts mobilized many who had never given to a political candidate in the past. Studies suggest that Internet donors are younger and less partisan than those who give through more traditional channels, and they are less affluent.[2] As use of the Internet for fund-raising grows, the pool of donors may become more diverse.

Dean's Internet fund-raising strategy contrasted sharply with President George W. Bush's focus on large-donor fund-raising dinners. For example, in 2003 when Bush interrupted a vacation for a fund-raising dinner with a goal of $1 million, Dean's camp challenged Bush's opponents online to match the $1 million mark without the fuss of dinner and shaking hands. Within a week, the Dean campaign had met its target (the average donation was reportedly $50)—all by means of the Internet.

Candidate Web sites feature an online subscriber route that allows supporters to authorize automatic monthly charges to their credit cards for donations. "Another successful technique involves polling members on a timely topic and then tying the expression of opinion to a request for funds to see opinion through to reality," adds Cornfield.

Fund-raisers use e-mail lists to solicit funds for candidates. In California's gubernatorial recall election of 2003, conservative groups e-mailed Internet links to special pages designed to receive contributions for Republican state senator Tom McClintock. MoveOn.org has sought to direct contributions to liberal candidates.

It is possible that the Internet will ultimately provide a route for younger and less affluent citizens to give small amounts to candidates. Yet it is also possible that the Internet will merely make it more convenient for candidates to collect pledged contributions immediately through a simple click of the mouse. At the very least, Internet fund-raising is much faster and far less expensive than traditional fund-raising. It is possible, however, that the Internet will create a major change in fund-raising and giving, much like computerized direct mail did in the 1970s.

1. Michael Cornfield, e-mail interview with Carin Larson, December 2003.

2. Eleanor N. Powell, Lynda W. Powell, Randall K. Thomas, and Clyde Wilcox, "Casting a Broader Net? Fundraising and Contributing through the Internet in the 2000 Presidential Election," paper presented at the annual meeting of the American Political Science Association, San Francisco, August 26, 2001.

money contacting their members and urging them to support particular candidates. Some conduct "nonpartisan" voter mobilization efforts such as the Christian Coalition's distribution of voter guides, and others engage in issue advocacy. In the 2004 campaigns, millions of dollars were spent by the existing interest groups and by newly formed groups to advocate the election or defeat of the two presidential candidates.[13] As noted earlier, these activities need not be financed by individual members of the PAC associated with the group, but can be paid for with any funds the group has.

Candidates ask PACs for money and ask interest groups for other types of support. Incumbent politicians direct their requests toward PACs that have business before their committees, PACs that usually support candidates from their party, PACs with special interests in their state or district, and sometimes PACs that fit none of these criteria. PAC directors are invited to cocktail parties or "meet and greet" sessions. During the vice-presidential debates in 1988, Democratic vice-presidential candidate Lloyd Bentsen admitted that as chair of the Senate Finance Committee he had hosted a series of PAC breakfasts so that those PACs that had given $10,000 to his re-election campaign could meet with him and express their views on tax issues.

Challengers face a more difficult time raising money from PACs, because they usually have no control over public policy and their odds of winning are slim. A core group of PACs does, however, back qualified challengers from a particular party or with a particular ideology. Labor union PACs will usually contribute to any Democratic challenger or, especially, open-seat candidate who seems viable, and some PACs do the same for Republicans. But first the candidates must convince PAC directors that they are viable. Usually candidates invest some of their own money, raise some more from friends and supporters, commission a poll, and then come to Washington with a "PAC Pack" of materials to be distributed to PAC directors. Nonincumbents usually benefit from a patron to host a meeting to introduce them to PAC directors—sometimes another politician from the state or a party leader. If polls show a contest narrowing, the challenger will usually find it easier to raise money. Because the number of competitive contests at all levels of government is limited, the candidates in these races can usually find someone willing to support them.[14]

Political Parties

In many countries, all campaign contributions are channeled through political parties. In the United States, parties play an important role, but they may actually compete with the candidates and interest groups in fund raising. Parties can help candidates in a variety of ways by

- making cash contributions to candidates, although these are limited by law
- offering in-kind assistance, including polls, research about the candidate's opponent, and help in crafting advertisements
- running generic ads that benefit the party
- running candidate-specific ads that are independent of the campaign
- mobilizing party supporters in get-out-the-vote drives that are coordinated with the party's candidates at various levels of government

Political parties form campaign committees at the national, state, and local levels. At the national level, both major parties have separate committees for House and Senate elections, as well as a general party committee. Although the national, state, and local party committees

frequently work together, they are not organized in a strict hierarchy, so that the national committee cannot order a state or local party committee to spend money in a particular way or to channel more support to a particular candidate.

Party resources are not infinite, and in most elections many more candidates seek full support than either party can afford to fund. Parties therefore allocate more of their resources to some candidates than to others. Parties generally seek to target their resources where they can do the most good—in close elections. They typically begin by protecting vulnerable incumbents, because these candidates have already proven that they can mount strong campaigns. Parties also offer resources to their competitive nonincumbents, and they may give limited support to candidates with little hope of winning. At the national level, party committees commission regular polls to see which races are close and which are not, and then they redirect their funds accordingly.

In recent years, Republican Party leaders in Congress have asked all safe incumbents in their party to contribute money to the national party committees and to contribute directly to candidates in close races. They also call on the party's most loyal individual and PAC donors to make last-minute contributions to campaigns in which they can do the most good.

Candidates running in contested primary elections do not usually receive support from the parties—the parties remain neutral until the winner is determined. As soon as the nominees are chosen, however, they contact party leaders for assistance. At times, party committees may support a candidate even without a request from the candidate. In 1998, for example, the Democratic Senatorial Campaign Committee ran soft money ads supporting incumbent senator Russell Feingold of Wisconsin, despite Feingold's explicit request that no soft money be used to support his campaign. Democratic activists feared that Feingold was in danger of losing the race and that the Republicans would capture the Senate as a result. Feingold went on to win a close election.[15]

Conclusion

U.S. elections are expensive, and candidates often need to raise substantial sums of money to introduce themselves to the voters, to articulate their issue positions, and to contrast their strengths with their opponents' weaknesses. The amount of money needed by a candidate to be competitive in an election varies widely, and it is not always true that the candidate who spends the most wins. But campaign costs have risen faster than the rate of inflation for many years, and anyone who seeks to win public office must spend at least some time raising money.

This campaign for resources is regulated at the national, state, and sometimes even local levels. These regulations define the rules of the game and help to channel the way money is raised and spent. At the national level, there are contribution limits, disclosure requirements, and partial public funding of presidential elections, but each of these elements presents problems in practice.

Candidates must assess their resources and then target their appeals to potential donors most likely to respond with contributions. Because many donors seek to invest in elections as a way to gain access to policy makers, incumbents have a huge advantage in fund-raising. But challengers who manage to mount competitive campaigns can usually raise enough money to get their messages out, often by appealing to donors who support their issue positions.

There are many established ways to raise money—through direct mail, individual networks, PAC events, and appeals to party leaders—but campaign finance is an ever-changing field. Campaigns are seeking to innovate and to push regulations to their limit in an effort to win. New technology such as the Internet may speed the pace of change in the campaign for resources.

Notes

1. Paul S. Herrnson, *Congressional Elections: Campaigning at Home and in Washington*, 4th ed. (Washington, D.C.: CQ Press, 2004).

2. Clyde Wilcox, "They Did It Their Way: Campaign Finance Principles and Realities Clash in Wisconsin 1998," in *Campaigns and Elections: Contemporary Case Studies*, 45–54 (Washington, D.C.: CQ Press, 2000).

3. Robert Boatright, Michael J. Malbin, Mark J. Rozell, Clyde Wilcox, and Richard Skinner, "Life after Reform: When the Bipartisan Campaign Reform Act Meets Politics," in *BCRA's Impact on Interest Groups and Advocacy Organizations,* ed. Michael J. Malbin (Lanham, Md.: Rowman and Littlefield, 2003).

4. Sidney Verba, Kay Schlozman, and Henry Brady, *Voice and Equality* (Cambridge, Mass.: Harvard University Press, 1995).

5. Soft money contributions could be made only to political parties, not to candidates. Yet very quickly presidential candidates began to raise soft money for their party, and they were then permitted to direct the spending of that money by the party committees.

6. The ability to give treasury funds greatly expanded the ability of corporations and unions to contribute to political campaigns. Companies limited to raising less than $50,000 from their employees through a PAC could suddenly give hundreds of thousands of dollars from their profits instead.

7. The Federal Election Commission makes this information available on its Web site, www.fec.gov. Other organizations such as Citizens for Responsive Politics (http://www.crp .org) organize the information differently and also make it available to citizens. These sites list the individuals and groups that have supported senators and members of the House, and the candidates to whom the National Rifle Association or the National Organization of Women, for example, have given. For a more complete discussion of transparency laws, see Clyde Wilcox, "Campaign Finance Disclosure: Lessons from the United States," paper presented at the Forum for Democracy and Political Finance, Seoul, Republic of Korea, 2001.

8. Clyde Wilcox and Keiko Ono, "Campaigning for Cash amid Chaos? George W. Bush, Campaign Finance Reform, and Presidential Fundraising in 2004," in *Understanding the Presidency,* 3d ed., ed. James P. Pfiffner and Roger Davidson (New York: Addison Wesley Longman, 2004).

9. For a discussion of campaign finance law and its impact on presidential funding, see the report of the Task Force on Financing Presidential Nominations, organized by the Campaign Finance Institute, April 12, 2005, www.cfinst.org/ presidential/index.html (accessed May 10, 2005).

10. For detailed discussions of donors, see Clifford Brown, Lynda Powell, and Clyde Wilcox, *Serious Money Fundraising and Contributing in Presidential Nominating Campaigns* (New York: Cambridge University Press, 1995); and Peter Francia, John Green, Paul Herrnson, Lynda Powell, and Clyde Wilcox, *The Financiers of Congressional Elections: Investors, Ideologues, and Intimates* (New York: Cambridge University Press, 2003).

11. For a description of these three groups of donors, see Francia et al., *Financiers of Congressional Elections.* Many donors give for a mix of motives. For example, a businesswoman might give to one candidate because he serves on a powerful committee in the House, and to a different candidate because of her position on environmental protection, and to still another candidate because they are old friends.

12. For a description of individual PACs and their decision-making strategies, see Robert Biersack, Paul S. Herrnson, and Clyde Wilcox, *Risky Business? PAC Decisionmaking in Congressional Elections* (Armonk, N.Y.: M. E. Sharpe, 1994).

13. Much of this activity was channeled through 527 committees, named after a provision in the U.S. Tax Code. Some of these committees were coalitions of preexisting groups; others were formed for the purposes of the 2004 election only.

14. In 2004 U.S. House races, for example, fewer than twenty-five races were identified in the spring as potentially competitive, but by the end of the campaign that list had shrunk to fewer than fifteen.

15. Wilcox, "They Did It Their Way," 45–54.

Suggested Readings

Biersack, Robert, Paul S. Herrnson, and Clyde Wilcox. *Risky Business? PAC Decisionmaking in Congressional Elections.* Armonk, N.Y.: M. E. Sharpe, 1994.

Boatright, Robert, Michael J. Malbin, Mark J. Rozell, Clyde Wilcox, and Richard Skinner. "Life after Reform: When the Bipartisan Campaign Reform Act Meets Politics." In *BCRA's Impact on Interest Groups and Advocacy Organizations,* edited by Michael J. Malbin. Lanham, Md.: Rowman and Littlefield, 2003.

Brown, Clifford, Lynda Powell, and Clyde Wilcox. *Serious Money Fundraising and Contributing in Presidential Nominating Campaigns.* New York: Cambridge University Press, 1995.

Francia, Peter, John Green, Paul Herrnson, Lynda Powell, and Clyde Wilcox. *The Financiers of Congressional Elections: Investors, Ideologues, and Intimates.* New York: Cambridge University Press, 2003.

Herrnson, Paul S. *Congressional Elections: Campaigning at Home and in Washington,* 4th ed. Washington, D.C.: CQ Press, 2004.

Magleby, David B., ed. *Financing the 2000 Election.* Washington, D.C.: Brookings, 2001.

Malbin, Michael. *Life after Reform: When the Bipartisan Campaign Reform Act Meets Politics.* Lanham, Md.: Rowman and Littlefield, 2003.

Rozell, Mark, and Clyde Wilcox. *Interest Groups in American Campaigns: The New Face of Electioneering.* Washington, D.C.: CQ Press, 1998.

Verba, Sidney, Kay Schlozman, and Henry Brady. *Voice and Equality.* Cambridge, Mass.: Harvard University Press, 1995.

Wayne, Stephen J. "Presidential Elections: Traveling the Hard and Soft Roads to the White House." In *The Interest Group Connection,* 2d ed., edited by Paul S. Herrnson, Ronald Shaiko, and Clyde Wilcox. Washington, D.C.: CQ Press, 2004.

Wilcox, Clyde. "Campaign Finance Disclosure: Lessons from the United States." Paper presented at the Forum for Democracy and Political Finance, Seoul, Republic of Korea, 2001.

———. "They Did It Their Way: Campaign Finance Principles and Realities Clash in Wisconsin 1998." In *Campaigns and Elections: Contemporary Case Studies,* 45–54. Washington, D.C.: CQ Press, 2000.

Wilcox, Clyde, and Keiko Ono. "Campaigning for Cash amid Chaos? George W. Bush, Campaign Finance Reform, and Presidential Fundraising in 2004." In *Understanding the Presidency,* 3d ed., edited by James P. Pfiffner and Roger Davidson. New York: Addison Wesley Longman, 2004.

CHAPTER 16

Polling and Research

Robert M. Eisinger

If elections are battles about political power, then polls are weapons in the candidates' arsenals. They help to determine what candidates say, when they speak, and to whom. When congressional or presidential candidates—regardless of party—visit a church, union hall, or local school auditorium to talk about their vision, values, and views for the future, there is a good chance that their uttered phrases are in part a product of polling or focus group research.

Likewise, the campaign ads run by candidates are the products of political consultants, who, working extensively with pollsters, attempt to forge a coherent, winning image. That image—the candidate's wardrobe, the background music, the kind of typeface used in a TV ad, the tone and accent of the voice on the radio commercial, even whether the candidate's spouse is seen or heard—may be determined by polling and market research.

This is not to say that candidates are beholden to polls or that they stick their fingers in the wind and decide what to say or believe based on the latest poll data. To the contrary, polling research is used to help market candidates. In this sense, it is the intersection of public opinion and public relations that is of special interest to political science students and scholars. Polling helps to identify the issues of interest to voters. Polling and focus group research helps to identify the phrases and messages that resonate with potential voters and those that they find particularly cacophonous or confusing.

This chapter presents an overview of polling and research and, in the process, highlights how political polling and campaign research are inextricably intertwined. Simply put, most successful campaigns use cutting-edge research; unsuccessful campaigns do not. Today, polling research has become a large part of campaign budgets. Those who can afford such research find themselves victorious, singing "Happy Days Are Here Again." Those who lack such resources may find themselves listening to "The Party's Over." Win or lose, candidates now consider polls to be an essential part of their campaigns.

Although some observers have decried polls and polling research as expensive luxuries that distort the political process, they should be viewed as tools by which candidates and their advisers can assess public opinion by using the most accurate and detailed information about citizens' attitudes and opinions. There is no doubt that this information on the pulse of the electorate, especially when it is gathered and analyzed properly, sometimes comes at an expensive price. Yet to run a successful campaign and to govern once elected, a politician must know how to communicate and how to discern what people believe.

The Development of Political Polling

Political polling is a twentieth-century phenomenon. The modern poll emerged in the 1930s, largely from pioneers Elmo Roper, Archibald Crossley, and George Gallup. But members of Congress showed great reluctance to use polls; they found them inaccurate and deleterious to representative democracy. Presidents showed no such resistance, arguably because they did not trust the other institutions that would gauge public opinion if polls were not used. Rather than rely on Congress, parties, the media, or interest groups, presidents seized the opportunity to use polls and led the way toward their becoming an integral part of American politics.

Before the advent of polls, presidents relied heavily on personal interactions, political parties, and the media to assess public opinion, both while campaigning and when governing. The line between campaigning and governing is a blurry one (see box 10-2). The campaigning done by presidents is not always electoral in nature; rather, their public persona demands that they advance their policies and themselves in a positive light at all times. The governing/campaigning distinction is therefore a matter of public relations. Presidents who understand how to assess public opinion are able to market their agendas, even when they are not officially campaigning in the traditional sense. President Abraham Lincoln, for example, described receptions with common people in the White House as his "public opinion baths," because he had "little time to read the papers and gather public opinion that way." He found that the receptions, even "though they may not be pleasant in all the particulars, the effect, as a whole, is renovating and invigorating to my perceptions of responsibility and duty." [1]

President Herbert Hoover had White House executive clerks Rudolph Forster and M. C. Latta measure public opinion by analyzing newspaper content. Forster and Latta read newspaper editorials about various issues, created categories of responses, tabulated how many newspapers shared that point of view, and then added the circulation of those newspapers. For example, in summarizing the editorials about the 1930 congressional elections Hoover's advisers listed eleven categories, one of which was "outcome is rebuke to administration." Fifty-three newspapers with a circulation of over 3.97 million were found to ascribe to that view.[2]

The tabulations of the Hoover White House were an important precursor of the rise of campaign polling. The circulation numbers attached to each issue position were only crude indicators of public opinion—surely not everyone who read a newspaper editorial shared that position. Yet the desire to quantify the qualitative strongly suggests that administration officials sought to measure public opinion, not ignore it. The Hoover archives also reveal the extensive use of straw polls (discussed later in this chapter). These polls were unscientific interviews with persons willing to answer questions about various issues before Congress. For example, passengers on train platforms were asked questions, and those responding were considered to be somewhat representative of a larger voting population. The Hoover archives also contain straw polls sent to the Hoover campaign, in which Hoover was pitted against potential Democratic rivals. These straw polls, and the confidential tabulations of newspaper readers, indicated that the Hoover White House solicited and received what it thought were the most scientific assessments of the public mood.

Invention of Modern Polling

It was not until the Franklin D. Roosevelt administration that the modern poll was invented. George Gallup, one of the pioneers of modern polling, predicted that the *Literary Digest* polls would inaccurately indicate that Republican Alfred Landon would beat Democrat Franklin Roosevelt in the 1936 presidential election. Gallup contended that the *Digest*'s straw polling methods—asking questions of magazine subscribers, automobile owners, and those with telephone service—was doomed to fail, because such persons did not reflect or represent a larger voting population.

In the end, Gallup, who predicted Roosevelt would win, was correct, and it was not long before the Roosevelt administration sought to use representative sampling methods to gauge the public's mood. Hadley Cantril, an-

other polling pioneer who was then director of the Office of Public Opinion Research at Princeton University, helped White House advisers to understand public opinion polls and educated them about where public opinion was located, enabling the administration to market specific policies to specific constituencies. FDR, through his private secretary, Grace Tully, commended Cantril for sending him poll reports, because they kept him "in touch with what people are thinking." [3]

Roosevelt's successor in office, Harry S. Truman, disdained polls, explicitly alluding to the failed *Literary Digest* poll in his *Memoirs:* "When those people vote, they are going to throw the Galluping polls right in the ashcan—you watch 'em. There are going to be more red-faced pollsters on November the 3rd than there were in 1936, when the *Literary Digest* said that Roosevelt shouldn't be elected." [4] Truman's penchant for straight talk did not mean that polls were to take a backseat in his presidential campaign. Rather, his 1948 presidential campaign reviewed media polls, which repeatedly showed Republican New York governor Thomas Dewey defeating President Truman. Yet the pollsters stopped polling a week or so before election day, and the result was the now famous and incorrect "Dewey Defeats Truman" headline. Truman won the election, reinforcing his negative views of polls.

In 1952 the Republican National Committee (RNC) hired advertising agency Batten, Barton, Durstein and Osborn (BBDO) to coordinate advertising for Dwight D. Eisenhower's presidential campaign. After Eisenhower's victory, the RNC contracted BBDO to provide weekly polls with samples of about a hundred persons. Here again, the polls were more primitive than sophisticated in that they asked respondents their vote preferences and a handful of questions about current events. The results of these polls were circulated in the White House.

The intersection between public relations campaigning and the public presidency was further blurred during the Eisenhower era. Sigurd "Sig" Larmon, president of the advertising firm of Young and Rubicam, was a friend of Eisenhower, his chief of staff, Sherman Adams, and pollster George Gallup. Larmon, and occasionally Gallup, provided the Eisenhower White House with Gallup poll data and with interpretations of the data. When Sen. John F. Kennedy considered running for president in 1960, his campaign enlisted pollster Lou Harris. Harris, like Kennedy, believed that a candidate's public image, projected by means of television, was replacing party identification as a primary determinant in how voters chose candidates. He also believed that Kennedy's Catholicism was important to many voters. Specifically, he argued that because party-line voting had waned, candidates such as Kennedy had the know-how to communicate with voters without relying on the party's get-out-the-vote apparatus—that is, the candidate's personality, style, and image would play a vital role in his campaign.

In the end, television, not parties, would get people to vote on election day.

By then, political polls had become a means by which presidential campaigns could develop and test various messages, and Harris tested his theories using polls. Should Kennedy downplay his Catholicism? To what extent should civil rights and the cold war be mentioned? To which audiences? Harris's polls emphasized these points, and his analyses repeatedly recommended ways for Kennedy to improve his already telegenic image. As for religion, Harris's polls asked questions designed to determine who was "bigoted" (Harris's term) and whether these individuals' views were malleable or entrenched. According to Harris, Kennedy could win only by tailoring his rhetoric and campaign strategy to the religious or prejudicial tenor of the state in which he was campaigning.

Harris and his protégé Oliver Quayle, who conducted polling for President Lyndon B. Johnson in 1964, provided detailed qualitative analysis to supplement the poll tabulations. This mixing of qualitative and quantitative analysis was an important juncture in the development of campaign polling and the institutionalization of polling more generally. Polls demand interpretation; pollsters know how to read poll data, but they also have to explain the importance of the numbers to campaign and policy advisers. By meshing the hard data with qualitative explanations, campaigns began to appreciate what polls provided and how they could be useful.

As polling technology advanced and as its currency became more common among political campaigns, parties and campaigns increasingly used polls in some form or another. Richard Nixon's campaign designed an image poll in 1968 to appraise and calculate how citizens viewed the candidate. Once elected in 1968, Nixon's use of polls increased as his administration began to look like a permanent presidential campaign. Polls became important instruments in advancing and marketing both Nixon and his agenda. Many of Nixon's advisers believed that polls were needed to shape the president's image, legislative strategy, and reelection campaign. All of these were intertwined through what Nixon did, with whom he did it, and how he and his agenda were presented in the media. Polls determined which constituencies needed wooing and which ones could be ignored.

President Gerald R. Ford's 1976 campaign further advanced campaign polling research, especially because his pollster used focus groups and dial response meters to evaluate the public mood. During the presidential debates between Ford and his challenger, former Georgia governor Jimmy Carter, focus group participants were given dials with knobs that they were to turn to the right when they liked what they were hearing and to the left when they disliked what they were hearing. The Ford campaign also used focus groups to explore what should be included in the campaign poll. According to Robert Teeter, President Ford's pollster, "The major purpose of

Robert Teeter was an influential pollster who played a major role in seven Republican presidential campaigns—from Richard Nixon's in 1968 to George Bush's reelection campaign in 1992. Source: Albion College Communications Office

the focus groups was to provide information for the development of the questionnaire for the national survey. Various subject areas were tested as to their importance to the group and their relevance to political attitudes. On this basis, the worth of each subject area for inclusion in the questionnaire was evaluated." [5] Teeter understood the importance of assessing public opinion quantitatively and qualitatively. Because of the scope of the presidential race, he had at his disposal the resources needed to employ novel methods to locate the depth of citizens' political attitudes.

Ford's opponent in the race, Jimmy Carter, hired Patrick Caddell, a twenty-five-year-old Harvard graduate who had worked on the George McGovern's campaign in 1972, to serve as his campaign pollster. When Carter won, Caddell became the White House pollster, receiving what was then considered unprecedented access to the Carter White House and Oval Office. As a presidential confidant and political consultant, Caddell provided lengthy poll summaries filled with campaign strategy and sometimes infused with arguments by academics.

The Growth of Campaign Polling

Carter's opponent in the 1980 race, former California governor Ronald Reagan, enlisted the expertise of Richard Wirthlin. Wirthlin's rise marked another critical juncture in the rise of campaign polling. Wirthlin, who

Patrick Caddell was only twenty-five years old when he became Democrat Jimmy Carter's campaign pollster in 1976. After his success in helping Carter to get elected president, he went on to do polling and strategy work for Democratic governors Mario Cuomo and Jerry Brown and senator Gary Hart. Source: Courtesy Jimmy Carter Library

emerged from academia, helped to develop the formal strategy for the 1980 presidential campaign, and, after Reagan won the election, he also directed the planning and strategy unit of the presidential transition. Wirthlin recognized that campaigns needed relevant, timely, and actionable data. In response to that need, he developed a political information system (PINS), which not only provided poll questions and answers, but also enriched that data by integrating historical vote data and demographic data and by employing modeling and simulation techniques to determine whether certain campaign strategies would be effective in increasing the vote for the Reagan-Bush ticket. Presidential campaigns were no longer about which candidate was preferred by citizens from Peoria or El Paso; campaigns now had at their fingertips sophisticated analyses by state, or sometimes even by congressional district or zip code. Wirthlin set the standard for how to run a presidential campaign that employs polling research.

President Bill Clinton took campaign polling to yet another height. According to former Clinton adviser Dick Morris, Clinton was an avid consumer of polls.[6] President Clinton's White House pollster Stanley Greenberg found focus groups "very important to listen to," because they helped him to appreciate the vernacular of the mass public. Greenberg also used dial groups, much like those used by Robert Teeter in the Ford White House, to help him "see people's 'gut' reactions to particular phrases or explanations." [7]

During the 2004 presidential campaign, both President George W. Bush and his Democratic challenger, Sen. John Kerry, used polling research, each seeking a comparative advantage in their search for a winning strategy. Local, state, and congressional candidates who could afford to hire pollsters also did so. It appears that John Kerry's early polling suggested that he exploit his military record. Indeed, the Democratic convention featured Kerry's participation in the Vietnam War. Similarly, President Bush's emphasis on national security and the war on terrorism in a post 9/11 world appears to be market-tested, especially when the media polls showed Bush with a significant advantage over Kerry on defense and security-related policies. Although the records are not yet publicly available, one can safely assume that both candidates poll-tested phrases and themes, not just for their conventions but throughout the fall campaigns. Failing to conduct polling research in an age of the permanent campaign cycle is nothing short of political suicide. Locating what resonates with voters and how to convey ideas—either via retail tactics at the coffee shop or wholesale on the Internet or through the airwaves—demands polling and market research. Born in market research and developed in presidential campaigns, the intersection between public opinion and public relations has become institutionalized and intertwined, perhaps in a Gordian knot. There is little evidence that this knot is going to be untangled, even as scholars debate whether it should be.

The Polling Process

This section outlines the various elements of a public opinion poll. Some of these elements are rooted in statistics (for example, margin of error). Other elements, such as question wording, are the by-product of imaginative minds seeking to devise an instrument that best gauges the opinions of citizens.

Sampling

A well-designed poll asks questions to a sample that represents a larger population. The sampling frame is the population from which a sample is drawn. Campaigns want to know not only what questions to ask, but also, and perhaps more important, whom should be asked. For example, it may be useful to ask questions to registered voters when determining the views of Democrats (or Republicans) in New Hampshire, because registered voters constitute the total universe of eligible New Hampshire primary voters. But do registered voters really vote? The answer is that some do, and many do not. As a result, campaigns screen for likely voters—that is, those people who repeatedly vote in primary and general elections. These voters are often targeted through polls in primaries, because campaigns cannot waste time attracting potential voters if their track records suggest that they are more likely to stay home than go to the polling place on election day.

At times, campaigns target a specific demographic population within a larger population. Some campaigns may wish to poll only African Americans or senior citizens or union members, in addition to or instead of likely voters. Results from these population-specific polls may be used in amending campaign advertisements or in tailoring the candidate's rhetoric to appeal to certain groups that campaign advisers have deemed necessary for victory. Targeting a specific population does not generate a definitive response from a campaign. If a poll shows support within a certain demographic segment, the candidate can opt to build that base or seek to garner votes from the segment in which he or she is less popular. For example, a candidate found to be more popular with middle-aged married men but not older women may decide to visit more senior citizens homes in the hope of generating support from elderly women. Alternatively, a candidate especially popular with middle-aged married men may concentrate on more public meetings with those already supportive married men.

Once a campaign determines what population to poll, it must generate the meaningful questions to be posed to a sufficient number of respondents. According to political scientist Herbert Asher, "Sample size is a major puzzle for Americans who wonder how a national sample of 1,500 respondents can accurately represent the views of 200 million adults. Contributing to the confusion is the fact that an equally accurate statewide survey requires a sample similar in size, even though any state's population is only a small proportion of the national total. . . . Statistical and probability theory explain why such small sample sizes generate valid results." [8]

Rather than explain statistical theory in detail, Asher notes that polls and sampling populations work a lot like blood tests; only a small amount of blood is needed to identify a medical ailment. Likewise, a sample of only a thousand adults provides a reasonable snapshot of a population that exceeds 100 million.

Margin of Error

Polls are not foolproof, nor are they intended to be. In fact, because polls are questions asked to samples of larger populations, there is the possibility that another poll, taken of a similar sample, could yield different results. The better the poll sample replicates the total population, the smaller will be the margin of error. For example, imagine a town named Smithville with a population of one thousand. Fifty percent of the population are women; 50 percent are men. If a pollster attempted to poll all one thousand residents, the poll sample would be identical to the total population.

If only a random sample of four hundred of Smithville's residents are polled instead of all thousand, it is reasonable to surmise that this new poll of four hundred respondents resembles the one thousand residents of Smithville, because the four hundred who are polled are located randomly. Yet even in a random sample, there is a slim possibility that the four hundred citizens polled do not represent all one thousand citizens. Perhaps there are more men in the sample of four hundred (such as 53 percent) than in the total population. If another poll were taken an hour later, with another random sample of four hundred Smithville residents (even if one includes the original four hundred residents who participated in the previous poll among those who could be polled), the question remains, how closely does the new poll of four hundred Smithvillites resemble the total (n = 1,000) population?

The closer the polling sample is to the total population, the lower is the margin of error. However, the margin of error does not have a simple linear relationship with the total population. In this case, the margin of error is defined as the likelihood that the results would be replicated if a poll with an identical sample were taken.

A poll with a margin of error of ± 4 percent means that there is a 95 percent probability that an identical poll, in which all respondents answered questions, would yield the same results, plus or minus four percentage points. Note the importance of how the margin of error is worded and the limitations of what the margin of error is and is not. First, a poll with a 95 percent confidence interval is not "95 percent accurate." Rather a poll with a ± 4 percent margin of error and a 95 percent confidence interval means that 95 out of 100 polls of the same population will generate results that are not necessarily identical to the previous poll, but are still within four percentage points of the theoretical response of the entire population. This also means that 5 percent of all polls taken of that same population may yield results that do not necessarily fall within four percentage points of the true population parameters. The important thing to keep in mind is that the margin of error refers to the margin around the true population parameters, not the results of the original poll. For a poll that looks at a fraction of the total sample population (say, just women), the margin of error is greater because the polled sample is smaller.

Professional public opinion organizations, such as the American Association for Public Opinion Research (AAPOR), the National Council of Public Polls (NCPP), and the World Association of Public Opinion Research (WAPOR), seek to educate journalists and students about what a sampling error is and what it means. Yet in the reporting of polls, margin of error continues to be mistakenly related to voter turnout or question wording.

Questionnaire Design

Asking meaningful campaign poll questions requires both imagination and creativity. Early campaign polls merely asked respondents which candidate they preferred. Today's polls are more sophisticated; in addition to asking the respondent's candidate preference, polls may ask a series of questions about the respondent's positions on certain issues, simultaneously inquiring whether the respondent is aware of the candidate's position on those issues. Polls may also ask whether a certain issue matters to a respondent. Respondents saying "yes" may be asked a series of follow-up questions about their position, and those saying "no" may be further questioned about why an issue is unimportant to them.

Pollsters must pay attention not only to what questions are asked, but also to the order in which they are asked. Question order effects may generate inaccuracies in attitudes. For example, a respondent asked a series of questions about violent crime such as rape and kidnapping may be more likely to respond that criminals deserve stern punishment than if first asked questions about civil liberties and protection of the innocent. Similarly, numerous questions about stresses on the family budget or government waste may harvest responses that favor tax cuts. However, prefacing the tax cut question with a series of questions about providing essential government services such as border protection may yield responses less favorable to tax cuts.

Good pollsters are keenly aware of order effects, and they seek to mitigate their adverse effects, either by randomly ordering lists of certain questions or by producing split ballots, in which part of a sample is polled with questions arranged in one order and another sample is polled with the questions listed in another order.

The wording of poll questions is also vital to the integrity of a poll. In a campaign poll, the question "Don't you think Candidate X has the traits essential to be a public servant?" is likely to evoke an affirmative response, but it is a useless question; campaigns are seeking true, accurate responses. Questions are therefore pretested and often vetted by several people, so they are not produced by one person with one point of view.

In the drafting of poll questions, a few common dos and don'ts endure. First, uneven and double-barreled questions should be avoided. "Do you believe that Candidate X is the best person for the job, or do you believe that all the candidates are worthy of acclaim?" is the type of imbalanced question that campaigns routinely avoid. Because this question comes in two parts, it is not clear from a yes or no answer which part of the question the respondent is answering. Second, poll questions should have a coherent purpose. Why is this question being asked? If the pollster (or the politician's advisers) cannot articulate why the question is asked, chances are that it is an extraneous question, best omitted. Third, poll questions should take into account that most respondents have a limited understanding of issues and of politics more generally. Therefore, questions must be easily understood (acronyms should be avoided whenever possible), and the context should be clear. For example, asking whether the state budget should be cut by 4 percent or by 5 percent is not likely to yield a meaningful response if the respondents do not know what those numbers mean in a context they can comprehend. The goal is to generate a meaningful answer that can be interpreted. Polls that yield a desired answer may appear to serve a public relations goal, but ultimately they have not served to gauge public opinion accurately and therefore must be disregarded as valuable instruments.

Argumentative questions are also discouraged. Pollsters provide respondents with information about an issue or candidate in the hope of educating them so they can provide a meaningful answer. But if the pollster provides too much information, and does so in a blatantly biased way, the pollster may both confuse respondents and prevent them from giving genuine, meaningful responses. The art of asking questions entails providing enough information about an issue or candidate so as to inform without prejudice or bias.

Interviewing

Interviewer effects also can affect the accuracy of a poll. In the early years of polling, interviews were conducted in person, frequently by housewives who knocked on the doors of residents. Today, fewer door-to-door interviews are conducted, and instead polls are often conducted via telephone. Computer-assisted telephone interviewing (CATI) is probably the most common method of conducting telephone interviews. Computers automatically and randomly dial potential respondents. Once the person called agrees to the interview, the interviewer reads the questions on the computer screen and then types the respondent's answers directly into the computer. If a respondent answers a particular question with an "Agree," the computer may automatically ask "Why?" or it may skip a series of questions to another topic. Computer-designed systems ensure that questions are being asked in the correct sequence and allow for faster analysis of results. As CATI systems advance, cost advantages also make CATI a preferred method for interviewing.

Analyzing Poll Data

Most candidates do not read polls; rather, campaigns are increasingly hiring professional pollsters whose sole job is to assess poll data, both from the campaign and from media organizations that conduct their own polls.

With few exceptions, internal poll data (poll data created by and for the campaign) are considered private information and are not released to the public. If a candidate is surging in a poll, then that candidate may wish to share that information with a journalist or reporter, who may disseminate it as news. Poll data that reveal a

DON'T FORGET THAT ELECTION YEAR IS ALSO LIE-TO-THE-POLLSTERS YEAR.

Reprinted by permission of the Detroit Free Press

weakness or shortcoming of the candidate are hidden, read only by the pollster, the key advisers, and consultants. Often, even the candidate is excluded from learning about poll results for fear that the results will prove distracting. Candidates do not live in an isolated bubble, however. By reading articles that describe media polls or listening to radio or television news stories that discuss such polls, candidates and their advisers have a keen sense of who is ahead and who is behind. By reading the nonverbal cues and applause levels of audiences, candidates often have a keen sense of which messages resonate and which ones either fall silent or result in confusion and cacophony. Some politicians, however, enjoy and appreciate poll data. Both Presidents Richard Nixon and Bill Clinton were poll consumers, occasionally providing insights after perusing a poll report.

Types of Polls

Not all polls are alike. Different polls serve different purposes. This section outlines the various types of polls, and their various functions. Note how some of the functions may overlap; campaigns employ these polls in order to gain a strategic advantage over their opponents. When both campaigns are using similar polls, the quality of the

sample, question wording and other elements of the poll (listed above) frequently determine which poll best assesses the public's opinions.

Benchmark Poll

A benchmark poll, the first one a candidate is likely to take, gives a campaign some sense of the contest ahead by answering questions such as: Do people know the candidate's name? What do they think of the candidate? What do they think of the incumbent, assuming there is one?

Often, a benchmark poll reveals that the candidate's name recognition is low, that the incumbent is relatively popular, and that if the election were held today the challenging candidate would lose. The benchmark poll is appropriately used as a guide, not as an instrument that determines the fate of a campaign. Candidates who think they can win will not be discouraged by a poll showing them behind. And challengers cannot expect to have the same high name recognition of an incumbent. Rather, poll readers, including the candidate, use benchmark polls as vehicles for assessing where the campaign has to go, not where it is.

One problem with benchmark polls is that their timing may explain their answers. For example, a nationwide poll taken in February 2001 by those who were running Democratic senator John Kerry's campaign for the presidency would have indicated low name recognition for Kerry (and for his running mate in 2004, Sen. John Edwards of North Carolina) and relative support for newly minted president George W. Bush, who would have been in office for about a month in the middle of what is known as the president's honeymoon period. By contrast, a benchmark poll taken in February 2003, two years after President Bush took office and after Senator Kerry had already crossed and recrossed the country trying to raise money for his presidential bid, probably would have noted slightly higher name recognition for Kerry.

Trend Polls

In pursuing successful execution of its strategy for winning an election, a campaign will design a survey instrument that asks specific questions repeatedly over the course of the campaign. The purpose of such a trend poll (also known as a brushfire poll) is to assess public opinion over time. Although a campaign's polls will ask different questions as the campaign evolves, the merits of asking the same question over time is that the campaign can monitor tendencies or developments in the thinking of the electorate.

The frequency of trend polls depends on how much money a campaign has to spend on polls. Frugal campaigns may monitor trends every three months. Well-bankrolled congressional, senatorial, gubernatorial, or presidential campaigns may poll monthly or almost weekly as the campaign evolves.

Good campaign managers will hire staff to assess cultural or political trends by reading academic and media polls. Sometimes, candidates may confirm their views about the opinions and outlook of the citizenry by reading certain poll questions. For example, a poll may reveal a resistance toward heavy taxation. But such resistance does not mean that citizens want to abolish taxes. A keen poll reader will assess how citizens are reacting to certain issues over time and perhaps detect a willingness to raise taxes for an impending crisis, such as a national security threat or a natural disaster. Similarly, attitudes about sexuality (premarital sex, homosexuality) have also changed drastically over time. A candidate who adopts a position about access to birth control for minors, for example, will benefit from appreciating that public opinion in the twenty-first century looks different than it did twenty or even fifteen years ago. The point here is that good campaigns evaluate poll trends to gauge broader political and social trends within the electorate.

Tracking Polls

Tracking polls are trend polls taken to the extreme. When a campaign wants to test campaign messages, especially as it is reaching its end, it will conduct surveys to see if its messages are being conveyed effectively. Take, for example, a candidate who wants to portray himself as "a man of new ideas" and his opponents as part of the Washington establishment. Convincing the electorate that he is a Washington outsider and that his opponents are Washington insiders will require carefully constructed speeches by the candidate and finely tuned advertisements. Gauging the effectiveness of this campaign strategy and the execution of it will require poll questions asked repeatedly and identically. Tracking polls are just that—questions intentionally asked identically over time, so that the interpretation of the poll results is not marred or subject to question wording. Because tracking attitudes and messages on a daily basis is expensive, some tracking polls employ rolling samples. Rather than poll four hundred persons a day (which is expensive), the campaign will poll one hundred persons each day and then analyze the last four days of results, which amount to a total of four hundred. According to Asher, "One danger of tracking polls is that any single day's interview could be highly aberrant; the candidate and campaign must be careful not to overreact to what might be only a statistical blip." [9]

Today, those campaigns that can afford to conduct tracking polls do so. Campaigns are largely interested in short-term trends and may ask questions such as:

- Will this radio advertisement make listeners think differently about the candidate?
- Will a major foreign policy address that was widely publicized in national newspapers and magazines make the potential voting public think of this presidential candidate as one who understands foreign policy?
- Do people associate the incumbent with a poor voting record after he was accused in a debate of setting the record for the most missed votes among anyone currently holding office?

Tracking polls that answer these questions serve as valuable aids in monitoring the effectiveness of one's campaign strategy.

Focus Groups

The presidential poll reports written in the 1960s by Lou Harris for President Kennedy and by Oliver Quayle for President Johnson often included verbatim passages by poll respondents. Why did these pollsters infuse their quantitative analyses with qualitative assessments? The answer is that the mere cross tabulations and percentage tables did not necessarily explain what respondents were thinking. A pollster who asks people for whom they will vote will get an answer. When a pollster asks why, the answer becomes even richer. When a pollster asks how intensely this opinion is held, the answer becomes even more nuanced. Focus groups, which are not polls, often provide the qualitative depth that underlies much of current survey research.

Focus groups are composed of seven to twelve persons, who talk about a particular issue or issues; a trained moderator facilitates and leads the discussion. The moderator does not try to sway the focus group members in any way, but rather wants them to feel comfortable articulating their views, even if others in the room disagree with that point of view. Because of their small size, focus groups are not a representative sample. A focus group of twelve senior citizens in Iowa, for example, cannot and should not be used to represent the views of all Iowa seniors. Rather, the responses of the focus group are intended to assist the campaign operatives and pollsters who are trying to make sense of poll answers or perhaps are deciding which topics are especially interesting to voters and therefore worth asking in a future poll. An optimal focus group has some sense of homogeneity. Perhaps the group will be composed of blue-collar working men, or stay-at-home women with young children, or senior citizens. Such homogeneity minimizes the factors that may separate members of the group and enhances their candor.

Pollsters and campaign managers sometimes use focus groups to pretest questions, ideas, or themes for a forthcoming campaign. Because focus groups can indicate how prospective voters might respond to alternate ways of phrasing the same political messages, campaigns also use them to plan advertising strategies. One famous focus group question asked group participants what they thought Bill Clinton's favorite color was. One woman

BOX 16-1
GLOSSARY OF POLLING TERMS

benchmark poll Large public opinion survey typically taken at the beginning of a campaign to gauge the initial party, candidate, and policy preferences of constituents. These polls help to shape campaign strategy, because they provide vital information about what kinds of messages will motivate the public.

confidence level Probability that a population parameter actually falls within the margin of error of a sample statistic.

dial group Small group of people who use devices that allow them to register their feelings during a speech, debate, or political advertisement. These groups may not be representative of a constituency or audience, but they can provide detailed information about the kinds of people who appear in the sample.

direct mail Surveys mailed (or e-mailed) to potential voters that rely on voluntary participation by the recipients. The recipients may not therefore be representative of the electorate. Because these polls are relatively inexpensive, public officials commonly use them to measure opinion in their states or districts.

exit poll Survey conducted by media outlets during primary and general elections to project the outcomes before the ballots are tallied. Questionnaires ask respondents about their vote choices, as well as about various demographic factors. The accuracy of these polls depends on the representativeness of both the precincts selected and the respondents at each precinct who participate.

focus group Group composed of seven to twelve persons, who converse about political issues with a trained moderator. The modest size of these groups does not permit a representative sample, but focus groups do provide more detailed information than that produced by traditional survey research. Because focus groups can indicate how prospective voters will respond to alternate ways of phrasing the same political messages, for example, campaigns use them to plan advertising strategies.

media rating Survey that provides information about television viewership in a market, as well as demographic information about the audience. Such ratings are used to determine the costs and target audiences for political television advertisements.

push poll Unscientific poll conducted by a political campaign under the pretense of objectivity. Although such polls may provide evidence about how constituents intend to vote in an upcoming election, the main purpose of these polls is to disseminate political propaganda that either benefits those conducting the poll or damages the campaign of an opponent.

recruitment survey Poll conducted by political parties very early in the campaign cycle to provide potential candidates with information about the viability of their candidacies.

sample Subset of observations or cases drawn from a specified population.

straw poll Although people use this term to refer generally to polls with a large but unscientific sample, the main usage in politics applies to surveys conducted among the membership of a political party. Because of this poll's sampling methods, its results cannot be generalized to the entire population, but they are useful for determining which issues, messages, or candidates can motivate the party faithful.

tracking poll Poll taken frequently during the latter stages of a campaign to monitor public reactions to various political events such as speeches and political advertisements.

trend poll Poll taken intermittently during a campaign after the benchmark poll. These polls examine changes in mood and issue and vote preferences that occur throughout the campaign process.

Sources: Jeffrey A. Fine and D. Stephen Voss, "Politics, Use of Polls in," *Encyclopedia of Social Measurement,* ed. Kimberly Leonard (San Diego, Calif.: Academic, 2003); Janet Buttolph Johnson, Richard A. Joslyn, and H. T. Reynolds, *Political Science Research Methods,* 4th ed. (Washington D.C.: CQ Press, 2001).

---

answered, "Plaid." This answer apparently was interpreted by many Republican operatives as indicating that President Clinton flip-flopped on issues and ultimately could not be trusted to give a straightforward answer. The answer by one woman did not, however, set off a firestorm or radical departure in the GOP's campaign strategy. Similarly, focus groups have revealed that the term *death tax* resonates more with Republicans than the term *estate tax*. Those who want to repeal this tax emphasize abolishing the death tax, in part because qualitative and quantitative analysis indicates that the term *death tax* generates more sympathy for its abolishment. Thus the "death tax" response from focus groups captured something deeper and more subtle—something that was not as readily identifiable by a poll question. Focus groups therefore serve as instruments for campaigns to locate (unrepresentative) attitudes and opinions, to test the intensity of existing attitudes, and to test-market phrases or campaign messages not yet in the field.

Exit Polls

Exit polls attempt to find out, once people leave the polls, how they voted. These polls also record the demographic characteristics—including gender, race, and age—of the respondents.

The merits of exit polls as instruments for media, scholarly, and campaign analyses are easily recognizable. Media pundits and political reporters assess who voted for whom, and they may use the exit poll data to predict the winner of a certain election (see chapter 13). Campaign operatives use exit polls as the ultimate test of their campaign strategy (for example, did farmers vote for candidate X or Y?). Political scientists and survey researchers use exit polls largely as trend polls, gauging, for example, whether the female electorate is becoming more Republican over time or whether union members are remaining loyal to Democratic Party candidates.

Exit polls generate controversy and at times contempt. In 1980 the exit poll results on election day showed Ronald Reagan defeating incumbent president Jimmy Carter. Media outlets announced the winner based on the exit poll returns, and President Carter conceded the election before some of the polls had closed on the West Coast. Some western Democrats blamed the media for announcing a Republican victory, and they blamed Carter as well. By not postponing his concession speech until all the voting had ceased, Carter may have hurt Democrats running for other state and local races, in which fewer persons vote than in presidential races.

In the 2000 election, the Voter News Service (VNS) conducted exit polls in Florida, and various media outlets sought to predict the outcome of the Florida vote, especially because the outcome of the presidential race between George W. Bush and Al Gore appeared to depend on the outcome in Florida (see page 226, *n*42). At first, the television networks declared Gore the winner in Florida. But later in the evening that projection was rescinded, and Bush was declared the victor. Still later in the evening, that prediction was also rescinded, leaving Florida as a toss-up, even as the polls were closing. The media's attempts to predict the Florida vote based on exit polls were controversial for several reasons. First, because of the closeness of the election, and of the Florida vote in particular, any projection was likely to anger or upset the opposition party. Second, VNS's survey methods were ultimately questioned. Meanwhile, pundits and commentators with little or no experience in understanding poll sampling found themselves relying on survey methodologists to explain how polls work and how they are not foolproof. Third, and perhaps most important, the media's desire to best each other at predicting and announcing the winner revealed itself before the world. Al-

though the media pollsters and VNS sought accuracy and excellence, the viewing public saw a crass race among networks to be first to predict a winner, even when, in hindsight, the Florida race looked like a tie. Despite the many reputable survey methodologists who worked at VNS, it ultimately disbanded, because the negative publicity and the ensuing controversy proved too much for it to endure.

Problems also plagued the 2004 exit polls, which were coordinated by Joe Lenski of Edison Media Research and Warren Mitovsky of Mitovsky International. Both Lenski and Mitovsky produced a report that details the human errors encountered in the 2004 exit poll sampling.[10] These dilemmas included the distance between the exit pollsters and the polling places and the pollsters' youth, which, it is believed, created a selection bias of who was polled and who was not.

Push Polls

Unscientific polls conducted by political campaigns under the pretense of objectivity are known as push polls. Unlike all of the other polls described in this chapter, the goal of a push poll is to disseminate negative information about an opponent under the guise of a legitimate poll rather than attempting to locate a genuine opinion. The poll itself becomes a piece of political propaganda, designed to manipulate the respondent in order to elicit a specific answer.

In a state legislative race in Oregon in 2002, for example, one candidate conducted a poll in which Republican primary voters were asked, "Would you vote for X if you knew he was for abortion for children?" Another question asked voters if they would vote for this candidate if they knew he was a gay rights advocate. The ethical nature of these questions was suspect largely because they suggested that the candidate advocated certain policies and subscribed to a particular point of view that he did not. It is possible that this campaign actually wanted to pretest a negative campaign message—that is, the campaign may have wanted to determine whether attacking its opponent for being soft on crime or weak on education issues would resonate with voters. But the push poll is in itself a negative campaign message. Having successfully raised questions to voters under the guise of a legitimate poll, the initiator of the push poll often demands that the push polling cease, leaving the victim of the push poll in a position of having to respond to the accusations or having to decry a method that is already being discredited by the campaign that used the push poll.

Push polls are easy to create, usually quick (under a minute), and have a large sample size in the hope of spreading the misinformation to as many citizens as possible. Such negative campaign tactics are increasingly common, even though the AAPOR, the NCPP, and the American Association of Political Consultants (AAPC) have all formally denounced push polls. There is a fine line between a legitimate poll that presents poll respondents with negative but accurate information and a push poll in which the information provided is factually dubious. As a result, push polls are often criticized and denounced, but all too often they are employed in close races in which a campaign seeks to discredit its opponent with little time for the opponent to respond.

Other Types of Research

Although the modern campaign employs more polls than ever, campaign research extends beyond polling. This section outlines the various types of campaign tactics that are related to polling. Each type of research is often used in tandem with polling, but it can be used separately as well. By learning about their opponents' pasts and the districts in which they are campaigning, political candidates seek to amass a sum of knowledge—positive and negative.

Opposition Research

Perhaps the most common form of research conducted in a campaign is that seeking information about the opponent to use to the advantage of the campaign. There are two forms of opposition research (also known as "oppo" or "OR")—political and personal.

Political Opposition Research

Anyone running for office wants to know as much about the opponent as possible. If the opponent has already held office, then opposition researchers will probe the opponent's voting record. Has the opponent voted inconsistently? Do votes on a specific issue reveal a pattern? If so, is this pattern inconsistent with the attitudes of the constituency or citizenry (that is, is it too liberal or too conservative)? State legislators and members of Congress, for example, vote frequently—sometimes thousands of times during each legislative session when subcommittee votes, full committee votes, and floor votes are included. Moreover, often legislators will vote for a bill in committee because of a deal struck to advance it to the full legislative body, only to vote against the bill in the floor vote. It is the job of opposition researchers to discover these ostensible "inconsistencies."

Much like campaign polling research, opposition research is a private enterprise that is rarely broadcast to a broader audience, unless doing so is part of a larger campaign strategy. A campaign may not immediately disseminate its findings, opting instead to inform the press when the campaign believes release of the information would most hurt the opponent (such as the day after the opponent holds a press conference aimed at scoring a campaign success).

In addition to locating inconsistent or difficult-to-explain votes, opposition researchers also look for votes not taken. Although all legislators miss votes, voters may view a pattern of absenteeism as indicative that an office-holder is not doing his or her job or is not taking it seriously. Explaining absenteeism is a challenge, because the response often sounds like an awkward justification or rationalization, even if the reason for not voting is legitimate.

Opposition research also entails identifying with whom a candidate has cosponsored legislation. Such information is vital if one campaign wants to insinuate that the opposition candidate is not a loyal party member. Although it was once common for senators to cosponsor legislation with members of the other party, today's politically charged atmosphere means that a Republican who cosponsors with a liberal Democrat runs the risk of being mocked by members of his or her own party. Likewise, a Democrat who crosses the aisle may be "guilty" of association with a conservative Republican. Nevertheless, members of the U.S. Senate frequently work with members of the opposite party to sponsor bills and pass legislation. Alleging that an incumbent has befriended or is too closely allied with a colleague who is an ideological rival may indicate the sense of collegiality and bipartisanship that traditionally has characterized the U.S. Senate rather than the notion that the incumbent is not a loyal party member. Although campaigns are not likely to be won or lost based on bill sponsorship, this form of opposition research, especially in primaries, is part of a larger campaign strategy designed to raise doubts about the credibility of the opponent.

Perhaps the most damaging form of political opposition research is the search for statements in the public record. Campaigns sift through public speeches, televised press conferences, off-the-cuff comments made at athletic events, casual remarks made to reporters, and any other form of articulated utterances that can be verified. One of the more telling examples of damaging information that emerged during the 2004 presidential race was Senator Kerry's description of legislation that came before the Senate about funding of the Iraq war. Before a crowd of supporters, Kerry noted that he had voted for the bill before he had voted against the bill. Talk radio hosts repeated Kerry's utterance as if it were manna from heaven, in part because it perpetuated the impression of Kerry as a flip-flopper. However, Senate experts, Democrats and Republicans alike, know that senators sometimes vote legislation out of committee, but then vote against it when it comes before the full Senate body. Senator Kerry did not intend his votes to be used as political dynamite, and he spent much of the fall campaign season decrying the Iraq war. Yet the damage to his campaign stemmed not just from his votes, but from his own words in attempting to explain his votes. In addition, some Vietnam veterans who opposed Kerry formed a group, the Swift Boat Veterans for Truth, who conducted opposition research about Kerry's Vietnam days. Some of the veterans interviewed questioned the veracity of statements made by Kerry years ago. Kerry's campaign then retaliated, contending that some of those interviewed who were refuting details about who was where and when were not actually at the specific locales in question and so could not definitively determine what transpired and when. The opposition research probably hurt Kerry more than his opponents, not because of the truth or untruth of the statements uttered, but because the opposition research by the anti-Kerry veterans, combined with Kerry's statements about his war-related votes, made Kerry's Vietnam service a polarizing issue and made undecided voters question Kerry's commitment to issues about war more generally.

Campaign finance is another ripe area for opposition research. The Federal Election Commission (FEC) requires federal candidates to declare the sources of all campaign contributions and how the money was spent. Opposition researchers thus spend hours combing the FEC records in the hope of finding a contribution made by a seedy character or by a questionable interest group. Here again, locating the "dirt" is all too easy, and sometimes reaches comical proportions. In 2004 the *New York Times* reported that Democrat John Edwards had announced that he had not taken a "dime" from lobbyists, when he received thousands of dollars from trial lawyers. Similarly, John Kerry made fighting special interests a key part of his stump speech, even though his campaign (and all of the Democrats running in 2004) received some funds from persons associated with advocacy causes and interests.

The best of opposition research is not amassed and then distributed via a press release. Instead, it is forwarded to a reporter, who then checks the facts and disseminates them in a modified context. By using the media as a vehicle to advance the opposition research, the campaign has legitimized the research without appearing to be soiling the opposition. Lee Atwater, former chair of the Republican National Committee, used to boast of his ability to locate damaging research about Democratic candidates. Atwater's acumen at identifying and procuring such information remains today the gold standard for all campaigns, regardless of party. Indeed, all campaigns at all levels thoroughly look into the sources of their opponents' campaign funds and attempt to discern if they jibe with the opponents' public records.

Personal Opposition Research

In addition to trying to learn more about opponents' political records, campaigns often investigate their opponents' personal lives. Did a candidate make claims about education or employment history that turned out to be exaggerated or untrue? Did a candidate who emphasizes family values commit adultery? There is limited evidence that citizens are turned off by this so-called dirty politics and its inclusion in political discourse. Nevertheless, such opposition research is not likely to go away, in part because citizens often admit that they vote for or against candidates because of these revelations despite their disdain for them.

In 1988 Sen. Joseph Biden of Delaware campaigned for the Democratic presidential nomination and gave several speeches that were similar to those made by Neil Kinnock, a Labour Party leader in England. Accusations that Biden plagiarized these speeches were compounded by a leak to the media by a law professor who claimed that Senator Biden had also plagiarized text when he was a law student at Syracuse University. Biden ultimately dropped out of the race.

Sometimes the personal information concerns a career path. The 2002 race between incumbent senator Max Baucus, a Democrat from Montana, and his Republican opponent, Mike Taylor, received widespread news coverage when the Baucus campaign distributed an unflattering feminine portrayal of Taylor wearing an anachronistic 1970s leisure suit when he was a hair stylist. Taylor ultimately dropped out of the race, and Baucus ran unopposed. Former Democratic senator Max Cleland of Georgia, campaigning for Senator Kerry in 2004, argued that President Bush's record during his National Guard service was a legitimate campaign issue. Although Bush's National Guard service record had been the subject of controversy for many years, Senator Cleland's public campaign proclamations legitimized the campaign strategy beyond rumors among journalists.

Drug use and sex are also considered fair game when trying to debilitate a campaign opponent. Examples abound. In 1988 Democratic presidential candidate Michael Dukakis found himself discussing his wife's addiction to pain killers. During the 1984 Democratic presidential nomination race, photos appeared of Colorado's Democratic senator Gary Hart aboard a boat called *Monkey Business* with a woman who was not his wife. Hart soon found himself answering questions about his marital fidelity. Bill Clinton's 1992 presidential bid was marked by the discovery of Gennifer Flowers, who alleged that she had sex with Clinton when he was governor of Arkansas. Clinton's campaign responded by denying what it called repeated "bimbo eruptions." During his 2000 presidential bid, George W. Bush was the subject of allegations of cocaine use. And then there was Louisiana governor Edwin Edwards, known in many circles to be fond of entertaining women. But Edwards made light of his behavior, once declaring that the only way for him to lose an election "was if they caught me in bed with a dead girl or a live boy." [11] Once again, many of these events may first have been revealed by hardworking journalists who, without any assistance from campaigns, dutifully investigated issues and brought them onto the national stage. Yet a successful opposition research campaign works through the media, further blurring the lines between public relations and public opinion, as well as the role of the press and the campaigns about which they are reporting.

Most candidates cannot afford to be as glib as Edwards (who later was sentenced to prison for taking kickbacks), nor do they possess his charisma, wit, and charm. Allegations of misconduct can ruin and end a previously viable campaign. Campaign advisers sometimes warn candidates fearful of revelations to come clean, hoping that voter exposure to the candidates' skeletons will immunize the candidates from further damage. Candidates rarely heed this advice, however, because they see what transparency yields—losing campaigns.

District Research

Not all research conducted by campaigns is confrontational, oppositional, or hostile in nature, but it can be tedious. Many of the student interns, volunteers, or paid staffers working on a campaign are often asked to research the campaign district itself. A mayoral candidate, for example, needs to know how many Democrats, Republicans, and independents live in the town or city. How many residents recently moved here? What is their party registration? How many people voted in the last election? In the last three elections? How many were Republicans? Democrats? Which precincts have the most registered Democrats? Republicans?

Such information is gathered by the County Board of Elections office, or perhaps by the local party organization. This information is vital for a successful campaign. A Republican campaign undertaking a door-to-door campaign during a primary season should not be canvassing neighborhoods with large numbers of Democrats (who will not be voting for the Republican candidates in the primary). If a campaign wants to target new immigrants, it needs to know where they are living, whether they are registering to vote, and, if so, under what party label. In congressional and statewide races, this information becomes invaluable, especially for tracing trends of what are becoming heavily Democratic or Republican neighborhoods.

Just as party registration and voting records are essential for a successful campaign, so too is demographic information (see Chapter 7). Successful candidates know their districts. How many seniors live in the campaign district? Women? Minorities? Farmers? The best way to know a district is to live in it. But because geographic boundaries make knowledge of a region difficult, a successful campaign must rely on information that the candidate cannot obtain from personal experience. A senator from New York, for example, may live in Manhattan or Buffalo, but cannot reasonably be expected to live in both places at the same time. That senator's campaign organization needs to know the demographics of the state, recognizing that this knowledge is no substitute for personally amassed data.

This information is employed in many different ways. Perhaps the campaign wants to target certain minority voters with a mailing and so it needs to know where they live. Perhaps the candidate has just spent time learning about a particular military issue, or has traveled abroad as part of a diplomatic mission. Knowing where the military bases are, where the American Legion hall is located, or whether the state's large employer is a defense contractor is necessary not just for a campaign but, once the candidate is elected, to be an effective legislator or chief executive.

Conclusion: The Strategic Uses of Research

Campaigns are rarely won or lost based on one nugget of information. Rather, they are a collective operation. A successful campaign must present a winning message in order to get voters to the polls to cast a ballot for its candidate. That message varies and ranges in tone: "I am more experienced than my opponents." "I am new; they are old." "It is time for change." "If it ain't broke, don't fix it." These are but a few of the campaign themes and messages that are evoked in campaigns, both the successful and unsuccessful (see Chapter 14).

A critical function of polling and research is to help develop those messages. A campaign with a detached, unintelligent candidate will have great difficulty winning, even with meticulous campaign research and the best pollsters. Deep pockets do not guarantee campaign victories either. Republican John Connolly of Texas ran for his party's presidential nomination in 1980 and spent $12 million, only to procure one GOP delegate.[12] In 1994 Michael Huffington, a California Republican, spent over $30 million in his unsuccessful bid for the U.S. Senate. Thus ample campaign funds do not necessarily translate into victory. Rather, the types of research described in this chapter reveal how polling, research, and message development are intertwined. A wise candidate with good ideas who does not know how to convey those ideas clearly to disparate audiences may lose the election. A campaign organization that knows the issues, knows detailed information about the other candidates, and appreciates how public opinion moves is more likely to find itself victorious.

Finally, no election district is homogeneous, either demographically or attitudinally. Campaign polling and research often break down the data—that is, assessing where the college students live, who the likely voters are, what they believe, and how their views differ from new voters or nonvoters. The research is used to help campaigns target various constituencies. Rather than thinking of a district as one space in which votes are to be tabulated, a keen pollster assesses a region (local, state, or nation) as a place to target messages to groups of voters. Seniors receive one mailing, immigrants perhaps another. Speeches on college campuses may emphasize one issue and addresses to veterans another.

The cynical or the disenchanted claim that such campaign tactics are the reason why people do not vote, or why they believe public servants are disingenuous. Political scientists and campaign managers, however, find the strategic use of polling and research to be a refined craft that enhances representative democracy.

In their ground-breaking 1940 work *The Pulse of Democracy: The Public-Opinion Poll and How It Works*, George H. Gallup and Saul Forbes Rae argued that polls would be the antidote to democratic woes.[13] Rather than rely on unrepresentative interest groups or ideologues, polls would ensure representativeness, because they would elicit the voice of the people. Scholars continue to debate whether Gallup and Rae's sanguine view of polling has endured, but polls are an endemic part of present-day campaigns, and opposition research has its place within every campaign operation.

Notes

1. Mario Cuomo and Harold Holzer, eds., *Lincoln on Democracy* (New York: HarperCollins, 1990), 285.

2. Robert M. Eisinger, *The Evolution of Presidential Polling* (New York: Cambridge University Press, 2003).

3. Franklin Delano Roosevelt Library Archives, PPF, Box 5470, 1943, Hyde Park, N.Y.

4. Harry S. Truman, *Public Papers of the Presidents of the United States: Harry S. Truman: 1945–1953* (Washington, D.C.: Government Printing Office, 1966), 920.

5. Gerald R. Ford Library, Forward and Overview (I), U.S. National Study, February 1975, Robert Teeter Papers, Box 51, Ann Arbor, Mich.

6. Dick Morris, *Behind the Oval Office: Winning the Presidency in the Nineties* (New York: Random House, 1997).

7. Greenberg quoted in James A. Barnes, "Polls Apart," *National Journal*, July 10, 1993, 1751, 1753.

8. Herbert Asher, *Polling and the Public: What Every Citizen Should Know*, 6th ed. (Washington, D.C.: CQ Press, 2004), 70.

9. Herbert Asher, *Polling and the Public: What Every Citizen Should Know*, 5th ed. (Washington, D.C.: CQ Press, 2001), 120.

10. This report is available at www.exit-poll.net (accessed May 13, 2005).

11. See John Maginnis, *The Last Hayride* (Baton Rouge, La.: Dark Horse Press, 1984).

12. See L. Sandy Maisel and Charles Bassett, eds., *Political Parties and Elections in the United States: An Encyclopedia* (New York: Garland Publishing, 1991), 190.

13. George H. Gallup and Saul Forbes Rae, *The Pulse of Democracy: The Public-Opinion Poll and How It Works* (New York: Simon and Schuster, 1940).

Suggested Readings

Asher, Herbert. *Polling and the Public: What Every Citizen Should Know.* 6th ed. Washington D.C.: CQ Press, 2004.

Barnes, James A. "Polls Apart." *National Journal*, July 10, 1993, 1750–1754.

Bishop, George F. *The Illusion of Public Opinion: Fact and Artifact in American Public Opinion.* Lanham, Md.: Rowman and Littlefield, 2005.

Cantril, Albert H. *The Opinion Connection: Polling Politics and the Press.* Washington, D.C.: CQ Press, 1991.

Eisinger, Robert M. *The Evolution of Presidential Polling.* New York: Cambridge University Press, 2003.

Gallup, George H., and Saul Forbes Rae. *The Pulse of Democracy: The Public-Opinion Poll and How It Works.* New York: Simon and Schuster, 1940.

Geer, John G. *From Tea Leaves to Opinion Polls.* New York: Columbia University Press, 1996.

Ginsberg, Benjamin. *The Captive Public: How Mass Opinion Promotes State Power.* New York: Basic Books, 1986.

Heith, Diane J. *Polling to Govern: Public Opinion and Presidential Leadership.* Stanford, Calif.: Stanford University Press, 2004.

Herbst, Susan. *Numbered Voices: How Opinion Polling Has Shaped American Politics.* Chicago: University of Chicago Press, 1993.

Hitchens, Christopher. "Voting in the Passive Voice: What Polling Has Done to Democracy." *Harper's*, April 1992, 45–52.

Jacobs, Lawrence R., and Robert Y. Shapiro. "The Rise of Presidential Polling: The Nixon White House in Historical Perspective." *Public Opinion Quarterly* 59 (1995): 163–195.

Moore, David W. *The Superpollsters: How They Measure and Manipulate Public Opinion in America.* New York: Four Walls Eight Windows, 1992.

Robinson, Matthew. *Mobocracy: How the Media's Obsession with Polling Twists the News, Alters Elections, and Undermines Democracy.* Roseville, Calif.: Prima/FORUM, 2002.

Roll, Charles W., Jr., and Albert H. Cantril. *Polls: Their Use and Misuse in Politics.* New York: Basic Books, 1972.

Stonecash, Jeffrey M. *Political Polling: Strategic Information in Campaigns.* Lanham, Md.: Rowman and Littlefield, 2003.

CHAPTER 17

Campaign Communications

Amy E. Jasperson

Mass media communications are important for setting a campaign agenda, framing a debate, and activating values and beliefs that serve as the foundation for evaluating candidates. Candidates give speeches and utilize extended and sophisticated political advertising plans. A variety of political actors, including candidates, interest groups, and parties, have become major players in the political communication game. Any complete explanation of the dynamics of campaigns must rely on a close look at the role that campaign communications play in the outcome of elections.

Based on the nature of campaigns today, it is difficult to realize that political communication did not begin with television. Since the speeches of the first political campaigns, mass media communications have evolved significantly in form and reach as the technology has changed with the times. The content and format of speeches have evolved to fit the medium through which the message is communicated. During the eighteenth and nineteenth centuries, candidate speeches and public debates between candidates were the primary methods for communicating messages to voters. For example, during the famous Lincoln–Douglas debates in the 1858 U.S. Senate race in Illinois, incumbent senator Stephen A. Douglas debated unknown challenger Abraham Lincoln in a series of seven debates across the state. The two candidates met head-to-head to argue differing positions on the issue of slavery. In each debate, the candidates spoke for one and a half hours, an amount of time unheard of in today's campaign context.

By the 1920s, debates were broadcast nationally on radio. The first significant televised debate took place in 1960 between presidential candidates Richard Nixon and John F. Kennedy. In the end, the interpretation of who won the debate depended on which medium—television or radio—voters were using. Those who watched the debate reported that Kennedy had won because he wore makeup, looked comfortable, and projected a confident, easy-going yet authoritative style. Those who listened on the radio felt that Nixon had won because they judged the event based solely on content. In this case, the television medium had a large impact on the perceptions of the public. Since that time, television has propelled the visual image into the forefront of modern-day campaign communications.

Advertising has undergone a similar transformation in response to advances in communications technology. As early as the 1800s, handbills and newspaper ads were used as the first form of political advertising. Because campaigns in that era were party-centered, campaign messages were strongly party-oriented; details about the traits of candidates were afterthoughts. Furthermore, candidates used very few advertisements—often just a single print ad for the shorter campaign season—during their campaigns. By contrast, modern campaigns employ a variety of advertising media over a much longer time period. In the 2002 election cycle, some candidates were already engaged in forms of political advertising nearly a year before election day.

By the 1950s, newspaper and radio were the primary vehicles for advertising. Early in this decade, 43 million homes had radios, making it the best medium for delivering controlled messages to a broad range of voters nationwide. Yet after the 1952 election, television advertising surged as the number of households with televisions increased to nineteen million, bringing candidates into living rooms and reinforcing the shift to candidate-centered campaigns: "The candidate changed from two-dimensional flatness to three-dimensional roundness, and from being distant to being close. . . . Television ads made the candidates and those personal qualities far more immediate and interesting." [1] By the 1970s, television had superceded other media as the dominant form of political advertising. In presidential primaries, candidates spent 70 cents of every advertising dollar on television spots.[2] Research on campaign spending for that decade indicates that during the general election a television ad typically ran five minutes. The thirty-second spot, which is the standard today, and the sixty-second spot were the popular formats during the primaries.[3]

By 1992, the greatest changes were apparent in new production techniques and the increased use of story-telling, a format well suited to the television medium. Although references to political parties in advertising had been declining, by the 1990s there were virtually no references to parties. In addition, scholars noted an increase in the use of negative political advertising against a candidate's opponent. In the 1990s, more than 50 percent of spots were negative in tone, and both incumbents and challengers employed such tactics. Furthermore, negative exposure was no longer being introduced only at the end of the campaign as a means of moving late-deciding voters. Some scholars pondered the impact of such campaign tone on democracy.[4] However, other research reveals that defining advertising in terms of simple negative and positive categories oversimplifies the nature and impact of the ads.[5]

The 1990s also saw the media increasingly covering political advertising messages as news stories (also see Chapter 13). In fact, print and television news created a new story format called the "ad watch" to evaluate the accuracy of political ads. Typically, ad watches focused on negative advertising, because media tended to concentrate on stories filled with drama and conflict. Ideally, the news would evaluate the credibility and accuracy of a message, but some studies showed that the news stories only amplified the sponsoring candidate's message. Other studies took issue with this conclusion, arguing that when the media do take a highly critical tone toward a candidate's negative ad campaign, the public may be more likely to punish the sponsoring candidate for "running a negative campaign."[6]

Meanwhile, political parties reasserted their role in campaigns by sponsoring ads paid for by "soft money," or money not regulated by federal law (see Chapter 6 for a full description of campaign finance). In addition, interest groups became involved in the campaign process by running ads advocating for particular issues rather than for candidates. Both types of ads have the effect of helping or harming political candidates.

This chapter examines the important role of mass media communications in political campaigns. In particular, carefully crafted speech content, presentation style, and audience targeting are essential for successful campaign outcomes. The effectiveness of political advertising messages also depends on the selection of venue, type of message, targeting of the audience, timing, and tone. Although speechmaking and advertising continue to change as communications technologies evolve, they will remain essential components of modern political campaigns. Future studies in mass media communications will continue to examine these factors as they trace the evolution of political campaigns over time.

Speechmaking

Speechmaking is the most fundamental form of campaign communication. Candidates are repeatedly called on to speak during their campaigns. Through personal speeches, candidates frame their messages and communicate directly with the voters. Campaign planners must decide whether candidates or their surrogates will speak, where candidates will speak, when they will speak, and to whom they will address their messages. All decisions are subject to careful consideration and planning, because the candidate's time and schedule are some of the most important resources of a campaign. The content of speeches is another important consideration. Particularly in campaigns for the higher levels of public office, the ultimate goal is to obtain "free media" or press coverage of a speech so that the candidate's message is communicated to a wider audience. If media coverage is possible, candidates and their campaign consultants must be aware that their message could be disseminated to a much wider audience than originally anticipated.

Precinct Targeting

In determining where to speak, candidates rely on voter statistics to target their likely support. Candidates want to concentrate most of their time in areas of party strength and in places with high percentages of swing, or persuadable, voters. Candidates are most likely to speak in the swing districts and to send surrogates to speak on their behalf in the areas in which voters are already strongly leaning toward the candidate. In the elections for lower levels of public office, such as city council or state legislative races, candidates can obtain targeting data to determine key precincts and then enjoy the benefit of being able to meet with constituents face-to-face, interacting and listening directly to them. In some areas, candidates and surrogates can even reach many constituents by knocking on doors. This type of communication provides a sense of responsiveness and gives voters personal knowledge of the candidate. The candidate's message then spreads through word-of-mouth communication between neighbors. In higher-level races, it is impossible to meet all constituents directly, and so candidates are more likely to think in terms of broad appeals to larger audiences through the media.

Whatever the level of the race, candidates rely on important party data about voters' past behavior in deciding where to spend their time speaking at events and how to focus their messages. Important data could include the percentage of Republican and Democratic voters per precinct, and past turnout figures from similar elections. These figures provide a sense of the general party breakdown for precincts and the percentage of turnout that can be anticipated (also see Chapters 7 and 8).

In general terms, candidates focus on the voters who will provide the 50 percent plus one of the vote needed to win the election, and they attempt to locate these voters in the most concentrated number of precincts. Another rule of thumb is that campaigns should target about 70 percent of precincts and ignore about 30 percent of the others based on party breakdown. Candidates focus their energies only where they have a reasonable chance of winning votes. For example, a Democrat will tend to speak in districts that vote moderately to heavily Democratic and will not waste his or her time in a precinct that is heavily Republican. Both candidates will, however, target swing districts—those with equal levels of voters from both parties.

Speech Content and Presentation

Once candidates have identified their key constituents, they must craft a persuasive message. In its most basic form, a speech is a conversation between the candidate and the voter. It should provide genuine insight into the values and motivations of the candidate—values and motivations that the candidate preferably shares with the audience. Especially in higher-level elections, candidates use public opinion polls to identify the issues and concerns of the electorate as well as to test the most effective arguments for persuading voters.

Although content is important for candidates' speeches, style is an often neglected factor for those who strive to be effective speakers. Experts in speech consulting offer three rules for successful speeches. First, establish a bond with the audience. Only 7 percent of candidates' messages are communicated through the *content* of speeches. Most of the message comes, instead, from body language and voice quality: "The successful candidate compels the audience to listen by projecting enough physical and vocal energy that it's virtually impossible for listeners to resist sending some of that energy back." [7] If the candidate establishes eye contact with a member of the audience between looking at the speech and delivering the line, the candidate is more likely to establish an authentic connection with the audience. Second, use personal stories and anecdotes. Third, use emotions to communicate expressively and signal passionate commitment to the issue at hand. But candidates must achieve a reasonable balance in applying this strategy; too much emotion could work against them. Although candidates make many speeches, their success will depend on how much they practice their delivery.

Speech Audience

Because candidates in higher-level races often receive free media coverage, their messages may reach well beyond the immediate audience. Such coverage can work against them if they tailor their message too closely to the audience, but it can also be used to their benefit if they make general statements that resonate with a larger group. One can ascertain which audience a candidate is trying to reach by investigating the contents of the candidate's message.

Candidates must, however, be careful about how narrowly they tailor their speeches, or they will fall prey to the practice of "tracking." Tracking refers to the practice of following the opponent to record audio or video footage of speeches for later use against him or her. Usually, this footage shows a candidate doing or saying something that would appeal only to a narrow audience. The footage is then used to expose a side of the candidate that would not be well received by a larger audience. Some trackers have attempted to provoke reactions from candidates and campaign staffs in order to get a hostile response on videotape. One such episode received unflattering media coverage in the 2002 election cycle when supporters of one candidate became upset with the opposing party trackers in the U.S. Senate race between incumbent Democratic senator Paul Wellstone of Minnesota and his Republican challenger Norm Coleman.

Media attention can be used, however, to a candidate's advantage. Candidates can deliver a controversial speech, knowing that although it may not resonate well with the immediate audience, it will gain media attention and be positively received by a broader one. For example, during his 1992 presidential campaign, Bill Clinton spoke before the Rainbow Coalition and criticized rap artist Sistah Souljah for making a racially insensitive comment. Although his rebuke of Souljah raised eyebrows in the black community, the message was intended to convey to white suburban voters that he could differ with his African American base.

Types of Speeches

The planning, timing, and content of campaign speeches are critical to the success of the campaign. Speeches may vary in content based on where, when, and to whom they are given, but they must always contain the candidate's fundamental message. Some scholars have pondered whether the dramatic drop in the length of the typical campaign speech has affected the quality of modern-day speeches. While reasoned arguments are still present in contemporary speeches, fewer arguments are addressed.

Announcement Speeches

An announcement speech serves several purposes. Its primary purpose is to declare the candidate's intention to run, and it thus represents an attempt to keep other potential competitors out of the race. The speech also explains why the candidate is running and what the candidate hopes to accomplish that cannot be accomplished by the others in the race. The main body of the speech should outline important themes of the campaign. As for the venue for the announcement, it should be relevant to the candidate's message. To demonstrate widespread support in the community, it is important to mobilize a crowd of supporters to appear with the candidate. Finally, in order to build on the momentum of the announcement, which serves as a rally of support, the campaign should follow up with paid or free media events. Careful timing is essential for a successful announcement. If a candidate announces his or her intentions too soon, the media may not be interested or will lose interest if the momentum of the campaign diminishes. If the delay in announcing is too long, other candidates can get ahead in organizing, fund-raising, gaining elite support, and drawing media attention.

Stock Speeches

Stock speeches refer to the central elements of the core message, which explains why the candidate is running for office and why he or she is the best candidate. These speeches must be adaptable to a variety of situations. Candidates often tailor the content of a stock speech to a given audience by using a speechwriting format called a "speech module." [8] These are short segments that a staff member prepares about each issue on the candidate's agenda. Each module is made up of an opening line, a discussion of the problem, a policy solution, and examples. Depending on the length of the speech, the candidate can combine a number of stock speech modules to fit a variety of audiences and lengths of speech. Political consultants recommend three different lengths to accommodate different types of events. A two-minute or five-minute speech could be used as the opening for a debate or a brief opportunity to address an audience; a twenty-minute speech would be appropriate for a longer, uninterrupted speaking opportunity. In each case, the speech should draw a contrast between the candidate and the opponent and should give the voter a clear reason to elect the candidate.

Acceptance Speeches

An acceptance speech is ritualistically given after the party organization has officially nominated a candidate to represent the party in the general election. The goal of this speech at this point in the campaign timeline is to thank supporters and invite others to join with the candidate. By unifying the party membership, candidates rally support for moving into the next battle against the opposing party. The most visible acceptance speeches are the presidential acceptance speeches given at the national party conventions after the parties' primaries. The nominee, as the now public leader of the party, uses this speech to generate enthusiasm for the general election. In their acceptance speeches, candidates may attack their opponents—a development in line with the movement from party-centered to candidate-centered campaigns. By "going negative" in speeches as well as in advertising, candidates immediately draw a contrast between themselves and their opposition.

News Conferences

Candidates, especially those in the higher-level races, give speeches in the form of news conferences when they want to draw attention to a special issue or event. The five potential audiences for a news conference are the public, the opposing campaign, staff, political elites (or opinion leaders, such as political experts that appear as guest commentators), and the media. Properly used, news conferences can increase coverage of the candidate's agenda by highlighting a timely issue or event, such as the release of a new television commercial. News conferences are more helpful than press releases (written statements focusing on a particular issue) in establishing personal relations with reporters.

The scheduling of news conferences must take into account media broadcast and print deadlines. During the conference itself, the candidate should open with a clear statement that sets the agenda and outlines the purpose of the event. Experts also recommend answering the media's questions and then adding an additional point from the candidate's agenda. To manage the event, staff members may plant questions with reporters before the event begins and selectively recognize some of them during questioning to encourage or reward particular ones. If problems arise, candidates should have an exit strategy, including possible intervention by a staff member to move the candidate to the next event.

Apologias

Apologias, or speeches made by candidates who want to express regret for a controversial statement or action, seem more prevalent in modern campaigns. Indeed, they have become a common form of campaign communication as the practice of reporting on the personal lives and mistakes of candidates has increased. Compared with other types of candidate speeches, these events are more likely to receive automatic coverage because of the media's interest in conflict and scandal. The primary purpose of this form of speechmaking is to remove the issue from the media's agenda and justify why it is no longer an important story. In this speech, candidates explain the situation in question and try to reduce fears that it will have an impact on their professional performance in office. By attempting to reframe their behavior, candidates can try to minimize the damage to their image.

Often when candidates directly address a scandalous issue, the act of bringing it into the open can allay fears in the mind of the public. For example, after the media revealed in 2000 that presidential candidate George W. Bush had been arrested for drunk driving when he was younger, he addressed the issue, admitted to having made mistakes in his past, and asserted that the issue was not a problem that would affect his current performance in office. Similarly, in 2004 when California gubernatorial candidate Arnold Schwarzenegger was accused of fondling women, he made a public apology, which deflated the issue for a portion of the public and the media.

Debates

Debates provide an interactive contrast for two or more candidates in a controlled message format, allowing voters to compare them on speaking style and substance (for a full description of debates, see Chapter 18). Candidates do not always choose to take part in debates, and, in fact, often it is preferable for candidates to avoid a debate. Candidates will debate only if they feel they are prepared and in control of the format, timing, location, and structure of the event. Incumbents are usually less likely to debate, because the debate will elevate the challenger to an equal level. Because incumbents have automatic and natural access to their constituents, they gain no real advantage from participating. In addition, as incumbents they have records of performance that could be called into question more easily than the challenger's record. Expectations are essential to interpreting performance during a debate. The lower the expectations of a candidate's performance before a debate, the greater the chance the candidate will receive positive reviews.

After the debate, campaign staffers work on spinning the media by claiming that their candidate won the debate. If the media pundits continually critique a particular point in a debate, the public may adopt that interpretation of the debate: "A massive and coordinated surrogate effort means that in the crucial post-debate hours, viewers and media representatives are hearing many respected figures present a cogent rationale of why their candidate did well in the debate. Often these interviews are widely reprinted and broadcast and may serve to influence audience perceptions of the debate." [9]

Overall, debates are dramatic, and they attract media attention at all levels. They also tend to reinforce the prior conclusions of partisans about the candidates rather than persuade significant numbers of voters. However, debates are a positive aspect of democracy; they can affect voters' images of the candidates and increase voter knowledge of issues if voters are tuned in and paying attention.

Political Advertising

Campaign advertising is the only way for candidates to reach a wide range of targeted voters, while exercising control over the content and timing of the message. In the most basic sense, political advertisements introduce candidates to voters and set the agenda for the campaign in repeated thirty-second spots. They connect candidates with the target audience by featuring issues that resonate with that audience and stressing the positive traits of the candidate. They also frame the debate in a manner that benefits the candidate and detracts from the opponent. Advertisements can activate particular values and beliefs already held by voters and make them important criteria for voters who are making decisions. By "priming" and "defusing" values and beliefs, advertising messages can alter the standards by which voters evaluate candidates. Ads may make some issues more salient and may deflate the importance of others. In other words, the messages

controlled by the candidates, parties, and interest groups through advertising can be the key to the success of their political campaigns, particularly during high-intensity, close races with evenly matched opponents.

Political advertising is one of the most significant forms of mass media communications, and it is a widely used tool for communicating with target voters. Advertising expenditures make up a significant amount of most campaign budgets, and research has shown that political advertising is important for increasing name recognition and enhancing voters' knowledge about candidates and campaigns.[10] Voters generally assess the candidates in the same way that they make a personal judgment of an acquaintance. They base such judgments on traits such as competence, experience, integrity, and empathy. Ads also provide information that is compacted into thirty-second segments that are easily digested by voters. However, this information can be vague on details, and thus scholars disagree about the true usefulness of the substance of political ads.

Political advertising is the most effective in lower-level races, campaigns with low voter involvement, nonpartisan races, and primaries. In all of these political contexts, few voters have already formed attitudes that guide their judgments about candidates or issues. Ads are also the main source of political information for uninvolved voters, and research finds that the influence of ads is greater when other sources of information are not readily available.[11] Because of the impact of ads in the absence of competing information, candidates have begun to air their advertisements earlier and earlier in the campaign season. Although ads may not define candidates later in the campaign process, they can activate or redefine perceptions of candidates or parties and can make a difference in hotly contested, close races.

Advertising Venues

Political advertising involves both push and pull media—those that push the message to the voters and those that pull the voters in to learn more. The choice of which medium to use in a given race will depend on which type is best suited for the level of race and which is the most cost-efficient way to reach the targeted voters. The venues discussed in this section differ in the types of audience they reach. Recent practices and technologies allow for "narrowcasting" or targeting messages to very specific groups. Each medium has its advantages and disadvantages, making it appropriate in some races and not in others.

Television

Many campaigns use television as a communication tool because it is found in most households across America. As one of the best ways to reach a broad audience, television advertising is essential for nationwide campaigns. Statewide races also use television advertising to reach corners of the state that the candidate would be unable to reach efficiently by other means. Television is an ideal medium for providing the desired emotional connection through moving visual images that resonate effectively with voters. Candidates are more easily able to establish a rapport when they appear in intimate color close-ups in viewers' living rooms. In addition, television is a story-telling medium in which producers, instead of listing a candidate's traits, can "develop a narrative, a mini-play, stressing the candidate's traits but arranging them much more inductively, using the convention of storytelling." [12] Production techniques also can heighten the visual impact of an ad. For example, President Lyndon B. Johnson's "daisy girl" ad was known for its dramatic visual impact during the 1964 presidential campaign. The ad begins with a young girl counting each petal that she pulls off a daisy. As she continues to pull petals and counts, her voice is overtaken by the dramatic voice of a man counting down to activate a nuclear bomb. The image of the girl is then replaced with the sound and image of an exploding mushroom cloud. Slow-motion techniques and dramatic music amplify the negative impact of the visual image.

Despite some communication advantages, television is not the best choice of medium for every race. It is the costliest form of political advertising, and the cost depends on variances within the media market—that is, the geographical area reached by a particular television station. States vary in the number and population of their media markets. For example, Texas has twenty-two media markets, and Massachusetts has only three. However, candidates can spend more money and potentially reach more voters in the Boston market than they could in the multiple rural Texas markets.

Campaigns that use broadcast television also incur production costs to create ad spots as well as "ad buy" costs—the price of airing ads during particular programs. Even though television reaches the largest and broadest audiences, its use may produce substantial waste, depending on the level of the race and the audience a candidate is trying to reach. For example, candidates in the New Hampshire presidential primaries have to buy airtime on Boston television as well as in New Hampshire, because the Boston media market reaches into New Hampshire. Thus candidates reach a large percentage of voters who cannot vote in New Hampshire.

With the advent of cable television, candidates were able to buy political advertising airtime at a lower cost to reach a more local, targeted audience. Cable allows more precise targeting by interest and background, because particular stations market their programming to specific demographic groups. For example, a candidate who wants to reach female voters would be advised to purchase spots on the Lifetime channel, whose primary audience is women. The practice of buying cable time in specific cities was especially popular during the 1992 presidential race. During the 1996 election cycle, 80 percent of congressional candidates used cable television as a

medium. As cable penetrates more and more households, this practice could continue to expand. [13]

Radio

Radio is much less expensive than television, and it, too, can reach a targeted audience. Like cable television stations, radio stations segment the audience and appeal to specific listener demographics. Radio is ideal for lower-level races and for reaching rural areas and large geographic areas in a cost-effective manner. This medium allows for a longer message and generally more variety in terms of the length of time that candidates can buy. Because people spend so much time listening to their radios, particularly while driving to and from work every day, radio can be effective. Stations may also offer less expensive daily specials that include drive time but extend through the entire day. If candidates want to reach conservative voters, they can run ads locally during a highly rated national talk show and have a high probability of reaching their target. In addition, candidates typically turn to radio first to run advertisements that attack their opponents, because there is no visual connection with a candidate and less chance of a backlash against the sponsor of such an ad.

Newspapers and Magazines

Print advertisements also allow candidates to target an audience based on demographic and geographic characteristics. Such ads are integrated easily into a campaign plan, because the space can be purchased ahead of time, and yet the actual copy can be provided just before printing. Because all of the content of a print ad appears in one visual, it is essential to design content that catches the eye of the reader. Newspaper ads can be produced more easily than television or radio ads, and such ads can be used to respond to attacks in low-level races. However, newspaper ads tend to be expensive. The usefulness of a paper or magazine will depend on its circulation and the area a candidate wishes to cover. Newspapers in smaller cities or suburban areas can be successful means of targeting well-educated, well-informed voters who are more likely to vote and keep up with current events. Magazines are also able to target audiences geographically, because they are sorted by region and zip code. For example, pro-gun candidates might want to advertise in the magazine *American Rifleman*.

Direct Mail

Direct mail is the best medium for targeting very specific audiences. Therefore, it is not surprising that more money is spent on direct mail than on television advertising in campaigns at all levels combined. Usually, a direct-mail piece will focus on one particular issue, such as education. Such a mailing, which would target only families with children in the school system, would provide a more detailed explanation of the policy proposals and solutions supported by the candidate that address this target audience's concerns.

Direct-mail pieces from the 2000 election cycle reveal that tone can often be much harsher in this medium than in the print or broadcast media. For example, groups have used dramatic graphics to criticize candidate support of abortion rights and gay rights. Because of the precisely targeted nature of these mailings, the risk of creating a backlash against the sponsoring candidate or group is somewhat lower than that of the other media, because these households have already been identified as sympathetic to the candidate's position on the issue. Strategists have also become increasingly savvy about creating interesting pieces, perhaps featuring a puzzle or a question that sparks voters' curiosity and entices them to open the piece and read further. Most pieces dispense with envelopes, because they add to the cost and may provoke the voter to throw the piece out. The voter will not take more than twenty seconds to a minute to read the piece, so the message must be short and focused on a narrow issue of concern for a particular audience. Experts recommend using professional mailing groups rather than dealing with bulk mail.

Direct mail is also used as a tool for raising money from sympathetic audiences. The fund-raising audience does not have to consist only of voters in the candidate's race. Some candidates, such as former first lady and Democratic senator Hillary Rodham Clinton of New York, have national visibility and a wide reach in fund raising—factors that can benefit them as well as their opponents. Likewise, Democrats sent out direct-mail fundraising solicitations to communities across the country in 1996 in an attempt to defeat Republican Speaker of the House Newt Gingrich in his reelection bid to represent his district in Georgia. Direct mail is particularly effective in raising funds from older voters. And once people become donors, chances are high that they will donate again, and so they receive repeat solicitations.

Direct mail is, however, a relatively expensive way to raise money. Yet it is usually ideal for lower-level races in which candidates would have to spend an exorbitant amount to penetrate the television or radio clutter during an election season. By investing in direct mail, the candidate can more carefully target the message to ensure that it reaches the intended household.

Display Graphics

Display graphics such as billboards, lawn signs, bumper stickers, and buttons appeal to mass audiences. Campaign buttons, which were some of the earliest display graphics used in campaigns, are ideal for establishing quick name recognition. Brief, catchy slogans also associate candidates with their messages and reinforce the larger themes of their campaigns. Billboards and lawn signs can help to create momentum and visibility in small areas.

One common tactic is to create a media blitz by installing multiple billboards at the same time. For example,

Political yard signs are an essential communication tool used by both small and large campaigns to raise candidates' name recognition and to get their messages in front of the voters. Source: Library of Congress/Photography by John Vachon

the San Antonio Smoke-Free Coalition, a group in Texas that wanted to strengthen the city's clean indoor air ordinance, installed in different parts of the city ten billboards in bright yellow and black that read "Second-hand Smoke Kills." These billboards communicated a simple message that raised awareness about the issue of second-hand smoke for those driving by each day on the highway as well as for the media. As for lawn signs, when volunteers, staff, and core supporters of a candidate or issue install lawn signs in unison, they are encouraging others to request signs, thus building momentum and creating the appearance of support. Despite their appeal, display graphics are expensive. Furthermore, such materials are easily wasted, and it is unclear that they are effective.

Telephone Contact

Because of advances in technology, telephone calling services can carefully target specific households, based on their demographic characteristics, with messages from candidates, interest groups, and the political parties. Candidates can leave prerecorded voice mail messages for voters that ask them to come out and vote on election day. They also can leave persuasive messages aimed at influencing voters to support their campaigns and at soliciting campaign donations. Professional call services can provide the necessities—the call script, the telephone callers, and a time-saving system for dialing calls—and the means of skipping over busy signals, answering devices, fax machines, and other obstacles. Generally, computerized calling systems result in double the number of completed calls and reduce the cost per call. In 2000, taped messages from Bill Clinton were phoned to predominantly African American districts on behalf of Al Gore and in 2004, Laura Bush "called" swing voters on behalf of President Bush. While these celebrity calls may be interesting, the general consensus among academics is that they are not effective.

The Internet

Unlike the push media described earlier, the Internet is a pull medium that has grown in the variety of functions it can provide during political campaigns. It plays such a central role in current campaigns that all candidates are expected to have a Web site. The primary function of the Internet in campaigns has been to communicate information directly to the public at an extremely low cost. Design, implementation, and maintenance are very inexpensive. Web sites can provide information on policy positions and on news events involving candidates. The sites also provide voters with practical election information such as polling sites, and they can assist campaigns in recruiting volunteers, mobilizing voters at events, requesting voter input, raising money, and attacking opponents. A drawback to the Internet is that the opposition can use it to gain access to the candidate's Web site, as the Bush–Cheney campaign learned during the 2004 presidential election. The campaign offered a "sloganator" on its Web site that invited supporters to suggest clever campaign slogans. However, when opponents entered unflattering, satirical slogans critical of the administration and its reelection bid, the function was promptly removed.

More recently, candidates and parties have been using the Web to mobilize activists with common interests. Democratic presidential candidate Howard Dean sparked a "Meet Up" frenzy in 2004, in which the Internet was used to set times and places for people to gather in person to discuss issues and provide his campaign with feedback. Other candidates and parties followed suit. The Web sites of news outlets and public interest groups such as Project Vote Smart offer campaign-related information as well. Citizens also tune in to news outlet Web sites as well as candidates' campaign sites for information.

Blogs (short for Web logs) are a new form of campaign communication that have risen in prominence since 1999. A blog is an online journal or diary that allows instant commentary or opinion on a particular topic. Blogs have become a primary tool in bringing new political information to light, in spinning breaking news events, and in keeping particular stories high on the media's agenda. As evidence of the importance of blogs as a form of campaign communication, both parties gave media credentials to bloggers at their national conventions during the 2004 presidential campaign.

Blogs have had an impact on both sides of the ideological spectrum. The controversy over the racial overtones of Mississippi senator Trent Lott's remarks on the occasion of the retirement of South Carolina Republican Strom Thurmond from the U.S. Senate may have been the first blog-driven conflict. In addition, bloggers were credited with exposing as forgeries documents used by CBS News in a 2004 story criticizing President George W. Bush's National Guard service. Blogs thus serve as an additional resource, providing evidence and commentary that is not necessarily emerging from mainstream media channels.

Types of Advertising

In addition to selecting the type of venue through which to communicate political advertising messages, campaigns also must decide on the content and tone of the messages they want to communicate. Generally, when scholars study political advertising, they use the individual television ad as the unit of analysis. However, an ad derives much of its meaning from its placement in the larger campaign plan and broader political context when it is aired. Academic studies have struggled with ways to classify ads meaningfully in order to determine their effects on voters and their impact on the larger democratic process (see Box 17-1).

Issue/Image Classifications

When searching for ways to understand the content of the advertising messages communicated to voters by candidates, scholars have distinguished between issue ads, which communicate some type of candidate issue position to the voters, and image ads, which focus on personality traits and character. Research has acknowledged the problem with this dichotomy, because issue and image components are interdependent and sometimes are inseparable parts of the same advertising message. Viewers of political ads do not distinguish between issues and images in political ads, probably because the political consultants who construct ads design them to merge or to "dovetail" the two constructs. Successful ads will use issues to help voters draw conclusions about a candidate's character or image.[14] However, one key enduring finding from these studies is that viewers find attacks against a candidate's stand on an issue more acceptable and fairer than attacks on a candidate's character. Character attacks are more likely to boomerang, whereas issue attacks are likely to produce the intended effects.[15]

Positive/Negative Classifications

Discussion of advertising tone dominates popular political discourse. Scholars, media pundits, and the public all simplify the discussion of ads by referring to tone in terms of positive and negative advertising. Yet a false dichotomy can obscure important distinctions in the impacts of ads on voters' attitudes. More nuanced categories are discussed in the rest of this section.

Positive or advocacy ads refer to the positive aspects of a candidate. In particular, these types of ads are important during primaries or the initial phase of a campaign, because they provide a biography of the candidate that helps to build a positive image with voters. These "i.d." spots are designed to identify the candidate, increase name recognition, and create a positive impression. Generally,

BOX 17-1
TYPES OF CAMPAIGN ADVERTISEMENTS
Megan Feehan

Television advertisements provide candidates with many different ways in which to express their campaign messages. Different types of ads serve different purposes, but all seek to give the candidate running the ad an advantage over the opponent.

One way to classify ads is by subject matter. Pure issue ads concentrate solely on public policy, while pure image ads focus exclusively on the candidate's character. Campaign ads also can be classified by tone. Advocacy ads are completely positive and attempt to put the sponsoring candidate in the best possible light. Many ads, however, have a negative tone, which can be expressed in a variety of ways. Some focus only on the opponent and directly attack him or her, whereas compare and contrast ads draw distinctions between two candidates based on issues or candidate traits. Response or rebuttal ads attempt to counteract criticism or allegations made by the opponent. Inoculation ads attempt to deal with potentially harmful information about oneself before the other side brings attention to it.

A successful campaign must use an array of these political advertisements—issue-based and image-oriented, positive and negative—to remain competitive in the dynamic environment of an electoral campaign.

Issue/Image Classifications

The following campaign ads—the first for Republican George W. Bush from the 2000 presidential campaign and the second for Democrat John Kerry from the 2004 presidential campaign—exemplify the distinction between a pure issue ad and a pure image ad. The Bush ad focuses entirely on the issue of prescription drugs, an issue that was highly salient in the 2000 campaign. The Bush campaign found it necessary to address what is often seen as a Democratic issue, albeit from a decidedly Republican perspective. The 2004 John Kerry ad ac-

centuates only Kerry's character traits, without any reference to the issues. The ad attempts to personalize the campaign by emphasizing leadership, a character trait that voters value. Although these examples illustrate a clear distinction between issues and images in campaign ads, these categories appear simultaneously—though in varying proportions—in most ads.

Pure Issue Ad

"Priority MD RNC" (George W. Bush, 2000)

[increasing graph of drug prices in relation to years on top of image of prescription bottles]
ANNOUNCER: Under Clinton/Gore, prescription drug prices have skyrocketed and nothing's been done.

[cut to George Bush at podium]
[supertext: THE BUSH PLAN]
FEMALE ANNOUNCER: George Bush has a plan.

[cut to several shots of George Bush with senior citizens]
ANNOUNCER: Add a prescription drug benefit to Medicare.

[cut to image of seniors, then to George Bush speaking at podium]
[supertext: AFFORDABLE RX PLAN]
BUSH: Every senior will have access to prescription drug benefits.

[cut to Al Gore speaking on television]
ANNOUNCER: And Al Gore, Gore opposed bipartisan reform. He's pushing a big government plan . . .
[supertext: OPPOSED BIPARTISAN REFORM]

[text: INTERFERE WITH DOCTORS]
ANNOUNCER: . . . that lets Washington bureaucrats interfere with what your doctors prescribe.

ANNOUNCER and supertext: The Gore prescription plan: bureaucrats decide.

[cut to George Bush shaking hands with supporters]
ANNOUNCER: The Bush prescription plan: seniors choose.

Pure Image Ad

"Heart" (John Kerry, 2004)

[uplifting music]
[John Kerry speaking, interspersed with pictures of his father, mother, and his time in the service]
KERRY: I was born in Fitzsimmons army hospital in Colorado. My dad was serving in the Army Air Corps. Both of my parents taught me about public service. I enlisted because I believed in service to country. I thought it was important if you had a lot of privileges as I had had, to go to a great university like Yale, to give something back to your country.

[cut to Del Sandusky, U.S. Navy]
DEL SANDUSKY: The decisions that he made saved our lives.

[cut to Jim Rassman, Army Special Forces]
JIM RASSMAN: When he pulled me out of the river, he risked his life to save mine.

[cut to black and white picture of John Kerry]
ANNOUNCER: For more than thirty years, John Kerry has served America.

[cut to Vanessa Kerry, interspersed with still pictures of John Kerry]
VANESSA KERRY: If you look at my father's time in service to this country, whether it's as a veteran, prosecutor, or senator, he has shown an ability to fight for things that matter.

[cut to still picture of John Kerry and Teresa Heinz-Kerry, then to Teresa Heinz-Kerry]

TERESA HEINZ-KERRY: John is the face of someone who's hopeful, who's generous of spirit and of heart.

[cut to John Kerry]
KERRY: We're a country of optimists. We're the can-do people. And we just need to believe in ourselves again.

[cut to John Kerry waving on stage]
ANNOUNCER: A lifetime of service and strength. John Kerry for President.

KERRY: I'm John Kerry and I approve of this message.

Positive/Negative Classifications

Positive/Advocacy Ads

The following 1984 ad for Ronald Reagan depicts renewed prosperity in the United States with scenes of a typical morning across America. The inspirational music, paired with the images of active citizens, leads the viewer to reflect positively on the previous four years under the Reagan administration. The ad enhances its optimistic tone with the inclusion of positive groups and symbols: children, seniors, and the American flag.

"Prouder, Stronger, Better" (Ronald Reagan, 1984)

[image of a city skyline at dawn]
MALE ANNOUNCER: It's morning again in America.

[cut to images of Americans going to work]
ANNOUNCER: Today more men and women will go to work than ever before in our country's history.

[cut to images of a family moving into a new home]
ANNOUNCER: With interest rates at about half the record highs of 1980, nearly two thousand families today will buy new homes, more than at any time in the past four years.

[cut to images of a wedding]
ANNOUNCER: This afternoon 6,500 young men and women will be married and with inflation at less than half of what it was just four years ago, they can look forward with confidence to the future.

[cut to image of Capitol building, then to children, a fire fighter, and a senior citizen, each raising the American flag]
ANNOUNCER: It's morning again in America and under the leadership of President Reagan our country is prouder and stronger and better. Why would we ever want to return to where we were less than four short years ago?
TEXT: President Reagan.

Negative Ads

Direct Attack

The following 1988 negative ad from Vice President George Bush directly attacks his Democratic opponent, Massachusetts governor Michael S. Dukakis, for his positions on various defense systems. The ad makes explicit reference to Dukakis while lacking any mention of Bush. The ad, with its disapproving tone juxtaposed with the comical images of Dukakis riding in a tank, portrays Dukakis as an incompetent—and therefore unacceptable—presidential candidate.

"Tank Ride" (George Bush, 1988)

[images of Dukakis riding in a military tank wearing a large helmet]
MALE ANNOUNCER: Michael Dukakis has opposed virtually every defense system we developed.

ANNOUNCER and supertext:
He opposed new aircraft carriers. He opposed antisatellite weapons. He opposed four missile systems, including the Pershing II missile deployment. Dukakis opposed the Stealth Bomber, a ground emergency warning system against nuclear attack. He even criticized our rescue mission to Grenada and our strike on Libya.

[cut to close up of Dukakis smiling and pointing from tank]
ANNOUNCER: And now he wants to be our commander in chief.

ANNOUNCER and supertext: America can't afford that risk.

Compare/Contrast

Bill Clinton's 1992 ad "Second" presents a direct contrast between Clinton and his opponent, George Bush. The ad specifically addresses both candidates by name and compares their positions on the issue of taxes. Presenting both sides of the issue—albeit in a way that benefits one candidate in particular—encourages viewers to make a choice between the two candidates.

"Second" (Bill Clinton, 1992)

MALE ANNOUNCER and title: The George Bush Promise.

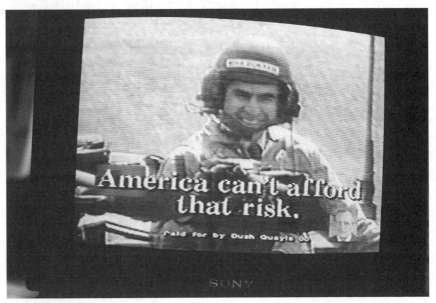

Michael S. Dukakis
Source: Republican National Committee

(Box continues on next page)

BOX 17-1 *(continued)*
TYPES OF CAMPAIGN ADVERTISEMENTS

George H.W. Bush
Source: Bush Presidential Materials Project

[cut to George Bush at podium]
BUSH (national address): Read my lips. No new taxes.

[supertext: Bush gave us the "second biggest tax increase" in American history. Congressional Budget Office Study 1/30/91. New York Times 8/7/92.]
ANNOUNCER: Then he gave us the second biggest tax increase in American history.

[cut to rising numbers on a gas pump, George Bush's face appears in background]
ANNOUNCER: Bush increased the gas tax by 56 percent. Can we afford four more years?

[cut to Bill Clinton touching hands of supporters]
ANNOUNCER: Bill Clinton—a different kind of Democrat.

[supertext: Arkansas has the "second lowest tax burden" in the country. State Policy Reports, 1/92, US Department of Commerce, 12/91]
ANNOUNCER: As governor,

Arkansas has the second lowest tax burden in the country.

ANNOUNCER and supertext: Balanced 12 budgets.

[cut to Al Gore and Bill Clinton on stage speaking to a crowd]
ANNOUNCER: You don't have to read his lips. Read his record.

ANNOUNCER and title: Clinton/Gore. For people. For a change.

Response or Rebuttal

In 1980, after President Jimmy Carter's attacks on his challenger, Republican Ronald Reagan, the Reagan campaign released an ad featuring Nancy Reagan. Mrs. Reagan defended her husband by refuting Carter's attacks and by making counterattacks of her own. This emotional response and hard-hitting rebuttal by the candidate's spouse helped the Reagan campaign to avoid potential damage from Carter's criticisms.

"Nancy Reagan" (Ronald Reagan, 1980)

[medium shot of Nancy Reagan addressing the camera]
NANCY REAGAN: I deeply, deeply resent and am offended by the attacks that President Carter has made on my husband, the personal attacks that he has made on my husband. His attempt to paint my husband as a man he is not. He is not a warmonger, he is not a man who's going to throw the elderly out on the street and cut off their Social Security. That's a terrible thing to do and to say, about anybody. That's campaigning on fear.

[cut to close-up of Nancy Reagan]
NANCY REAGAN: There are many issues that are at stake in this campaign. I would like Mr. Carter to explain to me why the inflation is as high as it is; why unemployment is as high as it is.

[cut to medium shot]
NANCY REAGAN: I would like to have him explain the vacillating, weak foreign policy so that our friends overseas don't know what we're going to do—whether we're going to stand up for them, or whether we're not going to stand up for them.

[cut to close up]
NANCY REAGAN: And the issue of this campaign is his three and a half year record.

ANNOUNCER: The time is now for strong leadership.

Inoculation

Although John F. Kennedy's religious background had not yet been directly addressed in public—at least by the candidates—in the 1960 campaign, it remained a significant factor on the minds of many Americans. In an attempt to confront and diminish these concerns, the Kennedy campaign released the following ad. By publicly dealing with his Catholicism and reiterating his commitment to the separation of church and state, Kennedy was able to move beyond the matter of his religious beliefs.

"Religion" (John F. Kennedy, 1960)

[image of a woman speaking on a microphone in a crowd]
WOMAN: You would be divided between two loyalties, to your church and to your state, if you were to be elected president?

[cut to JFK addressing the crowd]
JFK: The question is, whether I think that if I were elected president, I would be divided between two loyalties, my church and my state. Let me just say that I would not. I have sworn to uphold the Constitution, in the fourteen years I've been in Congress, in the years I was in the service. The Constitution provides in the First Amendment that Congress shall make no laws abridging the freedom of religion. I must say I believe in it; I think it's the only way that this country can go ahead. Many countries do not be-

lieve in it; many countries have unity between church and state. I would be completely opposed to it. And I say that whether I'm elected president, or whether I continue as a senator, or whether I'm a citizen. That is my view based on long experience. So in answer to your question, I would fulfill my oath of office, as I have done for fourteen years in the Congress. There is no article of my faith that would in any way inhibit, I think it encourages, the meeting of my oath of office. And whether you vote for me or not because of my competence . . .

[cut to image of crowd listening to speech]
JFK: . . . to be President . . .

[cut back to JFK]
JFK: . . .I am sure that no one believes that I'd be a candidate for the presidency if I didn't think I could meet my oath of office. Secondly, Article VI of the Constitution says there shall be no religious test for office. That's what was written in the Constitution: Jefferson, Washington, and all the rest.

They said that every American will have an opportunity. Now you cannot tell me that the day I was born it was said . . .

[cut to reporters taking notes on speech]
JFK: . . . I could never run for president because I wouldn't meet my oath of office.

[cut back to JFK]
JFK: I would not have come here if I didn't feel that I was going to get a complete opportunity to run for office as a fellow American in this state. I would not run for it if in any way I didn't feel that I could do the job. I come here today saying that I think that this is an issue . . .

[crowd cheering/clapping]

Source: American Museum of the Moving Image, "The Living Room Candidate: Presidential Campaign Commercials, 1952–2004," http://livingroomcandidate.movingimage.us/.

these types of ads use various familiar myths and symbols such as pride in country and the American dream to elicit a positive effect or emotion from the viewers.[16] The ultimate goals of such ads are to develop positive associations with leadership characteristics, to strike a responsive chord with the voter, and to link the candidate with positive groups and symbols such as children, war veterans, and the American flag. Humor can be another effective device in producing a positive image of the candidate, but it can also involve greater risk in that humor is subjective and different target audiences are going to differ in what they find to be humorous (see Box 17-2).

A negative ad can be defined as any ad that implicitly or explicitly criticizes the opponent or puts that opponent in an inferior position.[17] To understand the meaning and impact of negative ads, it is helpful to discuss them in terms of their specific purposes or functions. All of the ad types described in what follows can be classified as negative, and yet each is distinctive because of the manner in which negative information is utilized.

Direct attack ads specifically criticize opponents for perceived weaknesses. This type of publicity is effective in reaching and persuading the less educated voter. These ads also reinforce the positions of those who support the sponsor of the ad. Attacking a candidate's record is con-

sidered a fair attack. Any personal attack on the candidate or the candidate's family is generally considered unfair and can lead to a backlash. Personal attack ads are also known as assaultive ads.

Direct contrast ads make an explicit comparison between two candidates. Ads created in this format are persuasive, because it is thought that the process of making a vote choice is a comparative assessment in which voters choose the better of the two options. Direct contrast ads are understood to be most effective in lowering the evaluation of the opposing candidate. These ads are usually perceived to be more credible and fairer, because they contain positive information about the sponsoring candidate. Two-sided arguments also are more persuasive for highly educated voters.

Implied contrast ads highlight particular positive traits of the sponsor, but they do not refer explicitly to the opponent. These ads can be interpreted as positive ads, but the contrast is understood within the context of the larger campaign. In other words, "they are deductive in that voters must 1) infer who the opponent is and 2) understand how that candidate is being criticized." [18] Usually these ads are used in campaigns only after voters have a knowledge base on which to draw when processing the advertisements. Yet boomerang or unintended effects are more

BOX 17-2

THE USE OF HUMOR IN ADVERTISING:
JESSE VENTURA'S ACTION FIGURE AND HIS VICTORY RV

Political humor is subjective and therefore can be a risky proposition for an advertising strategy—what is humorous to political consultants may not be humorous to swing voters. Humor is temporally, regionally, and culturally defined. Certain types of humor are inappropriate in some political contexts, and candidates must therefore pay close attention to the attitudes of the target audience when determining the strategic uses of humor in the campaign. However, humor can serve as an effective way to take the edge off an attack, enabling a candidate to avoid the backlash that could accompany a direct attack. Humor also can increase the attention paid to and the likeability of advertising and can decrease irritation. Finally, some candidates, particularly challengers who have fewer resources, may use humorous ads in their campaigns to generate name recognition. The entertainment value of such ads often generates free media attention.

Jesse Ventura's run for governor of Minnesota in 1998 provides one such example. Ventura's advertising consultant, Bill Hillsman, first gained attention in 1990 when he was credited with creating the humorous, self-deprecating ad campaign for the Democratic senator Paul Wellstone of Minnesota. He also created the "Priceless" ad for third party candidate Ralph Nader during his 2000 presidential run. For Ventura's campaign, Hillsman came up with the idea of a Jesse Ventura action figure. The ads depicted kids playing with the action figure as a superhero of sorts as he rode in his recreational vehicle (RV) to search out and stop corruption and battle politicians favoring wasteful spending. Played against a backdrop of a remake of the theme song from the 1970s movie *Shaft*, the ads provided the entertainment value of a product ad and took on a humorous tone because the format was so unusual for a political advertisement.

These ads gained free media attention toward the end of the race, helping to increase Ventura's visibility in the race and providing a clear contrast between him and the other party candidates. Ventura surged past the Democrat and Republican candidates on election day to win with 37 percent of the vote in a state with same-day registration.

Thirty-Second TV Spot

"Action Figure"

Jesse Ventura for Governor

Produced by: North Woods Advertising

ANNOUNCER: New from the Reform Party.

BOYS: Yeahhh!!

ANNOUNCER: It's the new Jesse Ventura action figure! . . . You can make Jesse battle special interest groups.

BOY (imitating Jesse): I don't want your stupid money!

ANNOUNCER: And party politics!

BOY: We politicians have powers the average man can't comprehend.

ANNOUNCER: You can also make Jesse lower taxes, improve education, and fight for the things Minnesotans . . . really care about!

BOY (imitating Jesse): This bill wastes taxpayer's money! Redraft it!

ANNOUNCER: Don't waste your vote on politics as usual! Vote Reform Party candidate Jesse Ventura for Governor.

likely to occur when ads "offend the public's sensibilities" or violate the public's notion of good taste.[19] Moreover, negative attacks that are considered to be less relevant "mudslinging" are more likely to decrease turnout, whereas legitimate attacks can mobilize voters.[20]

If candidates do not plan a strategy for responding to a particular negative attack, they may be caught off-guard. In such cases, a candidate must determine how to react to the negative information that has been presented. There are a range of possible responses, including but not limited to *admission, denial, counterattack, refutation,* and *counterimaging.* Past lessons suggest that responding to an attack is more effective than silence. An admission means taking a stand; it says that the candidate is proud of his or her action. A denial turns the tables on the opponent and raises issues of credibility for the other side. A counterattack does not address the charge, but it places the candidate on the offensive by causing the candidate to criticize the opponent on another issue. The hope is that this action will distract the original attack. Refutations are the most convincing in that they reject the attack and provide contrary evidence. Counterimaging refers to a strategy in which candidates present a different image to the public to cancel out the image produced by the attack. Although these ads can be interpreted as positive spots for a candidate, with proper knowledge of the context of a race they are understood to be responsive ads.

Inoculation ads are defensive statements that candidates run in advance of attacks. If candidates are certain that particular attacks are forthcoming, they may want to raise those issues themselves before the opposition does, with the hope that it will neutralize or deflect the attacks. By exposing voters to a small amount of the damaging information, candidates hope that the release of the larger story will lessen the harm if the attacks do come or possibly convince opponents not to run the attacks.

Advertising Strategies and Tactics

Based on the different media venues and the different types of ads available to candidates, the candidates and their campaign managers make strategic decisions about how to combine these elements in an overall political advertising plan. The level of the race, a campaign's resources, the level of interest in the race, and the demographic and psychographic (personality) characteristics of the target voters will all influence a campaign's overall strategic plan. In higher-level campaigns such as presidential and Senate races, political advertising is important for setting an agenda laden with issues beneficial to the candidates and for framing issues in ways that give the candidates the advantage. In lower-level races, the candidates' goal is to place themselves first in the voters' minds when they make their vote choices. Higher-level races tend to make greater use of television, direct mail, and phone calling. Candidates in low-level races tend to direct their political advertising toward voter mobilization, concentrating mainly on targeting precincts. In this effort they are likely to rely on some direct mail or billboard media.

Message Targeting

The goal of message targeting is to reach the number of voters required to give a candidate the winning percentage at the polls. By strategically targeting the message through a variety of media, campaigns are able to spend limited resources most effectively. The nature of the race will determine which venues are most helpful. Generally, broadcasting reaches a wider audience at a higher cost. The process of narrowcasting allows a candidate to target a specific localized area and more efficiently reach that audience. For example, a candidate can buy a spot on a local cable station and reach a small but targeted audience for less money.

Candidates can fall into the trap of devoting a large portion of their budgets to television while excluding other media, but this tactic is dangerous because a range of media is often preferable for reaching all of a candidate's targets. For most lower-level races, cable television, radio, or direct mail are more effective than television for reaching the targeted voters, unless candidates are running in an inexpensive media market. If candidates do not have large budgets but are expected to run broadcast advertisements to compete effectively, they can produce one or two attention-grabbing or entertaining ads and then try to earn free media coverage for the ads. This strategy is used frequently by unknown and underfunded challengers.

Candidates who find themselves running in a district in a very expensive media market (such as a candidate running for a House seat near San Francisco or Los Angeles) may find cable television or radio to be a less expensive option. Radio allows greater flexibility, with less risk, for negative messages; the candidate can target the desired audiences through appropriate stations, including religious, news-talk, sports, hard rock, oldies, foreign language, and easy listening. The medium serves only as a tool for presenting the candidate's messages; it is up to the candidate's campaign to carefully monitor the content and tone of such messages.

Timing

In high-level campaigns, a strategic campaign plan is usually devised twelve to eighteen months before election day (see Chapter 14). However, candidates in lower-level races can plan early as well. A plan coordinates all aspects of the campaign, including targeting the paid media and devising fund-raising strategies to provide the budget for advertising. The most successful campaigns stick to the timing outlined in the plan. This strategy will tell the campaign when the money is needed to purchase various media and will suggest times to hold fund-raisers to ensure that the necessary funds are available for purchasing advertising. Before devising the strategy, each campaign should determine the cost of the available media and what coordination is needed between the media plan and other aspects of the campaign.

Generally speaking, candidates should start with positive or advocacy messages to introduce themselves to the voting public. In fact, positive ads should be run before attacks on the opponent. If the voters have not been convinced by enough positive image spots that the candidate is a likeable person, attacks against the opponent could backfire. Traditionally, contrast ads are run in the middle of the campaign, along with attack ads. Positive get-out-the-vote ads appear in the last week or two of the campaign as a way to mobilize voters. In recent years, campaigns have begun to air their advertising earlier. This practice creates a dilemma for delivering the message in new and fresh ways. Voters report suffering from advertising fatigue if they see the same ads aired more than a week to ten days in a row.

Some candidates with abundant resources begin their advertising campaigns early to entice their opponents to start spending money on ads. Opponents who find themselves in such a situation should resist the urge to run ads to match those of the better-funded candidates. When campaigns are lured into such a trap, they can run out of funds for the important ad blitz at the end of the campaigns. These final ads are generally positive in tone and designed to mobilize voters. Political parties can be useful allies in both situations—that is, by running early advertising to counteract an opponent and running ads designed to turn out the vote before the election. The parties may not, however, coordinate these activities with affiliated candidates' campaigns.

Finally, repetition of advertising over time will help to ensure that the voters are exposed to the message and that it remains salient. In order to achieve this repetition, some candidates purchase thirty-second spots of time and run three ten-second ads aimed at establishing the candidate's name recognition. The more these ads are repeated, the greater is the likelihood that they will achieve audience saturation to a point. Advertising professionals suggest that moderate levels of repetition are preferable to heavy levels. Otherwise, the repeated ads could begin to irritate the viewers.

Going Negative

Regardless of classification schemes, negativity in campaigning has increased in recent years. The values of news reporting are at least partly responsible for this. Journalists have tended to leap on any whiff of scandal or conflict related to a political campaign. In particular, with the advent of twenty-four-hour cable news, producers often feel forced to "feed the monster" and encourage reporters to cover every developing drama. Negative ads, such as the Swiftboat Veterans for Truth ads attacking John Kerry's Vietnam war record and medals in the 2004 presidential election, certainly qualify as such a drama that stretched on for weeks in the news media. Negative information figures prominently in campaigns, because it is used to point out to voters why an opponent should not be elected. Most political consultants agree that "going negative" works, because negative ads lower evaluations of the opponent and increase support for the candidate sponsoring the negative advertising. In the past, consultants rarely worried about a backlash against the sponsors of attack ads. But some consultants have become more sensitive to unintended effects in certain political climates and now concentrate more on contrast spots. Research has shown that types of negative messages must be chosen carefully, depending on the target audience. No single strategy will work for both base and swing voters.[21]

In general, psychological studies support the idea that negative information has a more forceful effect on the recipient than positive information.[22] Indeed, negative first impressions are harder to change than positive first impressions, and negative information has a greater capacity to alter existing impressions or to persuade voters. Yet large-scale studies of negative political advertising report no compelling evidence to confirm the finding that attack ads are more likely than advocacy ads to produce desired results.[23] When further studies are conducted to draw clear distinctions among the varieties of negative advertisements, perhaps clear indicators supporting the judgment of consultants will emerge. Although it is best to establish a positive image base with voters before attacking an opponent, it is better to define an opponent negatively before the opponent's positive message has gone on the air. Going negative in some fashion is more important for challengers, because they are making the case that an incumbent should be fired and that they should be hired instead.

Even though attack ads can backfire, such a boomerang effect is rarely seen when candidates use contrast spots.[24] It is more likely to occur when direct personal attacks or assaultive ads are used. If an opponent should level an attack, it is best to respond in the medium of the attack and to counterattack on issues potentially beneficial to the candidate. Finally, frequent repetition of harsh attack ads for an extended period of time can turn off voters, although a separate debate exists over whether or not negative attacks depress turnout (this issue is discussed later in this chapter).

Buying Advertising Time

In addition to the other strategic considerations, purchasing advertising airtime is an important calculation that affects the resonance of the message with the audience. Because candidates typically spend a large portion of their campaign budgets on political advertising, it is important to make sure that these ads are placed at times that will connect the candidates with the targeted voters (see Box 17-3). If at all possible, a candidate should buy time early to receive the most desirable time slots. The goal is to buy as much time as possible around television programming or during radio segments that reach the designated targets. For example, to reach viewers who are likely to vote,

---

BOX 17-3
UNDERSTANDING GROSS RATINGS POINTS (GRPs)

When a campaign outlines its advertising plan, it designs a strategy that will allow it to ensure that the target audience will be exposed to the candidate's message. In doing so, it relies on gross ratings points (GRPs), which are a measure of the reach and frequency for the campaign advertisement. "Reach" refers to the households out of all possible households in a given market that are tuned in to given program. "Frequency" refers to the average number of exposures for each household. Therefore, GRPs measure the ratings per program multiplied by the number of times a commercial is aired during that program. The cost per point (CPP) is the cost of a rating point for a specific media schedule. To estimate the total media expenditure, the media buyer will multiply the total GRPs by the CPP to get an estimate of the cost of the advertising schedule. Campaigns want to maximize GRPs for the least cost.

Each ratings point represents about one million households. Purchase of one hundred GRPs ensures that the entire television audience will see the ad once. Most consultants recommend showing an ad five times (the saturation level) or purchasing an ad buy of five hundred points.

A television station's rate card lists the costs of time slots during various programs. Prime-time slots cost thousands of dollars. Local stations may charge only $200 for a time slot during the afternoon soap operas, $40 for late-night movies. However, political candidates are given a break from paying the typical commercial rates. Thirty days before a primary and sixty days before a general election special regulations go into effect mandating that stations must offer political candidates the "lowest unit rate" —that is, the lowest rate the station would charge for the same class and amount of time for the period during which the candidate plans to buy time. The only drawback to selecting this discounted rate is that the time slot could be preempted. In other words, the station has the right to pull the slot for any reason, as long as it makes a concerted effort to provide a make good, by airing the ad in a slot similar to the one from which the ad was pulled. Because of this risk, candidates sometimes choose to pay higher rates to guarantee their time slots. In addition, stations are bound by law to give all candidates an equal opportunity to buy airtime.

The most effective advertising strategy is to amplify the message by purchasing a string of repeated spots, such as during the evening news for a week. After pollsters identify the audiences the campaign wants to target, the media buyer will make a buy based on these demographics. For example, many political campaigns target adults aged thirty-five and over. Or undecided or swing voters can be matched to audience profiles for particular programs. If a key persuadable or swing group for a candidate is suburban stay-at-home moms, the ad buyer can use this information to identify the television programs favored by this group.

Note: For more on GRPs, see Tobe Berkovitz, "Political Media Buying: A Brief Guide," 1996, www.ksg .harvard.edu/case/3pt/berkovitz.html (accessed May 22, 2005).

---

a candidate should buy time slots around the evening news, because the viewers who see these ads are more interested in public affairs. Candidates often track their opponents' ad buys to get a sense of the targeting, and often they will make parallel buys if they are targeting similar swing audiences. The mirroring of the opponents' ad buys also allows candidates to counteract any attack ads. Anyone can track candidate ad buys through the public file records (which include candidate invoices and ad buy schedules) available at all media outlets. However, interest group and political party records are not always made public by the stations, thereby making it more difficult to track these schedules and expenditures.

In high-level races such as presidential campaigns, candidates have begun to use a combination of national and local time buys that focus specifically on individual "battleground states." Campaigns adopt this strategy in order to use their money most efficiently, and they refrain from buying airtime in states that are clearly in their camps or their opponents' camps. In 1992 Bill Clinton took advantage of this dual strategy and targeted only eighteen states for local ad buys. His opponent, George Bush, used the markets in a subtle manner as well. He ran negative ads in local markets and stayed positive nationally toward the end of the race in order to attack his opponent under the radar of the national media.

Impact of Ads on Democracy

Most Americans report that ads do not affect their voting behavior. Yet research shows evidence of a positive relationship between ad expenditures and voter turnout. Moreover, ticket splitting, or voting for candidates of different parties in different contests, increases as voters are more exposed to political advertising.[25] This finding suggests that voters do go beyond partisanship to use the information provided in ads. In fact, R. A. Joslyn shows that exposure to television ads is the third most important criterion responsible for voters' defecting from their partisan leanings, behind the strength of a voter's party identification and the incumbency of the candidate.[26]

Despite concerns that advertising is bad for democracy, some studies show positive effects. Exposure to political advertising leads to more knowledge about a campaign. Indeed, those who are moderately to highly aware will gain important knowledge from advertising, although there appears to be a ceiling for this effect.[27] Voters also experience affective or emotional reactions to political advertising messages that can play a big role when they make their vote decisions. In fact, ads provide a personal, emotion-laden connection, and studies have shown that mere exposure to political ads will increase positive or negative feelings toward a candidate.[28]

However, different audiences are not equally receptive to political advertising messages. Simply assuming that a winning campaign had effective ads and that the losing campaign did not is a faulty generalization. Political ads have different effects on voters, depending on how receptive the voters are to the candidate's appeal. Receptivity depends on the levels to which voters pay attention to the information and how much prior knowledge they have to bring to their evaluations of the candidate or the race. Advertising messages are most likely to have the strongest impact when voters have little prior knowledge about the candidates. In such cases, ads are found to be more helpful than news in informing voters about new issues, because news tends to concentrate on the horse race—that is, who is ahead and who is behind at any given moment.

Finally, some studies have shown that negative political advertising has a detrimental impact on the democratic process, because it fosters a decline in political efficacy and voter turnout.[29] One analysis revealed that voters exposed to a single attack ad were about 5 percent less likely to vote in the next election than those who saw a single positive ad. The same 1995 study also found that turnout was about 4 percent lower in states that persisted in projecting a negative campaign tone. However, other studies have found higher levels of turnout in negative races because of the increased interest in the campaign created by the drama, while still others have shown no significant difference in turnout between highly negative and less negative races.[30] Clearly, further research is needed to address the most accurate way of classifying and measuring negative information in order to solve this puzzle.

Conclusion

This chapter has explored candidates' controlled messages in the form of campaign speeches and political advertising. These forms of communication set the agenda, frame the issues, and prime the considerations that voters use when evaluating candidates. Careful consideration of message content, style, and audience is essential for delivering persuasive speeches. Other important factors in launching a successful, controlled message from a candidate are advertising venues, message tone, and the strategies and tactics that increase the intended impact of advertising messages. Campaign communications do matter, and every strategic decision can have an impact, particularly in closely matched, high-intensity campaigns. Studies that ignore the role of mass media communications in campaigns are missing part of the story of the dynamics of campaigns and elections.

Notes

1. Kathleen E. Kendall, *Communication in the Presidential Primaries: Candidates and the Media, 1912–2000* (Westport, Conn.: Praeger, 2000), 125.

2. Ibid., 109.

3. Ibid.; Thomas Patterson and Robert D. McClure, *The Unseeing Eye: The Myth of Television Power in National Elections* (New York: Putnam, 1976).

4. Montague Kern, *Thirty-Second Politics: Political Advertising in the 1980s* (Westport, Conn.: Praeger, 1989).

5. Bruce Pinkleton, "The Effects of Negative Comparative Political Advertising on Candidate Evaluations: An Exploration," *Journal of Advertising* 26, no. 1 (1997): 19–29.

6. Stephen D. Ansolabehere and Shanto Iyengar, "Can the Press Monitor Campaign Advertising: An Experimental Study," *Harvard International Journal of Press/Politics* 1, no. 1(1996): 72–86; Kathleen Hall Jamieson and Joseph N. Cappella, "Setting the Record Straight: Do Ad Watches Help or Hurt?" *Harvard International Journal of Press/Politics* 2, no. 1 (1997): 13–22; Amy E. Jasperson and David P. Fan,

"News as Molder of Campaign Effects," *International Journal of Public Opinion Research* 16, no. 4 (December 2004); Darrell West, *Air Wars: Television Advertising in Election Campaigns, 1952–2000*, 3d ed. (Washington, D.C.: CQ Press, 2001).

7. Gary Genard, "Using Speeches to Gain Voters' Trust: Why What You Say Is Not Always as Important as How You Say It," *Campaigns and Elections Magazine* (October/November 2003): 30–32.

8. Judith S. Trent and Robert V. Friedenberg, *Political Campaign Communication: Principles and Practices*, 5th ed. (Westport, Conn.: Praeger, 2004).

9. Judith S. Trent and Robert V. Friedenberg, *Political Campaign Communication: Principles and Practices*, 4th ed. (Westport, Conn.: Praeger, 2000), 73.

10. On advertising expenditures and campaign budgets see, Darrell West, *Air Wars: Television Advertising in Election Campaigns, 1952–1996*, 2d ed. (Washington, D.C.: CQ Press, 1997); and on the importance of political advertising, see Patterson and McClure, *Unseeing Eye*, and Kern, *Thirty-Second Politics*.

11. On ads and uninvolved voters, see Kathleen Hall Jamieson, *Packaging the Presidency,* 2d ed. (New York: Oxford University Press, 1992). For research on the influence of ads when other sources of information are not available, see Marion Just, Ann Crigler, Dean Alger, Tim Cook, Montague Kern, and Darrell West. *Crosstalk: Citizens, Candidates, and the Media in a Presidential Campaign* (Chicago: University of Chicago Press, 1996).

12. Kendall, *Communication in the Presidential Primaries.*

13. Trent and Friedenberg, *Political Campaign Communication,* 5th ed., 363

14. Kern, *Thirty-Second Politics.*

15. Karen S. Johnson-Cartee and Gary A. Copeland, "Setting the Parameters of Good Taste: Negative Political Advertising," paper presented at the International Communication Association Convention, Montreal, 1987.

16. See Karen S. Johnson-Cartee and Gary A. Copeland, *Inside Political Campaigns* (Westport, Conn.: Praeger, 1997).

17. Ibid., 167.

18. Ibid., 149–184.

19. Karen S. Johnson-Cartee and Gary A. Copeland, *Negative Political Advertising: Coming of Age* (Mahwah, N.J.: Lawrence Erlbaum Associates, 1991), 41; and Johnson-Cartee and Copeland, "Setting the Parameters of Good Taste."

20. Kim Fridkin Kahn and Patrick J. Kenney, "Do Negative Campaigns Mobilize or Suppress Turnout? Clarifying the Relationship between Negativity and Participation," *American Political Science Review* 93 (December 1999): 877ff.

21. See Thomas L. Budesheim, David A. Houston, and Stephen J. DePaola, "Persuasiveness of In-Group and Out-Group Political Messages: The Case of Negative Political Campaigning," *Journal of Personality and Social Psychology* 70 (March 1996): 523–534; R. Faber, A. Tims, and K. Schmitt, "Accentuate the Negative? The Impact of Negative Political Appeals on Voting Intent," *Proceedings of the American Academy of Advertising* (1990): 10–16; G. Garramone, "Voter Responses to Negative Political Ads," *Journalism Quarterly* 61 (summer 1984): 250–259; S. Merritt, "Negative Political Advertising: Some Empirical Findings," *Journal of Advertising* 13, no. 3 (1984): 27–38.

22. M. Richey, H. Koenigs, H. Richey, and R. Fortin, "Negative Salience in Impressions of Character: Effects of Unequal Proportions of Positive and Negative Information," *Journal of Social Psychology* 97 (1975): 233–241.

23. Richard R. Lau, Lee Sigelman, Caroline Heldman, and Paul Babbitt, "The Effects of Negative Political Advertisements: A Meta-Analytic Assessment," *American Political Science Review* 93 (December 1999): 851–875.

24. Pinkleton, "Effects."

25. See the discussion in Johnson-Cartee and Copeland, *Inside Political Campaigns,* 153.

26. R. A. Joslyn, "The Impact of Campaign Spot Advertising on Voting Defections," *Human Communication Research* 7 (1981): 347–360.

27. Thomas Patterson and Robert D. McClure, "Television and the Less Interested Voter: The Costs of an Informed Electorate," *Annals of the American Academy of Political and Social Science* (1976): 88–97.

28. See the discussion in Johnson-Cartee and Copeland, *Inside Political Campaigns,* 153.

29. Stephen D. Ansolabehere and Shanto Iyengar, *Going Negative: How Negative Advertisements Shrink and Polarize the Electorate* (New York: Free Press, 1995); and see the replication study, Stephen D. Ansolabehere, Shanto Iyengar, and Adam Simon, "Replicating Experiments Using Aggregate and Survey Data: The Case of Negative Advertising and Turnout," *American Political Science Review* 93, no. 4 (December 1999): 901–909.

30. See Kahn and Kenney, "Do Negative Campaigns Mobilize or Suppress Turnout?"; and Martin P. Wattenberg and Craig Leonard Brians, "Negative Campaign Advertising: Demobilizer or Mobilizer?" *American Political Science Review* 93 (December 1999): 891–899.

Suggested Readings

Ansolabehere, Stephen D., and Shanto Iyengar. "Can the Press Monitor Campaign Advertising: An Experimental Study." *Harvard International Journal of Press/Politics* 1, no. 1 (1996): 72–86.

———. *Going Negative: How Negative Advertisements Shrink and Polarize the Electorate.* New York: Free Press, 1995.

Budesheim, Thomas L., David A. Houston, and Stephen J. DePaola. "Persuasiveness of In-Group and Out-Group Political Messages: The Case of Negative Political Campaigning." *Journal of Personality and Social Psychology* 70 (March 1996): 523–534.

Faber, R., A. Tims, and K. Schmitt. "Accentuate the Negative? The Impact of Negative Political Appeals on Voting Intent." *Proceedings of the American Academy of Advertising* (1990): 10–16.

Garramone, G. "Voter Responses to Negative Political Ads." *Journalism Quarterly* 61 (summer 1984): 250–259.

Genard, Gary. "Using Speeches to Gain Voters' Trust: Why What You Say Is Not Always as Important as How You Say It." *Campaigns and Elections Magazine* (October/ November 2003): 30–32.

Gronbeck, Bruce E. "The Rhetoric of Negative Political Advertising: Thoughts on Senatorial Race Ads in 1984." Paper presented at the Speech Communication Association Convention, Denver, 1985.

Gruner, C. R. "Wit and Humor in Mass Communications." In *Humor and Laughter: Theory, Research and Applications,* edited by Antony J. Chapman, Hugh C. Foote, and Peter Derks, 297–311. London: Wiley, 1976.

Jamieson, Kathleen Hall. *Packaging the Presidency.* 2d ed. New York: Oxford University Press, 1992.

Jamieson, Kathleen Hall, and Joseph N. Cappella. "Setting the Record Straight: Do Ad Watches Help or Hurt?" *Harvard International Journal of Press/Politics* 2, no. 1 (1997): 13–22.

Jasperson, Amy E., and David P. Fan. "An Aggregate Examination of the Backlash Effect in Political Advertising: The

Case of the 1996 U.S. Senate Race in Minnesota." *Journal of Advertising* 31 (spring 2002): 1–12.

———. "News as Molder of Campaign Effects." *International Journal of Public Opinion Research* 16, no. 4 (December 2004).

Johnson-Cartee, Karen S. and Gary A. Copeland. *Inside Political Campaigns*. Westport, Conn.: Praeger, 1997.

———. *Negative Political Advertising: Coming of Age.* Mahwah, N.J.: Lawrence Erlbaum Associates, 1991.

———. "Setting the Parameters of Good Taste: Negative Political Advertising." Paper presented at the International Communication Association Convention, Montreal, 1987.

Joslyn, R. A. "The Content of Political Spot Ads." *Journalism Quarterly* 57 (1980): 92–98.

———. "The Impact of Campaign Spot Advertising on Voting Defections." *Human Communication Research* 7 (1981): 347–360.

Just, Marion, Ann Crigler, Dean Alger, Tim Cook, Montague Kern, and Darrell West. *Crosstalk: Citizens, Candidates, and the Media in a Presidential Campaign*. Chicago: University of Chicago Press, 1996.

Kahn, Kim Fridkin, and Patrick J. Kenney. "Do Negative Campaigns Mobilize or Suppress Turnout? Clarifying the Relationship between Negativity and Participation." *American Political Science Review* 93 (December 1999): 877ff.

Kendall, Kathleen E. *Communication in the Presidential Primaries: Candidates and the Media, 1912–2000*. Westport, Conn.: Praeger, 2000.

Kern, Montague. *Thirty-Second Politics: Political Advertising in the 1980s*. Westport, Conn.: Praeger, 1989.

Lau, Richard R., Lee Sigelman, Caroline Heldman, and Paul Babbitt. "The Effects of Negative Political Advertisements: A Meta-Analytic Assessment." *American Political Science Review* 93 (December 1999): 851–875.

Merritt, S. "Negative Political Advertising: Some Empirical Findings." *Journal of Advertising* 13, no. 3 (1984): 27–38.

Patterson, Thomas, and Robert D. McClure. "Television and the Less Interested Voter: The Costs of an Informed Electorate." *Annals of the American Academy of Political and Social Science* (1976): 88–97.

———. *The Unseeing Eye: The Myth of Television Power in National Elections*. New York: Putnam, 1976.

Pinkleton, Bruce. "The Effects of Negative Comparative Political Advertising on Candidate Evaluations: An Exploration." *Journal of Advertising* 26, no. 1 (1997): 19–29.

Richey, M., H. Koenigs, H. Richey, and R. Fortin. "Negative Salience in Impressions of Character: Effects of Unequal Proportions of Positive and Negative Information." *Journal of Social Psychology* 97 (1975): 233–241.

Trent, Judith S., and Robert V. Friedenberg. *Political Campaign Communication: Principles and Practices*. 5th ed. Westport, Conn.: Praeger, 2004.

Wattenberg, Martin P., and Craig Leonard Brians. "Negative Campaign Advertising: Demobilizer or Mobilizer?" *American Political Science Review* 93 (December 1999): 891–899.

West, Darrell. *Air Wars: Television Advertising in Election Campaigns, 1952–2004*. 4th ed. Washington, D.C.: CQ Press, 2005.

CHAPTER 18

Debates

Nathan S. Bigelow

Since 1858 when nearly twenty thousand people showed up to witness Abraham Lincoln and Stephen A. Douglas square off in a series of public debates as they campaigned for the U.S. Senate in Illinois, debates have occupied an important substantive and symbolic place in American political campaigns. Whether political debates are held on elementary school stages in small towns or before television cameras broadcasting into millions of living rooms, candidates and their advisers recognize their importance in stimulating the electorate and winning important swing votes. Beyond the immediate political utility that debates hold for candidates, they also increase public deliberation and inform voters of the important political issues of the day. Debates have the unique ability to present candidates and their issues side by side, in a less scripted and less rehearsed setting. In short, debates hold the potential to improve the democratic system.

The public expects candidates to debate. At the presidential level, candidates debate several times in both the primary and general phases of the election. Yet presidential and vice-presidential debates represent only a small portion of the many political debates that take place for various offices across the nation. Although less visible, candidates for statewide or other high-profile offices are also expected to debate their opponents. In recent years, these debates have been reaching a larger audience. About 40 percent of all debates between candidates running for governor, the U.S. Senate, and the U.S. House of Representatives are now televised. Even nonpresidential debates, such as the 2000 U.S. Senate debates in New York between First Lady Hillary Rodham Clinton and Rep. Rick Lazio, can attract national attention. Despite how commonplace debates have recently become, however, only since 1976 have debates been a regular occurrence in presidential races.

This chapter describes the role that debates play in the campaign process. It begins by outlining the rules that govern presidential debates and important historical developments in those debates. The discussion of debate formats and candidate strategies that follows illustrates the intense preparation that candidates and their staffs undergo in their efforts to avoid potential pitfalls and to cap-

italize on as much as possible in debates. The chapter then considers the question of who "wins" debates, which requires some understanding of the way the media cover these events. Finally, the chapter discusses the effects debates have on the outcomes of elections and then speculates on the promise debates hold for improving the electoral process.

The Evolution of Debates

Largely for symbolic reasons, political debates trace their roots to the Lincoln–Douglas debates of 1858. Noted for their seriousness and articulation, Lincoln and Douglas delved deeply into the issues of slavery and westward expansion, charting out competing visions for the future of the country. This series of debates featured no moderator, set no agenda, attracted a raucous audience, and continued for hours on end. Critics of contemporary debates often cite the Lincoln–Douglas debates as examples of what contemporary debates are not. They argue that contemporary debates lack articulation and seriousness, and even go so far as to characterize them as "irrelevant, irritating, irascible squabbles over who did what to whom and how." [1]

Debates today, however, are fundamentally different than they were a century and a half ago, and comparisons with the Lincoln–Douglas debates may be unjustified. The most important differences stem from the extraordinary advances made in communications technologies. The advent of radio and especially television changed forever the nature of political campaigning in general and debates in particular. Instead of communicating to twenty thousand people without the benefit of a microphone, candidates today can reach hundreds of millions of voters simultaneously. The first televised presidential debate in 1960 between Democratic senator John F. Kennedy and Republican vice president Richard Nixon spawned much speculation about the influence of television on voters' perceptions. Television viewers judged Kennedy to be the winner, whereas radio listeners concluded that Nixon

DU PAGE COUNTY CENTENNIAL

LINCOLN ★ DOUGLAS

DEBATE

AUGUST · 27ᵀᴴ
WEST CHICAGO

The 1858 Illinois Senate campaign debates between Democrat Stephen A. Douglas and Republican Abraham Lincoln became a national dialogue on slavery and states' rights. Douglas prevailed in the election, but the seven landmark debates paved the way for Lincoln's election as president in 1860 and have since been reenacted over the years, as in Du Page County, Illinois. Source: Library of Congress

won the debate.[2] Since 1960, candidates and their advisers have had to manage both substantive and stylistic concerns when debating on television. Thus, even though Americans symbolically trace their debate roots to the Lincoln–Douglas debates, the true roots of contemporary debates are the Kennedy–Nixon debates of 1960 (see Box 18-1).

Some structural and legal barriers had to be overcome before debates could be broadcast over radio and television. The Equal Time Rule, passed as part of the 1934 Communication Act, requires broadcasters to treat legally qualified political candidates equally when it comes to selling or giving away airtime. When a station sells or gives time to Candidate A, it must sell or give the same amount of time (with the same audience potential) to all other candidates for the office. As such, at the time political debates violated the Equal Time Rule when they excluded minor-party candidates. Thus in 1960 Congress

had to suspend the rule so that the Kennedy–Nixon debate could take place without the inclusion of minor-party candidates Farrel Dobbs of the Socialist Workers Party, Eric Hass of the Socialist Labor Party, Orval Faubus of the States' Rights Party, as well as the Constitution and Prohibition Party candidates. The Federal Communications Commission (FCC) permitted the 1976 debates between Democrat Jimmy Carter and Republican Gerald R. Ford and the 1980 debate between Carter and Republican Ronald Reagan to go on under the technicality that they were "public meetings," which under the "regular news" exemption (meaning that the Equal Time Rule did not apply to on-the-spot news coverage) trumped the Equal Time Rule. In 1983 the FCC created a permanent exemption for political debates from Equal Time requirements, as long as the candidate selection process remained "nondiscriminatory."

In 1987 the nonpartisan Commission on Presidential Debates (CPD) was established to organize presidential debates. The CPD, which is chaired by former leaders of both the Democratic and Republican Parties, is charged with sponsoring all general election debates for presidential and vice-presidential candidates. Its stated purpose is to "ensure that debates, as a permanent part of every general election, provide the best possible information to viewers and listeners."

The CPD plays an important role as gatekeeper for would-be debate participants. In 2000 and 2004, for example, participants needed to fulfill three requirements to gain admission to the debates: (1) they had to be constitutionally eligible for the election; (2) they must have gained access to the ballot in enough states to have a mathematical chance of winning; and (3) they needed 15 percent of national support, as ascertained by the average polling results of five polling organizations. As a result of these rules, the 2000 debates featured only Texas governor George W. Bush and Vice President Al Gore, and the 2004 debates featured only President George W. Bush and Sen. John Kerry. Yet these requirements are open to change in each election cycle. In 1992 the commission stipulated that to participate in the presidential debate a candidate must have evidence of a national organization, signs of national newsworthiness and competitiveness, and indicators of national enthusiasm or concern. Despite some initial questions, the commission found that Reform Party candidate H. Ross Perot possessed each of these qualities. Affecting their decision to allow his participation was the fact that the campaigns of Democrat Bill Clinton and Republican George Bush did not object.

The Decision to Debate

The first strategic decision for candidates is whether to debate. Although presidential candidates Lyndon B. Johnson

BOX 18-1

MEMORABLE MOMENTS IN DEBATE HISTORY

Jeff Davis

1858: Lincoln–Douglas Debates

In 1858 Abraham Lincoln, a single-term Republican representative from Illinois, and Stephen A. Douglas, the state's incumbent Democratic senator, engaged in seven debates during their race for Douglas's U.S. Senate seat. Although senators were elected by state legislators at the time, Lincoln and Douglas used these debates to speak directly to the general public about the issues of slavery and states' rights. Lincoln spoke of the need for unity among the states on the eradication of slavery, while Douglas argued that each state ought to decide for itself how to resolve this volatile issue. On election day, the people cast their votes for the Illinois state legislators, who then reelected Douglas. Even though Lincoln lost this election, he gained so much popularity through his participation in the debates that the Republican leadership began to seriously consider him for their presidential nomination.

1960: Image, Image, Image

For the first time in political debate history, the presidential candidates faced the nation on radio and television during the 1960 campaign. In their four debates, Democrat John F. Kennedy and Republican Richard Nixon mainly addressed the issue of global communism, but the debates are often remembered for how the candidates appeared. In the first debate, Kennedy came across as energetic and composed, while the perspiring Nixon seemed pale and drab. Those who listened to the debate on the radio largely judged Nixon to be the winner, whereas those who watched it on television felt Kennedy had won. Candidates and consultants were quick to note that campaigning on television was fundamentally different from anything that had come

John F. Kennedy and Richard Nixon
Source: CBS/Landov

before. A carefully crafted message was no longer enough; a candidate had to be able to convey an image that felt comfortable to voters.

1976: The Power of the Political Gaffe

In the second debate between Republican president Gerald R. Ford and his Democratic challenger, Jimmy Carter, Ford made the mistake of stating something that was glaringly untrue: he claimed that "there is no Soviet domination of eastern Europe." Even after he was given an opportunity to correct his blunder, Ford refused. Almost a week later, Ford acknowledged his mistake, but the political gaffe had already damaged his campaign. Voters questioned Ford's competency, and in a later interview he pointed to his blunder as a major factor in his election defeat.

1980: Reagan's One-Liners

In 1980 incumbent president Jimmy Carter refused to participate in the first debate with his Republican op-

ponent, Ronald Reagan, because he was uncomfortable with the format. When he finally agreed to the debate, Ronald Reagan outperformed Carter. Reagan's memorable performance was attributed to his use of two famous lines. Whenever he believed Carter was misrepresenting his issue positions, Reagan repeatedly used the phrase "There you go again." Reagan also used what has perhaps become the most recycled question in presidential politics: "Are you better off now than you were four years ago?" The lines played well with the media, giving Reagan a clear edge over his opponent.

1984: Strategic Counterattacks

During his reelection campaign in 1984, President Ronald Reagan agreed to debate his Democratic challenger, Walter F. Mondale, despite the fact that Reagan was leading comfortably in the polls. The decision almost backfired as Mondale outperformed Reagan in the first

(Box continues on next page)

BOX 18-1 *(continued)*
MEMORABLE MOMENTS IN DEBATE HISTORY

Jimmy Carter (left) and Ronald Reagan
Source: AP Wide World Photos

debate. However, in the second debate Reagan rebounded when he tackled the issue of his advanced age by turning the issue around on Mondale, promising not to "exploit, for political purposes, my opponent's youth and inexperience." Reagan's clever response was effective in calming some of the concerns over his age.

1988: Do Not Compare Yourself to Jack Kennedy

The presidential debates were largely unmemorable in 1988, but some fireworks went off in the vice-presidential debate. After Republican senator Dan Quayle of Indiana likened himself to President John F. Kennedy, his Democratic opponent, Sen. Lloyd Bentsen of Texas, famously reminded Quayle, "I served with Jack Kennedy. I knew Jack Kennedy. Jack Kennedy was a friend of mine. Senator, you're no Jack Kennedy." The shocked and confused look on Quayle's face became one of the more memorable moments of the campaign, but the Bush–Quayle ticket went on to win in November.

2000: Lazio's Poor Presentation

Although the presidential race monopolized most of the media coverage in 2000, a series of debates in

New York between the U.S. Senate candidates, First Lady Hillary Rodham Clinton and Rep. Rick Lazio, captured national attention. In one of these debates, Lazio made a significant error in judgment by leaving his lectern, approaching Clinton, and, in an unusual and awkwardly aggressive manner, shoving in front of her a paper on which was written a promise not to spend "soft" (unregulated) money. The negative publicity from this action reinforced the idea that in debates the ways in which candidates present themselves can be as important as what they say.

Sources: Elihu Katz and Jacob J. Feldman, "The Debates in the Light of Research: A Survey of Surveys," in *The Great Debates, Background, Perspective, Effects,* ed. Sidney Kraus (Bloomington: Indiana University Press, 1962); Jim Lehrer, "Debating Our Destiny: President Gerald Ford Interview," November 11, 1989, www.pbs.org; "Ford, Gerald R(udolph)," *Microsoft Encarta Online Encyclopedia,* encarta.msn.com.

Rick Lazio (left) and Hillary Rodham Clinton
Source: Reuters/Pool/Landov

and Richard Nixon were able to opt out of debates un- scathed, the only other presidential candidate since 1960 to opt out of a general election debate was Jimmy Carter (although he did participate in a second debate). Carter went on to lose his bid for reelection in 1980. The political process has reached the point where candidates who would prefer not to debate often feel compelled to do so anyway. In 2000 the George W. Bush campaign consid- ered not participating in the debates, but in the end the costs would have been just too high. In down-ballot races (those for statewide office and Congress), the price of opt- ing out of debates may be smaller because of the relative lack of attention paid to these races.

Typically, debates take place when elections are close, both candidates hope to gain an advantage by debating, both candidates are confident in their debating skills, and the debate format offers minimal risk of potential gaffes. Debates are also more likely to occur when there is good possibility that the debate will receive media coverage, when candidates have low vulnerability levels because of the issues involved, when the formats and political cli- mate are favorable, and when the campaign is for a gen- eral, not a primary, election.[3]

Substantive and strategic concerns influence the deci- sion to include or exclude third party candidates. As a rule, the perceived front-runner promotes the inclusion of minor-party candidates, while the candidate trailing in the race prefers a one-on-one encounter. The logic behind this is that candidates leading in a race have little to gain from a one-on-one encounter and much to lose, with the opposite being true for a candidate who is trailing.[4]

The decision to allow third party participation also stems from a candidate's perceived competence. The "winner–loser" dichotomy of a two-person debate dimin- ishes with the inclusion of a third party candidate, and these debates present fewer questions and allot less time for answers, helping candidates who have a difficult time developing extended responses. Minor-party candidates also can change the tenor of debates, inserting ideological or issue-specific appeals that the major-party candidates would prefer to exclude from the campaign agenda. Fi- nally, once allowed to debate, a third party candidate may actually win the debate—thereby upsetting the prevailing campaign dynamic—and go on to victory in the election. This scenario occurs infrequently, but it is not without precedent. Jesse Ventura's successful gubernatorial cam- paign in Minnesota in 1998 is an example of the risks as- sociated with underestimating potential support for a spirited challenge from a third party candidate.

Debate Formats

Once candidates in an election decide to debate, they must determine the format of the debate. In their negotia- tions, the candidates and their advisers seek a format that highlights their strengths and reveals their opponents' weaknesses. For example, the conventional wisdom in the 2000 presidential race was that Vice President Gore would do best in a more formal, single-moderator format, because he and his advisers were confident about his for- mal debating abilities. In addition, there was considerable doubt about Governor Bush's abilities to perform well in a high-pressure and confrontational-style format. As it turned out, Bush, although probably outperformed by Gore, exceeded the expectations of the Gore camp, the media, and perhaps even his own campaign organizers. Nevertheless, the format is always a negotiable item that campaigns seek to use to their advantage.

Panel Format

The panel format is a popular and frequently used design for debates. In this design, a panel of experts, usually journalists, take turns questioning the candidates on a variety of issues. This format is especially popular in pri- mary debates in which there may be multiple candidates. The candidates may or may not be allowed to question each other, but they are usually allowed to respond to comments made by their opponents.

An advantage of the panel format, especially for the less confident debater, is that its barrage of questions on a variety of subjects is less formidable than a more thor- ough focus on a few issues. Its major disadvantage, from the perspective of viewers, is that it changes the nature of the adversarial relationship from politician to politician to questioner to politician.[5] Indeed, the experts and jour- nalists who act as questioners often seem to be participat- ing in a side competition to see who can do the best job of stumping the candidates. The panel format and the single-moderator format are considered to be the most confrontational debate formats.[6]

Single-Moderator Format

In the single-moderator format, the candidates usually stand at podiums, and a moderator asks them either preapproved questions, questions on agreed-upon topics, or perhaps questions on any subject at all. This format is often used when the field of candidates is limited to two or perhaps three. The single-moderator format is gener- ally the most successful at providing highly substantive debates, because in this format candidates have more time for their responses and moderators have more of an opportunity to follow up on the questions. Also, depend- ing on the candidate's predisposition, this format can be helpful because it produces less interaction between or among the candidates.

Town Hall Format

The town hall format, in which candidates respond almost entirely to questions asked by members of the audience, is another popular debate design. It appeals to candidates who are comfortable thinking on their feet, have the ability to interact well with different people, and can respond to a diverse set of questions. It is the most popular format with the public, because they feel candidates are less evasive when responding to questions from the audience.[7] This format, however, consumes large amounts of time that could be devoted to candidates' answers, and it can result in a barrage of questions that audience members cannot follow up. Audience reaction and rogue questioning are also difficult to control under this format. A candidate not adept at handling a heckler may wish to avoid this format.

Variations and Less Frequently Used Formats

Increasingly popular is the variation on the single-moderator format, which presents the debate in a news interview format. These *Meet the Press*–style debates have the benefit of putting candidates somewhat at ease and facilitating a more conversational debate, which the public seems to value but which forensic scholars find muffles the give-and-take between candidates. Another increasingly popular format is the variation on the single-moderator or panel format, in which the candidates sit at a table, a setting that typically facilitates a more conversational atmosphere. The 2000 vice-presidential debate between Richard B. Cheney and Sen. Joseph I. Lieberman was one of the more substantive, thoughtful, and collegial debates of recent times, probably because of the more relaxed seated format.

Less frequently used formats include the modified Ford–Carter format, which permits multiple rebuttals, counter-rebuttals, follow-ups, and lengthened time for responses. There is also the modified Lincoln–Douglas format, in which the debate revolves around lengthy answers to a specific policy question, and the policy address, in which a candidate delivers a long address that is followed up, perhaps the next day, by a long rebuttal address. Neither of these formats is particularly popular. They may result in more thoughtful responses from candidates, but they are less liked by viewers and require much more preparation by candidates.[8]

Technical Format Considerations

On a more technical level, the format decisions related to speaker time, rotations, opening and closing statements, rebuttals, the use of notes, microphones, staging, the use of reaction shots, camera movements, and the height of the podiums, among other things, are all vitally important. In 2004 the formal agreement between the Bush and Kerry campaigns was made public and offered great insight into the volume of considerations that candidates take into account when preparing for debates.[9] Some of the more obscure agreements formalized in this report include a precise time by which the coin toss must be completed before the beginning of the debate, an agreement to "maintain an appropriate temperature" in the hall,

and the precise procedures that the candidates' still photographers must follow.

Candidates must negotiate all of these aspects of the debate with their personal strengths and weaknesses in mind. How long does it take to deliver a position on an issue? Is a candidate more effective at leveling a charge or at responding to one? Should the candidates be able to interact directly? For a front-runner, direct questioning in debates is often a risky strategy. The desperate underdog, however, may be able to turn the tables on his or her opponent through direct questioning or by escalating emotion with all its attendant risks.

The moderator is also an important dimension of a debate. To what extent should the moderator be allowed to interject random subjects or pleas for clarification into the debate? Most candidates prefer rules that do not allow the moderator(s) to interrupt them and that tightly control the scope of the questioning.

Another important consideration is the role of the audience. Audience questioning poses the risk that an audience member may issue a statement instead of asking a question, begin to debate with the candidates, struggle for control with the moderator, or perhaps pursue an overly repetitive line of questioning. To avoid these situations, campaigns often opt to prescreen questions.

Scholars have taken note of the time constraints present in political debates. Kathleen Hall Jamieson and David S. Birdsell explain: "Debate values an advocate's ability to distill complex material into manageable blocks of time. Such a facility is valuable until the time pressures become so intense that slogans displace argument. In televised debates, candidates are asked to perform miracles of compression, explaining complex positions on major issues in less than a minute." [10]

Still, proposals to lengthen the time for answers have some drawbacks. First, modern audiences may not have the attention spans to listen to time-consuming answers. Second, few candidates use all the time allotted under current restrictions. Third, candidates might be unwilling to accept debate invitations if the time is extended. Debates that revolve around a stated proposition or issue are one possible remedy for improving the quality of discourse. However, campaigns typically shun proposition-centered debates, despite the fact that they are the standard for traditional forensic debates.[11]

Debate Strategy

Once candidates make the decision to debate, decide on participants, and agree to a format, they must develop their debate strategies. In doing so, a campaign must ask itself some questions: What should the candidate seek to accomplish during the debate? What are the strengths and weaknesses of the candidate and the opponent? Which audiences should be targeted? Is the debate strategy, once defined, compatible with the overall campaign strategy?

The Viewing Audience and the Target Audience

Candidates must know their audiences. Televised debates are fundamentally different from nontelevised debates. In the nontelevised debates, the audience is often partisan, and the most effective strategy is to reinforce the attitudes of supporters and, most important, to impress reporters who will inform the outside world of what transpired in the debate. In a televised debate, the strategy becomes more difficult. Candidates and their staffs must decide which viewers to target. This decision generally reflects a candidate's position in the race.

Front-runners are usually mainly concerned with appealing to their base by not saying anything that might jeopardize their support. Candidates trailing in the race must also appeal to the uncommitted and perhaps even the weakly committed opposition, whom debates are more likely to persuade. However, this approach can drain a campaign of core supporters and, as such, is regarded as a last-ditch strategy.

Image goals are central to the debate strategy. In well-funded campaigns, polls help campaigns craft the most effective candidate image possible. By querying people on the candidate's and opponent's "compassion," "intelligence," and other important characteristics, and cross-referencing the respondents' age, gender, race, income, education, and other demographic factors, campaigns can isolate target audiences and focus their messages accordingly.[12]

Relational Strategies

Relational strategies include attack, defend, sell, ignore, and "me too . . . me better" strategies. *Attack* is an offensive strategy in which the candidate assails the opponent's issues, party, or character. In a *defend* strategy, the candidate develops responses to anticipated attacks. *Sell* strategies allow the candidates to present their credentials for holding office or to show their accomplishments in office. In an *ignore* strategy, the candidates debate on their own terms, paying little attention to the opponents and the points the opponents are trying to make. The *"me too . . . me better"* strategy allows candidates to agree on an issue, but explain how they could handle the issue more effectively. Because candidates vying for their party's nomination often have similar issue positions, this strategy is common in primary election debates.

The candidate's status (as incumbent, challenger, or contestant for an open seat) and the competitiveness of the election influence the candidate's choice of relational strategy. Generally, nonincumbents or those trailing in the race are more attack-oriented because of the sizable incumbent advantage that challengers usually need to overcome. The hope of challengers is that, at a minimum, the attacks will plant a seed of doubt in the minds of voters and, in the best-case scenario, will draw the incumbent into a serious mistake. The goal of the incumbent is to keep the debate as uneventful as possible. An unplanned confrontation is not likely to have any positive effects. Incumbents or candidates in the lead are well advised to adopt the sell or defend strategies, because incumbents need to remind constituents of all the good things they have done and because challengers are likely to attack the incumbent's record. In open-seat races, the candidates of the out party are likely to tie their opponents to the incumbents' party and to engage in behavior similar to that of a challenger and vice versa.

The ignore strategy is effective when the debate format does not involve cross-examination or counter-rebuttals (features that make it difficult for candidates to avoid each other). A variation on the ignore strategy is the *above-the-fray* strategy. Most prevalent in multicandidate debates, this tactic allows the candidate in the lead to engage mainly in a sell strategy and occasionally to refer lightheartedly to the contention brewing among the other candidates.

Campaign advisers often instruct candidates to avoid specific answers to questions, because they do not have much to gain by offering detailed responses. Engaging in specificity is especially risky when a candidate does not know much about the issue in question, when making a policy commitment is politically dangerous, or when a specific approach to one issue consumes time better spent on other issues. Although it is strategically sound to avoid specificity, critics of contemporary political debates cite this avoidance as an important flaw in debates, claiming that it promotes a shallow discussion of the issues. Audiences, too, recognize overt evasion of the issues, which can affect their perceptions of a candidate's honesty. Candidates must therefore walk a careful line between overspecificity and overevasiveness in their answers.[13]

How the Media Cover Debates

The media are indispensable participants in political debates, first and foremost as facilitators. According to the Commission on Presidential Debates, the second debate of 1992 set the record with nearly seventy million viewers, and the average number of viewers for presidential debates remains about sixty million. Thus compared with regular prime-time programming on ABC, NBC, or CBS, for which the average audience is nine million, presidential debates are widely watched. The only regularly scheduled event that draws a larger audience is the Super Bowl.[14] Political debates would simply not be the significant events that they are without the participation, in a technical sense, of the media.

The media, however, do more than simply broadcast debates; they also provide postdebate commentary and

BOX 18-2
HOW TO HOST A LOCAL DEBATE
Jennifer Katkin

Although they are generally associated with presidential elections, political debates can also play an influential role at the local level. Candidates for local elective offices, such as county board members and school board members, may choose to participate in a debate in order to communicate their platforms to the electorate. These debates are frequently hosted by civic organizations as a way to generate discussion about particular issues. For example, the Florida Children's Campaign organizes local debates in order to raise concerns about the state's juvenile justice system, education policies, and family support programs.

Those organizing a debate at the local level must take many issues into account, including the participants, format, sponsorship, audience, and logistical matters. Organizers must first decide which candidates to invite, and then they must issue all of the invitations at the same time. The invitation should include the proposed details of the debate, such as the time, place, and format, although the organizers and candidates may negotiate these items later. One detail that is hotly negotiated is the proposed format of the debate. Format

considerations include various options for arranging the candidates, as well as a multitude of technical details such as time restrictions, rebuttal and counter-rebuttal rules, candidate interaction rules, and the inclusion or exclusion of opening and closing statements (see text for a more detailed description).

As a rule, candidates and their advisers try to negotiate more control into debates so that the candidates can avoid making mistakes or being caught off guard. Organizers should therefore act as a counterweight by always encouraging the most open and substantive debates possible, keeping in mind that they need to make the candidates comfortable enough to ensure their participation.

Sponsorship also plays an important role in a candidate's decision on whether to participate. If the debate organizers are strongly partisan, a candidate from the opposing party may refuse to attend. Candidates tend to believe that nonpartisan organizations such as the League of Women Voters and Project Vote Smart are more capable than some other organizations of hosting a fair debate. Likewise, the audience at a debate, if organizers choose to have one, should be a balanced mix of

supporters for each candidate. Audience members should always be prohibited from expressing their reactions to the candidates' statements.

The logistical matters to be settled for a debate include location, security, stage furniture, lighting, microphones, media kits, and the issuing of printed programs. Most organizers seek television coverage of a debate so that they can reach as many voters as possible. Television coverage, however, raises the costs of the event, as well as its complexity, because camera locations, equipment space, and power sources must be accommodated. Moreover, once candidates learn the event will be broadcast on television, they and their representatives become concerned about podium heights, camera angles, and other factors that could affect how they are perceived by viewers.

Sources: Ronald A. Faucheux, ed., *The Debate Book* (Washington, D.C.: Campaigns and Elections Publishing Company, 2003); "Guide to Hosting Your Own Debate," Commission on Presidential Debates, www.debates .org/pages/education.html (accessed June 28, 2004); Children's Campaign Inc., www.iamforkids.org (accessed November 3, 2004).

analysis. Voters are more likely to retain a memory of themes stressed by the media in postdebate coverage than information from the debate itself.[15] Postdebate commentators feel it is up to them to tell viewers who won the debate. Guided in part by immediate poll results, the media feel pressure to quickly establish a consensual answer to the "Who won?" question. This quickly reported "winner," in turn, guides public responses to subsequent questions about the winner, showing that people's responses solidify around a media-reported winner.[16] In addition to using instant polls, commentators also focus on who wins the one-liner battle—that is, they announce which candidate leveled the best, most creative, or most humorous verbal blow at the opponent. Such a postdebate assessment encourages candidates to score against one another rather than to focus on debating one another. The increas-

ing focus on the winner–loser dichotomy by postdebate commentators can reduce debates to mere horse race contests as opposed to helping debates live up to their billing as sources of political knowledge and improved public discourse. Similar to their approach to reporting election winners, news outlets have become slightly more responsible in recent years about pronouncing debate winners. They now often rely on a panel of television news personalities to prognosticate on who won.

The Effects of Debates

Most candidates and consultants agree that debates serve an important role in solidifying existing support among partisans and in capturing swing votes. Much of the political science literature, however, approaches debates, and other campaign activities, from the standpoint of assumed minimal effects—that is, the onus is on the researcher to prove that debates actually change something about the election. This task is difficult to carry out in a definitive sense, because a candidate would never agree to a researcher's request to refrain from entering a debate so that the researcher can assess whether the candidate would indeed lose as a result. Despite these difficulties, researchers have made important discoveries about the effects of debates on the electorate.

They do know that debates generate public interest in politics, especially when they are held in conjunction with close elections. Also, debates, especially those held early in an election cycle, play a role in informing the electorate.[17] Few studies, however, find a consistent relationship between performances in debates and vote choices in general elections.[18] Yet in primary debates the performance of a candidate is more likely to affect vote choice, because in those debates the candidates are of the same party, a factor that forces the audience to evaluate them without regard for party labels.[19]

Debates have separate effects on partisan and independent voters. Partisan voters find that debates activate their partisan predispositions and, through a process of selective reception and attention, reinforce those political attitudes.[20] Even if their candidate does poorly in a debate, partisans use the techniques of isolation, selective perception, and personalization to rationalize and forgive poor performance. Indeed, partisan voters become more committed to a candidate simply when the opposition presents information contradictory to their beliefs.[21] Independents, by contrast, are more likely to look to debates for information about the candidates' policy positions and to learn from them.[22] As such, debates influence the voting preferences of independents and so-called mismatched partisans (such as Bush Democrats and Kerry Republicans) to a greater extent than they affect partisans.[23]

The types of information that voters take away from debates fall into two main categories: the substantive information that voters learn from watching debates and the stylistic information that voters infer about the candidates. Debates transmit important substantive information to voters. They increase voters' awareness of political issues and of the candidates' positions. Likewise, those who watch debates are more likely to retain information on candidates' issue positions than those who do not.[24] Debates also reduce the "knowledge gap," as viewers with lower levels of political knowledge make strides to catch up with the better-informed citizens. Debates are especially useful for providing voters with knowledge about lesser-known candidates and their positions on issues. Indeed, for many underfunded candidates debates represent a rare free media opportunity. Debates also increase the salience of certain campaign issues.[25]

Debates are perhaps even better at conveying a candidate's style or personality. Television, to a greater degree than other communication medium, is especially suited to revealing candidates' personalities and thought processes.[26] Because most individuals have imperfect information about the candidates' positions, voters turn to other cues, such as the candidate's personality, appearance, or style, to form their voting decisions.[27] Indeed, television captured George Bush impatiently checking his watch and failing to connect with the "lay" questioners in the second 1992 debate. In the first debate of 2000, television noted every sigh that Al Gore let out and awkwardly accentuated each mention of his proposed Social Security "lockbox." In the second debate of 2000, Gore came across as overly passive, while in the final debate he managed to strike the right tone. This "Goldilocks" performance over the series of debates only reinforced the Bush campaign's claim that Gore liked to "reinvent" himself. In 2004 Sen. John Kerry jumped in the polls after coming across as "presidential" in the first debate, while George W. Bush seemed defensive, often scowling and hunching over his lectern. In the age of television politics, the visual message has at least as great an effect on viewers' impressions as the verbal arguments.[28]

Conclusion

Critics argue that debates fail to live up to their full potential. They contend that candidates in debates are more concerned with being elected and less concerned with political education, quality discourse, or any notion of the public good. They cite the prevalence of imagery, as opposed to substantive discussion, as evidence of this failure. Others argue, however, that all sorts of information that voters receive about candidates can be useful, whether the information focuses on substance or image. Adjustments to debate formats may hold the potential to improve the content of debates, making them more substance-based. Recent attempts to provide subpresidential campaigns with uniform and agreed-upon debate standards and formats are an example of efforts to improve the quality and frequency of debates.[29]

Despite these criticisms, debates remain major events in presidential election campaigns if for no other reason than because of their vast viewership. With the decreased relevance of party conventions, voters pay more attention to debates than to any other regularly scheduled event during presidential campaigns. In races for lower-level offices, the television coverage of debates has continued to increase. In these races, debates have the potential to spotlight campaigns that otherwise would receive only scant and sporadic media attention.

Debates serve an important democratic function. They clarify the choices available to the voter relative to the important issues of the day in an age in which campaigning is increasingly less personal. Because voters learn about candidates sporadically through conversations, pamphlets, posters, ads, and news, debates represent a rare opportunity for voters to receive information firsthand and unaltered—from the candidate's mouth. Sidney Kraus, a leading political debate scholar, notes that "democracy is essentially well served by televised debates.

They provide the American electorate, at their convenience and in their homes, with facts about candidates and issues. Debates on television should be institutionalized, if not by law, by public decree." [30] By increasing deliberation among voters and making them more aware of political issues and more politically active, debates help to make candidates more accountable to their constituencies.

Notes

1. Gus Tyler, "Democracy vs. Mediacracy," *New Leader,* May 28, 1984, 10.

2. For information on the Sindlinger and Company poll see Elihu Katz and Jacob J. Feldman, "The Debates in the Light of Research: A Survey of Surveys," *The Great Debates,* ed. Sidney Kraus (Bloomington: Indiana University Press, 1962). Recent research questions the validity of these findings. See James N. Druckman, "The Power of Television Images: The First Kennedy-Nixon Debate Revisited," *Journal of Politics* (2004): 65, 559–571.

3. Robert V. Friedenberg, " 'We Are Present Here Today for the Purpose of Having a Joint Discussion': The Conditions Requisite for Political Debates," *Journal of the American Forensic Association* (1979): 1–9, 16.

4. Myles Martel, *Political Campaign Debates* (New York: Longman, 1983).

5. Kathleen Hall Jamieson and David S. Birdsell, *Presidential Debates* (New York: Oxford University Press, 1988).

6. Diana Prentice Carlin, Charles Howard, Susan Stanfield, and Larry Reynolds, "The Effects of Presidential Debate Formats on Clash: A Comparative Analysis," *Argumentation and Advocacy* (winter 1991): 27, 126–136.

7. Ibid.

8. Martel, *Political Campaign Debates.*

9. "Memorandum of Understanding," news.findlaw.com/nytimes/docs/election2004/debates2004mou.html (accessed May 14, 2005).

10. Jamieson and Birdsell, *Presidential Debates,* 196.

11. Martel, *Political Campaign Debates.*

12. Myles Martel, "Political Campaign Debates: Images, Issues and Impact," *Campaigns and Elections* (winter 1984).

13. Ibid.

14. Thomas E. Patterson, "Election 2000: How Citizens 'See' a Presidential Debate," Press Release: A Product of the Vanishing Voter Project, Joan Shorenstein Center on the Press, Politics and Public Policy, Harvard University, Cambridge, Mass., October 3, 2000. It must be kept in mind, however, that the presidential debates appear simultaneously on all of the major network channels.

15. Arthur H. Miller and Michael MacKuen, "Informing the Electorate: A National Study," in *The Great Debates: Carter vs. Ford, 1976,* ed. Sidney Kraus (Bloomington: Indiana University Press, 1979).

16. David O. Sears and Steven Chaffee, "Uses and Effects of the 1976 Debates: An Overview of Empirical Studies," in

The Great Debates: Carter vs. Ford, 1976, ed. Sidney Kraus (Bloomington: Indiana University Press, 1979).

17. On these points, see, respectively Robert E. Denton and Gary C. Woodward, *Political Communication in America* (New York: Praeger, 1990); and Thomas M. Holbrook, "Political Learning from Presidential Debates," *Political Behavior* (1999): 21, 67–89.

18. But see John G. Geer, "The Effects of Presidential Debates on the Electorate's Preferences for Candidates," *American Politics Quarterly* (1988): 16, 486–501.

19. Mike Yawn, Kevin Ellsworty, Bob Beatty, and Kim Fridkin Kahn, "How a Presidential Primary Debate Changed Attitudes of Audience Members," *Political Behavior* (1998): 20, 155–181.

20. Geer, "Effects of Presidential Debates"; David J. Lanoue and Peter Schrott, *The Joint Press Conference* (New York: Greenwood Press, 1991).

21. On the first point, see Kurt Lang and Gladys Lang, "Ordeal by Debate: Viewer Reactions," *Public Opinion Quarterly* (1961): 25, 277–288. On the second, see David O. Sears, Jonathan C. Freedman, and Edward F. O'Connor, "The Effects of Anticipated Debate and Commitment on the Polarization of Audience Opinion," *Public Opinion Quarterly* (1964): 28, 615–627.

22. Lang and Lang, "Ordeal by Debate"; Steven H. Chaffee, "Presidential Debates—Are They Helpful to Voters?" *Communication Monographs* (1978); Holbrook, "Political Learning from Presidential Debates."

23. D. Sunshine Hillygus and Simon Jackman, "Voter Decision Making in Election 2000: Campaign Effects, Partisan Activation, and the Clinton Legacy," *American Journal of Political Science* (2003): 43, 583–596.

24. Chaffee, "Presidential Debates"; Lanoue and Schrott, *Joint Press Conference.*

25. On these three points, see, respectively, Thomas M. Holbrook, "Presidential Campaigns and the Knowledge Gap," *Political Communications* (2002): 19, 437–454; Holbrook, "Political Learning from Presidential Debates"; Diana Prentice Carlin, "Presidential Debates as Focal Points for Campaign Arguments," *Political Communications* 9 (1992): 251–265.

26. Jamieson and Birdsell, *Presidential Debates*; James N. Druckman, "The Power of Television Images: The First Kennedy–Nixon Debate Revisited," *Journal of Politics* (2003): 65, 559–571.

27. Arthur H. Miller, Warren E. Miller, Alden S. Raine, and Thad A. Brown, "A Majority Party in Disarray: Policy Polarization in the 1972 Election," *American Political Science Review* (1976): 70, 753–778.

28. Susan A. Hellweg, Michael Pfau, and Steven R. Brydon, *Televised Presidential Debates* (New York: Praeger, 1992).

29. Ronald A. Faucheux, *The Debate Book: Standards and Guidelines for Sponsoring Political Candidate Debates in Congressional, State and Local Elections* (Washington, D.C.: Campaigns and Elections Publishing Company, 2003).

30. Sidney Kraus, *Televised Presidential Debates and Public Policy* (Mahwah, N.J.: Lawrence Erlbaum Associates, 2000).

Suggested Readings

Carlin, Diana Prentice. "Presidential Debates as Focal Points for Campaign Arguments." *Political Communications* 9 (1992): 251–265.

Carlin, Diana Prentice, Charles Howard, Susan Stanfield, and Larry Reynolds. "The Effects of Presidential Debate Formats on Clash: A Comparative Analysis." *Argumentation and Advocacy* 27 (winter 1991): 126–136.

Chaffee, Steven H. "Presidential Debates—Are They Helpful to Voters?" *Communication Monographs* 45 (1978): 330–346.

Denton, Robert E., and Gary C. Woodward. *Political Communication in America.* New York: Praeger, 1990.

Druckman, James N. "The Power of Television Images: The First Kennedy–Nixon Debate Revisited." *Journal of Politics* 65 (2003): 559–571.

Faucheux, Ronald A. *The Debate Book: Standards and Guidelines for Sponsoring Political Candidate Debates in Congressional, State and Local Elections.* Washington, D.C.: Campaigns and Elections Publishing Company, 2003.

Friedenberg, Robert V. " 'We Are Present Here Today for the Purpose of Having a Joint Discussion': The Conditions Requisite for Political Debates." *Journal of the American Forensic Association* 16 (1979): 1–9.

Geer, John G. "The Effects of Presidential Debates on the Electorate's Preferences for Candidates." *American Politics Quarterly* 16 (1988): 486–501.

Hellweg, Susan A., Michael Pfau, and Steven R. Brydon. *Televised Presidential Debates.* New York: Praeger, 1992.

Hillygus, D. Sunshine, and Simon Jackman. "Voter Decision Making in Election 2000: Campaign Effects, Partisan Activation, and the Clinton Legacy." *American Journal of Political Science* 47 (2003): 583–596.

Holbrook Thomas M. "Political Learning from Presidential Debates." *Political Behavior* 21 (1999): 67–89.

———. "Presidential Campaigns and the Knowledge Gap." *Political Communications* 19 (2002): 437–454.

Jamieson, Kathleen Hall, and David S. Birdsell. *Presidential Debates.* New York: Oxford University Press, 1988.

Katz, Elihu, and Jacob J. Feldman. "The Debates in the Light of Research: A Survey of Surveys." In *The Great Debates,* edited by Sidney Kraus. Bloomington: Indiana University Press, 1962.

Kraus, Sidney, ed. *The Great Debates.* Bloomington: Indiana University Press, 1962, 1979.

———. *Televised Presidential Debates and Public Policy.* Mahwah, N.J.: Lawrence Erlbaum Associates, 2000.

Lang, Kurt, and Gladys Engel Lang. "Ordeal by Debate: Viewer Reactions." *Public Opinion Quarterly* 25 (1961): 277–288.

Lanoue, David J. "The 'Turning Point': Viewers' Reactions to the Second 1988 Presidential Debate." *American Politics Quarterly* 19 (1991): 80–95.

Lanoue, David J., and Peter Schrott. *The Joint Press Conference.* New York: Greenwood Press, 1991.

Martel, Myles. *Political Campaign Debates.* New York: Longman, 1983.

———. "Political Campaign Debates: Images, Issues and Impact." *Campaigns and Elections* (winter 1984).

Miller, Arthur H., and Michael Mackuen. "Informing the Electorate: A National Study." In *The Great Debates: Carter vs. Ford, 1976,* edited by Sidney Kraus. Bloomington: Indiana University Press, 1979.

Miller, Arthur H., Warren E. Miller, Alden S. Raine, and Thad A. Brown. "A Majority Party in Disarray: Policy Polarization in the 1972 Election." *American Political Science Review* 70 (1976): 753–778.

Patterson, Thomas E. "Election 2000: How Citizens 'See' a Presidential Debate." Press Release: A Product of the Vanishing Voter Project. Joan Shorenstein Center on the Press, Politics and Public Policy, Harvard University, Cambridge, Mass., October 3, 2000.

Sears, David O., and Steven Chaffee. "Uses and Effects of the 1976 Debates: An Overview of Empirical Studies." In *The Great Debates: Carter vs. Ford, 1976,* edited by Sidney Kraus. Bloomington: Indiana University Press, 1979.

Sears, David O., Jonathan C. Freedman, and Edward F. O'Connor. "The Effects of Anticipated Debate and Commitment on the Polarization of Audience Opinion." *Public Opinion Quarterly* 28 (1964): 615–627.

Tyler, Gus. "Democracy vs. Mediacracy." *New Leader,* May 28, 1984, 10–12.

Yawn, Mike, Kevin Ellsworth, Bob Beatty, and Kim Fridkin Kahn. "How a Presidential Primary Debate Changed Attitudes of Audience Members." *Political Behavior* 20 (1998): 155–181.

CHAPTER 19

Voter Mobilization

Jan E. Leighley and Tetsuya Matsubayashi

For most political consultants and campaign managers, voter mobilization is at the heart of their campaign activities.[1] This makes sense from the perspective of campaign professionals. Simply put, their job is to win elections, which means getting at least one more vote than their opponent. As described in Chapter 14, in the early stages of campaigns candidates seek to make their names recognizable to voters, create a positive image, and establish a broad base of support through direct mail, phone calls, and television and radio ads. But if supporters fail to show up at the polls on election day, these efforts to persuade *voters* would be completely worthless. So getting out the vote on election day is absolutely essential for victory.

As one might expect, then, candidates, political parties, and interest groups sometimes invest substantial time and money in mobilizing voters. This means that some citizens, in some elections, are deluged with news stories and political ads on television or the Internet, many of which may encourage viewers to go to the polling booth on election day. Candidates for lower offices also may phone or go door to door to hand out campaign information and ask citizens to vote. But sometimes candidates, political parties, and interest groups do not attempt to mobilize voters. Thus in some states during presidential elections, or in some districts during congressional elections, citizens may see candidates' ads only if they look for them on the Internet, and no one knocks on their doors. These varying levels of campaign mobilization reflect candidates', parties', and other groups' decisions about how valuable mobilization is in any one race.

This chapter describes how and why political elites, such as candidates and political parties, try to influence who votes by engaging in voter mobilization campaigns. It focuses primarily on *direct mobilization*—that is, when politicians organize door-to-door canvassing, telephoning, mailing, and leafleting efforts focused on asking citizens to vote. Elites use, and campaigns are also influenced by, *indirect mobilization,* in which voters are mobilized through their social networks or the campaign environment. For example, voters may be encouraged to vote by family members, coworkers, friends, or neighbors who have been directly contacted by political candidates or parties.

Persuasion versus Mobilization

In direct or indirect mobilization, the distinction between persuasion (convincing someone to vote for a particular candidate) and mobilization (convincing someone to vote) may be difficult to maintain. Indeed, the strategies for voter mobilization may not differ significantly from the ones for voter persuasion—that is, who is targeted and the message they receive may be developed with both goals in mind. For example, door hangers that lead with the message "Your vote can make a difference . . ." could be used to convince citizens that showing up at the polls is worth their efforts—but it also could be used to highlight how voting for the correct candidate can matter for policy outcomes. Furthermore, the effectiveness of the message might well depend on when and where the door hangers are distributed. When distributed to a highly partisan neighborhood, they might spur a boost in turnout; when distributed in highly competitive precincts, they might persuade independent voters to make the "right choice" (also see Chapter 7 on the electorate and party identification).

Campaign organizations typically focus on persuasion in the early stages of the campaign and then shift to mobilization as election day approaches. However, this shift will depend on the perceived competitiveness of the campaign and whether finances allow a last minute "push" for voter turnout activities. For the typical local, state, or congressional campaign, resources are quite limited and remain so for the life of the campaign. This is a constraint that successful political consultants work around by making careful, conscious choices about how they use the campaign's resources. Consultants are keenly aware that it costs much more to persuade a voter—that is, to convince one to support their candidate rather than the opponent—than it costs to ensure that supporters with a history of voting go to the polls on election day. Therefore, most get-out-the-vote (GOTV) campaigns target known supporters who have demonstrated their willingness to vote in elections. This, in fact, is the "dirty little secret" of practical campaign politics: the goal is not to increase overall turnout (which is too expensive and does not necessarily mean that the campaign's candidate is more likely to win) but to mobilize enough of the candidate's supporters to win the election.

One indicator of the value that candidates place on voter mobilization efforts is how much they spend on them.[2] In the 1992 House races, incumbents devoted 19.95 percent of their total expenditures to mailings, rallies, GOTV drives, and other mobilization activities, whereas challengers devoted 26.4 percent, and candidates for open seats 32.3 percent. In the 1992 Senate races, incumbent candidates spent 7.9 percent of their total expenditures on mobilization activities, challengers spent 8.6 percent, and candidates for open seats spent 8.5 percent.[3] Because media expenditures on advertisements that call for voter turnout are reported separately from these categories to the Federal Election Commission (FEC), these expenditure levels indicate that campaigns clearly care who votes.

In making such expenditures, candidates seek "contact" of various sorts, and national surveys confirm that the money is getting candidates the contact they want. Some 20 to 25 percent of the voting-age population in the United States reports being contacted by political parties during presidential election campaigns, although this number varies from election to election. For example, recent research by Peter W. Wielhouwer suggests that 36 percent of adults were contacted by the major parties in 2000, which is the highest level of reported contact over the past five decades.[4]

Intuitively, one would think citizens would respond positively to voter mobilization efforts. At a minimum, whether citizens end up voting or not, they might feel flattered for having been asked. This point was driven home to former House Speaker Thomas P. "Tip" O'Neill, a Democrat from Massachusetts, during his first campaign. When O'Neill saw a neighbor he had known for a long time, she told him, "Tom, I'm going to vote for you tomorrow even though you didn't ask me to." O'Neill was surprised at her remark, because he had always assumed that she was going to vote for him. In response to his surprise, the woman explained, "Let me tell you something: people like to be asked." [5]

The effect of elite mobilization on voters has been observed in most presidential elections since the early 1950s. Although technological innovations—and the heavy reliance on direct telephone marketing—may not make everyone happy (when they are inundated with telephone calls at the dinner hour or in the middle of a favorite program), research repeatedly shows that elite mobilization increases voter turnout on election day. In fact, the more money spent by candidates, the higher voter turnout will be. Survey-based research also demonstrates that contacted voters are more likely to turn out. Thus mobilization plays a significant role in electoral politics not only because it helps a candidate to win, but also because it encourages citizens to vote.

Theories of Voter Turnout and Elite Mobilization

The political consultants who plan campaign strategy and the political scientists who study the effects of campaigns typically recognize that citizens' decisions to vote or not reflect the costs and benefits of doing so. In the same way that college students (and their parents) decide that going to college is "worth it" because a college degree confers particular benefits, citizens think about whether there is a "payoff" in going to the polls. One of the implications of this rational choice theory of voter participation is that the cost of voting (such as the travel time to the polls, time spent collecting campaign information, registration) often discourages citizens from voting.

Scholars argue that elite mobilization reduces that cost, which, in turn, encourages people to vote. Mobilizing agents usually provide voters with information on the campaign and voting procedures. Citizens who learn the location of their polling places and the voting hours will incur lower costs of participating than those who must independently track down that information. Citizens contacted directly through face-to-face canvassing or through direct mail also may learn something about what policy issues are significant or who is running for office. Without investing any of their own time or resources, these citizens might have a better sense that the election is personally meaningful for them and thus be more likely to vote. Generally, then, efforts to reduce the information costs associated with an election increase voters' incentives for going to the polls.

Scholars Sidney Verba, Kay Schlozman and Henry Brady have observed that elite mobilization is one of the three critical factors that determine voter turnout.[6] First, citizens go to the polls if they "can"—that is, if they have the resources to meet the cost of participation. Citizens with more education, higher income, and more political information are most likely to vote on election day (see Chapter 8). Second, citizens go to the polls if they "want to." Those who are interested in politics and feel they can make a difference in politics are more likely to cast ballots. Finally, citizens go to the polls if they "are asked." Those who report they have been contacted by candidates or political parties during a campaign are more likely to vote. Each of these three factors figures in the costs and benefits of voting and who can "afford" to do so.

In their study of elite mobilization and voter turnout, Steven J. Rosenstone and J. Mark Hansen demonstrate the critical importance of elite mobilization for voter turnout.[7] They asked themselves why, even as education levels have increased and voter registration has become easier, voter turnout has declined in every type of U.S. election since the 1960s? These patterns are exactly the opposite of those that might be expected under the "costs and benefits" theory of voter turnout, in which highly educated people incur fewer costs in voting and therefore vote more often than less educated people.

Rosenstone and Hansen argue that the decline in voter turnout between 1952 and 1988 stemmed primarily from a decline in elite mobilization activity. They show that the number of voters who receive requests from political parties has declined at the same time that political leaders have shifted their mobilization strategy from activity "on the ground" (face-to-face, mail, and telephone contacts) to media advertisements (television). Because mobilization activity on the ground is more effective than it is on the air, voters have become less likely to cast a vote on election day.

Strategies of Elite Mobilization

Mobilizing citizens to vote is not a new feature of democratic politics in the United States. For decades, politicians, political groups, and political parties have tried to win elections by getting their supporters to the polls. But who has invested the most in mobilization efforts and how they have done so have changed over time. This section reviews who mobilizes voters in contemporary politics, how they try to persuade citizens to vote, and which citizens they target to get to the polls on election day.

Who Mobilizes Voters?

Who mobilizes voters depends in large part on features of the electoral system. In many advanced democracies, voters cast ballots for parties rather than candidates, and thus parties play a dominant role in voter mobilization. In the United States, voters choose a candidate for each office being contested, and thus candidates play a central role in mobilizing voters. Over the last few decades in the United States, candidates have become critical actors in electoral politics, and political parties have lost the significance they had as campaign organizations in the 1920s and 1930s. In presidential elections, for example, the presidential candidates, not the major-party committees, decide how and where to spend campaign money or other details of the campaign such as which states or cities they will visit. The role of candidates has strengthened relative to that of political parties in part because the number of independents, voters who have no partisan attachment, has grown.

Candidates' campaign organizations are more visible as mobilizing agents in local and nonpartisan elections than in state or national elections. Political parties tend not to be highly organized or active at the local level in most areas, and public finance laws are either nonexistent

Republican National Committee chair Ed Gillespie attends a voter registration drive at the GOP headquarters in the Washington Heights neighborhood of New York City on March 9, 2004. Using a semitruck named "Reggie the Registration Rig," Republicans undertook in March 2004 a week-long voter registration drive with the goal of registering one million new voters in all fifty states. National Voter Registration Week was part of the RNC's unprecedented commitment to registering three million voters by election day 2004. Source: Miguel Rajmil/EPA/Landov

or irrelevant to who spends money for what purposes. Thus if candidates want to get elected, they must put their own independent organizations together and get their supporters to the polls.

Yet the "candidate-centered" nature of campaigns in the United States does not mean that the parties play no role in mobilizing voters. Local party organizations may be able to provide substantial resources in the form of recruiting campaign volunteers or setting up phone banks. State and national party organizations also provide candidates with services such as training sessions, monetary assistance, and (partisan) voter data. Not surprisingly, congressional candidates report that the assistance provided by local and state party organizations is moderately important. In summary, although the role of political parties in mobilizing voters on the ground may be less salient to electoral outcomes than in the past, the parties are still players in the mobilization game.

Interest groups give candidates physical and monetary assistance and also conduct their own mobilization activities. The extent to which interest groups become involved in mobilization activity depends on the type, size, and composition of the group. Two major groups, labor unions and faith-based organizations, have energetically engaged in voter mobilization in recent elections. One of the advantages of churches and labor unions in delivering votes (or voters) is that they are organized on a local basis. This factor strengthens their ties to candidates at all levels who are running within their communities and translates into more efficient mobilization efforts.

Labor unions have been one of the most significant driving forces of voter mobilization for Democratic candidates. Their strength is in their numbers. According to one AFL-CIO leader, "Big businesses have got the money, but we've got the people." [8] Yet unions often provide candidates with both the manpower *and* the money for grassroots activity such as knocking on doors. In addition to helping candidates, unions conduct their own mobilization activity by targeting union members and their households. These activities are especially visible in unions that have large, homogeneous memberships, which in the past has meant high proportions of Democratic voters. New unions, such as those representing teachers and public sector employees, have more diverse memberships and may be less likely to engage in voter mobilization activities, because it may not be clear which candidate their members will support once they go to the polls.

Faith-based organizations, whether local church congregations or religious groups such as Focus on the Family, also draw their strength from their membership numbers and personal networks, which allow their leaders to conduct massive, systematic mobilization activities. African American churches have historically played an important role in mobilizing their members by issuing explicitly political messages through their leaders or through fellow congregants. The Christian Right has recently become notable for its ability to deliver voters to the polls on election day, possibly influencing election outcomes in everything from congressional contests to school board races.

Other political organizations—civil right groups, environmental groups, and business associations—are more limited in their abilities to mobilize their members and the electorate at large, because their memberships are often dispersed across the country. In fact, because of the small number of votes (or voters) that they can deliver in any one race, they usually do not devote a high level of resources to get-out-the-vote activities. Instead, they typically focus on communicating with their members by mailing voter guides or endorsement cards.

Although occasionally constrained by federal and state campaign finance or tax laws, candidates, political parties, and interest groups sometimes coordinate their efforts within and between organizations. For example, in the 2001 Los Angeles mayoral election a variety of labor unions that normally operate separately organized their mobilization efforts into a single, coordinated activity in order to concentrate their resources and avoid wasting them. Coordination across labor unions allowed union leaders to use a larger number of volunteers and to distribute them to precincts more efficiently than in previous elections. Organized labor also coordinated its effort with the Democratic candidate's campaign organization: labor unions and the Democratic Party took responsibility for mobilization activity on the ground, while the candidate largely devoted his resources to advertisements on the air.

How Much Effort?

Most political campaigns are run with very limited budgets. Within this general constraint, several factors shape the amount of effort that elites put into get-out-the-vote activities (as distinct from other campaign expenses). For one thing, mobilization efforts are constrained by the resources (such as money, time, or human capital) available to mobilizing agents. In general, challengers spend much less on mobilization activities than incumbents and candidates for open seats. The differences in spending are attributed to the limited amount of campaign funds available to the challengers.

Cost-benefit calculations also shape how much candidates invest in mobilization activities. If the cost of mobilization activity is not worth the number of votes it yields, campaigns stop making phone calls, sending direct mails, and knocking on doors. For example, if a hundred phone calls produce one additional vote and each phone call costs $1, a candidate needs $100 to mobilize just one vote. If the mobilizing agents conclude that $100 per vote is not cost-effective (that is, they do not have enough money to raise the number of votes needed to make a difference in the election outcome), they stop making calls.

Sometimes, it is difficult for mobilizing agents to estimate exactly how much money they have to spend or how many votes they need to make a difference, but this estimate is a critical aspect of campaign strategy. It is clear, however, that voter mobilization efforts are less efficient in elections in which one candidate is expected to win by a substantial margin than in a close election. There is, then, a strong relationship between election closeness (or competitiveness) and candidate spending: candidates spend when it can make a difference in the election outcome.

Another important aspect of deciding how much to invest in voter mobilization activities is the campaign's knowledge of who its supporters are and how likely they are to vote absent any mobilization efforts. In general, the

Republican Party receives support from high-income citizens, who are more likely to vote on election day, and the Democratic Party tends to draw its support from low-income individuals, who are less likely to vote. Thus Democrats are more likely to view voter mobilization efforts as efficient: the more they invest in voter mobilization, the higher the turnout of their supporters. Overall, the increased turnout levels attributed to voter mobilization activities are greater for Democrats than for Republicans.

The greater "yield" of voters for Democratic mobilization efforts as compared with that for Republican mobilization efforts helps to explain why local Democratic Party leaders emphasize the importance of increasing voter turnout as an organizational priority. Consistent with these reports from Democratic leaders, Democrats are more likely to engage in mobilization activities such as registration drives and transportation services on election day than are Republican leaders. For example, 62.3 percent of Democratic county party chairs in Texas report providing transportation for voters on election day compared with only 35.7 percent of Republican chairs, and 54.7 percent of Democratic chairs report offering transportation to early voting sites compared with 30.9 percent of Republican chairs. Democrats are also significantly more likely than Republicans to provide citizens with registration materials (62.3 percent versus 35.7 percent).[9]

Whom to Target

The primary electoral goal of candidates, political parties, and interest groups is to win elections. To do so, they need to have more supporters than opponents show up at the polls. One possible strategy is to mobilize all potential supporters in a district by contacting them directly. But this strategy is both very difficult and costly to pursue in a campaign world of scarce resources. Even a lot of volunteers may not be enough for a campaign to knock on every door. And not everyone will respond by showing up at the polls, even if visited by a volunteer.

In response to these problems, mobilizing agents use a strategy called "targeting mobilization"—that is, campaigns target a limited number of people who are chosen because they possess specific desirable political and personal characteristics. Campaigns are most interested in those characteristics that best predict whether an individual is a likely voter and who the individual will vote for.

Determining who are likely voters is critical, because elections are won on the basis of votes cast—that is, the choices made by the individuals who go to the polls on election day. Even if candidates and political parties identify a set of prospective supporters (through the use of a public opinion survey, for example), unless those supporters cast ballots, their opinion is irrelevant to the election outcome. Thus mobilizing agents have to find not only prospective supporters, but also prospective voters.

Determining who are likely supporters is also important, because the primary goal of voter mobilization efforts is to get people to the polls rather than to change their political attitudes or persuade them to vote for a particular candidate. It is rare that mobilizing agents intentionally contact those who support their opponent, because they know that it is very difficult to change political attitudes by a brief contact and that their efforts to persuade are most likely a waste of resources. Furthermore, mobilization activity that targets those who support an opponent may encourage them to vote, which is not a good thing for the candidate. Thus mobilizing agents have to identify those who support or are likely to support them, and they usually rely on partisanship—the extent to which a person reports identifying with, or voting for, one party or the other—in identifying their supporters. On a broader level, an electoral jurisdiction (precinct, neighborhood, subdivision) with a higher percentage of votes for Democratic (Republican) candidates in the previous elections is more likely to have the higher percentage of Democratic (Republican) voters in future elections. Mobilizing agents therefore often concentrate their efforts on geographical areas with high densities of partisan supporters.

A critical resource for campaigns seeking to identify partisan supporters is the official list of registered voters, a public record available from county governments. This official list includes basic information such as the names, addresses, and voting histories of registered voters, from which additional indirect information such as a voter's gender or partisanship can be gleaned. In states with closed party primaries, the record of elections in which the individual has voted provides a good clue about his or her partisanship. Using this official list, mobilizing agents can easily learn where many prospective supporters and voters live and target efforts to specific individuals. This helps to explain why Democratic (Republican) voters are more likely to be contacted by the Democratic (Republican) Party prior to election day.

Swing voters—individuals without strong partisan attachments—often receive great attention from the mass media in the national elections, but mobilizing agents may or may not focus their effort on their behavior. Because swing voters are more likely to be in a competitive district or jurisdiction, mobilizing agents have incentives to mobilize them as potential supporters. Yet there is no official record that tells mobilizing agents who and where swing voters are. And so these agents cannot *target* these voters on the ground. Moreover, because swing voters are less likely than partisan voters to show up on election day, mobilization directed toward them may not be rewarded.

In addition to political traits, some demographic characteristics also provide mobilizing agents with valuable information for targeting. Race and ethnicity are often significant pieces of information that help campaigns to know where supporters reside. Democrats especially recognize the importance of mobilizing African American voters, because African Americans have been allied with the Democratic Party since the New Deal and have formed a significant support base for it. Not surprisingly, then, the Democratic Party is much more likely than the Republican Party to contact black voters. Minority candidates also tend to target minority voters, because such voters are more responsive to requests from a candidate who belongs to the same racial/ethnic group. On a broader level, this tendency results in significantly more mobilization of minority voters who live in areas with a high percentage of minority residents than minority voters who live in areas with a low percentage of minorities.

Education, income, and age are demographic characteristics that help campaigns to identify likely voters. The conventional wisdom is that wealthier, better educated, and older people are more likely to go to the polls. Thus mobilizing agents tend to target areas where the percentages of the affluent, the educated, or older citizens are high. The demographic makeup of each geographical jurisdiction is easily available from official records such as U.S. Census data.

The critical importance of demographic characteristics for campaign strategies is evident in the increased efforts of both parties to invest in research operations that purchase and update lists of potential supporters who have the relevant political or social characteristics. These efforts are labeled "geodemographics," because the party lists include demographic and social characteristics organized by geographical location. Using this combination of characteristics, state and, especially, national parties can then provide both national and local candidates with vital information on the voter profiles in particular geographical locations (see Box 19-1).

Group memberships help both interest groups and other mobilizing agents to target supporters. Labor unions and faith-based organizations utilize their lists of members in identifying targets. Membership lists are also valuable to candidates and political parties, because those active in organizational activities are more likely to participate in politics and to have strong feelings about political issues and candidates. Liberal Democratic candidates target union members, who are expected to be responsive and supportive to their request. Conservative Republican candidates target the members of faith-based groups, who are also responsive.

Occasionally, campaigns are not able to use the sources just described. Instead, they must invest in efforts tailored to their specific needs and collect new information that distinguishes prospective supporters and voters from nonsupporters and nonvoters. This situation arises most often in local elections in which the number of citizens (and likely voters) in a district is especially small. Yet congressional and statewide campaigns also utilize this technique in which a campaign begins by making a complete list of voters in the district. The next step is to contact people by means of phone calls and door knocking and evaluate their response to the campaign's visit. Those classified as supporters or prospective supporters (who have not made up their minds) are kept on the list, and those who are considered nonsupporters are dropped from the list. Although this information might be useful, it is also extremely expensive to collect.

How to Contact?

Once mobilizing agents decide whom to mobilize, they must plan how to contact them. Face-to-face canvassing, telephoning, mailing, leafleting, and transportation to the polls are the major techniques used in contemporary campaigns for direct personal mobilization. In addition, mobilizing agents have recently begun using the Internet, especially e-mail, as another way of contacting potential voters.

The amount of resources available to mobilizing agents constrains what and how much they can do during a campaign. For example, a campaign with just a small number of volunteers is not able to conduct a massive face-to-face canvass in precincts. Likewise, a small interest group cannot afford to buy a service from a telephone marketing company. Thus resources are a significant factor in deciding which types of mobilization techniques to use during a campaign.

Precinct characteristics also shape the selection of mobilization techniques. Techniques are selected on the basis of precinct features—previous voting records, demographics, and geography. One campaign consultant suggests that a campaign use the more effective (and more expensive) mobilization techniques in areas in which the candidate's support level is lower, and rely on the less effective (and less expensive) mobilization techniques in those areas in which support is strong regardless of additional mobilization efforts.[10] So, for example, in areas that highly favor a candidate's party and that have high levels of voter turnout, candidates might use direct-mail techniques rather than more costly face-to-face contacting to encourage supporters to vote. In suburban areas, face-to-face canvassing is even less cost-effective, because canvassers need more time to walk from house to house than in urban areas. It is not surprising, then, that as the suburbs have grown over the past several decades, reliance on phone banks and direct mail has increased.

The rest of this section describes a few things campaigns must keep in mind as they choose among get-out-the-vote methods.

Face-to-Face Canvassing

Canvassing—visiting targeted households and asking for a vote in person—depends heavily on volunteers. "Door knockers" are usually campaign workers, union and religious activists, and volunteers for other interest groups. In local elections, the candidates themselves sometimes go to precincts and knock on doors. Some campaigns hire workers to go door to door. Other than precinct visits made to compile a list of voters for targeting, face-to-face

BOX 19-1
LIST BUILDING

The 2000 presidential election in Florida was one that scholars, campaign consultants, and citizens alike will not soon forget. To many citizens, the election became an unwanted civics lesson about the workings of the electoral college, election administration, and the state and federal court system. But scholars and political consultants learned a different lesson: they were reminded that even in presidential elections the outcome can be close—and that voter turnout matters in who wins.

For Democrats, the election and its aftermath underscored the importance of having extensive and accurate lists of potential supporters to use in their get-out-the-vote efforts. After all, the numbers speak for themselves: Florida's electoral votes went to Republican George W. Bush because he won the state's popular count by 537 votes in an election in which the Democratic Party did not contact nearly 1.5 million Democrats simply because they did not have their correct addresses and phone numbers! Not surprisingly, then, the Democrats responded to the 2000 election by investing more heavily in its list-building efforts. Terence R. McAuliffe, who became the Democratic National Committee chair in 2001, substantially increased the resources devoted to maintaining and enhancing the party's state-by-state voter files. The 2004 presidential election was therefore the first in which both parties used their enhanced databases ("DataMart" for the Democrats, "VoterVault" for the Republicans) as part of their get-out-the-vote strategies.[1]

The parties rely on various sources for their databases, including local, state, and national party records on campaign contributors and activists, purchased demographic information from commercial marketing firms, and their own in-house telephone banks, which routinely contact households on the list to verify and update existing information.

The household-specific information in these databases is mostly demographic, along with party registration in states that require registration by party and individuals' vote histories. For a given household, then, the parties are likely to know the age and gender of each occupant, along with party registration (in states that require it) and the number of local, state, and federal elections in which each person voted. These demographic and political data are typically available from public voter registration records.

This publicly available information is used primarily by parties and candidates to identify likely voters and likely supporters. From it, parties and candidates also guess what type of information might be useful to gain undecided voters' support. Borrowing from marketing strategies, the parties develop voter profiles based on demographics, geography, and public records and then make some guesses about the political tendencies of households. According to McAuliffe, "You could ask me about any city block in America, and I could tell you how many on that block are likely to be health care voters, or who's most concerned about education or job creation." But note that even McAuliffe describes the lists as indicating which individuals are *likely* to be health care voters—whether the issue of health care is a deciding factor for any individual voter cannot be known with complete confidence based on these databases.

What is not available from public records is how the individual voted in past elections. Parties can guess the partisanship of many households by identifying precincts, neighborhoods, or counties that vote predominantly Democratic or predominantly Republican. But the odds of guessing correctly about the partisanship of any given household are much lower in areas in which the two parties are more competitive—which, of course, are the very areas where campaign targeting is most critical.

More accurate information on individuals' partisanship or issue priorities can be obtained in most cases by talking to voters (or households) individually. Parties use their phone banks to contact households and gather information on their likelihood of voting, partisan leanings, and candidate evaluations or issues, and responses to those phone solicitations are incorporated into the database. For example, if the response to a party mobilization call is "I wouldn't vote Republican (Democratic) on my deathbed!" the Republican (Democratic) Party is quick to note that in its records, because the response suggests that contacting that person again is not worth the time or effort.

The bottom line on the importance of list building by the major parties is a function of their goal of winning elections with minimal resources. Widespread voter mobilization is extremely expensive and not necessarily related to winning. But targeting messages to identified supporters to get them to the poll is a necessary, if not sufficient, strategy in winning elections today.

1. Paul Fahri, "Parties Square Off in a Database Duel," *Washington Post,* July 20, 2004.

canvassing is usually conducted at the final stage of the campaign or on election day. Campaign leaders send their door-to-door workers into areas in which their efforts might deliver the greatest payoff.

Telephoning

In recent years, technological innovations have increased the popularity of telephoning as a mobilization technique. Because computer-assisted calling has reduced the cost of telephone canvassing, mobilizing agents are able to call a huge number of citizens repeatedly. This technology has also changed the potential nature of the contact. In the 2000 presidential campaign, for example, a recorded message by former first lady Barbara Bush asking Republicans to get out and vote on election day was played to thousands of households across the country. This "personal" touch was intended to convince people uncertain about whether they would vote to go to the polls and vote for her son.

Telephone canvassing is conducted using professional phone banks, robo calls (automated calling systems that deliver a prerecorded message), or volunteer phone banks. In recent elections, many mobilizing agents have used commercial telemarketing companies and robo calls to lower the cost (time and money) of telephone canvassing. Volunteer phone banks operated by mobilizing agents have many things to do: recruit volunteers, set up a location and phones, prepare a script, train and organize callers, and supervise them. However, these efforts are most likely worthwhile; telephone canvassing with volunteer phone callers is more effective than the canvassing with professional phone banks and robo calls (as discussed later in this chapter). Like door knocking, telephone canvassing is usually done close to election day.

Mailing

Technological innovations have also spurred more campaigns to use direct mail as a campaign technique. By using mail, candidates, parties, and especially interest groups whose activity is not based locally are able to contact many voters repeatedly and do so at a relatively low cost. Targeted mailing requires only creating a message, printing it on a card, stamping the card, and sending the card out. Mail canvassing is conducted by either volunteers and campaign workers or professional direct mail companies, relying on lists of identified supporters or lists that target particular geographical areas with a high proportion of known partisans. Because of the low cost and easy implementation of this method, mailings are often repeated to targeted citizens throughout a campaign.

Leafleting

Leafleting refers to a broad category of activities in which campaigns distribute written material. Campaigns using this technique must decide what kind of leaflet will be used, the substantive message to include on the hand-outs, and how to distribute them. "Door hangers" are leaflets designed to be left on the front doors of people who do not respond to a knock or doorbell (see Box 19-2). Additional important decisions in leafleting are the neighborhoods or other locations (such as shopping malls or public buildings) in which to distribute the hand-outs and how many volunteers to place in the chosen location. Leafleting is probably used the most, and the most effectively, in local races in which voting records are not easily accessible, or when a campaign finds it easy to identify the key locations for distribution.

Effectiveness of Elite Mobilization Efforts

How effective are these mobilization techniques? Although candidates, campaign officials, and political parties rely more on advertisements on the air in contemporary campaigns, they still claim that mobilization activity on the ground has an influence on voter turnout. Anecdotes from the 2000 presidential election offer the state of Florida as an example of a state in which the lack of get-out-the-vote efforts in the final days of the campaign led to a much narrower victory in the state than the polls predicted. By contrast, in Georgia, where the state and national parties invested in last-minute, face-to-face get-out-the-vote efforts, George W. Bush held onto a substantial lead on election day.

In 2004 Ohio was a key battleground state, and the political parties, presidential campaigns, and local organizations sent groups out to knock on citizens' doors and encourage them to vote even as late as on election day. Phone banks, too, were busy in the last hours of the campaign calling (and calling again) households to remind them to vote for their preferred candidate. In the end, Republicans appear to have had the more effective get-out-the-vote operation as President Bush captured Ohio's electoral votes.[11]

Research by political scientists Donald P. Green and Alan S. Gerber seems to confirm these anecdotal claims. Using a large-scale field experiment, Green and Gerber have examined the effectiveness of the mobilization techniques used in election campaigns.[12] A field experiment is different from a laboratory experiment in that the field experiment is conducted during the course of a real electoral campaign. To study whether face-to-face contacting is effective at increasing turnout in a mayoral election, for example, researchers would first identify the population of registered voters in the city and randomly choose some of them as a sample. The sample would then be divided into a treatment group and a control group. During the actual mayoral election, trained canvassers would contact households in the treatment group. After the election, official election records would be used to determine who voted. If citizens in the treatment group voted at a higher rate than citizens in the control group, then it could be

BOX 19-2
DOOR HANGERS

Most discussions of political "marketing" focus on televised political advertising because of its dominance in presidential campaigns and its great expense to candidates. Yet recently the national parties and candidate organizations have come to believe that advertising is not enough and that more personal mobilization techniques are better. Dan Balz and David S. Broder, writing about partisan mobilization efforts in the 2000 presidential election, reported that "Republicans say they mistakenly believed that 'GOTV' meant 'get on television,' not 'get out the vote,' and therefore they redirected their efforts away from hi-tech approaches in the 2002 and 2004 campaigns."[1]

A critical part of the new "ground game" is a return to door-to-door solicitation efforts, which may include talking to potential voters directly, leaving door hangers with a campaign message, or both. As discussed in this chapter, political scientists Donald P. Green and Alan S. Gerber have produced some evidence that face-to-face canvassing and leafleting are actually more cost-effective in yielding votes than telephone or mail contacts.[2]

Examples of the ground game are shown in the accompanying photos. These pieces of campaign literature were distributed in two different neighborhoods in the 2004 congressional election contest between Democrat Chet Edwards and Republican Arlene Wohlgemuth of Texas. Edwards was the incumbent

Chet Edwards
OUR CONGRESSMAN

GETTING RESULTS FOR BRAZOS COUNTY.

Chet Edwards is our independent Congressman who puts Brazos County families above partisan politics and delivers for our area.

Aggie Values

Chet is a 1974 graduate of Texas A&M, where he received the prestigious Earl Rudder Award. Texas A&M has had a profound impact on Chet's life and his values of personal responsibility, hard work and of giving something back to his community and country. That is why, as one of only three Aggies in Congress, Chet will continue to work hard for Brazos County.

Fighting for Texas A&M and Blinn College

Chet is a strong supporter of the federal student loan program and Pell Grants, which are so important in helping students at A&M and Blinn College offset rising tuition costs. He has used his experience in Congress on the key House Appropriations Committee to secure tens of millions of dollars in federal funding for A&M, including its Army tank modernization program with Ft. Hood, the George Bush fellowship program and numerous engineering and agriculture research programs in the A&M System.

Recently, Chet helped secure $20 million to train our nation's first responders at A&M's Emergency Response and Rescue Training Center to protect our homeland.

Improving Transportation

Chet knows that transportation is one of the most pressing priorities for Brazos County. With his seniority and position on the Appropriations Committee, Chet is in a key position to see that Brazos County gets its fair share of federal transportation funds. In the last two years, Chet has secured $23.3 million for transportation and highway projects in his district and he secured $3 million to widen University Drive.

in the eleventh district, which became the new seventeenth district after the Republican-controlled state legislature redistricted the state. The newly created district splits the military vote from Fort Hood and McClennan County, and it includes the cities of College Station (Brazos County) and Waco. College Station is home to Texas A&M University, whose students tend to vote Republican. Waco is home to Baylor University and Fort Hood.

The district is predominantly Anglo, with 15.4 percent Latino and 10 percent African American resi-

concluded that canvassing is an effective mobilization technique. If there is no difference in turnout between the treatment and control groups, then the conclusion is that face-to-face canvassing has no impact on voter turnout.

Green and Gerber's extensive, large-scale studies of voter mobilization techniques have led them to conclude that face-to-face contacting has the greatest effect on voter turnout per contact. Based on their numerous field experiments, they estimate that every fourteen contacts made by canvassers produced one additional vote. By contrast, phone canvassing, direct mail, and leafleting had a much weaker effect on turnout; fifty volunteer calls, 133 (nonpartisan) mailings, and sixty-six leaflets each produced one additional vote.

Campaigns with limited resources, however, have to make decisions based not just on this "yield" ratio, but

BUSH ★ CHENEY
Wohlgemuth

A winning team for Texas

LEADERSHIP

That is what we need in our next Congressman and that's exactly what we will get from Arlene Wohlgemuth.

Representative Arlene Wohlgemuth is a proven conservative who throughout her service in the Texas Legislature has been a leader in the fight to protect our values and our hard-earned tax dollars.

Whether working hand-in-hand with then-Governor George W. Bush to pass the largest tax cut in the history of our state or standing firm in the fight to protect the traditional values of faith, family, and freedom, Arlene Wohlgemuth is recognized across Texas as a leader who says what she means, does what she says, and get things done.

Now, Arlene wants to take her proven leadership to Washington D.C. and put it to work for you and your family as a member of the United States Congress.

As your Congressman, Arlene Wohlgemuth will once again work with George W. Bush to lower your tax burden, cut the federal bureaucracy, defend human life, protect our borders from those who seek to do us harm, defend our 2nd Amendment rights, and stand firm against the liberal special interests who want more taxes and more government and less freedom and individual responsibility.

election, Chet Edwards beat Republican challenger Farley 52.3 percent to 47.7 percent. In the 2004 election, Chet Edwards found himself a Democrat in a district even more Republican than the one he represented previously.

The Edwards flyer was distributed in a College Station neighborhood consisting primarily of rental homes and duplexes sometime in September. Polling in the race at the time suggested that the College Station vote was up for grabs. By mid-October, when the Wohlgemuth campaign distributed its door knocker in one of the most Republican neighborhoods in town, Wohlgemuth had fallen behind in the polls. Edwards's "obvious" strategy of not indicating his party affiliation on his flyers made sense in the newly redrawn, and more heavily Republican, district. Wohlgemuth, trying to unseat a fairly popular incumbent, did not have quite as obvious a strategy but chose to target Republicans to get them to the polls. Perhaps Edwards's victory in the race, which he won 52.2 percent to 47.4 percent, is in part attributable to these strategic campaign choices.

1. Dan Balz and David S. Broder, "Close Election Turns on Voter Turnout," *Washington Post,* November 1, 2002, A1.

2. Donald P. Green and Alan S. Gerber, *Get Out The Vote! How to Increase Voter Turnout* (Washington D.C.: Brookings, 2004).

dents. Significant employers include Texas A&M University, Baylor University, Sanderson Farms, and L-3 Communications, a major defense contractor. In College Station, a substantial proportion of residents are associated with the university as faculty, staff, or students. In the 2000 presidential election, nearly three-fourths of Brazos County voted for Republican George W. Bush. In the 2002 congressional (eleventh district)

also controlling for the widely differential costs of undertaking each activity. Although the costs of these activities vary (sometimes dramatically) depending on location and other resources, Green and Gerber provide a sense of the cost-effectiveness of each technique by using "reasonable" estimates of the costs that typical campaigns would incur for each activity and predicted impacts of mobilization techniques from their experiences. These estimates follow:

- Face-to-face canvassing: $18.67 for one additional vote (if canvassers are paid $16 an hour)
- Telephoning (professional): $45 for one additional vote ($1.50 per call)
- Telephoning (paid volunteer): $35 for one additional vote ($16 an hour per paid volunteer)
- Mailing: $59 for one additional vote ($0.50 per partisan mailing)

- Leafleting: $14 for one additional vote ($13 to canvassers plus printing fees)

These calculations suggest that telephoning and mailing are not as cost-effective as face-to-face and leafleting techniques in mobilizing voters—that is, Green and Gerber's findings suggest campaigns could mobilize more votes for less money if they rely more heavily on face-to-face and leafleting mobilization techniques rather than telephoning and mailing. This conclusion is ironic because the most attention and expenditures in election campaigns are devoted to telephoning and mailing techniques, perhaps not because they are most effective, but because they are the conventional wisdom in campaign politics.

Mobilization Challenges and Implications

Voter mobilization is important for political leaders and individual citizens alike. For political leaders, the probability of winning an election depends on how successfully they mobilize prospective supporters. For citizens, elite mobilization gives them a reason to turn out on election day. Thus, although voter mobilization rarely leads in campaign news these days, it is nevertheless fundamentally important to understanding elections and electoral campaigns in the United States.

Beyond the particulars of voter mobilization, however, is the broader picture of how elite mobilization in the United States structures who participates—and therefore who is elected and who elected officials respond to as their constituents. It is important to note, however, that it is not just the *number* of citizens contacted, but also *how* they are contacted, that matters. According to Rosenstone and Hansen, as mobilizing agents have shifted their efforts from traditional efforts on the ground to advertising on the air, the number of citizens personally contacted to vote has declined and voter turnout has fallen. Although Green and Gerber conclude that the number of contacted citizens has not dramatically changed over time, they argue that a decreased emphasis on face-to-face mobilization has resulted in a decline in turnout. This decline results at least in part from elites using the less effective techniques of mail and telephone contacting.

Another practical aspect of campaign strategy that also might contribute to lower levels of voter turnout is the campaigns' increasing reliance on registered voter lists. As noted at the beginning of this chapter, elites do not seek to increase overall turnout; they seek to mobilize supporters. And they try to be most efficient in their efforts by focusing on individuals who have some record of voting previously because their mobilization efforts might well return

these citizens to the polls. Advances in technology have allowed campaigns to tailor their targeting efforts more than ever, and, as a consequence, the proportion of nonvoting citizens contacted has decreased. Contacting individuals who "almost always" vote may yield candidates and parties few "new" votes, but this yield might be greater than the yield associated with efforts associated with creating voters from (habitual) nonvoters. This approach also provides the advantage of mobilizing known supporters. The disadvantage is that the shift of elites toward mobilizing those who already vote does not necessarily result in higher overall turnout.

Related to the question of who participates—and how political mobilization influences such participation—is a concern about whether the voting population is representative of citizens as a whole. To the extent that strategic elite mobilization is effective and targets some individuals to the exclusion of others, this important aspect of campaign politics may enhance political inequality.[13] It is known that well-off individuals are more likely to vote than those who are less well-off, in part because the former can meet the cost of participation while the latter cannot. As a result, citizens with more education and higher income are overrepresented as voters, and those with less education and lower income are underrepresented. In short, better educated, higher-income individuals make up a greater proportion of the population of voters than the population of citizens.

Political scientists argue that political leaders' strategic choices of those who receive their messages enhance overrepresentation of those citizens who have more education and income. Candidates and political parties target people who are accessible, identifiable, and responsive to their request—that is, better-off individuals. Thus these individuals are much more likely to vote on election day. By contrast, mobilizing agents ignore those who are not accessible, identifiable, and responsive—that is, less well-off individuals. Thus their probability of voting remains constant. In sum, strategic mobilization, based largely on social status and past voting behavior, might well make electorates in the United States less representative than they would be if elites did not mobilize strategically.

Although this finding may seem to point to a pessimistic conclusion about the normative implications of voter mobilization, only the creativity and ambitions of those running for office make it so. True, "mainstream" normal politics may produce less representative electorates. But there is always the possibility that electoral challengers (candidates, parties, or groups) will take advantage of recent advances in mobilization technology to deliver new votes on election day, and perhaps new elected officials as well.

Notes

1. Will Robinson, "Organizing the Field," in *Campaigns and Elections: American Style,* ed. James A. Thurber and Candice J. Nelson (Boulder, Colo.: Westview Press, 1995).

2. All references to campaign spending data in this chapter are taken from Dwight Morris and Murielle E. Gamache, *Handbook of Campaign Spending: Money in the 1992 Congressional Races* (Washington D.C.: CQ Press, 1994), chap. 1.

3. Ibid.

4. Peter W. Wielhouwer, "In Search of Lincoln's Perfect List: Targeting in Grassroots Campaigns," *American Politics Research* 31, no. 6 (2003): 632–669.

5. Tip O'Neill, with William Novak, *Man of the House* (New York: Random House, 1987), 26.

6. Sidney Verba, Kay Lehman Schlozman, and Henry Brady. *Voice and Equality: Civic Voluntarism in American Politics* (Cambridge, Mass.: Harvard University Press, 1995).

7. Steven J. Rosenstone and John Mark Hansen, *Mobilization, Participation, and Democracy in America* (New York: Macmillan, 1993).

8. Steven Rosenthal, "Building to Win, Building to Last: The AFL-CIO Political Program," in *Not Your Father's Union Movement,* ed. Jo-Ann Mort (New York: Verso, 1998), 100.

9. Jan E. Leighley, *Strength in Numbers: The Political Mobilization of Racial and Ethnic Minorities* (Princeton, N.J.: Princeton University Press, 2001), 63.

10. Robinson, "Organizing the Field."

11. Matt Bai, "Who Lost Ohio?" *New York Times Magazine,* November 21, 2004.

12. Donald P. Green and Alan S. Gerber, *Get Out the Vote! How to Increase Voter Turnout* (Washington D.C.: Brookings, 2004).

13. Rosenstone and Hansen, *Mobilization.*

Suggested Readings

Green, Donald P., and Alan S. Gerber. *Get Out The Vote! How to Increase Voter Turnout.* Washington D.C.: Brookings, 2004.

Leighley, Jan E. *Strength in Numbers? The Political Mobilization of Racial and Ethnic Minorities.* Princeton, N.J.: Princeton University Press, 2001.

Morris, Dwight, and Murielle E. Gamache. *Handbook of Campaign Spending: Money in the 1992 Congressional Races.* Washington D.C.: CQ Press, 1994.

Robinson, Will. "Organizing the Field." In *Campaigns and Elections American Style,* edited by James A. Thurber and Candice J. Nelson. Boulder, Colo.: Westview Press, 1995.

Rosenstone, Steven J., and John Mark Hansen. *Mobilization, Participation, and Democracy in America.* New York: Macmillan, 1993.

Rosenthal, Steven. "Building to Win, Building to Last: The AFL-CIO Political Program." *Not Your Father's Union Movement,* edited by Jo-Ann Mort. New York: Verso, 1998.

Verba, Sidney, Kay Lehman Schlozman, and Henry Brady. *Voice and Equality: Civic Voluntarism in American Politics.* Cambridge, Mass.: Harvard University Press, 1995.

Wielhouwer, Peter W. "In Search of Lincoln's Perfect List: Targeting in Grassroots Campaigns." *American Politics Research* 31, no. 6 (2003): 632–669.

PART VI
Specific Campaigns

CHAPTER 20

Presidential Campaigns

Richard S. Conley

U.S. presidential historian Theodore H. White once said, "There is no excitement anywhere in the world, short of war, to match the excitement of the American presidential campaign." [1] Indeed, for voters and political observers alike the process leading up to that fateful Tuesday once every four years is the pinnacle of national political spectacle all wrapped up in a single event. Americans have come to expect nothing less in the competition for the most coveted elective office in the nation. Underlying the jockeying, posturing, and debating that define the long campaign leading the victor to the White House is a core belief that presidential elections matter. As commander in chief, chief diplomat, and "chief legislator," the president makes decisions and takes stances that fundamentally shape national and foreign policy and leave lasting imprints on history.

The stability of quadrennial elections, a cornerstone of the Constitution, does not imply that presidential campaigns have remained static since the founding of the Republic in 1789. Significant technological and structural changes in the electoral process have altered campaign strategies during the last fifty years. Presidential campaigns in the post–World War II period are best understood as combining essential republican features reflected in the founders' desire for *indirect* democracy with pressures for democratization and citizen participation. This evolution has produced a unique amalgam of features and a new set of challenges for presidential contenders in their bids for the Oval Office.

This chapter considers the basic characteristics and processes surrounding contemporary presidential campaigns. The first section examines the characteristics of presidential challengers. The second section surveys the complexities of the nominating system, from primary elections and caucuses to national party conventions. It is followed by an overview of general campaign dynamics and then a brief discussion of identifiable patterns of voting behavior in presidential elections. The concluding sections assess the impact of campaigns on governance, giving particular attention to the concept of presidential "mandates," and examine calls for reforms aimed at redressing dysfunctions of the current system.

Candidate Characteristics

It is an axiom of American politics that in the contest for the White House "many are called but few are chosen." Primary elections and caucuses are structured to narrow the field of contenders for the nomination to a single nominee by the time the two parties hold their national conventions in summer of the election year. But even a year before the first primary or caucus an identifiable pool of candidates usually emerges and begins to consider a run for the White House. This "invisible primary" constitutes efforts to gain name recognition, media attention, and the national spotlight well in advance of the first-in-the-nation New Hampshire primary and the Iowa caucuses.

At this early stage of the presidential campaign the parties may field a dozen or more hopefuls for the White House. Several factors may contribute to the magnitude of contestants who decide to get into the race (see Table 20-1, which accentuates several patterns). First, the "out party"—that is, the party that does not currently hold the White House—is much more likely to attract a sizable number of candidates when the incumbent of the opposition party is seeking reelection. In 1972 and 1976, for example, a large number of Democrats lined up to challenge Richard Nixon and Gerald R. Ford, respectively. Similarly, Democratic President Bill Clinton's reelection bid in 1996 drew competition from no less than twelve Republican contenders, and ten Democrats stood ready to square off against incumbent president George W. Bush a full year before the 2004 presidential election. Second, the party faithful are less inclined to challenge an incumbent president seeking reelection. Neither Ronald Reagan (1984) nor George W. Bush (2004) faced an in-party challenge in their reelection bids. When serious challenges to incumbent presidents have occurred in either party, such as Massachusetts senator Edward M. Kennedy's effort to overtake Jimmy Carter for the Democratic nomination in 1980 or former California governor Ronald Reagan's attempt to beat Gerald Ford for the 1976 Republican nomination, the sitting president has always prevailed.

315

Table 20-1 Presidential Candidates by Party and Type of Race, 1960–2004

Year	Democrats	Republicans	Incumbent/open race
1960	4	2	Open[c]
1964	1	5	Democratic incumbent
1968	5	4	Open[c]
1972	12	3	Republican incumbent
1976	12	2	Republican incumbent
1980	3	7	Democratic incumbent
1984	8	1	Republican incumbent
1988	8	6	Open
1992	6	3	Republican incumbent
1996	1	12	Democratic incumbent
2000	2	11[a]	Open[c]
2004	10[b]	1	Republican incumbent

Source: Adapted by author from Robert E. DiClerico, "In Defense of the Presidential Nominating Process," in *Choosing Our Choices: Debating the Presidential Nominating Process,* ed. Robert E. DiClerico and James W. Davis (Lanham, Md.: Rowman and Littlefield, 2000), 56.

[a] Includes Sen. Robert Smith of New Hampshire, who first ran as a Republican and then changed to independent.

[b] Includes the Democratic candidates who had announced by September 2003 (Wesley Clark, Howard Dean, John Edwards, Richard A. Gephardt, Bob Graham, John Kerry, Dennis Kucinich, Joseph I. Lieberman, Carol Moseley-Braun, and Al Sharpton).

[c] In all open presidential races between 1960 and 2004, the incumbent vice president won his party's nomination. Only George Bush (1988) was successful in his bid for the White House. Richard Nixon (1960), Hubert Humphrey (1968) and Al Gore (2000) were defeated.

Americans are prone to complain about their presidential candidate choices. But it is difficult to make the case that the vast majority of nominees are unqualified. The "job experience" of competitors in presidential campaigns has been both substantial and remarkably stable in the last half-century. About half of presidential candidates have been lawyers and served in Congress, and most of the others have held state or local elected offices. And, occasionally, celebrities, entrepreneurs, and political activists vie for the Democratic and Republican Party nominations. Indeed, a favorite tactic in modern presidential politics is to run against Washington as an "outsider," even though candidates generally need to have "insider" experience to win the party nomination. The eventual nominees of both parties have had significant executive experience in either national or state government or legislative experience in Congress. In fact, between 1960 and 2000 Democratic nominees had an average of fifteen years of combined executive, congressional, or gubernatorial experience. Republicans boasted a combined average of seventeen years.[2]

State governorships, the vice presidency, and, especially, the U.S. Senate are the most important launching pads for successful presidential contenders (Table 20-2). Between 1960 and 1996 over one-third of those contesting the presidency and just less than a quarter of those

Table 20-2 Backgrounds of Presidential Candidates, 1960–1996 (percent)

Last office held	Contenders	Nominees	Winners
President	5.0	28.6	40.0
Vice president	6.5	28.6	30.0
Governor	23.0	19.1	20.0
Senator	36.7	23.8	10.0
Representative	10.8	0	0
Activist/celebrity	9.4	0	0
Other	8.6	0	0

Source: Adapted by author from Barry C. Burden, "United States Senators as Presidential Candidates," *Political Science Quarterly* 117, no. 1 (2002): 95.

who were nominated as their party's standard-bearer in the general election had Senate experience. These candidates include Republicans Barry Goldwater (1964) and Robert J. Dole (1996) and Democrats Lyndon B. Johnson (1964), George McGovern (1972), Walter F. Mondale (1984), and Al Gore (2000). Republican Gerald Ford is an anomalous case because he served twenty-four years in the House of Representatives. But Ford was elected to neither the presidency nor the vice presidency.

President Ronald Reagan waves to onlookers during a "whistle-stop" train tour as part of his 1984 reelection campaign. As a former actor and Republican governor of California, Reagan capitalized on his celebrity status and his executive background to win two terms in office. Source: Courtesy Ronald Reagan Library

don Johnson, Richard Nixon, and George Bush, won the White House (Nixon failed in 1960, but prevailed in his second try in 1968). Vice-presidential candidates often face the unique dilemma of needing to support, while simultaneously distinguishing themselves from, their predecessors. The point is underscored by the conundrum of Democratic candidate Hubert H. Humphrey (1968), who sought to distance himself from Lyndon Johnson's unpopular policies in the Vietnam War without undermining Johnson's authority. Similarly, Democrat Al Gore (2000) attempted to take credit for the successful economic policies of Clinton's presidency while detaching himself from the scandals that clouded Clinton's two terms. Even successful vice-presidential candidates are not immune from the quandary. Republican George Bush was victorious in 1988 after Ronald Reagan's two terms, although his promise of a "kinder, gentler America" seemingly called into question the "Great Communicator's" legacy and drew the ire of many conservative Republicans.

The public often equates executive experience at the state level with that at the national level. State governorships are the second largest source of presidential candidates. Between 1960 and 1996, nearly a fifth of nominees held governorships. States are often considered "laboratories of democracy," and shrewd governors can build name recognition and media attention for innovativeness and leadership. As governor of Arkansas for thirteen years, Democrat Bill Clinton earned the national spotlight as president of the National Governors Association prior to his bid for the White House in 1992. Republican Ronald Reagan served eight years as governor of the most populous state in the nation, California, and Democrats Michael Dukakis of Massachusetts and Jimmy Carter of Georgia served ten and four years, respectively, as governor of their home states. Republican George W. Bush was elected twice to the Texas governorship and touted his record of working in a bipartisan spirit with Democrats in the state legislature. Howard Dean, the early front-runner for the Democratic nomination in 2004, served as governor of Vermont for over eleven years. One common link between all these candidates is that they appealed to voters to recognize that their economic management and experience at the state level enabled them to apply expertise to national policies.

Vice presidents form a small number of overall contenders but a higher percentage of eventual nominees. Most vice-presidential candidates also have had prior congressional experience. Table 20-2 reveals that just less than a third of vice-presidential nominees, including Lyn-

The Nominating System: From Primaries and Caucuses to the Convention

The complicated process that eventually yields the parties' nominees is tedious, challenging, and costly for presidential aspirants (see Chapter 5 for a description of the nominating process). Unlike most parliamentary democracies such as Great Britain and Canada, the United States has no legally sanctioned "campaign period" that guides the process for choosing the American national executive. Federalism plays a pivotal role. Constitutionally, it is the states, not the federal government, that determine how and when delegates to the national party conventions are chosen. The majority of states hold *primary elections* beginning in January of the presidential election year. These elections give voters an opportunity to express their candidate preference. The tabulation of these preferences translates into a share of delegates for each candidate from the states to the national party conventions. The party's standard-bearer is ultimately chosen through a roll call vote of those delegates. Other states hold *caucuses,* which are local or statewide meetings of party activists. Party members then cast votes for delegates of their preferred candidate to the state and national conventions. Thus primary elections and caucuses have popular participatory components but retain an important element of indirect democracy.

The primary season that begins in January of the presidential election year and ends with the parties' summer conventions serves a vital purpose in presidential selection. On a fundamental level, the nominating process provides a framework for legitimization of presidential candidates and facilitates mass electoral choice, which is the lifeblood of representative democracy. The system is aimed at winnowing the field of contenders, producing a candidate with the greatest level of consensus in each party, and giving voters the tools they need to make informed choices. The primary season furnishes contestants with a forum in which to debate current policy issues, critique one another as well as candidates or the incumbent from the other party, and make their stances known to the public while enabling the press and the public to scrutinize their platforms. The objective of each party is to produce the most qualified candidate for the nation's highest office and close ranks by the end of the summer national convention, which signals the beginning of the general election campaign.

The Dynamics of the Nominating Process: Historical and Contemporary Perspectives

The various types of nominee selection processes have produced various campaign tactics for winning the parties' nominations. Primary elections grew out of Progressive era reforms of the early 1900s as a means of redressing corrupt and authoritarian nineteenth-century practices at state and national conventions. Presidential nominees were often "insiders" chosen by party elites, with little popular participation, either in Congress or through caucuses (meetings of state party leaders). Wisconsin instituted the first presidential primary in 1905. By 1912 eleven other states had followed suit. It was not until the 1970s, however, that a majority of states began to adopt primaries. Until that point, presidential candidates shied away from entering primaries, and party leaders continued to exercise substantial control over the choice of the nominee at the national conventions.

Figures 20-1a and 20-1b reveal that the percentage of delegates chosen through presidential preference primaries grew rapidly through the 1970s. Today, 60–75 percent of the delegates to the two parties' conventions are routinely chosen through popular means, and four of every five states hold a primary election. The year 1968 proved to be a watershed in the development of presidential primaries. The raucous Democratic convention in Chicago, at which protestors clashed with police when anti–Vietnam War protestors could not gain access or influence over the convention proceedings, precipitated important reforms. The delegate selection reforms were so sweeping that most Democratic state parties abandoned the caucus in favor of presidential primaries. And the national party organization could enforce the new rules, because it seats the state delegates at the national convention.

After the 1968 convention, the Democrats constituted the McGovern-Fraser Commission (named for Sen. George McGovern of South Dakota and Rep. Donald Fraser of Minnesota), which was charged with developing rules to open up the delegate section process to as many voters as possible. The reforms set quotas for the number of delegates constituting minorities and women, as well as younger voters. The Republican Party established its own Delegates and Organization Committee that pursued similar modifications. The net effect of this reformist impulse in both parties was a decisive end to the era of brokered conventions by limiting the influence of party leaders and extending popular control over nominations through primaries. By 2004 only four states—Alaska, Colorado, Nevada, and Utah—did not have some form of a presidential preference primary.

The consequences of the proliferation of primaries for presidential contestants are manifold from a strategic perspective. Candidates must pay close attention to the electoral timetable. Advance planning is essential. Months before the primary season, they must assemble a core campaign organization to help raise money, develop a campaign strategy, craft a message, and recruit staff and volunteers to organize states for the upcoming primaries and caucuses. Such groundwork includes currying favor with the media, attempting to obtain positive press coverage, conducting polling on policy ideas, and networking with local and state party organization leaders and activists.

Nowhere is the need for early planning more evident than in fund-raising. Candidates able to bankroll large sums of money solidify their status as a serious challenger and can create an image as an early front-runner by drawing media attention to substantial financial backing. Although a large campaign war chest does not guarantee success, it may help a candidate who has survived an early defeat compete in later primary contests.

One important decision candidates must make is whether to accept federal matching contributions. Federal law provides that if candidates raise a total of $100,000 by collecting $5,000 in individual contributions of no more than $250 each in at least twenty states, they can receive matching federal funds. Matching contributions are provided by taxpayers who voluntarily check off a box on their annual federal income tax returns. The trade-off is that if candidates accept federal money, they face spending ceilings and must comply with federal reporting and auditing requirements. In 2004 candidates receiving federal matching funds had to limit primary campaign spending to about $45 million and no more than $50,000 from personal funds. Spending caps for the general election were fixed at $74 million, excluding unregulated contributions (often referred to as "soft money") such as those from state and party organizations and political action committees (PACs).

Many recent presidential candidates have decided to reject federal funding, because they can raise far more for their campaign war chests through individual contributions, and accepting federal funds may place their campaigns at a disadvantage. In 2000 George W. Bush's

Figure 20-1a Number of Democratic Presidential Primaries and Percentage of Delegates Selected through Primaries, 1968–2000

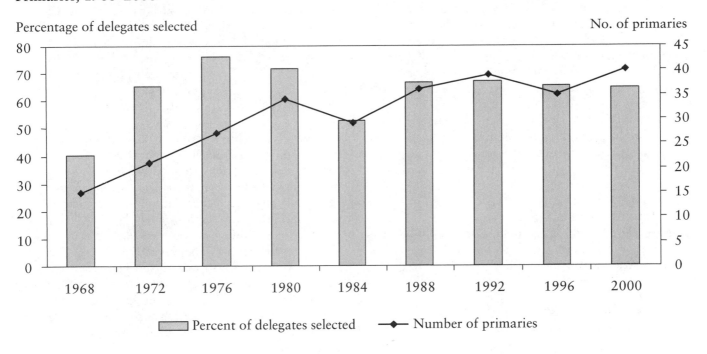

Figure 20-1b Number of Republican Presidential Primaries and Percentage of Delegates Selected through Primaries, 1968–2000

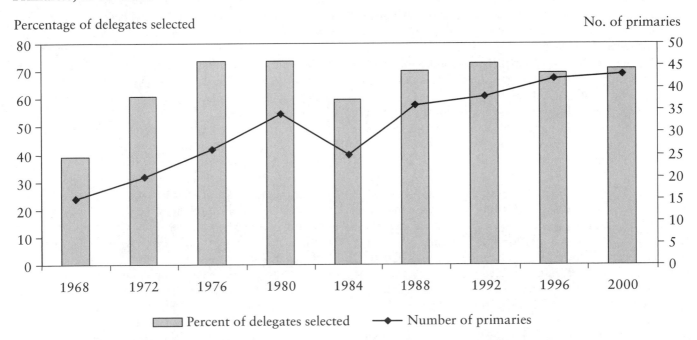

Source: Adapted by author from *Presidential Elections 1789–2000* (Washington, D.C.: CQ Press, 2002), 99.

campaign made a conscious decision to forgo federal matching funds and concentrate instead on raising "hard money" (individual contributions). Robert Dole's experience in 1996 was not lost on the Bush campaign. Dole, the Republican nominee, had accepted federal matching con-

tributions but had spent heavily in the primaries against wealthy businessman Steve Forbes. As a result, Dole's campaign approached spending limits well in advance of the general election. In the 2004 election cycle, the early Democratic primary front-runner, Howard Dean, similarly decided to decline federal matching funds, preferring to amass individual contributions he estimated would exceed federal limits. In the primary election, both Bush and the Democratic nominee, John Kerry, did as well.

In tailoring their messages to primary voters and caucus participants, candidates must be mindful of their audience. By their very nature, caucuses draw committed party activists who tend to be more ideological than general election voters. And though turnout for primary elections tends to be much lower than in the general election, those who do go to the polls tend to be more ideologically committed, dyed-in-the-wool party supporters. Thus candidates in both parties have incentives to try to mobilize the ideological extremes of the primary electorate. For Democrats, these supporters may include party loyalists such as African Americans and union members. For Republicans, committed party supporters may span social conservatives to business leaders. The first test of candidates' appeals to core supporting groups comes in New Hampshire and Iowa.

Iowa, New Hampshire, and Front-Loading

The first battleground for the presidential nomination of each party is New Hampshire and Iowa, and presidential candidates ignore the New Hampshire primaries and the Iowa caucuses at their own risk. These two states traditionally hold the first-in-the-nation tests for presidential aspirants. Iowa Democrats, who had rushed to implement the McGovern-Fraser Committee reforms four years ahead of schedule, held the state's first caucuses in 1972. New Hampshire held its first primary contest in 1952, and a provision of the state constitution mandates that its primary come before all others in the Union.

The New Hampshire primary has taken on mythical qualities. Between 1952 and 1988, no candidate successfully won the White House without prevailing in the Granite State's primary. Only in the last decade has New Hampshire's crystal ball for the White House proven incorrect. In 1992 Bill Clinton lost the New Hampshire primary but won the Democratic nomination and later defeated incumbent president George Bush. In fact, the Clinton campaign attempted to spin the early defeat in New Hampshire into a victory, arguing that the "Comeback Kid" did better than expected against favorite son Paul Tsongas, a veteran U.S. senator from neighboring Massachusetts. In 2000 Republican John McCain ran a spirited, centrist campaign and outpaced George W. Bush by eighteen points in New Hampshire. Bush, who was victorious in many later primaries and won the Republican nomination decisively, dismissed the loss by contending that "New Hampshire has long been known as a bump in the road for front-runners."[3]

Do the New Hampshire primary and Iowa caucuses give the two states too much influence in the early race for party nominations? Critics allege that New Hampshire and Iowa are not politically, economically, or so-

cially representative of the country. Both states are rural, have few minority voters, and are more conservative than larger, more populous states such as New York, California, Texas, and Florida. Moreover, the frenzied national media coverage that follows candidates to Iowa and New Hampshire is biased toward the horse race. The focus is less on candidates' policy positions and much more on which candidate is the front-runner and prognostications about who will come out ahead when the vote counting ends (see Chapter 13 on the media).

Regardless of the merits of these critiques, candidates spend much time visiting the two states, cultivating contact with party activists, and reaching out to voters months before any voting occurs. These early contests are bellwethers that place candidates under heightened public and media scrutiny. And winning the New Hampshire primary or the Iowa caucuses provides pivotal momentum to the victor that produces mutually reinforcing effects. Prevailing in the Iowa and New Hampshire contests buttresses the victor's image as the front-runner, attracts media attention, and facilitates fund-raising for the next round of contests, which increasingly are coming earlier and earlier in the winter and early spring of the general election year.

Because other states have envied the privileged and allegedly disproportionate role played by Iowa and New Hampshire in the presidential selection process, many have moved their primary or caucus dates up in the election season in order to maximize leverage over the choice of the nominee. This dynamic of front-loading primaries on the electoral calendar produces the parties' nominees much earlier in the general election year as leading candidates rack up the necessary delegates to prevail in the summer conventions.

States' attempts to gain influence over nominations through the electoral calendar and compete with Iowa and New Hampshire have grown in the last several decades. In 1988 southern Democrats, disappointed by the liberal nominees George McGovern in 1972 and Walter Mondale in 1984, pressured their state legislatures to hold primaries on the same day in March, dubbed "Super Tuesday," in order optimize regional clout. In 1996 the California legislature, unhappy that the presidential nominees in both parties were a foregone conclusion by the time voters in the Golden State were able to cast their ballots, moved the state's presidential primary data from June to March. California's decision had a ripple effect as other states jockeyed to position their primaries earlier in the season and carry substantive influence over the nominees. Also in 1996, several Midwestern and New England states coordinated their primaries on the same day. In 2002 the Democratic Party moved up its 2004 primary schedule to concur with the Republican calendar. The goal was to avoid a detrimental month-long pause in election dates in 2000 that had given more media attention to the George W. Bush campaign.

Figure 20-2 The Front-Loaded Presidential Primary Season, Selected Years (percent of primaries held before April 1)

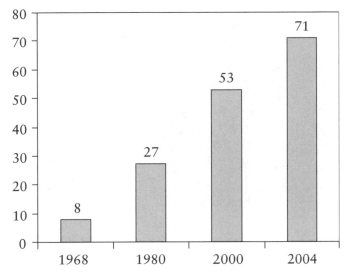

Source: Adapted by author from www.vote-smart.org and Rhodes Cook, *Race for the Presidency: Winning the 2004 Nomination* (Washington, D.C.: CQ Press, 2004).

The compound effect of front-loading, as Figure 20-2 makes clear, is an extremely compressed campaign schedule. Figure 20-2 shows the rising frequency of presidential primaries held before April 1 in the election year. In 1968 only one state, New Hampshire, held its primary by April 1. The percentage of states holding early primaries doubled between 1980 and 2000, and in 2004 nearly three-quarters of all primaries were held before April 1.

Front-loading raises some normative concerns. One is that the overwhelming number of early primaries depresses voter turnout in later contests. Another is that front-loading forces candidates to raise greater sums of money earlier in the process. This dynamic may give a distinct strategic advantage to the front-runner, who is better able to marshal the necessary resources to compete effectively in the contests that follow Iowa and New Hampshire. Finally, the compressed elections schedule may only encourage the media coverage to focus on the horse race rather than the substantive aspects of primary contests.

Critics worry that the media may fail to vet candidate qualifications adequately and early "knockouts" may rob voters of choices. In the 2000 primary season, for example, Republican challenger John McCain and Democratic challenger Bill Bradley quit their bids for the White House in March, five to six months before the party conventions. The dynamics of 2004 confirmed the degree to which even long-standing front-runners can rapidly fall victim to defeat in the Iowa caucuses and New Hampshire primary. For months, former Vermont governor

Howard Dean led the Democratic pack, yet Massachusetts senator John Kerry earned a surprise victory in Iowa. The negative media coverage of Dean's controversial "rebel yell" to supporters in Iowa after his third-place showing there seemed to be the death knell for his campaign. Dean placed a distant second in New Hampshire and managed only single digits in the South Carolina primary that followed. He dropped out of the race just one month after the Iowa caucuses, in a bow to his failure to win a single state's primary.

National Conventions: What Role?

The front-loading of primary elections and party caucuses enables front-runners to accumulate enough delegates to wrap up their nominations months before the parties hold their national conventions in July or August of the election year. Since the significant reforms of the 1970s, the choice of the presidential nominee has been a foregone conclusion; both parties' nominees have been chosen on the first ballots of the delegates assembled at the conventions. So why do the parties continue to hold national conventions?

Conventions play several useful roles. First, each party ratifies its policy platform at its national convention. When there are disagreements about the platform, the convention provides a forum for airing the issues, resolving them, and consensus building.

Second, it is during the convention proceedings that each party formally nominates its presidential candidate after a vote of the delegates. The delegates also formally select the vice-presidential running mate, although the presidential nominee, by tradition, makes the choice. Ticket "balancing" is often a factor in the selection of the vice-presidential nominee. Such balancing reflects a conscious choice by the party to ensure regional diversity, generational diversity, policy expertise, or some combination thereof. In 2000, for example, George W. Bush chose former Wyoming representative Richard B. Cheney, who brought significant private and public sector experience to the Republican ticket. Cheney had served as chief of staff to President Gerald R. Ford and defense secretary under George Bush, and he had headed a Fortune 500 energy corporation. Similarly, Democratic nominee Al Gore chose Connecticut senator Joseph I. Lieberman to provide regional balance to the campaign; Lieberman, a Jew, also brought religious diversity to the ticket by representing a core Democratic constituency.

Finally, the nominating convention marks the official kickoff of the general election campaign. The fanfare of conventions draws media attention that the parties attempt to utilize as free advertising. Although a party cannot guarantee which parts of its convention the national or local television media will cover, the carefully scripted speeches by party notables and well-planned festivities are aimed at providing a favorable public image and campaign boost to the presidential candidate. Nevertheless, the parties face a dwindling audience for televised coverage of the conventions. A 1996 survey, for example, revealed that only about a sixth of all households watched either convention, and three-fifths of respondents did not even know when the Republican convention was being held.[4]

The Political Environment and Presidential Campaigns

After the primary season, nominees face various strategic considerations in their bids for the White House. First, they must settle quickly on a calculus to win 270 votes in the electoral college—the magic number for election. Their anticipated geographical distribution of support becomes paramount in this numbers game. Second, the candidates must decide which groups they want to target as they attempt to construct broad coalitions of supporters in the electorate. They must simultaneously tailor their mes-

In a parody of all four presidential candidates in 1860, a map of the United States is being torn apart by three of the candidates. Republican Abraham Lincoln (far left) and northern Democrat Stephen A. Douglas vie for the West, as southern Democrat John Breckinridge (center) goes for the South. Constitutional Union candidate John Bell stands on a stool trying to glue together the Northeast. Source: Library of Congress

sages to the voters and fix the tenor of their campaigns, carefully searching for the appropriate balance in criticizing their opponents and elaborating their own policy goals. In this process, challengers and incumbents seeking reelection face different constraints and opportunities.

Mapping an Electoral College Strategy

Americans do not vote for their preferred presidential candidate directly. When they enter their polling places on the first Tuesday following the first Monday in November every four years, they are actually casting their votes for a slate of electors in their state who have pledged support to one or another candidate. Winning the presidency is not contingent on winning the national popular vote. Instead, a candidate needs a majority 270 of the 538 votes in the electoral college.

In the electoral college, each state has a number of electoral votes equal to its number of senators (two) and members of the House of Representatives (the District of Columbia has three electoral votes). In all states but Maine and Nebraska, the "unit rule" applies—that is, the candidate who receives a plurality of the statewide vote receives all of that state's electoral votes. Maine and Nebraska partition electoral votes according to candidate pluralities in congressional districts, with the two "at large" votes awarded to the candidate who wins a plurality of the statewide vote. Because of the predominance of the winner-take-all system, the net effect of the electoral

college is that it typically exaggerates the victor's margin compared with the national popular vote.

The selection of the president by the electoral college method is best understood as a compromise among the founders. They sought to strike a balance between those who favored Congress's choosing the executive and those who feared that direct election could lead to demagogues capturing the White House. The result was a truly federal arrangement in which states are free to decide for themselves how electors are chosen and apportioned. Satisfying those with a Madisonian preference for legislative government in the situation in which no candidate receives a majority in the electoral college, the Constitution calls for the House of Representatives to select the president (and the Senate the vice president). In the House, each state delegation casts a single, unified vote among the top three presidential contenders.

Many critics charge that the electoral college is an archaic institution that should be replaced by direct election of the president. Twice, in 1800 and 1824, a presidential election has been thrown into the House in the absence of an electoral college majority. And three times—in 1876, 1888, and 2000—the winner of the electoral college narrowly lost the popular vote. The calls for reform of the electoral college system are examined in greater detail at the end of this chapter.

For the moment, the import of the electoral college system is that it forces candidates to map out a general election strategy that targets a set of states and not one that necessarily maximizes popular votes across the nation. In this sense, George W. Bush was correct in 2000 when, after prevailing in the Florida recount controversy but losing the popular vote nationally, he noted that had he sought to increase his popular vote tally he would have campaigned more extensively in his native Texas where his popularity as governor was strong.

Table 20-3 shows that since the 2000 census a candidate can obtain a majority in the electoral college by winning only eleven states. Five of those states—California, Texas, Florida, Georgia, and North Carolina—have experienced heavy population growth in the last two decades, bolstering their importance in a presidential candidate's campaign strategy. With its fifty-five electoral votes, California is the richest electoral prize followed by Texas (thirty-four), New York (thirty-one), and Florida (twenty-seven). A candidate likely to lose one or more of these populous states must devise a compensatory strategy by attempting to prevail in another set of states with fewer electoral votes each. Thus forecasting electoral college votes becomes a critical enterprise for the nominees' campaigns.

Nominees can draw upon past history as a guide to their electoral college strategy. Figure 20-3 presents the basic geographic electoral trends of the last decade. States backing the Democratic candidate in the 1992, 1996, and 2000 elections are concentrated on the West Coast (California, Oregon, Washington), the upper Midwest (Minnesota, Michigan, Wisconsin, Illinois), and the East Coast (New York, New Jersey, Pennsylvania). Together, the states that supported Bill Clinton in 1992 and 1996 and Al Gore in 2000 had 260 electoral votes after the 2000 census. Republican strength is, by contrast, concentrated in Texas, the Rocky Mountain West (Idaho, Utah, and Wyoming), parts of the Midwest (North and South Dakota, Nebraska, Kansas, Indiana), and much of the South (Virginia, North and South Carolina, Alabama, Mississippi). The states voting consistently in favor of the Republican standard-bearer from 1992 to 2000 together have 135 electoral votes.

Presidential campaigns traditionally have concentrated their resources on a relatively small number of competitive states while ignoring states that appear to strongly favor one candidate over the other. "Swing states"— states that have alternated support for the parties' nominees in the last decade—play a pivotal role in handing the presidency to the nominee of one or the other party (Figure 20-3). To secure an electoral college victory, candidates must pay particularly close attention to courting voters in these states. Of the states that have thrown support behind Republican candidates in two of the three elections from 1992 to 2000, Florida, with its twenty-seven electoral votes, is the largest prize. Conversely, those states that supported Clinton in 1992 and 1996 all went for Bush in 2000. Of these nine states, Ohio was the

most important, with its twenty electoral votes at present. Bush won both Florida and Ohio in 2004, solidifying his popular vote margin in both states compared with 2000.

Secular Realignment, Electoral Coalitions, and Incumbent/Challenger Strategies

Figure 20-3 implicitly conveys the importance of the geographic realignment of the national electorate for the parties' nominees. Although Pacific Coast states have become more Democratic in recent presidential elections, southern states began their much longer-term transition toward support of the Republican Party nearly half a century ago. The breakup of the once solid Democratic South can be traced to South Carolina governor Strom Thurmond's "states' rights" Dixiecrat campaign in 1948. In 1964 Lyndon Johnson failed to carry five states in the South due to his strong support of civil rights. This facilitated Alabama governor George C. Wallace's successful independent campaign in the Deep South and Nixon's victories in the "outer South" and border states in 1968, fueling a critical transition. Finally, in-migration to the Sun Belt states of the South and social and religious conservatives' increasing support of Republicans fueled the party's breakthrough in 1994. Riding on southerners' support of GOP congressional candidates, Republicans gained control of the House of Representatives after a forty-year hiatus. In the intervening period, southerners had often split their vote between Republican presidential candidates and conservative Democratic congressional candidates, who had seniority on key committees and could bring significant benefits to their constituents.

If current trends continue in the new century, the secular geographic realignment presages closer presidential races in the electoral college, as evidenced by Florida's determinant role in 2000 and Ohio's in 2004. With a large number of states solidly Democratic or Republican, a smaller number of states may ultimately hold sway over the outcome. Increasingly competitive elections oblige nominees to craft their appeals to targeted groups in the electorate. As noted in Chapter 14 on campaign strategy, candidates first need to encourage a high turnout and loyalty among their party's base. For Republicans, supporters may include social conservatives, wealthy voters, Protestants, and whites. For Democrats, core supporters tend to be lower-income voters, African Americans and other minorities, educators, and Jews. The second objective of nominees is to broaden their supporting coalitions as widely as possible. For most presidential campaigns, this strategy entails fine-tuning their policy positions toward the center of the electorate without alienating the loyal primary voters who enabled them to capture their party's nomination. Political scientists often speak of "coalitions in the electorate" that nominees constructed to win the Oval Office. Examples include Franklin D. Roosevelt's 1932 New Deal coalition, which included blacks, southerners, business interests, and

Table 20-3 States' Electoral Votes by Magnitude, 1981–2010 (ranked by current magnitude after 2000 U.S. Census)

State	1981–1990	1991–2000	2001–2010	State	1981–1990	1991–2000	2001–2010
California	47	54	55	**Virginia**	12	13	13
Texas	29	32	34	Massachusetts	13	12	12
New York	36	33	31	Indiana	12	12	11
Florida	21	25	27	Missouri	11	11	11
Pennsylvania	25	23	21	Tennessee	11	11	11
Illinois	24	22	21	Washington	10	11	11
Ohio	23	21	20	**Arizona**	7	8	10
Michigan	20	18	17	Maryland	10	10	10
Georgia	12	13	15	Minnesota	10	10	10
New Jersey	16	15	15	Wisconsin	11	11	10
North Carolina	13	14	15	Alabama	9	9	9
Total	*266*	*270*	*271*	Colorado	8	8	9
				Louisiana	10	9	9
				Kentucky	9	8	8
				South Carolina	8	8	8
				Connecticut	8	8	7
				Iowa	8	7	7
				Oklahoma	8	8	7
				Oregon	7	7	7
				Arkansas	6	6	6
				Kansas	7	6	6
				Mississippi	7	7	6
				Nebraska	5	5	5
				Nevada	4	4	5
				New Mexico	5	5	5
				Utah	5	5	5
				West Virginia	6	5	5
				Hawaii	4	4	4
				Idaho	4	4	4
				Maine	4	4	4
				New Hampshire	4	4	4
				Rhode Island	4	4	4
				Alaska	3	3	3
				Delaware	3	3	3
				D.C.	3	3	3
				Montana	4	3	3
				North Dakota	3	3	3
				South Dakota	3	3	3
				Vermont	3	3	3
				Wyoming	3	3	3
				Total	*272*	*268*	*267*

Source: Compiled by author from the Federal Election Commission data, www.fec.gov/pages/elecvote.htm.

Note: States shown in **boldface** have consistently increased their number of electoral college votes over the last two decades.

Figure 20-3 States Won by Democratic and Republican Candidates, 1992, 1996, and 2000

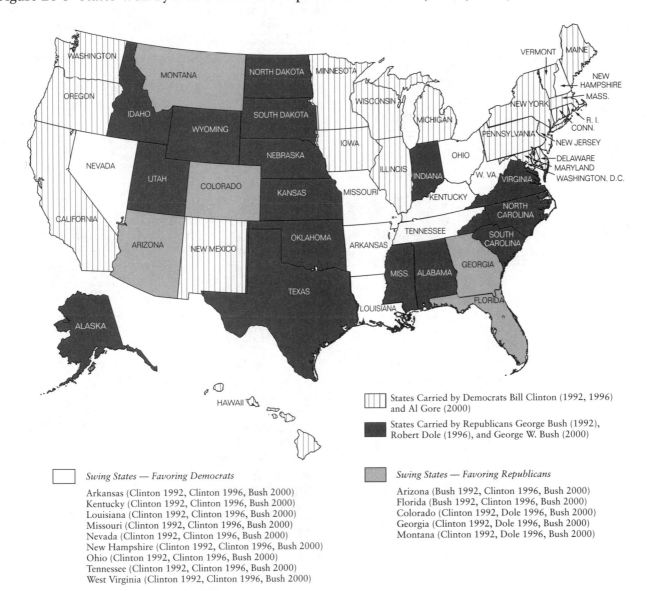

States Carried by Democrats Bill Clinton (1992, 1996) and Al Gore (2000)

States Carried by Republicans George Bush (1992), Robert Dole (1996), and George W. Bush (2000)

Swing States — Favoring Democrats

Arkansas (Clinton 1992, Clinton 1996, Bush 2000)
Kentucky (Clinton 1992, Clinton 1996, Bush 2000)
Louisiana (Clinton 1992, Clinton 1996, Bush 2000)
Missouri (Clinton 1992, Clinton 1996, Bush 2000)
Nevada (Clinton 1992, Clinton 1996, Bush 2000)
New Hampshire (Clinton 1992, Clinton 1996, Bush 2000)
Ohio (Clinton 1992, Clinton 1996, Bush 2000)
Tennessee (Clinton 1992, Clinton 1996, Bush 2000)
West Virginia (Clinton 1992, Clinton 1996, Bush 2000)

Swing States — Favoring Republicans

Arizona (Bush 1992, Clinton 1996, Bush 2000)
Florida (Bush 1992, Clinton 1996, Bush 2000)
Colorado (Clinton 1992, Dole 1996, Bush 2000)
Georgia (Clinton 1992, Dole 1996, Bush 2000)
Montana (Clinton 1992, Dole 1996, Bush 2000)

Catholics, and the Reagan coalition of 1980, which comprised middle-class voters, disaffected Democrats, and social conservatives.

Challengers and incumbent presidents seeking reelection face different constraints and opportunities in the general campaign. Voters know who the president is and what he and his party did during the previous four years. Presidential campaigns provide little new information about the incumbent. The domestic economy and foreign policy issues figure most prominently in voters' retrospective evaluations of sitting presidents. Presidents can take credit for successes in both domains, but they cannot escape blame for failures.

Economic and foreign policy issues have cut both ways for incumbent presidents. Robust economic growth and successful handling of foreign policy crises in the Suez and China propelled Dwight D. Eisenhower to a landslide re-election victory in 1956 on the theme of "peace and prosperity." Ronald Reagan's reelection in 1984 hinged on economic prosperity, captured by television ads touting "It's morning again in America." Similarly, Bill Clinton crafted his successful reelection campaign in 1996 by attributing strong economic growth to his administration's policies that would enable him to build "a bridge to the twenty-first century."

Other incumbent presidents have fared less well. The domestic backlash against the unpopular war in Vietnam shaped Lyndon Johnson's decision not to seek reelection in 1968. High unemployment and spiraling inflation, combined with the image of a weak president in his dealing with the Iranian hostage crisis, thwarted Jimmy Carter's reelection bid in 1980. In that election, challenger Ronald Reagan asked voters, "Are you better off now than you were four years ago?" A majority answered

During her run for the 2004 Democratic presidential nomination, Carol Moseley Braun poses with David H. Swinton, president of Benedict College, a historically African American school in Columbia, South Carolina. Such colleges have become an important stop for Democratic candidates hoping to gain support from the state's minority voters in the first primary in the South. Source: Lou Krasky/AP Wide World Photos

"No." And in 1992 George Bush's widespread popularity after the victory in the Persian Gulf War was precipitously eclipsed by a downturn in the economy that ultimately cost him reelection. Bush was hammered by Democratic nominee Bill Clinton and by millionaire Reform Party candidate H. Ross Perot for the stagnating economy.

A challenger's campaign needs to run on a theme emphasizing change. Challengers for the presidency have no record in the White House on which to run; they can only make promises. Although former governors and members of Congress can tout their prior policy records at the state level or in the national legislature, all such challengers are nevertheless asking voters to judge their future agendas. It is little wonder, then, that challengers go out of their way to highlight the theme of "change" in their campaigns. In 1976 the Carter campaign ran under the banner "A leader, for a change"; in 1984 Walter Mondale ran against Ronald Reagan by suggesting "America needs a change"; and in 1992 the Clinton campaign's informal slogan—"It's the economy, stupid!"—aimed to remind staffers (it was taped on the wall of the Little Rock campaign headquarters) to portray incumbent George Bush as out of touch with voters and convey the message that Clinton would make economic growth a priority. Clinton simultaneously told voters, "Don't stop thinking about tomorrow," as he detailed plans to launch an unprecedented overhaul of the national health care system.

In each election since 1960, when incumbent presidents have served out two terms or have chosen not to seek re-

election (Johnson, 1968) the incumbent vice president has won the party's nomination (Nixon, 1960; Humphrey, 1968; Bush, 1988; Gore 2000). But vice-presidential candidates confront special challenges. They must stress continuity with the past administration's successful policies while carving out their own vision of the future. In his unsuccessful run for the White House in 1960, for example, Richard Nixon accentuated the economic and civil rights policies of the Eisenhower administration. Hubert Humphrey promised to further the Johnson administration's progress on the domestic front (the Great Society). Similarly, George Bush emphasized his role in Reagan's economic and defense policies and pledged to "stay the course." By most accounts, however, the 1988 campaign was one of the most negative in the past half-century. The Bush campaign's steadfastly harsh portrayals of Michael Dukakis as "soft" on crime and defense, exemplified by television advertisements criticizing the Massachusetts governor's furlough program and questioning his ability to act as commander in chief, infuriated Democrats. The Dukakis campaign responded with a series of ads reproving Bush's plans for tax cuts that would putatively benefit only the "top 1% of taxpayers."

Although the Bush-Dukakis campaign may have been notable for the intensity with which both camps leveled negative charges and personal attacks at one another, the basic themes form a leitmotiv in presidential contests in the postwar period. Democrats often paint their Republican opponents as catering to wealthy voters and business interests. In 1956, for example, Democratic standardbearer Adlai Stevenson criticized Eisenhower's tax cuts, which he contended aided the well-to-do and left the middle class behind. Similarly, in the 2000 campaign Al Gore charged that George W. Bush's tax cut plans would benefit only the wealthiest taxpayers and corporations. Republicans have frequently accused their Democratic challengers of a laxity on national defense and poor economic management. In 1964 Barry Goldwater charged Lyndon Johnson with "weak and vacillating leadership" on foreign affairs; in 1972 Richard Nixon criticized George McGovern's defense cut plans as potentially ruinous to the military; and in 1996 Robert Dole accused Bill Clinton of allowing the nation's military to fall into disarray.

Although many Americans view negative campaigning and personal character attacks as distasteful, such tactics are as old as the Republic itself. The extreme enmity between John Adams and Thomas Jefferson in 1796 and 1800, in which even the virtue of the candidates' wives was trampled underfoot, is a case in point. Why then does negative campaigning persist? The answer is simple: *it is highly effective.* Negative portrayals of opponents have considerable influence in shaping undecided voters' views and reinforcing party loyalists' voting intentions, and they have substantial staying power. In the television era of sound bites and thirty-second spot ads, candidates find it much easier to paint a negative image of their opponents than elaborate the details of their policy positions.

Presidential Voting

A comprehensive analysis of presidential voting patterns is beyond the scope of this chapter. However, well-established models of presidential voting emphasize basic factors that shape the contours of turnout and voter choice, particularly the impact of socioeconomic status, age, race, religion, and gender (see Chapters 7 and 8). These factors merit a brief discussion because presidential campaigns must pay close attention to the loci of their potential support.

Determinants of Turnout

The turnout in U.S. presidential elections usually exceeds that in the midterm congressional elections by some 10 to 20 percent. Still, voters who go to the polls every four years to elect the president represent, on average, only about half of the eligible electorate. Even in 2000, the closest presidential election in the last several decades, only 51 percent of eligible voters nationally cast ballots.

There is a certain historical irony to the lack of voter participation in the United States. Over the years, the franchise has been extended to once excluded groups, including women (Nineteenth Amendment), African Americans (Voting Rights Act of 1965), and eighteen-year-olds (Twenty-Sixth Amendment), yet fewer Americans exercise that right on a whole. Which factors account for this vanishing electorate? Structural barriers to voting, such as voter registration requirements that vary widely in the states, may be one reason for low turnout. Efforts to make registration easier, such as the 1993 "Motor Voter" act that enables citizens to register to vote at state motor vehicle offices have not significantly boosted turnout. Other Western industrialized nations have adopted compulsory voting requirements, and they often make election day a paid holiday—factors that increase turnout significantly. U.S. elections are held on weekdays, which may complicate some voters' abilities to get to the polls.

Sociological models of voting emphasize various interrelated factors that affect turnout in U.S. presidential elections. Such factors are borne out in statistics compiled by the U.S. Census Bureau for the 2000 presidential election. One of the most important factors is *age*. In presidential elections, older Americans go to the polls in far greater numbers than younger Americans. The Census Bureau reports that in 2000 only 32 percent of eligible voters eighteen to twenty-four years of age cast votes, whereas 74 percent of Americans aged sixty-five to seventy-four turned out. Younger voters increased their turnout figures to just under 47 percent in 2004, but they were outpaced by seniors aged sixty-five to seventy-four, 73 percent of whom went to the polls.[5] This turnout rate marks a significant increase over the rate for 2000, but the *proportion* of younger Americans in the electorate remained flat because voter turnout increased across all age groups—and seniors are a much

more significant voting bloc.[6] "Demobilization" among younger voters may stem from a variety of sources, such as alienation from political parties or dissatisfaction with candidate choices. Older Americans, particularly retirees, may have more free time to go to the polls. But they also may feel a greater stake in the outcomes of presidential elections because of the programs that directly affect them such as Social Security and Medicare. Because older Americans represent a highly mobilized voting group, it is little wonder that presidential candidates pay close attention to the issues affecting this age group in their campaigns.

The combined impact of *education and income* on voter turnout accentuates the importance of social class in voting participation. Well-educated, upper-income voters are typically the targets of campaign appeals dealing with tax, health, and social policy. Social groups with the lowest voter turnout include the unemployed, less educated Americans, and minorities. By contrast, the most mobilized voters are employed, college-educated, white Americans. In 2000 only 27 percent of eligible voters with less than a ninth-grade education went to the polls, while just less than half of high school graduates cast ballots. By contrast, 70 to 75 percent of voters with a bachelor's or advanced degree turned out for the 2000 presidential election. Similarly, less than a third of eligible voters whose income fell below the poverty line (approximately $8,900, depending on family size) voted in the 2000 presidential election. Nearly two-thirds to three-quarters of voters with incomes above $50,000 took part. The dynamic was repeated in 2004. About 39 percent of eligible voters with less than a ninth grade education took part in the election, while 78 to 84 percent of eligible voters with an undergraduate or advanced degree cast votes.

Race and ethnicity also substantively affect voter turnout. Nationally, Hispanics have the lowest voter turnout among ethnic groups.[7] In the 2000 election, just a little more than a quarter of eligible Hispanics went to the polls. By contrast, 60 percent of eligible white voters cast ballots. In 2004, 47 percent of eligible Hispanics voted, the lowest rate of any ethnic group. Turnout among whites increased to just over 65 percent. Participation among African Americans remains lower overall compared with that of whites. However, the long-term impact of passage of the Voting Rights Act of 1965 for African American turnout cannot be underestimated. Some 25 million new African American voters were registered by 1968, enabling that community to surmount barriers to voting that many states had implemented dating to Reconstruction. Today, there is some evidence that mobilization among blacks is approaching parity for whites. In the 2000 presidential election, overall turnout among African Americans stood at 54 percent, just six points lower than that of whites. The gap narrowed to 5 points in 2004, when 60 percent of African Americans went to the polls.

Voter Choices

Party registration and loyalty are the most telling indicators of how individuals are likely to vote in presidential elections. Typically, 70 to 90 percent of registered Democrats vote for the Democratic standard-bearer, and the same dynamic holds for Republicans. Presidential candidates on both sides of the political spectrum attempt to curry favor with the shrinking number of swing voters, who frequently alter their support between candidates of the two parties, and with voters who consider themselves independents.

Still, many of the factors that affect turnout in presidential elections also condition voter choice. *Race, religion, and economic status* are particularly noteworthy factors. African Americans are the most loyal supporters of Democratic candidates. In the 2000 election, 90 percent of blacks voted for Al Gore, whereas 83 percent voted for Bill Clinton in 1992 and 84 percent in 1996. Exit polls suggest that blacks remained the most loyal Democratic group in 2004, because 88 percent of African Americans voted for John Kerry.[8] The conservative views of many Republicans on affirmative action and economic policies have alienated all but a tiny minority of African American voters. Hispanics also form a core Democratic group, though not as uniformly as blacks. Republican candidates culled about a quarter of the Hispanic vote between 1992 and 2000, and George W. Bush, as governor of Texas, sought to attract significant support from Hispanic voters in his home state and elsewhere in the nation. Bush improved his margin by 9 percent among Hispanics between 2000 and 2004, earning 44 percent of the group's vote nationally in 2004.

A person's *religious affiliation* also conditions party identification and voting. White Protestants, particularly southern evangelicals, tend to be the bedrock of Republican support. Over 60 percent of white Protestants backed George W. Bush in 2000. By contrast, Jews, who tend to be more liberal on social issues, overwhelmingly support Democratic candidates. In 2000 Al Gore marshaled the support of nearly 80 percent of Jewish voters. Finally, Catholics are somewhat more supportive of Democratic candidates overall, but show evidence of more significant cleavages in recent elections. Forty-nine percent of Catholics supported Gore in 2000, and 47 percent supported Bush. Social policy issues and abortion, in particular, tend to split Catholics.

Not surprisingly, income has a strong impact on presidential voting. Republican candidates' calls for tax cuts, smaller government, and regulatory reform tend to resonate most with upper-income voters. From 1992 to 2000, voters with annual incomes exceeding $50,000 consistently backed Republican candidates more than their Democratic rivals. By contrast, Democratic candidates' greater emphasis on government services and social programs more consistently resound with voters under the $30,000 threshold.[9]

The impact of a voter's gender on presidential voting has recently piqued the interest of scholars and elections observers. Many analysts speak of a contemporary gender gap in presidential contests in which, increasingly, men are tending to support Republican candidates more than Democratic candidates, while the inverse is true for women. The elections in 1996 and 2000 evidenced the largest gender gaps in recent times—11 and 10 percent, respectively. In 1996 Bill Clinton won the support of 54 percent of women voters compared with only 43 percent of men. According to some analysts, women's stronger support of Clinton facilitated his victory over Robert Dole.[10] Similarly, in 2000 George W. Bush garnered the support of 53 percent of men and only 43 percent of women. In 2004 the gender gap weakened somewhat. Bush marshaled 55 percent of the male vote and 48 percent of the female vote.

The issues highlighted by presidential candidates may explain, in part, the existence of the gender gap. Gore's emphasis on health care and education may have appealed more to women, who tend to be the primary caregivers of children. By contrast, men, as the primary income earners in family settings, may have preferred Bush's accent on taxes and the economy.[11] Yet the 2004 election provided insight into the gender gap that is at odds with the media focus on Democratic-leaning "soccer moms" and Republican-leaning "NASCAR dads." Critics of the existence of a gender gap contend that the phenomenon disappears if the women's vote is disaggregated by race.[12] Indeed, exit polls show that 55 percent of white women voted for George Bush in 2004, whereas 75 percent of nonwhite women voted for John Kerry.

The Mandate Controversy

Do presidential campaigns bestow "mandates" on elected presidents to carry out policy reforms and their preferred agendas? Presidents routinely claim to have mandates regardless of whether they won by large or narrow margins or whether voter turnout was comparatively high or low. Some scholars question the very concept of mandates from the perspective of the constitutional coequality of the presidency and Congress. Among the others, there is little consensus on the empirical conditions that might confer a mandate on an elected president.

Robert A. Dahl, one of the foremost theorists of American politics, opposes the concept of mandates. His central objection is that mandates presuppose a type of *institutional partisanship* that "when conflicts over policy arise between the president and Congress, the president's policies ought to prevail."[13] Such a notion assumes that Congress and its 535 elected members should subordinate themselves to the executive and disregard the legislature's constitutional status as a coequal branch of govern-

Table 20-4 First-Term Presidents and the Question of Mandates

President	Year	Turnout (%)	Popular vote (%)	Electoral college (%)	Coattails (House)	First pres. approval poll (%)	Unified/divided government	Midterm election (House)
Eisenhower	1952	58	55.1	63.2	+22	68	Unified	−18
Kennedy	1960	61	49.7	56.4	−20	76	Unified	−4
Johnson	1964	61	61.1	90.3	+37	75	Unified	−47
Nixon	1968	60	43.4	55.9	+5	59	Divided	−12
Carter	1976	55	50.1	55.2	+1	71	Unified	−15
Reagan	1980	53	50.7	90.9	+34	51	Divided	−26
G. Bush	1988	53	53.4	79.2	−3	57	Divided	−8
Clinton	1992	56	43.0	68.8	+10	58	Unified	−52
G. W. Bush	2000	51	49.9	54.0	−2	53	Unified[a]	+6

Sources: Data gathered by author. "First pres. approval poll" for the period 1953–1993: Lyn Ragsdale, *Vital Statistics on the Presidency* (Washington, D.C.: CQ Press, 1998); turnout and popular vote: Federal Election Commission.

[a] Republicans controlled both the House and Senate after the 2000 elections. However, within a few months Vermont senator James Jeffords left the Republican Party and became an independent who caucused with the Democrats, thereby giving Senate Democrats the de facto majority.

ment. Dahl disputes claims that presidential elections convey information about voter preferences for the president's program worthy of elevating the presidency over Congress. Citing interview data from two landslide election victories in the last half-century—that of Democrat Lyndon Johnson in 1964 and Republican Richard Nixon in 1972—Dahl provides evidence that no more than a fifth of all voters actually cited Johnson's or Nixon's policy program in their vote choices. Dahl concludes that presidents refer to mandates for politically self-serving ends. "No elected leader," he admonishes, "including the president, is uniquely privileged to say what an election means nor to claim that the election has conferred on the president a mandate to enact the particular policies the president supports."[14]

Yet pundits, political scientists, and, most particularly, presidents themselves do attempt to surmise the significance of presidential elections and the national electoral trends connected to them. In 1960 John F. Kennedy prevailed over rival Richard Nixon by one of the narrowest margins in modern electoral history—just 119,000 votes. But Kennedy implicitly rejected the idea that the election failed to produce a mandate. "There may be difficulties with Congress," Kennedy reputedly said, "but a margin of only one vote would still be a mandate."[15] Kennedy molded much of his real or perceived mandate in his inspiring, inaugural speech with the refrain "ask not what your country can do for you, ask what you can do for your country." Similarly, George W. Bush, who lost the popular vote to Al Gore in 2000 by over 500,000 votes but prevailed in the electoral college after the recount controversy in Florida, dismissed the notion that he had no mandate. Although some observers contended Bush's

only mandate could be to govern from the center, the president set his administration's policies on a decidedly conservative path in domestic and foreign affairs. After he won 51 percent of the popular vote in his 2004 reelection campaign, Bush evoked the mandate concept when he said, "I earned capital in the campaign—political capital. And now I intend to spend it." He proceeded to make far-reaching Social Security and tax reform agenda priorities in his second term.[16]

The evidence on mandates and the conditions that might allow presidents to claim a mandate are open to interpretation. Table 20-4 assesses various indicators for first-term presidents. Higher voter turnout should indicate greater voter interest in the presidential campaign and bolster the victor's claims to a mandate. Although the winner-take-all nature of the electoral college inflates the victor's margin in that body, the president's popular vote is pivotal in such claims. Furthermore, the length of the presidential "coattails"—the number of seats the president's party gains in the House of Representatives—can buttress assertions of a mandate and reflect the president's popularity in members' districts, which can translate into bargaining leverage for the president. Elections to the House are used as a bellwether because all 435 seats are up for election every two years. Presidents can more credibly claim a mandate when their party controls both chambers of Congress (unified government) rather than when control of the presidency and Congress is split (divided government). The president's first postelection approval rating can also reinforce claims to a mandate if the president is riding high in the court of public opinion. Finally, although most presidents suffer the phenomenon of "midterm loss"—that is, the president's party loses seats in the House of Representatives in the midterm elections—the magnitude of the seat loss, or a surprise gain, can signal the degree of unhappiness with, or continued voter support of, the president's agenda.

The overall evidence for presidential mandates presented in Table 20-4 is decidedly mixed. On the basis of the data, two elections represent particularly strong cases. The first, Lyndon Johnson's 1964 victory over Republican standard-bearer Barry Goldwater, stands out. With strong voter turnout, Johnson gained over 61 percent of the popular vote—a figure higher than those of all other postwar presidents. Johnson brought thirty-seven Democrats into Congress on his coattails, most of whom shared enthusiasm for his Great Society agenda. With his initial public approval rating at 75 percent, Johnson had a surfeit of public good will, though that reservoir would dry up by the midterm elections of 1966, reflecting the backlash against the Vietnam War. The second election was Dwight Eisenhower's landslide victory in 1952 with 55 percent of the popular vote, and he swept enough Republicans onto Capitol Hill that the GOP captured majorities in the House and Senate. Eisenhower also enjoyed strong public support after the election; 68 percent of the citizenry approved of his job as chief executive. However, Eisenhower may not have used perceptions of a mandate to his benefit. He did not have much of a legislative agenda. In fact, he did not even present one to Congress until his second year in office when urged to do so by his staff.

The case of Ronald Reagan is complex. Reagan's landslide victory in the electoral college in 1980 was tempered by a popular majority that was barely over 50 percent. Moreover, although Reagan's victory helped to give Republicans a majority in the Senate, his coattails of thirty-four seats in the House were not long enough to prevent Democrats from retaining control of that chamber as they would for both of his terms in office. Yet Reagan was highly popular in some Democratic districts, particularly in the South, and his electoral popularity gave him strong leverage during his first two years to accomplish much of his agenda. Still, the gains the GOP made in the House in 1980 were erased two years later as voters registered their dissatisfaction with a recessionary economy.

Other cases for a mandate are less compelling. Presidents Kennedy, Nixon, Clinton, and George W. Bush (2000) marshaled only a plurality, not a majority, of the popular vote behind their campaigns, and Carter won a very close race against Republican incumbent Gerald Ford. With the exception of 1960, voter turnout was well below 60 percent. Except for Carter, none of these presidents' first approval ratings was above 58 percent. Moreover, the coattails of these presidents were minimal or "negative." John Kennedy (1960), George Bush (1988), Bill Clinton, and George W. Bush (2000) saw their party's number of seats in the House fall with their election victory, complicating efforts to posit a mandate. For all first-term presidents but George W. Bush, the erosion of party strength in Congress was compounded in the midterm elections.

Beyond these objective data, a persuasive case for a mandate may depend significantly on the nature of the issues that infuse the presidential campaign. There are actually several different categories of mandates.[17] Non–policy-focused campaigns that center more on candidate qualities and personalities, particularly with narrow electoral margins, may produce a victory without a mandate. The Kennedy–Nixon (1960), Carter–Ford (1976), and Bush–Dukakis (1988) contests seem to conform to this scenario quite well. *Popular mandates* are most likely to follow issue-based campaigns, a large victory margin or at least a majority of the popular vote, and long coattails in Congress. Eisenhower's promise in 1952 to "go to Korea," Lyndon Johnson's tireless campaign for the "Great Society," and Ronald Reagan's sharp critiques of Jimmy Carter on taxes and foreign policy, followed by their electoral victories, are the best examples of presidents who were credibly able to argue that the outcomes had conferred more than a modicum of popular support for their agendas. Finally, falling into the intermediate category of *bargained mandates* are perhaps those presidents who win by narrow margins, have variable coattails, but run an issue-oriented campaign. Along with his plurality popular vote victories, President Clinton's focus in 1992 on the economy and health care, and later in 1996 on moderating the Republican congressional majority's domestic policies, gave him some if not always a lot of leverage over defining the national agenda.

Mandates are clearly in the eye of the beholder. Andrew Jackson was the first president to claim a popular mandate a century and a half ago. Modern presidents have carried on the tradition, in large measure because persuasively laying claim to a mandate may be a vital mechanism for gaining influence in Congress and surmounting the obstacles of the constitutional separation of powers.

Reforming Presidential Campaigns and Elections

Presidential campaigns have been an integral part of the evolution of the American democracy and are fundamental to shaping national governance. As this chapter has emphasized, the history of presidential campaigns and elections has been one of increasing pressures for mass participation in the choice of chief executives. What is perhaps most striking is that this challenge has been met thus far in the Republic's history without altering the basic form of the Constitution.

Still, critics suggest the nation may be at a crossroads and that more drastic reforms may now be required to redress the inherent dysfunctions of the presidential selection process. For example, the United States has one of the poorest voter turnout rates of the Western industrialized countries—it is some 10–30 percent lower than that for comparable elections in Canada, France, or the United Kingdom. And other important calls are being made to reform primary elections and the electoral college. The potential advantages and shortcomings of such reforms must be weighed carefully and objectively.

Dysfunctions of the Nominating Process and Possible Remedies

There is no shortage of critiques of the presidential primary process. Detractors contend that divisive primaries can breed in-fighting and place a party's eventual nominee in a particularly difficult situation in the general election. Many scholars lament that the growth of primaries has precipitated the weakening of state party organizations and party leaders' influence, enabling outsider and comparatively unknown candidates to win nominations, often with disastrous results (for example, McGovern in 1972 and Dukakis in 1988). And the net impact of the front-loading of primaries, combined with fund-raising prerequisites and media coverage dynamics, has reinforced candidate-centered, not party-centered, campaigns from the early primaries through the general election.

The proliferation of primaries since the reforms of the 1970s has spawned an important debate about whether divisive intraparty primaries wind up damaging a party's eventual nominee in the general election. The hypothesis is that candidates' personal attacks on one another and the exposure of internal strife over policy questions can spur "fratricide." Factionalism, while a part of the winnowing process, may give rise to negative media coverage on candidate controversies, provide fodder for the other party's campaign, and permanently damage candidates' chances by driving disgusted voters away from the polls. Recently, colorful and memorable disputes between primary contenders have included Republican George Bush's charge in 1980 that Ronald Reagan's agenda amounted to "voodoo economics," the protracted dispute between Democratic incumbent Jimmy Carter and Sen. Edward Kennedy in 1980, and Republican Robert Dole's warning to rival George Bush in 1988 to "stop lying about my record." Moreover, contenders may have to spend large sums of money to ward off challengers before the general election campaign, depriving the eventual nominee of vital resources. The example of Dole's primary contests against Pat Buchanan and Steve Forbes in 1996, mentioned earlier, is a case in point. Finally, in-fighting may irreparably harm the parties' abilities to arrive at a consensus when the convention meets, because some groups who supported losing contestants may feel slighted and be unwilling to support the eventual nominee.

It seems unlikely that the parties will do away with primaries and restore party leaders to an exalted position

in nominee selection. Such a move could remedy the problem of divisive primaries, but it would be contrary to the general thrust toward greater inclusion and popular participation in the presidential selection process. Also, scholars may have overestimated the relative effects of divisive primary campaigns. Recent evidence suggests that "out groups"—that is, those whose candidate lost in a divisive primary campaign—do return to the party fold by the general election. Their concern shifts from their preferred candidate's agenda in the nominating process to which party will ultimately control the White House.[18] Moreover, by another line of reasoning the competitive nomination process is a healthy one, because it encourages candidates to reach out to and mobilize new constituencies during the primary process.[19] Another positive effect of a tough primary campaign is to adequately prepare the eventual nominee to do battle with his or her opponent in the general campaign.

Several proposed reforms aimed at improving the quality of the early presidential campaign process have targeted the recent phenomenon of states front-loading the electoral calendar. The objective is to shorten the campaign season in order to garner voters' sustained interest and nullify states' timing advantage through early primaries. One idea is to institute regional or "time zone" primaries that group primaries and caucuses by one of these factors and schedule them one month apart. The proposal would displace the allegedly disproportionate importance of Iowa and New Hampshire in the primary process, encourage candidates to launch broader appeals, and equalize the weight of the more and less populous states in nominee selection. Other proposals suggest a set of staggered regional primaries, or a blanket national primary held on the same day, to accomplish the same goal.

The institution of such reforms would depend on states' willingness to agree on a date for a set of regional primaries or a national primary. Otherwise, codifying such reforms would require a constitutional amendment. As noted earlier, southern, New England, and midwestern state legislatures have agreed at various times to hold regional primaries, so such an "informal" reform is not without precedent. Yet states are scarcely homogeneous. Population centers and ethnic, social, and occupational diversity vary greatly, complicating efforts to classify states neatly into specific regions. In addition, it is doubtful that Iowa and New Hampshire would willingly forgo the media attention and tourist dollars spent by candidates and reporters that accompany their first-in-the-nation tradition. Currently, no constitutional proposals mandating regional or national primaries are pending in Congress.

The Electoral College: An Antiquated Institution?

The issue of reforming the electoral college was thrown into the spotlight once again after the contentious presidential balloting in Florida in 2000. Perhaps what was most surprising in 2000 was not the closeness of the popular vote between George W. Bush and Al Gore, or even Bush's loss of the popular vote to Gore, but the extremely narrow margin for the victor in the electoral college. There, the outcome hinged on a single state, and Bush ultimately prevailed by only two votes.

Critics contend that the 2000 outcome is evidence that the electoral college is anachronistic. The central concern is that the system undermines popular sovereignty in presidential selection. Apart from the possibility that a candidate who loses the popular vote can win the electoral college, detractors point to the nefarious prospects of the "faithless elector" problem. Hypothetically, an elector, although pledged to a particular candidate, could decide to throw his or her support to another candidate. What if such support were enough to alter the outcome in a close electoral college race? Although such a scenario has not occurred, some electors have made the theoretical point by purposefully reneging on their vow to a particular candidate. In 2000 Barbara Simmons, a Democratic elector from the District of Columbia who was pledged for Al Gore, left her ballot blank to protest the District's lack of voting representation in Congress. And in 1988 Margaret Leach, a Democratic elector from West Virginia, switched her vote to support vice-presidential candidate Lloyd Bentsen for president instead of Michael Dukakis in order to draw attention to the faithless elector question. In other cases, electors may have simply confused the ballot. In 2004 an unknown Democratic elector from Minnesota may have unintentionally cast one of the state's ten ballots for John Edwards, the vice-presidential candidate, instead of John Kerry by confusing the first and last names.

Other critics are uncomfortable with the possibility that a presidential election could be thrown to the House of Representatives if no candidate receives a majority in the electoral college. This scenario has occurred twice in the nation's history—once in 1800 and again in 1824. The wheeling and dealing in Congress that awarded the White House to John Quincy Adams in 1824 was broadly viewed as illegitimate and cast a pall over his troubled presidency. In more recent times, the concern is that because of the "unit rule" in forty-eight states (winner-take-all systems), a regional or third party candidate could draw enough electoral college support to rob one of the two major-party candidates of a majority and leave the House to decide the victor.

By contrast, some critics of the electoral college support its demise precisely *because* the institution discriminates against third party presidential candidacies. George Wallace, who ran a spirited independent campaign in 1968 on segregation and law and order, won 13.6 percent of the popular vote. Because his support was regionally concentrated in the Deep South, he won forty-six electoral college votes. He was the last third party candidate to earn any electoral college votes. In 1992 and 1996, Ross Perot garnered 18.9 percent and 8.4 percent

of the popular vote, respectively, but he won no electoral college votes because his support was geographically diffuse. Such electoral college dynamics may lead some supporters to believe that supporting even a serious third party challenger results in a "wasted vote."

The most radical proposal to reform the electoral college calls for its abolishment through a constitutional amendment that would institute direct election of the president. The simplest plan would hand the presidency to the candidate who wins the most votes. Other plans call for direct election of the president under a system that resembles the French two-ballot system. A minimum threshold for victory (either a plurality or a majority) must be met by the winning candidate. If no contestant attains the minimum, a runoff would be held between the top two candidates.

Other proposals seek to make the electoral college outcome roughly proportionate with the popular vote and target the faithless elector problem. These "mend it, don't end it" proposals suggest variants of the systems in place in Maine and Nebraska in which electoral votes are apportioned according to which candidate prevails in each congressional district, with the two "at large" electoral votes determined by the candidate who receives a plurality in the statewide vote. Other plans would simply apportion electoral college votes according to the popular vote in each state. In either type of plan, removing the faithless elector problem could be achieved by automatically awarding electoral votes to the candidates.

Scholars and the general public are divided on electoral college reform, and the 2000 election controversy did not produce a real or perceived constitutional crisis leading to serious calls for the institution's abolition. After the 2000 election fracas in Florida, polls suggested that Americans favored eliminating the electoral college by a 60–40 margin. Yet that figure was actually less than the figures produced by surveys conducted since the 1960s. And post–2000 election polls showed that, by broad margins, Americans believed Bush's accession to the presidency and the Supreme Court's intervention in the Florida recounts were legitimate.[20]

Still, proponents of electoral college reform or abolition point to the advantages of such steps. First, direct election, proportional schemes, or district plans would ensure that presidents would carry the popular vote. Second, such reforms also might increase voter turnout by encouraging third party candidates. Third, larger metropolitan areas would have greater political clout than they do under the current system. Finally, such reforms are in keeping with the historical drive toward democratization of presidential selection.

The concerns about direct election are, however, numerous. Some people worry that direct election would destabilize the federal system by encouraging the proliferation of minor parties. Candidates might choose to launch regional, rather than national, appeals and move the nation toward unnecessary sectional conflicts. Candidates also might have incentives to campaign primarily in the most populous states at the expense of small states and ignore issues of importance to minority voters. Finally, the financial and human costs of imposing a uniform, national voting system could be quite significant.

Whatever the merits of the arguments for and against electoral college reform, constitutional amendments have repeatedly failed to find support in Congress. Americans have amended the Constitution only twenty-seven times in over two centuries. Given this reticence to alter the basic structure of the Constitution, substantive changes to the apportioning of electoral votes may be most likely to emanate from the states and come in piecemeal fashion. The Maine and Nebraska district plans are among the most feasible options for reform, major constitutional change notwithstanding.

Conclusion

"Every vital question of state," Alexander Hamilton forecast in the debates over the adoption of the Constitution, "will be merged in the question, 'Who will be the next president?'" Hamilton's wisdom still echoes today. Though not without controversy, complexity, and some level of dysfunction, presidential campaigns are dynamic and central to the American democracy. Their evolution at the dawn of the nation's third century will depend on the character, determination, and democratic spirit of the candidates who run for the nation's highest office and the expectations and evaluations of voters who engage and select them.

Notes

1. Theodore H. White, quoted in *Simpson's Contemporary Quotations,* com James B. Simpson (New York: Harper, 1997).

2. Figures were calculated by author from data reported by Robert E. DiClerico, "In Defense of the Presidential Nominating Process," in *Choosing Our Choices: Debating the Presidential Nominating Process,* ed. Robert E. DiClerico and James W. Davis (Lanham, Md.: Rowman and Littlefield, 2000), 069; data were updated by author for the 2000 election, and the averages included "accrued" years of experience by incumbent presidents seeking reelection.

3. Associated Press Wire, "McCain Revels in Decisive Win, Bush Looks Down the Road," February 1, 2000, www.primarymonitor.com/news/stories/aej_2100mccainreax .shtml (accessed September 14, 2003).

4. Martha T. Moore, "Networks Return to Convention Coverage," *USA Today,* July 27, 2000, www.usatoday.com/news/opinion/e2429.htm (accessed May 15, 2005).

5. See Current Population Survey, 2004, at www.census .gov/population/www/socdemo/voting.html (accessed June 23, 2005).

6. The *Washington Post* reported that the overall estimated voter turnout increased from 54.3 percent in 2000 to 60.7 percent in 2004; see Brian Faler, "Election Turnout in 2004 Was Highest Since 1968," *Washington Post,* January 15, 2005, A5. Also see Tucker Sutherland, "Seniors Are Consistent Voters and Increasingly Large Share of Vote," *Senior Journal,* October 28, 2004, www.seniorjournal.com/NEWS/Politics/4-10-28SeniorVote.htm (accessed May 15, 2005); and Nicole Yinger, "Are Young Voters Has-Beens?" November 20, 2004, www.cbsnews.com/stories/2004/11/20/politics/main656805 .shtml (accessed May 15, 2005).

7. The exception is Cuban Americans in South Florida. In addition, unlike Hispanics in other parts of the country, Cuban Americans tend to vote Republican, especially older voters. See Richard S. Conley, *Florida 2002 Elections Update* (Boston: Pearson, 2002), chap. 1.

8. In this section, exit poll and other results of the 2004 election, unless otherwise indicated, are taken from www

.cnn.com/ELECTION/2004/pages/results/states/US/P/00/epolls .0.html (accessed May 15, 2005).

9. Statistics for the 2000 election in this section are drawn from Gerald M. Pomper, "The Presidential Election," in *The Election of 2000,* ed. Gerald M. Pomper (Chatham, N.J.: Chatham House, 2001).

10. For an in-depth analysis, see Susan J. Carroll, "The Disempowerment of the Gender Gap: Soccer Moms and the 1996 Elections," *PS: Political Science and Politics* (March 1996).

11. Pomper, "Presidential Election," 139–140.

12. "Gender Gap Myths and Legends" (editorial), *Washington Post,* December 19, 2004, p. B2.

13. Robert A. Dahl, "The Myth of Presidential Mandate," in *Understanding the Presidency,* ed. James Pfiffner and Roger H. Davidson (New York: Longman, 1997), 65.

14. Ibid., 69.

15. Theodore Sorenson, quoted in R. W. Apple Jr., "News Analysis: Recipe for a Stalemate," *New York Times,* November 9, 2000.

16. Bill Sammon, "Bush Pushes New Agenda," *Washington Times,* November 5, 2004.

17. Patricia Heidotting Conley, *Presidential Mandates: How Elections Shape the National Agenda* (Chicago: University of Chicago Press, 2001).

18. Lonna Rae Atkeson, "From the Primaries to the General Election: Does a Divisive Nomination Race Affect a Candidate's Fortunes in the Fall?" In *In Pursuit of the White House 2000: How We Choose Our Presidential Nominees,* ed. William G. Mayer (New York: Chatham House, 2000).

19. See Walter J. Stone, Lonna Rae Atkeson, and Ronald B. Rapoport, "Turning On or Turning Off? Mobilization and Demobilization Effects of Presidential Nomination Campaigns," *American Journal of Political Science* 36 (1992): 665–691.

20. Frank Newport, "Americans Support Proposal to Eliminate Electoral College System," Gallup Poll Release, January 5, 2001. For an overview, see Karlyn Bowman, "Vote of Confidence," *Public Perspective,* March/April 2002, www.aeipoliticalcorner.org/KB%20Articles/kb02marchapril .pdf (accessed May 17, 2005).

Suggested Readings

Campbell, James E. *The American Political Campaign: U.S. Presidential Campaigns and the National Vote.* College Station: Texas A&M University Press, 2000.

DiClerico, Robert E., and James W. Davis, eds., *Choosing Our Choices: Debating the Presidential Nominating Process.* Lanham, Md.: Rowman and Littlefield, 2000.

Jackson, John S., and William Crotty. *The Politics of Presidential Selection,* 2d ed. New York: Longman, 2001.

Nelson, Michael, ed. *The Elections of 2004.* Washington, D.C.: CQ Press, 2005.

Shumaker, Paul D., and Burdett A. Loomis, eds. *Choosing a President: The Electoral College and Beyond.* New York: Chatham House, 2002.

Wayne, Stephen J. *The Road to the White House 2004.* New York: Wadsworth, 2003.

CHAPTER 21

U.S. House Campaigns

Paul S. Herrnson and Peter L. Francia

Candidates running for a seat in the U.S. House of Representatives must compete in two campaigns: one for resources and one for votes. The campaign for votes is the campaign that generally comes to mind when people think about congressional elections. For this campaign, a candidate must assemble an organization and use that organization to target key groups of voters, select a message they will find compelling, communicate that message, and get supporters to the polls on election day.

For the other campaign, which is based largely in Washington, D.C., candidates must convince the party operatives, interest group officials, political consultants, and journalists who play leading roles in the nation's political community that their races will be competitive and worthy of support. Gaining the backing of these various groups is a critical step toward attracting the money and campaign services available in the nation's capital and in other wealthy urban centers. These resources enable the candidate to run a credible campaign back home. Without them, most congressional candidates would lose their bids for election.

This chapter describes House campaigns, and especially the campaigns for resources and for votes. It begins with an overview of the legal and political context that surrounds House campaigns. This overview is followed by a description of the major players in those campaigns, which include the candidates, political parties, and interest groups. Finally, it reviews the critical features of the campaign for resources and the campaign for votes.[1]

The Legal and Political Context

Congressional elections in the United States, more than elections in other modern industrialized democracies, center on the candidates. Federal and state laws contribute to the candidate-centered nature of congressional elections. Originally, federal law regulated few aspects of congressional elections; it specified only the number of representatives a state was entitled to elect. States held congressional elections at different times, used different methods of election, and set different qualifications for voters. Some states used multimember at-large districts, a practice that awarded each party a share of congressional seats proportional to its share of the statewide popular vote. Others elected their House members in odd years, which minimized the ability of presidential candidates to pull House candidates of their own party into office on their coattails. The financing of congressional campaigns was virtually unregulated for most of the nation's history.

Over the years, Congress and the states passed legislation governing the election of House members that further reinforced the candidate-centered nature of congressional elections at the expense of parties. The creation of geographically defined, single-member, winner-take-all congressional districts was particularly important in this emphasis on the candidate. In response to the shift to these districts, which were mandated by the Apportionment Act of 1842, individual candidates began to build locally based coalitions. Such districts gave no rewards to candidates who came in second, even if their party performed well throughout the state or in neighboring districts. Thus candidates of the same party had little incentive to work together or to run a party-focused campaign. Under the multimember district or general ticket systems that existed in some states prior to the act (and that continue to be used in most European nations), members of parties that finished lower than first place received seats in the legislature. Candidates had strong incentives to run cooperative, party-focused campaigns under these systems, because their electoral fortunes were bound together.

The timing of congressional elections also helps to produce a candidate-centered system. Because the dates are fixed, with House elections scheduled every two years and roughly one-third of the Senate up for election every two years, many elections are held when there is no burning issue on the national agenda. Without a salient national issue to capture the voters' attention, House and Senate candidates base their campaigns on local issues or on their personal qualifications for holding office. Incumbents stress their experience, the services they provide to constituents, or their seniority. Challengers, by contrast, attack their opponents for casting congressional roll call votes that are out of sync with the views of local voters, for pandering to special interests, or for "being part of the problem in Washington." Open-seat races—that is, those in which the incumbent declines to run for reelection—focus mainly on local issues, the candidates' political experience, or character issues. Systems that do not have fixed election dates, including most of those in Western Europe, tend to hold elections that are more national in nature and centered on political parties.

Because the boundaries of congressional districts rarely match those for statewide or local offices and because the terms for the House, the Senate, and many state and local offices differ from one another, a party's candidates often lack incentives to work together. House candidates consider the performances of their party's candidates statewide or in neighboring districts to be a secondary concern, just as the election of House candidates is usually not of primary importance to candidates for state or local offices. Differences in election boundaries and timing also encourage a sense of parochialism in party officials similar to that of their candidates. Cooperation among party organizations can be achieved only by persuading local, state, and national party leaders that working together is in their mutual best interest. Cooperation is often heightened during elections that precede or follow the decennial U.S. Census, when politicians at all levels of government focus on the imminent redrawing of election districts or on preserving or wresting control of new districts or those that have been significantly altered.

The Federal Election Campaign Act (FECA), its amendments, regulatory rulings, and court decisions also contributed to candidate-centered congressional elections. The original law, passed in 1971 and amended significantly in 1974, placed strict limits on the amount of money parties could contribute to or spend in coordination with their congressional candidates' campaigns. Many of these limits remained in place in 2004. The FECA further limited the parties' involvement in congressional elections by placing ceilings on individual contributions and an outright ban on corporate, union, and trade association contributions to the accounts the parties used to contribute to or expressly advocate the election or defeat of federal candidates. Moreover, with the exception of subsidies for the parties' presidential nominating conventions, the FECA provided no special support for generic, party-focused campaign activity.

The law's provisions for political parties stand in marked contrast to the treatment given to parties in other democracies. Most of these countries give the parties subsidies for campaign activities and for activities undertaken between elections. The United States is the only democracy in which parties do not receive free television and radio time. The support that other democracies give to parties is consistent with the central role parties play in those democracies' elections, government, and society, just as the lack of assistance afforded to American political parties is consistent with the candidate-centered system that has developed in the United States.

Lacking independent sources of revenue, local party organizations are unable to play a dominant role in the modern cash-based system of congressional campaign politics. The national and state party committees that survived the reform movements and changes in federal election laws simply do not have sufficient funds or staff to dominate campaign politics. Perhaps even more important, party leaders have little desire to do so in most cases. Most believe a party should bolster its candidates' campaigns, not replace them with a campaign of its own.

American political culture also reinforces the candidate-centered system. Historically, U.S. political culture has supported a system of candidate-centered congressional elections in many ways, but its major influence stems from its lack of foundation for a party-focused alternative. Americans have traditionally held a jaundiced view of political parties. *Federalist* No. 10 and President George Washington's Farewell Address are evidence that the framers and the country's first president thought a multitude of overlapping, wide-ranging interests were preferable to class-based divisions represented by ideological parties. The framers designed the political system to encourage pragmatism and compromise in politics and thus to mitigate the harmful effects of factions. Although neither the pluralist system championed by the framers of the Constitution nor the nonpartisan system advocated by Washington has been fully realized, both visions of democracy have found expression in candidate-centered campaigns.

The Players

During the golden age of political parties, from the post–Civil War era through the 1940s, party bosses were able to steer their preferred candidates into the races for Congress. In many places, the bosses' control over the party apparatus was so complete that, when in agreement, they could guarantee the nomination to the person they wanted to run. Moreover, receiving the nomination was usually tantamount to winning the election, because strong political machines typically were located in one-party areas.

After the golden age, party leaders had less control over the nominating process and less ability to ensure that the individuals they recruited would in fact win the nomination. Today, the parties are no longer the primary recruiters of congressional candidates. They continue to play a role in encouraging some individuals to run for office and in discouraging others, but they, along with interest groups, serve more as vehicles that self-recruited candidates use to advance their careers than as organizations that can make or break those careers.

Republican candidate Katherine Harris waves to potential Florida voters at an intersection in Sarasota during her successful 2002 campaign for an open House seat. Harris, who as Florida's secretary of state played a major role in the Bush-Gore recount controversy in 2000, was also a state senator before being elected to the U.S. House. Source: Charles Luzier/Reuters/Landov

The Candidates

The Constitution, state laws, and the political parties pose few formal barriers to running for Congress, enabling virtually anyone to become a candidate. Members of the House are required to be at least twenty-five years of age, to be a U.S. citizen for at least seven years, and to reside in the state they represent. Some states bar prison inmates or persons who have been declared insane from running for office, and most states require candidates to pay a small filing fee or to collect anywhere from a few hundred to several thousand signatures in order to have their names placed on the ballot.

Although the formal requirements are minimal, other factors related to the candidate-centered nature of the electoral system favor individuals with certain personal characteristics. Strategic ambition—which is a combina-

tion of a desire to get elected, a realistic understanding of what it takes to win, and an ability to assess the opportunities presented by a given political context—is one such characteristic that distinguishes most successful candidates for Congress from the general public. Most successful candidates are also self-starters, because the electoral system lacks a tightly controlled party recruitment process or a well-defined career path to the national legislature. And, most important, because the electoral system is candidate-centered, the desire, skills, and resources that candidates bring to the electoral arena are the most important criteria separating serious candidates from those who have little chance of getting elected.

Ambitious candidates, sometimes called strategic, rational, or quality candidates, are political entrepreneurs who make rational calculations about when to run. Rather than plunge right in, they assess the political waters in which they would have to wage their campaigns, consider the effects that a bid for office could have on their professional careers and families, and carefully weigh their prospects for success.[2]

Strategic politicians examine many institutional, structural, and subjective factors when considering a bid for Congress. The institutional factors include filing deadlines, campaign finance laws, nominating processes that allow or prohibit preprimary endorsements, and other election statutes and party rules. The structural factors include the social, economic, and partisan composition of the district; its geographic compactness; the media markets that serve it; the degree of overlap between the district and lower-level electoral constituencies; and the possibilities for election to some alternative office. One structural factor that greatly affects the strategic calculations of nonincumbents is whether an incumbent plans to run for reelection. Potential candidates also assess the political climate in deciding whether to run. Strategic politicians focus mainly on local circumstances, particularly whether a seat will be vacant or whether the results of the previous election suggest that an incumbent is vulnerable.[3]

National forces, such as a public mood that favors Democrats or Republicans, challengers or incumbents, are usually of secondary importance. The convergence of local and national forces can have a strong impact on the decisions of potential candidates. For example, the widespread hostility the public directed at Congress and its members played a major role in influencing who ran in the 1994 and 1996 primaries and general elections.

These forces motivated many House incumbents to retire and encouraged many would-be House members to believe that a seat in Congress was within their reach. Favorable circumstances and these candidates' positive self-assessments encouraged them to think they could win the support of local, state, and national political elites; raise the money; build the name recognition; and generate the momentum needed to propel them into office. In 1998 and 2000, the nation's overall prosperity and the public's positive feelings toward incumbents had the opposite effect—it discouraged would-be office seekers. The same is true of pro-incumbent redistricting and other national and local factors in 2002. The effects of redistricting also reverberated in 2004. The ongoing wars in Iraq and on terror may have discouraged some potential candidates from running, perhaps because they believed that voters may have been reticent to change leaders in times of war.

A final set of subjective assessments involve a potential candidate's professional and personal circumstances. Before politicians decide to contest a House seat they usually weigh the costs and benefits. Among the factors they consider are the impact that losing would have on their political careers, the effect that mounting a congressional campaign would have on their employment situations or businesses, and whether they are ready to subject themselves and their families to the rigors of a campaign and the intense scrutiny that accompanies it. Of course, many also usually ponder the impact that winning could have on their families, because being a member of Congress requires all but a small number of legislators to reside in both their home in the district and a residence in Washington, D.C.

Political Parties

Political parties in the United States have one overriding goal: to elect their candidates to public office. Policy goals are secondary to winning control of the government. Nevertheless, the parties' electoral influence has waxed and waned as a result of the legal, demographic, and technological changes in U.S. society and the reforms instituted by the parties themselves. During the golden age of political parties, local party organizations dominated elections in many parts of the country. They picked the candidates, gauged public opinion, raised money, disseminated campaign communications, and mobilized voters, most of whom had strong partisan allegiances.

By the 1950s, most state and local party organizations had been ushered to the periphery of the candidate-centered system. Party organizations at the national level had not yet developed into repositories of money and campaign services for congressional candidates. Most contenders for the House and Senate were largely self-recruited and relied on campaign organizations that they themselves had assembled to wage their bids for office. Professional consultants helped to fill the void left by deteriorating party organizations by providing advice about fund-raising, media, polling, and campaign management to clients willing to pay for it.

During the late 1970s and early 1980s, first Republican and then Democratic national party organizations in Washington, D.C., began to adapt to the contemporary candidate-centered system by emphasizing campaign activities requiring technical expertise and in-depth research. Many candidates, especially nonincumbents running for the House, lacked the money or professional know-how needed to run modern congressional campaigns. Candidates' needs created the opportunity for party organizations to assume a more important role in congressional elections. The national parties responded to these needs by assuming a more important role in the candidate-centered election system, not by doing away with it.[4]

The national parties also adapted to changing circumstances during the late 1990s, particularly the rise of "soft" (unregulated) money and the issue advocacy advertisements that emerged after the weakening of federal campaign finance laws (see Chapter 6). Both of the major parties and many interest groups began to conduct so-called independent, parallel, or coordinated campaigns that consumed millions of dollars in spending on television, radio, direct mail, mass telephone calls, and other communications and voter mobilization efforts. By carefully tailoring these activities to meet the needs of a small number of competitive congressional elections, parties have greatly increased their influence in those contests, thereby assuming an even greater role in the candidate-centered system.

Interest Groups and Political Action Committees

During the earliest days of the Republic, the leaders of agricultural and commercial groups influenced who was on the ballot, the coverage they received in the press, and the voting patterns that determined election outcomes. As the electorate grew and parties and candidates began to spend more money to reach voters, steel magnates, railroad barons, and other captains of industry expanded their roles in political campaigns. Labor unions counterorganized with manpower and dollars. Religious and ethnic groups also influenced elections, but their financial and organizational efforts paled next to those of business and labor.

Interest groups continued to flourish at the close of the twentieth century, but several developments significantly affected their roles in congressional elections. The growth in the number of organizations that located or hired representatives in Washington led to the formation of a community of lobbyists that was, and continues to be, attuned to the rhythms of legislative and election politics. The enactment of the FECA and the creation of the Federal Election Commission (FEC), the agency charged with enforcing federal campaign finance laws, led to the development of the modern political action committee (PAC)—the organizational entity that most interest groups use to carry out the majority of their federal campaign activities. Court decisions and FEC rulings handed down in recent years have allowed interest groups to use new approaches, including issue advocacy advertising, to spending money in congressional elections.

The Campaign for Resources

The legal and political context of House campaigns places candidates in a central position of influence, and parties and interest groups each play a supporting role in congressional elections. However, to win office candidates must clear several hurdles. The first major test for a candidate is to demonstrate an ability to raise money.

Indeed, raising the funds needed to run for Congress has evolved into a campaign in and of itself. Part of this campaign takes place in the candidate's state or district, but many candidates are dependent on resources from party committees and PACs located in and around Washington, D.C., and from wealthy individuals who typically reside in major metropolitan areas. The campaign for resources begins earlier than the campaign for votes. The candidate must attract the support of sophisticated, goal-oriented groups and individuals who have strong preconceptions about what it takes to win a congressional election. Theoretically, all congressional candidates can turn to the same sources and use the same techniques to gather campaign funds and services. In fact, however, candidates begin and end on uneven playing fields. The level of success that candidates achieve with different kinds of contributors or fund-raising techniques depends largely on whether they are incumbents, challengers, or contenders for open seats. It also depends on the candidates' party affiliation and on whether they are running for the House or the Senate, among other factors.

Overall, the rise of national party organizations, PACs, and other Washington-based cue givers, as well as the Federal Election Campaign Act's ceilings on campaign contributions, have led to the replacement of one type of fat cat with another. Individuals and groups that gave candidates tens or hundreds of thousands of dollars directly have

Figure 21-1 Sources of House Incumbents' Campaign Receipts, 2002 Elections

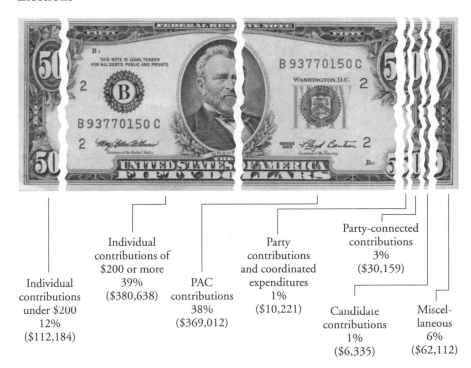

Individual contributions under $200 12% ($112,184)

Individual contributions of $200 or more 39% ($380,638)

PAC contributions 38% ($369,012)

Party contributions and coordinated expenditures 1% ($10,221)

Party-connected contributions 3% ($30,159)

Candidate contributions 1% ($6,335)

Miscellaneous 6% ($62,112)

Source: Compiled from Federal Election Commission data.

Note: The dollar values in parentheses are averages. PAC contributions exclude contributions by leadership PACs. Candidate contributions include loans candidates made to their own campaigns. Party-connected contributions are made up of contributions from leadership PACs, candidates, retired members, and members of Congress not up for reelection in 2002. Miscellaneous sources include interest from savings accounts and revenues from investments. Figures are for general election candidates in major-party contested races, excluding those in incumbent-versus-incumbent races (those in which redistricting places two members of Congress in the same district and forces them to run against each other). Percentages do not add to 100 percent because of rounding. $N = 300$.

been replaced by new sets of elites who help candidates raise these sums rather than contribute them directly.

House Incumbents' Fund-Raising Activities

Incumbents routinely complain about the time, effort, and indignities associated with raising funds. Their lack of enthusiasm for asking people for money figures prominently in how they raise campaign contributions (see Figure 21-1). A fear of defeat and a disdain for fundraising have two principal effects: they encourage incumbents to place the bulk of their fund-raising in the hands of others, mainly professional consultants, and to raise large amounts of money. Forty-six percent of all major-party House incumbents devote at least a quarter of their personal campaign schedule to raising funds. Seventeen percent devote more than half of their schedule to asking others for money.[5]

Most incumbents develop permanent fund-raising operations. They hire direct-mail specialists and PAC finance directors to write direct-mail appeals, update contributor lists, identify and solicit potentially supportive PACs, script telephone solicitations, and organize fund-raising events. These operations enable incumbents to limit their involvement to showing up at events and telephoning potential contributors who insist on having a direct conversation with them before making a large contribution.

Incumbents raise small contributions by making appeals through the mail, over the telephone, at fund-raising events, and via the Internet. Direct mail can be a relatively reliable method of fund-raising for an incumbent, because solicitations are usually made from lists of previous donors that indicate which appeals garnered earlier contributions. Most direct-mail and telephone solicitations generate contributions of less than $100 and are targeted at the candidate's constituents. However, many prominent House members, including Speaker J. Dennis Hastert, Republican from Illinois, and former Democratic Congressional Campaign Committee chair Patrick Kennedy of Massachusetts, have huge direct-mail lists that include hundreds of thousands of people from across the United States and even a few from abroad. A significant portion of these individuals contribute large sums. In 2004 Hastert raised almost $865,000 and Kennedy raised more than $1,173,000 in individual contributions of $200 or more from outside their respective states (representing roughly 33 percent and 81 percent, respectively, of these candidates' individual large contributions).[6] Had either of these members faced serious competition, they would have undoubtedly raised even more money from out-of-state (and other) donors.

The Internet emerged as an important fund-raising tool during the 1998 congressional elections. By 2002, 57 percent of all House candidates in major-party contested races and virtually every Senate candidate were using Web sites or e-mail to solicit funds. Some sites directed supporters to where they might send their checks, and others instructed donors how to make contributions online using a credit card.

Candidates who used e-mail to solicit contributions relied on e-mail addresses purchased from Internet providers and other companies as well as addresses collected from people who logged on to their Web sites. E-mail lists of individuals who share a candidate's issue concerns are a potential source of monetary and volunteer support, especially among computer-literate youth. The greatest advantage of e-mail and Internet fund-raising is that the solicitation is delivered for free, compared with the $3 to $4 per piece cost of sending out one first-class direct-mail solicitation. The trade-off for e-mails is that they are not always appreciated. Mass-distributed e-mails, often referred to as "spam," are frequently deleted without being read, the electronic equivalent of tossing an unopened piece of direct mail into the trash or hanging up on a telemarketer.

Traditional fund-raising events are another popular means of raising small contributions. Local cocktail parties, barbecues, and picnics with admission costs from $10 to $50 are useful ways to raise money. They are also helpful in generating favorable press coverage, energizing political activists, and building goodwill among voters.

Incumbents can ensure the success of local fund-raising events by establishing finance committees made up of business executives, labor officials, civic leaders, or political activists who live in their districts. These committees often begin with a dozen or so supporters who host "low-dollar" receptions (where individuals usually contribute from $20 to $100) in their homes and make telephone solicitations on the candidate's behalf. Guests at one event are encouraged to sponsor others. In time, small finance committees can grow into large, pyramid-like fund-raising networks, consisting of dozens of finance committees, each of which makes a substantial contribution to the candidate's reelection efforts. Most House and Senate incumbents have fund-raising networks that extend from their district or state to the nation's capital.

Individual large contributions and PAC money are also raised by finance committees, at fund-raising events, and through networks of supporters. Events that feature the president, congressional leaders, sports heroes, or other celebrities help to attract individuals and groups willing to contribute anywhere from a few hundred dollars to the legal maximum of $1,000 (in 2002) for each stage of the race. Some of these events are held in the candidate's state, but most are held in political, financial, and entertainment centers such as Washington, D.C., New York City, and Hollywood. In 2002 those few Republican incumbents who were the beneficiaries of a visit by President George W. Bush raised 144 percent more than did other GOP incumbents.

Traditional fund-raising events can satisfy the goals of a variety of contributors. They give donors who enjoy the social side of giving, including the proximity to power, a chance to speak with members of Congress and other celebrity politicians. Persons and groups that contribute for ideological reasons are able to voice their specific issue concerns. Individuals and organizations motivated by material gain, such as a tax break or federal funding for a project, often perceive these events as opportunities to build relationships with members of Congress.[7]

In raising individual large contributions, House members have advantages over challengers that extend beyond the prestige and political clout that come with incumbency and an ability to rely on an existing group of supporters. Incumbents also benefit from the fact that many wealthy individuals have motives that favor incumbents over challengers. About 25 percent of all individuals who contribute $200 or more to a congressional candidate do so mainly because they wish to gain access to the people who will be in a position to influence legislation once the election is over—mainly incumbents. Roughly 36 percent of donors give contributions mainly for broad ideological reasons or because of their positions on specific, highly charged issues. These donors tend to rally around incumbents who champion their causes. Another 24 percent are motivated to contribute primarily because they enjoy attending fund-raising events and mixing with incumbents and other elites who attend these functions. The final 15 percent are not strongly motivated by access, ideology, or the social side of contributing. Although they contribute for idiosyncratic reasons, they, like other donors, primarily support incumbents. Another advantage enjoyed by incumbents is that the information mailed by the parties and PACs to their big donors often focuses on the campaigns of endangered incumbents, further leading some wealthy individuals to contribute to those campaigns instead of to hopeful challengers and open-seat candidates.

Incumbents consciously use the influence that comes with holding office to raise money from PACs and wealthy individuals who seek political access. Legislators' campaigns first identify potential donors who are most likely to respond favorably to their solicitations. These include PACs that supported the incumbent in a previous race, lobbyists who agree with an incumbent's positions on specific issues, and others who are affected by legislation that the incumbent is in a position to influence. Members of Congress who hold party leadership positions, serve on powerful committees, or are recognized entrepreneurs in certain policy areas can easily raise large amounts of money from wealthy, interest group–based financial constituencies. It is no coincidence that the eight House incumbents who raised more than $1 million in interest group PAC contributions in 2002 each enjoyed at least one of these assets.[8]

Once an incumbent has identified his or her financial constituency, the next step is to ask for a contribution. The most effective solicitations describe the member's background, legislative goals, accomplishments, sources of influence (including committee assignments, chairmanships, or party leadership positions), the nature of the competition faced, and the amount of money needed. Incumbents frequently assemble this information in the kits they mail to PACs. Solicitations also take into account the potential donors' motives for contributing.

Some of the PACs that agree to contribute will require a candidate to meet with one of their representatives, who personally will deliver a check. A few will require incumbents to complete questionnaires on specific issues, but most PACs will rely on members' prior roll call votes or interest group ratings as measures of their policy proclivities. Some PACs, particularly ideological committees, will want evidence that a representative is facing serious opposition before giving a contribution. Party leaders and the party's congressional campaign committee staff are sometimes called to bear witness to the competitiveness of an incumbent's race.

Parties are another source of money and campaign services, especially for vulnerable incumbents. The parties' congressional campaign committees have most of the information they need to make a determination about vulnerability, but incumbents can give details on the nature of the threat they face that might not be apparent to a party operative who is unfamiliar with the nuances of a member's seat. The National Republican Congressional Campaign Committee gives incumbents who request extra party support the opportunity to make their case before a special Incumbent Review Board composed of GOP members. Once a party's congressional campaign committee has made an incumbent a priority, it will go to great lengths to supply the candidate with money, campaign services, and assistance in collecting resources from others.

Subject to only two-year terms, House incumbents usually begin raising money almost immediately after they are sworn into office. Sometimes, they have debts to retire, but often they use money left over from previous campaigns as seed money for the next election. More than 23 percent of all House incumbents began the 2002 election cycle with more than $400,000 left over from their previous campaigns. In turn, over 28 percent of all successful 2002 House candidates completed their campaigns with more than $400,000 in the bank, including thirty-two incumbents who had amassed more than $1 million.[9] These funds undoubtedly provided useful seed money for their reelection campaigns in 2004 or bids for some other office.

Early fund-raising is carried out for strategic reasons. Incumbents build substantial war chests early in the election cycle to try to deter potential challengers. An incumbent who had to spend several hundred thousand or even millions of dollars to win by a narrow margin in the last election will have a greater compulsion to raise money earlier than someone whose previous election was a landslide victory. Once they have raised enough money to reach an initial comfort level, however, incumbents appear to be driven largely by the threat posed by an actual challenger.[10] Incumbents under duress seek to amass huge sums of money regardless of the source, whereas those who face weak opponents can afford to pick and choose whom they solicit. A typical incumbent's campaign—one waged by a candidate who does not face stiff competition in either the primary or the general election—will generally engage in heavy fund-raising early and then allow this activity to taper off as it becomes clear that the candidate is not in jeopardy. Incumbent campaigns typically begin the election season with more money in the bank than do challengers, who usually start fund-raising much later. Thus the campaign for resources is usually a campaign among unequals.

House Challengers' Fund-Raising Activities

Challengers have the greatest need for money, but they encounter the most difficulties raising it. The same factors that make it difficult for challengers to win votes also impede their ability to collect campaign contributions. A lack of name recognition, limited campaign experience, a relatively untested organization, and a high probability of

Figure 21-2 Sources of House Challengers' Campaign Receipts, 2002 Elections

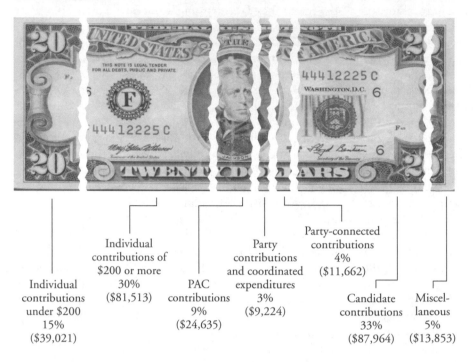

Individual
contributions
under $200
15%
($39,021)

Individual
contributions of
$200 or more
30%
($81,513)

PAC
contributions
9%
($24,635)

Party
contributions
and coordinated
expenditures
3%
($9,224)

Party-connected
contributions
4%
($11,662)

Candidate
contributions
33%
($87,964)

Miscel-
laneous
5%
($13,853)

Source: Compiled from Federal Election Commission data.

Note: See note, Figure 21-1. N = 300.

defeat discourage most contributors, especially those who give large amounts in pursuit of access, from supporting challengers. The fact that their opponents are established Washington operators who possess political clout does not make challengers' quests for support any easier.

Incumbents may find fund-raising a disagreeable chore, but at least their efforts are usually met with success (see Figure 21-2 for a breakdown of House challengers' campaign receipts). Challengers put in just as many long, hard hours on the money chase as incumbents, but they clearly have less to show for their efforts. Most challengers start raising early money at home. They begin by donating to or loaning their campaigns the initial funds needed to solicit contributions from others. They then turn to relatives, friends, professional colleagues, local political activists, and virtually every person whose name is in their personal organizer or, better yet, on their holiday card list. Some of these people are asked to chair fund-raising committees and host fund-raising events. Candidates who have previously run for office are able to turn to past contributors for support. Competitive challengers frequently obtain lists of contributors from members of their party who have previously run for office or from private vendors. Some of these challengers will receive lists from party committees or PACs. However, most of these organizations mail fund-raising letters on behalf of selected candidates rather than physically turn over their contributor lists.

Only after enjoying some local fund-raising success do most nonincumbents set their sights on Washington. Seed money raised from individuals is especially helpful in attracting funds from PACs, particularly for candidates who have not held elective office. The endorsements of local business, labor, party, or civic leaders have a similar effect, especially if they can be persuaded to serve on a fund-raising committee. If it can be obtained, the assistance of congressional leaders or members of a candidate's state delegation can be helpful to challengers who hope to raise money from their party's congressional campaign committee, PACs, or individual large contributors. When powerful incumbents organize luncheons, attend "meet-and-greets," and appear at fund-raising events for nonincumbents, contributors usually respond favorably. Contributors also look favorably on events attended by high-ranking executive branch officials, particularly the president.

Unfortunately for most challengers, their long odds of success make it difficult for them to enlist the help of incumbents. House members prefer to focus their efforts on candidates who have strong electoral prospects and may someday be in a position to return the favor by supporting the member's leadership aspirations or legislative goals in Congress.

Challengers' fund-raising prospects are enhanced when they understand how party leaders and PAC managers make contribution decisions. Political experience and a professional campaign staff are often helpful in gaining this understanding. Candidates who put together feasible campaign plans, hire reputable consultants, and are able to present polling figures indicating that they enjoy a reasonable level of name recognition usually attract the attention of party officials, PAC managers, generous contributors, and the inside-the-Beltway journalists who handicap elections. By contrast, political amateurs who wage largely volunteer efforts usually cannot.

One way in which challengers can increase their chances of success in raising money from PACs is to identify the few committees likely to give them support. For Democrats, these committees include labor groups. Democratic challengers can improve their prospects of attracting labor PAC money by showing they have strong ties to the labor community, have previously supported labor issues in the state legislature, or support labor's current goals.

Challengers from both parties may be able to attract support from PACs, particularly ideological committees, by convincing PAC managers that they are committed to the group's cause. A history of personal support for that cause is useful. Challengers, and in fact most nonincumbents, typically demonstrate this support by pointing to roll call votes they cast in the state legislature, or to the backing of PAC donors or affiliated PACs located in their state or district, or to the support of Washington-based organizations that share some of the PAC's views.

Nonincumbents who make a PAC's issues among the central elements of their campaign message and communicate this information in their PAC kits enhance their odds of winning a committee's backing. Properly completing a PAC's questionnaire or having a successful interview with a PAC manager also is extremely important. Taking these steps can help a challenger to obtain a contribution and endorsement from a PAC and to gain assistance in raising money from individuals and other PACs with shared policy concerns.

Political experience and professional expertise also can help a nonincumbent raise PAC money. In 2002 challengers who had previously held office raised an average of $46,800 from PACs, roughly $13,700 more than the typical unelected politician (who may not have held elected office but has had an opportunity to develop political skills and contacts while working as a political aide, political appointee, political consultant, or party official) and $34,900 more than the typical rank amateur. Challengers who hired a professional fundraiser raised, on average, about $53,500 more than those who relied on volunteers.

Ideological causes have been at the forefront of many candidates' PAC fund-raising strategies during the past few decades. Women challengers have been able to attract large amounts of money and campaign assistance from EMILY's List (which supports pro-choice Democratic women), the WISH List (the Republican counterpart of EMILY's List), and other pro-women's groups. Challengers who take a stand on either side of the abortion issue are frequently able to raise money from PACs and individual donors who share their positions. By taking a side on emotionally laden issues, such as handgun control or support for Israel, some challengers are able to attract the contributions of ideological PACs and individuals who identify with those causes. However, the most important factors that challengers bring to bear on the fund-raising process are their prospects for success and their political clout.

Open-Seat Candidates' Fund-Raising Activities

Candidates for open seats put the longest hours of all House contestants into fund-raising and, as noted earlier,

Figure 21-3 Sources of House Open-Seat Candidates' Campaign Receipts, 2002 Elections

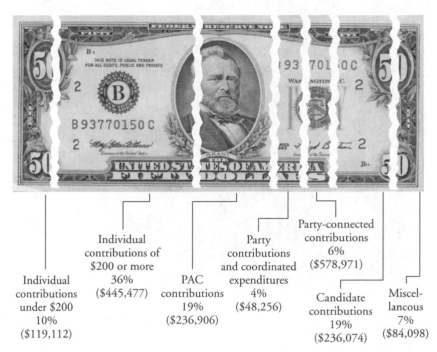

Individual contributions under $200 10% ($119,112)

Individual contributions of $200 or more 36% ($445,477)

PAC contributions 19% ($236,906)

Party contributions and coordinated expenditures 4% ($48,256)

Party-connected contributions 6% ($578,971)

Candidate contributions 19% ($236,074)

Miscellaneous 7% ($84,098)

Source: Compiled from Federal Election Commission data.

Note: See note, Figure 21-1. N = 94.

with considerable success (see Figure 21-3 for a breakdown on their campaign receipts). Just over 60 percent devote more than a quarter of their personal campaign schedule to attending fund-raising events, meeting in person with potential donors, and dialing for dollars. These candidates help their cause by telling potential contributors about the experience and organizational assets they bring to the race, but these factors have less effect than others, such as the partisan makeup of the district, on the fund-raising abilities of open-seat candidates.

Elected politicians raised the most party money in 2002, averaging about $53,900, or about $5,000 more than that collected by the typical unelected official and about $31,500 more than that raised by the typical amateur. Elected politicians also raised the most party-connected contributions, averaging $90,000, or roughly $16,900 more than that raised by the typical unelected official and $52,500 more than that garnered by the typical amateur. Mounting a professional campaign also helps open-seat candidates attract more party support. In 2002 open-seat candidates who hired professional fund raisers collected an average of $44,300 in party money and $78,200 in party-connected contributions, in contrast with the $32,880 and $47,800, respectively, raised by candidates who relied mainly on campaign volunteers.

Open-seat contestants who have political experience and have assembled professional campaign organizations are better able to meet the campaign objectives set by the

Democrat Doris Matsui raised almost $700,000 in the six-week special election campaign in California's Fifth Congressional District to succeed her late husband, Rep. Robert Matsui. She won the election with more than 70 percent of the vote and joined Republican Mary Bono of Palm Springs and Democrat Lois Capps of Santa Barbara as the third member of California's U.S. House delegation to take office after a husband's death. Source: Courtesy Office of Rep. Doris O. Matsui

parties' congressional campaign committee staffers. As a result, they are among the top recipients of party money, campaign services, and fund-raising assistance. Receiving the endorsements of their state's congressional delegations and other incumbents can also help open-seat contestants to attract party funds.

Winning support from PACs can be a little more challenging. Although open-seat candidates use the same techniques as challengers to identify interest group constituencies and to campaign for PAC support, they usually have greater success than challengers. Because their odds of victory are better, open-seat candidates have an easier time than challengers gaining an audience with PAC managers and are able to raise more PAC money. Open-seat candidates also are able to point to the same kinds of information used by challengers to make the case that their campaigns will be competitive. Experienced open-seat contestants and those who wage professional campaigns collect more PAC money than do amateurs. In 2002 open-seat candidates who had previously held elec-

tive office raised, on average, almost $273,300, about $27,100 more than the typical unelected politician and almost $179,600 more than the typical amateur. Open-seat candidates who hired professional fund-raisers collected $79,400 more in PAC money than those candidates who relied largely on volunteers.

Thus candidates for open seats typically raise about the same amount as incumbents. But open-seat candidates, compared with challengers, are more likely to wage campaigns that are financially competitive with those of their opponents. Nonincumbents who have significant political experience or who have assembled professional campaign organizations typically raise more money—especially from parties, members of Congress, other party leaders, and PACs—than amateur candidates who assemble unprofessional campaign organizations.

The Campaign for Votes

Although raising money is important, House candidates must ultimately win votes for election to office. But first they must survive the nomination battle within their own party, so they can compete in the general election against a candidate of the opposing political party.

The Nomination Campaign

There are two ways to win a major-party nomination for Congress: in an uncontested nominating race or by defeating an opponent. It is not unusual for incumbents to receive their party's nomination without a challenge. Even in the 1992 elections, which were marked by a record number of nonincumbent candidacies, 52 percent of all representatives and 42 percent of all senators who sought reelection were awarded their party's nomination without having to defeat an opponent. In 2002 the numbers were even greater: 71 percent of all representatives and 69 percent of all senators seeking reelection faced no primary opponent.

Incumbent Victories in Uncontested Primaries

Victories by default occur mainly when an incumbent is perceived to be invulnerable. The same advantages of incumbency (including the outreach activities members of Congress routinely conduct as part of their jobs) that make some incumbents confident of reelection make them seem invincible to those contemplating a primary challenge. Good constituent relations, policy representation, and other job-related activities are sources of incumbent strength. A hefty campaign account is another.

The loyalties of political activists and organized groups also discourage party members from challenging their representatives for the nomination. While in office, members of Congress work to advance the interests of those who supported their previous election, and in return they

Table 21-1 Number of Unchallenged and Defeated House Incumbents, 1982–2002

	1982	1984	1986	1988	1990	1992	1994	1996	1998	2000	2002
Incumbents unchallenged by major-party opposition in general election	49	63	71	81	76	25	54	20	94	63	78
Incumbents defeated											
In primary	10	3	3	1	1	19	4	2	1	3	8
In general election	29	16	6	6	15	24	34	20	6	6	8

Sources: Compiled from various editions of *CQ Weekly* and *Congressional Roll Call* (Washington, D.C.: CQ Press). The primary and general election results are from Norman J. Ornstein, Thomas E. Mann, and Michael J. Malbin, *Vital Statistics on Congress, 2001–2002* (Washington, D.C.: AEI Press, 2002), 69.

Note: The 1982, 1992, and 2002 figures include incumbent-versus-incumbent races (those in which redistricting places two members of Congress in the same district and forces them to run against each other).

routinely receive the support of these individuals and groups. With this support comes the promise of endorsements, campaign contributions, volunteer campaign workers, and votes. Would-be primary challengers often recognize that the groups whose support they would need to win the nomination are usually among the incumbent's staunchest supporters.

Senior incumbents benefit from the clout—real and perceived—that comes with climbing the ranks of congressional leadership. Junior incumbents rarely have the same kind of clout in Washington or as broad a base of support as senior legislators, but because they tend to devote a great deal of time to expanding their bases of support, they, too, typically discourage inside challenges. Junior members also may receive special attention from national, state, and local party organizations. Both the Democratic Congressional Campaign Committee (DCCC) and the National Republican Congressional Committee (NRCC) hold seminars immediately after the election to instruct junior members on how to use franked mail (free postage given to members of Congress for communicating with their constituents and for other official business), town meetings, and the local press to build voter support. Prior to the start of the campaign season, these party committees advise junior members on how to defend their congressional roll call votes, raise money, and discourage opposition. State party leaders also give junior members of Congress advice and assistance. Yet such considerations of teamwork rarely protect House members who are vulnerable because of scandal. These incumbents face stronger challenges from within their own party than do others. Experienced politicians often are willing to take on an incumbent who is toiling under the cloud of scandal.

Contested Primaries with an Incumbent

When incumbents do face challenges for their party's nomination, they almost always win (see Table 21-1). Of the 115 House members who were challenged for their party's nomination in 2002, only eight lost: five lost to other incumbents who shared their districts as a result of redistricting, and three—Gary Condit, D-Calif.; Earl Hilliard, D-Ala.; and Cynthia McKinney, D-Ga.—were defeated because of their implication in political scandals. With the exception of House members who are forced to run against each other, typically only those members of Congress who have allegedly committed an ethical transgression, lost touch with their district, or suffer from failing health run a significant risk of falling to a primary challenger.

What kinds of challengers succeed in knocking off an incumbent for the nomination? The answer is those who have had significant political experience. Only 22 percent of the 2002 challengers who sought to defeat an incumbent in a primary had been elected to a lower-level office and 25 percent had other significant forms of political experience. Yet these elected officials and unelected politicians accounted for all of the primary challengers who wrested a party nomination away from an incumbent that year. Experienced candidates typically succeed where others fail because they are able to take advantage of previous contacts to gain the support of the political and financial elites who contribute to or volunteer in political campaigns. Elected officials can make the case that they have represented some of the voters in the district and know what it takes to get elected. Some of these candidates consciously use a lower-level office as a stepping-stone to Congress.

Types of Primaries

An *opposing-incumbent primary* is one in which contestants seek the nomination of their party in order to run against the incumbent of the opposing party who decided to seek reelection (also see Chapter 5 for a description of the nominating process). An *open-seat primary* is held in districts in which no incumbent is seeking reelection.

Both types of primaries attract more candidates than do contests in which a nonincumbent must defeat an incumbent to win the nomination, but opposing-incumbent primaries are usually the less hotly contested of the two.

In opposing-incumbent primaries, political experience is frequently a determining factor. Elected officials do well in such primaries; in 2002 they made up about one-fifth of all of the candidates and one-fifth of the winners in these races. Democratic elected officials enjoyed a nomination rate of 80 percent, and their Republican counterparts had a success rate of 85 percent. Because more unelected politicians of both parties ran in opposing-incumbent primaries in 2002, it is not surprising that they won more nominations than did primary candidates with officeholding experience. Political amateurs typically outnumber politically experienced candidates, and, as a consequence, they win more primaries. The 2002 contests were no exception, but the success rates of the amateurs were substantially lower than those of more experienced primary contestants.

Open-seat primaries are the most competitive of all nominating contests. They typically attract many highly qualified candidates, often pitting one elected official against another. A relatively large number of candidates with officeholding experience ran for open seats in 2002. Elected officials of both parties made up most of the primary winners and had the highest primary success rates. Unelected politicians also did well, achieving higher success rates than did political amateurs.

The General Election

Once candidates have earned their party's nomination, they must begin to mount a general election campaign. This involves developing an overall strategy, gauging public opinion, deciding which voters to target, and crafting a message and selecting issues that will appeal to them.

Crafting a Campaign Strategy

Candidates who have emerged from their primaries victorious must craft a strategy to win the general election against a candidate from the opposing party. Most candidates rely heavily on political consultants in crafting their strategy in the campaign for votes (see Chapters 10 and 14).

Candidates and political consultants generally do not plan election campaigns on the basis of abstract political theories. Rather, they draw on a body of knowledge about how people make their voting decisions (see Chapter 8). Politicians' notions about voting behavior agree to some extent with the findings of scholarly research—for example, (1) most voters have only limited information about the candidates, their ideologies, and the issues; (2) voters are generally more familiar with and favorably predisposed toward incumbents than toward challengers;

and (3) voters tend to cast their ballots in ways that reflect their party identification or previous voting behavior. Candidates and consultants also believe that a campaign sharply focused on issues can be used both to motivate supporters to show up at the polls and to win the support of undecided voters. They try to set the campaign agenda so that the issues that politically informed voters use as a basis for casting their ballots are the most attractive issues for their candidate.

Politicians' beliefs account for some of the differences that exist among the campaigns waged by incumbents, challengers, and open-seat candidates as well as many of the differences that exist between House and Senate campaigns. Generally, members of Congress use strategies that capitalize on the advantages of incumbency. They discuss the services and the federal projects they have delivered to their constituencies. They focus on elements of their public personas that have helped to make them popular with constituents and draw on strategies they have used successfully in previous campaigns.[11]

Some incumbents capitalize on their advantages in name recognition and voter approval by virtually ignoring their opponents. They deluge the district with direct mail, radio advertisements, television commercials, yard signs, or other communications that make no mention of their opponents in order to minimize the attention the challengers receive from the local media and voters. An alternative strategy is to take advantage of the challengers' relative invisibility by attacking their inexperience, qualifications, or positions on the issues early in the campaign. Incumbents who succeed in defining their opponents leave them in the unenviable position of being invisible to most voters and negatively perceived by others.

House challengers are in the least enviable position of any candidates. Not only are they less well known and less experienced, but they are also without the campaign resources of their opponents. To win, challengers have to force their way into the voters' consciousness and project a message that will give voters a reason to cast a ballot for a little-known candidate.

Many challengers make the election a referendum on some negative aspect of the incumbent's performance. They may portray the incumbent as incompetent, corrupt, an extreme ideologue, or out of touch with the district, and they may magnify the impact of any unpopular policy or scandal with which the incumbent is associated. Challengers often try to link the current officeholder to unpopular policies or trends and to tout themselves as agents of change, using negative or comparative ads to do so.

Lacking the advantages of an incumbent or the disadvantages of a challenger, both candidates in an open-seat race face the challenge of making themselves familiar to voters and becoming associated with the themes and issues that will attract electoral support. They also have an opportunity to define their opponents. Some open-seat candidates seek to define themselves and their opponents on the basis of issues. Others, particularly those running in districts that favor their party, emphasize partisan or ideological cues.

Gauging Public Opinion

Campaigns use many different tools to take the public's pulse. Election returns from previous contests are analyzed to locate pockets of potential strength or weakness. Geodemographic analysis (that is, analysis of demographic and social characteristics organized by geographical location) enables campaigns to identify individuals who voted in previous elections and to classify them by gender, age, ethnicity, race, religion, occupation, and economic background. By combining geodemographic information with polling data and election returns, candidates are able to identify potential supporters and to formulate messages that will appeal to them (also see Chapter 19).

Polls are among the tools most commonly used to gauge public opinion (see Chapter 16). Roughly three-quarters of all House campaigns take at least one poll to learn about voters. *Benchmark polls,* which are taken early in the election season, inform candidates about the issue positions, partisanship, and initial voting preferences of people living in their state or district. House campaigns commonly commission benchmarks a year before the election, and Senate candidates have been known to commission them as early as three years before election day. Benchmark polls also measure the levels of name recognition and support that the candidates and their opponents or prospective opponents enjoy. They help campaign staff to learn about the kinds of candidates voters prefer, the types of messages that are likely to attract support, and to whom specific campaign advertisements should be directed.

Campaigns also use benchmark polls to generate support. Challenger and open-seat candidates disseminate favorable benchmarks to attract press coverage and the support of campaign volunteers and contributors. Incumbents typically publicize benchmarks to discourage potential challengers. When poll results show a member of Congress to be in trouble, however, the incumbent quietly uses them to convince parties, PACs, and other potential contributors that he or she needs extra help to win.

Trend polls are taken intermittently throughout the campaign season to gauge changes in voters' attitudes (some senators use them to chart their public approval throughout their six-year terms). These polls are more narrowly focused than benchmarks. They feature detailed questions designed to reveal whether a campaign has been successful in getting voters to associate its candidate with a specific issue or theme. Trend polls help a campaign to determine whether its candidate has been gaining or losing ground with different segments of the electorate. They can reassure a campaign that its strategy is working or indicate that a change in message is needed.

Just as trend and benchmark polls present "snapshots" of public opinion, *tracking polls* provide campaigns with a "motion picture" overview. These polls typically assess the reactions of samples of 150–200 voters to a few key advertisements, issue statements, or campaign events. Each night, a different group of voters is interviewed. The interviews are then pooled and used to calculate "rolling averages" based on the responses from the three most recent nights. Changes in rolling averages can be used to reformulate a campaign's final appeals. Because tracking polls are expensive, most House campaigns wait until the last three weeks of the campaign to use them.

Candidates may supplement their polling with *focus groups.* These groups usually consist of one to two dozen participants and a professional facilitator, who meet for a two- to three-hour session. The participants are selected not to be a scientifically representative sample but to represent segments of the population whose support the campaign needs to reinforce or attract. Campaigns use focus groups to learn how voters can be expected to respond to different messages or to pretest actual campaign advertisements. Some high-priced consultants employ computerized audience response techniques to obtain a precise record of how focus group participants react to specific portions of campaign advertisements. These techniques enable an analyst to plot a line that represents the participants' reactions onto the ad itself, pinpointing exactly which portions participants liked or disliked. Focus group research is useful in fine-tuning the visuals and narratives in television communications.

Finally, candidates learn about public opinion through a variety of approaches that do not require the services of public opinion experts. Newspaper, magazine, radio, and television news stories provide information about voters' positions on major issues. Exchanges with local party leaders, journalists, political activists, and voters can also help candidates to get a sense of the public mood.

Targeting Voters

Campaigns are not designed to reach everyone. Targeting involves categorizing different groups of voters, identifying their political preferences, and designing appeals to which they are likely to respond. It is the foundation of virtually every aspect of campaign strategy. Candidates and campaign managers consider many factors when devising targeting strategies, including the underlying partisan and candidate loyalties of the groups that reside in the district, the size and turnout levels of those groups, and the kinds of issues and appeals that will attract their support.[12] Using this information, they formulate a strategy designed to build a winning coalition.

In most campaigns, partisanship is the number-one consideration in targeting voters; it subsumes all other factors. Incumbents, in particular, focus on individuals who identify with their party and independent voters.

Challengers in uncompetitive races are the most likely to target voters who identify with the opposing party. Many of these candidates recognize that the one-sidedness of their districts makes it impossible for them to compete without winning the support of some of the opposing party's supporters. Some likely-loser challengers do not even have the resources needed to carry out a basic party-oriented targeting strategy. Lacking a poll or a precinct-by-precinct breakdown of where Republican, Democratic, and independent voters reside, some amateurs resort to unorthodox strategies, such as focusing on precincts that had the highest turnout levels in the previous election.

Other factors that campaigns consider when designing targeting strategies are demography and political issues. Many House campaigns target demographic, geographic, or occupational groups; some concentrate on specific ethnic, racial, religious, gender, or age groups; and a small number focus on counties, suburbs, cities, or other geographic locations. Issues and political attitudes, including voting intentions and partisanship, also play a central role in the targeting strategies of House campaigns.

Group-oriented and issue/attitudinal-oriented targeting strategies each offer campaigns some distinct advantages. The group-oriented, or geodemographic, approach is based on the idea that there are identifiable segments of the population whose support the campaign needs to attract and that specific communications can be tailored to win that support. Just as soliciting money from a readily identifiable fund-raising constituency is important in the campaign for resources, communicating a message to identifiable groups of supporters and undecided voters is important in the campaign for votes. Campaigns that use group-based targeting strategies emphasize different aspects of their message, depending on the intended audience for a particular campaign advertisement. By tailoring their messages to attract the votes of specific population groups, these campaigns hope to build a winning coalition. During the 1990s, many campaigns stressed the effect of the economy on children and families in literature that was mailed to middle-class and working women, whereas they emphasized tax cuts and economic growth issues in literature mailed to business executives and upper-class and upper-middle-class voters.

The issue/attitudinal strategy is based on the premise that issues and ideas should drive the campaign. Campaigns that target voters on the basis of specific policies or a broad ideology, such as conservatism or progressivism, hope to win the support of single-issue or ideological voters who favor these positions. Often, one or two specific issues are emphasized in order to attract the support of swing voters, whose support, the candidate believes, will be a deciding factor in the election outcome. Some candidates targeted pro-life or pro-choice voters in the 1990s, believing their support would be decisive. Others targeted pro-environment or anti–gun control voters. Republicans who employed these strategies focused primarily on voters who were concerned about the deficit, taxes, the size of government, government regulation, and crime. Democrats who employed them focused on voters who cared about public education, jobs, the environment, health care, and the protections and services that government provides for the elderly, children, and underprivileged groups.

Targeting strategies based on issues or voter attitudes more readily lend themselves to the communication of a coherent campaign message than do group-oriented strategies. They are especially effective at mobilizing single-issue voters and political activists who have strong ideological predispositions. Yet such strategies run the risk of alienating moderate voters who agree with the candidate on most policy matters but disagree on the issues the campaign has chosen to emphasize. Campaigns waged by policy amateurs and ideologues are the most likely to suffer from this problem. Often these candidates become boxed in by their own message; they are labeled "ultra-liberals" or "right wingers" by their opponents, and ultimately they lose.

Incumbents target demographic, geographic, and occupational groups more than do challengers and open-seat candidates. Most incumbents have a detailed knowledge of the voting blocs that supported them in the past and target constituents who belong to them. Many challengers, especially those unable to mount competitive campaigns, do not have this information. Lacking good voter files, and recognizing the need to peel away some of their opponents' supporters, they target on the basis of issues.

Delivering a Campaign Message

The message delivered by a candidate gives substance to the candidate's campaign and helps to shape the political agenda, mobilize backers, and win votes (see Chapter 14). In a well-run campaign, the same coherent message pervades every aspect of the candidate's communications—from paid television advertisements to impromptu remarks. Campaign messages can be an essential ingredient of victory in close elections, because they activate supporters and strongly influence the decisions of persuadable voters.

Campaign messages rely heavily on imagery. The most successful campaigns weave the candidate's persona and policy stances into thematic messages. These form the core of the image the candidate seeks to project. According to Joel Bradshaw, president of the Democratic consulting firm Campaign Design Group, good campaign messages are clear and easy to communicate, short, convey a sense of emotional urgency, reflect voters' perceptions of political reality, establish clear differences between the candidate and the opponent, and are credible.[13]

The precise mix of personal characteristics, issues, and broad themes that candidates project depends on their political views, the groups they target, and the messages they anticipate their opponents will communicate. Good strategic positioning results in the transmission of a message that most voters will find appealing. When both candidates achieve this result, an election becomes what strategists refer to as a "battle for the middle ground." In designing a message, campaign decision makers consider a variety of factors, which Fred Hartwig of Peter Hart and Associates refers to as "the Seven P's of Strategy": performance, professional experience, positioning, partisanship, populism, progressivism, and positivity.[14] Virtually all consultants emphasize the importance of consistency. The different components of the message must add up to a coherent public image.

Campaigns endeavor to create a favorable image for their candidates by identifying them with decency, loyalty, honesty, hard work, and other cherished values. Campaign communications interweave anecdotes about a candidate's personal accomplishments, professional success, family, or ability to overcome humble origins to portray him or her as the living embodiment of the American dream—someone the voters would be proud to have represent them in Washington. Campaigns frequently emphasize elements of their candidate's persona that point to an opponent's weakness. Veterans who run against draft evaders, for example, commonly emphasize their war records.

Incumbents frequently convey image-oriented messages. They seek to reinforce or expand their base of support by concentrating on those aspects of their personas that make them popular with constituents. Their messages convey images of competent, caring individuals who work tirelessly in Washington to improve the lives of the folks they represent back home. Incumbents' campaign communications often describe how they have helped constituents to resolve problems, brought federal programs and projects to the district, and introduced or cosponsored popular legislation. Some discuss their efforts to prevent a military base or factory from closing. Those whose districts have experienced the ravages of floods, earthquakes, riots, or other disasters almost always highlight their roles in bringing federal relief to victims.

Many challengers and open-seat contestants also seek to portray themselves as caring, hard-working, and experienced. Nonincumbents who have previously held elective office frequently contrast their accomplishments with those of their opponent. During the elections held in the early and mid-1990s, many challengers who were state legislators blamed their opponents for contributing to the federal deficit, while pointing to their own budget-cutting efforts.

Political amateurs usually discuss their successes in the private sector, seeking to make a virtue of their lack of political experience. Many blame the "mess in Washington" on the "career politicians" and claim that someone who has succeeded in the private sector is needed to make government work for the people again. Still, a challenger who focuses on experience rarely wins because a current officeholder almost always has more experience.

Taking a Stand on the Issues

Most House candidates and campaign aides maintain that the bulk of their messages focus on policy concerns rather than the candidate's personality—a claim that has been borne out by examinations of their campaign materials.[15] Candidates in competitive contests run the most issue-oriented campaigns, reflecting the fact that they view their policy stances as a way to attract the support of undecided voters. Challengers run the most opposition-oriented campaigns. They point to incumbents' ethical lapses, congressional roll call votes that are out of sync with constituents' views, or federal policies that have harmed local voters or the national interest. The incumbents holding marginal seats may respond in kind by pointing to unpopular aspects of their challengers' backgrounds or issue positions.

Almost all candidates take policy stands that identify them with "valence" issues—such as a strong economy, job creation, domestic tranquility, and international security—which are universally viewed in a favorable light. Some make these issues the centerpieces of their campaigns. They either ignore or soft-pedal "positional" issues (sometimes referred to as "wedge" issues), which have two or more sides.[16] When both candidates campaign mainly on valence issues, the dialogue can be likened to a debate between the nearly identical Tweedledee and Tweedledum.

When candidates communicate dissimilar stands on positional issues, however, political debate becomes more meaningful. Issues such as the economy, taxes, gun control, crime, abortion, and civil rights have for several years had the potential to draw the attention of voters and affect elections. Scandals, health care, environmental issues, and social entitlement programs also have the ability to influence elections.

Challengers are especially likely to benefit from emphasizing positional issues. By stressing points of disagreement between themselves and the incumbents, challengers can help to crystallize their images, attract media attention, and strip away some of their opponents' support. Incumbents may not derive the same electoral benefits from running on positional issues, because they are usually evaluated in personal terms.[17] Candidates who campaign on positional issues hope to attract the support of single-issue or ideological voters or to overcome some weakness in their images. Some liberal Democrats emphasize crime to project a "tougher" image. Some conservative Republicans discuss health care to show their compassionate side. Both groups of candidates seek to convince centrist voters that they share their concerns.

Before taking a strong policy stance, candidates try to anticipate the issues their opponents will emphasize. For example, candidates who run against police officers rarely mount "law and order" campaigns because of the obvious disparities in credibility that they and their opponents have on crime-related issues. Candidates who learn that their opponents are vulnerable on a salient issue generally try to make it a major focus of their campaigns in order to win the support of independents or pry voters from their opponents' camps. Democrats and some moderate Republicans lure women's votes by making abortion rights a major part of their campaign platforms. In 1992 and 1996, Democrats who adopted this position received the added benefit of being able to coordinate their message with the Clinton-Gore campaign. Divisions within the Republican Party made abortion an issue to avoid for many GOP candidates. Women who run against men are the most likely to campaign as pro-choice and discuss women's concerns, but some male candidates also stake out pro-choice positions to attract the support of women and liberal voters.

Economic issues—whether they be inflation, unemployment, taxes, jobs, the federal budget, or the national deficit—have been the number-one concern of voters in most elections since the Great Depression. Virtually all candidates in the 1980s and 1990s made some aspect of the economy part of their campaigns. Democratic candidates often discuss the economy as a fairness issue. In 1992 many Democrats followed the Clinton-Gore campaign's lead in pointing to the increased tax burdens that Reagan-Bush policies placed on the middle class and the tax breaks they gave to wealthy Americans. In 1996 and 1998, many Democratic candidates again adopted the Clinton-Gore campaign's message. They claimed credit for the nation's booming economy and for creating new jobs. They also chastised Republicans for proposing to cut popular social safety net programs in order to give a tax break to the rich.

Republican candidates usually focus on economic growth and the deficit. Throughout the 1980s and early 1990s, they sought to blame the economic woes of the country on wasteful government subsidies, excessive regulation, and profligate pork-barrel spending approved by the Democratic-controlled Congress. Their message gained supporters in 1994, as Republican candidates proclaimed that tax cuts were the crown jewel of their vaunted Contract with America.[18] Later in the decade, the Republican argument for tax cuts and a balanced budget amendment lost much of its persuasiveness as a result of the nation's improved economy.

Political reform was also an important issue for both Republicans and Democrats in the 1990s, reflecting the anti–Washington establishment mood of the country. Many House challengers concentrated on term limits,

campaign finance reform, and "reinventing government," often contrasting their reform positions with their opponents' votes for a congressional pay raise and dependence on PAC contributions. Incumbents address political reform differently. Some candidates seek to defend Congress, while others try to impress upon voters that they are part of the solution and not the problem—they argue that they are working to improve government from the inside. An opponent may be content to merely lob stones from a distance. Another popular incumbent strategy is to campaign for reelection to Congress by attacking the institution itself. The Republicans' success in making political corruption a campaign issue in 1994 and their lengthy investigations of the Clinton administration and Democratic fund-raising activities in 1996, combined with repeated calls by members of both parties for revamping the campaign finance system, suggest reform will play a prominent role in future congressional elections.

Conclusion

Contemporary congressional elections are waged primarily by candidate-centered organizations that draw on the expertise of political consultants for polling, mass media advertising, and other specialized functions. Few candidates depend on parties and interest groups to carry out many campaign activities. However, parties and interest groups do supplement candidate efforts and can play important supporting roles in House campaigns.

Candidates must survive several tests to win a seat in the U.S. House. Indeed, they must succeed at two distinct campaigns—the campaign for resources and the campaign for votes. The campaign for resources requires a candidate to win the backing of the power brokers in Washington, D.C., including party operatives, interest group officials, and political consultants. The campaign for votes requires a candidate to form a campaign organization that can communicate the candidate's message, reach the proper target audience, and mobilize supporters on election day. The candidates who can succeed in both campaigns are ultimately the ones who win office.

Notes

1. This chapter is drawn primarily from Paul S. Herrnson, *Congressional Elections: Campaigning at Home and in Washington,* 4th ed. (Washington, D.C.: CQ Press, 2004).

2. Gary C. Jacobson and Samuel Kernell, *Strategy and Choice in Congressional Elections* (New Haven, Conn.: Yale University Press, 1983), chap. 3; William T. Bianco, "Strategic Decisions on Candidacy in U.S. Congressional Districts," *Legislative Studies Quarterly* 9 (1984): 360–362; David T. Canon, *Actors, Athletes, and Astronauts: Political Amateurs*

in the United States Congress (Chicago: University of Chicago Press, 1990), 76–79; L. Sandy Maisel, Walter J. Stone, and Cherie Maestas, "Quality Challengers to Congressional Incumbents," in *Playing Hardball: Campaigning for the U.S. Congress,* ed. Paul S. Herrnson (Upper Saddle River, N.J.: Prentice Hall, 2001).

3. Gary C. Jacobson and Samuel Kernell, "National Forces in the 1986 U.S. House Elections," *Legislative Studies Quarterly* 15 (1990): 65–87; Canon, *Actors, Athletes, and Astronauts,* 106–108.

4. Joseph A. Schlesinger, "The New American Political Party," *American Political Science Review* 79 (1985): 1151–1169; Paul S. Herrnson, *Party Campaigning in the 1980s* (Cambridge, Mass.: Harvard University Press, 1988), chaps. 2–3.

5. Figures are compiled from Paul S. Herrnson, *The Campaign Assessment and Candidate Outreach Project, 2000 Survey* (College Park, Md.: Center for American Politics and Citizenship, University of Maryland, 2000).

6. Center for Responsive Politics, www.opensecrets.org.

7. Peter L. Francia, John C. Green, Paul S. Herrnson, Lynda W. Powell, and Clyde Wilcox, *The Financiers of Congressional Elections: Investors, Ideologues, and Intimates* (New York: Columbia University Press, 2003), esp. chap. 3.

8. The figure for PACs excludes contributions by leadership PACs, which are PACs sponsored by members of Congress, congressional retirees, or other politicians. The members were Roy Blunt, R-Mo. (chief deputy whip and member, Energy and Commerce Committee); Shelley Moore Capito, R-W.Va. (vice chair, Congressional Caucus for Women's Issues); John D. Dingell, D-Mich. (ranking member, Energy and Commerce Committee); Richard A. Gephardt, D-Mo. (House minority leader); Dennis Hastert, R-Ill. (Speaker of the House); Nancy L. Johnson, R-Conn. (chair, Health Subcommittee of the Ways and Means Committee); Earl Pomeroy, D-N.D. (member, Ways and Means Committee); and Karen Thurmon, D-Fla. (member, Ways and Means Committee).

9. The fund-raising figures for incumbents, challengers, and open-seat candidates are from Herrnson, *Congressional Elections,* chap. 6.

10. Gary C. Jacobson, *Money in Congressional Elections* (New Haven, Conn.: Yale University Press, 1980), 113–123; Jonathan S. Krasno, Donald Philip Green, and Jonathan A. Cowden, "The Dynamics of Fundraising in House Elections," *Journal of Politics* 56 (1994): 459–474.

11. David R. Mayhew, *Congress: The Electoral Connection* (New Haven, Conn.: Yale University Press, 1974); Stephen Ansolabehere, James M. Snyder Jr., and Charles Stewart III, "Old Voters, New Voters, and the Personal Vote," *American Journal of Political Science* 44 (2000): 17–34; Richard F. Fenno Jr., *Home Style: House Members in Their Districts* (Boston: Little, Brown, 1978), 3, 4.

12. See, for example, Robert Axelrod, "Where the Votes Come From: An Analysis of Presidential Election Coalitions, 1952–1968," *American Political Science Review* 66 (1972): 11–20.

13. Joel C. Bradshaw, "Who Will Vote for You and Why: Designing Campaign Strategy and Theme," paper presented at the Conference on Campaign Management, American University, Washington, D.C., December 10–11, 1992.

14. Fred Hartwig, vice president, Peter Hart and Associates, presentation to the Taft Institute Honors Seminar in American Government, Flushing, N.Y., June 15, 1993.

15. See Peter Clarke and Susan H. Evans, *Covering Campaigns: Journalism and Congressional Elections* (Stanford, Calif.: Stanford University Press, 1983), 38–45.

16. On the differences between valence issues and positional issues, see Donald E. Stokes, "Spatial Models of Party Competition," in *Elections and the Political Order,* ed. Angus Campbell, Philip E. Converse, Warren E. Miller, and Donald E. Stokes (New York: Wiley, 1966), 161–169.

17. See, for example, Gary C. Jacobson, *The Politics of Congressional Elections,* 4th ed. (New York: Longman, 1997), 112–116.

18. James G. Gimpel, *Fulfilling the Contract: The First 100 Days* (Boston: Allyn and Bacon, 1996); Robin Kolodny, "The Contract with America in the 104th Congress," in *The State of the Parties,* ed. John C. Green and Daniel M. Shea (Lanham, Md.: Rowman and Littlefield, 1996), 314–327.

Suggested Readings

Canon, David T. *Actors, Athletes, and Astronauts: Political Amateurs in the U.S. Congress.* Chicago: University of Chicago Press, 1990.

Herrnson, Paul S. *Congressional Elections: Campaigning at Home and in Washington.* 4th ed. Washington, D.C.: CQ Press, 2004.

Jacobson, Gary C. *Money in Congressional Elections.* New Haven, Conn.: Yale University Press, 1980.

Jacobson, Gary C., and Samuel Kernell. *Strategy and Choice in Congressional Elections.* New Haven, Conn.: Yale University Press, 1983.

CHAPTER 22

U.S. Senate Campaigns

Nicol C. Rae

The United States has one of the very few genuinely bicameral (two-chamber) legislatures among modern democracies. For the framers of the U.S. Constitution, the Senate had two principal roles within the new constitutional system. First, the Senate was to represent the states equally in the federal government (and in keeping with this role, senators were to be chosen by the state legislatures). In fact, equal representation in the Senate regardless of population was one of the essential conditions imposed by the states in agreeing to ratify the 1787 Constitution. Second, the Senate was to act as a check on the directly elected House of Representatives.

The passage in 1913 of the Seventeenth Amendment, which called for direct election of the Senate by the voters rather than the state legislatures, reinforced the legitimacy of the chamber in an increasingly democratic age and enhanced the Senate's power in relation to that of the House. Yet the vast disparity in state populations has meant that the smaller and less urban states are overrepresented in the Senate. This disparity also has implications for Senate campaigns. Very different kinds of Senate campaigns can be run in, say, Vermont or Wyoming than in the large, populous states of California, Texas, or Florida. Overall, however, Senate campaigns have become increasingly nationalized and partisan in recent years.

This chapter examines the legal and political context of Senate campaigns, the conduct of these campaigns, and the factors that determine the outcome of Senate elections. The chapter concludes with some observations about the impact of Senate election campaigns on the contemporary Senate as a representative and governing institution.

The Legal and Political Context

Because senators enjoy a six-year term in office, they are more insulated from direct electoral pressure than House members, whose terms are only two years. Unlike the House, the Senate is a continuous body; only one-third of senators are up for election at any one time (Senate reelec-

tion classes are arranged so the two Senate seats from a state never are up for election in the same year). As a result, it is, in theory, somewhat more difficult in the Senate than in the House to change partisan control of the chamber in any one election. In practice, other factors leading to greater volatility in modern Senate elections cancel out this advantage for Senate incumbents and the controlling party. One thing is certain: party leaders in the Senate, like those in the House, must be continually mindful of the electoral clock.

When election campaigns are under way, several Senate traditions are usually observed. For example, when the two senators from the same state are from opposing parties, they do not openly campaign against each other, and when the two senators from the same state are from the same party, they keep some distance from each other's campaigns. Senators from opposing parties in a state have little motivation to strive too overtly for the defeat of one another, because if the incumbent is reelected they will have to work together in the future on matters important to their state. The possibility that an incumbent colleague from the same party might be defeated by a challenger from the other party, with whom the other senator would then have to work, similarly discourages senators from working too hard to reelect their partisan colleagues.

States as Election Constituencies

The Senate is unusual among chambers directly elected by the people in that the electoral constituencies—in this case, U.S. states—vary tremendously in size. At the two extremes are Wyoming with a population of just below 0.5 million and California with its almost 34 million inhabitants.[1] Yet both states carry the same weight in Senate elections. This situation leads to curious anomalies such as the Republicans gaining control of the Senate by winning twenty-two of the thirty-four Senate seats at stake in 1980 (a net gain of twelve), while the Democrats won a majority of the total national votes cast in Senate elections because of the landslide reelection of Sen. Alan Cranston in populous California.[2] The variations in state size have serious implications for Senate elections from the point of view of both incumbent senators and party leaders seeking strategies for Senate campaigns.

In small states, senators are likely to be familiar to most of the electorate, perhaps even on a personal basis. Because of this name recognition, as well as the fewer and smaller media markets in those states, incumbent senators from small states, like House incumbents in their districts, are better able to manage their visibility and public profile back home.[3] The intimacy of small-state contests may also serve to mitigate partisanship and further emphasize the need for senators, even from different parties, to get along and work together for the mutual benefit of the state. Small-state electorates, which tend to be fairly homogeneous, are therefore also likely to frown on overtly partisan elections and focus more on what the incumbents or challengers have done or can do for the state. Small-state contests are a relative boon for the national party committees and Senate campaign committees because they get more for their money—a Senate victory in a small-state is just as significant as one in a large state such as California in securing Senate control and far cheaper to fund. Nevertheless, these committees have to be wary of threatening the relationships that small-state voters may have with their senators and respectful of the traditions of decorous campaigning in these homogeneous political environments.

In the medium-size to larger states, Senate election campaigns are an altogether different game.[4] Senators can no longer rely entirely on personal ties and a reputation for protecting the state's interests in Washington for election and reelection. The electorates are too diverse (see next section), and the potential electoral and resource base is much greater. Indeed, the larger the state population, the more evident are class, racial, ethnic, religious, and cultural differences. Such diverse states are almost always the scene of competitive Senate elections between the candidates of the major parties.

Meanwhile, the national Senate campaign committees must make strategic decisions on where to deploy their resources in Senate contests, and differences in the campaign costs among states factor into decisions on candidate recruitment and where to deploy resources late in the campaigns. States such as New York and California are expensive not only because of their large populations, but also because campaigns there are fought on television and advertising rates in their major media markets are among the most expensive in the nation. Thus in those states only wealthy candidates or those with proven abilities to raise large amounts of cash quickly are likely to be viable.

Internal Diversity of States

The high degree of social, economic, and geographic diversity of most state electorates poses a particular challenge for Senate election campaigns (see Chapter 7). Viable candidates in both the primary and general elections have to accommodate this diversity and devise electoral strategies attuned to it. Moreover, socioeconomic, racial/ethnic, or religious cleavages may well map onto a long-standing regional cleavage within a state. A division between a state's major economic and industrial urban center and its suburban/rural hinterland is common—New York City and upstate New York, Chicago and downstate Illinois are two examples. In states with more than one major urban center, the situation becomes even more complex. Senate candidates in Pennsylvania must face the long-standing rivalry between Philadelphia and Pittsburgh, just as candidates in Missouri must deal with the similar competition between the St. Louis and Kansas City metropolitan areas.

The Sun Belt megastates of California, Texas, and Florida are characterized by their geographical diversity, multiple urban centers, and rapid population growth. In these states, Senate election campaigns must deal with an even greater degree of diversity and present a variety of distinctive themes that target each electoral constituency. California's traditional north/south divide has been complicated by the emergence of new economic and political power centers—such as Silicon Valley and San Diego—within the traditionally antagonistic sections. In addition, the Central Valley, with its rapidly growing cities and conservative Republican politics, is becoming economically, socially, and politically distinctive from the increasingly liberal Pacific Coast.

Texas has four highly distinctive urban centers—Dallas–Fort Worth, Houston, Austin, and San Antonio—and its subregions, such as the Panhandle and the Rio Grande Valley, have differing interests that Senate campaigns must attempt to balance.

Florida, whose electorate had doubled in size since the 1970s, is a good example of how a state's internal heterogeneity affects Senate elections and how such heterogeneity can be consistently overcome by a clever incumbent. The Sunshine State has four major metropolitan areas—Miami–Fort Lauderdale–Palm Beach, Tampa–St. Petersburg–Clearwater, Orlando, and Jacksonville—and ten media markets.[5] The state has six socially and culturally distinctive regions. Northeast Florida and the Panhandle resemble the Deep South; Central Florida along Interstate 4 from Tampa Bay to Cape Canaveral is suburban and heavy with theme parks, voters, and migrants; Southwest Florida is wealthy and heavy with retirees, largely from the Midwest; and Southeast Florida centered on Miami looks toward Latin America and the Caribbean and is heavy with Jewish Democrats and Cuban Republicans. Tensions between the regions pervade state politics and statewide campaigns, but Democrat Bob Graham, first as governor and later as a U.S. senator (1987–2005), was a master at balancing these demands. Graham had roots in South Florida, but he talked like a North Floridian. He was culturally moderate (if not liberal), which appealed to African American, Jewish, and women voters, but economically conservative, which appealed to the wealthy retirees and the middle-class suburbanites worried about their tax burden. He was "strong" on defense (essential for a state with many military bases and infrastructure), an enemy of Cuban dictator Fidel Castro, and an unswerving friend of Israel.

Graham succeeded politically by offending no significant economic interest, region, or segment of the state electorate. His much publicized "workdays" (he regularly worked for a day in various jobs around the state) and his excellent state constituency service operation allowed him to remain visible throughout the state and to highlight his empathy with Florida's diverse constituencies and his achievements for the state in Washington. It was also clear that the senator and his staff were highly sensitive to what was going on in the state at any particular time. One possible downside for Graham was that the need to devote so much of his time and energy to his politically eclectic home base left him little time for significant legislative achievement and visibility in Washington. Such a situation would seem to be an inevitable danger for senators from large, internally complex states.

Money

Money is a key element of Senate campaigns and has been so for most of U.S. history (campaign finance is covered more fully in Chapter 6). In the nineteenth century, the party machine bosses provided the largesse to elect the state legislatures that selected senators. But once direct election came into effect, party machines became less powerful, and electoral constituencies became larger and more diverse, Senate races almost inevitably relied on either the personal wealth of candidates or funding from wealthy individuals.

In the modern era, Senate elections are regulated by the Federal Election Campaign Act (FECA) of 1974 and subsequent court decisions and amendments, including most recently the 2002 Bipartisan Campaign Reform Act (BCRA). Individuals are limited to donating no more than $2,000 to a Senate candidate, and political action committees (PACs) are limited to a maximum of $5,000 in donations to any one campaign (because primary and general elections are counted as separate campaigns, contributors can contribute twice the sums just listed during an election cycle). Political party committees can make a maximum direct contribution of $17,500 to a Senate candidate during an election cycle. The FECA also allows party committees to spend money "on behalf of" a Senate candidate. The limit on such "coordinated spending" is indexed for inflation and varies according to state population, with California the highest at $1.78 million.[6] Party leaders and other prominent members of Congress also regularly form their own political action committees—called leadership PACs—and members of Congress in safe races can transfer money from their accounts to members in marginal races in coordination with the

Table 22-1 Sources of Campaign Funding, 2002 Senate Elections

Source	Average campaign funding[a]	Percentage of total funding
Individual contributions (maximum $1,000)	$2,914,537	60
Political action committees	788,690	16
Candidate contributions	375,123	8
Party contributions and coordinated spending	236,396	5
Party-connected contributions[b]	114,086	2
Miscellaneous	401,084	8

Source: Federal Election Commission data adapted from tables in Paul S. Herrnson, *Congressional Elections: Campaigning at Home and in Washington,* 4th ed. (Washington, D.C.: CQ Press, 2004).

[a] Average for general election candidates in contested races.
[b] Leadership PACs, other candidates, members, and retired members.

party's leadership and campaign committees. Table 22-1 lists the sources of direct or "hard money" funding for Senate campaigns in 2002.

In 1976 the Supreme Court ruled in *Buckley v. Valeo* that any limits on what candidates spend of their personal funds on their own campaigns were unconstitutional. PACs were permitted to spend as much money as they wished on individual campaigns, provided none of the spending was directly coordinated with any candidate's campaign—the so-called independent expenditures loophole. Subsequent federal legislation also allowed state and national parties to raise unlimited and unrestricted amounts of money—so-called soft money—which they channeled back into national races, including Senate campaigns. In the 2002 election cycle, the Republican Senate campaign committee spent $44 million in soft money on Senate races and the Democrats spent $52 million.[7] But by then soft money had become so politically controversial that it was prohibited entirely by the 2002 BCRA.

The effects of the campaign finance system on Senate election campaigns are discussed in greater depth in the next section. It is possible to conclude here, though, that Senate elections continue to hinge on candidates' personal wealth or their access to large donations from parties, interest groups, and committed individuals (generally party activists). The ability to raise money in itself is a major factor in the viability of Senate candidacies and, indeed, in the initial decisions made about whether to mount a Senate campaign. Incumbent senators thus devote a great deal of time to maintaining a large campaign war chest in order to deter potential challengers.

Table 22-2 Reelection Rates of Senate Incumbents, 1980–2004

Year	Number seeking reelection	Defeated in primary election	Defeated in general election	Total defeated	Reelection rate (percent)
1980	29	4	9	13	55
1982	30	0	2	2	93
1984	29	0	3	3	90
1986	28	0	7	7	75
1988	27	0	4	4	85
1990	32	0	1	1	97
1992	28	1	4	5	82
1994	26	0	2	2	92
1996	21	1	1	2	91
1998	29	0	3	3	90
2000	29	0	6	6	79
2002	27	1	3	4	85
2004	26	0	1	1	96

Sources: Adapted from tables in Norman J. Ornstein, Thomas E. Mann, and Michael J. Malbin, *Vital Statistics on Congress, 2001–2002* (Washington, D.C.: AEI Press, 2002); 2004 data: *CQ Weekly,* November 6, 2004.

The Players

The players in Senate election campaigns are not only the candidates, but also political parties, interest groups, and, not least, the news media. Today, television serves as the critical arena of Senate campaigns; candidates devote most of their campaign budgets to television ads, and television news and televised debates help to frame the contests for the overwhelming majority of voters.

Candidate Emergence and Recruitment

When senators were elected by state legislators, many Senate candidates were already members of their legislature, or they were prominent political figures within their state. As party machines developed and gained control over legislatures, party bosses—such as Senators Thomas Platt of New York and Matthew Quay of Pennsylvania—often awarded themselves a U.S. Senate seat to solidify their control over federal patronage in their respective fiefdoms. However, with the onset of the direct election of senators in 1914 and the atrophy of party machines over the course of the twentieth century, Senate candidates became largely self-selected and self-sustaining. In today's era of relatively weak party loyalties, any person who has access to the key resources of money and organization can mount a credible U.S. Senate campaign without having to undergo any "peer review."

Incumbency is probably the most significant single factor governing Senate elections. Although Senate incumbents are reelected at a somewhat lesser rate than their House counterparts, the reelection rates are still impressive (see Table 22-2).

Because mounting a Senate campaign takes considerable resources, senators tend to be independently wealthy individuals or those with access to ample money and resources. For the latter, resources will flow more readily if they have an established political profile. For U.S. House members, their district is their base of support. Governors and other statewide elected officials—lieutenant governors, attorneys general, and state secretaries of state—generally make formidable Senate candidates, because they have already run successfully in a statewide election. Indeed, previous officeholding is the greatest indication of candidate "quality" and electoral success in congressional elections.[8] Table 22-3 shows the prior professions of senators in the 107th Congress (2001–2002). As might be expected, lawyers, businessmen, and elected officials feature prominently.

The campaign finance laws place no restrictions on the amount of their personal wealth that Senate candidates may spend on their own campaigns. This is a particular advantage for unknown or inexperienced candidates who can deploy their personal wealth to overcome the disadvantages of lack of name recognition. California Republican Michael Huffington, a U.S. House member who spent $28.4 million on his unsuccessful challenge of California's Democratic senator Dianne Feinstein in 1994, is a conspicuous example.[9] His personal fortune allowed the relatively unknown and politically inexperienced Huffington (who was serving his first term in the U.S. House) to secure the Republican nomination from more

Republican nominee Mel Martinez steps off his tour bus to vote in the 2004 U.S. Senate election in Florida. Martinez, who defeated Democrat Betty Castor, is the first Cuban American to serve in the Senate. As George W. Bush's former secretary of the Department of Housing and Urban Development, Martinez was heavily recruited by the White House to run. Source: Reuters/Kevin Kolczynski/Landov

Outsider candidates can run successfully for the Senate, even without vast personal wealth, if they can capitalize on a particular issue relevant to the state or that can be used against a weak incumbent. Former senator Carol Moseley Braun of Illinois defeated incumbent Democratic senator Alan Dixon in the 1992 Democratic primary by focusing on Dixon's vote to confirm controversial Supreme Court nominee Clarence Thomas. In 1990 Democrat Paul Wellstone of Minnesota upset the Republican Senate incumbent, Rudy Boschwitz, in the general election with a shoestring budget but a highly amusing and effective media campaign.

The Parties

The parties' Senate campaign committees—the National Republican Senatorial Committee (NRSC) and the Democratic Senate Campaign Committee (DSCC)—are largely responsible for the day-to-day conduct of national party activity in U.S. Senate campaigns. The two committees help to recruit candidates, provide the candidates with campaign resources, and develop a national party strategy for Senate election campaigns (also see Chapter 11).

Because national party funding may be critical in close races, the principal activity of the parties' Senate campaign committees is fund-raising. In 2002 the DSCC raised $126 million and the NRSC $143 million.[11] Each party's senators elect the chair of their committee, who is regarded as a member of the Senate leadership. The post tends to rotate among senators, and few take it for more than two terms because of the arduous demands of constant fund-raising.

Early in the election cycle, the committee leaders and their senior staff plan their campaign strategy by deciding which races are likely to be closely contested. At this stage, they may also join with other party leaders—including the incumbent president—to recruit strong candidates for these races ("strong" refers generally to elected officeholders in the state in question or those with the ability to raise a great deal of money) or to persuade incumbent senators of their party not to retire. At this point, and throughout the election cycle, the parties' Senate campaign committees will conduct and commission polls. On this basis, they will decide where to switch or allocate their resources during the campaign, and they will plan visits to critical states by party leaders or incumbent presidents. The national campaign committees will also advise PACs and other large contributors to the party where their resources might be beneficial to the overall effort. Finally, the national campaign committees and the national party committees will encourage activities such as registration and get-out-the-vote drives to help their strongest challengers or most vulnerable incumbent senators.

seasoned opponents and to almost defeat a popular Senate incumbent. In 2000 Huffington's spending record was easily overtaken by another political neophyte, Wall Street magnate Jon Corzine. He overwhelmed more politically experienced Democratic opponents in the primary and a Republican opponent in the general election by spending $60.2 million of his own money to secure a New Jersey Senate seat.[10] Interestingly, both of these examples occurred in states in which elections are primarily fought through television advertising and that include the most expensive media markets in the nation. In such circumstances, personal wealth can be a decisive factor.

Although candidates can and do jump into Senate races unbidden, national party committees and even incumbent presidents encourage potentially strong candidates to run for Senate seats they believe the party has a chance of winning. In the 2004 election cycle, the George W. Bush White House and the national Republican Party committees took considerable trouble to encourage Housing and Urban Development Secretary Mel Martinez and former congressman John Thune to run for the Senate, because they judged (correctly as it turned out) that these candidates could win important Senate races in Florida and South Dakota, respectively. Interest group allies of the parties—such as labor unions for Democrats and the Christian Coalition for Republicans—might also encourage sympathetic candidates to run with promises of organizational support.

Table 22-3 Prior Occupations of U.S. Senators, 107th Congress (2001–2002)

Occupation	Number of senators
Actor/entertainer	1
Aeronautics	1
Agriculture	6
Business or banking	24
Clergy	1
Education	16
Journalism	7
Labor leader	1
Law	53
Medicine	3
Military	1
Professional sports	1
Public service/politics	28
Real estate	4

Source: Adapted from tables in Norman J. Ornstein, Thomas E. Mann, and Michael J. Malbin, *Vital Statistics on Congress, 2001–2002* (Washington, D.C.: AEI Press, 2002).

Note: Senators can report more than one occupation.

In terms of resources, the national party committees operate under the restrictions of the FECA and the *Buckley v. Valeo* amendments in raising the funds (hard money) they can contribute directly to candidates' campaigns. As mentioned earlier, the 2002 BCRA (largely upheld by the Supreme Court in its 2003 *McConnell v. FEC* decision) now prohibits the party committees from raising soft (unregulated) money, which will likely lead to a somewhat reduced role for the national political parties in Senate campaigns.

Political Action Committees

Interest groups, like the parties, are critical actors or intermediaries between voters and candidates in Senate election campaigns (see Chapter 12). They raise and spend large sums of money on senatorial candidates through PACs. In 2002 some four thousand registered PACs spent a total of $59 million in Senate elections—$25 million to Democrats and $34 million to Republicans.[12] These PACs can be grouped into various categories: single corporations, trade and professional associations, labor, and public interest groups (ethnic, religious, lifestyle, environmental, and other single-issue "cause" groups, usually called "nonconnected PACs"). The biggest contributors to Senate campaigns in 2002 were the corporate, labor, and trade and professional groups, with the public interest groups close behind (Table 22-4).

PACs can contribute to Senate campaigns in a number of ways. The first and most common route is through direct contributions—limited to $5,000 each for the primary and general election. Corporate and trade and professional PACs favor these kinds of PAC contributions—a limited amount distributed very widely among candidates and across party lines, sometimes even to both candidates in the same race. These PACs spread the net widely, because they are "buying" access. Should they ever have any relevant business before the Senate, they want their lobbyists' calls returned and an opportunity to meet with the member. Corporate PACs tend to give to incumbent candidates (see Table 22-5), thereby reinforcing the incumbency advantage in Senate elections.

In addition to direct contributions, public interest groups, which care passionately about which party controls the Senate, strongly favor independent expenditures, the loophole opened up by the Supreme Court's 1976 *Buckley v. Valeo* decision. Under this provision, PACs may spend as much as they please "on behalf of" their chosen candidates, so long as there is no "coordination" with those candidates' campaigns.

Some groups tend to favor candidates from one party (see Table 22-5). Corporate PACs were very even-handed in their giving while Democrats controlled Congress from 1955 to 1994. But since the Republicans gained control of the Senate in the 1994 midterm elections, corporate PACs have shifted toward their natural Republican allies. Trade and professional PACs tend to follow a similar pattern, but labor PACs are heavily aligned with the Democrats and have been major contributors to Democratic Senate campaigns in terms of both money and workers on election day. As for the nonconnected groups, feminist, gay

Table 22-4 Political Action Committee (PAC) Contributions to 2002 Senate Campaigns

Type of PAC	Amount (millions)	Percentage of total PAC contributions to Senate campaigns
Corporate	$23.42	40
Trade/membership/ health	14.27	24
Labor	7.53	13
Leadership	6.40	11
Nonconnected	6.06	10
Nonstock corporations	1.02	2
Cooperative	.52	1
Total	59.22	

Source: Federal Election Commission data adapted from tables in Paul S. Herrnson, *Congressional Elections: Campaigning at Home and in Washington*, 4th ed. (Washington, D.C.: CQ Press, 2004).

Note: Second column does not add up to 100 because of rounding.

Table 22-5 Pattern of PAC Spending by Incumbents versus Nonincumbents and by Party, 2002 Senate Elections (percent)

Type of PAC	Incumbents	Nonincumbents[a]	Democratic candidates	Republican candidates
Corporate	88	13	29	70
Trade/membership/health	67	4	34	66
Labor	63	37	92	8
Nonconnected	52	47	46	53

Source: Federal Election Commission data adapted from figures in Gary C. Jacobson, *The Politics of Congressional Elections,* 6th ed. (New York: Pearson Longman, 2004).

[a] Challengers and open-seat candidates.

and lesbian, and environmental PACs give overwhelmingly to Democrats, whereas Christian Right, anti–gun control, antiabortion, and small business groups are overwhelmingly aligned with Republican candidates. These "cause" groups are now so aligned with their respective parties that the national parties and congressional campaign committees serve virtually as coordinating and holding operations for the greater cause.

The real winners in the PAC contribution game are incumbents. Most PAC money comes from corporate and trade PACs, and they like to make a safe bet on the "devil they know." The pattern of PAC contributions thus enhances the advantages of incumbents in Senate campaigns.

News Media

After parties and interest groups, the third important intermediary political organization in Senate election campaigns is the news media (also see Chapter 13). In the nineteenth century, voters generally had to rely on party machines for political information. Since the advent of the telegraph, mass literacy, and advances in printing technology in the early twentieth century, however, voters have received most of their information about politics from the mass news media, initially mass-circulation newspapers and then radio and television. Most recently, the Internet has become a significant new medium of political information and communication.

The news media at all levels tend to cover Senate campaigns more extensively and intensively than House races. One reason is that media markets map more easily onto states than onto congressional districts. Senators are also more prestigious and politically visible, and, for the national media, covering thirty-four Senate races is far more feasible than covering well over four hundred races for the U.S. House. Senate elections also attract better-quality challengers, and thus they tend to be more competitive and newsworthy.

Senate campaigns today are by necessity media campaigns. Campaign events are geared toward favorable "free" news media coverage, and campaign strategists devote a considerable amount of time to trying to "spin" the media in their direction and create the impression of

momentum. Media outlets conduct polls in the major races that let the voters and parties know the state of the race and where the parties need to concentrate their resources. Televised debates are also critical to the outcomes of Senate races these days.

But candidates cannot rely just on free media coverage. Candidates and PACs spend heavily on television advertising during a Senate campaign. Often this advertising is crucial to building name recognition for little-known challengers. "Paid" media are regarded as less reliable than free media by the voters, but candidates can also use their paid TV advertising to frame the public's overall view of them and to attack their opponents. One cardinal rule of modern Senate campaigns is that attack advertising must be answered fully and rapidly.

The impact of the Internet on Senate campaigns is not yet clear. Because cyberspace is a good mechanism for communications among the like-minded, the medium should serve as an excellent fund-raising and voter mobilization device for public interest groups and partisans, perhaps reinforcing an apparent tendency toward more partisan and ideological Senate candidates and campaigns.

Campaigns

This section describes how the major actors in Senate campaigns interact with each other from the emergence of the candidates until general election day.

The Primary Phase

The introduction of direct Senate elections in 1914 coincided with the introduction of one of the major Progressive reforms of the American electoral process—the direct primary. Intended to reduce the control of party machine bosses over nominations, the primary is now used almost universally for choosing major-party candidates in Senate elections (see Chapter 5). Thus Senate candidates must run two campaigns—one in the primary and the general election campaign. For incumbents, the primary election is generally an easy win (see Table 22-2). Even senators in a relatively weak political position can usually rely on their party to rally around in an effort to save these Senate seats.

There are exceptions, however. As mentioned earlier, in 1992 Democratic senator Alan Dixon, who had become seriously out of touch with his party's activist base in his home state of Illinois, lost his Democratic primary. More recently, Republican senator Bob Smith of New Hampshire was defeated in the 2002 Senate primary by U.S. Rep. John Sununu. Smith owed his defeat to a reputation for erratic political behavior—most notably a quixotic 1996 presidential campaign and his subsequent temporary departure from the Senate Republican caucus—and the availability of an ambitious, articulate, and youthful challenger in Sununu, the son of a former New Hampshire governor and White House chief of staff. The younger Sununu was also widely regarded as a potentially stronger candidate than the incumbent against the certain Democratic nominee, Democrat Jean Shaheen, as later proved to be the case.

In primaries involving an incumbent, the incumbent is likely to face a serious challenge only on grounds of competence, age or infirmity, scandal, extreme political weakness, or severe alienation of the party base. The very existence of a serious primary challenge to an incumbent is in itself a sign of electoral weakness, because consolidation of one's own party base is a prerequisite for success in modern American elections. Moreover, even if the incumbent senator survives the challenge, some damage has already been done. The case laid out against the incumbent by the challenger from his or her own party in the primary helps to undermine the incumbent with the general electorate, and it also provides the other party's candidate with valuable ammunition for the general election campaign. Few senators survive a major primary challenge and then proceed to easy reelection.

In open-seat races or in primary contests to decide on the incumbent's general election opponent, the primary is every bit as serious an affair as the general election. During the primary campaign, challengers hone their theme and message for the general election. The primary campaign differs from that for the general election in two significant ways, however. First, the primary turnout is invariably lower than general election turnout—indeed, sometimes less than 20 percent of the eligible electorate turns out for the primary. Thus only the most committed and most ideological partisans are likely to turn out for primary elections. The primary electorate is also likely to be better educated and better off than the general electorate.[13]

The second critical factor is that only a plurality is required to win a primary in most states—the exceptions are the nine southern and border states that still require a runoff election if no candidate receives over 50 percent of the vote (40 percent in North Carolina) in round one. It is therefore possible for candidates to win primary elections with the support of only a relatively small portion of the state's primary electorate and an even smaller portion of the potential general electorate. Extreme candidates closely tied to one or two committed interests or to the party's base voters thus have an advantage in primary contests. In relatively small states that lean heavily toward one major party, the divergence between the two electorates may not be so great, but in larger, diverse states a primary winner will invariably have to move somewhat toward the center for the general election while holding on to the party base. If the primary contest has been particularly bitter, holding on to the party base may prove to be very difficult. In general, one rule applies to both incumbents and challengers in primary elections: the narrower the margin of victory, the harder the fall campaign is likely to be. Unopposed incumbents whose challengers have to secure their party's nomination in a bitter primary have the best of both worlds.

One final important aspect of primary elections is the fact that it counts as a single election from the point of the campaign finance regulations. Thus individuals and PACs may double the amount they give to candidates who win primaries by making another maximum donation—$2,000 for individuals, $5,000 for PACs—in the general election. The rules on independent spending by PACs apply equally to primaries. Therefore, incumbents unopposed in primaries once again have an obvious advantage. They can raise money for a purely nominal "election" that can then be transferred directly into their general election account.

Despite their role in recruiting candidates, parties at the state and national levels play no formal role in primary elections these days. In fact, the national party committees have a rule of strict neutrality in primary elections, even for candidates they have recruited. Informally, the party and its elected officials, including campaign committee chairs, Senate leaders, and even presidents, can exercise influence to discourage candidacies and pave the way for a chosen favorite, although this influence might backfire if exercised in too heavy-handed a fashion.

Most Senate candidacies die at the primary stage, which whittles down the field in most races to the two major-party contenders. The extent of primary competition and the margin of victory, however, may give a very strong indication of the general election outcome and the themes of the fall campaign.

Campaign Management

Modern Senate campaigns are vast, complex operations, and candidates have neither the time nor the inclination to manage their campaigns themselves. Because of the decline of party machines and the restrictions imposed by the campaign finance laws, candidates can no longer rely on their parties to manage their campaigns. Those factors, as well as the advent of television as the primary arena of Senate election campaigns, have given rise to that modern political phenomenon the professional campaign consultant (see Chapter 10). Since the 1950s, political consulting has developed into a major profession and industry in its own right, and now all serious Senate candidates hire professionals to manage and run their campaigns. Today, most major political consultants and consulting firms tend to be more associated with one of the major political parties, although a few notorious freelancers continue to work for both.

The campaign manager's job is essentially to run the campaign on a day-to-day basis, keep the campaign dollars flowing in, come up with themes for the candidate's media campaign, and devise and approve campaign advertising. A campaign manager also interprets polls with the help of a pollster or polling firm and offers advice on how the campaign should be structured for maximum effect and utilization of resources. Rather than delegating all management responsibilities, candidates may prefer to entrust a good friend or family member, or someone familiar with the politics of the state, with the formal job of campaign manager or chair. An overreliance on national consulting firms and campaign "gurus" might actually backfire if their methods are ill-attuned to the culture of the state—particularly small states in which politics is by its nature more intimate and in which bare-knuckled Washington attitudes may be frowned upon.

Because an inefficient and disorganized campaign reflects badly on the candidate, it is essential that candidates structure their campaigns so that consultants, pollsters, and the candidate's personal and local supporters are all in harmony or, in modern political parlance, "on message." Today, successful Senate campaigns consist largely of hammering home a few well-tested themes with monotonous regularity, responding rapidly to any direct attacks from the opposition, and making maximum use of the resources available—including national party and interest group help.

Fund-Raising

Fund-raising is a major consideration for most Senate campaigns, except for those candidates who can rely on their own great personal wealth and who therefore are essentially self-financing. Other candidates must establish campaign committees and start to raise contributions from individuals and PACs. In doing so, candidates will need to tap into the fund-raising networks of their parties or like-minded interest groups or collect dollars from state and local business interests. Again, this is an area in which a candidate's previous officeholding experience becomes critical. Candidates who have served in the U.S. House or run a statewide campaign will already have a fund-raising network in place from their last campaigns. By comparison, political neophytes—unless wealthy enough to self-finance—are in a much weaker position as Senate candidates.

In the primary, candidates have to compete with each other for the financial support of the party base and allied interests, but in the general election such support should be available for the nominees, especially non–self-financing candidates who will require injections of party money and uncoordinated independent spending by interest groups. The 2002 BCRA eliminated soft money entirely and forbids interest groups to run ads expressly advocating the election of a candidate in the thirty days prior to a primary and sixty days prior to the general election, but large, unlimited contributions are now finding their way to ideological, party-related, tax-exempt organizations—commonly called "527 committees" after a provision in the U.S. Tax Code. How effectively these organizations can legally channel their funds to help individual Senate campaigns is not yet clear.

Effectiveness in raising money early and consistently throughout the election has become a major test of the virility of a campaign. When the media point out that a campaign is short of money, it is a sure sign of failure. But if candidates can demonstrate competitiveness and momentum, the dollars will come both from personal and ideological allies and also from those with likely future business before the Senate.

Polls and Polling

Opinion polls are a vital component of modern Senate campaigns (also see Chapter 16). Serious candidates hire a pollster to conduct polls for the campaign, and the media use polls to gauge the state of the race from the days leading up to the primaries through the general election. In fact, regular statewide polling on the popularity of incumbent senators plays a role in deciding whether they will face a strong challenge at election time. Weak public approval ratings indicate vulnerability and will spur the opposite party to find strong challengers. As a general rule, an approval rating of less than 50 percent is regarded as a danger signal for incumbents.

Candidates use polls to identify the most important issues on the minds of voters and therefore the themes the candidates will accentuate in their campaigns, as well as their strengths and weaknesses among particular categories of voters. In addition to formal polls, some Senate campaigns use small groups of voters, or "focus groups," to test out candidate messages and themes and even commercials. Polls also indicate which voters are most likely to actually show up at the polls on election day, and candidates specifically target these voters for appeals, because contemporary U.S. elections are in large part a mobilization exercise.[14]

Opinion polls are indispensable to the managers of Senate campaigns, but the danger to candidates is that they become too dependent on polls and focus groups, thereby following an inchoate public opinion rather than attempting to lead. Yet because candidates depend strongly on their party's core ideological voters to get elected, the chance of their overall messages being lost in a fog of poll and focus group-driven messages appears remote. In most modern Senate campaigns, it is abundantly clear what policies Republican and Democratic candidates represent.

Polling, then, may be used to frame the overall message or attune it to particular segments of the electorate and to modify the candidate's own personal style.

Media Strategies

Devising a media strategy is largely the job of the campaign manager, who is likely a political consultant, and the campaign's pollster—or they may be the same person. Together, they seek advertising spots that emphasize the strengths of their candidate and, if necessary, undermine those of their opponent. To capture free media coverage, the campaign stages events likely to attract the media's attention and coincide with evening news cycles. Because of the importance of getting the candidate's message out to the media in a positive manner and responding to attacks from the media or the opposition, the job of press officer/communications director is critical to Senate campaigns. Anyone filling this position must know how the media operate and what journalists need from the campaign, and must be able to put a positive spin for the campaign on all developments.

Media strategies must be extremely flexible so that a campaign can respond rapidly to political attacks or any developments during the campaign. All modern Senate campaigns have a section that deals with "opposition research"—that is, a section that combs through all aspects of the opponent's political career in a search for damaging information or statements that might be useful. If the opposition goes negative, it is important to respond rapidly with effective statements and commercials. Some political consultants have perfected this art, even producing commercials in twenty-four hours or less to address any attacks before they can do any lasting damage.

Voter Mobilization

Steven E. Schier has argued that contemporary American politics is largely a politics of mobilization—getting voters to the polls on election day.[15] Thus it is particularly important for campaigns to identify the party faithful and ascertain their voting records, make sure these voters know who the candidate is, and get them to the polls. These voters are therefore bombarded with regular and electronic mail, phone calls, and recorded messages from party luminaries as election day approaches.

In the run-up to the election, the candidates of both major parties will encourage voter registration drives and get-out-the-vote efforts. The 1993 "Motor Voter" federal legislation requiring states to offer voter registration when citizens apply for or renew their driver's licenses allow these efforts to be regularly combined. Meanwhile, Democrats have found African American churches and labor unions to be particularly effective in mobilizing voters. For Republicans, faith-based organizations have played a similar role.

In the era of machine politics, state and local party machines were the primary agents of voter mobilization,

and, judging by electoral turnouts in the late nineteenth century, they were quite effective at it, even though some of their methods would not pass legal or ethical muster today. In contemporary elections, this role has devolved upon national parties to some extent, but more frequently upon interest groups, who are interested only in selective mobilization of the "committed." This situation has implications for the representativeness of the Senate and the effectiveness of American government in general.

Senate Election Outcomes and Determinants of Voting Behavior

Like most elections, those to the U.S. Senate are determined by various factors ranging from international politics to candidate personalities. In general, these factors fall into two categories: (1) macro-level national and international factors, and (2) micro-level factors specific to the individual contest or state. Most Senate races are probably determined by a combination of both factors, although the extent to which either predominates will vary from year to year and state to state.

National and International Factors

Senate elections can be governed by national and even international factors, in part because of the Senate's constitutional powers to ratify treaties (requiring a two-thirds majority) and to confirm judicial nominations, which bring foreign policy, national security, and cultural issues into play in Senate campaigns. For example, the political fallout from the battle to confirm Supreme Court justice Clarence Thomas in 1992 had a significant impact on several Senate races in 1992. In 2002 Democratic opposition in the Senate to some aspects of President George W. Bush's proposal for a Department of Homeland Security was probably a factor in several close Senate races.

Despite the advantages of incumbents, then, Senate contests are not immune to national trends. Partisan control of the presidency also seems to have considerable influence on Senate elections. The president's party almost invariably loses seats in Senate elections, with losses tending to be particularly significant in the sixth year (or second midterm election) after a party's candidate has taken control of the White House (1958, 1966, 1974, 1986). Yet the midterm Senate elections in 1998 and 2002 departed from the norm, with countervailing national forces—the likely impeachment of President Bill Clinton in 1998 and the continuing fallout from the terrorist attacks on the United States of September 11, 2001—prevailing over the trend in each instance.

Recent decades have revealed little evidence of significant presidential coattails, although Republican presidential candidates Dwight D. Eisenhower in 1952 and

Ronald Reagan in 1980, both of whom won the presidency by a large margin, undoubtedly helped to turn over power in the Senate to their party. Yet the active involvement of incumbent presidents in Senate elections has usually had little direct impact on races or has even backfired. Franklin D. Roosevelt's effort to purge recalcitrant conservative Democrats in the 1938 Senate primaries was an abysmal failure, and hard campaigning by the popular Ronald Reagan in 1986 could not prevent the Democrats from winning almost all of the close Senate races and regaining control of the chamber. A rare instance of presidential popularity apparently working to his party's benefit was the 2002 midterm election, in which President George W. Bush's continued high personal popularity after September 11, 2001, undoubtedly contributed to the gains that helped his party to regain control of the Senate.

But presidential popularity and approval are themselves contingent on diplomatic and military success abroad and the state of the economy back home—factors that inevitably come into play in Senate races. Major-party Senate candidates thus have to adjust their campaign strategies to these national factors in deciding whether they should try to focus the election on national issues in order to capitalize on presidential popularity or unpopularity or to localize it in order to try to neutralize these factors. Because political events can change so quickly and the election cycle is long, candidates sometimes switch from one approach to the other during a single campaign.

State- or Contest-Specific Factors

The most important of the state- or contest-specific factors is incumbency, the most significant determinant of Senate election outcomes. However, specific incumbents may be vulnerable, depending on how well they have conducted themselves in representing their state in the Senate, how they have voted, and how well they have generated federal benefits. A reputation for eccentric behavior, an impression of growing incapacity, or a hint of scandal can neutralize all the advantages of incumbency and open opportunities for the challenger. Particularly appealing challengers with name recognition and proven electability in the state (principally governors and other statewide elected officials) can make a Senate race more competitive than it otherwise might have been. Factors specific to the state can also be decisive. For example, although the national economy may be prosperous, the state's economy may be in recession, or the incumbent president may be particularly unpopular in the state because of factors such as its cultural or ideological profile. In small states, personal interaction with the candidates become more likely, and thus television campaigns are perhaps less decisive factors in an election.[16]

In the end, because of the complicated mix of macro- and micro-level issues that might influence a race, it is often hard to know which factors might be decisive in Senate elections. The curious nature of the Senate itself complicates any attempt to interpret the results of elections, because a switch of a small number of seats in certain states can bring about a shift of partisan control in the chamber, which occurred in 2002. Political scientists and pundits will strive to discern national trends from Senate elections, but often these may originate more in the interpretation of the result by the relevant political actors in Washington than in the reality of the totality of individual Senate races in any given year.

Senate Campaigns: Implications for Representation and Governance

Since 1980, the margin of control in the U.S. Senate has been relatively close. As a result, the biennial elections for control of the Senate have been strongly contested by the national political parties and interest groups. In fact, Senate elections as a whole have become more nationalized than they used to be in every sense. Although idiosyncratic factors and personalities—and the overwhelming fact of incumbency—still matter, the macro-level factors described earlier are increasingly dominating elections.

This shift reflects in part the nationalization of government since the New Deal and the national focus of the major news media, and in part the strength of ideological party and interest group activists nationwide. Increasingly, the same groups are active in behalf of the candidates of one party or the other in each state. Labor unions, teachers' unions, feminists, environmentalists, African Americans, Hispanics, and gay and lesbian activists strongly back Democratic candidates. Large and small business interests, church-goers, white males, gun owners, and married voters with children back the Republicans. This division is as true of Massachusetts as it is of Texas; the proportions of each group in the electorate simply vary state by state.

These groups make a major contribution to Senate races in money, but, more important, in organization and voter mobilization. Their activists vote and vote consistently, constituting a disproportionate element of the general electorate (where turnout varies between around 50 percent in presidential years to under 40 percent in midterm years) and even more so of the primary electorate. Candidates thus have to pay particular attention to these groups and deviate from their agendas at their own peril if they wish to secure party nominations. All of this has the effect of leading to partisan and ideological polarization in Senate campaigns.

Much has been made of the rising rates of candidate personal spending and campaign spending in Senate elections. But in view of the high costs of television advertising—the principal medium of Senate campaigns these days—the trend toward greater spending is not so surprising, and the spending per voter in the United States is still relatively low. The trend toward wealthy self-financed candidates is growing stronger and is unlikely to diminish, because such candidates have the ability to spend what it takes to win with little regulation. This trend, however, has some disturbing implications for American democracy and the representativeness of the Senate. The heavy spending and giving by political action committees in Senate races also have the somewhat unwholesome consequence of enhancing the access of these groups to the legislative process.

Overall, however, the polarization between the parties engendered by the electoral process is a more serious problem for the contemporary Senate than any "corruption" that may enter in through the financing of campaigns. With senators beholden to their partisan core voters, largely funded by the interest groups that sustain their party, and advised by political consultants and pollsters also closely associated with the party, the chamber that prides itself on its deliberation and the independent-mindedness of its members is becoming a partisan battleground.[17] This unhealthy development is reflected in the rising levels of party unity on Senate votes. It has been accompanied by increasingly partisan rhetoric on the Senate floor and more partisan charges levied in the press by Senate party leaders. The escalation in partisanship is hardly surprising, however, in view of the increasingly bitter, personalized, attack-oriented nature of Senate campaigns.

That said, the level of partisanship and polarization in the Senate has not reached the extraordinary levels of the U.S. House. The more ideologically diverse electorates of most states and the norms of the chamber still militate against that. Yet the current election process has driven the Senate into a degree of polarization that makes the chamber extremely difficult to operate on a day-to-day basis. Unlimited debate or the "filibuster," previously a weapon of last resort, has now become commonplace, because the minority party cannot afford to let down its grass-roots partisans on any significant issue before the Senate. With sixty votes required to cut off debate, the tactic is generally successful if the minority party is united, which these days, because of the factors just described, it generally is on most matters.

The Senate was intended to be the chamber that encouraged reflection, prolonged deliberation, independence, and the tempering of popular passions in the forging of legislation. Because of the evolution of the electoral process, the contemporary Senate reflects and even encourages such passions rather than restraining them.

Notes

1. Michael Barone and Richard E. Cohen, *The Almanac of American Politics, 2004* (Washington, D.C.: National Journal, 2003).

2. Gary C. Jacobson, *The Politics of Congressional Elections,* 6th ed. (New York: Pearson Longman, 2004).

3. Frances E. Lee and Bruce I. Oppenheimer, *Sizing Up the Senate: The Unequal Consequences of Equal Representation* (Chicago: University of Chicago Press, 1999).

4. Ibid., and Jacobson, *Politics of Congressional Elections.*

5. Kevin A. Hill, Susan A. MacManus, and Dario Moreno, eds., *Florida's Politics: Ten Media Markets, One Powerful State* (Tallahassee: Florida Institute of Government, 2004).

6. Jacobson, *Politics of Congressional Elections.*

7. Ibid.

8. Gary C. Jacobson and Samuel Kernell, *Strategy and Choice in Congressional Elections,* 2d ed. (New Haven, Conn.: Yale University Press, 1983).

9. Jacobson, *Politics of Congressional Elections,* 84.

10. Paul S. Herrnson, *Congressional Elections: Campaigning at Home and in Washington,* 4th ed. (Washington, D.C.: CQ Press, 2004), 160.

11. Ibid., 92.

12. Ibid., 145.

13. Barry C. Burden, "The Polarizing Effects of Congressional Primaries," in *Congressional Primaries and the Politics of Representation,* ed. Peter F. Galderisi, Marni Ezra, and Michael Lyons (Lanham, Md.: Rowman and Littlefield, 2001), 95–115 .

14. Steven E. Schier, *By Invitation Only: The Rise of Exclusive Politics in the United States* (Pittsburgh: University of Pittsburgh Press, 2000).

15. Ibid.

16. Lee and Oppenheimer, *Sizing Up the Senate.*

17. Alan I. Abramowitz, "Party Realignment, Ideological Polarization, and Voting Behavior in U.S. Senate Elections," in *U.S. Senate Exceptionalism,* ed. Bruce I. Oppenheimer (Columbus: Ohio State University Press, 2002) , 31–44; Jacobson, *Politics of Congressional Elections.*

Suggested Readings

Abramowitz, Alan I. "Party Realignment, Ideological Polarization, and Voting Behavior in U.S. Senate Elections." In *U.S. Senate Exceptionalism,* edited by Bruce I. Oppenheimer, 31–44. Columbus: Ohio State University Press, 2002.

Barone, Michael, and Richard E. Cohen. *The Almanac of American Politics, 2004.* Washington, D.C.: National Journal, 2003.

Burden, Barry C. "The Polarizing Effects of Congressional Primaries." In *Congressional Primaries and the Politics of Representation,* edited by Peter F. Galderisi, Marni Ezra, and Michael Lyons, 95–115. Lanham, Md.: Rowman and Littlefield, 2001.

Herrnson, Paul S. *Congressional Elections: Campaigning at Home and in Washington.* 4th ed. Washington, D.C.: CQ Press, 2004.

Hill, Kevin A., Susan A. MacManus, and Dario Moreno, eds. *Florida's Politics: Ten Media Markets, One Powerful State* Tallahassee: Florida Institute of Government, 2004.

Jacobson, Gary C. *The Politics of Congressional Elections.* 6th ed. New York: Pearson Longman, 2004.

Jacobson, Gary C., and Samuel Kernell. *Strategy and Choice in Congressional Elections.* 2d ed. New Haven, Conn.: Yale University Press, 1983.

Lee, Frances E., and Bruce I. Oppenheimer. *Sizing Up the Senate: The Unequal Consequences of Equal Representation.* Chicago: University of Chicago Press, 1999.

Schier, Steven E. *By Invitation Only: The Rise of Exclusive Politics in the United States.* Pittsburgh: University of Pittsburgh Press, 2000.

Sinclair, Barbara. "The '60-Vote Senate': Strategies, Process, and Outcomes." In *U.S. Senate Exceptionalism,* edited by Bruce I. Oppenheimer, 241–282. Columbus: Ohio State University Press, 2002.

CHAPTER 23

Gubernatorial Campaigns

Gary F. Moncrief

Just as the office of governor has changed over the years, so have campaigns for that office. Gubernatorial campaigns in virtually every state are media-driven, expensive races, requiring a complex organization that seeks to reach and persuade a statewide audience. But not all gubernatorial campaigns are the same. There are variations born of the differences in the legal and political context from state to state and of the circumstances surrounding the array of candidates and issues in any given election.

The Legal Context

Candidates running for various political offices in the United States must meet any legal constraints imposed on the office. One obvious constraint is the minimum age requirement found in state constitutions. These range from eighteen years (in six states, including California and Ohio) to thirty-one years (Oklahoma). Over half of states set the minimum age at thirty. In 2003 the youngest governor in the United States was forty years old (Democrat Brad Henry of Oklahoma), and only three others were forty-five or younger.

Some states also impose minimum residency requirements. In three states (Alabama, Alaska, and Tennessee), one must be a citizen of the state for a minimum of seven years. In Rhode Island, by contrast, one can run for gubernatorial office after establishing residency for thirty days. The reality, however, is that most serious gubernatorial candidates are longtime residents of their state.

Other legal constraints also affect the office of governor, some of which have changed substantially in many states over the years.

Terms of Office

One of the obvious changes in the office of governor is the length of the term of office (see Table 23-1). A century ago, the term of office for most governors was one or two years. As recently as fifty years ago, governors in seventeen states served two-year terms. Today, only two states, Vermont and New Hampshire, still have a two-year term

for their governors; all other states have four-year terms. Also years ago, many states limited their governor to one term. Now, only Virginia imposes a single term of office, although about 75 percent of states limit the governor to two consecutive terms.[1] About a dozen states currently permit unlimited tenure for governors, including Illinois, Massachusetts, New York, and Texas.

The upshot is that governors tend to stay in office for longer periods today than previously—on average about twice as long. This longer tenure not only frees governors from constant reelection concerns, but also gives them more time to build a policy record in office. Consequently, the office is more attractive today than in earlier times. Noting the move toward four-year gubernatorial terms from two-year terms and toward more than one term in office, Stephen Salmore and Barbara Salmore point out that "part of the advantage of incumbency is related to structural enhancements of the office. . . . A clear correlation exists between the strengthening of the governor's position and the proportion of incumbents both seeking reelection and gaining it." [2]

Campaign Finance Laws

Because the governorship is a state office, it is subject to state campaign finance laws, which vary substantially from state to state (see Table 23-2). For example, in Alabama, Pennsylvania, and about a dozen other states, there are no limits on how much an individual or PAC (political action committee, the funding mechanism for interest groups) can contribute to a candidate. In Montana, an individual or PAC can give a maximum of $800 to a candidate—$400 for the primary and $400 for the general election. In Florida, the limit is $1,000 ($500 for the primary and $500 for the general election). In some states, then, a candidate must tap many small contributors in order to build an adequate campaign fund, while in other states a candidate's campaign can be financed by just a few large donors.

States may vary in their laws on contribution limits, but the U.S. Supreme Court ruled in *Buckley v. Valeo* in 1976 that no legal limit can be placed on the amount a candidate may spend. A few states, however, have

Table 23-1 Change in Length of Governors' Term of Office: 1904, 1954, 2004

Term of office	1904 (45 states)	1954 (48 states)	2004 (50 states)
One year	2	0	0
Two years	21	17	2
Three years	1	0	0
Four years	21	31	48

Source: Calculated by author from data in Congressional Quarterly, *Gubernatorial Elections, 1787–1997* (Washington, D.C.: CQ Press, 1998), 2.

Note: Arizona, New Mexico, and Oklahoma were admitted to the Union between 1907 and 1912; Alaska and Hawaii were admitted in 1959.

adopted a "clean elections" system, in which candidates can voluntarily choose to limit their spending in exchange for public funding, largely freeing the candidates from the need to raise money from individuals and PACs. In Arizona, these public funds come from a voluntary income tax checkoff and surcharges on traffic fines and other court fines. In the 2002 election in Arizona, most of the gubernatorial candidates (including the winning candidate) opted for the public funds and voluntary spending limits.

Although about fifteen states now employ some measure of public funding for gubernatorial elections, making useful generalizations is difficult because the state public funding laws are quite different.[3] For example, substantial public funding for gubernatorial campaigns is in place today in several states, including Arizona, Maine, Minnesota, Kentucky, and Vermont, whereas other states have a more limited system involving only small amounts of money that go only to the political parties, not the candidates. Often in these instances the public funds generated are quite small.

Recent research on the effects of public financing in governor's races has uncovered mixed results. For example, Donald Gross and Robert Goidel found that the system worked very well in Kentucky in 1995—the election was more competitive than past ones and spending was contained—but that it did not achieve its goals in the 1999 election.[4] Overall, their assessment is that public

Table 23-2 Campaign Contribution Limits for Gubernatorial Elections

	Individual	PAC	Political party
$1,000 or less	Alaska, Fla., Maine, Mass., Mont., S.Dak., Vt.	Alaska, Colo., Fla., Maine, Mass., Mont., Vt.	
$1,001–$5,000	Ariz., Ark., Conn., Del., Kans., Ky., Md., Mich., Minn., Mo., Nev., N.H., N.J., Ohio, R.I., S.C., Tenn., Wash., W.Va., Wyo.	Ariz., Ark., Conn., Del., Ky., Mich., Minn., Mo., N.H., Ohio, R.I., S.C., Wash., W.Va.	Mass., W.Va.
$5,001–$10,000	Colo., Hawaii, Idaho, La., Ga., N.C., Okla.	Ga., Hawaii, Idaho, La., Md., Nev., N.C., Okla.	Ark., Ga., Hawaii, Idaho, Md., Nev.
$10,001–$50,000	N.Y., Wis.	Calif., N.J., N.Y., Tenn., Wis.	Fla., Mo., Minn., Mont., R.I.
$50,001–$100,000			Alaska, Ariz., Del., Mich., Okla., S.C.
$250,000–$1,100,000			Colo., Neb., Ohio, Tenn., Wash., Wis.
Unlimited	Ala., Calif., Ill., Ind., Iowa, Miss., Neb., N.Mex., N.Dak., Ore., Pa., Tex., Utah, Va.	Ala., Ill., Ind., Iowa, Miss., Neb., N.Mex., N.Dak., Ore., Pa., S.Dak., Tex., Utah, Va., Wyo.	Ala., Calif., Conn., Ill., Ind., Iowa, Kans., Ky., La., Maine, Miss., N.H., N.J., N.Mex., N.Y., N.C., N.Dak., Ore., Pa., S.Dak., Tex., Utah, Vt., Va., Wyo.

Source: Figures calculated by the author from data available from the National Conference of State Legislatures.

Note: Figures are for electoral cycle (includes primary and general election). Some states distinguish between "small donor," "regular," and "super" political action committees (PACs). Figures in the table are for regular PACs.

financing, under the right conditions, can help to level the playing field between candidates in campaign spending. This is largely because public financing allows challengers, who are usually at a distinct fund-raising disadvantage compared with incumbents, to somewhat close the spending gap. Gross and Goidel also find some evidence that public funding leads indirectly to more competitive elections (the vote margin between winners and losers is less) and a small increase in voter turnout. They are careful to note, however, that most of these consequences are relatively minor. Because few gubernatorial elections are substantially publicly financed, firm conclusions about the effect of public financing cannot yet be made. Moreover, as Michael Malbin and Thomas Gais demonstrate, spending limits linked to public funding for candidates cannot control independent spending by individuals or PACS.[5]

The Political Context

Like the legal issues, the political context surrounding gubernatorial campaigns differs from state to state. In those states in which one party is dominant, the minority party may have difficulty finding a qualified candidate to run. By contrast, the dominant party may have an abundance of candidates, leading to a crowded primary contest. The timing of elections and the nominating processes also vary from state to state.

Separating State from National Elections

An important change in the political context of gubernatorial elections is the trend toward moving elections for statewide office away from the presidential election year. It has been suggested that this "decoupling" from the national elections has been part of an effort to unhitch the gubernatorial election from the issues and events surrounding the presidential election.[6] Until the 1930s, about 70 percent of the states held their election for governor in the presidential election year; now only about 20 percent do so. A few states (Kentucky, Louisiana, Mississippi, New Jersey, and Virginia) hold their statewide elections in odd-numbered years, distancing themselves from even congressional elections.

The Nominating Process

One of the more distinctive characteristics of the U.S. electoral system is the widespread use of primary elections to select each party's nominee for the general election. The idea behind holding a primary election is to allow input into the nominating process by a large group of voters rather than leaving the selection up to a small group of the party leaders. The trend toward primary elections began in the states roughly a century ago as a cornerstone of the Progressive reform movement. Within

fifty years, almost all states were using primaries as a mechanism for gubernatorial nominations, and today all states use primaries (also see Chapter 5, which describes in detail the nominating process).

But not all state primary electoral systems are alike. The most important difference is that a handful of states—such as Colorado, Connecticut, and New York—use a mechanism known as the "preprimary endorsement." The endorsement occurs in a party convention some time prior to the primary election. It allows the party elite (those party members most active in and committed to the welfare of the political party) to indicate on the primary ballot which candidate is the party's nominee. The convention delegates "are usually party activists, persons who work frequently in local, state, or national campaigns."[7]

The endorsement mechanism permits the party elite to influence, but not absolutely determine, the outcome of the nominating process. In recent decades, the endorsed candidate has won the primary about 75 percent of the time, often because no other candidate will challenge an endorsed candidate in the primary.[8] The endorsed candidates are likely to be longtime party "insiders" who have held elective office. The importance of the endorsement mechanism is that it often gives the endorsed nominee a fund-raising advantage and organizational support that makes it more difficult for party mavericks to win the nomination in the primary.

For a candidate seeking a party's endorsement, the process adds another phase to the campaign that requires the candidate's time, energy, and organizational resources. The tactics used in seeking an endorsement differ from those used in the primary election (or general election, for that matter). Candidates must rely on their personal contacts and reputation among the party elite. The campaign is one in which the candidate must contact individual caucus or convention delegates and argue persuasively why the delegate's support is warranted. The type of media campaign evident in the primary election, and especially in the general election, will not be found at this stage. Money is not the immediate issue; ideology, the candidate's relationship and standing within the party, and the candidate's potential to win in the general election are the critical concerns.

Overall, the value of the party endorsement appears to have declined. At one time, 90 percent of endorsed candidates won the party primary. It appears now, however, that self-financed, wealthy "outsiders" can occasionally overcome the advantages of the party endorsement. Sometimes, it is not an outsider but another insider who decides to challenge the convention endorsement. This is precisely what happened in Minnesota in 1998 among the Democrats (known in Minnesota as the Democratic Farm Labor Party), when five well-known candidates sought the endorsement. The party rules stipulated that to obtain an endorsement a candidate must receive 60 percent of

BOX 23-1
PROFILES OF FOUR GUBERNATORIAL RACES
Jeff Davis

The job description and power of the chief executive position differ in each of the fifty states, but gubernatorial campaigns nationwide are similar in many ways. For example, a candidate generally needs considerable name recognition to become governor—that is, a candidate whose name is familiar to the public before the campaign does better on election day. Thus, governors who have already served their states for at least one term are likely to be reelected. Likewise, those candidates with previous lawmaking experience have an advantage over less experienced candidates.

The following case studies describe four recent gubernatorial races. Some of these cases illustrate the attributes that most elections for governor have in common. Others are examples of exceptions to the rule. Either way, each case sheds light on the complexities of these kinds of elections and what it takes to become governor.

1994 Texas Gubernatorial Campaign

Before he was elected president in 2000, George W. Bush was governor of Texas.[1] To win that office, Bush had to oust the incumbent, a task that often proves to be a challenge. In this case, the incumbent was a popular Democrat, Ann Richards, who had served as governor for four years.

After an unsuccessful bid for Congress in 1978, Bush returned to politics in 1994 to run against Richards as she sought a second term. In a highly competitive race that gained national attention, Bush raised more

money than any candidate for any office in Texas history. The campaign was one of the most expensive in the country, with the candidates spending together more than $26 million.

A year before the election, Richards seemed sure to win another term. She led Bush in all the polls and enjoyed support throughout the state. But Bush's name and celebrity status as the owner of the Texas Rangers baseball team began to fuel his campaign. Taking advantage of the trend of conservatism across the state and the nation, Bush was able to turn voters' attention away from Richard's popularity and the state's stable economy.

By means of television commercial spots and other expensive campaign tools, Bush attacked Richards's inaction on crime, while Richards defended her record and called Bush a bad businessman. In the end, Bush outlined a clear plan of what he

Texas Governor Ann Richards
Source: G. Reed Schumann/Reuters/Landov

would do in office and Richards's support faded away. Bush easily beat Richards with 54 percent of the vote to Richards's 45 percent.

1998 Minnesota Gubernatorial Campaign

In 1998 the people of Minnesota shocked the nation when they elected Jesse Ventura as the state's governor.[2] Ventura's win stunned so many people across the country not just because he had run on a Reform Party ticket, but also because he was a former professional wrestler. The governor's race was open after the former governor chose not to seek reelection. This left Ventura to face Democrat Hubert "Skip" Humphrey III and Republican Norm Coleman. Humphrey, the state's attorney general and son of the late vice president, was the early front-runner because of his name recognition. Coleman was the mayor of St. Paul.

The campaign received attention nationally, because Ventura brought a young and enthusiastic edge to the race. He was one of the first candidates to use the Internet to his advantage, maintaining a Web site and using e-mail to gather and contact thousands of volunteers. This campaign style attracted many young voters, and the uniqueness of the race brought out more voters than usual to vote—a 61 percent turnout compared with a 37 percent national average. Ventura won by only three percentage points. Many political analysts point to the state's young voters as the reason for his narrow victory.

The campaign's fund-raising also bucked national trends. Both Humphrey and Coleman raised $2.5 million, and their parties and political action committees spent several million dollars more. Although more money generally gives candidates an advantage in gubernatorial races, Ventura spent just $500,000 and went on to win.

2000 Indiana Gubernatorial Campaign

After serving as lieutenant governor of Indiana from 1988 to 1996 and then as governor for four years, Democrat Frank O'Bannon launched a bid for reelection in March 2000.[3] Riding on the popularity of his first term in office, O'Bannon ran his campaign on promises to maintain a strong economy. To challenge the incumbent, Republican David McIntosh promised to cut property taxes by 25 percent. He even vowed not to run for a second term if he did not live up to this goal. McIntosh chose to battle O'Bannon for governor instead of running for a fourth term in Congress, a race that would have proven much easier than unseating the popular incumbent.

Even with his platform of cutting taxes, McIntosh was unable to diminish O'Bannon's support. Many Republicans who normally would have backed the candidate promising lower taxes supported O'Bannon. The incumbent held a steady lead in the polls throughout the campaign, and in November O'Bannon easily won reelection with 56 percent of the vote. McIntosh earned 42 percent, and libertarian candidate Andrew Horning won 2 percent. O'Bannon's win extended the Democratic control of the governor's office to sixteen years. This was the longest stretch of the party's power since the Civil War.

2002 Massachusetts Gubernatorial Campaign

Mitt Romney became governor of Massachusetts in 2002 after enduring

Massachusetts gubernatorial candidate Mitt Romney
Source: *Brian Snyder/Reuters/Landov*

a tight race that was the most expensive in the state's history.[4] Romney, a Republican who had served as chair of the 2002 Salt Lake City Winter Olympics, won his first political position after defeating Democratic state treasurer Shannon O'Brien. The candidates spent $50 million on the race, mainly on campaign commercials.

Romney's win continued the Republicans' control of the governor's office, which the party had held for the last twelve years. Democrats in Massachusetts outnumber Republicans by nearly three to one, and O'Brien campaigned to the largely liberal population of the state in the hope that Democrats could take back the governorship and add to the party's control of the state House and Senate.

The GOP's efforts to maintain control of the state's executive office were extensive. The acting governor, Republican Jane Swift, withdrew from the Republican primary in response to Romney's popularity and prospects of winning. She noted that her withdrawal would give the party a better chance of retaining control of the governor's office. Although the race was close and O'Brien led in the polls prior to the election, Romney

came back from behind to win the general election.

1. This section relies on coverage by CNN, www.cnn.com/ELECTION/ 2004/special/president/candidates/ bush.html (accessed May 2, 2005); Anne Pressley, "Bush Defeats Richards for Texas Governorship," *Washington Post*, November 9, 1994, A27; and R. G. Ratcliffe, "Bush Sweeps by Richards; Close Race Crumbles as Republican Scores Easy Win," *Houston Chronicle*, November 9, 1994, A1.

2. www.politicsonline.com/coverage/ nytimes2/06campaign.html (accessed May 2, 2005), and CNN, www.cnn .com/ALLPOLITICS/stories/1998/11/ 03/election/governors/minnesota/ (accessed May 2, 2005).

3. This section relies on coverage by the *Indianapolis Star*, www.indystar .com/library/factfiles/gov/politics/ election2000/gov-race.html (accessed May 2, 2005).

4. This section relies on coverage by CNN, www.cnn.com/2002/ ALL POLITICS/03/19/massachusetts .governor/ (accessed May 2, 2005), and PBS, www.pbs.org/newshour/ vote 2002/races/ma_gov_11-6.html (accessed May 2, 2005).

the convention delegate votes. On the tenth ballot, Mike Freeman reached the 60 percent threshold and received the party's endorsement. But all four of the nonendorsed candidates remained in the primary race—essentially challenging the party endorsement—and Hubert "Skip" Humphrey III won the nomination with 37 percent of the total primary vote. Three other candidates, including Freeman, received between 18 and 19 percent of the vote each, and the fifth candidate received 7 percent. As Jacob Lentz notes, "In terms of choosing a nominee, the endorsing convention was completely ineffectual." [9]

Another major distinction in the nominating process is whether the primary is "open" or "closed." The difference is largely one of who is allowed to vote in the party primary. Generally, in a closed primary system only those registered Republicans can vote in the Republican primary, and only registered Democrats can vote in the Democratic primary. Independents are excluded. In an open primary system, any voter can vote in either party primary. Thus eligible voters without a party affiliation can vote and influence the choice of nominee in one of the party primaries. Moreover, a Republican voter could vote in the Democratic primary or a Democrat in the Republican primary, although there is not much evidence that it happens regularly.

The practical implication of the two kinds of primaries for candidates is that somewhat different segments of the electorate may be targeted in an open primary than in a closed primary. In open primaries, the introduction of independent voters into the equation may mean that moderate candidates are more likely to be nominated, whereas in the closed primaries the more extreme factions of each party may have a greater influence. Although this assumption is logical, there does not appear to be much empirical evidence to either support or dispute it. Moreover, one might expect open primaries, which could potentially draw more eligible voters than closed primaries, to generate a higher voter turnout. Yet again, there does not seem to be much evidence one way or the other.

The Candidates

"Quality candidates" find the governorship an attractive office. As chief executive, the governor is the single most influential policy maker in the state. Moreover, recently most states have substantially increased the compensation of their governors. Only three states—Arkansas, Maine, and Nebraska—pay their governors less than $80,000 a year, whereas another three states—California, Michigan and New York—pay their governors at least $175,000 a year. Most states compensate their governors more than $100,000. Although these figures are clearly not on a par with what chief executive officers make in

Thomas Jefferson of Virginia was the first of seventeen state governors who went on to become president. Since 1977, all presidents except George H. W. Bush have been former governors. Source: Library of Congress

the private sector, they are a substantial improvement over the gubernatorial salaries of twenty years ago.

Another reason the governorship is attractive is that it often serves as a springboard to federal offices such as the U.S. Senate or a cabinet-level position. Except for the administration of George Bush (1989–1993), a former governor has occupied the White House since 1977.

Over time, those seeking governorships have followed fairly predictable career paths. The most common historically is service in the state legislature—about half of all governors have served in those bodies. About one in three began public service in local offices such as mayor, city councilor, or district attorney. But where they began is not as instructive as where they were immediately before their election to the governorship. Thad Beyle reports that of the governors in office in 2003, seventeen held some other statewide office (such as lieutenant governor or attorney general) just prior to winning the governor's office. Nine had been in the U.S. Congress, and seven moved up from the state legislature.[10] Thus these statewide or legislative offices are the most common springboard from which to mount a successful run for the governor's office.

Yet holding statewide office is no guarantee of a successful run for the governorship. In fact, many such candidates lose in either the primary or the general election. According to Beyle, more than 60 percent of lieutenant governors, attorneys general, state auditors, and treasurers lose in their bids for the governor's office.[11]

Two recent trends in career paths bear mentioning. First, a slightly larger proportion of governors are coming directly from the U.S. Congress than was the case previously. This trend probably reflects the recent greater role for the states in federalism and the belief of some in Congress that they can more fully accomplish their policy goals as an executive rather than a legislative official. The second trend is the increase in the number of those who have no political experience who have run successfully for the governor's office. By late 2003, nine governors had held no prior elective office. Many of these individuals were quite wealthy, suggesting that the higher cost of running for office made them more viable candidates than in the past.

Voting in Gubernatorial Elections

Voter turnout in gubernatorial elections varies widely from state to state. In those states (about forty) that hold gubernatorial elections in nonpresidential years, the average voter turnout was from 41 to 46 percent between 1978 and 1998.[12] As might be expected, states that hold their gubernatorial elections in presidential years experience a higher turnout by about 10 to 12 percent.

Differences in turnout from state to state are influenced by other factors as well, including party competition, region, and political culture. Between 1978 and 1998, voter turnout averaged about 65 percent in Montana, South Dakota, and Utah, and was almost 60 percent in Washington and Missouri. At the other end of the spectrum, the average turnout in the southern states of Georgia, Kentucky, South Carolina, Tennessee, and Texas was 35 percent or less during the same twenty-year period.

A relatively small but growing body of research exists on the factors that affect the vote for governor. This question has become more important in recent years, as the prestige and importance of the office of governor has grown. Most of the research takes a macroanalytic approach—that is, it looks at the effect of *aggregate* measures on the vote shares received by candidates. Some research, however, takes the form of microanalysis—that is, asking *individual* voters how they voted and why. The answers to these two types of questions should be related, but there are some inconsistencies in findings. For example, there is some disagreement as to whether national economic forces or state-level economic forces have the greater influence on voters' decisions in gubernatorial elections.[13] Nevertheless, virtually all the studies agree that the single most important variable is partisan loyalty. Individual voters who strongly identify with one of the

two major political parties are less likely to "defect" and vote for a gubernatorial candidate from the other party. It makes sense, then, that states in which one party enjoys a substantial advantage in party registration or identification are more likely to show some consistency in the vote patterns for governor. But this situation provides only an advantage, not a guarantee. Idaho is an example of a state in which the Republican Party enjoys a substantial advantage in partisan identification, but Democratic candidates won six consecutive gubernatorial elections from 1970 through 1990. Another example is Massachusetts, which is predominantly Democratic and yet has had three Republican governors since 1991. Thus, although partisanship is the single strongest correlate of the vote, other factors are clearly involved, including voter reaction to the characteristics of candidates and the issues at the forefront of the election.

The Incumbent Advantage

One of the most important factors in any gubernatorial race is the presence or absence of an incumbent—incumbent governors have a clear advantage, winning about 80 percent of the time. Indeed, incumbency is an advantage in virtually all U.S. elections because of name recognition, the ability to command media attention, the opportunity to establish a record of achievement, and experience in running campaigns, including how to put together a campaign organization and how to raise funds. All of these factors mean that for incumbent governors, the race for reelection is theirs to lose.

But the advantage of incumbency can be overcome. In 1990 six of the twenty-three incumbent governors (26 percent) who ran for reelection lost. As Malcolm Jewell and Sarah Morehouse note, "Governors have no choice but to run on their record; sometimes this is a major asset and sometimes it is a burden."[14] The public may hold the governor responsible for any personal actions such as ethical breaches. And certainly the voters can hold the incumbent responsible for the handling of specific policies, such as education reform or a tax increase. For example, incumbent New Jersey governor James J. Florio was defeated in 1993 after he pushed through a tax increase. Apparently, this is not an isolated case. There is evidence that governors who raise taxes are indeed punished in subsequent elections.[15] Voters also may hold governors responsible for events that occur on their administrative "watch," even though governors may not have had much control over those events.

Challenger Quality

Sometimes, an election is determined as much by who stays out of the race as by who chooses to run. Good potential candidates may choose not to run under several, relatively predictable circumstances. For example, knowing that incumbents are difficult to beat, some potential candidates will stay out of the race, biding their time until the incumbent vacates the office. These potential candidates are behaving "strategically," waiting until the odds of winning shift. Peverill Squire has demonstrated that open-seat races draw higher-profile candidates than does the role of challenger when an incumbent is running.[16] But he also found that these strategic politicians may enter the race if they think economic conditions have made the incumbent vulnerable. Others have noted that the governor's party is likely to take an electoral hit if taxes were increased during the governor's administration.[17] Strategic politicians may be more likely to enter the fray against an incumbent when taxes were raised.

The Role of National Issues in Gubernatorial Elections

Presumably, one of the main arguments for moving statewide (including gubernatorial) elections to nonpresidential years was that this "decoupling" would mute the effect of national issues on state elections. Nevertheless, it appears that gubernatorial elections cannot entirely escape national issues. Particularly relevant here is "retrospective voting," the phenomenon by which voters cast their ballots on the basis of their assessments of economic conditions.

There is evidence that the gubernatorial candidate from the president's party is rewarded or punished by voters based on their assessment of the condition of the national economy.[18] But other research finds that national trends are less important in retrospective voting than the economic trends within the state.[19] Recent researchers find a connection between a state's economic conditions and popularity of its governor, which, presumably, would affect the vote in the gubernatorial election.[20]

At least one study finds that the connection between a state's economic conditions and its gubernatorial vote applies only under conditions of unified government—that is, when the governor and the legislative majority are of the same party.[21] In other words, voters are more likely to affix economic responsibility to the governor's party when the governor has a majority to work with in the legislature. Under circumstances of divided government—that is, when one party controls the governor's office and the other controls the legislature—it is harder to hold the governor responsible for economic conditions.

Does the Governor Have Coattails?

Some political observers believe that a successful gubernatorial candidate can help fellow party members running for lower state offices (so-called down-ballot candidates) win election. The theory is that voters who turn out to elect a particular candidate for governor may be more likely to vote for candidates from the governor's party in races for other offices such as state legislator. Nu-

merous journalistic analyses indicate such a coattails effect, but the empirical evidence is quite limited; there simply has not been empirical research on the subject. On the one hand, the prevalence of divided government (one party controls the legislature, the other party controls the executive branch) at the state level suggests that gubernatorial coattails are quite limited—otherwise, one would expect the governor's party to win legislative majorities.[22] As campaigns become more candidate-centered and less party-oriented, it is only logical that coattails will be less important. On the other hand, there is some limited evidence that the gubernatorial vote provides a modest increase in the vote share for legislative candidates of the same party.[23]

Running a Statewide Campaign

By now it should be clear that a serious run for the governorship must be considered within the political context of the state. States vary in degree of party competition, campaign finance rules, and nominating systems. All of these factors affect campaign strategy. States also vary in demographics, which, too, affects how campaigns are run. For example, in Minnesota 80 percent of the population lives within the Minneapolis–St. Paul media market, so a candidate would concentrate television media buys in the Twin Cities area. The same scenario applies in Utah and the Salt Lake City metropolitan area. In New Jersey, most of the major television outlets that reach the state are actually in New York or Pennsylvania, which means that television advertising is extremely expensive, and much of it is "wasted" in that it reaches viewers who cannot vote in the New Jersey gubernatorial election. In Wyoming, candidates must travel long distances to reach relatively small numbers of potential voters.

In some states, important regional differences in partisanship and political culture shape where a candidate spends campaigns and what issues the candidate emphasizes. For example, in Washington State the Cascade mountain range represents a basic ideological divide; the eastern part of the state is far more conservative than the coastal area. Similar ideological and political watersheds are found in Illinois between Chicago and "downstate" and in Tennessee, between the eastern and western parts of the state.

Putting Together a Campaign Team

Volumes have been written about how political campaigns have changed in the United States (also see Chapters 14–19 in this volume). The most important changes of relevance here are (1) the current greater reliance on a campaign team put together by the candidate rather than the traditional party organization; (2) the prevalence of mass media advertising in efforts to reach voters; and (3) the increased specialization of campaign tasks and the professionalization of those who manage those tasks. The three trends are related.

With the possible exception of those in a few rural states, gubernatorial campaigns today are media-driven. Media advertising costs make up perhaps 70 to 75 percent of the expenditures of a typical gubernatorial campaign. The reasons are not hard to discern. With the decline in strong party identification about a generation ago in the United States came a decline in the ability of the political party to mobilize large numbers of volunteers to work on campaigns. At about the same time, television became a commonplace item in America's living rooms and therefore an efficient (albeit an expensive) way to reach potential voters. Later, new computer and communications technologies enhanced the ability of campaigns to efficiently reach individual voters through direct mail and automated telephone banks. As television advertising and new technologies gained use and party organizations atrophied, candidates began to hire professionals to manage aspects of their campaigns. Thus campaigns were transformed from party-organized affairs to specialist-organized and candidate-centered endeavors.

Almost any viable statewide campaign today will include the following professionals: a campaign manager, pollster, media consultant, fund-raiser, event scheduler, press relations specialist, and field organizer (these positions are described more fully in Chapters 14–19).[24] The campaign manager runs the day-to-day operations and is usually the person in closest contact with the candidate. The pollster designs, implements, and analyzes benchmark polls (early surveys to determine a candidate's name recognition and assessment by potential voters) and tracking polls (daily polls conducted toward the end of a campaign to assess the effects of a candidate's issue positions and campaign tactics) in order to gauge how the campaign is resonating with likely voters. The media consultant designs radio and television ads and negotiates the purchase of airtime (media buys) with television and radio stations. Because statewide campaigns are expensive, professional fund-raisers are hired to solicit campaign contributions. The event scheduler often works closely with the fund-raiser to organize fund-raising events such as dinners and cocktail parties and also schedules the candidate for rallies, speeches, and media events. A press relations specialist drafts and distributes press releases and works to ensure that events and speeches at which the candidate appears receive television and newspaper coverage. A direct-mail specialist may also be hired to manage the direct-mail campaign—the variety of brochures and flyers sent to targeted voters. Finally, the field organizer directs the network of volunteers in the different communities of the state. Sometimes, but not always, the field organizer will be working with local party officials.

Most, if not all, of the people hired for these positions are professional consultants (see Chapter 10). Many of these consultants work only for candidates of one particular party. Their allegiance is short-term (basically from date of hire to election day), and they work for the candidate, not the party organization. In this sense, they operate as free agents, hiring on during the campaign and then moving on to another campaign the next year or election cycle—for example, they may work on a gubernatorial campaign in Virginia one year and a Missouri congressional campaign the following year.

Similarities and Differences between Gubernatorial and U.S. Senatorial Campaigns

The campaigns for governor and U.S. senator are similar in some ways. The most obvious one is the electoral constituency; both are statewide elections. Both offices are also highly visible, attracting more attention than elections for other statewide offices such as state attorney general or secretary of state. As Peverill Squire and Christina Fastnow point out, "Both are high profile offices whose occupants are regularly viewed as national leaders and potential presidential candidates."[25] For these reasons, the costs and tactics of campaigning are comparable. Both kinds of races require similar campaign organizations, and they must run statewide media campaigns, relying heavily on television to reach the voters.

But there are some differences as well. First, the issues on which the gubernatorial and Senate campaigns are run are often different, because the governor, as a state executive officer, is more concerned with issues at the state level, such as education and the local economy, and a senator is a member of the federal legislature and so is more concerned with national issues such as foreign relations. Second, incumbent governors are somewhat more vulnerable to electoral defeat; throughout the latter part of the twentieth century, incumbent governors averaged about a 5 percent smaller vote margin than incumbent U.S. senators. Third, governors, who are generally better known to the voters than are U.S. senators from the state, are often held more responsible for the condition of the state economy than U.S. senators are held accountable for the condition of the national economy.[26]

Comparing campaign costs between gubernatorial and Senate races is a little risky. With so few races (between thirty and forty) for each office in any given electoral cycle, average spending may vary widely from year to year because of idiosyncratic factors. That said, it is probably safe to say that gubernatorial campaigns are generally more expensive than U.S. Senate races because of the more competitive nature of most governors' races and because more gubernatorial races are open-seat contests

Table 23-3 Top Ten Most Expensive Races for U.S. Senate and Governor, 2000 and 2002

Governor		U.S. Senate	
State and year	Amount ($ millions)	State and year	Amount ($ millions)
New York, 2002	$146.7	New York, 2000	$91.8
California, 2002	109.5	New Jersey, 2000	78.9
Texas, 2002	105.5	North Carolina, 2002	29.3
Pennsylvania, 2002	65.1	Minnesota, 2000	29.3
Illinois, 2002	48.6	Virginia, 2000	27.0
New Jersey, 2001	37.4	Minnesota, 2002	24.5
Virginia, 2001	34.6	Michigan, 2000	22.5
Massachusetts, 2002	30.6	Pennsylvania, 2000	22.4
South Carolina, 2002	29.6	New Jersey, 2002	22.3
North Carolina, 2000	29.3	Washington, 2000	21.0

Sources: Gubernatorial data: www.southnow.org; data compiled by Thad Beyle and Jennifer Jensen for *The Book of the States* (Lexington, Ky.: Council of State Governments, annual). Senate data: Center for Responsive Politics, "Most Expensive Races," www.opensecrets.org/.

Note: Figures represent total spending by all candidates.

(most governors are limited to two terms). In 2000 and 2002, only two U.S. Senate races exceeded $30 million in total spending: those in New York, $92 million, and New Jersey, $79 million (see Table 23-3). But in eight states gubernatorial candidates spent more than $30 million on their campaigns, and those in California, New York, and Texas spent over $100 million. There are exceptions, however. For example, candidates in the 2002 U.S. Senate race in Minnesota spent $24.5 million, whereas campaign spending in the governor's race in the same year was $6 million. Nevertheless, it is generally true that more money is spent in the governor's race.

The cost of running for office in the United States, including governorships, continues to rise. Over the past twenty years, gubernatorial election spending has increased by about 60 percent more than the rate of inflation. Yet the increase is *less* than the increase in spending for U.S. House and Senate races.[27] The next section examines spending of another kind—that incurred in removing a governor from office.

Recalling Governors

Although virtually all states may remove governors (and other state officials) through the impeachment process, only eighteen states recall by election. It is largely a western (nine states) and midwestern (five states) phenomenon. Only two southern states (Georgia and Louisiana) and two eastern states (New Jersey and Rhode Island) allow for recall elections.[28]

On October 7, 2003, California voters participated in one of the most bizarre elections in U.S. history. Gov. Gray Davis was recalled from office a mere eleven months after winning election to a second term. The recall was extraordinary for several reasons. First, Davis was not charged with any illegal or unethical behavior. Instead, the recall was motivated by a combination of frustration over the stagnant economy and unhappiness with specific policies of the Davis administration such as the electrical utility package brokered by Davis, his call for a hike in car license taxes, and his support for granting driver's licenses to undocumented immigrants. Partisan motivations were evident as well; the recall effort was largely funded and organized by Republican member of Congress Darrell Issa.

Second, the recall election actually involved two simultaneous votes: one vote on whether to recall and one vote on a "replacement"—that is, a vote for a specific candidate to replace the governor if indeed the recall vote was successful. Thus even voters who voted "no" on recall were asked to vote on a replacement. This decision structure is a highly unusual one in U.S. elections.

Third, the percentage of valid petition signatures necessary to trigger the recall election was relatively low—12 percent of the votes in the previous gubernatorial election.

Fourth, the rules for declaring candidacy as a replacement governor were quite open. Essentially, anyone who gathered sixty-five signatures and paid a filing fee of $3,500 could become a candidate. These rules resulted in a colorful field of 135 candidates that included Hollywood action-film star Arnold Schwarzenegger, author and political columnist Arianna Huffington, former commissioner of major league baseball Peter Ueberroth, former television star Gary Coleman, and the creator of the "Ask Jeeves" Web site search engine, Garrett Gruener.

Finally, the length of the campaign was relatively short by American standards—seventy-seven days from acceptance of the recall petition to election day. And it was conducted under new state campaign finance laws passed in California in 2000 but not in effect until after the 2002 election. The new campaign finance system established limits on how much an individual could contribute to a replacement candidate's campaign and also established a system of public funding for candidates who agreed to accept spending limits.

This combination of factors led to a situation in which wealthy candidates were advantaged by their ability to self-finance their campaigns (if they declined to accept public funding in exchange for spending limits). Thus, although the law encouraged a multitude of candidates to enter the race, it favored the few wealthy candidates who ran. The short time frame, coupled with the presence of several wealthy candidates and a large field of other candidates, led to "one of the most intensive expenditures of campaign money in U.S. political history."[29] About $80 million was spent during the campaign, or about $1 million a day.

The campaign itself was clouded by numerous lawsuits seeking to delay the date of election for a variety of reasons. At one point the federal Ninth Circuit Court of Appeals issued an injunction, effectively delaying the election until the spring of 2004. This decision was overruled four days later, however, and the campaign continued apace toward the October 7 election date.

The vote in favor of a recall was 55 percent to 45 percent, making Gray Davis the first California statewide official ever to be recalled. Republican Arnold Schwarzenegger received almost 49 percent of the "replacement" votes, beating Democratic lieutenant governor Cruz Bustamante (31 percent) and Republican state senator Tom McClintock (13 percent). No other candidate received as much as 3 percent of the replacement vote. Current estimates are that Schwarzenegger's campaign spent more than $21 million (including $11 million of Schwarzenegger's own money). Other wealthy candidates such as Darrell Issa and Peter Ueberroth spent over $1 million of their own money, but their campaigns never caught fire and both dropped out by September.

One of the most remarkable things about this election was the voter turnout—over 61 percent of registered voters went to the polls. The previous gubernatorial election in 2002 drew less than 51 percent of registered voters. Because of the high profile of this race and the successful recall effort, one could wonder whether such recall attempts against governors are more likely to occur in other states.

In fact, there was such an effort in Nevada at about the same time the California events were unfolding. In response to Gov. Kenny Guinn's support of a tax increase package, the Committee to Recall Governor Guinn was formed. The group failed, however, to obtain the number of petition signatures required to trigger a recall election. The standards for initiating a recall are higher in Nevada and other states that allow recalls than in California, which is one reason, among others, that it is unlikely that the California scenario will be played out in very many other states.

Indeed, of the states that do permit the recall of statewide officials California's requirement is the easiest to meet (signatures equal to 12 percent of the vote in the last gubernatorial election). Most of the other states require valid signatures totaling at least 25 percent of the votes cast in the previous election. Moreover, the time allowed for circulation of petitions in most states is 60 to 90 days; in California it is 160 days. Thus the supporters of the California recall were advantaged by a lower threshold of signatures and a longer time frame in which to gather those signatures than is the case for other states. Finally, California is one of only six states that allow for recall and replacement elections to be held concurrently. In the vast majority of states, if the governor is recalled, the successor is chosen in a later election or by appointment.

Conclusion

The differences in the partisan contexts, electoral rules, and campaign finance laws from state to state affect the nature of gubernatorial campaigns. The last third of the twentieth century also saw a major change in how campaigns are conducted for the office of governor in almost all states. Gubernatorial campaigns today are highly professional, media-driven endeavors.

For most states, they are also highly competitive. Incumbency is an important factor, but perhaps not as important as it is for many other offices. Governors are subject to retrospective voting, especially on the condition of the state economy and taxes, and they may even be subject to retrospective voting on the condition of the national economy. Because incumbent governors are at slightly more electoral risk than many officeholders, they tend to attract quality challengers. Moreover, the pool of candidates has changed a bit over time. Increasingly, federal officeholders may return to their home state and make a bid for the governor's office. And there appears to be an upsurge in the number of "outsiders"—those who have name recognition or wealth but little previous political experience—making serious runs for the office.

The governorship is an important position in the U.S. electoral system. Governors can leave lasting policy legacies, and they can use their experience to run for other offices, including the presidency. But there are no guarantees. As Gray Davis discovered, the tide can turn quickly.

Notes

1. States with a two-term limit vary on the specifics. Some impose a lifetime limit of two terms; others impose a limit of two consecutive terms, but allow a return after sitting out for four or eight years. States with no term limits for governors are Connecticut, Idaho, Illinois, Iowa, Minnesota, New Hampshire, New York, North Dakota, Texas, Utah, and Vermont.

2. Stephen Salmore and Barbara Salmore, "The Transformation of State Electoral Politics," in *The State of the States*, 3d ed., ed. Carl Van Horn (Washington, D.C.: CQ Press, 1996), 55.

3. Michael Malbin and Thomas Gais, *The Day after Reform* (Albany, N.Y.: Rockefeller Institute Press, 1998).

4. Donald Gross and Robert Goidel, *The States of Campaign Finance Reform* (Columbus: Ohio State University Press, 2003).

5. Malbin and Gais, *Day after Reform*.

6. Salmore and Salmore, "Transformation of State Electoral Politics," 56.

7. Malcolm Jewell and Sarah Morehouse, *Political Parties and Elections in American States*, 4th ed. (Washington, D.C.: CQ Press, 2001), 108.

8. Ibid., 109.

9. Jacob Lentz, *Electing Jesse Ventura* (Boulder, Colo.: Lynne Rienner, 2001), 21.

10. Thad Beyle, "The Governors," in *Politics in the American States*, 8th ed., ed. Virginia Gray and Russell Hanson (Washington, D.C.: CQ Press, 2004), 197.

11. Ibid., 198.

12. Gross and Goidel, *States of Campaign Finance Reform*, 88.

13. See, for example, John E. Chubb, "Institutions, the Economy, and the Dynamics of State Elections," *American Political Science Review* 82 (1988): 133–154; Craig Svoboda, "Retrospective Voting in Gubernatorial Elections: 1982 and 1986," *Political Research Quarterly* 48 (1995): 135–150; and Lonnie Rae Atkeson and Randall Partin, "Economic and Referendum Voting: A Comparison of Gubernatorial and Senatorial Elections," *American Political Science Review* 89 (1995): 99–107.

14. Jewell and Morehouse, *Political Parties*, 146.

15. Richard Niemi, Harold W. Stanley, and Ronald Vogel, "State Economies and State Taxes: Do Voters Hold Governors Accountable?" *American Journal of Political Science* 39 (1995): 936–957.

16. Peverill Squire, "Challenger Profile and Gubernatorial Elections," *Western Political Quarterly* 45 (1992): 125–142.

17. Susan Kone and Richard Winters, "Taxes and Voting: Electoral Retribution in the American States," *Journal of Politics* 55 (1993): 22–40.

18. Chubb, "Institutions"; Robert Stein, "Economic Voting for Governor and U.S. Senator: Electoral Consequences of Federalism," *Journal of Politics* 52 (1990): 29–53.

19. Niemi, Stanley, and Vogel, "State Economies"; Randall Partin, "Economic Conditions and Gubernatorial Elections," *American Politics Quarterly* 23 (1995): 81–95; Svoboda, "Retrospective Voting."

20. See Susan Hansen, " ' Life Is Not Fair': Governors' Job Performance Ratings and State Economies," *Political Research Quarterly* 52 (1999): 167–188; Deborah Orth, "Accountability in a Federal System," *State Politics and Policy Quarterly* 1 (2001): 412–432; and, to some extent, Greg Adams and Peverill Squire, "A Note on the Dynamics and Idiosyncrasies of Gubernatorial Popularity," *State Politics and Policy Quarterly* 1 (2001): 380–393.

21. Kevin Leyden and Stephen Borrelli, "The Effect of State Economic Conditions on Gubernatorial Elections: Does Unified Government Make a Difference?" *Political Research Quarterly* 48 (1995): 275–290.

22. See Morris Fiorina, *Divided Government*, 2d ed. (Boston: Allyn and Bacon, 1996), on the causes and consequences of divided government.

23. Robert C. Lowry, James E. Alt, and Karen E. Ferree, "Fiscal Policy Outcomes and Electoral Accountability in American States," *American Political Science Review* 92 (December 1998): 759–774; Michael John Mayo, "The Relationship between an Incumbent Governor's Popularity and State Legislative Election Outcomes: A Contemporary Assessment of the Coattails Phenomenon," Virginia Tech Political Science Department, Blacksburg, 2004.

24. L. Sandy Maisel, *Parties and Elections in America*, 3d ed. (Lanham, Md.: Rowman and Littlefield, 1999), 233–241.

25. Peverill Squire and Christina Fastnow, "Comparing Gubernatorial and Senatorial Elections," *Political Research Quarterly* 47 (1994): 705–720.

26. Ibid.

27. Gross and Goidel, *States of Campaign Finance Reform*, 36–37.

28. See National Conference of State Legislatures, "Recall of State Officials," www.ncsl.org. Virginia allows a recall trial, not election. Thirty-six states allow the recall of local elected officials.

29. Dan Thompson and Tom Chorneau, "Recall Campaign Spending Follows Familiar Patterns," *Contra Costa Times* (California), October 17, 2003.

Suggested Readings

Adams, Greg, and Peverill Squire. "A Note on the Dynamics and Idiosyncrasies of Gubernatorial Popularity." *State Politics and Policy Quarterly* 1 (2001): 380–393.

Atkeson, Lonnie Rae, and Randall Partin. "Economic and Referendum Voting: A Comparison of Gubernatorial and Senatorial Elections." *American Political Science Review* 89 (1995): 99–107.

Beiler, David. "The Body Politic Registers a Protest." In *Campaigns and Elections: Contemporary Case Studies*, edited by Michael Bailey, Ronald Faucheaux, Paul Herrnson, and Clyde Wilcox. Washington, D.C.: CQ Press, 2000.

Beyle, Thad. "The Governors." In *Politics in the American States,* 8th ed., edited by Virginia Gray and Russell Hanson. Washington, D.C.: CQ Press, 2004.

Carsey, Thomas. *Campaign Dynamics: The Race for Governor.* Ann Arbor: University of Michigan Press, 2000.

Carsey, Thomas, and Gerald Wright. "State and National Factors in Gubernatorial and Senatorial Elections." *American Journal of Political Science* 42 (1998): 94–102.

Chubb, John E. "Institutions, the Economy, and the Dynamics of State Elections." *American Political Science Review* 82 (1988): 133–154.

Congressional Quarterly Inc. *Gubernatorial Elections, 1787–1997.* Washington, D.C.: CQ Press, 1998.

Fiorina, Morris. *Divided Government.* 2d ed. Boston: Allyn and Bacon, 1996.

Gross, Donald, and Robert Goidel. *The States of Campaign Finance Reform.* Columbus: Ohio State University Press, 2003.

Hansen, Susan. " 'Life Is Not Fair': Governors' Job Performance Ratings and State Economies." *Political Research Quarterly* 52 (1999): 167–188.

Hedge, David. *Governance and the Changing American States.* Boulder, Colo.: Westview Press, 1998.

Kone, Susan, and Richard Winters. "Taxes and Voting: Electoral Retribution in the American States." *Journal of Politics* 55 (1993): 22–40.

Lentz, Jacob. *Electing Jesse Ventura.* Boulder, Colo.: Lynne Rienner, 2001.

Leyden, Kevin, and Stephen Borrelli. "The Effect of State Economic Conditions on Gubernatorial Elections: Does Unified Government Make a Difference?" *Political Research Quarterly* 48 (1995): 275–290.

Malbin, Michael, and Thomas Gais. *The Day after Reform.* Albany, N.Y.: Rockefeller Institute Press, 1998.

Mayo, Michael John. "The Relationship between an Incumbent Governor's Popularity and State Legislative Election Outcomes: A Contemporary Assessment of the Coattails Phenomenon." Virginia Tech Political Science Department, Blacksburg, 2004.

Morehouse, Sarah McCally, and Malcolm Jewell. *State Politics, Parties and Policy.* 2d ed. Lanham, Md.: Rowman and Littlefield, 2003.

Niemi, Richard, Harold W. Stanley, and Ronald Vogel. "State Economies and State Taxes: Do Voters Hold Governors Accountable?" *American Journal of Political Science* 39 (1995): 936–957.

Orth, Deborah. "Accountability in a Federal System." *State Politics and Policy Quarterly* 1 (2001): 412–432.

Partin, Randall. "Economic Conditions and Gubernatorial Elections." *American Politics Quarterly* 23 (1995): 81–95.

Salmore, Stephen, and Barbara Salmore. "The Transformation of State Electoral Politics." In *The State of the States,* 3d ed., edited by Carl Van Horn. Washington, D.C.: CQ Press, 1996.

Squire, Peverill. "Challenger Profile and Gubernatorial Elections." *Western Political Quarterly* 45 (1992): 125–142.

Squire, Peverill, and Christina Fastnow. "Comparing Gubernatorial and Senatorial Elections." *Political Research Quarterly* 47 (1994): 705–720.

Stein, Robert. "Economic Voting for Governor and U.S. Senator: Electoral Consequences of Federalism." *Journal of Politics* 52 (1990): 29–53.

Svoboda, Craig. "Retrospective Voting in Gubernatorial Elections: 1982 and 1986." *Political Research Quarterly* 48 (1995): 135–150.

CHAPTER 24

State House and Local Office Campaigns

Gary F. Moncrief and Peverill Squire

Within the general populace, there is the perception that even campaigns for state and local offices are so expensive that all candidates for such offices must be independently wealthy. This perception is clearly illustrated by the experience of Rev. Madison Shockley, a recent candidate for the Los Angeles City Council. As Shockley explains, "My son went to elementary school each day, came back telling me 'dad, everybody thinks we're rich.' I said, why in the world would they think that? 'Because you're running for office.' There is this impression that you have to be personally wealthy to be involved in politics. And, surprising to me, that's not true. I'm certainly not personally wealthy, but I was able to raise money from people who believed and shared in my cause in order to get the ball rolling in the political campaign."[1]

Although candidates for state and local offices do not have to be personally wealthy, it certainly costs a lot of money to run a competitive campaign in a big city such as Los Angeles. The same is true for a state legislative race in California, where Assembly races can easily cost $500,000 and Senate races might top $1 million. But these are the exceptions, not the rule.

The nature of campaigns for local government offices varies considerably by community. In the United States, the term *local government* usually refers to five types of jurisdictions: city (municipality), county, school district, special district (such as a parks and recreation district), and township. But in this chapter a state legislative office is considered a local office. It is "local" in the sense that it is not a statewide or federal office; officeholders are elected from legislative districts. Moreover, most, but certainly not all, legislative districts represent fewer than sixty thousand people. In this sense, running for legislative office is often similar to running for mayor in a midsize city, for a city council seat in a moderate-to-large municipality, or for commissioner or supervisor in many counties.

Admittedly, there are important exceptions. Districts range in size from 3,000–4,000 in New Hampshire and Vermont House races to more than 670,000 in Texas and California state Senate districts. The latter are actually larger than U.S. House districts. Overall, however, about 70 percent of the 7,500 state legislative districts in the United States have populations of under 60,000.

Most local elections occur in even smaller jurisdictions. For example, of the over 19,400 cities in the United States, only 601 (3 percent) have populations of 50,000 or more. Most locally elected officials thus conduct small-time, small-town, traditional campaigns. These campaigns are a far cry from the type of campaign waged in New York City, where Michael Bloomberg spent almost $70 million in the race for mayor in 2001.

Electoral Rules and Their Implications for Campaigning

The over 500,000 locally elected officials in the United States are elected under a variety of rules. For the purposes of this chapter, these rules fall into three broad categories: district magnitude, partisan or nonpartisan, and electoral formula.[2] *District magnitude* refers to the number of people being elected for office in a specific electoral district. In many instances, local officials are elected in *single-member districts*—one mayor, one city councilor, or one state senator is elected from the area. The *multimember districts* in some localities may elect several members of the state house of representatives or city council members from the same district. Often, for example, the entire city council or county commission is elected "at large," which means that there are multiple seats to fill and everyone in the city or county votes for multiple candidates. But this electoral scenario may have an effect on campaigning. It is often more expensive to campaign in multimember districts and at-large elections, because candidates must reach more voters than they would have to reach in single-member districts. Therefore, in some multimember districts several candidates may run as a "team," pooling some of their resources and running coordinated campaigns.

The second factor, or set of rules, affecting elections is whether they are partisan or nonpartisan. For example, almost all candidates for county offices (including supervisors, commissioners, sheriffs, and prosecuting attorneys) are chosen in partisan elections—that is, they campaign as a member of a particular political party, and their party affiliation appears on the ballot with their name. With the exception of Nebraska's, all state legislative elections in the United States are partisan.

Yet a multitude of local officials, including many mayors and city councilors as well as most school and special district board members, are elected in nonpartisan elections, in which candidates run without the benefit (or burden) of party affiliation. Candidates cannot rely on party identification as a voting cue or on assistance from the local party organization. Generally speaking, nonpartisan elections are truly candidate-centered. Without the aid of party identification, candidates must find ways to distinguish themselves from the others in an effort to attract votes. The campaign organization becomes distinctly personal, relying heavily on friends, personal supporters, and perhaps volunteers from specific interest groups. In other words, the candidate must build a campaign organization without the cadre of local party volunteers that might be available in a partisan election.

Although almost all local elections suffer from low voter turnout, this is particularly true of nonpartisan races, in which turnout may be only about 25 percent. Without the party labels as a voting guide, potential voters must engage in a more elaborate search for information in order to vote intelligently, and for many potential voters that increased effort is enough to keep them from voting. It is widely recognized that a higher proportion of voters in nonpartisan elections hold middle and upper socioeconomic status.

The third set of rules applies to how a winner or winners are determined. Most elections in the United States are held under a *plurality* rule; whoever gets more votes—even if it is less than 50 percent of the votes cast—wins. For example, four candidates are in a race in a single-member district. If candidate A receives 36 percent of the vote, candidate B 34 percent, and candidates C and D each 15 percent, then candidate A wins the election, even though candidate A received far fewer than a majority of the total votes cast (in fact, 64 percent of voters chose someone other than candidate A). If the electoral system operates under a *majoritarian* rule, a candidate wins the seat only if he or she receives more than half of the total votes cast.

Campaign strategies may be quite different under plurality versus majoritarian rules, especially when four or five candidates are in the race. In a majoritarian system, candidates must seek the middle ground; in a plurality system with numerous candidates, the winner may be successful by appealing to a smaller but very active segment of the electorate. In many American cities, the electoral rule is essentially majoritarian; if no candidate receives more than half the votes cast, then a second election, a runoff, must be held between the two top vote-getting candidates. Some states such as Alabama and Georgia use this double-ballot system for state legislative primary elections. Thus under this system a candidate may have to conduct three campaigns—primary, runoff primary, and general election—in order to win a seat.

A few local jurisdictions, including San Francisco, have adopted a system known as *instant runoff voting* (IRV). The IRV system allows voters to rank-order candidates by preference by placing a "1" next to the name of the preferred candidate, a "2" next to the name of the second choice, and so forth. If no one receives a majority of first-place votes, then the candidate with the fewest votes is dropped and the second-place votes on those ballots are allotted to the remaining candidates. This process continues until one candidate receives a majority of votes. Proponents of this system argue that it leads to a more "conciliatory" method of campaigning; candidates do not want to alienate voters by attacking opponents because the candidate may eventually need that opponent's second-place votes.[3]

Another system used in a handful of places in the United States, most commonly in New Mexico and Texas, is *cumulative voting* (CV). This system is designed to facilitate minority representation in at-large electoral systems. If, for example, five city council seats are up for election, each voter receives five votes to allocate in whatever manner he or she chooses—perhaps five times for one candidate, or one time for each of five candidates, or three times for one candidate and twice for another. The idea is that voters can express their intensity of support for a candidate by placing all votes on one candidate. Minorities have a much better opportunity to elect at least one candidate of their choice under this system, but the system requires coordination among potential candidates and clear communication with the voters.

Aside from the implications of the electoral rules, the most important factor for the type of campaign to be waged is population. Regardless of whether the election is for a city, county, school district, or state legislative office, campaigns in small districts are run in about the same way. Legislative and local campaigns in districts with populations of fewer than about fifty thousand tend to be conducted in a more grass-roots, door-to-door, face-to-face style. This type of campaign is often referred to as a traditional campaign, or "old politics," because it relies largely on time-honored practices and techniques, or it is called *retail* politics, suggesting the main feature of this style is communicating with potential voters one-on-one.

Candidates running in larger districts tend to pursue a *wholesale* campaign strategy, which relies heavily on media advertising, polling, and sophisticated direct-mail techniques to contact large groups of potential voters. This type of campaign, often referred to as "professional campaigning," "high-tech campaigning," or simply the "new politics," is a much more expensive endeavor, usually requiring the assistance of professional consultants (also see Chapter 10).[4] These sophisticated, professional campaigns are the norm in federal and statewide elections and have been for some time. Their use in local campaigns is both more recent and far from universal.

Much of the discussion in the rest of this chapter focuses on state legislative races, but most of the observations apply equally to local offices. Where differences do exist, they are a product of the differences in electoral rules, as described earlier. For all local and state legislative offices, however, the single most important variable is district population.

Size of the Electoral District

State legislative districts vary in two fundamental ways: population size (the number of people in a district) and geographical size (the number of square miles in a district). Each has important consequences for the conduct of the legislative campaigns.

The campaign implications of district population size are obvious. As Table 24-1 reveals, state legislators represent an enormous range in number of people. At the extremes are the New Hampshire House of Representatives and the California state Senate. The four hundred members of the New Hampshire House each represent about three thousand people. This small size allows candidates to engage in "retail" politics, personally interacting with most of the voters. One incumbent representative in New Hampshire, for example, recently claimed that he knew 60 percent of the people in his district.[5] It seems plausible, in fact, that in a district of three thousand people a legislator might actually know eighteen hundred of them. But contrast that situation with the one facing a California state senator. Each state senator in California represents some 875,000 people, almost 200,000 more people than represented by the average member of the U.S. House of Representatives. It is, of course, unrealistic to think that a California state senator can know 60 percent of his or her constituents. Indeed, a California state senator will know very few of those constituents, which

Table 24-1 District Population in State House and Senate Districts, 2002

State	Senate	House	State	Senate	House
Alabama	127,060	42,253	Montana	18,044	9,022
Alaska	31,347	15,673	Nebraska	34,924	Unicameral
Arizona	171,021	171,021	Nevada	95,155	47,578
Arkansas	76,383	26,734	New Hampshire	51,491	3,089
California	846,791	423,396	New Jersey	210,359	210,359
Colorado	122,893	66,173	New Mexico	43,311	25,986
Connecticut	94,599	22,553	New York	311,089	126,510
Delaware	37,314	19,112	North Carolina	160,986	67,078
Florida	399,559	133,186	North Dakota	13,106	13,106
Georgia	146,187	45,840	Ohio	344,035	114,678
Hawaii	48,461	23,756	Oklahoma	71,889	34,165
Idaho	36,970	36,970	Oregon	114,047	57,023
Illinois	210,496	105,248	Pennsylvania	245,621	60,498
Indiana	121,610	60,805	Rhode Island	20,966	10,483
Iowa	58,526	29,263	South Carolina	87,218	32,355
Kansas	67,210	21,507	South Dakota	21,567	21,567
Kentucky	106,362	40,418	Tennessee	172,403	57,468
Louisiana	114,589	42,562	Texas	672,639	139,012
Maine	36,426	8,443	Utah	77,006	29,776
Maryland	112,691	37,564	Vermont	20,294	4,059
Massachusetts	158,727	39,682	Virginia	176,963	70,785
Michigan	261,538	90,349	Washington	120,288	120,288
Minnesota	73,425	36,713	West Virginia	53,187	18,083
Mississippi	54,705	23,317	Wisconsin	162,536	54,179
Missouri	164,565	34,326	Wyoming	16,459	8,230

Source: National Conference of State Legislatures.

means that a candidate running for the state Senate in California will campaign in a very different way than a candidate running for the state House in New Hampshire. The New Hampshire candidate campaigns by meeting with voters, while the California candidate must rely on more impersonal means of persuasion. The same is true at the local government level. Running for mayor in Cleveland, Texas (population 7,605), is a lot different than running for mayor in Cleveland, Ohio (population 467,851).

Although the effect of the geographical size of a district on campaigning has received relatively little scholarly attention, it is possible to conclude that campaigning in large districts differs from that in small districts. The most extreme case is Alaska's state Senate District C, which covers the sparsely populated rural areas of the state and encompasses more than 240,000 square miles, making it almost the same size as Texas. Campaigning in District C is challenging. Candidates have to travel by car, airplane, and ferry, and with bad weather, visits to some communities may take days or even weeks. Moreover, when the candidate arrives the locals have certain expectations. As one candidate described it, "They don't expect you to go in and spend 15 minutes and you're out of there. That's rather insulting. They expect you to spend the night." [6] And the distances to be covered are vast. A few years back, the incumbent senator tried to visit every town in her district, but after three months she had managed to visit only about 75 percent of them.

Most states in the western part of the United States also have very large legislative districts representing rural populations. Candidates seeking to represent those kinds of districts realize the difficulties—the long car or plane trips just to meet with small groups of voters. Candidates running for legislative seats in more densely populated eastern states run different kinds of campaigns. A member of the Rhode Island House, for example, told her colleagues, "I learn by listening and I listen to my voters over the fence, at the swimming pool. . . . My office is a shopping cart on Sunday afternoon at Stop & Shop." [7] It is hard to imagine many of her colleagues from large districts in the West making the same claims.

Legislative Professionalization and Candidate Recruitment

States vary in levels of legislative professionalization as defined by members' salaries, level of staffing, and length of the legislative session. Professionalization in this sense measures how closely a state legislature resembles the U.S. Congress. Only a handful of states are considered reasonably professionalized—notably, California, Michigan, and New York. These state legislatures, like Congress, pay their legislators well, provide them with good facilities, and meet full time. A few other states, such as New Jersey and Florida, are well on the way to professional status. Most states, however, little resemble Congress. Their legislatures pay their members very little, do not have long sessions, and provide virtually nothing in the way of staff or other resources.

What effect does legislative professionalization have on the campaign process? There is evidence that it influences the recruitment process. For one thing, the kind of people serving in a state legislature vary with the body's level of professionalization.[8] Women, for example, are more likely to serve in less professionalized legislatures than in more professionalized legislatures. Recruitment efforts in more professionalized legislatures are usually extensive, with party and legislative leaders working hard to find candidates to run for office.[9] Those in the less professionalized legislatures are less well organized or energetic. For example, in New Hampshire, the state at the bottom of the professionalization rankings, parties do not devote much effort to candidate recruitment.[10]

Salary is an especially important component of professionalization, and one that can alter the recruitment landscape. In 1998, for example, a Colorado legislative leader observed that more people were running for the state legislature than in previous years because the salary had increased substantially, from $17,500 to $30,000, beginning with the 1999 legislative session. Money gives at least some people an incentive to run, such as one Colorado candidate in 1998, a single parent, who said, "I couldn't run before because $17,500 was too low." [11]

More highly professionalized state legislatures are also often associated with intense party competition for control of the chambers, motivating the parties or the state legislative leadership to be very active in the recruitment process. Legislative campaign committees, for example, are more active in professional legislatures than they are in less professionalized bodies.[12]

Finally, legislative professionalization may have a differential effect on the recruitment patterns of Democrats compared with those of Republicans. Some scholars contend that Republicans are less likely to find full-time legislative service enticing, because often they must give up lucrative professional positions in the private sector to serve in a full-time, professional state legislature.[13]

Candidate Qualifications

The current age qualifications for service in state legislatures vary. In lower houses, the minimum age requirements range from eighteen years in thirteen states to twenty-five years in three states. The range in upper houses is even greater, from eighteen years in thirteen states to thirty years in five states. The age requirement is the same for both chambers in twenty-seven states. In the other twenty-two bicameral states, different age qualifications are imposed on the two houses, but always with the older qualification being put on the upper house. The greatest gap in age minimums is in New Hampshire, where a member of the lower house may be only eighteen years old, but an upper house member must be at least thirty years old.

The trend over time has been for lower age requirements, often in tandem with lower age requirements for voting. But lower age requirements may not always be popular. In 2002 Oregon voters were asked to amend the state constitution to lower the minimum age to serve in the legislature to eighteen from twenty-one. The amendment was placed on the ballot, as Measure 17, by overwhelming votes in both houses of the state legislature after the Oregon secretary of state was asked by a Portland Community College student why eighteen-year-olds could run for offices such as secretary of state and attorney general but not for the legislature. Unexpected organized opposition to the measure surfaced in the form of fundamentalist Christian groups, which interpreted the Bible as saying that ruling positions should be held only by men and women thirty or older. In the end, the constitutional amendment to lower the minimum age for legislative service failed, receiving only 27 percent of the vote.

State constitutions also impose state and district residency requirements for legislative service. Every state currently has some residency standard in place. To serve in the lower houses of six states, a candidate need only be a resident of the district at the time of the election. Most states, however, use more stringent standards, requiring district residency from thirty days in Nevada to two years in Illinois and Mississippi. In addition to district residency, state residency ranging from a single year to five years is required in over half of states.

Residency standards are even higher for service in several state senates. Every state requires residency in the senate district, although the time needed to establish residency varies from a loose day-of-the-election standard to two years in Illinois and Mississippi. State residency requirements also are stringent. At the most extreme, the state residency standard to qualify for service in the New Hampshire state senate is seven years.

Questions are raised from time to time about whether candidates or members have met state residency requirements. For example, in West Virginia in 2002 a House of Delegates candidate learned that he did not live in the district in which he was running—as required by state law—when his opponent raised the issue during a debate. The opponent worked for the candidate's mother, prompting the unlawful candidate to observe, "So he knew exactly what part of the county I lived in more than me."[14] Not surprisingly, most state legislative candidates are long-time district residents.[15]

Recruitment Patterns

Because the pay is low and the demands on time are high enough that most people must leave their current employment to serve, recruiting candidates for the state legislature is often difficult. Spiraling campaign costs and the time and effort required to raise money also may discourage people from running. And then there is the daunting reality of running for legislative office in the United States: when a challenger takes on an incumbent, the incumbent almost always wins. Overall, then, the appeal of being a state legislator is limited.

In many districts in many states, the sad reality is that nobody opts to run for the legislature (as in contests for many local offices, particularly for school boards). Table 24-2 gives some sense of the level of political competition for the state legislature in twelve states in 2002. Most strikingly, it reveals that a vast number of seats go uncontested by one of the two major parties. In Massachusetts, for example, in 59 percent of the contests for the state House of Representatives only one candidate was on the ballot. In another 10 percent of races a major-party candidate faced only a minor-party candidate. On average in these twelve states, over four out of every ten elections were uncontested. Only in California and Minnesota did voters have a high probability of being able to vote in a contested race for the lower house.

The findings in Table 24-2 are consistent with those reported in an extensive study of uncontested seats in state legislative elections over a longer time period.[16] That study found that uncontested seats are, at the aggregate level, a function of the value of the seat to potential candidates and the electoral environment in each state. As noted earlier, state legislatures vary substantially in what they pay their members and in their levels of legislative professionalization. Not surprisingly, as member pay increases, the percentage of uncontested seats declines. Likewise, the more professionalized the legislature, the fewer legislative races are uncontested. Clearly, then, the higher the value of a seat—in either political or financial terms—the more people are willing to bear the costs of candidacy for a chance to win it.

States also vary in the level of electoral competition they enjoy. In states in which partisan competition for elective office is keen, a lower percentage of seats are uncontested than in states in which competition is lacking. For example, in the 2002 elections in Arkansas where Democrats dominate, fifty-four Democrats enjoyed uncontested races for the state House of Representatives, whereas only thirteen Republicans faced no opponent. Similarly, in Idaho where the GOP prevails, the 2002 elections for the lower state house saw eighteen Republicans and only four Democrats with no major-party opposition. These results suggest that in the aggregate, potential candidates for state legislative office behave rationally. They

Table 24-2 Party Competition in Selected Lower-House Races, 2002 (percent)

State (number of legislative seats)	Races with only major-party candidates on ballot	Races with two major-party candidates and at least one minor-party candidate on ballot	Uncontested races: only one major-party candidate on ballot	Uncontested races: one major-party candidate and at least one minor-party candidate on ballot
Alaska (40)	25	20	38	18
Arkansas (100)	32	1	67	0
California (80)	48	43	5	5
Colorado (65)	29	40	14	17
Georgia (180)	38	1	59	2
Idaho (70)	41	27	21	10
Iowa (100)	55	7	36	2
Massachusetts (160)	23	8	59	10
Minnesota (134)	64	30	5	1
Pennsylvania (203)	50	8	38	4
Tennessee (99)	39	14	41	6
Texas (150)	35	10	42	13

Source: Calculated by authors from official state legislative election returns.

run when they have a good chance to win, and they opt out of races in places in which their prospects are dimmer. Thus competition begets competition.

Finally, there is less competition in the South than in the rest of the country, even when other state legislative and electoral characteristics are controlled. Although the Republican Party is strong in the South, the level of competition for office is still weaker there than in the rest of the country. At the state legislative level, at least, region continues to matter.

Who does run for the state legislature? State legislative candidates are not a random sample of the general population. For example, women constitute only about a quarter of legislative candidates; more than nine out of every ten candidates for the legislature are white; and the majority of candidates are middle-aged, and they tend to be better educated and somewhat wealthier than the population at large. Even though most state legislative candidates are well rooted in their communities, candidates are drawn from a wide range of occupations. Only 10 percent of state legislative candidates are lawyers; business employees, business owners, and retirees actually run in larger numbers.[17]

By and large, candidates for the state legislature enter the race with some political experience under their belts. Only about a quarter currently hold some other elective office, and even fewer hold an appointed office at the time of the race for the legislature. A majority of legislative candidates have held a party office, and most have been active in campaigns at the local, state, and national levels.

About a third of legislative candidates are self-starters, who run without any prompting or encouragement from the party. About half of candidates had toyed with the idea of running, but they required some nudge to enter the race. A serious recruitment effort was required to get the other 20 percent of candidates to toss their hats in the ring. In this one area a significant difference appears between men and women as candidates. Men are far more likely than women to jump into a campaign on their own initiative. Women tend to be more selective in the races they undertake and often require more encouragement to enter.

Political parties are the most active recruitment agents in state legislative campaigns. About 40 percent of candidates for the state legislature report having been encouraged to run by local party leaders, officials in the state party, and state legislative leaders. Other recruitment agents are less active but still important. Many candidates are urged to run by family members, friends, and acquaintances from civic organizations, churches, and other groups.

Funding Campaigns

Many legislative and local races today are still grassroots campaigns that make limited use of professional

---

BOX 24-1
CAMPAIGN EXPENDITURES VARY

In 2000 New York state senator Guy Velella spent $2 million to retain his District 34 seat, or more than twice what the average incumbent spent in a U.S. congressional election. His opponent spent $500,000 in a losing cause. In the same year, three state Senate candidates spent over $1 million each, and two Assembly (lower-chamber) candidates spent more than $600,000 apiece.[1]

In 1998 the average cost of running for a state Senate race in California was $509,000; in the lower house it was $244,000. In Kentucky, where the control of the Senate was in doubt, over half of all Senate candidates spent at least $100,000 in 2000, including one Senate candidate who spent $637,000.[2] By contrast, only four candidates spent as much as $40,000 for any of the 105 seats in the Idaho legislature in 2002. Most candidates spent less than $20,000. One candidate defeated both primary and general election opponents in an open-seat race and spent only $3,612.

1. Jill Schneeback and R. Kirsch, "The Wealth Primary," Public Policy and Education Fund of New York, New York, 2001.

2. Mark Chellgren, "2000 Legislative Campaign Costs Skyrocketed," *Courier-Journal* (Louisville, Ky.), July 11, 2001.

---

consultants and television campaigns. Thus most local races are still relatively inexpensive. One recent survey revealed that more than half of the state legislative candidates questioned hired no professional campaign consultants.[18] But that is not true everywhere. Probably half the state senate campaigns and 30 percent of the house campaigns employ some of the professional services that tend to drive campaign costs up. According to Ron Faucheaux and Paul S. Herrnson, $50,000 seems to represent an important threshold in characterizing a campaign: "The dividing line between professional and amateur campaigns is at the $50,000 spending level: many of the candidates above it run media and research-driven campaigns that utilize paid consultants and sophisticated vote-getting techniques; the vast majority of those below it run volunteer-driven grassroots campaigns."[19]

Many mayoral and county commissioner races, and a few city council campaigns, also use these modern-day techniques, and therefore they can be quite expensive. For example, sophisticated campaign techniques such as targeted direct mail, radio and television ads, and polls are becoming a prevalent feature of mayoral campaigns in mid-sized (over fifty thousand population) cities.[20]

At least two factors help to explain the costs of campaigning at the local level. The most important factor is

district size—the more people to be reached with campaign communications, the more expensive the race. In turn, the larger the target population, the more likely it is that television advertising is cost-effective. The second factor is the *competitiveness* of the race. Open-seat races are more competitive than races in which there is an incumbent. Elections right after a redistricting cycle also tend to be more competitive, because the district boundaries may have changed and even incumbents are unknown by some of the new voters in the district. Finally, in state legislative races competitiveness for *control of the chamber* can make a big difference. When only a few seats separate the majority party from the minority party, spending tends to spike because control of the chamber can shift from one party to the other and every seat becomes crucial. For these reasons, there are tremendous differences in the spending on state legislative races, as described in Box 24-1.

Comprehensive, state-by-state campaign expenditure figures are extremely difficult to obtain because of different reporting requirements and variation in the accessibility of those data from one state to another. However, the Institute on Money in State Politics has collected data for almost all states on the total amount raised by each candidate during the 2000 electoral cycle. The data are reported as state averages.[21] The median state for house races is South Carolina, where an average of $29,000 was raised. The median for senate races is Arkansas at $58,000. These figures are probably fairly accurate measures of a "typical" legislative campaign budget. Nevertheless, the funds raised and spent vary tremendously—state by state and, within a state, district by district.

This variation is even more substantial at the local level, where some city council or school district races cost almost nothing, whereas mayoral races in large cities can cost millions. For example, Antonio Villaraigosa spent $7 million in his bid to become mayor of Los Angeles in 2001, but he lost. In the same year, billionaire Michael Bloomberg spent ten times that amount in his successful campaign for mayor of New York City.

As for the specific campaign finance laws in force, state legislative and local offices are mostly governed by state laws. Such state laws are often very different from the federal campaign finance laws that apply to congressional races (see Chapter 6). For example, individual contributions are limited to $2,000 per election for U.S. House races, and some states do not limit individual contributions at all to state legislative candidates (see Table 24-3). The same is true of contributions by political action committees (PACs). The role of political parties in funding legislative candidates varies by state.

Recent changes in federal law, such as enactment in 2002 of the Bipartisan Campaign Reform Act (BCRA), may have an important impact on state legislative campaigns. In the past few electoral cycles (until 2004), so-called soft money (unregulated funds) from the national

Michael Bloomberg, Republican candidate for mayor of New York City, talks with family members as they watch televised reports of the Republican primary results on September 25, 2001. The primary was delayed by the September 11, 2001, attacks on New York's World Trade Center. Bloomberg, a billionaire media mogul, won both the primary and the general election after spending a total of $70 million to succeed outgoing mayor Rudolph Giuliani.
Source: Reuters/Landov

party organizations was funneled to state races. In some states, the amount of money was substantial, and it almost certainly contributed to the increase in state legislative campaign spending. In 2002 national political party committees contributed more than $10 million in soft money to state party committees in each of ten states—Arkansas, Florida, Georgia, Iowa, New Hampshire, Minnesota, Missouri, South Dakota, Texas, and Virginia.[22] Although much of that money was used to support congressional candidates in those states, some of the funds probably helped state legislative candidates as well.

The BCRA eliminates this funneling process, but it does not necessarily affect the ability of state political parties to obtain soft money elsewhere. As one report cautions, "While the BCRA ban on soft money closes one fund-raising door at the federal level, 50 other doors remain wide open in the states. Those doors lead to a financial arena governed by 50 different sets of laws and regulations."[23] Whether states can replace the hundreds of millions of dollars of national party soft money, and, if they can, how many of those replacement dollars flow to state legislative candidates, remain to be seen.

In some states, *independent expenditures* have become a dramatic part of the legislative campaign scene. Independent expenditures are money spent by interest groups in an effort to help elect or defeat a specific candidate. Such expenditures are protected under the First Amendment to the U.S. Constitution and are outside the control of the candidate. It is unlikely that the BCRA will have much of an effect on this trend in the states. For example, in Wisconsin interest groups spent more than $650,000 in independent spending in one 1998 state Senate race,

while the candidates themselves spent less than $500,000. As one of the candidates later said, "The campaign was totally out of my control . . . I was a bit player."[24] In the Los Angeles city elections of 2001, independent expenditures totaled more than $3 million.

The Advantages of Incumbency

Students of congressional elections assert that the advantages of incumbency account for the extraordinary reelection rates witnessed over the last several decades. Scholars point to publicly financed trips back to the district, constituent newsletters, the availability of staff to help solve constituents' problems, and other advantages enjoyed by incumbents as the likely explanation for why over 90 percent of congressional incumbents are successful in their reelection efforts. Intuitively, the claims make sense; incumbents use such resources to become known and liked by the voters. State legislative incumbents also benefit from high reelection rates, but most have few if any resources they can exploit for their electoral benefit.

Yet some state legislators do receive the same kinds of wherewithal enjoyed by members of Congress. For example, when Hilda Solis moved from the California state Senate to the U.S. House after the 2000 elections, she "decided to keep the same field offices, in El Monte and East Los Angeles, to provide continuity to her constituents."[25] More typical, however, is the situation faced by state legislators in Wyoming. They do not have offices in either the district or the state capitol building. They simply have a desk on the floor of the chamber and a file cabinet drawer or two in a committee meeting room.

Although most state legislators are successfully reelected, there is evidence that those who serve in more professionalized bodies have enhanced electoral prospects for several reasons. Incumbents in more professionalized legislators are able to devote more time to pursuing reelection than are their counterparts in less professionalized bodies. They also have more travel money to use in maintaining contact with constituents, and they perform more constituent casework.[26]

An example of the advantages enjoyed by legislative incumbents is a directory of public officials that was sent to households in the district of a state senator in Washington. On the top of a directory sent to one of the senator's constituents, the voter wrote, "I like this booklet so much I remember [the senator's] name." Such sentiments are, of course, exactly what elected officials who provide their constituents with such items hope they will produce. Their colleagues with fewer such resources are hard-pressed to become known and liked by the voters.

Table 24-3 Contribution Limits to House Candidates per Election Cycle

	Individual contributions	PAC contributions	Political party contributions
Under $300	Colo., Mont., S.Dak., Vt.	Mont., Vt.	
$300–$1,000	Ariz., Conn., Fla. Kans., Maine, Mass., Mich., Minn., Mo., R.I., Wis.	Alaska, Ariz., Colo., Conn., Del., Fla., Kans., Maine, Mass., Mich., Minn., Mo., R.I., Wis.	Mont.
$1,001–$3,000	Ark., Alaska, Del., Hawaii, Idaho, Ky., N.H., S.C., Tenn., Wash., W.Va., Wyo.	Ark., Hawaii, Idaho, Ky., N.H., S.C., Wash., W.Va.	Del., Hawaii, Mass., N.H., W.Va.
$3,001–$5,000	Ga., La., Md., N.J., Ohio	Ga., La., Ohio	Ark., Ga., Idaho, Mich., Minn.
$5,001–$10,000	Calif., Nev., N.C., N.Y., Okla.	Calif., Md., N.C., Nev., N.Y., Okla., Tenn.	Ariz., Ark., Md., Mo., Nev., S.C.
$10,001–$50,000		N.J.	Colo., Fla., Neb., Okla., R.I., Tenn., Wash., Wis.
Over $50,000			Ohio
No limits	Ala., Ill., Ind., Iowa, Miss., Neb., N.Mex., N.Dak., Ore., Pa., Tex., Utah., Va.	Ala., Ill., Ind., Iowa, Miss., N.Dak., N.Mex., Ore., Pa., S.Dak., Tex., Utah, Va., Wyo.	Ala., Calif., Conn., Ill., Ind., Iowa, Kans., Ky., La., Maine, Miss., N.C., N.Dak., N.J., N.Mex., N.Y., Ore., Pa., S.Dak., Tex., Utah, Va., Vt., Wyo.

Source: National Conference of State Legislatures, August 2003.

Note: In some states the limit is per year; in others it is per election (separate for primary and general elections, and for runoff elections where applicable). Where limits are per election, yearly totals are calculated by adding the primary and general election limits.

In many states, contribution limits for senate candidates are higher than the limits for house candidates.

There is no specific limit on how much an individual political action committee (PAC) can give in Nebraska, except that candidates are limited to $36,500 in total PAC contributions.

The laws governing political party contributions vary in the specifics: some limits are aggregate for all party committees; others are limits for each national, state, or local party. Some limits are calculated as a specific amount per registered voter. In these cases, the estimated number of registered voters in an average house district was multiplied by the amount allowed per registered voter.

Minor Parties in State Legislative Elections

Members of minor political parties currently hold almost no state legislative seats. In 2004 only 21 of the 7,333 state legislators elected by party were elected as something other than a Republican or a Democrat. Yet, as Table 24-2 reveals, in many states minor-party candidates are a regular feature of state legislative elections. Over half the contests in Colorado and almost half of the races in California and Idaho in 2002 involved at least one minor-party candidate. But almost no minor-party candidates were found on the ballots in Arkansas or Georgia.

Along demographic dimensions, minor-party candidates look much like their major-party counterparts. The candidates of minor parties are slightly less well educated than major-party candidates, and they tend to have lower incomes. The major differences appear in political credentials. Minor-party candidate have less experience in politics; they have been involved in fewer campaigns and have held far fewer elective and appointed offices. And, because of a lack of party organizations in most cases, it is not surprising that minor-party candidates are far more likely than major-party candidates to have entered the race on their own initiative and without consulting party officials.[27]

Campaign Techniques

Because most state legislative campaigns do not involve huge sums of money or large numbers of voters, they do not resemble races for Congress. In most state legislative races, for example, television advertising is an unaffordable luxury. According to a survey conducted by Faucheux and Herrnson, only 13 percent of campaigns spending less than $50,000 run ads on broadcast television stations and only 19 percent run ads on cable television programs.[28] Among wealthier campaigns—those spending in excess of $50,000—well under 50 percent run ads on either broadcast or cable television.

Other research supports this point. Robert E. Hogan found that less than 10 percent of general election expenditures were devoted to television ads in the five states he surveyed in 1994–1996. Jonathan Smith, using data from Georgia, and South and North Carolina from the 2000 electoral cycle, reported that 23 percent of the candidates used broadcast television, and 36 percent used cable television. Presumably, most of those candidates who reported using cable ads were in the Atlanta, Georgia, area. Owen Abbe and Paul S. Herrnson found that less than 25 percent of the nine hundred state legislative candidates they surveyed nationally in 1999 said they had hired professional consultants to help them with media advertising.[29] Most state legislative or local candidates simply cannot afford to use television to reach potential voters.

But expense is not the only reason that state legislative campaigns shy away from television advertising. In most legislative districts, television advertising is a very inefficient way to contact voters. Because media markets usually encompass a large number of state legislative districts, candidates opting to use television in them run the risk of paying large sums of money to run advertising seen mostly by people who do not live in their districts. For example, in the Pennsylvania House of Representatives contest in the Philadelphia area in 2000, the Democratic candidate—a former local TV news reporter—ran commercials on a broadcast TV station in Philadelphia, only to be mocked by her Republican opponent for spending large sums of money to talk "to all those people in [neighboring] New Jersey who can't vote for her." [30] Generally, state legislative campaigns take to the broadcast airwaves only when the media market is congruent with the district.[31]

Nicole LeFavour places a sign in a supporter's yard during her 2004 campaign for the Idaho House of Representatives. In her winning effort, LeFavour employed two campaign techniques common among state and local candidates—putting up yard signs and ringing door bells. Source: Matt Cilley/AP Wide World Photo

Other forms of mass media are more commonly employed in state legislative campaigns. Just under half of less well-funded campaigns and two-thirds of wealthier campaigns use radio advertising as part of their strategy—it is a much less expensive alternative to television. Newspaper ads are used by about three-quarters of all state legislative candidates. But, again, most state legislative candidates run into the same concerns about efficiency in using radio and newspapers that they run up against in using television.

Most legislative and local candidates also seek "free media"—that is, opportunities to get the candidate's name in the news. One time-honored approach is to ask supporters to write letters to the editor in the local newspapers. Another is creating "media events," such as announcing a candidacy in front of city hall or holding a press conference to discuss the campaign platform.

The most common campaign techniques used in state legislative campaigns are direct mail, literature drops, billboards and signs, and doorbelling. Direct mail, which can be targeted to potential voters, is used by 75 percent of low-budget campaigns and every large-budget effort. Smith found that 82 percent of the southern legislative candidates he surveyed used direct mail; 29 percent claimed to have sent out at least seven different mailings.[32] Direct mail has become a staple of almost all legislative and many local campaigns. Although many candidates use volunteer help to produce mailings, almost 34 percent of candidates say they have hired professional help with their direct mail.[33]

Similarly, the vast majority of candidates use literature drops—that is, campaign workers leave campaign brochures on doorsteps. Billboards and yard signs are a common feature of virtually all state legislative and many local campaigns. Many incumbents even save money on their reelection campaigns by reusing yard signs from previous runs.

In doorbelling, a traditional form of campaigning, a candidate walks the district and knocks on the doors of people's homes. This form of person-to-person campaigning is popular because it is inexpensive, and many candidates think it is the best way to connect with potential voters. But doorbelling does take a toll. After knocking on seven thousand doors in his quest to win a seat in the Indiana House, one candidate told doubters of his efforts, "I've got the blisters and the worn-out shoes to prove it." [34] A candidate for the West Virginia House noted another problem. After knocking on seven thousand doors in her district, she lamented, "I got bit by a dog on Friday and I got bit by a dog Saturday." [35]

Because most candidates do not have the money to use the mass media in their campaigns and they are unable to generate much coverage from the free media, they have to employ other techniques to get their names before the voters. Thus many candidates find themselves doing the kinds of things undertaken by an incumbent state senator in Oregon: "Republican incumbent Eileen Qutub planted herself in a median at a busy entrance to the Washington Square Mall parking lot, waved a sign and gave the thumbs-up to drivers. At her feet was Mr. Tibbs, a rat terrier who wore a fleece-lined cloak with a Qutub bumper sticker." [36]

The Internet is the most recent campaign innovation in state legislative elections; state legislative candidates are increasingly promoting their candidacies with a Web site.

Indeed, in some campaigns the Internet plays a critical role. When Mary Beth Williams first announced her candidacy for the Maine House of Representatives in early 2004, her campaign foundered. But once she announced that she was running on her Web blog, a site dedicated to promoting "progressive politics, Indian issues, and autism advocacy," she tapped into several groups of people willing to help elect her to office.[37] The specific role the Internet plays in state legislative campaigns is still evolving, but it may become a more important tool in large population districts because, as a candidate for the Texas legislature noted, "There are only so many doors I can knock on. If I can talk to people online, that's an advantage." [38]

Conclusion

There is little doubt that some campaigns for state legislature and local offices have become more professional and use the more specialized and expensive communications techniques associated with polling, media advertising, and direct mail. Currently, however, this new style of campaigning is generally confined to larger legislative districts and municipalities. Most candidates for state legislatures, and the vast majority of those running for local office, still rely on the more traditional grass-roots methods of campaigning. Nevertheless, the "new style" will continue to seep deeper into the layers of local levels. Indeed, as one scholar has pointed out, there is an arms race mentality to campaigning; once one candidate for an office adopts the more sophisticated and more expensive techniques, others will soon follow.[39] The old style will not altogether disappear, however. New-style techniques rarely supplant the old grass-roots efforts; they supplement them.

Notes

1. Los Angeles City Ethics Commission, "Campaign Finance Reform: Lessons from Los Angeles," October 12, 2001, transcript.

2. This is a slight modification of Douglas Rae's classic distinction of the components of electoral systems, because the primary interest here is on the implications for campaigning. See Douglas Rae, *The Political Consequences of Electoral Laws* (New Haven, Conn.: Yale University Press, 1967).

3. Douglas Amy, *Behind the Ballot Box* (Westport, Conn.: Praeger, 2000), 53–54.

4. L. Sandy Maisel, *Parties and Elections in America,* 3d ed. (Lanham, Md.: Rowman and Littlefield, 1999), 222.

5. Norma Love, "Remap Threatens New Hampshire's Folksy Politics," September 16, 2002, www.stateline.org (accessed May 24, 2005).

6. Bill McAllister, "Alaska Senate District Tests Candidates' Stamina," *Stateline.org,* October 17, 2002, stateline.org (accessed April 13, 2005).

7. State of Rhode Island and Providence Plantations, *Journal of the House of Representatives,* May 31, 2000.

8. Peverill Squire, "Legislative Professionalization and Membership Diversity in State Legislatures," *Legislative Studies Quarterly* 13 (1992): 65–81.

9. Gary F. Moncrief, Peverill Squire, and Malcolm E. Jewell, *Who Runs for the Legislature?* (Upper Saddle River, N.J.: Prentice Hall, 2001).

10. Michelle Fistek, "New Hampshire: Is the Granite Grip of the Republican Party Cracking?" *Polity Special Supplement* (1997): 50–51.

11. Moncrief, Squire, and Jewell, *Who Runs for the Legislature?* 22.

12. Daniel Shea, *Transforming Democracy: Legislative Campaign Committees and Political Parties* (Albany: State University of New York Press, 1995).

13. Alan Ehrenhalt, *The United States of Ambition* (New York: Random House, 1991); Morris Fiorina, *Divided Government* (Boston: Allyn and Bacon, 1996).

14. *Charleston Gazette,* "Candidate Files for House but in the Wrong District," April 26, 2002.

15. Moncrief, Squire, and Jewell, *Who Runs for the Legislature?* 35.

16. Peverill Squire, "Uncontested Seats in State Legislative Elections," *Legislative Studies Quarterly* 25 (2000): 131–146.

17. The remainder of this section is based on Moncrief, Squire, and Jewell, *Who Runs for the Legislature?* 34–38, 43, 102.

18. Owen Abbe and Paul S. Herrnson, "Campaign Professionalism in State Legislative Elections," *State Politics and Policy Quarterly* 3 (2003): 231–232.

19. Ron Faucheux and Paul S. Herrnson, "See How They Run: State Legislative Candidates," *Campaigns and Elections* (August 1999): 25.

20. J. Cheri Strachan, *High Tech Grass Roots* (Lanham, Md.: Rowman and Littlefield, 2003), 40.

21. Institute on Money in State Politics, "2000 State Election Overview," 2002, www.followthemoney.org (accessed May 25, 2005). These figures probably overestimated the true "normal" amount raised, because averages (means) are sensitive to the effect of a few extraordinarily high values. In reporting measures of central tendency for campaign finance data, median figures are often a truer reflection of the situation. For example, Jonathan Smith ("Professionalization of State Legislative Campaigns in South Carolina, North Carolina and Georgia," paper presented at the annual meeting of the Southern Political Science Association, Atlanta, November 2001, 11) reports total contributions for legislative candidates in three southern states in which the mean contribution for senate candidates was $85,761, but the median figure was $63,000—a difference of more than 25 percent. For a more detailed discussion of this issue, see Gary F. Moncrief, "Candidate Spending in State Legislative Races," in *Campaign Finance in State Legislative Campaigns,* ed. Joel Thompson and Gary Moncrief (Washington, D.C.: CQ Press, 1998), 39.

22. Denise Barber, "Life before BCRA," Institute on Money in State Politics, Helena, Mont., December 2003.

23. Ibid., 4.

24. Alan Ehrenhalt, "Political Pawns," *Governing* (July 2000): 20–23.

25. Jean Merl, "Solis Prepares to Take Another Step Up," *Los Angeles Times,* December 28, 2000.

26. On professionalized legislators, see John Carey, Richard Niemi, and Lynda Powell, *Term Limits in the State Legislatures* (Ann Arbor: University of Michigan Press, 2000). On travel money, see Thomas M. Holbrook and Charles M. Tidmarch, "Sophomore Surge in State Legislative Elections, 1968–86," *Legislative Studies Quarterly* 16 (1991): 49–63. And on constituent casework, see Gary W. Cox and Scott Morgenstern, "The Increasing Advantage of Incumbency in the U.S. States," *Legislative Studies Quarterly* 18 (1993): 495–514; and George Serra and Neil Pinney, "Casework, Issues, and Voting in State Elections: Bridging the Gap between Congressional and State Legislative Research," paper presented at the annual meeting of the American Political Science Association, 2001.

27. Moncrief, Squire, and Jewell, *Who Runs for the Legislature?* 110–113.

28. Faucheux and Herrnson, "See How They Run."

29. Robert E. Hogan, "Voter Contact Techniques in State Legislative Campaigns: The Prevalence of Mass Media Advertising," *Legislative Studies Quarterly* 22 (1997): 551–571; Smith, "Professionalization of State Legislative Campaigns in South Carolina, North Carolina and Georgia"; Abbe and Herrnson, "Campaign Professionalism in State Legislative Elections."

30. Ken Dilanian and Thomas Fitzgerald, "Pa. House Candidates Seek an Edge on Region's Airwaves," *Philadelphia Inquirer,* October 20, 2000.

31. Hogan, "Voter Contact Techniques in State Legislative Campaigns."

32. Smith, "Professionalization of State Legislative Campaigns in South Carolina, North Carolina and Georgia."

33. Abbe and Herrnson, "Campaign Professionalism in State Legislative Elections," 232.

34. Kevin Corcoran, "District 89 Exemplifies Emerging Uncertainty," *Indianapolis Star,* October 2, 2000; John Fritze, "Voter Rolls Are Rising, as Turnout Declines," *Indianapolis Star,* October 9, 2000.

35. *Charleston Gazette,* "Legislative Hopefuls Struggle to Get Attention," November 6, 2000.

36. Lisa Grace Lednicer and Tomoko Hosaka, "Weekend Scramble for Votes," *Oregonian,* November 6, 2000.

37. Alex Irvine, "Candidate Blog," *Portland Phoenix,* February 27, 2004.

38. Thomas E. Weber, "In Texas Hill Country, Getting Out the Vote Means Going Online," *Wall Street Journal,* September 18, 2000.

39. Strachan, *High Tech Grass Roots.*

Suggested Readings

Abbe, Owen, and Paul S. Herrnson. "Campaign Professionalism in State Legislative Elections." *State Politics and Policy Quarterly* 3 (2003): 223–245.

Amy, Douglas. *Behind the Ballot Box.* Westport, Conn.: Praeger, 2000.

Barber, Denise. "Life before BCRA." Institute on Money in State Politics, Helena, Mont., December 2003.

Carey, John, Richard Niemi, and Lynda Powell. *Term Limits in the State Legislatures.* Ann Arbor: University of Michigan Press, 2000.

Cox, Gary W., and Scott Morgenstern. "The Increasing Advantage of Incumbency in the U.S. States." *Legislative Studies Quarterly* 18 (1993): 495–514.

Ehrenhalt, Alan. "Political Pawns." *Governing* (July 2000): 20–23.

———. *The United States of Ambition.* New York: Random House, 1991.

Faucheux, Ron, and Paul S. Herrnson. "See How They Run: State Legislative Candidates." *Campaigns and Elections* (August 1999).

Fistek, Michelle. "New Hampshire: Is the Granite Grip of the Republican Party Cracking?" *Polity Special Supplement* (1997): 50–51.

Hogan, Robert E. "Voter Contact Techniques in State Legislative Campaigns: The Prevalence of Mass Media Advertising." *Legislative Studies Quarterly* 22 (1997): 551–571.

Holbrook, Thomas M., and Charles M. Tidmarch. "Sophomore Surge in State Legislative Elections, 1968–86." *Legislative Studies Quarterly* 16 (1991): 49–63.

Maisel, L. Sandy. *Parties and Elections in America.* 3d ed. Lanham, Md.: Rowman and Littlefield, 1999.

Moncrief, Gary. "Candidate Spending in State Legislative Races." In *Campaign Finance in State Legislative Campaigns,* edited by Joel Thompson and Gary Moncrief. Washington, D.C.: CQ Press, 1998.

Moncrief, Gary F., Peverill Squire, and Malcolm E. Jewell. *Who Runs for the Legislature?* Upper Saddle River, N.J.: Prentice Hall, 2001.

Serra, George, and Neil Pinney. "Casework, Issues, and Voting in State Elections: Bridging the Gap between Congressional and State Legislative Research." Paper presented at the annual meeting of the American Political Science Association, 2001.

Shea, Daniel. *Transforming Democracy: Legislative Campaign Committees and Political Parties.* Albany: State University of New York Press, 1995.

Smith, Jonathan. "Professionalization of State Legislative Campaigns in South Carolina, North Carolina and Georgia." Paper presented at the annual meeting of the Southern Political Science Association, Atlanta, November 2001.

Squire, Peverill. "Legislative Professionalization and Membership Diversity in State Legislatures." *Legislative Studies Quarterly* 13 (1992): 65–81.

———. "Uncontested Seats in State Legislative Elections." *Legislative Studies Quarterly* 25 (2000): 131–146.

Strachan, J. Cherie. *High Tech Grass Roots.* Lanham, Md.: Rowman and Littlefield, 2003.

CHAPTER 25

Judicial Elections

Roy A. Schotland

Campaigns come in many styles, but judicial election campaigns have always been unique. It has been said that "political campaigns for judicial posts are generally about as exciting as a game of checkers . . . [p]layed by mail." [1] Indeed, they have been "low-key affairs, conducted with civility and dignity." [2] With the unprecedented rise in competitiveness and spending in the 2000 election, however, judicial elections have become more like other kinds of elections, and whether one deplores or applauds the changes, there is no question that judicial election campaigns are drawing more attention than ever.

This chapter looks at the lesser-known contests for elected office—those for judgeships. It begins by explaining the political and legal context of judicial elections—how many states have judges facing election and at what levels, how judicial campaigns are conducted, and what makes judicial campaigns different from other types of campaigns. The chapter then explores what happened in the 2000 Ohio judicial campaigns to illustrate why Ohio has been viewed as the "poster child" of the new judicial election scene. The third section demonstrates that events in Ohio are not isolated but part of a trend, and it presents cases, including seldom studied lower-court races, from other states in which judicial campaigns have become more like those for other offices. Next, the chapter considers the unique role of candidate name familiarity in judicial elections. The final two sections put recent events into context and summarize the kinds of efforts under way to reform judicial campaigns.

Political and Legal Context of Judicial Elections

Thirty-nine states have judicial elections, and eleven states are strictly appointive. In twenty states, all or some judges run in nonpartisan elections; in sixteen all or some run in partisan elections; and in nineteen all or some face "retention" elections in which the voters either keep or fire an incumbent judge (see Table 25-1). Nationwide, of the almost 1,500 state appellate judges (those sitting on

courts with jurisdiction to review lower-court or executive decisions) and over 11,000 state trial judges (general jurisdiction), 87 percent face elections of some type. In fact, in some states far more judicial candidates than legislative candidates are listed on the ballot. For example, Florida has 160 legislators and 536 judges; Illinois has 177 legislators and 556 judges; and Ohio has 132 legislators and 445 judges.

Campaign rules for judicial candidates differ greatly from those regulating candidates for other offices, and the differences stem from an array of constitutional provisions that preserve the distinctive role of the judiciary.[3] Those provisions, which would be unthinkable for other elected officials in the legislative and executive branches, are meant to meet the unique challenges that judicial elections present—the "fundamental tension between the ideal character of the judicial office and the real world of electoral politics." [4]

Judicial candidates' fund raising has been uniquely constrained. In over thirty states, campaign contributions cannot be solicited by judicial candidates personally—only by their campaign committees. Another unique aspect of their elections is that judicial candidates may not seek support by making promises about how they will perform. Also, because of the nature of their job judges may not cultivate and reward support by working with their supporters and their communities to advance shared goals. Unlike judges, nonjudicial elected officials often work unreservedly toward change and are free to meet—at any time, openly or privately—with their constituents or anyone who may be affected by their actions in pending or future matters. Nonjudicial officials also participate in diverse, and usually large, multimember bodies.

Although electoral contests are held more frequently for supreme court seats than for the lower-court positions, a study of high-court elections from 1980 to 1995 found that 48 percent of incumbent justices were not challenged.[5] Even in states that have elections, roughly half of all judges, especially on the lower courts, initially reach the bench by appointment to fill vacancies.[6] Few lower-court judges are challenged, although information about lower-court elections is sparse (as noted more fully

Table 25-1 States and Types of Judicial Elections Held for Some or All Judges

Partisan[a]	Retention[b]	Nonpartisan	No judicial elections[c]
Alabama	Alaska	Arizona[d]	Connecticut
Idaho[d]	Arizona[d]	Arkansas	Delaware
Illinois[d]	California[d]	California[d]	Hawaii
Indiana[d]	Colorado	Florida[d]	Maine
Kansas[d]	Florida[d]	Georgia	Massachusetts
Louisiana	Illinois[d]	Idaho[d]	New Hampshire
Maryland[d]	Indiana[d]	Indiana[d]	New Jersey
Michigan[d]	Iowa	Kentucky	Rhode Island
Missouri[d]	Kansas[d]	Michigan[d]	South Carolina
New Mexico[d]	Maryland[d]	Minnesota	Vermont
New York[d]	Missouri[d]	Mississippi	Virginia
Ohio	Nebraska	Montana	
Pennsylvania[d]	New Mexico[d]	Nevada	
Tennessee[d]	Oklahoma[d]	North Carolina	
Texas	Pennsylvania[d]	North Dakota	
West Virginia	South Dakota[d]	Oklahoma[d]	
	Tennessee[d]	Oregon	
	Utah	South Dakota[d]	
	Wyoming	Washington	
		Wisconsin	

Source: Compiled by author.

[a] In Ohio, judicial candidates appear on the general election ballot without party labels, but their selection and campaigns are otherwise partisan. In Michigan, the same is true of supreme court candidates, but others are nonpartisan. In Maryland, trial judges face contestable elections that were deemed nonpartisan until the Maryland Supreme Court held in November 2004 that they are partisan. In New York, high-court judges are appointed.

[b] In Illinois and Pennsylvania, judges are initially elected in partisan elections, but their continuance is determined in retention elections; New Mexico has a uniquely hybrid process.

[c] Included here are Connecticut, Maine, South Carolina, and Vermont, which elect probate judges. Otherwise, this table includes only appellate and general-jurisdiction trial judges.

[d] In these states, different judges face different types of elections.

later in this chapter).[7] This relative lack of competitiveness is, again, one of the most important distinctions between judicial elections and elections for other offices.

Until recently, even very competitive high-court contests have drawn little media attention, although high-court races are often near the top of the ballot. In many states, exit polls have revealed voters' extreme unawareness of the judicial candidates. This finding is hardly surprising, because lack of media attention is routine for most down-ballot or lower-office contests.

What singles out judicial campaigns was captured by California consultant Joe Cerrell when he said, "Our [state] senators have a political operation for use in retaliation. For the most part, judges are standing naked in the political process not knowing what, when, or how to do anything."[8] Judicial campaigns are unique in part

because a judge's job is so different from those of nonjudicial elected officials and in part because of the way judicial races are run.

What Happened in Ohio

In November 2002, two days after the election, Chief Justice Thomas Moyer of Ohio said, "Candidates were outraged. Citizens were outraged. I am outraged. Anybody who places his or her trust and confidence in a constitutional democracy should be outraged."[9]

The source of Moyer's outrage was the hottest of all of Ohio's elections that year—the contests for two supreme court seats—and the influence of the television ads sup-

---

OFFICIAL GENERAL ELECTION BALLOT
BREVARD COUNTY, FLORIDA
NOVEMBER 2, 2004

- TO VOTE, COMPLETELY FILL IN THE OVAL ● NEXT TO YOUR CHOICE.
- Use a black or blue pen (not red) or a black pencil to mark your ballot.
- If you make a mistake, don't hesitate to ask for a new ballot. If you erase or make other marks, your vote may not count.
- To vote for a candidate whose name is not printed on the ballot, fill in the oval, and write in the candidate's name on the blank line provided for a write-in candidate.

PRESIDENT AND VICE PRESIDENT		NONPARTISAN
(Vote for One)		Shall Justice Raoul G. Cantero, III of the Supreme Court be retained in office?
○ George W. Bush Dick Cheney	REP	
		○ YES
○ John F. Kerry John Edwards	DEM	○ NO
		DISTRICT COURT OF APPEAL
○ Michael A. Peroutka Chuck Baldwin	CPF	Shall Judge Jacqueline R. Griffin of the Fifth District Court of Appeal be retained in office?
○ Michael Badnarik Richard V. Campagna	LIB	○ YES
		○ NO
○ David Cobb Patricia LaMarche	GRE	Shall Judge David A. Monaco of the Fifth District Court of Appeal be retained in office?
○ James Harris Margaret Trowe	SWP	○ YES
		○ NO
○ Walter F. Brown Mary Alice Herbert	SPF	Shall Judge Earle W. Peterson, Jr. of the Fifth District Court of Appeal be retained in office?
○ Ralph Nader Peter Miguel Camejo	REF	○ YES
		○ NO
CONGRESSIONAL		Shall Judge Winifred J. Sharp of the Fifth District Court of Appeal be retained in office?
UNITED STATES SENATOR (Vote for One)		○ YES
		○ NO
○ Mel Martinez	REP	Shall Judge Vincent G. Torpy, Jr. of the Fifth District Court of Appeal be retained in office?
○ Betty Castor	DEM	
○ Dennis F. Bradley	VET	○ YES
○ _____ Write-in		○ NO
REPRESENTATIVE IN CONGRESS **15TH CONGRESSIONAL DISTRICT** (Vote for One)		**CITY OF MELBOURNE**
○ Dave Weldon	REP	**MAYOR** (Vote for One)
○ Simon Pristoop	DEM	
LEGISLATIVE		○ Harry C. Goode, Jr.
STATE REPRESENTATIVE **31ST HOUSE DISTRICT** (Vote for One)		○ Ed Palmer
		○ William Perry

A portion of a November 2, 2004, general election ballot from Brevard County, Florida, lists six judges subject to a thumbs-up or thumbs-down vote in nonpartisan retention elections.
Source: Supervisor of Elections, Brevard County, Florida

porting each of the candidates. Republicans—one an incumbent, the other the lieutenant governor—won both races. Although Ohio's ballots have no party label for any judicial candidate, making these offices nominally nonpartisan, the candidates are nominated in partisan primaries, they run as partisans, and they often have direct party support. For example, the 2002 winners received $229,000 from their state party, and the losers received $231,736 from theirs. The winning incumbent raised more than any other judicial candidate in the nation in 2002, almost $1.9 million; the other winner came in second nationally with about $1.8 million. Their opponents raised, respectively, about $1.35 million and $1.2 million.[10]

The candidates adhered to tradition by not taking stands on issues lest they prejudice or preclude their sitting in cases involving those issues (this situation is examined later in this chapter in connection with the June 2002 U.S. Supreme Court decision that found unconstitutional the limits placed by some states on how judicial candidates campaign). What made the Ohio races so notable were the television ads by business groups on one side and trial lawyers on the other. Citizens for an Independent Court, a committee of trial lawyers and unions, ran an ad mocking the incumbent, Evelyn Lunberg Stratton, whose own campaign was calling her the "velvet hammer." The group's ad featured an Ohioan who had won an appeal of a negligence case against his employer over Stratton's dissent. "Yeah, corporations get the velvet, Ohio families get the hammer. . . . [The GOP candidates] put large corporations ahead of working families. . . . [The Democratic candidates] put people ahead of profits . . . they're on our side." On the other side, Competition Ohio, a business-supported group, ran an ad about a pending telephone company request to raise phone rates, praising the GOP candidates for "standing up for Ohio consumers and small business." And Informed Citizens of Ohio defended the incumbent justice with an ad saying that "doctors are disappearing from the state of Ohio . . . because frivolous lawsuits are forcing them to leave." Stratton's record "shows that she understands the need to stop lawsuit abuse." Other ads were in the same vein.

The candidates themselves forcefully protested the ads, and a state bar committee on judicial election conduct deplored such ads as injurious to the judicial system, because they imply that judges have made up their minds before cases are presented. It was these ads, and the overall campaign conduct by the noncandidate groups, that drew Chief Justice Moyer's powerful condemnation.

Two years earlier, in 2000, Ohio had had two seats up on the court up for election—one held by a GOP incumbent, the other by a Democratic incumbent who had authored a 4–3 decision striking down an important tort reform statute (tort reform is a movement to reduce the amount of tort litigation, usually involving legislation that caps settlement amounts for injuries and medical malpractice). Tort reform, more than any other issue, has in many states fueled the increased funding and heat in recent judicial campaigns, with business interests on one side and plaintiff trial lawyers and sometimes unions on the other.

In that 2000 election, the Ohio Chamber of Commerce spent $5–$6 million backing the GOP incumbent, and its television ad against Democratic incumbent justice Alice Resnick became the event of the campaign.[11] The ad featured a statue of Lady Justice peeking underneath her blindfold as piles of special interest money tip her scales and as a voiceover states that Justice Resnick ruled nearly 70 percent of the time in favor of trial lawyers who have given her more than $750,000 in campaign funds since 1994. The announcer concluded: "Alice Resnick. Is justice for sale?"

The ad was at once strongly attacked as inappropriate by the state bar president, and Resnick went on to retain her seat. But the ad did have one constructive result: the state bar formed a diverse, representative campaign conduct oversight committee for the 2002 elections, when it found itself once again attacking campaign ads as inappropriate, this time with much more press coverage than in 2000. In 2004, although more money than ever was spent in the Ohio judicial races, not a single ad was problematic, probably because the oversight committee was on the job.

In Ohio, the extent to which the campaigns were affected, if not dominated, by noncandidate groups comes through most clearly by comparing the spending by the candidates and by those groups. In 2002 the candidates raised $6.2 million, roughly doubling the 2000 figure; the prior record was $4.6 million in 1992. (The political parties contributed $884,000 to the candidates in 2002. Although no party contribution totals are available for 2000, the Democratic Party that year spent directly at least $470,000 on express advocacy television ads and also ran some issue ads.) By contrast, in 2002 the noncandidate groups, split almost equally between business groups and coalitions of unions and trial lawyers, spent an estimated $5 million on television, and in 2000 such groups spent more than double the candidates' funds—roughly $7.5 million—mostly from an Ohio Chamber of Commerce affiliate and the U.S. Chamber of Commerce.[12]

Judicial elections are not the only contests experiencing major participation by outside groups, with the candidates elbowed aside. But in judicial elections, such participation dominates or verges on dominance, not only because of the relative sums involved—in Ohio in 2000 the candidates' spending totals were less than half the outsiders' spending just on TV—but also because judicial candidates take few if any positions on issues. Thus,

apart from the candidates' personalities and records, the contests can be shaped by the outsiders.

The National Picture

In 2000 Ohio was one of five states—the others were Alabama, Illinois, Michigan, and Mississippi—in which supreme court races were unprecedentedly expensive and fiercely contested. Funding records were set in ten of the twenty states holding such elections that year. Nationally, candidates' campaign chests rose to $45.6 million, which was 41 percent above the previous peak in 1998, for an average cost per seat of $995,999 (46 seats), or nearly double the 1990–1999 per seat average of $540,067 (189 seats).[13] The 2002 and 2004 campaigns were calmer: new records were set in the eighteen states that have supreme court races, and the national total spending was lower. However, television ads were run by candidates and others in more than twice as many states as in 2000, although the total spending was lower.

One recent major change is that never before have noncandidates been significant in judicial elections (except for spending by political parties in the states in which judges were facing partisan elections). In 2000 roughly $16 million was spent by noncandidates in just four of the five states with the most competitive races, although little or none was spent elsewhere. Yet in 2002 outside those four states, it appears that less than $250,000 was spent by noncandidates, and, although there is almost no information on earlier years, it is likely that even smaller sums were spent then.

Out-of-state intervention cost Mississippi's Chief Justice Lenore Prather her seat in 2000. The U.S. Chamber of Commerce itself, not a local affiliate, spent about $958,000 on TV ads on behalf of the chief justice, two other incumbents, and one challenger. The chief justice asked the Chamber to halt the ads, but without success. The Chamber's intervention was a major cause of her upset defeat. Her challenger, who had raised only $9,000 as of mid-October, attacked the chief justice's support by the Chamber, an "outside" national organization, and her "liberal" participation in reversal of criminal convictions. The chief justice had served fifteen years and had never been opposed, but she lost the election 48 percent to 52 percent.

The change in judicial elections from quiet and usually uncontested races to lively and even heated ones in a steadily increasing number of states began in 1978 when Los Angeles County deputy district attorneys actually advertised to find candidates to oppose unchallenged incumbent trial judges. The prosecutors were opposed to the approaches of many judges appointed by Democratic governor Jerry Brown, and their advertising and support helped to defeat an unprecedented number of these judges. In the 1980s, the Texas Supreme Court races—fiercely fought between tort plaintiffs and defense lawyers—involved unprecedented levels of campaign spending. Because the Texas developments gained national notoriety by means of a *60 Minutes* broadcast in 1987, for years most of the few people who paid any attention to judicial elections ignored the spreading changes, arguing, "Well, that's just Texas." In 1990 the American Judicature Society's national project aimed at reducing the problems in judicial elections brought together in Little Rock, Arkansas, an impressive array of people who could not have been more interested—or, as they made clear, more certain that the problems could not happen in Arkansas. But by unhappy coincidence their next election, between two very well-qualified candidates, was by far the most expensive and least restrained in Arkansas history.

As for Texas, its elections have become very quiet for two reasons. First, since 1999 its supreme court has been all Republican, and the justices' positions are so secure that in 2002 Chief Justice Tom Phillips (running for the fourth time) was endorsed by the head of the plaintiff's trial lawyers' organization. In 2000 the three incumbents up for reelection faced only $14,000 in spending against them in the primaries, and in the general election they faced only three nonspending Libertarians and one Green Party candidate.[14] The incumbents spent a total of $1.2 million, two-thirds by Justice Alberto Gonzales, who was appointed U.S. attorney general by President George W. Bush in 2004. His 58 percent to 42 percent primary election margin was the closest of any incumbent. The second reason Texas judicial races no longer see Texas-sized spending is Chief Justice Phillips's 1995 success in winning enactment of the nation's only rigorous regulation of campaign finance in judicial elections, capping not only individuals' contributions, but also aggregate contributions by law firms.

In the 2000 judicial elections in Michigan, Democratic Party ads featured animated trees shuddering about the incumbent supreme court justices as a voiceover said the court had "ruled against families and for corporations 82 percent of the time." That claim was reviewed by the *Detroit Free Press,* which found that it "borders on the bogus," because in fourteen of the forty-three "antifamily" cases, the Democratic justices had agreed with the result, to which Democratic Party officials replied that "defining a family or corporate entity [is not] an exact science." [15] On the other side, a GOP ad attacked a challenger (who was an intermediate appellate judge) for having joined in upholding a light sentence for a pedophile. The *Free Press* reported that in the ad "the word 'pedophile' in huge type flashes close to the judge's name." When the ad was attacked, the GOP replied, "We don't call him [a pedophile]."

For simplicity of message, it is hard to beat the now-famous (or infamous) Alabama trial judge who won that state's chief justiceship in 2000. Judge Roy Moore had gained national notice for posting the Ten Commandments in his courtroom and refusing to remove them despite court orders. In 2004 Moore was removed from the supreme court after he placed a four-foot-high, 5,280-pound Ten Commandments monument in the court's lobby without consulting any of his colleagues.

All of the races just described are those for supreme court seats rather than the lower courts for two reasons. First, high-court seats are more likely to be contested. Second, only limited, often episodic information is available, and there is almost no campaign finance data on lower-court campaigns. Data on the latter have been gathered for a few states, but only the Florida figures are notable, and they are striking indeed. In 2002, with 277 trial court seats up and 43 contested, candidates raised over $16 million, and in 2000, with 182 seats up and 17 contested, they raised over $8 million.[16] (Florida's appellate judges do not face contestable elections; they are appointed and subject to retention votes.)

Two other snapshots of lower-court races are also significant. Texas has partisan elections, meaning that a strong presidential or gubernatorial candidate may heavily affect down-ballot races. As for Texas's lower-court campaign funding, the average spending in the races for fifteen contested intermediate appellate seats in 2000 was $308,000; one candidate spent $681,000 and lost the general election, and one trial court candidate spent $633,000 to win in the primary, which included a runoff. The average spending in the twelve trial court races in major cities was $314,000.[17]

Political Consultants and the Role of Name Familiarity

A rarely noted aspect of judicial campaigns is raised by the Florida data just presented: the role of campaign consultants (also see Chapter 10). California spawned the first consultant specializing in judicial campaigns, Joe Cerrell, who has advised several hundred judicial candidates. Today, Miami-Dade County in Florida seems to be the jurisdiction with the most active consultants for judicial campaigns. They even specialize along ethnic lines—at least one consultant specializes in Hispanic candidates and another in African American candidates. In Miami-Dade, potential challengers often hire a consultant and remain as "floaters" until moments before the deadline for filing to be a candidate, so that they can see which incumbents have no challenger or no strong challenger (the same practice prevails in Cook County, Illinois). One consultant even assures any potential client who is an incumbent that none of his "floater" clients will run against another of his clients.

Campaign consultants figured importantly in a Texas legislative effort in 2003–2004 in which the Senate had passed a bill to change most judgeships from elective to appointive positions and the House was about to vote. The proposed change ran into two hurdles. For one thing, it was not popular with substantial elements of the GOP grass roots, especially abortion opponents, who believed that they would have less impact if judges were appointed. Also, House members received calls from their own campaign consultants—many of whom also worked in judicial campaigns—saying that if the member voted for the bill, she or he was likely to have opposition in the primary. The House did not bring the bill up for a vote.

Another unusual aspect of judicial campaigns is how hugely candidates' names matter. Name familiarity is important in all kinds of campaigns, but in judicial campaigns it is especially important, because these candidates have low visibility and sometimes names are the only voting cue that most citizens have when trying to decide for whom to vote. In 1990 in Washington State, the highly regarded chief justice Keith Callow was defeated by an unknown Tacoma lawyer who won 53 percent of the vote, even though he spent only $500 on the race and did not campaign—he had the same name as Tacoma TV news anchorman Charley Johnson. The same year in San Antonio, Texas, a popular and highly respected judge was defeated for a supreme court nomination by a lawyer new to the area, a recent retiree from the army whose name was Gene Kelly. In 1998 in North Carolina, a primary election cost one of the state's most respected appellate judges his seat. The trial judge who defeated him had twice been censured by the supreme court for improper conduct, but he had the same name as a recent former governor and used campaign signs that looked like the governor's. Finally, a 1982 Alabama supreme court primary was narrowly won by the incumbent, Oscar Adams, the state's first black justice. The challenger, a three-year practitioner from an unaccredited law school, had the same name as a well-known local company. The justice said, "Our surveys showed a substantial number favored him [the opponent] because they thought he was the bakery man." [18]

Recent Events in Perspective

The first U.S. Supreme Court decision about judicial campaigns (*Republican Party of Minnesota v. White*) was handed down on the last day of the Court's term in June 2002. The Court held 5–4 that Minnesota could not prohibit a judicial candidate from "announc[ing] his or her views on disputed legal or political issues." That limit was law in only eight states, because in 1990 the Model Code of Judicial Conduct[19] had been amended (precisely because that old limit was deemed constitutionally questionable) and so the other states had limits barring candidates from any "pledges or promises of conduct in office other than the faithful performance of the duties of the office"[20]—a limit that, as the Court noted, had not been challenged. Where that limit stands after the *White* decision is unclear; a number of states have revised their codes, but none except North Carolina repealed anything other than the "announce" clause. However, later in 2002 the Eleventh Circuit went beyond *White* in holding unconstitutional a limit (which is law in over thirty states) that bars judicial candidates from *personally* soliciting campaign contributions.[21] That issue is pending now in an Eighth Circuit *en banc* consideration of the remand in *White*. Also at issue now is a challenge to limits on partisan activity in judicial elections, which are law in eight states.

Susan Burke, candidate for the Hennepin County (Minn.) Fourth District judgeship in 2004, participates in a campaign debate. Burke, who opposed the discussion of disputed legal and political issues during judicial campaigns, went on to win the seat on the bench. The election closely followed the Supreme Court's 2002 decision in Republican Party of Minnesota v. White *that the state could not prohibit a judicial candidate from "announc[ing] his or her views on disputed legal or political issues." Source: Minneapolis Labor Review*

Perhaps in future campaigns judicial candidates will exercise less restraint in their statements, but so far *White* has had surprisingly little effect on judicial campaigns. It is unknown whether the outcome of Pennsylvania's 2003 supreme court race stemmed from the losing Republican's adherence to the traditional restraints or from the winning Democrat's efforts to speak out on positions. In fact, whether that difference mattered is unknown. What is known about that election is, as one judicial reformer put it, "turnout, turnout, turnout." The mayor of Philadelphia was running for reelection, his office had been wiretapped by the Federal Bureau of Investigation (FBI), and a new "shadow" Democratic group conducted unprecedentedly successful registration and turnout drives. In 2004 in Ohio, the only one of seven candidates who took positions on issues lost by the widest margin.[22]

In addition to the frequent use of messages conveying positions on some issues, very rough campaigning has sullied the civility and dignity traditionally associated with judicial campaigns. The most notorious campaign occurred in a 1996 retention election in Tennessee in which a supreme court justice was defeated because of the opposition of the Republican Party and one interest group. Six weeks before the election, a Nashville newspaper displayed the headline "Court Finds Rape, Murder of Elderly Virgin Not Cruel. Tennessee Conservative Union Says 'Just Say No to Justice White.'" The Tennessee Supreme Court had agreed unanimously with the lower court that the defendant was entitled to a new sentencing hearing. Three justices, including the one up for retention, wrote that the evidence was insufficient to show an aggravating circumstance beyond a reasonable doubt, as required by law. Then, the Tennessee Conservative Union sent faxes to its members that opened with a description of the crime:

> 78 year old Ethel Johnson lay dying in a pool of blood. Stabbed in the heart, lungs, and liver, she fought back as best she could. Her hands were sliced to ribbons as she tried to push the knife away. And then she was raped.
>
> Savagely. . . .
>
> But her murderer won't be getting the punishment that he deserves.
>
> Thanks to [Justice] Penny White.

In the end, Justice White's opponents—whose campaign had not been expected—defeated her with very little money, using mainly faxes.

Crime has long been the leading subject of many judicial campaigns. According to Oregon Supreme Court Justice Hans A. Linde,

> Every judge's campaign slogan, in advertisements and on billboards, is some variation of "tough on crime." The liberal candidate is the one who advertises: "Tough but fair." Television campaigns have featured judges in their robes slamming shut a prison cell door. . . . Most judges may see themselves as umpires between the state and the citizen, but many citizens regard judges as part of law enforcement, and plenty of candidates will offer themselves for that role. A conscientious judge who imposes less than the maximum possible sentence in cases evoking public outrage invites a bidding war with future opponents.[23]

Prospects and Reform

Anyone trying to predict whether campaigning and campaign spending will be more unrestrained than in the past may find it best to hide behind Samuel Goldwyn's obser-

vation that "predicting is hard, especially the future." What is not hard to predict is that judicial elections will be around for a while (see Box 25-1).

The British publication *The Economist* has described the situation in the United States as follows: "Back in 1906 Roscoe Pound, a scholar at Harvard Law School, started a campaign to have judges appointed by saying: 'Putting courts into politics, and compelling judges to become politicians, in many jurisdictions has almost destroyed the traditional respect for the bench.' When he spoke, eight in ten American judges stood for election. Today, the figure is 87 percent. Americans are still reluctant to accept that politicians should be chosen by the people, but not judges."[24] And, indeed, voters in a number of states have rejected efforts to end contestable elections. For example, in 2000 Florida voters overwhelmingly defeated a ballot proposition that would have provided a local option on whether trial courts would move from an elective system to appointive-cum-retention system. The highest vote the proposition won in any county was 39 percent; the average affirmative vote was 26 percent. In 2004 South Dakota voters defeated a similar proposal two to one. Ohio voters did the same in 1987.

Three types of efforts are under way to change the judicial election scene: legal reforms, unofficial efforts to reform campaign conduct, and direct responses to inappropriate conduct. These efforts are described in the rest of this section.

Legal Reforms

Among the legal reforms have been efforts to replace contestable judicial elections with a system of appointments followed by retention elections. As noted earlier, such efforts are not faring well. In some states such as Pennsylvania and Illinois, efforts to end contestable elections are hardy perennials, with constant calls for change in editorials, bills, and articles. But as *The Economist* reported, the resistance to change has been strong and pervasive.

One remedy advocated is official disciplinary action against judges or judicial candidates—even the removal of a Florida judge who "was charged with making explicit campaign promises to favor the state and the police and side against the defense in court proceedings; making unfounded attacks on an incumbent county judge and the local court system and local officials, and improperly presiding over a court case in which he had a direct conflict of interest."[25]

Longer judicial terms, the major reform effort being pressed by Ohio's chief justice, Thomas Moyer, would reduce the number of campaigns and the need for campaign funds, and such a measure would make judicial positions more attractive (the overriding goal of all of these reforms is to get and keep the best possible judges.) Ohio judges have six-year terms, which is shorter than those of 55 percent of state appellate judges and 45 percent of

BOX 25-1
JUDICIAL SELECTION IN THE UNITED STATES: A SPECIAL REPORT

Larry C. Berkson

Historically there has been considerable controversy about how American judges should be chosen. During the colonial era, they were selected by the king, but his intolerably wide powers over them was one of the abuses that the colonists attacked in the Declaration of Independence. After the Revolution, the states continued to select judges by appointment, but the new processes prevented the chief executive from controlling the judiciary.[1]

Gradually, however, states began to adopt popular election as a means of choosing judges. For example, as early as 1812 Georgia amended its constitution to provide that judges of inferior courts be popularly elected. In 1816, Indiana entered the Union with a constitution that provided for the election of associate judges of the circuit court. Sixteen years later, Mississippi became the first state in which all judges were popularly elected. Michigan held elections for trial judges in 1836.

By that time the appointive system had come under serious attack. People resented the fact that property owners controlled the judiciary.[2] They were determined to end this privilege of the upper class and to ensure the popular sovereignty we describe as Jacksonian Democracy.

During the next decade, there was little opposition to those who advocated popular elections. For example, in the New York Constitutional Convention of 1846 there was not even a lengthy discussion of the subject. As one writer has stated:

> The debates on an elective judiciary were brief; there was apparently little need to discuss the abuses of the appointive system, or its failures, or why election would be better. A few delegates argued cogently for the retention of the old system, and indeed forecast the possible evils if the judiciary fell under political domination . . . . But the spirit of reform carried the day.[3]

New York's adoption of an electoral system signaled the beginning of this trend. By the time of the Civil War, 24 of 34 states had established an elected judiciary with seven states adopting the system in 1850 alone.[4] As new states were admitted to the Union, all of them adopted popular election of some or all judges until the admission of Alaska in 1959.

No Panacea

Within a short time, however, it became apparent that this new system was no panacea, and the need for reform again was recognized. For example, as early as 1853 delegates to the Massachusetts Constitutional Convention viewed the popular election of judges in New York as a failure and refused to adopt the system. One delegate claimed that it had "fallen hopelessly into the great cistern" and quoted an article in the *Evening Post* that illustrated that judges had become enmeshed in the "political mill."[5] By 1867, the subject was a matter of great debate in New York, and in 1873 a proposed amendment to return to the appointive system gained strong support at the general election.[6]

One of the main concerns during this period was that judges were almost invariably selected by political machines and controlled by them. Judges were often perceived as corrupt and incompetent. The notion of a judiciary uncontrolled by special interests had simply not been realized. It was in this context that the concept of nonpartisan elections began to emerge.

The idea of judicial candidates appearing on the ballot without party label was used as early as 1873 in Cook County [Chicago], Illinois. Interestingly, it was the judges themselves who decided to run on a nonpartisan ballot rather than doing so pursuant to a statute or some other authority. Elections in 1885 and 1893 were also nonpartisan (Cook County subsequently returned to partisan elections). By the turn of the century the idea of nonpartisan judicial elections had gained strength, and several states had adopted the idea. By 1927, 12 states employed the nonpartisan idea.[7]

Once again, criticism of nonpartisan elections arose almost as soon as such elections began. As early as 1908 members of the South Dakota Bar Association indicated dissatisfaction with how the idea was working in their state. By 1927, Iowa, Kansas, and Pennsylvania had already tried the plan and abandoned it.[8] The major objection was that there was still no real public choice. New candidates for judgeships were regularly selected by party leaders and thrust upon an unknowledgeable electorate, which, without the guidance of party labels, was not able to make reasoned choices.

The Rise of Commission Plans

While others attacked nonpartisan elections, a number of well-known scholars, judges and concerned citizens began assailing all elective systems as failures. One of the most outspoken critics, Roscoe Pound, delivered a now classic address to the American Bar Association in 1906 on "The Causes of Popular Dissatisfaction with the Administration of Justice." He claimed that "putting courts into politics, and compelling judges to become politicians in many jurisdictions . . . [had] almost destroyed the traditional respect for the bench." [9]

Several years later in a speech before the Cincinnati Bar Association, William Howard Taft claimed that it was "disgraceful" to see men campaigning for the state supreme court on the ground that their decisions would have a particular class flavor. It was "so shocking, and so out of keeping with the fixedness of moral principles," he said, that it ought to be "condemned." [10]

Reformers claimed that the worst features of partisan politics could be eliminated through what they called a "merit plan" for selecting judges. The plan would expand the pool of candidates to include persons other than friends of politicians. Selectors would not consider inappropriate partisan factors such as an individual's party affiliation, party service, or friendship with an appointing executive so the most distinguished members of the bar, regardless of party, could be elevated to the bench.[11]

Origins of the plan are usually traced to Albert M. Kales, one of the founders of the American Judicature Society. Versions of his proposal were introduced in state legislatures throughout the 1930s. The American Bar Association endorsed a merit plan in 1937, and in 1940 Missouri became the first state to put one into effect. Today it is variously known as the Kales plan, Missouri plan, merit plan, or commission plan.

Almost none of the state plans are identical, but they do share common features. Most include a permanent, nonpartisan commission composed of lawyers and nonlawyers (appointed by a variety of public and private officials) who actively recruit and screen prospective candidates. The commission then forwards a list of three to five qualified individuals to the executive, who must make an appointment from the list.

Usually the judges serve a one- or two-year probationary period, after which they must run unopposed on a retention ballot. The sole question on which the electorate votes is: "Shall Judge ____ be retained in office?" A judge must win a majority of the vote in order to serve a full term.

Judicial Selection Today

Today the combination of schemes used to select judges is almost endless. Almost no two states are alike, and many states employ different methods of selection depending upon the different levels of the judiciary, creating "hybrid" systems of selection. It is possible, however, to classify selection methods in the states. The most frequently used classification differentiates between states that appoint their judges and states that elect their judges. The two groups turn out to be fairly equal in number.

1. Eight of the original 13 states vested the appointment power in one or both houses of legislature. Two allowed appointment by the governor and his council, and three vested appointment authority in the governor but required him to obtain consent of the council. Escovitz, *Judicial Selection and Tenure* (Chicago: American Judicature Society, 1975), 4.

2. Niles, "The Popular Election of Judges in Historical Perspective," *The Record of the Association of the Bar of the City of New York* (November, 1966), 523.

3. Ibid., 526.

4. Escovitz, 6, n. 1.

5. Niles, 528, n. 2.

6. Ibid., 535, n. 46.

7. Aumann, "Selection, Tenure, Retirement and Compensation of Judges in Ohio," 5 *University of Cincinnati Law Review* 412, n. 11 (1931).

8. Ibid.

9. Pound, *"The Causes of Popular Dissatisfaction With the Administration of Justice,* 20 *Journal of the American Judicature Society* 178 (February, 1937).

10. Taft, "The Selection and Tenure of Judges," 38 *American Bar Association* Rep. 418 (1913).

11. Kales, *Unpopular Government in the United States* (Chicago: University of Chicago Press, 1914), chap. 17. *See also* Harley, "Taking Judges Out of Politics," in *Public Administration and Politics* (Philadelphia: The American Academy of Political and Social Science, 1916); and Winters, "Judicial Selection and Tenure," in Winters (ed.), *Selected Readings: Judicial Selection and Tenure,* (Chicago: American Judicature Society, 1973).

Source: Elliot E. Slotnick, ed., *Judicial Politics: Readings from Judicature* (Washington, D.C.: CQ Press, 2005), 50–52. This article originally appeared in Volume 64, Number 4, October 1980, pages 176–193, and was updated in August 2004. It is condensed from a larger study by the American Judicature Society (www.ajs.org), *Judicial Selection in the United States: A Compendium of Provisions* (Chicago: American Judicature Society, 1980).

state trial judges. Lengthening terms stirs some opposition, however. In 2000, when Mississippi's chief justice succeeded in getting a ballot proposition before the voters to lengthen judges' four-year terms, it was defeated by a vote of 63 percent to 37 percent. As the editor of the *Clarion Ledger* (Jackson, Mississippi) commented, "They'd vote on the mailman if they could." [26]

Public financing of campaigns for some offices is the law in twenty-three states, but for judicial campaigns it has been available only in Wisconsin and, starting in 2004, in North Carolina. When public financing of judicial campaigns was proposed in Ohio, one justice said it had less likelihood of passage than a bill to mandate the leashing of cats. Wisconsin's public financing began in 1979 and worked well in its early years, but since 1995 the public funds have accounted for only about 3 percent of candidates' total campaign funds. Reform groups are working to revitalize the system. In North Carolina's 2004 election, almost every judicial candidate chose to participate in the public funding system, but the funds available were sparser than hoped for, and it is too early for evaluation.

Two other legal efforts are significant. In all down-ballot races, not only those for the courts, voters have little or no information about candidates. For many years, five states—Alaska, California, Colorado, Oregon, and Washington—have mailed official voter pamphlets describing the candidates to all registered voters; different "editions" are published for different parts of each state. This source of information is especially valuable for judicial elections, and in 2000 a summit conference of seventeen chief justices from states with judicial elections recommended that states create and distribute voter pamphlets and that Congress provide a free-mailing privilege.[27] The other effort, fuller disclosure by "independent spenders" about their contributions, is so far only a proposal. It involves the far more general problem of issue ads. The 2002 Bipartisan Campaign Reform Act calls for the disclosure of the sources of funding for such ads in federal campaigns, a disclosure model Ohio has just adopted.

Unofficial Reform Efforts

Over the years, codes of conduct for various kinds of campaigns have been discussed. For judicial campaigns, however, some jurisdictions have long had in place citizen committees composed of representative community leaders who work to encourage candidates to avoid problematic advertising, such as a campaign poster that says "Vote for Judge X," even though "Judge X" is not a judge or has not been one for many years. If such an ad or a problematic statement is issued, such committees go public, exercising their own free speech to explain why they find the conduct inappropriate. Such committees, which were first established in California's San Mateo County in 1976 and have been active in Columbus, Ohio, and

Florida's Miami-Dade County, have spread to many jurisdictions since 2000 because of the recommendations by the state chief justices and the American Bar Association.

Response to Inappropriate Conduct

In the Supreme Court's *White* decision, Justice Anthony Kennedy concurred separately, expressing more readiness than the majority to treat judicial elections like all other elections. However, he also said: "The legal profession, the legal academy, the press, voluntary groups, political and civic leaders, and all interested citizens can use their own First Amendment Freedoms to protest statements inconsistent with standards of judicial neutrality and judicial excellence. Indeed, if democracy is to fulfill its promise, they must do so." [28] Justice John Paul Stevens made the same point, adding that even official disciplinary bodies "may surely advise the electorate that [announcements of the candidate's views on issues that may come before the court] demonstrate the speaker's unfitness for judicial office. If the solution to harmful speech must be more speech, so be it."

After the *White* decision, the Missouri Supreme Court noted which of its limits on campaign conduct would no longer be enforced and which remained, and then went on to say: "Recusal [of the judge from a pending matter], or other remedial action, may nonetheless be required of any judge in cases that involve an issue about which the judge has announced his or her views as otherwise may be appropriate under the Code of Judicial Conduct." [29]

Efforts to have judges withdraw from cases because of previous campaign statements are bound to increase. Thus the overwhelming majority of candidates who want to campaign judiciously may find themselves saying such things as "I know what you'd like me to say, but if I go into that then I'll be unable to sit in just the cases you care about most." Also, any candidate whose opponent has pushed the envelope (with some variant of "I'll hang them all" or "I believe that anyone convicted of child abuse should receive the maximum sentence allowed by law" or "I'm a tenant, not a landlord") may respond by saying, "My opponent has told you what he thinks you want to hear, but he hasn't told you that he won't be able to deliver—he'll be disqualified from the cases you care about." Indeed, in Justice Kennedy's opinion in *White*, which supports the striking down of state limits on judicial candidates' campaign speech, he added that states "may adopt recusal standards more rigorous than due process requires, and censure judges who violate these standards." [30]

Despite the growing resemblance of judicial elections to nonjudicial races—greater spending and competition, noncandidate involvement, and the use of negative ads—the nature of judgeships and constitutional preservations of the integrity of the judiciary mean that many of these campaigns will probably continue to be "checkers by mail" contests, as they have been called. The most important "reform" is to increase public understanding of what judges do, why their job is different from the jobs of other elected officials, and thus why their campaigns need to be different. Without that greater understanding, ef-

forts to make changes in the laws on judicial selection are unlikely to succeed—but with more public understanding, there will be less need for any other changes.

Notes

1. William C. Bayne, "Lynchard's Candidacy, Ads Putting Spice into Justice Race; Hernando Attorney Challenging Coff," *Commercial Appeal,* October 29, 2000.

2. Peter D. Webster, "Selection and Retention Judges: Is There One 'Best' Method?" *Florida State University Law Review* 23 (1995): 1, 19.

3. The states with judicial elections have an array of constitutional provisions that make it clear that their choice of elections does not mean they will not treat the judicial branch as unique. For example, in all states with judicial elections judges' terms are longer than those of any other elective officials (55 percent of appellate judges have terms longer than six years; 20 percent of appellate judges have ten-year or longer terms; and 27 percent of trial judges have terms longer than six years). In thirty-seven of these states, only judges are subject to both impeachment and a special disciplinary process. In thirty-three, judges are the only elective state officials subject to requirements of training or experience or both (but in ten the attorney general is subject to similar requirements). In twenty-one, only judicial nominations go through nominating commissions; in six, this applies even to interim appointments. Finally, in eighteen states only judges cannot run for a nonjudicial office without first resigning.

4. *Chisom v. Roemer,* 501 U.S. 380, 400 (1991).

5. Melinda Gann Hall, "State Supreme Courts in American Democracy: Probing the Myths of Judicial Reform," *American Political Science Review* 95 (2001): 315.

6. See American Judicature Society, "Survey of Thirteen Elective States," September 10, 2001 (on file with author). Minnesota initially appoints 90 percent of its judges; Alabama, 49 percent; Georgia, 71 percent; Michigan, 44 percent; Nevada, 33 percent; North Dakota, 30 percent; Texas, over 40 percent; and Washington State, about 75 percent. Such appointees must face election soon after going on the bench.

7. Texas seems typical: of the 481 judges sitting in 1993 "over 80 percent . . . were unopposed in both the primary and general election when they first sought reelection. And in bids for subsequent terms, that trend accelerates. . . . [O]f those . . . who initially reached the bench by appointment, . . . 55 percent have never had an opponent . . . either in a primary or a general election." Chief Justice Thomas R. Phillips, "Address to the Joint Session of the 73rd Legislature," February 23, 1993 (on file with author).

8. Cerrell is mentioned in Larry J. Sabato, *The Rise of Political Consultants: New Ways of Winning Elections* (New York: Basic Books, 1981), 12–13. The quote is from Roy A. Schotland, "Elective Judges, Campaign Financing: Are State Judges' Robes the Emperor's Clothes of American Democracy?" *Journal of Law and Politics* 2 (1985): 57.

9. Moyer made these comments in a talk to the Ohio Council of Retail Merchants, November 7, 2001. Quoted in

Roy A. Schotland, "2002 Judicial Elections and State Court Reforms," *The Book of the States* 35 (2003): 233.

10. Ibid. and data collected by author.

11. Sources cited in Roy A. Schotland, "Financing Judicial Elections, 2000: Change and Challenge," *Michigan State University–Detroit College of Law Law Review* (2001): 849, 872.

12. Because most of those groups disclose neither their spending nor contributors (even litigating their right to continue that way), these are well-based estimates. See Jack Torry, "Ohioans Endured the Most TV Ads," *Columbus Dispatch,* November 21, 2002; and ibid., 875–876.

13. The averages for candidates' campaign chests exclude candidates who raised nothing, which is far more common in judicial than nonjudicial elections. In 2002, 35 percent raised no funds. All data on the candidates are for funds raised, which for judicial races are almost never significantly different from funds spent. Data, unless otherwise indicated, are from the National Institute on Money in State Politics, followthemoney.org/database/NationalOverview/index.phtml (accessed May 20, 2005).

14. Schotland, "Financing Judicial Elections, 2000," 881.

15. Ibid., 871–872.

16. Division of Elections, Florida Department of State, elections.dos.state.fl.us.

17. Data compiled by the Texas Administrative Office of the Courts from Texas Ethics Commission reporting forms (on file with author).

18. Schotland, "Elective Judges, Campaign Financing," 89.

19. The code, which is promulgated by the American Bar Association, has been adopted or adapted in almost all states. See Jeffrey M. Shaman, Steven Lubet, and James J. Alfini, *Judicial Conduct and Ethics,* 3d ed. (Charlottesville, Va.: Lexis Law Publishers, 2000); and Peter Moser, "The 1990 ABA Code of Judicial Conduct," *Georgetown Journal of Legal Ethics* 4 (1991): 731.

20. *Republican Party of Minnesota v. White,* 536 U.S. 765 (2002), 770. Many states also bar candidates from making "statements that commit or appear to commit the candidate with respect to cases, controversies or issues that are likely to come before the court" (id. at 775, n. 5). Both the "pledge/ promise" clause and the "commit" clause are now under attack as unconstitutional in litigation in four states.

21. *Weaver v. Bonner,* 309 F. 3d 1312 (2002).

22. After a complaint about that candidate's conduct was filed, the candidate won a federal court injunction to stop any proceeding against him. David B. Rottman and Roy A. Schotland, "2004 Judicial Elections," *Spectrum* 78 (2005): 17–19.

23. "Elective Judges: Some Comparative Comments," *Southern California Law Review* 61 (1988): 1995, 2000.

24. "Guilty, Your Honour?" *The Economist,* July 24, 2004, 28–29.

25. *Inquiry re Matthew E. McMillan,* 797 So. 2d 560, 562 (Fla. 2001). See also the Florida Supreme Court opinion reprimanding a judge for misconduct in his campaign—the finest statement about judicial elections ever written anywhere—in "Court publicly reprimands Judge Angel," *Florida Bar News,* July 1, 2004, 31.

26. This comment was made in a phone call to the author.

27. This was one of twenty recommendations made for judicial election reform; see "Call to Action," *Loyola (L.A.) Law Review* (2001): 1353, 1357. In 2004 North Carolina became the first state east of the Mississippi to send its voters a voter guide—this one on judicial elections.

28. *Republican Party of Minnesota v. White,* 795.

29. *In re Enforcement of Rule 2.03, Canon 5.B.(1)(c),* July 18, 2002. More than half of Missouri's trial judges run in partisan elections.

30. *Republican Party of Minnesota v. White,* 792, 794.

Suggested Readings

American Bar Association. *Report and Recommendations of the Task Force on Lawyers' Political Contributions (Part One): Regarding Contributions to Judges and Judicial Candidates.* Chicago, ABA, 1998.

Atchison, Amy B., et al. "Judicial Independence and Judicial Accountability: A Selected Bibliography." *Southern California Law Review* 72: 723 (1999).

Champagne, A., and J. Haydel, eds. *Judicial Reform in the States.* Lanham, Md.: University Press of America, 1993.

Dubois, P. *From Ballot to Bench: Judicial Elections and the Quest for Accountability.* Austin: University of Texas Press, 1980.

———. *The Politics of Judicial Reform.* Lexington, Mass.: Lexington Books, 1982.

Goldberg, D., C. Holman, and S. Sanchez. *The New Politics of Judicial Elections: How 2000 Was a Watershed Year for Big Money, Special Interest Pressure, and TV Advertising in State Supreme Court Campaigns.* Washington, D.C.: Justice at Stake Campaign, 2002.

Goldberg, D., S. Sanchez, and B. Brandenburg, eds. *The New Politics of Judicial Elections 2002: How the Threat to Fair and Impartial Courts Spread to More States in 2002.* Washington, D.C.: Justice at Stake Campaign, 2004.

McFadden, P. *Electing Justice: The Law and Ethics of Judicial Election Campaigns.* Chicago: American Judicature Society, 1990.

Schotland, R. "Elective Judges, Campaign Financing: Are State Judges' Robes the Emperor's Clothes of American Democracy?" *Journal of Law and Politics* 2 (1985): 57.

———. "Financing Judicial Elections, 2000: Change and Challenge." *2001 Michigan State University–Detroit College of Law Law Review* 849 (2001): 875–876.

———. "To the Endangered Species List, Add: Nonpartisan Judicial Elections." *Willamette Law Review* 39 (2003): 1397.

"Symposium on Judicial Campaign Conduct and the First Amendment, The Way Forward." *Indiana Law Review* 35 (2002): 649ff.

"Symposium on Judicial Election, Selection, and Accountability." *Southern California Law Review* 61 (1988): 1555ff.

"Symposium: Summit on Improving Judicial Selection: Call to Action." *Loyola (L.A.) Law Review* 34 (2001): 1353, 1357.

CHAPTER 26

Initiatives and Referenda

Eric R. A. N. Smith

Questions about how democracy should be designed have been posed since before the American Revolution. Political thinkers ponder these matters because there are many ways in which a democracy could be set up. One of the fundamental decisions is whether to allow the people to rule directly by putting questions to them in elections or have the people elect legislators and other officials who will decide policy questions for them. For the most part, Americans have opted for the second choice—electing legislators in a republican form of government. Some states, however, have adopted the tools of direct democracy— the initiative, the referendum, and the recall.

The initiative and referendum—procedures that allow citizens to vote on proposed laws—are the basic forms of direct legislation. Under the direct initiative, citizens can draft a proposed law or constitutional amendment and place it on the ballot if they collect enough valid signatures on a petition. The indirect initiative allows citizens to draft a proposal and—again with a sufficient number of signatures—submit it to the state legislature. If the state legislature fails to act on it, the measure is placed before the voters in the next election. Both of these processes give voters a way to get around a legislature when the legislature refuses to pass laws the public wants.

The referendum process allows state legislatures to put measures before the voters for their approval. Almost all states allow their constitutions to be amended in this way. In addition, many states require voter approval for tax increases or bond sales (the mechanism by which states borrow money for construction projects and other uses). Some state legislatures put other questions to voters as well. This process limits legislatures and gives power to the voters, because voter approval is required for raising taxes, borrowing money, and some other changes in state and local laws.

The protest referendum, also called the citizen petition referendum, allows citizens to challenge laws passed by their state legislature. Those who object to a law can circulate a petition demanding that the law be nullified. If they gather a sufficient number of signatures, the question of whether to nullify the law goes to the voters.

Again, this is a mechanism for limiting the power of state legislatures and placing control in the hands of the voters.

Finally, the recall process allows voters who are dissatisfied with the performance of a public official to demand that the officeholder face election before the expiration of his or her term in office. As with the other forms of direct democracy, this process requires petitions with a minimum number of valid signatures. Also like the other forms of direct democracy, the recall provides voters with a means of controlling elected officials once they are in office.

Every state but Alabama uses the referendum or initiative in some fashion. Alabama alone does not even allow voters to approve state constitutional amendments. Beyond approval of constitutional amendments, twenty-nine states have adopted at least some other form of referendum or initiative. In most of these states, these forms of direct democracy operate at both the state and local levels. For example, in states with the initiative process statewide voters can use the process to pass state laws, and local voters can use the process to pass laws in cities or counties. Table 26-1 shows the types of procedures each state allows, including whether the state allows elected officials to be recalled.

Together, these mechanisms allow the people a measure of direct control over government. Indeed, the laws establishing direct democracy were passed by reformers who wanted to take power away from corrupt legislators and wealthy business interests and give it back to the people. How well they have succeeded, and whether the benefits of direct democracy outweigh the costs, are matters of debate to this day.

This chapter reviews the history of the initiative and referendum, and it describes the processes required to qualify ballot measures in different states, the limits placed on the uses of direct legislation, and the constitutional protections guaranteed to users of direct democracy procedures. The chapter then focuses on the initiative and referendum campaigns themselves, first examining campaign spending and then turning to campaign strategy. A discussion of the need to defend successful ballot propositions against attacks in state legislatures and the courts

---

BOX 26-1

THE FORMS OF DIRECT DEMOCRACY

"**D**irect democracy" refers to the processes by which voters make public policy decisions by voting on public policy proposals in elections and by which they decide whether to remove elected officials without waiting for the next regularly scheduled election. Direct democracy procedures are in place in many states and in local governments. There are five basic forms of direct democracy:

Direct initiative Citizens vote on a proposed law that is placed on the ballot by petition of registered voters.

Indirect initiative Citizens present a proposed law to a local or state legislature by petition of registered voters. If the legislature fails to pass the law, it is put before voters as a ballot measure in the next election.

Referendum Legislatures or local governments put a proposed law on the ballot for the voters to accept or reject in an election.

Protest referendum, or citizen petition referendum A petition of registered voters requires that a law recently passed by a state or local government be put to a vote of the citizens before it becomes law.

Recall Citizens present a petition to the government to require an elected official to stand for election before his or her regular term of office expires.

---

follows. The chapter concludes with a discussion of direct legislation and proposed reforms.

The History of Direct Democracy

How did the states arrive at a system that puts legislative power directly in the hands of the voters? This section begins with a look at the origins of the initiative and referendum, and then it describes state laws as they stand today.

Origins of Direct Democracy

The origins of direct democracy lie in ancient Greece. In Athenian democracy, thousands of citizens would come together periodically to discuss issues and vote. But it was hardly a perfect democracy. Slaves, women, minors, and foreigners could not vote, and turnout among eligible citizens was low. Nevertheless, Athens gave the world the central concepts of democracy and direct control of government by the people.

Direct democracy appeared again in colonial era New England town meetings. Adult men—and at times adult women—came together to discuss and decide local laws and policies. The referendum was first used by the Massachusetts Bay Colony, when it put a question to voters in 1640. In the years that followed, the use of town meetings to decide law spread throughout New England, but it was already in decline by the time of the American Revolution. As towns grew in population, representative democracy began to replace direct democracy.

Although the framers of the Constitution debated whether to include an initiative process, they opted instead for representative democracy. Nevertheless, both Massachusetts and New Hampshire used referenda to establish their state constitutions during the Revolutionary War. Over the next twenty years, the practice spread to other New England states, and by the 1830s the referendum process was used by several states outside of New England for constitutional changes and sometimes other issues. In the 1840s, several states added provisions to their constitutions requiring a vote by the people for the states to borrow money.

In the years after the Civil War, dissatisfaction with government corruption grew. Many westerners directed their anger at the railroad companies, which used their near-monopoly control of commercial transportation to charge western producers painfully high prices to ship goods east. The railroad companies also used some of their enormous profits to corrupt state legislators. That corruption fueled the populist movement.

In their search for reforms to limit the power of railroads and other moneyed interests, Populists looked to the system of direct democracy that the Swiss had developed in the mid-1800s. From Switzerland, the Populists borrowed the ideas of the initiative, a vastly expanded referendum, and the recall. A handful of activists began advocating direct democracy in the late 1880s, and in 1898 they won their first major victory when South Dakota voters passed constitutional amendments establishing the initiative and protest referendum.

As the Populist movement waned in the late 1800s, the Progressive movement flourished. The political bases of the Populists and Progressives differed enormously. The Populists were predominantly western agrarian activists; Progressives were primarily eastern and middle or upper class. Nevertheless, they agreed on some of their complaints about government corruption, and they agreed on one of the solutions—direct democracy. Thus as the Populist movement abated, the Progressives took up the cause and pushed through direct democracy in almost half the states. Figure 26-1 shows the spread of the initiative and referendum, from their start in South Dakota in 1898 through 1918, by which time nineteen states had adopted some form of initiative process and twenty-two had adopted the referendum.

Table 26-1 Direct Democracy Procedures by State

State	Changes to state constitution			Changes to state laws				Recall
	Initiative		Referendum legislative	Initiative		Referendum		
	Direct	Indirect		Direct	Indirect	Legislative	Citizen protest	
Alabama								
Alaska			*		*		*	*
Arizona	*		*	*		*	*	*
Arkansas	*		*	*		*	*	
California	*		*	*		*	*	*
Colorado	*		*	*		*	*	*
Connecticut			*					
Delaware			*			*		
Florida	*		*					
Georgia			*					*
Hawaii			*					
Idaho			*	*		*	*	*
Illinois	*		*	*		*		
Indiana			*					
Iowa			*					
Kansas			*					*
Kentucky			*			*	*	
Louisiana			*					*
Maine			*		*	*	*	
Maryland			*			*	*	
Massachusetts		*	*		*	*	*	
Michigan	*	*	*		*	*	*	*
Minnesota			*					*
Mississippi		*	*					
Missouri	*		*	*		*	*	
Montana	*		*	*		*	*	*
Nebraska	*		*	*			*	
Nevada	*		*	*	*	*	*	*
New Hampshire			*					
New Jersey			*					*
New Mexico			*			*	*	
New York			*					
North Carolina			*					
North Dakota	*		*	*		*	*	*
Ohio	*		*	*	*	*	*	
Oklahoma	*		*	*		*	*	
Oregon	*		*	*		*	*	*
Pennsylvania			*					
Rhode Island			*					*
South Carolina			*					
South Dakota	*		*	*			*	
Tennessee			*					
Texas			*					
Utah			*	*	*	*	*	
Vermont			*					
Virginia			*					
Washington			*	*	*	*	*	*
West Virginia			*					
Wisconsin			*					*
Wyoming			*		*		*	
Number of states	16	3	49	17	9	22	24	18

Source: The Book of the States 2000–2001 (Lexington, Ky.: Council of State Governments, 2000), 233, 248–249.

Note: Direct initiatives are measures placed on the ballot.
Indirect initiatives are submitted to the state legislature and are placed on the ballot only if the state legislature declines to act.
Legislative referendums are measures placed on the ballot by the legislature.
Some measures, such as borrowing money and constitutional amendments, must be placed on the ballot.
Some states allow the legislature to place a measure on the ballot if it wishes.
Citizen petition referenda (col. 1) are measures placed on the ballot to allow the voters to repeal a law passed by the state legislature.

Figure 26-1 The Spread of Initiatives and Referenda, 1898–1918

Number of states

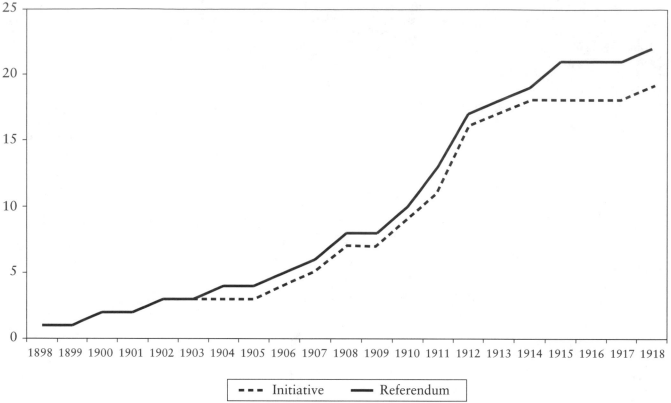

Source: Richard J. Ellis, *Democratic Delusions: The Initiative Process in America* (Lawrence: University Press of Kansas, 2002), fig. 2.1, 35.

Since 1918, a trickle of states have adopted the initiative: Alaska when it became a state in 1959, Florida and Wyoming in 1968, Illinois in 1970, and Mississippi in 1992. Moreover, in recent years movements have emerged in over a dozen states to establish the initiative and referendum or expand their use. Because public opinion polls show that about two-thirds of the American public supports some version of an initiative for their states, it seems likely that more states will eventually adopt some form of direct democracy.

The Use of Initiatives and Referenda

Initiatives and referenda have covered a wide range of topics, including abortion, affirmative action, civil rights, gay and lesbian rights, gun control, insurance reform, nuclear power, pesticide use, tax reform, and tobacco use. They are not, however, without limits.

Half of the states with an initiative process restrict the number of subjects addressed by an initiative. The most common restriction is that an initiative may address only a single subject—that is, an initiative that combines, say, restrictions on abortion and increased public spending on K–12 education would be nullified by the courts. Several explanations have been offered for this restriction. Some

scholars have argued that the point of restricting initiatives to a single subject is to prevent complicated initiatives that would confuse voters. Others have suggested that single-subject restrictions are intended to prevent logrolls such as mixing abortion restrictions (which would appeal to conservatives) with increased school spending (which would appeal to liberals).

In practice, whether an initiative violates the single-subject requirement is often a close call. In 2000, for example, the Arizona Supreme Court removed Proposition 107 from the ballot because it banned individual and corporate state income taxes, required a public vote on the new taxes or fees that would be needed to replace the lost income taxes, and allowed candidates for federal office to sign a pledge to eliminate the federal income tax. The proposition's defenders argued that these provisions comprised a single set of reforms ending the income tax and moving toward other revenue sources. The court, however, saw three separate issues in a single initiative.

Several states limit the extent to which initiatives can change their state constitutions. California's constitution, for example, says that the legislature may call a "convention to revise the Constitution," and in the next section it says, "The electors may amend the Constitution by initiative." Nothing in the wording of the California constitution suggests how to interpret the words "revise" and "amend," but the California courts have ruled that revisions refer to large-scale changes, whereas amendments refer to small-scale changes.[1] Using that reasoning, the courts have denied the voters the right to make sweeping changes in the constitution through the initiative process. Other states have developed similar doctrines and have occasionally nullified initiatives on the grounds that they were amendments, not revisions.

Other restrictions in some states include bans on appropriating money and on passing laws to address "administrative" issues. Most restrictive of all, Illinois allows only initiatives that change the legislative process. Despite these limitations, initiatives have been used to modify a huge range of policies and have caused political earthquakes such as a tax revolt and term limits for legislators.

Since their introduction at the turn of the twentieth century, the number of initiatives has varied widely over time. Immediately after the initiative was adopted, attempts to pass laws using it surged (see Figure 26-2). From 1910 to 1918, an average of fifty-four initiatives were put to a vote every two years. This surge was the result of the frustrated demand to change government, coupled with widespread distrust of politicians. As the United States entered World War II, however, attention turned elsewhere and use of the initiative dropped. Even

after the war, initiative use continued to drop through the 1960s, when the average number of initiatives was only nineteen every two years. During these years, Americans trusted their government, according to public opinion polls. When they had problems, they turned to legislatures to solve those problems rather than trying to go around the legislatures by filing initiatives.

In the late 1960s and 1970s, trust in government fell sharply as the nation faced the struggle over civil rights, urban riots, the Vietnam War, and President Richard Nixon's Watergate scandal. New political movements— most prominently the women's movement and the environmental movement—emerged and placed new demands on government. The United States had entered a period of political upheaval and reform not seen since the Progressive era at the turn of the century. Along with the reform zeal of the 1960s and 1970s came another surge in the use of initiatives.

Just as important as the increase in dissatisfaction with government and increased demand for new policies was the beginning of the modern campaign industry in the 1970s (see Chapter 10). Political consultants set up campaign firms that offered a wide range of services, including qualifying initiatives for the ballot and running campaigns for or against initiatives and referenda. With easy access to professionals who could launch initiatives and manage campaigns, many groups turned to direct legislation to achieve their goals. The dissatisfaction with

Figure 26-2 Initiative Use by Decade, 1900s–2000

Average number of initiatives per two-year election cycle

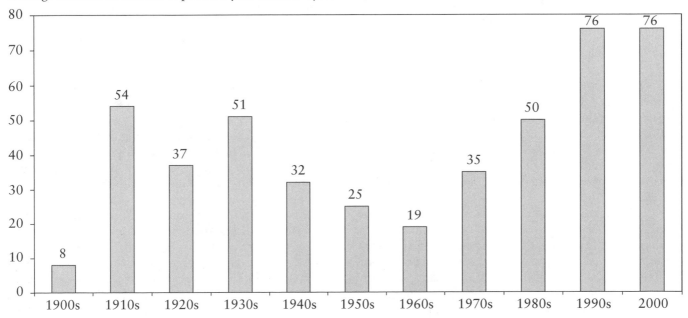

Source: Richard J. Ellis, *Democratic Delusions: The Initiative Process in America* (Lawrence: University Press of Kansas, 2002), fig. 2.1, 35.

government, together with the existence of an industry ready to help initiative backers, sent the average number of initiatives skyrocketing to an average of seventy-six every two years.

The Qualifying Stages

Qualifying a referendum or initiative for the ballot is no easy matter. Persuading the state legislature to place a referendum on the ballot is essentially a lobbying task, and, like persuading a legislature to pass any law, it is difficult and time-consuming. Putting together an organization to draft a proposed initiative and gathering the signatures to place it on the ballot are even more daunting tasks. Although the original supporters of direct democracy thought of their reforms as means of giving the mass public control over their governments, the key players in these efforts are typically well-connected political activists and leaders. Merely having a good idea for a law is not enough.

Persuading State Legislatures to Qualify Referenda

Although dealing with legislators on proposed referenda is a matter for professional lobbyists, it is often a fairly routine matter. Legislatures are required to put some types of issues up for a statewide vote whenever they arise. The decision to issue state bonds to borrow money for construction projects, for example, must be approved by voters in almost all states with referendum processes. Many states also require voter approval for some types of tax increases. Local governments, for example, usually must seek voter approval to increase property taxes and sale taxes to pay for schools or other needs.

Beyond these routine measures lies a range of constitutional amendments from the trivial to the controversial. In 2002 the California state legislature was forced to ask voters to approve a plan to consolidate parts of the state court system. Although many voters chose to skip this question, those who did vote easily passed the measure. At the opposite extreme, a few state constitutions require that laws dealing with certain, often controversial, moral issues be put before the voters. Louisiana and Massachusetts, for example, require votes on approval of gambling and race-track betting.

Almost all issues that state legislators place before voters are put on ballots because state constitutions require voter approval for passage. In most states with the referendum process, if the state legislators wish to put controversial proposals before voters—even if state constitutions do not require them to do so—they can. In practice, however, state legislators rarely choose to do so. If citizen groups cannot persuade state legislators to pass laws, they must almost always turn to the initiative process.

Legal Issues Involved in Qualifying Initiatives

Several steps are required to qualify an initiative for the ballot. The details—especially the number of signatures required—vary from state to state, but the qualification processes are all similar.

Drafting the initiative is the first step. Because of the potential for confusing language, several states require people working on initiatives to meet with state officials to refine the language of the initiative. No state with the initiative process, however, requires the approval of state officials for an initiative to go forward.

The next step is where political battle often begins. After drafting an initiative, the supporters must submit the initiative to a state official (usually the attorney general), who prepares a ballot title and short description—both of which appear on the ballot. Those titles and descriptions are critical, because they influence citizens' voting choices. Consider the proposed initiative in Oregon that would have prohibited the state from making sexual preference the basis for civil rights protection. The proponent of the initiative wanted the title to be "Amends Constitution: Prohibits Minority Status Based on Sexual Behavior, Desires." The American Civil Liberties Union sued, requesting that the title be "Amends Constitution: Forbids Civil Rights Protection Based on Homosexuality." Eventually, the Oregon Supreme Court rejected both titles and ruled that the title should be "Amends Constitution: Restricts Local, State Government Powers Concerning Homosexuality." [2] Clearly, each side was arguing for a title that would gain it votes. Because some voters know very little about the measures on which they are voting, the wording of the ballot title and description may determine whether an initiative wins or loses.

The title and description of an initiative, because of their importance, are often the target of lawsuits in which initiative supporters and opponents argue that some aspect of the title or description is biased or misleading. Oregon may lead the nation in this area. From 1998 through 2000, 92 of the 146 ballot titles written by the state attorney general were the targets of legal action, and one-fifth of the Oregon Supreme Court's decisions addressed initiative ballot titles.

In addition to preparing a title and description, most states prepare a summary of the propositions, which are put together in a voter handbook, along with the text of the propositions, and mailed to all voters. Most states also allow proposition supporters and opponents to include brief arguments for and against the ballot measures.

Once the title and description have been approved, initiative proponents may begin to gather signatures of registered voters to qualify their initiative for the ballot. Oklahoma allows the shortest time for this process, a mere ninety days, while Arkansas, Idaho, Nebraska, Oregon, and Utah place no limits on how long initiative supporters have to gather the required number of signatures. The average time is one year.

Table 26-2 Signature Requirements for Initiatives

State	Basis for required signatures	Signatures needed (percent)	
		Statute	Constitutional amendment
Alaska	No. of voters in last election	10	–
Arizona	Vote for governor	10	15
Arkansas	Vote for governor	8	10
California	Vote for governor	5	8
Colorado	Vote for secretary of state	5	5
Florida	Vote for president	–	8
Idaho	No. of eligible voters	6	–
Illinois	Vote for governor	–	8
Maine	Vote for governor	10	–
Massachusetts	Vote for governor	3	3
Michigan	Vote for governor	8	10
Mississippi	Vote for governor	–	12
Missouri	Vote for governor	5	8
Montana	Vote for governor	5	10
Nebraska	No. of eligible voters	7	10
Nevada	No. of voters in last election	10	10
North Dakota	Resident population	2	4
Ohio	Vote for governor	3	10
Oklahoma	Vote for office receiving most votes	8	15
Oregon	Vote for governor	6	8
South Dakota	Vote for governor	5	10
Utah	Vote for governor	10	–
Washington	Vote for governor	8	–
Wyoming	No. of voters in last election	15	–

Source: The Book of the States 2000–2001 (Lexington, Ky.: Council of State Governments, 2000), 236–237.

Note: – Not applicable.

States use different numbers as the basis for arriving at the number of required signatures. Most use a percentage of the number of votes cast for the office of governor in the most recent election, but others use a percentage of the number cast for another office or the total number of votes, or some other standard (see Table 26-2). Massachusetts has the lowest threshold—only 3 percent of the gubernatorial vote in the last election for either a statute or a constitutional amendment. At the other end, Wyoming has the highest threshold, 15 percent of the number of people who voted in the most recent general election.

Nine states also have some type of geographical distribution requirements for signatures. For example, Massachusetts requires that no more than 25 percent come from any single county. States established these requirements with the intention of making initiative backers write their proposals with an eye toward appealing to the entire state, not just narrow interests. In Massachusetts,

initiative backers cannot just obtain signatures from Boston and its suburbs; they have to reach out to the less populous counties as well.

Although signature requirements may have posed serious difficulties for initiative proponents early in the century, the modern signature-gathering industry has substantially reduced the difficulty of qualifying initiatives. If sufficient campaign funds are available to qualify a ballot initiative, the professionals can usually get the job done.

The Business of Signature Gathering

Although direct democracy was supposed to be a way to minimize the use of money in politics, paid signature gatherers have helped to qualify initiatives since the early 1900s. In Oregon between 1904 and 1912, for example, initiatives containing some of the most important pieces of the Progressive agenda were put on ballots by campaigns that hired people to collect signatures in addition to relying on campaign volunteers. From the very start, politicians working to qualify initiatives realized that paying people to collect signatures was good politics.

Concern about paid signature gatherers appeared almost as soon as the practice began. Critics argued that it took power from the people and gave it to wealthy interests. As early as 1909, attempts were being made to pass laws preventing campaigns from paying their signature gatherers. By 1914, Ohio, South Dakota, and Washington had passed such laws, and other state legislatures had considered them. When the first professional campaign management firms appeared in the 1930s, collecting signatures for initiatives was one of the services they provided, and the debate was renewed.

The bans on paying for signatures did not pass in most states, because initiative supporters believed such laws would make it far harder to qualify initiatives. Modern evidence supports their concerns. A study by Richard J. Ellis found that paid signature gatherers were far more successful in qualifying initiatives than volunteers. Among the 255 initiative campaigns launched in Oregon from 1988 through 2000, 42 percent of those that used paid signature gatherers qualified, but only 12 percent of those that relied on volunteers succeeded.[3] Although campaign money could not guarantee ballot access, it could certainly make access far easier to achieve.

The debate on paying people to collect signatures ended abruptly in 1988. In *Meyer v. Grant* (1988), the U.S. Supreme Court held that banning paid petition gatherers was unconstitutional. The Court declared that "the circulation of a petition involves the type of interactive communication concerning political change that is appropriately described as 'core political speech.' " [4] The decision explained that refusing to permit initiative supporters to pay workers to gather signatures restricts political speech in two ways. It limits the number of potential circulators who will tell voters about the initiative, which reduces the number of people who hear about the initiative, and it lessens the likelihood that the initiative will qualify for the ballot, which limits statewide discussion of the issue.

In *Buckley v. American Constitutional Law Foundation* (1999), the Court extended protection for paid petition circulators. Colorado had passed a state constitutional amendment requiring that initiative petition circulators be registered voters, that they wear identification badges showing their names, and that the campaign report the names and addresses of all paid circulators and the amount paid to each one. The Court held that all three restrictions unconstitutionally limited speech. Thus, although paying campaign workers to gather signatures may seem inconsistent with the concept of direct democracy, it is a practice that is here to stay.

Campaign Spending

The initiative and referenda processes were originally designed to limit the influence of corporate money on government. The reformers hoped that by creating a process to bypass corrupt legislators, the influence of moneyed interests would be neutralized. Paradoxically, the most frequent complaints about direct democracy today are that wealthy interests have too much power, and that money has corrupted the process.

This section looks at why money plays such a significant role in direct legislation campaigns. It first considers U.S. Supreme Court interpretations of the First Amendment, and then turns to the use and influence of money in campaigns.

Constitutional Limits on Campaign Spending Laws

The barrier to campaign finance laws limiting the influence of money in initiatives and referenda consists of a series of U.S. Supreme Court decisions. Beginning with

Buckley v. Valeo (1976), the Court developed an interpretation of the First Amendment that would allow restrictions on donations *only* in races with candidates (see Chapter 2). When the Court took up questions of campaign financing for ballot measures in later cases, it followed the reasoning initially stated in *Buckley* and blocked efforts to limit donations or spending.

The critical aspect of *Buckley* was the Court's conclusion that large campaign donations posed a threat of real or perceived bribery. The Court stated: "To the extent that large contributions are given to secure political *quid pro quo's* from current and potential office holders, the integrity of our system of representative democracy is undermined. . . . Of almost equal concern as the danger of actual *quid pro quo* arrangements is the impact of the appearance of corruption stemming from public awareness of the opportunities for abuse inherent in a regime of large individual financial contributions." [5] In addition to establishing the potential for corruption as the foundation for *Buckley,* the Court rejected the notion of any standard of equality in campaign funding. In other words, if one candidate raised more than another, the better-funded candidate presumably was preferred by more donors or wealthier donors—the issue was irrelevant. The Constitution, according to the Supreme Court, does not require an even playing field when it comes to campaign cash. Limits can be placed on donations, but no limits can be placed on campaign expenditures.

When the Court faced a case that tested the right of states to limit campaign donations in direct legislation campaigns, it simply applied the *Buckley* reasoning. In *First National Bank of Boston v. Bellotti* (1978), the Court nullified a Massachusetts law that banned corporate donations in initiatives. The Court ruled that because there were no candidates, there was no opportunity for quid pro quo corruption. Lacking that justification, Massachusetts had no right to ban corporate donations.

The Supreme Court followed *Bellotti* with a decision in *Citizens Against Rent Control (CARC) v. City of Berkeley* (1981) saying that not only could states not ban corporate contributions, but they also could not limit them. More recently, in *Buckley v. American Constitutional Law Foundation* (1999), the Court reaffirmed its *Meyer* decision.

State Laws and Regulations

Because they lack means of limiting campaign donations or expenditures, campaign finance regulations for initiatives and referenda are quite minimal. By far the most common type of law is one that requires campaigns to disclose information about their finances. The underlying idea is that if voters know what people or organizations favor or oppose a ballot measure, that knowledge will help guide their voting decisions. For example, if voters understood that an initiative to reform state regulations on nuclear power plants was favored by the corporations that build nuclear power plants but opposed by environmental groups, then voters could grant their approval or disapproved based on their knowledge of the supporters and opponents rather than on the technical details about nuclear power plants.

Although almost every state has some form of campaign finance disclosure for initiatives and referenda, many state laws are not very useful to voters. Some states put the names of donors and the amounts they donated on the Web, but most do not. Instead, most states maintain written records at the state capital, thereby making it difficult for voters or journalists to learn who is supporting or opposing ballot measures.

Another aspect of some state disclosure laws is that campaigns may not disclose the original campaign donors. In California, for example, people may donate to a political committee, which in turn will donate to a campaign on behalf of a ballot measure. The official campaign donation records show only the political committee that acted as the intermediary, and the original sources of the money are hidden.

In states that allow campaigns to hide the original sources of their funds, the courts have observed that two conflicting values need to be weighed. On the one hand, the public may benefit by learning who donated to various campaigns. On the other hand, the individuals who donated may suffer if their donations are made public. The courts must therefore weigh the public benefits of disclosure against the privacy rights of donors. Decisions have come down on both sides of this question in different states.

How Much Money Is Spent?

In most states, no useful records on campaign spending on ballot measures were kept before the 1970s. Moreover, because of the difficulties in comparing states, useful summary statistics are not even available for the years after the 1970s. Nevertheless, it is possible to state that the amounts of money spent on ballot measures range from little or no money to staggering sums—far greater than those spent in most campaigns for public office.

Because the initiative and referendum processes were created by reformers who wanted to curtail the power of moneyed interests, one might suspect that money would play a small role early in the 1900s and that the use and influence of money would grow slowly over time. Indeed, some political observers have claimed that wealthy interests took over direct democracy in the 1980s and 1990s. Although those claims sound persuasive, the evidence does not support them. Money has always played a prominent role in direct legislation.

Early records indicate that at least some initiative campaigns drew substantial spending from the start. For example, in a 1922 fight over the proposed Water and Power Act in California, public utilities and their opponents spent $660,000. Adjusting for inflation, that figure amounts to $7.1 million in 2002 dollars—a huge expenditure in a largely rural state before the advent of high-cost campaign technology such as television.

By the 1930s, spending on ballot measures had clearly risen to modern-day levels. The California partnership of Whitaker and Baxter, often credited with being the first professional campaign management firm, led the way to high-cost campaigns. California records show that the two sides disputing a 1936 proposition on retirement benefits spent about $1 million, and the two sides fighting over a proposal to tax chain stores spent $1.2 million. In 2002 dollars, those campaigns cost $13 million and $15.6 million, respectively.

Another Whitaker and Baxter proposition would have created a California Oil and Gas Conservation Commission in 1956. Its oil industry backers described it as a way to increase oil production. Its critics countered that it would open up the California coast to more oil production and would lead to increases in imported oil. The two sides spent $4.9 million, or slightly over $32 million in 2002 dollars, as the measure went down to defeat. This measure was hardly typical—it set a spending record that lasted through 1978—but it shows that big-money campaigns are not a recent development.

To put these numbers in context, David B. Magleby notes that from the 1950s through the 1970s spending on initiatives occasionally exceeded spending on all statewide and legislative offices in California.[6] By another standard, spending on both the 1936 and 1956 propositions just described would rank among the top ten most expensive races for the U.S. Senate in 2000. To summarize, since the 1920s spending on statewide ballot measures has at least occasionally reached modern levels. Direct democracy and big money have gone hand in hand for decades.

That huge sums are spent on ballot measures should not surprise anyone. Some measures strike emotional hot buttons and draw reactions from both sides. A proposal to ban affirmative action in state hiring and college admissions, for example, is a cause over which many people are willing to fight bitterly. Other measures can create huge profits or losses for businesses or entire economic sectors. The 1956 oil conservation measure was supported by the major oil companies with a flood of campaign cash because it would have enormously increased their profits. When the costs of campaign donations are far smaller than the potential gains or losses to a firm, businesses often donate lavishly to support their interests.

Does Money Buy Victory?

Probably the foremost concern of critics of direct legislation is that wealthy interests allegedly dominate the process. Many people believe that groups with access to a great deal of campaign money—usually business interests—can qualify their initiatives for the ballot, and win changes in laws or even state constitutions, just because they have a lot of money.

To some extent, they are right; money clearly has an influence on election outcomes. Studies have shown that the side that significantly outspends the other has a better chance of winning. Moreover, the side that spends the most generally wins. However, these facts can be misleading, because they hide a critical distinction—whether the campaigns funds were spent for or against passage of a measure.

The most important finding about campaign spending is that money spent in opposition to a ballot measure is more effective than money spent in favor of it. In his classic study of direct legislation, Magleby discovered that initiative supporters who outspent their rivals two to one or better won less than 50 percent of their campaigns, while opponents who held a two-to-one spending edge won nearly 90 percent of their campaigns.[7] In practical terms, this finding means that when supporters and opponents each spend an equal amount of money, the initiative will likely fail.

Why money spent against initiatives gains more votes than money spent in favor is unclear. The most likely explanation seems to be that the threshold of persuasion is lower for initiative critics than for supporters. If a campaign against an initiative can raise serious doubts about the measure, voters—following the logic "better safe than sorry"—will send the measure to defeat.

A related finding is that as the amount of spending rises, measures become more likely to go down to defeat—even if supporters outspend opponents. The explanation for this peculiar pattern emerges when considering races for the U.S. House of Representatives. An incumbent who represents a safe district and does not have a serious challenger can run a modest campaign and expect to win by a landslide. By contrast, an incumbent who represents a marginal district and is faced with a high-quality challenger must run as hard as possible to win, including raising and spending as much money as possible in order to fend off the challenger. Thus a serious threat forces the incumbent to spend more campaign money, but it also means that the incumbent is likely to be in a close race. The peculiar result is that the more an incumbent spends, the fewer votes the incumbent is likely to win on election day.

The same pattern appears with campaign spending and voting in direct legislation. Uncontroversial measures are often poorly funded, but they generally win by large margins. In March 2002, for example, Californians gave 69 percent of their vote to Proposition 41, a $200 million bond issue for modernizing voting machines. The supporters raised only $205,000 in campaign funds; there was no organized opposition. In the general election that year, Proposition 48—a measure to consolidate state courts—passed with 73 percent of the vote. Supporters of the measure raised a mere $10,099; again, there was no organized opposition. Uncontroversial, good government measures such as Propositions 41 and 48 often appear on state ballots. Because they lack controversy, they generally pass with little or no spending on either side. Controversy, however, draws campaign donations.

A final set of important findings about money and direct legislation elections is that economic groups are less successful than citizens groups in their efforts to pass initiatives. Researchers have defined economic groups as organizations of people who come together because of their business, union, or professional group associations, or because of some other occupational connection. Citizens groups consist of people who join for reasons unrelated to their occupations—reasons such as their ideologies or beliefs about religion, gun control, education, or environmentalism. Although one can certainly find cases in which narrow economic interests have successfully pushed through initiatives, those interests have a significantly lower success rate than citizens groups. Moreover, when an economic group and a citizens group take opposite sides, the citizens group is likely to prevail. In short, critics' concerns about wealthy economic groups taking over government by running initiatives are just not supported by the record.

Campaign Strategy Issues

One of the earliest and most influential models of how voters choose candidates identified three primary influences on voting decisions—party identification (the strongest influence); candidate characteristics such as experience, intelligence, speaking style, race, and religion; and the issue stands of the voter. In initiative and referendum elections, the first two of those three influences are missing. As a result, campaign strategy in direct legislation elections differs sharply from the strategies followed in contests with candidates.

Approaches to Campaigning on Initiatives and Referenda

The first barrier that every direct legislation campaign must confront is public ignorance. The two major political parties in the United States have existed for over 150 years, and many political candidates have been in the public eye for years or even decades. The same is not true of initiatives and referenda, which appear only months before an election. Getting the public to learn something about them is a formidable task.

A study of voter awareness of ballot propositions in California from 1956 through 2000 illustrates the problem.[8] The state's leading poll asked whether voters had heard of the most prominent initiatives during those years. The number of voters who said "yes" ranged from 17 percent for an initiative limiting lawyers' contingency fees to 97 percent for a gun control initiative. The average level of awareness was only 64 percent. These numbers are far below those found for parties or statewide candidates. A review of the many sources of information on ballot measures—ballot titles and descriptions, voter handbooks, newspaper endorsements, news coverage by the mass media, and the campaigns themselves—offers a view of how supporters and opponents can craft their campaigns.

The basic information that all voters see is the ballot title and description printed on the ballot. Indeed, this is the only information some voters see before voting. Whether an initiative is titled "Prohibits Minority Status Based on Sexual Behavior, Desires" or "Forbids Civil Rights Protection Based on Homosexuality" may decide which side wins or loses. The one- or two-sentence descriptions that also appear on the ballot can have similar effects, although research indicates that the descriptions are often framed in language that is too confusing to be clearly understood by many voters. That is why the ballot title, and sometimes the description, are worth fighting over in court.

The voter handbook that state governments send out to voters typically includes the text of the measure, a summary of what the measure will do (written by state election officials), and arguments for and against the measure. Although such a handbook might seem to be an excellent source of information for voters as well as a way in which campaigns can influence voters, it is not as useful as many observers might suspect for two reasons. First, many—perhaps most—voters do not read the voter handbook. One study found that only 13–33 percent of all voters claimed to have read their handbooks. Another study, an exit poll run by the Massachusetts secretary of state, found that 59 percent of Massachusetts voters used the secretary of state's voter handbook.[9] Because some of the survey respondents may have claimed that they read the handbook in order to appear to be good citizens, the lower figures are probably more accurate. Second, the handbooks are typically written in sophisticated language that most voters find hard to understand. One study estimates that in a sample of voter handbook descriptions from California, Massachusetts, Oregon, and Rhode Island, two-thirds of voters could not understand the official descriptions of the measures, and half of voters could not understand the pro and con arguments from the campaigns.[10] Thus despite the fact that all voters receive handbooks in most states, the handbooks are mentioned by few voters as one of their top information sources. Voters are even less likely to actually read the ballot measure itself (see Box 26-2).

Newspaper endorsements offer another source of information on ballot propositions. The few studies of the effects of newspaper endorsements on ballot measure elections consistently show that endorsements have an effect. The great advantage of newspaper endorsements is that they are typically printed a few days before an election, and voters can easily take the list of endorsements with them when they vote. However, now that absentee voting is becoming more widespread, newspaper endorsements may be losing some of their influence, because newspapers must either list their endorsements long before election day or risk publicizing their endorsements after many people have voted. Nevertheless, influential or not, newspaper endorsements remain a prize for campaigners.

News coverage of ballot measures provides the most important source of information other than the campaigns themselves. The news media, however, generally cover only high-profile, controversial issues. Except for major regional newspapers, they give little or no coverage to minor ballot propositions. The characteristics that draw media attention to ballot measures are high levels of campaign spending and conflicting endorsements by prominent politicians or media stars. When the campaigns are low-key, poorly funded efforts, the news media generally do not step in to fill the void, and voters are left with few sources of information.

When the news media do cover issues, voters pay attention. Several surveys have shown that 30–45 percent of voters say that newspapers and television news are important sources of information for them, and 20–25 percent of voters identify radio news and talk shows as important sources. Although campaigning via the Internet has become more popular in recent years, no studies have addressed the role of the Internet as a source of information about ballot measures. Nevertheless, because voters must actively seek out information on the Internet—unlike the readily available news provided by newspapers or television—it seems unlikely that the Internet is a major source of information in ballot measure campaigns.

Another important point about news media coverage is that the well educated are far more likely than the poorly educated to use the media to learn about ballot measures. The better educated a voter is, the more likely it is that the voter will make use of many sources of information. In addition, the well educated are more likely to rely on newspapers than on television, whereas the less well educated turn to television more often. Campaigners often take these patterns into account when they design their media appeals.

The final sources of information for voters are the campaigns for and against the measures. Because propositions have no party labels or candidates with personal characteristics, the campaigns largely focus on the merits of the proposed policies.

However, a key element of many ballot measure campaigns is the set of endorsements on either side. Support from well-known politicians or other prominent citizens, as well as organizations, can often sway voters. After all,

SORTING OUT THE TRUTH—
CALIFORNIA'S RACIAL PRIVACY INITIATIVE

In 2003 California voters were given an opportunity to amend their state constitution to prevent the state, local governments, the university system, and the contractors who worked for them from gathering information about people's race or ethnicity. The ballot measure, Proposition 54, would end the practice of having government employees and students fill out information cards identifying their racial backgrounds.

Advocates of Proposition 54 argued that the measure promoted civil rights, because it would help society move beyond racial labels. They also pointed out that the initiative contained exceptions for police work, medical research, and federal laws that required the collection of racial data. Critics of Proposition 54 argued that the measure harmed civil rights, because it would prevent the state from gathering the data needed to find and prevent racial discrimination. They also argued that the measure would damage many types of research efforts in areas ranging from education to medicine, because the necessary records with racial labels would not exist.

Like many ballot measures, Proposition 54 presented voters with a confusing choice, and the campaign consisted of claims and counterclaims. How did voters sort out the truth? The answer is not that they read the measure (see below) and analyzed the impact themselves, but that they listened to campaign ads and news and decided how to vote based on which people and organizations were lining up on each side of the debate. During the campaign, many conservative political organizations supported Proposition 54, while most civil rights organizations and university research groups opposed it. In the end, Proposition 54 was defeated 63.9 to 36.1 percent.

To understand why voters generally do not read and analyze the text of ballot initiatives, consider the text of Proposition 54:

Section 32 is added to Article I of the California Constitution as follows:

Sec. 32. (a) The state shall not classify any individual by race, ethnicity, color or national origin in the operation of public education, public contracting or public employment.

(b) The state shall not classify any individual by race, ethnicity, color or national origin in the operation of any other state operations, unless the legislature specifically determines that said classification serves a compelling state interest and approves said classification by a ⅔ majority in both houses of the legislature, and said classification is subsequently approved by the governor.

(c) For purposes of this section, "classifying" by race, ethnicity, color or national origin shall be defined as the act of separating, sorting or organizing by race, ethnicity, color or national origin including, but not limited to, inquiring, profiling, or collecting such data on government forms.

(d) For purposes of subsection (a), "individual" refers to current or prospective students, contractors or employees. For purposes of subsection (b), "individual" refers to

Source: Denise Mock/
ACLU of Northern California

persons subject to the state operations referred to in subsection (b).

(e) The Department of Fair Employment and Housing (DFEH) shall be exempt from this section with respect to DFEH-conducted classifications in place as of March 5, 2002.
(1) Unless specifically extended by the legislature, this exemption shall expire ten years after the effective date of this measure.
(2) Notwithstanding DFEH's exemption from this section, DFEH shall not impute a race, color, ethnicity or national origin to any individual.

(f) Otherwise lawful classification of medical research subjects and patients shall be exempt from this section.

(g) Nothing in this section shall prevent law enforcement officers, while carrying out their law enforcement duties, from describing particular persons in otherwise lawful ways. Neither the governor, the legislature nor any statewide agency shall require law enforcement officers to maintain records that track individuals on the basis of said classifications, nor shall the governor, the legislature or any statewide agency withhold funding to law enforcement agencies on the basis of the failure to maintain such records.

(k) For the purposes of this section, "state" shall include, but not necessarily be limited to, the state itself, any city, county, city and county, public university system, including the University of California, California State University, community college district, school district, special district, or any other political subdivision or governmental instrumentality of or within the state.

Note: Other sections of the measure (not shown) say that if federal law or valid court orders require racial data, then those data will be collected.

the decisions voters face at the polls are often technically complicated. Are pesticides safe to use, or should the state regulate their use in new ways? Should nuclear power plant regulations be changed to make them safer? Will an increase in the state's minimum wage help or harm the state's economy? When faced with such questions, advice from trusted leaders is particularly important to voters. They can decide based on endorsements rather than on their own evaluations of the proposed policies.

In 1986, for example, actor Charlton Heston endorsed a "right-to-work" law in Idaho. In a television advertisement, Heston said, "I've played men like Tom Jefferson, Andrew Jackson, Lincoln—all heroes defending American freedom. There are Americans still carrying on that fight in Idaho, where citizens want the right to work without being forced to join a union. As a former union president, I believe Americans should be free to choose. We're watching, Idaho. Strike a blow for freedom. Vote Yes on Referendum I." [11] That endorsement by Heston, along with others by President Ronald Reagan and actor Clint Eastwood, carried the day for the antiunion measure in the relatively conservative Idaho. In general, endorsements such as Heston's simplify matters for voters and offer them guides to voting that do not require them to evaluate complicated questions.

The use of elite endorsements also shows why it would be wrong to describe direct legislation campaigns as only being about the merits of the issues. The issues certainly play the leading roles in initiative and referendum campaigns, but parties, candidates, and other political leaders play roles as well.

Evil Twins

One of the most effective strategies for defeating a ballot initiative is to propose a "counterinitiative," or an "evil twin" as it is sometimes known. The counterinitiative is another initiative or referendum that addresses the same issue as an initiative that has already qualified for the ballot, but it offers an alternative policy proposal. In some instances, supporters of the counterinitiatives actually want them to win; more commonly, however, counterinitiatives are launched with the intent of defeating an initiative or referendum that has already qualified for the ballot.

The key to the counterinitiative strategy is voter confusion. When voters are faced with a pair of large, complicated measures and with advocates on both sides making claims and counterclaims, they tend to become unsure about what the proposed laws will do and so they vote no. Overall, the record shows that when an initiative faces a counterinitiative on the same ballot, both measures are likely to lose.

An example of the initiative-counterinitiative strategy is the fight between environmentalists and the agriculture industry in California in 1990. Proposition 128, or "Big Green" as it was called, was a proposal to regulate the pesticides and chemicals that were ending up in the food

supply and to tighten clean water and air standards associated with agricultural pollutants. The agriculture industry responded with a $22 million campaign against Proposition 128 and with a counterinitiative, Proposition 135. Their initiative also dealt with pesticide regulation, but the standards were far laxer, and there were many loopholes. The environmentalists fought back, labeling Proposition 135 "Big Brown," but in the end both initiatives lost—which was exactly what the agriculture industry wanted.

Pressuring State Legislatures

Another strategic approach to initiatives is to use them as a means of pressuring the state legislature. When groups sponsor initiatives, they almost always speak boldly about the campaign to come and the victory they expect to achieve. Yet sometimes they actually hope to achieve victory without the cost and bother of the campaign by pressuring state legislatures.

Campaigns are generally more expensive than lobbying efforts. If a group thinks it can achieve its policy goals by lobbying the legislature, that is the path it normally takes. A group may decide, however, that the threat of an initiative is needed to prod a legislature to action. Although the group may have to pay the costs of qualifying an initiative for the ballot, it may be able to save the cost of the campaign if the legislature acts.

The 2003 drive for a financial privacy law in California is an example of using an initiative to lobby a state legislature. A group of consumer advocates had been unsuccessfully lobbying the legislature for a bill that would restrict the ways in which corporations could distribute financial information about their customers. After the consumer advocates gathered 600,000 signatures to qualify an initiative with even tougher restrictions than the ones under consideration in the state legislature, the legislature acted, quickly passing the bill. In response, the consumer advocates declared victory and announced that they would not be filing the petitions for the election.

Because legislatures can act far more quickly than voters can through the initiative process, initiative opponents have an opportunity to respond before the election. If an initiative seems likely to succeed, the opponents may be able to avoid complete defeat by pushing a compromise measure through the state legislature. This strategy does not always work because it requires the legislature to go along, but it is attempted regularly.

In a variation on this pattern, legislatures sometimes act on issues even after initiatives have failed. If an initiative receives enough votes to persuade the legislature that a second, revised effort might prevail, the legislature may act to prevent the second attempt. For example, in 1996 Californians voted down two propositions designed to regulate health maintenance organizations (HMOs). Although the initiatives failed, they revealed substantial public dissatisfaction with HMOs, and they persuaded the legislature that something had to be done. A few months after the election, the legislature responded by tightening regulations on HMOs.

Overall, the fact that initiatives are occasionally used to pressure state legislatures shows that initiatives can have impacts on public policy, even when they are not successful. The mere existence of initiatives as a tool of direct democracy makes legislatures more accountable to the public.

Using Initiatives to Help Candidates

Sometimes candidates or parties have found it in their interest to propose ballot measures as a means of winning elections. Candidates and parties can benefit from ballot measures in several ways. A proposition can be used as a "wedge issue" to divide one's opponents, as a platform around which a candidate can build a campaign for public office, or as an inducement for a party's supporters to turn out on election day.

Politicians have at times proposed initiatives with the hope of dividing supporters of the opposition party. An example of such a wedge issue is California's Proposition 209, a 1996 initiative designed to end affirmative action in state hiring and contracting and in college admissions. The strongest supporters of affirmative action are African Americans and Latinos; many working-class whites, however, are strong opponents of affirmative action. All of these groups lean heavily toward the Democratic Party. The California Republican Party donated almost $1 million to the Yes on Prop. 209 Committee because it realized that no matter what stand Democratic politicians took, they would offend at least some of their Democratic followers. This situation, Republican leaders hoped, would help Republican candidates in November.

Some candidates build their campaigns around initiatives. For example, California Proposition 187 was written to discourage illegal immigration by denying health services to illegal immigrants, by denying the benefits of public school to their children, and by requiring state, local government, and school employees to report suspected illegal immigrants to the authorities. Gov. Pete Wilson helped launch the initiative in 1994 both to help with his reelection bid and to bolster his image with conservatives around the nation in preparation for a bid for the 1996 Republican presidential nomination.

Proposition 187 also serves as an example of an initiative that was intended to gain a turnout advantage by appealing to voters who favored one political party over the other. Governor Wilson believed it would bring a greater number of conservatives to the polls without having much effect on Democratic turnout. Although the initiative won with 59 percent of the vote, it eventually backfired on its Republican backers. Because the measure targeted Latinos, it persuaded many legal residents to apply for citizenship and many nonvoting Latino citizens to start voting. Together with Proposition 209 in 1996 and

Proposition 227 in 1998 (a measure that banned bilingual education in the public schools), Proposition 187 is credited with creating a surge of Latino voters who turned California into a Democratic state.

Postelection Defense

Once an initiative or referendum has passed, the fight is not necessarily over. The people may have spoken, but they do not always have the last word. The state legislature or the courts may change or even block measures passed by the people. Thus the last step in winning a change in a state law or constitution is often the postelection defense.

Defending Initiatives from Legislative Changes

Legislatures in every state but California have the right to modify changes in state laws passed by voters. This right extends only to changes in laws, not to changes in state constitutions, but it is a substantial power nevertheless. Most states require more than a simple majority to overrule the people—typically, a supermajority of two-thirds is required. A few states also have time limits for changes. By some means, therefore, laws passed by the voters are at the mercy of the state legislature and the governor.

Legislative efforts to change measures passed by the people are, however, uncommon. Most important, a legislature has apparently never directly defied the will of the people by reversing the outcome of an election shortly after the election. To do so would seem undemocratic, and it would almost certainly lead to the defeat of anyone who supported a reversal. When state legislators do attempt to change laws passed by the people, they usually seek only minor modifications. As years pass, of course, revising the product of direct legislation becomes easier. In effect, what started out as a law passed by the people becomes just another law, subject to normal legislative politics.

Defending Initiatives in the Courts

Legislative challenges to initiatives passed by the people are relatively easy to fend off; legal challenges are not. When opponents of a measure lose at the polls, often their next step is to turn to the courts. No studies have recorded how many initiatives have been partly or fully overturned in the courts, but the answer is certainly a great number.

Legal challenges can be mounted on many bases. Propositions passed by voters may violate state or federal constitutions or federal law. Even if there is no federal law on the particular issue covered by an initiative, the courts may rule that jurisdiction in the area lies exclusively with the federal government and that no state laws are allowed. The single-subject requirement offers another avenue for attacking initiatives. Finally, opponents

*In February 2002, New Orleans voters passed Proposition A,
establishing a citywide livable minimum wage. The Louisiana
Supreme Court later dismissed the election result on the ground
that it violated a state ban on cities' establishing minimum wages.*
Source: J. Scott/ACORN

of an initiative may argue that the election process was
flawed in some fashion and that the results of the election
must be nullified.

California's Proposition 187 offers a classic example of
how a popular initiative can be defeated in the courts.
One provision of the measure declared that children of illegal immigrants were not eligible to attend K–12 public
schools. That provision was struck down because it violated a 1982 U.S. Supreme Court decision that the children of illegal immigrants had a right to attend school.
The Court had argued that children were in the country
because of their parents. Therefore, the children were not
at fault and should not be punished. Other provisions of
Proposition 187 prevented illegal immigrants from receiving welfare or publicly funded health care. These provisions were struck down on two grounds. First, when the
federal government revised the welfare system in 1994 it
addressed immigration issues in the law, and therefore it
preempted state legislation that addressed similar questions. Second and more broadly, immigration is a policy
area that falls exclusively within federal jurisdiction, and
states may not pass laws that influence immigration policy. Some minor aspects of Proposition 187 were left in
place, but the core of the initiative was defeated in court.

The single-subject requirements of many states give
the courts substantial power to block initiatives. A few
legal scholars have argued that single-subject restrictions
effectively allow courts to veto laws they do not like.
These critics maintain that virtually all laws can be interpreted as covering two or more subjects, because no state
constitution offers a definition of what constitutes a "single subject."

A 1994 Florida Supreme Court decision offers an example of a controversial single-subject decision. A group

opposed to giving new rights to gays and les-
bians tried to put a constitutional amendment
on the ballot that would bar the state legislature
from passing antidiscrimination laws that applied to any group except those characterized by
"race, color, religion, sex, national origin, age,
handicap, ethnic background, marital status, or
familial status." [12] Supporters of the amendment argued that it covered only one subject—
discrimination—and they maintained that their
amendment would restrict new antidiscrimination laws only to groups already protected
under current law. The Florida Supreme Court
ruled that the proposed amendment actually
covered ten subjects—the ten protected characteristics—and therefore could not be placed on
the ballot.

When the courts do act, they need not strike
down entire laws. They have the option to
strike down or modify only the portions of
laws that fail legal tests. Nevertheless, unlike
state legislatures, state and federal courts have
defied public opinion by voiding laws or important portions of them on many occasions.

Initiatives, Referenda, and Democracy

Critics have sounded warnings about direct democracy
since the ideas were first proposed. Three central questions have been raised. First, do the people know enough
to vote wisely on policy issues? Second, do the people respect the constitutional protections guaranteed to minorities? Third, can special interests unfairly manipulate the
process by spending their way to victory? After a hundred years of experience with direct democracy, political
observers continue to debate these questions.

Do the People Know Enough?

It is well established that the American public is poorly
informed about politics. Survey findings revealing ignorance are commonplace. For example, in 2000 only 62
percent of the public knew that the Republican Party held
a majority in the House of Representatives; only 30 percent could correctly identify J. Dennis Hastert as Speaker
of the House; and only an abysmal 8 percent could identify William H. Rehnquist as chief justice of the United
States. With such a record, should people be expected to
vote intelligently on issues such as pesticide regulation or
a plan to regulate HMOs? Critics of direct democracy
argue that such issues exceed people's technical competence; they simply do not know enough about the risks
posed by certain chemicals or about the economics of the
health care industry to choose wisely. It would be better,
the critics maintain, to return to a republican form of

government. Voters choose legislators whom they trust, and the legislators spend the time to become experts on technical matters and then make choices on the public's behalf.

Defenders of direct democracy offer two arguments in rebuttal. First, voters do not have to evaluate all the technical issues themselves; they can rely on trusted leaders to advise them on their voting choices. For example, if the Republican governor of Florida proclaims that a proposed initiative to reform the board of regents overseeing Florida's public universities is bad and Democratic leaders say it is good, then voters know enough to make up their minds about the plan. Elite cues provide enough guidance to make direct democracy work.

Second, legislators sometimes refuse to do what the public wants, and direct democracy offers a way in which the public can force its preferences to be enacted into law. Legislators may believe that a proposed measure would harm them, or they may vote against their constituents because of large campaign donations, or they may simply disagree with their constituents on ideological grounds. For whatever reason, legislators do occasionally refuse to do what the public wants. Direct legislation offers the public a means to force its will on recalcitrant legislators.

The history of term limit measures offers a good example of disagreements between legislators and their constituents. In 1990 political groups in three states put initiatives on the ballot that would limit the number of terms that a legislator could hold. The proposal in Oklahoma—the first state to limit its legislators' time in office—allowed its legislators to serve no more than a total of twelve years in the state House and Senate combined. Other proposals limited the number of terms a legislator could serve. Most state legislators opposed these initiatives, because the limits forced them out of office. The public, however, strongly supported term limits.

The first three initiatives passed in 1990, and, fueled by widespread distrust of politicians, a term limits movement swept the nation. By 1994, with the exception of Utah and Mississippi, every state that allowed its constitution to be changed by initiative had passed term limits. Although public opinion surveys showed that the term limits were popular all across the nation, no other state passed them through the legislative process. For term limits, then, the public forced a change on its state legislatures, which the legislatures resisted.

Both sides in the debate over direct democracy have valid points. Deciding the question is a matter of weighing the damage inflicted by a public that does not know enough about the issues against the benefits of allowing the public to control public policy.

Do the People Respect Constitutional Limits?

Another criticism of direct democracy is that voters occasionally pass initiatives that violate constitutional protec-

tions for minorities. U.S. democracy is a combination of majoritarian rule and minority rights—that is, on most issues majorities rule through elections; on some issues, however, individuals have rights that prevail over majority preferences. The rights to freedom of speech and freedom of religion, for example, cannot be overturned with either a law passed by Congress or a majority vote on an initiative.

Critics of direct democracy point to cases in which majorities passed initiatives that violated individual rights. For example, some initiatives have been struck down by the courts because they unconstitutionally restricted a woman's right to have an abortion. Other initiatives have been held unconstitutional because they allowed discrimination in housing, public accommodations, and public schools, and because they unconstitutionally required all public employees to speak only English on the job. To some observers, in these initiatives the public was engaging in tyranny of the majority, only to be stopped by the courts. The inevitable concern, therefore, is whether the courts will always stand up to the public when necessary to protect minority rights.

Defenders of direct democracy respond that the courts have blocked the public will in the past, and they will likely do so again in the future when needed. They also point out that voters are not alone in failing to respect constitutional limits; legislatures, too, have passed laws unconstitutionally limiting individual rights. Thus turning all decisions over to legislatures does not guarantee that individual rights will always be protected.

Once again, both sides in the debate over direct democracy have valid points. The question remains how to balance the benefit the public gains from being able to control public policy against the possible damage the public may do to individual rights.

Can Special Interests Buy Victory at the Polls?

The most common complaint about direct democracy is that special interests abuse the system by spending huge amounts of money on initiatives to pursue their goals at the ballot box. The fact that some interest groups raise and spend huge amounts of money is indisputable. As explained earlier, money does influence voting, but when narrow economic interests use the initiative process, they generally lose because the public usually reacts negatively to the pleas of special interests. Yet the debate does not end there.

Although economic interests usually lose, they do not always lose. In some cases, voters have successfully been persuaded to pass initiatives that conferred special economic advantages on business interests. In 1992, for example, Californians passed Proposition 163, which eliminated the sales tax on candy and junk food. But economic interests do not always try to pass initiatives; sometimes they try to defeat them. As noted earlier, money spent in opposition to ballot measures is generally more effective than money spent in support of measures. Indeed, finding cases in which economic interests were able to defeat initiatives or referenda that would have harmed them is easy. For example, voters in both California and Oregon defeated measures that would have blocked the construction of more nuclear power plants—the opposition campaigns were largely funded by the nuclear power industry. Thus even though narrow economic interests cannot always buy victory, critics point out, they may sometimes be able to buy victory—and that, some critics say, should be a matter of concern.

All this said, the focus on economic "special interests" begs the question of fairness. Critics and defenders of direct democracy disagree about what constitutes a special interest and whether economic interests should be singled out for criticism because of their wealth. The questions about limiting nuclear power posed to California and Oregon voters were technical questions about nuclear power plant safety. The fact that the nuclear power industry spent a lot of money on the campaigns did not necessarily mean that it was wrong about the engineering. More broadly, arguments about the proper role of money in elections are often made by people with strong preferences about election outcomes. Business critics often see campaign spending as a problem for democracy; business supporters generally do not see any problem. Once more, sorting out the best way to run a democracy is not merely a matter of getting the facts right.

Reform Proposals

Many reform proposals have been offered for improving the initiative and referendum processes. This chapter has already touched on the reasons behind the major proposals. Foremost among the complaints about direct democracy is that the people do not know enough to decide about ballot measures, that people often fail to recognize or respect constitutional limits when they vote, and that money and special interests have too much influence in direct legislation elections.

Reformers who complain about voter competence have suggested various ways to make ballot measures easier to understand or to increase the amount of information available to voters. Some states have passed laws requiring that the official ballot descriptions and handbooks be written in plain language that can be easily understood. Although these measures may have some effect, they are not likely to have large ones, both because many—perhaps most—voters are not likely to read ballot handbooks and because many ballot questions are inherently complex and cannot easily be understood.

The complaint that voters do not recognize or respect minority rights dates from the days in which the U.S.

Constitution came into being. *The Federalist Papers* (especially *Federalist* No. 10), which explained the thinking behind the design of the Constitution, warned against the tyranny of the majority and argued that the republican form of government was best suited to avoid it. The strongest proposal to prevent such abuses has been the suggestion that the courts be allowed to intervene before an election rather than respond only after the fact. Pre-election review would have both advantages and disadvantages. On the positive side, it would be easier for the courts to reject proposals before they have the weight of an electoral majority behind them, and it would reduce the frustration of the voters who supported a measure that was nullified by the courts. On the negative side, the courts have traditionally responded only when necessary to correct constitutional abuses rather than intervening in the midst of electoral or legislative disputes. Many political observers find the idea of giving the courts a more active role in deciding the results of the democratic process worrisome. They argue that making it too easy for the courts to intervene would damage U.S. democracy by turning more power over to a group of appointed judges with no direct electoral responsibility. Whatever the outcome of these reform proposals, this is a problem that will never go away. As long as elections exist, majorities will from time to time pass legislation that denies some people their rights. In the end, the courts will be faced with decisions about whether to frustrate an electoral majority or to uphold constitutional rights.

Yet another major complaint about direct legislation is that it is too easily influenced by money and special interests. Whatever the merits of this complaint, there are few avenues for addressing it. The U.S. Supreme Court has ruled that almost every aspect of the direct legislation process is protected by the First Amendment. Signature gatherers are protected during the qualification process, and both donations and expenditures cannot be limited in campaigns. Reformers are left with little room to limit the influence of money at any point in the direct legislation process.

One avenue open to reformers is expansion of disclosure laws. Many states still have relatively limited financial disclosure laws, which make it difficult for people to find out who is supporting a measure financially. Some reformers advocate requiring more frequent reporting, making the reports available on the Internet, and preventing various schemes to launder donations and hide the original sources of the funds. All of these steps pass constitutional review, but persuading state legislatures to enact them has been difficult.

Although the debate about the merits of direct democracy has been lively and various reforms have been proposed, the prospects for any major changes seem slim. Direct legislation has been in place for a hundred years, and it seems likely to be part of the U.S. democratic system for the foreseeable future.

Notes

1. See *Amador Valley Joint Union High Sch. Dist. v. State Bd. of Equalization* (1978).

2. Richard J. Ellis, *Democratic Delusions: The Initiative Process in America* (Lawrence: University of Kansas Press, 2002), 150.

3. Ibid., 51.

4. *Meyer v. Grant*, 486 U.S. 414 (1988).

5. *Buckley v. Valeo*, 424 U.S. 1 (1976), 26–27.

6. David B. Magleby, *Direction Legislation: Voting on Ballot Propositions in the United States* (Baltimore: Johns Hopkins University Press, 1984), 149.

7. Ibid., 146–148.

8. Stephen Nicholson, "Political Environment and Ballot Proposition Awareness," *American Journal of Political Science* 47 (2003): 403–410.

9. Thomas E. Cronin, *Direct Democracy: The Politics of Initiative, Referendum, and Recall* (Cambridge, Mass.: Harvard University Press, 1989), 82.

10. Magleby, *Direction Legislation,* 118–119, 136–139.

11. Quoted by J. Kent Marlor and A. Robert Inama in "The 1986 Right-to-Work Campaign in Idaho: An Evaluation of Direct Democracy in Action," paper delivered at the annual meeting of the American Political Science Association, Chicago, September 1987, 20; also quoted by Cronin, *Direct Democracy,* 118–119.

12. *In re Advisory Opinion*, 632 So. 2d 1018 (1994), quoted in Caroline J. Tolbert, Daniel H. Lowenstein, and Todd Donovan, "Election Law and Rules for Using Initiatives," in *Citizens as Legislators: Direct Democracy in the U.S.,* ed. Shaun Bowler, Todd Donovan, and Caroline J. Tolbert (Columbus: Ohio State University Press, 1998), 42.

Suggested Readings

Bowler, Shaun, Todd Donovan, and Caroline J. Tolbert, eds. *Citizens as Legislators: Direct Democracy in the United States.* Columbus: Ohio State University Press, 1998.

Cronin, Thomas E. *Direct Democracy: The Politics of Initiative, Referendum, and Recall.* Cambridge, Mass.: Harvard University Press, 1989.

Ellis, Richard J. *Democratic Delusions: The Initiative Process in America.* Lawrence: University of Kansas Press, 2002.

Gamble, Barbara W. "Putting Civil Rights to a Popular Vote." *American Journal of Political Science* 41 (January 1997): 245–269.

Gerber, Elisabeth R. *The Populist Paradox: Interest Group Influence and the Promise of Direct Legislation.* Princeton, N.J.: Princeton University Press, 1999.

Magleby, David B. *Direct Legislation: Voting on Ballot Initiatives in the United States.* Baltimore: Johns Hopkins University, 1984.

Mendelsohn, Matthew, and Andrew Parkin, eds. *Referendum Democracy: Citizens, Elites and Deliberation in Referendum Campaigns.* New York: Palgrave, 2001.

Piott, Steven L. *Giving Voters a Voice: The Origins of the Initiative and Referendum in America.* Columbia: University of Missouri Press, 2003.

Sabato, Larry J., Howard R. Ernst, and Bruce A. Larson, eds. *Dangerous Democracy: The Battle over Ballot Initiatives in America.* Lanham, Md.: Rowman and Littlefield, 2001.

PART VII
Campaign Reform

CHAPTER 27

Reform

Paul S. Herrnson

As noted in Chapter 1, political campaigns are a necessary condition for democratic politics. Campaigns increase citizens' interest in elections, give voters the information they need when deciding how to cast their ballots, and motivate many people to go to the polls. Campaigns are designed to build coalitions of diverse groups of voters in support of specific candidates and causes. Although candidates and campaign aides are primarily interested in winning elections, an important by-product of their efforts is the meaning with which they imbue elections and the democratic process. Without campaigns, voters would have little foundation on which to cast their ballots, and representation and accountability in government would suffer. Democracy also would fall short of the mark in other ways.

As described in the chapters of this volume, contemporary campaigns have many virtues as well as some shortcomings. In view of those shortcomings, this chapter takes up the thorny issue of reform. It briefly contrasts some of the ideals that democratic theorists posit for election campaigns with the reality of contemporary elections, provides an overview of the relationships between election rules and reform, reviews some current reform proposals, and describes some of the challenges that face reformers.

Democratic Theory and Reality in Contemporary Campaigns

Traditional democratic theory makes some big demands on what is to be expected from citizens, and by extension it sets very high standards for political campaigns. Citizens are expected to be knowledgeable about the candidates and the issues and capable of using that knowledge to determine which candidates most accurately represent their views and are likely to govern in the nation's best interests. Once voters have gone to the trouble of gathering and processing this information, they are expected to be motivated enough to cast a ballot. By implication, politi-

cal campaigns are expected to provide voters with user-friendly information they can utilize to make informed judgments about candidates and issues. But campaigns are not supposed to just inform voters; they also must be vibrant enough to capture voters' attention and motivate them to go to the polls.

Citizens, however, fall short of the high standards established by political theorists. Most voters have relatively limited information about candidates and the issues, and they possess neither the interest in nor the commitment to weighing the pros and cons of the choices they make on election day. The full body politic, including nonvoters, is, in general, even less concerned than voters about elections, as is demonstrated by their lower levels of information and participation. The fact that only about 50 percent of the adult population participates in presidential elections and only 40 percent votes in midterm congressional elections does not paint a picture of the United States as a particularly vibrant participatory democracy.

Contemporary campaigns also frequently fail to live up to the lofty principles espoused in traditional democratic theory. Campaigns are concerned first and foremost with winning elections. Candidates, political consultants, political parties, interest groups, and the vast majority of activists who participate in campaigns keep their gaze firmly affixed on this goal. They are rarely distracted by the more altruistic and abstract goal of improving democracy. As such, campaigners do not seek to provide voters with complete, unbiased, and factual information. Nor do they aim to inspire voters across the board to show up at the polls. Instead, campaigns seek to control the flow of information, so that voters receive flattering communications about their candidates and less-than-positive messages about their opponents. Chapter 14 on the strategic and tactical aspects of campaigns reveals that campaigns use sophisticated targeting techniques to mobilize their supporters and sometimes engage in tactics designed to discourage voters who are supportive of their opposition. Recent campaigns have minimized discussion of the issues. Instead they have wrapped their candidates in positive symbols, including the American flag, and have attacked those who disagree with them as captured by special interests or even unpatriotic. Some elections are now so rife with personal attacks that they degenerate into little more than mudslinging contests that not only fail to provide voters with the information favored by democratic theorists, but also encourage feelings of apathy and distrust to develop within the electorate.

Other aspects of campaigns and elections that fall short of the ideals articulated by theorists are the inability of some candidates to garner the resources needed to communicate with voters, the ways in which votes are aggregated and counted, how party nominees are selected, how elections are funded, and the unwillingness of many highly talented prospective candidates to run for office. Many of these deficiencies contribute to a more fundamental weakness of American democracy: a lack of competition in the electoral process.

Election Rules and Reform

Some of the shortcomings of elections—both real and perceived—are rooted in causes that are deeper than the failings of contemporary citizens and campaigners. These deficiencies are embedded in the political institutions, laws, administrative decisions, and court rulings that structure elections. Even though electoral arrangements must never be intentionally designed to favor certain candidates, political parties, interest groups, or voters, such arrangements are never neutral. The rules governing elections influence who wins and loses, which organized groups and less organized blocs of voters receive better representation in the policy-making process, and ultimately the policies that govern a nation. A simple example illustrating the importance of electoral rules is that in 2000 the Republicans were able to win the presidency and retain control of the U.S. House of Representatives despite the fact that GOP candidates did not win a majority of either the presidential or the congressional vote. The result has been that interests aligned with the Republican Party have benefited from access to policy-making circles in Washington, D.C., and from a policy windfall they would have not received under a Democratic administration or a Democratic-controlled Congress.

Politicians are fully aware of the potential impact of electoral arrangements on their election prospects. Candidates, parties, and others involved in election campaigns plan and execute their strategies with the goal of maximizing their advantages under the electoral institutions and laws under which they must compete. For example, when mounting their 2000 presidential campaigns, both Texas governor George W. Bush and Vice President Al Gore devised strategies designed to win a majority of the electoral college vote instead of those designed to maximize their total popular vote nationally.

Campaign officials also recognize that the rules governing elections can be changed in ways that work to or against their advantage. For example, in 2002 Republican leaders in the House of Representatives opposed the Bipartisan Campaign Reform Act (BCRA), which sought to alter certain aspects of the financing of federal campaigns, because they believed the reform would favor Democrats and thus could endanger the Republicans' congressional majority. Their attempt to defeat the bill was, however, unsuccessful.

The fact that the BCRA may ultimately work to the advantage of Republican candidates calls attention to another aspect of electoral arrangements: election reform and reform more generally. Reforms instituted to change election campaigns can have unanticipated consequences. Some of these may be apparent soon after the reforms are implemented. Others may become apparent only after political campaigns have become accustomed to the new electoral rules. Still other unanticipated consequences may emerge after a reform has been in effect for some time. These consequences are often brought about by challenges to the reform by those governed by it or by the decisions of administrators and judges who implement or interpret the law. These realities suggest that campaign reform should be an ongoing process in which new regulations are instituted to meet new challenges.

Current Reform Proposals

A wide array of election reforms have been proposed in recent years. Many reforms are intended to address obvious biases in the system. Abolishing the electoral college and doing away with single-member, simple-plurality (SMSP) or winner-take-all legislative elections, for example, could lead to a more accurate system of representation. Lowering the barriers to minor-party and independent candidacies or substituting proportional representation or some other vote-counting procedure for SMSP elections also would have significant implications for representation. Other reforms, such as revamping the presidential nominating process, promise to reduce the time and money needed to run for election. Proposals such as campaign finance reform and changing redistricting procedures could increase electoral competition. New approaches to voter registration could improve the nation's anemic voter turnout. Changes in voting technology promise to lead to fewer errors and greater accuracy in counting ballots. Strategic issues involving campaign conduct, while more difficult if not impossible to change legislatively, also are worthy of discussion. In the descriptions of these proposals that follow, it becomes clear that each one is associated with some predictable benefits and costs.

Abolishing the Electoral College

The electoral college is one of the most unusual and frequently criticized political institutions in the United States. Under the electoral college system, candidates who did not win a majority of the popular vote have won the presidency four times, the most recent in 2000. Reformers have frequently proposed modifying the system or replacing it. Among the more modest changes put forth is doing away with the "electors" who officially cast their states' electoral college votes. Such a change would prevent the "faithless elector" problem, which occurs when electors vote as they wish rather than cast their ballots as instructed by the voters in their states. Yet faithless electors have appeared only eight times in U.S. history, and so passing a constitutional amendment to make this change hardly seems worth the effort.

A more substantial set of proposals, which could be enacted by the individual states, calls for changing the way in which the popular votes cast in the states are translated into electoral college votes. One recommendation is to change the winner-take-all formula used at the state level to a system that aggregates votes within congressional districts and gives one electoral college vote to the presidential candidate who wins the most votes in each district. Some reformers advocate treating the two remaining electoral votes as a bonus awarded to the candidate who wins the most popular votes. This system would result in seemingly closer races, because it would reduce the magnification of the winner's victory margin produced by the electoral college vote. But it also would introduce a new set of biases into the vote totals, because, as pointed out later in this chapter, the vast majority of congressional districts emerge from a partisan redistricting process. Yet another approach, which involves distributing electoral votes in direct proportion to the number of popular votes a candidate wins statewide, would lead to a more accurate representation of state voter preferences in the presidential contest, but it, too, would result in close election outcomes. Moreover, if prominent third party candidates find their way onto most state ballots, the possibility that no candidate receives a majority of the electoral college votes becomes greater.

Direct election of the president is the simplest and most frequently discussed approach to reforming the electoral college. The major advantage to this approach is it most accurately represents the ballots cast by voters nationwide. Among the biggest disadvantages of this system is that it would lead to closer elections and more uncertain outcomes, and it would increase the possibility that presidential elections would have to be decided by the House of Representatives—unless some runoff system is also adopted. Moreover, because a direct election would not require candidates to build an electoral college majority out of electoral victories in a large number of states, it would likely encourage "sectional" campaigns that ignore entire states, regions, and population groups.

Adopting an Alternative System of Counting Votes

Any reform that replaces the current SMSP system of voting used in most American elections with some other system of aggregating votes, such as a proportional representation (PR) system, could change representation in Congress and other legislatures. Because under a PR system legislative seats are distributed to candidates on the basis of the number of votes their political parties win, minor parties—which rarely win legislative seats under the SMSP system—would have far better opportunities to elect their members. For example, a minor party that wins 10 percent of the statewide congressional vote in Massachusetts would win one of the state's congressional seats, whereas under an SMSP system it would win no seats if that vote were spread out over several districts, as is usually the case. Adoption of a PR system also would enable minor parties to attract voter support, because the argument that such parties act as "spoilers" for the major-party candidates would be rendered moot by the fact that they could realistically elect some of their own candidates.

The advantage that a PR system affords in terms of minor-party representation is considered a liability by those who oppose the system. They point out that minor parties divide opposition to incumbents in elections, and they make it more difficult for the largest party in the legislature to form coalitions, especially if that party does not hold a majority of seats. Thus the more accurate representation that is associated with PR is offset to some degree by a reduction in electoral accountability and greater potential instability in the legislative process, which in turn could enhance the power of the executive branch at the expense of the legislature. Substituting PR systems (or other forms of voting) for SMSP systems would require action by the states or perhaps lower-level governments; it would not require an amendment to the U.S. Constitution.

Revamping the Presidential Nominating Process

The presidential nominating process has been criticized for its length, expense, and propensity to grant some states and voters more influence than others. It also has been disparaged for its lack of peer review—that is, unlike in most other democracies, officeholders and party officials have little to no formal role in selecting presidential candidates. The process officially begins about ten months before election day, making it the longest nominating process for the chief executive of any modern democracy.

It is also more expensive. During the 2004 primary and caucus season, presidential candidates raised a combined total of $674.2 million in pursuit of their parties' nominations. These figures, which exclude the massive independent spending by interest groups and the $172.3 million the parties spent on their conventions, dwarf the

$351.6 million raised in 2000. The major explanation for the massive bump in fund raising is that President George W. Bush, Democratic governor Howard Dean of Vermont, and Democratic senator John Kerry of Massachusetts (the Democratic Party's eventual nominee), all decided to decline public funding so they could avoid the spending limits that accompany it. Unless the system is reformed, it is possible to predict with confidence that the leading nomination candidates will continue to decline public subsidies in favor of private dollars and that the costs of these contests will continue to climb.

The presidential nominating system has also come under criticism for granting a disproportionate influence to voters in early caucus and primary states, particularly Iowa and New Hampshire, which, respectively, host the first caucuses and primary. The early states have an important role in determining who the early leaders are and in winnowing the field of candidates. Many candidates drop out or are declared "long-shots" before some of the more populous states hold their nominating contests. Under the current system, the nominating schedule forces candidates to hopscotch across the country in order to win convention delegates. In some recent contests, the de facto nominee was selected before some large states, including California, got to vote.

Another criticism of the present nominating system is that it takes the decision out of the hands of party leaders and puts it in those of registered party voters, and in some cases independents, whose support must be won through a national political campaign. The system eliminates peer review, gives the media a greater role in determining the candidates each party selects, and places a premium on fund raising. It also has resulted in the nomination of some candidates who do not have much political experience at the national level.

Reformers have proposed various measures for changing the presidential nominating system. Some focus on the schedule. The National Association of Secretaries of State has proposed instituting a regional primary schedule. States in each of four regions—East, South, Midwest, and West—would hold their primaries on the same day in March, April, May, and June, and the order in which the regions vote would rotate. The "Delaware Plan" also calls for four days of primary voting spread out over three to four months, but it would divide the states into four groups by size and have the smallest states vote first. A third plan calls for holding all state primaries or caucuses on one day in the late spring. It is believed that all of these systems would extend the length of time candidates stay in the race, giving voters in more states an opportunity to vote for them. Although these proposals are likely to accomplish this goal, they, and especially the national primary, may make it difficult for a candidate to win enough votes to win the nomination outright. As such, the nominee would have to be chosen at the convention, which, while allowing more peer review, might make it difficult for the eventual nominee to unify the party behind his or her general election candidacy.

Some reform proposals focus more on who selects the nominee and advocate more peer review. For most of U.S. history, political parties did not use participatory primaries or caucuses to select their presidential nominees. Instead, they assigned this task to their congressional delegations, state legislative caucuses, or national convention delegates who were selected by the leaders of local party organizations. It was not until 1972 that participatory primaries and caucuses were widely used to select convention delegates and presidential nominees. Numerous democracies use elite-based procedures similar to those used in the United States prior to 1972, and some reformers advocate incorporating elements of those systems back into the U.S. system to increase the amount of peer review in the process.

Reforming the presidential nominating process requires the approval of a variety of organizations, but it is not as daunting a task as passing some other reforms, because it does not require a constitutional amendment. The process is governed by various factors, including state law, state and local party rules, and national party rules. Who may participate also has been influenced by state and federal court rulings. Thus changing some aspect of the process could require the approval of a state government, state or county party central committee, or national party. Major change, such as switching to a one-day national primary, would be difficult to bring about, but tinkering with the rules has become a quadrennial event.

Campaign Finance Reform

The financing of political campaigns is one of the most hotly debated subjects in reform politics. Critics of current election financing have many complaints. Among other things, they claim that (1) campaigns cost too much; (2) the ability of wealthy individuals and organized interests to contribute and spend large sums of money corrupts the political process; (3) candidates must spend too much time raising money; (4) the vast inequalities in the distribution of money among candidates result in uncompetitive elections; and (5) all of the problems just described discourage talented and qualified individuals from running for office.

As noted in Chapter 6, federal law strictly regulates the sources and amounts of contributions for federal candidates, allows presidential candidates to accept partial public funding during the nominating races and full public funding for the general election, and requires the disclosure of most campaign transactions. Nevertheless, one murky area of campaign finance that is exempt from federal campaign finance regulations allows interest groups to make unlimited candidate-focused political expenditures up to thirty days before a primary and sixty days before the general election.

State and local campaign finance laws vary, because they are subject to regulations enacted at those levels of government. Some states apply minimal regulation to campaign financing. Many others have strict regulations in place. Maine and Arizona allow voluntary full public funding for legislative races. Several others—most notably, Hawaii, Minnesota, and Wisconsin—have provisions for partial public funding for such contests. Maryland, Minnesota, and eleven other states permit publicly funded gubernatorial elections. Ten states have public funding programs for political parties.[1] Some other states and localities also have had or plan to initiate public funding programs.

Campaign finance reform proposals range from eliminating all private money from elections to removing the contribution and expenditure limits that currently govern campaign finance. Those who prefer the former approach would reduce the roles of the wealthy individuals and organizations that spend money in politics and equalize campaign spending by providing candidates with public funding. Those who advocate the latter are uninterested in equalizing political influence or campaign resources. They would allow the market to operate unfettered, enabling wealthier individuals, parties, and interest groups to spend as much as they please. In between these two extremes is a variety of reform proposals, including some that call for partial public funding of political campaigns and others that call for providing candidates or parties with free or subsidized television, radio, or postage to be used for campaign purposes. Other approaches suggest giving tax incentives to encourage more individuals to make campaign contributions and prohibiting incumbents from carrying over large war chests from one election to the next.

Enacting campaign finance reform has proven to be a major challenge in most jurisdictions, because most incumbents prefer not to give up the tremendous financial advantages they have over their opponents. In addition to the normal obstacles associated with passing legislation, reformers have routinely found their work challenged in the courts. The Supreme Court has equated election spending with free speech, establishing a significant barrier for those wishing to regulate the role of campaign money in politics.

Redistricting

The ways in which election districts are drawn has a tremendous impact on representation and political competition. Districts that strongly favor one party over another discourage individuals from challenging incumbents or from running in some open seats, resulting in many uncontested congressional and state legislative races. Lopsided districts also reduce the competition for seats contested by candidates of both major parties. For example, during the 2002 elections (the first to follow redistricting) eighty-eight House seats were uncontested,

and, in a recent record, 75 percent of all House races contested by major-party candidates were decided by vote margins of 20 percent or larger. The reason for this lack of competition is that redistricting is a political process in most states, and incumbents use it to improve or maintain their reelection prospects and to advance the prospects of their party's nonincumbents.

Reformers advocate improving the redistricting process by taking it out of the hands of elected officials and other partisans and placing it in the hands of a redistricting commission that ignores issues of partisanship or incumbency. Iowa is an example of such a state. During the 2002 elections, four of its five congressional districts were won by fewer than fifteen points in contrast to California, where three of its fifty-three congressional elections were decided by a vote margin of twenty points or less. Redistricting reform could be accomplished at the state level.

Voter Registration and Turnout

One explanation for the low voter turnout in the United States is that the American political system erects barriers that discourage voting. Most states require prospective voters to register in advance of an election, making it impossible for citizens who become interested in voting in the closing days of an election to cast a ballot. Voter apathy also produces low voter turnout. Many of those eligible to vote, particularly young people, feel disconnected from the political system. They believe their participation in elections would make no difference. Sometimes, they are correct; the one-sided partisan competition of most political jurisdictions and disparities in campaign finance among candidates render most elections uncompetitive. In view of the costs and benefits associated with voting, many citizens believe the former outweigh the latter and opt not to exercise their right to vote.

Reform proposals have been put forward to address these issues. To deal with legal barriers, some states have enacted voting procedures that allow their citizens to vote at convenient locations over an extended period before election day. Oregon has moved to voting exclusively by mail, and many other states have made it easy to vote using absentee ballots. Some of these measures have resulted in higher turnout, but their effects are generally modest because those who take advantage of them often would have voted anyway. More radical solutions, which probably would not be accepted in the United States, include placing the onus of voter registration entirely on the government, like in Britain, or making voting compulsory, like in Australia. Even efforts to make election day a national holiday have met with stiff resistance from U.S. politicians.

Voter apathy can be addressed in different ways, including through civic education initiatives. Most of these seek to connect citizens to their government. Many civic initiatives enlist musicians, actors, and other celebrities to appear at venues popular with youths and minorities to encourage them to become politically involved. Personal contact is another tool used by candidates and political parties to urge citizens of all ages to vote. However, these efforts will have only limited effects when individuals believe that the political system does not respond to people like them.

One of the most important factors related to voting is political competition. When elections are close fought and the stakes are high, voter turnout tends to increase. Both campaigns in a competitive race are generally well funded, and they undertake substantial efforts to mobilize their supporters and win over undecided voters. Party activity, interest group efforts, and media coverage in these elections are also often high. All of these factors come together to produce an environment rich in political information. And they combine to encourage voters to believe that each of their votes matter. Increasing voter turnout through boosting political competition is a laudable goal, but it would require reforms to address major issues such as redistricting, inequities in campaign finance, and perhaps some larger structural changes in political institutions.

Improving the Way Americans Vote

The 2000 presidential election showed that something was amiss with how Americans vote (see Chapter 4). Problems with voter registration rolls and long lines at the polls were blamed for many instances of nonvoting, and faulty voting technologies, including ballots and election machines, resulted in the loss of millions of votes. The entire process, including the de facto determination of the winner by the U.S. Supreme Court, left many people disturbed.

In 2002 Congress responded to public pressure for reform by passing the Help America Vote Act (HAVA), which provides federal funding for states to replace outdated voting machines, address flawed registration rolls, improve voter education, and train poll workers. Nevertheless, HAVA depends on the state and local governments that administer elections (mostly counties) and the private manufacturers that design voting equipment and ballots. Whether the problems that arose in 2000 will reemerge or new shortfalls will arise remains an unanswered question.

Campaign Conduct

One area of U.S. elections requiring improvement cannot be fully addressed by legislation or an infusion of new resources. That area is how campaigns are actually conducted. Citizens and trained political observers have been critical of several aspects of contemporary campaigns. First, they have complained about the negativity infusing those campaigns. Most campaigns meticulously research the opponents' personal backgrounds and attack the opposition on the basis of personal characteris-

tics rather than discuss their own or their opponents' issue stances. Second, campaigns have been criticized for presenting short sound bites and manipulating emotionally charged symbols, such as the flag, instead of presenting informative discussions of policy issues. Third, critics bemoan the few opportunities given voters to make side-by-side comparisons of the candidates. Fourth, they point out that most political campaigns employ strategies and tactics that ignore significant numbers of potential voters.

It would be impractical to try to correct these shortcomings legislatively. Efforts to improve campaign conduct must instead take the form of showing candidates, party officials, and others that it is in their best interests to wage better campaigns—that is, campaigners must be convinced that taking the high road can help them to win—or, at the very least, that it will not harm their prospects. Some foundations, most notably the Pew Charitable Trusts, have invested substantial resources in funding the systematic study of campaigns and in determining whether some of the campaign practices just described do indeed improve a candidate's electoral prospects. The findings of these projects are that most candidates are willing to attack an opponent's position on the issues and performance in office but not to attack a candidate's personal characteristics;[2] most consultants agree with these tactics;[3] negative campaigning is not significantly related statistically to the number of votes candidates win;[4] most televised negative campaigning is conducted by political parties and interest groups; and face-to-face campaigning is an effective tool to get first-time voters to the polls.[5] Although these studies have been disseminated at many campaign training seminars and trade magazines, their impact has been limited.

Challenges Faced by Reformers

Because election rules are not neutral, because reform has the potential to advantage some candidates, parties, groups, and voters over others, and because not all of the consequences of reform can be anticipated, it should come as little surprise that campaign reforms are difficult to enact. The fact that the incumbents who would be reforming campaign laws are the very same people who have already won office under them poses additional obstacles to reform. More than two decades elapsed between Congress's passage of the Federal Election Campaign Act of 1979 and its successor, the BCRA—an apt illustration of the time it often takes to address shortcomings that may emerge in the campaign process. The courts and the Federal Election Commission made several important decisions about the regulation of money and politics in the interim and Congress considered many bills, but no legislation was forthcoming.

Sen. Paul Wellstone of Minnesota was an outspoken advocate of campaign finance reform. He was a promoter of public financing for campaigns as the lead sponsor of the Clean Money/Clean Elections Act, and he cosponsored the Bipartisan Campaign Reform Act of 2002, which bans soft money contributions. Wellstone was killed in a plane crash on October 25, 2002, while campaigning for reelection. Source: Patrick Ryan/Reuters/Landov

Not surprisingly, a great deal of the activity surrounding campaign reform is more indicative of an incumbent's survival instincts than a desire to improve the political system. Most officeholders who participate in the reform process routinely portray themselves as reformers while advocating changes that reflect their own self-interest. Incumbents are preoccupied with protecting elements of the system that benefit them, and most challengers are just as vocal about passing reforms to remove those advantages. Most Republicans prefer high contribution limits or no limits at all, because such limits would enable them to take advantage of their superior fund-raising prowess and larger donor base. Democrats are typically more favorably disposed toward public funding for campaigns and free media time and postage, which would reduce the impact of the Republicans' financial advantages.[6]

Members of the two chambers of Congress also have divergent points of view, reflecting differences between running in a House district and running in a statewide Senate campaign. Variations in legislators' opinions about reform also stem from the demands that campaigning makes on different types of candidates. Women, African Americans, ethnic minorities, and members of other traditionally underrepresented groups that depend on national donor networks have preferences that differ from those of most white male candidates. Candidates' opinions about campaign reform further vary according to the nature of their constituencies. Candidates from wealthy urban seats tend to have fund-raising opportunities, spending needs, and views on reform that differ from those of candidates from poor rural states or districts. But not all differences

are grounded in personal or partisan advantage. Philosophical principles are also important. As noted earlier, Republicans tend to favor marketplace approaches, and Democrats generally prefer regulatory measures accompanied by public subsidies.

Finally, many legislators and others are skeptical about the government's ability to regulate the flow of political money. Some believe in the "hydraulic theory," which maintains that money, like water, will flow through other existing channels or find new ones if an existing route is closed. They believe that any campaign finance reform will have only a limited effect at best. Others have embraced what might be called the "principle of inadequate results." They contend that a reform law that fails to accomplish all of its supporters' goals is not worth enacting. The skepticism of still others originates from the well-established "law of unintended consequences," which holds that once a reform is passed the unexpected is bound to happen.

Faced with skepticism, a diversity of opinion, and a complex issue, legislators are hard-pressed to find the common ground needed to pass meaningful campaign reform. The sometimes inflammatory rhetoric of reform groups occasionally widens the gaps between political decision makers. Not surprisingly, legislators find it challenging to move beyond public posturing to engage in serious reform efforts. Between 1979 and 2002, House members and senators of both parties introduced an estimated nine hundred campaign finance bills.[7] Some of these were sincere attempts to improve the campaign finance system. Others were less sincere. Legislators who knew their bills would never be adopted by their own chamber or Congress's other chamber, would never survive a conference committee, and would never be signed into law by the president introduced them to provide political cover for themselves rather than to actually enact reform.

Conclusion

Campaign reform is a complex subject, because any change is likely to favor one set of candidates, parties, or interests over others and because its results are somewhat difficult to predict and unlikely to accomplish all of the stated goals of the reformers. Moreover, advocating change in the way officials are elected is not a good vocation for the impatient or for those who are easily discouraged, because the forces opposing reform are strongly entrenched. Nevertheless, as long as some participants in the political process perceive a disconnection between the values underlying democracy and the electoral process, reform is worth pursuing. Reformers do the nation a service by pointing out weaknesses in its political institutions, and some of their recommendations occasionally become the law of the land. The U.S. political system has benefited from numerous advancements since its founding, including improvements in the ways in which its campaigns and elections are conducted. The efforts of political reformers are part of the process by which the nation moves closer to embodying the lofty ideals on which it was founded.

Notes

1. Public funding programs in some states are inactive.

2. See Ron Faucheux and Paul S. Herrnson, eds., *The Good Fight: How Political Candidates Struggle to Win Elections without Losing Their Souls* (Washington, D.C.: Campaigns and Elections, 2001); and Ron Faucheux and Paul S. Herrnson, eds.*Campaign Battle Lines* (Washington, D.C.: Campaigns and Elections, 2002).

3. Candice J. Nelson, David A. Dulio, and Stephen K. Medvic, *Shades of Gray: Perspectives on Campaign Ethics* (Washington, D.C.: Brookings, 2002).

4. Ibid.

5. Donald P. Green and Alan S. Gerber, eds., *Get Out the Vote! How to Increase Voter Turnout* (Washington, D.C.: Brookings, 2004).

6. Paul S. Herrnson, *Congressional Elections: Campaigning at Home and in Washington,* 4th ed. (Washington, D.C.: CQ Press, 2004), 282–283.

7. Colton Campbell, Congressional Research Service, personal communication, February 29, 2004.

Suggested Readings

Anthony Corrado, Thomas E. Mann, Daniel R. Ortiz, and Trevor Potter. *The New Campaign Finance Sourcebook.* Washington, D.C.: Brookings, 2004.

CQ Researcher. Various articles on election reform are available (by subscription) at library2.cqpress.com/cqresearcher.

Donovan, Todd, and Shaun Bowler. *Reforming the Republic: Democratic Institutions for the New America.* Upper Saddle River, N.J.: Prentice Hall, 2004.

Green, John C., and Paul S. Herrnson, eds. *Responsible Partisanship? The Evolution of American Political Parties since 1950.* Lawrence: University Press of Kansas, 2002.

Herrnson, Paul S. *Congressional Elections: Campaigning at Home and in Washington.* 4th ed. Washington, D.C.: CQ Press, 2004.

Malbin, Michael, ed. *Life after Reform: When the Bipartisan Campaign Reform Act Meets Politics.* Lanham, Md.: Rowman and Littlefield, 2003.

Selected Bibliography

BOOKS

PART I OVERVIEW OF POLITICAL CAMPAIGNS

Campbell, Angus, Philip E. Converse, Warren E. Miller, and Donald E. Stokes. *The American Voter.* New York: Wiley, 1960.

CQ Press. *Guide to U.S. Elections.* 5th ed. Washington, D.C.: CQ Press, 2005.

Fiorina, Morris P. *Retrospective Voting in American National Elections.* New Haven: Yale University Press, 1981.

Herrnson, Paul S. *Congressional Elections: Campaigning at Home and in Washington.* 4th ed. Washington, D.C.: CQ Press, 2004.

———. *Party Campaigning in the 1980s.* Cambridge: Harvard University Press, 1988.

Holbrook, Thomas M. *Do Campaigns Matter?* Thousand Oaks, Calif.: Sage Publications, 1996.

Jacobson, Gary C. *The Politics of Congressional Elections.* 6th ed. New York: Longman, 2004.

Johnson, Dennis W. *No Place for Amateurs: How Political Consultants Are Reshaping American Democracy.* New York: Routledge, 2001.

Maisel, L. Sandy, ed. *The Parties Respond: Changes in American Parties and Campaigns.* 4th ed. Boulder, Colo.: Westview Press, 2002.

Medvic, Stephen K. *Political Consultants in U.S. Congressional Elections.* Columbus: Ohio State University Press, 2001.

Ornstein, Norman J., and Thomas E. Mann, eds. *The Permanent Campaign and Its Future.* Washington, D.C.: American Enterprise Institute for Public Policy and the Brookings Institution, 2000.

Patterson, Kelly D. *Political Parties and the Maintenance of Liberal Democracy.* New York: Columbia University Press, 1996.

Polsby, Nelson W., and Aaron Wildavsky. *Presidential Elections: Strategies and Structures of American Politics.* 10th ed. New York: Chatham House, 2000.

Sabato, Larry J. *The Rise of Political Consultants: New Ways of Winning Elections.* New York: Basis Books, 1981.

Stanley, Harold W., and Richard G. Niemi. *Vital Statistics on American Politics 2005–2006.* Washington, D.C.: CQ Press, 2005.

Thurber, James A., and Candice J. Nelson. *Campaigns and Elections American Style.* 2nd ed. Boulder, Colo.: Westview Press, 2004.

Wayne, Stephen J. *The Road to the White House 2004.* New York: Wadsworth, 2003.

PART II LAWS AND REGULATIONS GOVERNING CAMPAIGNS

Canon, David T. *Race, Redistricting, and Representation: The Unintended Consequences of Black Majority Districts.* Chicago: University of Chicago Press, 1999.

Ceaser, James W. *Presidential Selection.* Princeton: Princeton University Press, 1979.

Corrado, Anthony, Thomas E. Mann, Daniel R. Ortiz, and Trevor Potter. *The New Campaign Finance Sourcebook.* Washington, D.C.: Brookings Institution, 2004.

Cox, Gary W., and Jonathan N. Katz. *Elbridge Gerry's Salamander: The Electoral Consequences of the Reapportionment Revolution.* New York: Cambridge University Press, 2002.

Galderisi, Peter F., Marni Ezra, and Michael Lyons, eds. *Congressional Primaries and the Politics of Representation.* Lanham, Md.: Rowman and Littlefield, 2001.

Heard, Alexander. *The Costs of Democracy.* Chapel Hill: University of North Carolina Press, 1960.

Magleby, David B. *Financing the 2000 Election.* Washington, D.C.: Brookings Institution, 2002.

Malbin, Michael J., ed. *Life after Reform: When the Bipartisan Campaign Reform Act Meets Politics.* Lanham, Md.: Rowman and Littlefield, 2003.

Malbin, Michael J., and Thomas L. Gais. *The Day after Reform: Sobering Campaign Finance Lessons from the American States.* Albany, N.Y.: Rockefeller Institute Press, 1998.

Sorauf, Frank J. *Inside Campaign Finance: Myths and Realities.* New Haven: Yale University Press, 1992.

Wayne, Stephen J. *Is This Any Way to Run a Democratic Election?* 2nd ed. Boston: Houghton Mifflin, 2003.

Winger, Richard. "More Choice Please! Why U.S. Ballot Access Laws Are Discriminatory and How Independent Parties and Candidates Challenge Them." In *Democracy's Moment,* edited by Ronald Hayduk and Kevin Mattson, 45–59. Lanham, Md.: Rowman and Littlefield, 2002.

PART III VOTERS AND VOTING

Campbell, Angus, Philip E. Converse, Warren E. Miller, and Donald E. Stokes. *The American Voter.* New York: Wiley, 1960.

Fiorina, Morris P. *Retrospective Voting in American National Elections.* New Haven: Yale University Press, 1981.

Flanigan, William H., and Nancy H. Zingale. *Political Behavior of the American Electorate.* 10th ed. Washington, D.C.: CQ Press, 2002.

Green, Donald, Bradley Palmquist, and Eric Schickler. *Partisan Hearts and Minds: Political Parties and the Social Identities of Voters.* New Haven: Yale University Press, 2002.

Keith, Bruce E., David B. Magleby, Candice J. Nelson, Elizabeth Orr, Mark C. Westlye, and Raymond E. Wolfinger. *The Myth of the Independent Voter.* Berkeley: University of California Press, 1992.

Layman, Geoffrey. *The Great Divide: Religious and Cultural Conflict in American Party Politics.* New York: Columbia University Press, 2001.

Nie, Norman H., Sidney Verba, and John R. Petrocik. *The Changing American Voter.* Cambridge: Harvard University Press, 1976.

Patterson, Thomas E. *The Vanishing Voter: Public Involvement in an Age of Uncertainty.* New York: Knopf, 2002.

Putnam, Robert D. *Bowling Alone: The Collapse and Revival of American Community.* New York: Simon and Schuster, 2000.

Rosenstone, Steven J., and John Mark Hansen. *Mobilization, Participation, and Democracy in America.* New York: Macmillan, 1993.

Sundquist, James L. *Dynamics of the Party System: Alignment and Realignment of Political Parties in the United States.* Rev. ed. Washington, D.C.: Brookings Institution, 1983.

Wattenberg, Martin P. *Where Have All the Voters Gone?* Cambridge: Harvard University Press, 2002.

Wolfinger, Raymond E., and Steven J. Rosenstone. *Who Votes?* New Haven: Yale University Press, 1980.

PART IV THE PLAYERS

Berry, Jeffrey M. *The Interest Group Society.* New York: Longman, 1997.

Biersack, Robert, Paul S. Herrnson, and Clyde Wilcox. *Risky Business? PAC Decisionmaking in Congressional Elections.* Armonk, N.Y.: M. E. Sharpe, 1994.

Canon, David T. *Actors, Athletes, and Astronauts: Political Amateurs in the United States Congress.* Chapel Hill: University of North Carolina Press, 1990.

Dautrich, Kenneth, and Thomas H. Hartley. *How the News Media Fail American Voters: Causes, Consequences, and Remedies.* New York: Columbia University Press, 1999.

Day, Christine L., and Charles D. Hadley. *Women's PACs: Abortions and Elections.* Upper Saddle River, N.J.: Prentice Hall, 2005.

Dulio, David A. *For Better or Worse: How Political Consultants Are Changing Elections in the United States.* Albany: State University of New York Press, 2004.

Farnsworth, Stephen J., and S. Robert Lichter. *The Nightly News Nightmare: Network Television's Coverage of U.S. Presidential Elections, 1988–2000.* Lanham, Md.: Rowman and Littlefield, 2003.

Fowler, Linda L., and Robert D. McClure. *Political Ambition: Who Decides to Run for Congress?* New Haven: Yale University Press, 1989.

Goldstein, Kenneth M., and Patricia Strach. *The Medium and the Message: Television Advertising and American Elections.* Upper Saddle River, N.J.: Prentice Hall, 2004.

Green, John C., and Paul S. Herrnson, eds. *Responsible Partisanship? The Evolution of American Political Parties Since 1950.* Lawrence: University Press of Kansas, 2002.

Green, John C., and Rick Farmer. *The State of the Parties.* 4th ed. Lanham, Md.: Rowman and Littlefield, 2003.

Herrnson, Paul S. *Party Campaigning in the 1980s.* Cambridge: Harvard University Press, 1988.

Herrnson, Paul S., Ronald G. Shaiko, and Clyde Wilcox, eds. *The Interest Group Connection.* 2nd ed. Washington, D.C.: CQ Press, 2005.

Hershey, Marjorie Randon, and Paul Allen Beck. *Party Politics in America.* 10th ed. New York: Longman, 2003.

Jewell, Malcolm E., and David M. Olson. *Political Parties and Elections in American States.* 3rd ed. Chicago: Dorsey Press, 1988.

Jacobson, Gary C., and Samuel Kernell. *Strategy and Choice in Congressional Elections.* 2nd ed. New Haven: Yale University Press, 1983.

Johnson, Dennis W. *No Place for Amateurs: How Political Consultants Are Reshaping American Democracy.* New York: Routledge, 2001.

Just, Marion, Ann Crigler, Dean Alger, Tim Cook, Montague Kern, and Darrell West. *Crosstalk: Citizens, Candidates, and the Media in a Presidential Campaign.* Chicago: University of Chicago Press, 1996.

Maisel, L. Sandy, ed. *The Parties Respond: Changes in American Parties and Campaigns.* 4th ed. Boulder, Colo.: Westview Press, 2002.

Medvic, Stephen K. *Political Consultants in U.S. Congressional Elections.* Columbus: Ohio State University Press, 2001.

Moncrief, Gary F., Peverill Squire, and Malcolm Jewell. *Who Runs for the Legislature?* Upper Saddle River, N.J.: Prentice Hall, 2001.

Rozell, Mark J., and Clyde Wilcox. *Interest Groups in American Campaigns: The New Face of Electioneering.* Washington, D.C.: CQ Press, 1999.

Sabato, Larry J. *The Rise of Political Consultants: New Ways of Winning Elections.* New York: Basis Books, 1981.

Shea, Daniel. *Transforming Democracy: Legislative Campaign Committees and Political Parties.* Albany: State University of New York Press, 1995.

Thurber, James A., and Candice J. Nelson. *Campaign Warriors: Political Consultants in Elections.* Washington, D.C.: Brookings Institution, 2000.

PART V CAMPAIGNING

Ansolabehere, Stephen, and Shanto Iyengar. *Going Negative: How Political Advertisements Shrink and Polarize the Electorate.* New York: Free Press, 1995.

Buchanan, Bruce. *Presidential Campaign Quality.* Upper Saddle River, N.J.: Prentice Hall, 2004.

Brown, Clifford, Lynda Powell, and Clyde Wilcox. *Serious Money: Fundraising and Contributing in Presidential Nominating Campaigns.* New York: Cambridge University Press, 1995.

Eisinger, Robert M. *The Evolution of Presidential Polling.* New York: Cambridge University Press, 2003.

Francia, Peter L., John C. Green, Paul S. Herrnson, Lynda W. Powell, and Clyde Wilcox. *The Financiers of Congressional Elections.* New York: Columbia University Press, 2003.

Geer, John G. *From Tea Leaves to Opinion Polls.* New York: Columbia University Press, 1996.

Green, Donald P., and Alan S. Gerber. *Get Out the Vote! How to Increase Voter Turnout.* Washington, D.C.: Brookings Institution, 2004.

Hart, Roderick P. *Campaign Talk: Why Elections Are Good for Us.* Princeton: Princeton University Press, 2000.

Herbst, Susan. *Numbered Voices: How Opinion Polling Has Shaped American Politics.* Chicago: University of Chicago Press, 1993.

Herrnson, Paul S. *Congressional Elections: Campaigning at Home and in Washington.* 4th ed. Washington, D.C.: CQ Press, 2004.

————., ed. *Playing Hardball: Campaigning for the U.S. Congress.* Upper Saddle River, N.J.: Prentice Hall, 2001.

Jamieson, Kathleen Hall. *Eloquence in an Electronic Age: The Transformation of Political Speechmaking.* New York: Oxford University Press, 1988.

————. *Packaging the Presidency.* 3rd ed. New York: Oxford University Press, 1996.

Jamieson, Kathleen Hall, and David S. Birdsell. *Presidential Debates.* New York: Oxford University Press, 1988.

Kahn, Kim Fridkin, and Patrick J. Kenney. *No Holds Barred: Negativity in U.S. Elections.* Upper Saddle River, N.J.: Prentice Hall, 2004.

Kern, Montague. *Thirty-Second Politics: Political Advertising in the 1980s.* Westport: Praeger, 1989.

Kraus, Sidney, ed. *The Great Debates: Background, Perspective, Effects.* Bloomington: Indiana University Press, 1962.

Leighley, Jan E. *Strength in Numbers? The Political Mobilization of Racial and Ethnic Minorities.* Princeton: Princeton University Press, 2001.

Moncrief, Gary F., Peverill Squire, and Malcom E. Jewell. *Who Runs for the Legislature?* Upper Saddle River, N.J.: Prentice Hall, 2001.

Patterson, Thomas, and Robert D. McClure. *The Unseeing Eye: The Myth of Television Power in National Elections.* New York: Putnam, 1976.

Powell, Larry, and Joseph Cowart. *Political Campaign Communication: Inside and Out.* Boston: Allyn and Bacon, 2003.

Rosenstone, Steven J., and John Mark Hansen. *Mobilization, Participation, and Democracy in America.* New York: Macmillan, 1993.

Shea, Daniel M., and Michael J. Burton. *Campaign Craft: The Strategy, Tactics, and Art of Political Campaign Management.* Rev. ed. Westport: Praeger, 2001.

Stonecash, Jeffrey M. *Political Polling: Strategic Information in Campaigns.* Lanham, Md.: Rowman and Littlefield, 2003.

Thurber, James A., and Candice J. Nelson. *Campaigns and Elections American Style.* 2nd ed. Boulder, Colo.: Westview Press, 2004.

West, Darrell M. *Air Wars: Television Advertising in Election Campaigns, 1952–2000.* 3rd ed. Washington, D.C.: CQ Press, 2001.

West, Darrell M., and John Orman. *Celebrity Politics.* Upper Saddle River, N.J.: Prentice Hall, 2003.

PART VI SPECIFIC CAMPAIGNS

Ahuja, Sunil and Robert Dewhirst, eds. *The Roads to Congress, 2000.* Belmont, Calif.: Wadsworth/Thomson Learning, 2000.

Beito, Gretchen Urnes. *Coya Come Home: A Congresswoman's Journey.* Los Angeles: Pomegranate Press, 1990.

Buchanan, Bruce. *Presidential Campaign Quality.* Upper Saddle River, N.J.: Prentice Hall, 2004.

Cronin, Thomas E. *Direct Democracy: The Politics of Initiative, Referendum, and Recall.* Cambridge: Harvard University Press, 1989.

Dubois, P. *From Ballot to Bench: Judicial Elections and the Quest for Accountability.* Austin: University of Texas Press, 1980.

Gerber, Elisabeth R., Arthur Lupia, Mathew D. McCubbins, and D. Roderick Kiewet. *Stealing the Initiative: How State Government Responds to Direct Democracy.* Upper Saddle River, N.J.: Prentice Hall, 2001.

Herrnson, Paul S. *Congressional Elections: Campaigning at Home and in Washington.* 4th ed. Washington, D.C.: CQ Press, 2004.

Jacobson, Gary C. *The Politics of Congressional Elections.* 6th ed. New York: Longman, 2004.

Jacobson, Gary C., and Samuel Kernell. *Strategy and Choice in Congressional Elections.* New Haven: Yale University Press, 1981.

Kahn, Kim Fridkin, and Patrick J. Kenney. *No Holds Barred: Negativity in U.S. Elections.* Upper Saddle River, N.J.: Prentice Hall, 2004.

Mitchell, Greg. *The Campaign of the Century: Upton Sinclair's Race for Governor of California and the Birth of Media Politics.* New York: Random House, 1992.

————. *Tricky Dick and the Pink Lady: Richard Nixon vs. Helen Gahagan Douglas—Sexual Politics and the Red Scare, 1950.* New York: Random House, 1998.

Moncrief, Gary F., Peverill Squire, and Malcolm Jewell. *Who Runs for the Legislature?* Upper Saddle River, N.J.: Prentice Hall, 2001.

Polsby, Nelson W., and Aaron Wildavsky. *Presidential Elections: Strategies and Structures of American Politics.* 10th ed. New York: Chatham House, 2000.

Sabato, Larry J., Howard R. Ernst, and Bruce A. Larson, eds. *Dangerous Democracy: The Battle over Ballot Initiatives in America.* Lanham, Md.: Rowman and Littlefield, 2001.

Simmons, Donna. "The Contested Vote for Mississippi Governor." In *Campaigns and Elections: Issues, Concepts, Cases,* edited by Robert P. Watson and Colton C. Campbell, 131–138. Boulder, Colo.: Lynne Rienner Publishers, 2003.

Wayne, Stephen J. *The Road to the White House 2004.* New York: Wadsworth, 2003.

PART VII   CAMPAIGN REFORM

Champagne, A., and J. Haydel, eds. *Judicial Reform in the States.* Lanham, Md.: University Press of America, 1993.

Corrado, Anthony, Thomas E. Mann, Daniel R. Ortiz, and Trevor Potter. *The New Campaign Finance Sourcebook.* Washington, D.C.: Brookings Institution, 2004.

Donovan, Todd, and Shaun Bowler. *Reforming the Republic: Democratic Institutions for the New America.* Upper Saddle River, N.J.: Prentice Hall, 2004.

Green, John C., and Paul S. Herrnson, eds. *Responsible Partisanship? The Evolution of American Political Parties Since 1950.* Lawrence: University Press of Kansas, 2002.

Malbin, Michael J., ed. *Life after Reform: When the Bipartisan Campaign Reform Act Meets Politics.* Lanham, Md.: Rowman and Littlefield, 2003.

Malbin, Michael J., and Thomas L. Gais. *The Day after Reform: Sobering Campaign Finance Lessons from the American States.* Albany: Rockefeller Institute Press, 1998.

WEB SITES

Annenberg Political Fact Check: http://www.factcheck.org

Brookings Institution Campaign Finance Web page: http://www.brookings.org/gs/cf/cf_hp.htm

Campaigns and Elections magazine: http://www.campaignline.com

Campaign Legal Center, Campaign Finance Guide: http://www.campaignfinanceguide.org

Center for American Politics and Citizenship: http://www.capc.umd.edu/research.asp

CQ Press Voting and Elections Collection: http://library.cqpress.com/elections/index.php

Democratic National Committee: http://www.democrats.org

Federal Election Commission: http://www.fec.gov

Green Party: http://www.gp.org

Libertarian Party: http://www.lp.org

The Living Room Candidate: Presidential Campaign Commercials 1952–2004: http://livingroomcandidate.movingimage.us/index.php

National Election Studies, Center for Political Studies: http://www.umich.edu/~nes

Project Vote Smart: http://www.vote-smart.org

Reform Party: http://www.reformparty.org

Republican National Committee: http://www.rnc.org

U.S. Census Bureau Voting and Registration Data (Current Population Survey): http://www.bls.census.gov/cps/cpsmain.htm

Index

Boxes, figures, notes, and tables are indicated by b, f, n, and t. Italics indicate illustrations.